Micro-Economics

George Leland Bach

FRANK E. BUCK PROFESSOR OF ECONOMICS AND PUBLIC POLICY, STANFORD UNIVERS

PRENTICE-HALL, INC., ENGLEWOOD CLIFFS, NEW JERSEY 07632

2ND EDITION

CRO—
OMICS

Analysis and Applications

WITH THE ASSISTANCE OF David J. Teece

Library of Congress Cataloging in Publication Data

BACH, GEORGE LELAND, (date)
  Microeconomics.

  Selections from the author's Economics, 10th ed.,
1980.
  Includes bibliographical references and index.
  1. Microeconomics.   I. Title.
HB171.5.B132 1980   330   79-25137
ISBN 0-13-581298-4

To Christopher, Barbara, Susan, and Timothy

2nd Edition
MICROECONOMICS:
Analysis and Applications
George Leland Bach

© 1980 and 1977

*This material also appears in Economics: An Introduction to Analysis and
Policy, 10th Edition, by George Leland Bach
© 1980, 1977, 1974, 1971, 1968, 1966, 1963, 1960, 1957, and 1954
by Prentice-Hall, Inc.*

Printed in the United States of America
10 9 8 7 6 5 4 3 2 1

Editorial/Production Supervision by Colette Conboy
Interior and Cover Design by Janet Schmid
Composition by Typothetae Book Composition
Interior Illustrations by Fine Line Illustrations, Inc.
Acquisition Editor: David Hildebrand
Manufacturing Buyer: Edmund W. Leone

Prentice-Hall International, Inc., *London*
Prentice-Hall of Australia Pty. Limited, *Sydney*
Prentice-Hall of Canada, Ltd., *Toronto*
Prentice-Hall of India Private Limited, *New Delhi*
Prentice-Hall of Japan, Inc., *Tokyo*
Prentice-Hall of Southeast Asia Pte. Ltd., *Singapore*
Whitehall Books Limited, *Wellington, New Zealand*

ONTENTS

LIST OF END-OF-CHAPTER CASES

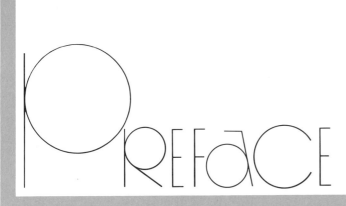

Preface

We live in an economic world of constant change. In the 200 years since Adam Smith's *Wealth of Nations* founded modern economics in 1776, we have built up a great deal of understanding of how our economy works. But it is a rare generation that hasn't had to face new problems that call for rethinking what we thought we knew before.

The 1970s were such a period, and the economics of the 1980s will be significantly different from the ideas that have dominated our thinking since World War II. Government deficit spending that was supposed to cure unemployment seems instead to produce ever-worsening inflation. The "Great Society" programs of the 1960s generated more disappointment than joy in the perspective of the 1970s. A tax revolt has swept the nation, against an ever-bigger and more intrusive government. Many of the government regulations aimed to produce a better life instead have had perverse results, and demands for deregulation have swept the land.

Economics has been undergoing a basic reassessment, which has produced a "new look" on important points and issues. This new, 1980 edition is written in this spirit of reassessment. It has much that is unchanged, but also much that marks the "new economics." For example:

1. *The tax revolt—the role of government.* The tax revolt is everywhere. Citizens and politicians are calling for constitutional amendments to require a balanced budget annually, or a tight ceiling on government spending. How to check big government is a pervasive question. Thus, in this edition, I have emphasized a thorough analytical comparison of markets versus the political process as mechanisms for allocating resources and incomes. Government income transfers are the core of the new public sector.

2. *Big business, consumerism, government regulation—the location of power in the modern economy.* During the post-World II decades, government regulation of economic activity, and especially of big business, expanded rapidly. Consumer protection, led by Ralph Nader, has become a major goal of government. The Johnson "Great Society" programs of the 1960s saw the peak of a parallel direct government intervention in economic life, especially in redistributing income. But achievements fell short of expectations, and deregulation is now moving to center stage. Modern micro economics can provide a more thorough analysis of "market failures" and of the effects of detailed, intrusive government regulation. I have woven the huge

corporation, consumerism, and other economic "pressure groups" more actively into the entire analysis of micro economics. The whole micro analysis is thus both more rigorous and broadened to recognize the central role economic and political power plays in many current policy issues.

3. *Slowing U.S. growth, the savings shortage, and the puzzle of poor productivity.* The rate of U.S. growth in output per capita, and hence in the American standard of living, has slowed dramatically in recent years. Why? Is the problem permanent or transient? Again, a "new look" from the economics of supply comes to the fore in helping to provide answers.

4. *A new overview of comparative economic systems and ideologies.* This weaves together Marxist and "New Left" criticisms of the American economy with a comparison of the performance of market- and non-market-directed economies on the modern world scene.

Like its predecessors, this is a book focused on what the *student* does. The evidence is overwhelming that students retain little of what they learn in college economics courses unless they become interested enough to continue to use it as they read the newspaper and vote in elections, after they leave the classroom. If the text and the class does not kindle a real interest in economics, and give them concepts and methods that they can use *for themselves* after the course is over, students will retain little. This is my educational philosophy. Thus the emphasis is on:

- *A set of key concepts, principles, and models —the core, no more, of essential theory; and*
- *Helping students learn to apply these analytical tools themselves to big and little real-world problems.*

Learning to apply theory in complex, real-world situations turns out to be more difficult for most students than learning the theory per se. Thus, to aid both students and instructors, I have added more new, real-world cases to the highly-successful ones included in the preceding edition; the user mail from both students and teachers has been most satisfying. This book now includes 31 such cases, each attached to a chapter where it shows the student how to apply the concepts and principles developed in that chapter. In addition, there are *Suggestions for Analysis* for most cases, segregated at the end of the book, so that students can check their own reasoning and understanding of the concepts and principles involved. Some of the cases are simple applications; others involve more complex decisions on public policy or managerial problems; still others raise broad issues for analysis and discussion, where answers hinge on value judgments and the weighting of goals as well as on economic analysis. They are real cases, not arithmetical problems. Some of the cases have no *Suggestions for Analysis,* so they can be used as examinations or homework by teachers who want students to deal with the cases entirely on their own.

The complete cases are listed in the Table of Contents. A sample:

- *Campus parking*
- *How much for auto safety?*
- *The price of pears*
- *Polly Poet's problem*
- *The battle of the supermarkets*
- *The economics of minimum-wage laws*
- *The voucher education plan*
- *How much social security can we afford?*
- *The energy problem*
- *Multinational corporations*

This book thus offers a variety of lively applications from which instructors can choose to fit the interests of their students.

I have also indicated a "Minimum Essentials Track" in micro theory for those instructors who want to develop only the bare-bones essentials of theory and to stress primarily the applications. (See the opening pages of Part 2.)

Because I think instructors and students have a right to know what educational theory a textbook author is using, I venture to repeat some simple notes on learning theory from the preface to the first edition;

Clear focus on objectives what the student should learn and retain; see the Chapter Previews and new end-of-chapter summaries and lists of key concepts.

Student motivation cases and big and little applications throughout, to involve students and let them see how they can *use* what they are learning.

Learning retention through repeated explicit *use* of the concepts and principles.

Feedback suggestions for analysis of cases, at the end of the book, let students know how they are doing and provide help in applying the theory in the text to the cases.

Beyond these, the new edition again offers a package of up-to-the-minute teaching aides for both students and teachers:

Instructors Manual and Test Bank about 2,000 easy-to-grade objective and discussion questions; plus possible examinations and suggestions on how to use the text and the new cases in and out of class. It includes special cases for homework and examination use, in addition to those in the text. Free to instructors on adoption.

A lively new improved and updated student Workbook and Study Guide (by Michael Block and Henry Demmert), which includes a programmed review of every chapter, more objective questions, cases, and dozens of imaginative new problems and crossword puzzles, for all chapters. Answers are included for student self-grading and quick feedback.

Black and white transparency masters for all charts and major tables. Free to instructors on adoption.

My indebtedness to colleagues and friends for assistance on succeeding editions is so great that it is patently impossible to list all those who deserve credit. For this edition, however, my greatest debt is to Professor David Teece of Stanford for help and suggestions on a wide range of topics; I have acknowledged this help more formally on the title page. In addition, a number of economists at different institutions made especially helpful suggestions for improvements. I thank especially Kenneth Alexander (Michigan Technical University); Christopher Bach (U.S. Department of Commerce); Tom Bible (Oregon State); Michael Boskin (Stanford); Conrad Caligaris (Northeastern University); Richard Cooke (Cincinnati); Curtis Cramer (Wyoming); John Dahlquist (University of Alameda); Larry DeYoung (Cincinnati); Walter Falcon (Stanford); Deric Jennings (Tufts); Florence Jaffy (College of San Mateo); Allen Kelley (Duke); Bruce Kutnick (Northeastern University); Stewart Lee (Geneva College); Adolph Mark (DePaul); Gerald Meier (Stanford); William Moffat (Stanford); Phillip Saunders (Indiana); Gail and Michael Shields (Southern Illinois); Francis Shieh (Prince Georges Community College); Stanley Steinke (Community College of Philadelphia); Myra Strober (Stanford); and Arthur Welch (Joint Council on Economic Education). Professor Michael Lovell of Wesleyan University continues to share authorship of the mathematical appendixes. The usual warning that only I am responsible for the final outcome needs to be added, however, for I have accepted only some of the suggestions advanced. Lastly, my special thanks go to Colette Conboy of Prentice-Hall who has shepherded the book through the whole production process and helped in innumerable other ways; to David Hildebrand, Janet Schmid and Rita DeVries of Prentice-Hall for wise advice, design of the book, and editing the manuscript; to Deborah Nichols for infallibly good-natured secretarial help above and beyond the call of duty; and to Lynda Thoman for preparing the index and reviewing key chapters of the manuscript.

G. L. B.

Part 1

Some Foundations

NOTE: Some instructors may prefer to change the order of Chapters 1, 2, and 3. They are written to be usable in any order.

Scarcity, Private Wants, and National Priorities

CHAPTER 1

ow is it that we in America are, by and large well fed, well clothed, and well housed, while over two-thirds of the world's population is desperately poor—over 2 billion people living on per capita incomes of less than $30 per month? What explains the incomes we receive—$1 million for basketball star Bill Walton, $75,000 for a typical physician-surgeon, $30,000 for a master plumber, $3,000 for an itinerant fruitpicker? Why are we plagued by repeated inflations and unemployment? Why do we have air and water pollution, when almost everyone agrees that we need a cleaner environment? How can we have a better life for all, in the United States and in the rest of the world?

These are questions of economics, these and many others like them. There are no simple answers to most of the questions. But even though economics can't give simple answers to such complex questions, it can go a long way in helping you understand the economic world in which you live and the issues on which you will have to take positions and vote.

WHAT IS ECONOMICS?

Economics is the study of how the goods and services we want get produced, and how they are distributed among us. This part we call economic analysis. Economics is also the study of how we can make the system of production and distribution work better. This part we call economic policy. Economic analysis is the necessary foundation for sound economic policy, and this book is about both economic analysis and policy.

Another, slightly different, definition of economics, favored by many economists, is this: Economics is the study of how our scarce productive resources are used to satisfy human wants. This definition emphasizes two central points. First, productive resources are scarce, in the sense that we are not able to produce all of everything that everyone wants free; thus, we must "economize" our resources, or use them as efficiently as possible. Second, human wants, if not infinite, go so far beyond the ability of our productive resources to satisfy them all that we face a major problem in "economizing" those productive resources so as to satisfy the largest possible number of our wants. Indeed, most major economic problems arise from this fact of scarcity, and the need to make effective use of our resources to satisfy our wants. If there were plenty of everything for everyone to have without working or paying for it, there would be no economic problem. But, alas, this is not the state of the world, even in the affluent American society, and certainly not in the poorer nations that contain most of the world's people. Hence the title "Economics" for this field of study.

SCARCITY AND AFFLUENCE

The United States is an affluent society. We are rich by comparison with other nations. In 1978, the prodigiously productive American economy turned out over $2 trillion of goods and services, about 25 percent of the total production in the entire world, even though less than 6 percent of the world's people live in the United States. Table 1–1 shows per capita output of goods and services in the United States as compared with a dozen other nations. With several of the Western European democracies, we lead most other nations by a wide margin. Our lead over the so-called developing countries is enormous. (Such international comparisons are very rough, and the ranking depends on the measurement method used, but they suffice to suggest orders of magnitude. We will examine them in detail later.)

TABLE 1–1
World Output Per Capita, 1976*

United States	$7,900	Italy	$3,800
Canada	7,200	Brazil	2,300
Sweden	6,800	Mexico	2,000
France	6,100	Egypt	800
Germany	6,000	Kenya	500
Israel	5,000	India	400
Japan	4,900	Bangladesh	200

* Rough estimates, in 1976 U.S. dollars, by author, based on U.N.-sponsored study by I. Kravis and others, *Economic Journal*, June 1978. For estimates for more countries, for 1977, based on official exchange rates among the various national currencies, see Table 29–1, and the notes there on the roughness of such comparative estimates. Estimates in either table should be considered only order-of-magnitude figures.

In 1978, the median family income in the United States was about $17,200, half of all families received more and half less than this amount. (This is considerably less than output per family, because a large amount of total production goes into building factories, replacing worn-out productive machinery and housing, and the like that are not directly income to families. It is more than the average income per worker because many families include more than one worker.) But not all Americans are affluent. Figure 1–1 shows the distribution of income in America in 1978. About 12 percent of all families were classified as "poor" by official government statistics; a typical four-person family living in a city was considered poor if its income was $6,200 or less. By contrast, the average income of about half the world's population, about 2 billion people, was less than $200.

What did our huge gross national product of $2 trillion in 1978 include? We produced one-half billion loaves of bread and 160 billion passenger-miles of air travel; about $3 billion worth of books, $6 billion worth of frozen fruits and vegetables, $3 billion worth of toys and games, $180 billion worth of health services

(over $3,000 per family), and about $100 billion worth of educational services. The auto industry turned out about 11 million cars, bringing the total on the road to over 100 million. We built 2 million new housing units, and over 95 percent of all existing housing had inside plumbing, a rarity among the world's nations. The economy provided 96 million jobs, an increasing proportion of them in retail and wholesale trade, government, and other service occupations, in contrast to agriculture and manufacturing, which had earlier provided most of the nation's jobs. Figure 1–2 presents a summary picture of what has happened to the composition of jobs in the American economy over the past century; the total number of jobs over the same period has risen by over 500 percent, from about 18 million in 1869.

With all this productivity, the American economy has also produced some of the world's largest slums in our central cities, widespread air and water pollution that threatens our health and the natural beauty of the land, and wide discrepancies in the quality of education provided to students of different races and different locations. The average black family income was only 60 percent of that of whites, although blacks' incomes have risen more rapidly since World War II than those of whites, and young, well-adjusted blacks have almost caught up with comparable whites. Defense spending in 1978 totaled about $115 billion, enough to eliminate poverty and provide drastically improved housing and education for the American people if those resources could have been allocated to peaceful purposes.

Looking at these shortcomings, many Americans call for a redirection of our national priorities. They say we are using our resources for the wrong purposes. They call for less emphasis on the "quantity" of GNP and more on the "quality" of life. Some radicals in the "New Left" argue that modern American society is a mess, characterized by inequality of income and opportunity, alienation, capitalist imperialism internationally, and a topsy-turvy set of values. Although most Americans find these criticisms grossly overdrawn, many feel that we do need to reassess our national priorities, without giving up the demonstrated virtues of the American mixed-capitalist type of economy.

FIGURE 1–1

Family Incomes in 1978

The United States has a wide range of family incomes. Each bar represents one-fifth of all families. About two-thirds of all families had incomes in 1978 between $7,000 and $28,000. Half got more than $17,200, half less. (Source: U.S. Department of Commerce; preliminary estimates for 1978 by author.)

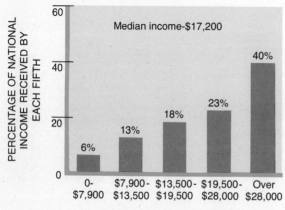

RANGE OF FAMILY INCOMES

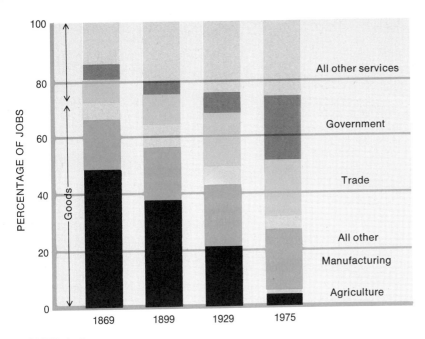

FIGURE 1–2
The Changing Pattern of Jobs
The past century has seen a dramatic change in the way Americans earn their livings. Less than 25 percent now work in manufacturing, nearly 70 percent in service industries. Note the decline in agriculture. (Sources: National Resources Committee and U.S. Department of Commerce.)

PROBLEMS OF THE 1980s

Looking to the new decade, the pollsters have asked many Americans what they think will be the main national problems of the 1980s. Although the answers depend in part on how the question is asked, a sampling of the polls shows results something like this:

1. Inflation
2. Maintaining peace—avoiding war
3. Crime and lawlessness
4. The high cost of health care, especially for the aged
5. Unemployment, especially for young minority groups in the cities—stimulation of economic growth and progress
6. Big government
7. The quality of life—environmental pollution
8. The problems of the cities
9. The power of big business and big labor
10. Poverty and inequality
11. The energy crisis

From a personal point of view, you might add, "Will I be able to get a job?" Economics is about your personal problems, the allocation of your resources and rewards to your actions, as well as about national problems and the use of resources at the national level.

It is clear that these problems range beyond economics. Maintaining peace, for example, is a complex problem, in which economics plays a role, but only one role among many. This is true of most of the problems listed—they are partly economic and partly non-economic. So it is with the world. It is very difficult to separate the economic from other forces at work. Crime and lawlessness provide another example. Surely the forces at work are sociological, political, and legal, but they are also economic (crime rates are highest in the city slums and ghettos).

5

Thus, economics turns up in almost every aspect of modern life, and we shall look at the economics of the problems listed above. But to see only the economic aspects of such problems can be seriously misleading. This is a book about economics, but we shall try to keep the economics in perspective. It is very definitely a book about political economy—about economic policy, which usually involves the political process as well.

WHAT ARE OUR NATIONAL GOALS?

What are our national goals? Are we producing the right things with our productive resources? Do we have our priorities straight?

Unless we have at least a rough idea of what we want the economy to achieve for us, it is impossible to judge meaningfully whether or not it is doing a satisfactory job, and how we might improve it. Moreover, since different people have different goals for the economy, it is particularly difficult in our individual-oriented system to agree on how well the economy is performing. Economists, focusing on the economic aspects of the system, often list a set of goals like these:

1. Progress—a rising average standard of living for the people
2. Production in accordance with individual (consumer) preferences
3. Equitable distribution of income and opportunities
4. Economic security—avoidance of economic fluctuations and inflation, and participation (a sense of belonging) in the system
5. Individual freedom

Other groups—for example, President Eisenhower's Commission on Goals for Americans, and the Department of Health, Education and Welfare's distinguished Task Force on Social Goals in the 1960s—have recommended quite different sets of national goals, putting more emphasis on non-economic factors. But in all, one central question is how much stress should be placed on improving the economic standard of living of the American people and how much on other priorities that are only partially economic—for example, social mobility, health, reducing alienation, and the like. More-

over, there may be conflicts between the goals listed—for example, between progress and security. In such cases, we can have more of one only by having less of the other. Further, words like "freedom" mean different things to different people. Setting out an agreed list of overriding national goals is a far more difficult task than it seems at first glance. Everyone is in favor of a better life. But just what that means is highly debatable when it hits our individual lives.

PERSONAL WANTS, NATIONAL GOALS, AND PRIORITIES

If nature somehow provided free everything each of us wants, there would be no need to economize—no need to choose among alternative uses of resources. But, alas, nature is niggardly. Affluent though we are by historical and comparative standards, our resources are far short of assuring that each of us can have all he wants without working for it. In this fundamental sense, our productive resources (often categorized as land, labor, and capital) are scarce—limited in relation to our wants. Given limited resources, we must choose what to have and what to forego, at both personal and national levels. We must establish priorities.

Consider housing, for example. Housing has become very expensive, and at the personal level, one of your biggest problems for the 1980s may be how to afford a house of your own. If you buy or rent a nice house, you may have painfully little income left for other purposes. At the national level, America still has vast slums. We might set as a national goal a modest $50,000 house for each family in the United States, a small and certainly not luxurious home. But to achieve merely this one national goal would require over $1 trillion worth of new housing—the equivalent of over thirty years of our total housing production at peak construction rates. To achieve this goal in only one year or in a few years is obviously impossible, even if we cut back dramatically our other goals.

Consider another goal that seems less far-fetched. One thing the typical American wants is lots of electricity. He has a passion for gadgets that freeze, defrost, mix, blend, toast, roast, iron, sew, wash, dry, open garage doors, trim hedges, entertain with sound and picture, heat his house in winter, and cool it in summer. Residential use of electricity has grown at nearly 10 percent per year, to which must be added the increases for industrial and commercial use. The whole north-eastern section of the country was shut down for hours in the great electric blackout of 1965, and temporary brownouts now threaten every summer in wide areas of the country.

To increase electric-generating capacity to meet these soaring demands will require huge outlays—resources that cannot then be used for something else. Unfortunately, moreover, electric generating plants can be unsightly and may pollute the air and water around them. Electric transmission lines cut great scars across the countryside. Nuclear and fossil-fuel plants occupy scenic sights along the rivers and shores because their condensers require huge amounts of cooling water. The growth in private demand for electricity alone will, by 1985, mean that an amount equal to one-sixth of all fresh flowing water in the United States will pass through, and be heated by, the condensers of generating plants. How many new plants shall we build? Actually, at a high enough cost, we can have both—all the electricity people want to buy, and clean air and water around the plants—but the resources diverted from other uses would be huge.

So it is with myriads of other things we want. Rich as this nation is, we can't have them all. We must choose. We face tradeoffs at every turn.

How Shall We Set Our Priorities?

The market. Many believe that the happiness and welfare of the individual are the primary ends of social policies. In day-to-day life, we register our personal priorities by what we buy in the markets—pizzas, automobiles, ballet tickets, haircuts. How much we spend on each is a measure of how badly each of us wants that good or service. In earning our incomes, if we prefer money to leisure we register our own priorities by taking jobs where the pay is high even though the hours are long. When markets add together these actions of over 200 million individuals in the United States today, markets are the priority-registering mechanism for most of our economic activity.

To go back to the examples at the beginning

of the chapter, who decided in 1978 that we should produce a half-billion loaves of bread? Answer: Millions of individual housewives voted with their dollars at their local groceries; and a complex list of farmers, truckers, bankers, and supermarkets, all actuated by the profit motive, cooperated to meet those demands. And so it is for most of the things we produce in our economy. Over three-fourths of all the goods and services are produced in response to private demands expressed through the marketplace. Less than a quarter is in response to spending by federal, state, and local governments. Thus, for the most part, our national economic priorities are set by millions of individual market preferences, not by some formal national-decision-voting process.

With over 200 million consumers, no one person has much individual market power over what gets produced. Indeed, one of the virtues of the market system is that each dollar spent counts as much as every other. The "common man" who has only a few dollars can still register his priorities by spending those dollars, and those priorities will be met by the market if the price he is willing to pay is higher than the cost of producing what he wants to buy—not precisely nor in every case, but by and large. Conversely, if consumers decide, for whatever reason, that they don't want to buy something—say, cigarettes—profits in the cigarette industry will fall, and fewer resources will be devoted to cigarette production. Thus, in the private sector of the economy, the market process automatically provides direct representation of majority and minority views. There is no formal ranking of national goals, no formal ranking of alternatives, but the result seems to many observers an impressively effective one in meeting individual priorities.

But these descriptions of the market process make it sound more effectively democratic than it is. In the marketplace, big corporations and big unions exert market power that sometimes overrides the wishes of consumers. The power of a billion-dollar corporation or a million-member union is constrained by competition in the market, but it is by no means eliminated. Advertising can sway and shape consumer preferences. Big business and big labor unions sometimes grab off for themselves more of the increase in consumer spending than is justified by the working of competitive markets. As we shall see, the market process doesn't work satisfactorily when big "externalities" exist—for example, where the production of some good (say, steel) involves social cost (dirt and smoke in the surrounding neighborhood) not included in economic costs paid by the producers and hence not included in the price of steel to consumers. Thus, the market process reflects individuals' priorities and wants only imperfectly. In such cases, people tend to turn to the government to enforce their priorities—a better deal for consumers, controls on big business and big labor, regulations to control pollution.

The political process. The other main approach to determining priorities is through the political process. We vote for representatives who will support those goals we consider most important. If your senator or representative votes to spend what you think is too much on national defense and not enough on urban reconstruction, you can vote for his opponent in the next election. You, plus 100 million or so other voters, hold the ultimate power to determine what the government should or should not do, how much of the national output shall be devoted to priorities determined through the government and how much left in private hands. For when the government taxes income away from us and uses the money to buy highways, education, and moon shots, it is in that way determining national priorities—theoretically reflecting the collective wishes of all citizens.

Once in a while, the president will establish a major national objective and mass support behind it—for example, President Kennedy's statement in 1961 that we would send a man to the moon before 1970. But mainly, the political process operates through adjustments at the margin—more for educational benefits next year, less for dams and highways, an increase in the income tax on high-income groups, a decrease on low-income groups. Unfortunately, it provides no simple process for reflecting minority votes on particular issues. You vote for Jones or Smith as your senator, and you have to take the bundle of preferences that is the winner, even though you like some and dislike others. If your senator and others vote for space exploration, you must pay your share of the taxes used, whether or not you approve—indeed, whether or not you even voted for the senator.

Similarly, governments, and the bureaucracies that often control them, also have a power of their own. They may be unresponsive to voter wishes, especially those of minorities. "The public" is vast but generally unorganized. The political process is *ad hoc,* pragmatic. Those who are most concerned over issues take steps to get their viewpoints across to Congress and the administration, and to state and local governments. Those who feel helpless or who don't care so much are apt to be silent. The net result is very uneven.

Which is better? Which way reflects our individual interests better? Clearly, neither the market nor the political process represents a neat, simple way of establishing and implementing our private and national priorities. Both the American economy and the American political system are pragmatic, adaptive mechanisms. With over 200 million people, they both disperse power widely among many individuals and groups—although in the eyes of some, not widely enough. In the market, Madison Avenue is said to have too much power to mold consumer preferences. In the political process, legislators and bureaucrats seem inadequately responsive to what the people want.

Many who support the market deny that it is meaningful to formally list "national goals" at all in a nation where individual freedom is the overriding goal. If individual freedom is dominant, the only meaningful national goals are those that arise out of the combined free actions of individuals acting in accord with their own wishes. But others reply that somehow this doesn't get a lot of the most important things done very well—rebuilding the cities, protecting the environment, eliminating poverty, and so on—and that we need to rely on government more.

In the following chapters, we shall examine these arguments carefully. But whichever alternative you prefer, remember that the fundamental problem is one of choice. Since we don't have enough resources to produce all of everything everyone wants, somehow we have to establish priorities as to what shall be done with our productive resources. The more efficiently we use them, the better off we will all be. This is the basic problem of "economizing."

OBJECTIVES OF THE BOOK

If you're going to spend several months or a year studying a book, you deserve to know what the author is trying to accomplish. Some of the flavor of this book has been given in the preceding pages, and Chapters 1–3 are largely devoted to providing this background. The book is a mixture of analysis and policy. Specifically, it has these objectives:

1. To provide an overview of the way our individualistic, largely private-enterprise but mixed economic system works.

2. To focus attention on the big problems faced by our economic system, and to arouse an interest in these problems that will last after you leave college. If your use of the concepts and theory in this book ends with the final exam, the book will have failed. Its real goal is to help you read the newspaper, argue understandingly with your neighbor, and vote intelligently on economic issues over the years ahead.

3. To provide a few fundamental analytical concepts and principles that will stick with you and help you in thinking about economic problems. You need an economic tool kit.

4. To help you develop an orderly, systematic way of thinking through economic problems—of applying the concepts and theories in your economic tool kit. There's nothing unique about straight thinking in economics. But straight, clear thinking anywhere takes some real mental discipline.

5. To provide enough descriptive material on the present economic system to give you a foundation for understanding what the problems are. Without understanding a problem in its whole setting, there's little chance of solving it effectively. And knowing the crucial facts is a first step. But the book takes the position that your main job is to learn how to think straight for yourself, not to cram your head full of facts. A mind cluttered with transient details seldom sees the major issues. And few things will be more obsolete ten years from now than many of today's facts. In any case, the evidence is clear that we don't remember most of the facts we memorize anyway. So learn the main outlines of the economic system and the facts you need to understand each problem that you study. But don't make a fetish of facts.

SOME SUGGESTIONS ON HOW TO USE THE BOOK

There are some tricks in using a book like this that may help you do a better job than just plowing through each assignment.

1. *Know where you're going before you start reading.* Before you start a chapter, look carefully at the "Preview" on the first page. Then skim through the chapter itself. Every chapter is organized so that the major headings mark off the main parts. These headings are designed to provide an outline of the chapter to help you keep the main points in focus. With this framework in mind, then study the chapter thoroughly.

2. *As you read, keep asking yourself, "What is the main point of this paragraph and of this section?"* Try to put the ideas in your own words. Some sections are largely descriptive. Some are full of tightly reasoned analysis, usually supplemented by an example of how the analysis might apply. It's important to remember that the analysis is the main point; don't let the example become the center of your attention, except as an example. To help you, main ideas are set in blue type so they will stand out. In addition, the old-fashioned device of underscoring main points in the text can help you in studying and reviewing throughout the book.

3. *Much of economics is cumulative.* So if you don't understand a paragraph or a section the first time you read it, don't kid yourself. Be sure you understand as you go along. Otherwise, as the course goes on, things are likely to get progressively foggier, not clearer.

4. *When you've finished reading, review to see what you've really learned.* The brief summary at the end of each chapter should help. A tough but useful test is to shut the book, put aside any notes you have taken, and then write down in a few sentences the fundamental points of the chapter. If you can do this, you've read the right way—concentrating on the fundamentals and using the rest of the chapter as a setting for understanding them. If it takes you more than a page, you may have read the chapter well, but you had better recheck to be sure you have the central points clearly in mind.

SUMMARY AND REVIEW

At the end of each chapter, you will find a brief summary of the main points in the chapter and a list of key concepts introduced in that chapter, to help you review the main ideas and concepts. But don't let these become a substitute for studying the chapter yourself. They are an aid, not a substitute for study.

1. Economics is the study of how the goods and services we want get produced, and how they are distributed among us (economic analysis). Economics is also the study of how we can make the system of production and distribution work better (economic policy).

2. Since productive resources are scarce relative to our wants, the central problem of economics is "economizing" our productive resources so as to satisfy the largest possible number of our wants.

3. Although America is rich in comparison to most of the rest of the world, we still face the central problem of economizing. Our productive resources fall far short of meeting all our wants.

4. In an individual-oriented society, national goals should reflect the wishes of individuals in that society. We rely mainly on two processes—the market and the political process—to reflect individual wishes and respond to them in using our resources. In the market process, individual preferences are indicated by the dollars consumers spend on different goods and services. In the political process, they are indicated by citizens' voting for representatives, who in turn make decisions as to what shall be done through the government. Both processes have strengths and weaknesses, but many economists believe that the market process provides stronger incentives and generally reflects minority views better.

New Concepts to Remember

scarcity
economize
national goals

personal wants
priorities

For Analysis and Discussion

Throughout the text, the end-of-chapter questions are designed as a basis for class and out-of-class analysis and discussion. They are "think" questions. Drill and self-test questions and problems, to test whether you understand the mechanics of the theory presented and its use, are available in Michael Block and Henry Demmert, *Workbook in Economics* (Englewood Cliffs, N.J.: Prentice-Hall, Inc., 1980), designed specifically for use with this text.

1. Do you believe the uses of our productive resources (bread, autos, and so on) in 1978, described at the beginning of the chapter, were optimal? Who decided these were the right things to produce? What should we have produced?
2. What is your list of major national goals?
3. Can you establish priorities among those goals? If so, what are they?
4. What are your personal economic priorities? Are they different from the national priorities you list? If so, why are they different?
5. How should we as a nation set our national goals and establish operational priorities among them? Who should determine the goals and priorities? Should we use the market or the political process?
6. Is it inconsistent to say that we are one of the world's wealthiest nations but that scarcity is still the fundamental economic problem we face?
7. Are you more likely to achieve your personal economic goals if we rely on the market or on the political process to establish our national priorities?

CASE 1

HOW MUCH FOR AUTO SAFETY?

In 1978, more than 50,000 persons were killed in automobile accidents. Over 2 million were injured. On the other hand, of the 200 million Americans who rode in autos that year, over 98 percent went through the year with no auto-accident injury. Until 1972, Americans were free to decide for themselves whether or not to invest in such auto passenger-safety equipment as seat belts, which had been available as optional equipment on new U.S.-made cars since the 1950s, and the vast majority decided not to. But in 1972, seat belts, padded dashboards and visors, and safety-glass windshields became mandatory equipment on all new cars; and soon, automatically inflatable air bags will also be required in all new cars unless Congress modifies its recent legislation. Together, all the required passenger-safety features have probably raised total cost, and hence the price, by perhaps $300–$400 per car. The new air bags will cost an additional $100–$200 per car.

Congressional action to require this safety equipment reflected widespread demands from consumer-safety advocates that Congress "do something to end this needless slaughter on the highways." Ralph Nader was a leading critic of the auto manufacturers, whom he accused of being concerned only with profits, not with the welfare of auto buyers. Opponents agreed that consumers should have the option of buying such safety equipment on their cars, but denied that the equipment should be mandatory. Consumer advocates' answer to this was that experience shows that many buyers would fail to specify the safety equipment, and the accident death toll would remain astronomical, whereas it could readily be reduced by adding more new safety equipment on all cars. The result was a congressional requirement that new-car buyers each year spend $3–$4 billion on seat belts, better bumpers, safety glass, and other safety features that, by the test of the pre-legislation market, most would not buy voluntarily. (New-car sales are about 10 million annually.)

Is the new auto-safety legislation desirable? Should Congress now decide for all new-car buyers that they must spend $1–$2 billion more annually for air bags to protect themselves against injury in possible auto accidents? Or should each citizen be free to decide for himself in the market how much he wants to spend to protect himself? Should this "national goal" be set by individual consumers in the marketplace, or by the political process?

A subsidiary question: Should the auto manufacturers voluntarily include air bags on all new cars as a matter of social responsibility, even though they are not required by law to do so?

Stop and analyze the issue for yourself before you go further. To help you, there are at the end of the book, for this and for each case, suggestions to help you with your analysis. But this case and all the others that follow are primarily designed to get you to use independently the concepts and principles in the chapter each follows. You will probably learn most if you work the cases through yourself, possibly in discussion with others, before you check your solution against the suggestions for analysis.

The Methods
of Economics:
Facts
and Theory

CHAPTER 2

Chapter 1 laid out some of the main problems of economics. We need now to examine briefly how economists go about analyzing economic problems and the economy. That is the purpose of this chapter.

STRAIGHT THINKING IN ECONOMICS

Straight, clear thinking is hard work. Few of us have acquired the careful, orderly mental habits and discipline demanded by such thinking.

For many people, straight thinking is especially difficult in economics. Not that economics is inherently more difficult or more complex than many other fields. But economics is so mixed up with our everyday lives that, without realizing it, most of us have accumulated a mass of opinions, ideas, hearsay, and half-truths that subtly dominate our minds when economic questions arise.

It's not surprising then that most people have views on economic questions. They are mentioned in the newspapers every day, and stressed in every election campaign. Moreover, the fact that economics is close to the pocketbook makes it especially hard to be objective. But merely living in the economic world doesn't make us experts on how the economy operates, any more than having teeth makes us experts on dental health and how to fill cavities. Few people consider themselves experts on bridge building just because they use a bridge every day driving to work, or on physics just because they live in the physical world. Yet many people somehow feel that anyone who has "met a payroll" is an expert on economics. Alas, it ain't necessarily so!

Economics as an Empirical Science

Modern economics is an empirical science; it is concerned with real-world data. Like other sciences, it has to develop theories about the complex world in which we live. But these theories, if they are to be useful, must rest on validated facts and relationships about the world they are analyzing.

The most apparent fact about economic reality is its complexity. There are millions of businesses, over 200 million consumers, hundreds of thousands of different products, multiple stages in the production of nearly every product. Faced with this overwhelming complexity, we obviously have to find some way of simplifying things to manageable proportions. Thus, the first job is to simplify.

Use of Simplified Models: Theory

In order to simplify, the economist, like other scientists, begins by developing an analytical framework, or model, of the reality he wants to analyze. This model focuses on the main elements and relationships he is studying. Such simplified models are often called "theories." They make no pretense of being accurate descriptions of the economy. If they were completely accurate, they would defeat their own purpose by getting back to all the detail. Instead, they are intended as simplified abstractions of the main elements of the reality to which they apply.

The notion of a model or theory can be illustrated by a non-economic example. Suppose you want to understand how a bicycle works—a theory of its operation. You could study every detail of a single bicycle, or of a large number of them, examining the tires, the handlebars, the sprocket, the paint, and so on. But if you could instead get a simple diagram, or a stripped-down working model of a bicycle, you'd get to the essentials quicker. This diagram wouldn't be concerned with all the details of paint, style, quality of steel, and so on. Instead, it would show the fundamental parts of the bicycle—wheels, frame, sprockets, driving chain, brake—and the basic relationships among these parts.[1] People have used such a model of a bicycle many times, and its predictions have been thoroughly validated by empirical evidence. The theory, or model, is thus a good one in that it helps us to understand the way a bicycle works and to predict the consequences of changing the main variables—for example, the sizes of the two sprocket wheels. The theory "works."

---

[1] In terms of basic physics, it might help to explain that the principles of mechanical advantage are used, with the pedal being a second-class lever and the relative sizes of the gear wheels being crucial in determining the speed and power resulting from any given foot pressure on the pedals.

So it is in economics. A model is a simplified diagram indicating the main elements in any situation, and the main interactions among these elements. The more firmly validated these relationships are by empirical observation of many cases, the safer we feel in using them in our model. Some models are very sketchy, merely identifying the main elements and loosely stating their interrelationships. Others are more elaborate.

An economic model may be stated as a diagram, and many graphs are used in the pages ahead. It may be stated in words, as in the bicycle case here. Or it may be stated in mathematical terms, but except for some simple algebra and geometry used in the diagrams, we shall use little mathematics.[2] Most economic models can be stated in any of these three ways.

Last, it is important to emphasize that the economist doesn't apologize for the fact that his theories don't describe the real world precisely. On the contrary, like any other scientist, he says that any theory is a skeleton, a framework, to help simplify the intricate complexity he is attempting to understand and predict.

"Other Things Equal" and "Equilibrium"

The real world is far too complex to analyze everything in it at once. Thus, in common with many other scientists, economists hold "other things equal" in their models in order to analyze the effects of one thing at a time.

In the chemistry laboratory, we hold "other things equal" through controlled experiments. We put two elements (say, hydrogen and oxygen) together in a test tube under controlled conditions, and get water if the proportions are 2 to 1. In the bicycle example above, we hold friction, gravity, air pressure, and various other factors constant as a first approximation (or assume them away altogether) in analyzing the way the bicycle works.

So it is in economics. One of the simplest and most fundamental theories in economics is that people will, other things equal, buy more of any good or service at a lower price than at a higher

one. If the price of T-bone steak goes up, consumers will buy less steak. Housewives will complain bitterly, blame the greedy butcher or farmer, and switch to lower-priced alternatives.

But note that this is a safe prediction only if other things are equal. Suppose at the same time you get a big raise. Then you may well buy *more* T-bones, even at the higher price. Or suppose the prices of pork, veal, and fish (substitutes for beef) all go up even more than steak. Again, you may buy more beef even at the higher price. Obviously, the "other things equal" assumption is critical. In the real world, other factors may not stay constant; but by assuming temporarily that they do, we can analytically isolate the effects of the higher price for steak.

This idea is closely related to the concept of equilibrium, which is also widely used by other scientists. In chemistry, for instance, after we've combined hydrogen and oxygen to form water, this equilibrium state is maintained until something disturbs it. In the same way, economists generally think of the economic system or parts of it as tending to move toward a new equilibrium whenever some disturbing change occurs. In talking about equilibrium, scientists are nearly always holding many other things constant to focus on the equilibrium of some part of the total system.

Consider a simple example. In economics, we generally theorize that people spend their incomes to get the greatest possible satisfaction from their expenditures. (Any other assumption obviously raises difficult questions as to why they don't switch to a satisfaction-maximizing spending pattern.) If people are allocating their incomes to maximize their satisfaction, given their incomes, we say they are "in equilibrium." Now, suppose the government cuts taxes, so everyone's after-tax income rises. Consumers will now be out of equilibrium. With larger spendable incomes, they will start spending more, and probably saving more as well, until their new spending pattern again maximizes their satisfactions, given their new higher incomes—that is, they adjust their spending and saving until they are again in equilibrium.

Another example: Suppose you are in equilibrium, buying four pizzas per week, and the price of pizzas goes up sharply. You are thrown out of equilibrium and will presumably cut back your weekly pizza consumption, substituting

---

[2]However, there is a set of special mathematical appendixes at the end of the book for students familiar with calculus. References are indicated in the chapters to which these appendixes apply.

some other, stable-priced goody to restore your equilibrium. By equilibrium, we mean a situation in which those involved are satisfied to keep on doing what they are doing. In equilibrium, there's nothing at work to change the economic behavior under consideration.

To repeat, "equilibrium" and "other things equal" are purely analytical concepts. No one believes that in the real world, "other things" do always stay equal when we are trying to analyze the behavior of the economy, or that economic units are always in equilibrium. Use of these concepts simply helps us to trace through what would happen if all "other things" in the economic system remained unchanged until the disturbance (for example, the higher price for steak) had fully worked itself out. But don't think that this makes economic analysis just an intellectual game. Such analysis can give us powerful conclusions as to the direction in which consumers, businesses, and the economy will move in response to different private or government actions, even if it can't tell us precisely what the end result will be in the complex real world.

Assumptions, Theory, and Facts in Economics

The social scientist, unfortunately, can seldom run controlled experiments to validate his theories. We can't get everything else in the economy to stand still while we lower income taxes 10 percent to see what would happen. Nor can we get reliable results by putting a sample of a few people in a closed room and lowering their income tax 10 percent.[3] So how can economists be sure their theories are right?

---

[3]Actually, economists have recently begun to run "controlled experiments" in a few cases. For example, a "negative income tax" has been proposed, whereby every family would be given a minimum annual income of, say, $4,200 to eliminate poverty, if it doesn't already earn that much. One theory was that this would lead recipients to give up working or looking for jobs; another was that the recipients would continue to work or seek jobs if unemployed. To test the conflicting theories, the government financed five three-year experiments for different groups in different areas. Which won? By and large, the theory that said people would go on working and looking for jobs even if they were assured a minimum $4,200 family income without working. But about 20 percent would not, and results varied for different groups of people and in different regions. The economists studying the results found that many variables played important roles, so there was no simple answer.

Suppose, for example, we theorize ("hypothesize") that the amount people spend on goods and services in any year will depend stably on the after-tax, or disposable, income they have in that year. We hypothesize that consumer spending is a "function of" disposable income—that consumer spending depends on, or is predictably related to, the disposable income consumers receive. Economists write this functional relationship:

$$C = f(DI)$$

where C stands for consumption, f for "a function of," and DI for disposable income. To say that C is a function of DI means that it depends on DI. Is this theory right?

There are two ways to answer. One is to examine the assumptions on which the theory rests and the internal logic that it builds on those assumptions. The other is to make a pragmatic test of how well the theory actually predicts in the real world.

In the first approach, we ask two questions: (1) Do the assumptions of the theory correspond to the reality to which it is being applied? (2) Is the internal reasoning of the theory logically correct? If both these conditions are met, the theory should be useful for explanation and prediction.

But there are problems. Most important, the world is so complex that it is hard to be sure that our assumptions are correct and that they are the relevant ones for our problem. Remember all those "other things" that are assumed constant in most theories. There is always the painful possibility that we are holding one of the really critical variables constant, and as a result are getting a misleading theory.

Suppose, for example, another group theorizes that, instead, changes in the amount of money in the economy determine changes in consumer spending—that is, that $C = f(M)$—and they report a close relationship between changes in the amount of money and consumer spending since World War II. The $C = f(DI)$ theory has left out the most important determinant of all, they say.

Many modern economists rely more on the second test—how well does the theory actually predict the final variable in which we are interested?—than on the accuracy of the assumptions.

So they might well say, How well does each theory predict?

Suppose we get records showing the disposable incomes and consumption spending of a large number of families over the past ten years. Looking at these records, we find that most families have spent 90–95 percent of their disposable incomes on consumption in most years, but there are many exceptions. For example, young families seem consistently to spend more, families in their fifties spend less, and retired families spend more. (These differences make sense: Young families are just starting out, buying new durable goods and raising babies, so they are able to save little; older families, once their homes are established and their children raised, find it easier to save out of their incomes; retired families have reduced incomes and must spend their past savings.) We also find that in years when incomes have risen rapidly, the percentage spent on consumption falls below 90. (Again, this seems reasonable, because it takes time for people to adjust their spending to new, higher incomes.) And so we might find other special forces at work. But overall, for the average of all families in periods of reasonably stable, prosperous times, consumption hovers around 92–94 percent of disposable income.

From this statistical analysis, we could certainly not safely predict the behavior of any particular family without knowing a lot about that family. But on the hypothetical evidence cited, we would be increasingly comfortable in using our theory to predict that, other things equal, in reasonably stable, prosperous periods, consumers as a group will spend about 93 percent of their disposable income on goods and services, given a reasonable amount of time to adjust to the new income.

Using Theories to Predict

This evidence, which doesn't even mention money, certainly casts doubt on our simple money-spending theory above. But the monetary evidence similarly casts doubt on our disposable-income-spending theory. Which one predicts spending better is a pragmatic test to apply in choosing between them. But if, as is true in the real world, neither predicts perfectly, it is clear that we need a more complete knowledge of the variables involved and their relationships for a satisfactory theory of what determines total spending. We must use both tests—how well does the theory predict, and how accurate are the underlying assumptions—to get a satisfactory theory in most real-world cases.

Both our theories above are oversimplified. But the example suggests the way in which we must go about building up empirical evidence on economic behavior to form and modify theories. Actually, as we shall see later, consumer behavior is more complex than either theory above suggests, and we need a more elaborate theory, incorporating both of them, to explain and predict spending satisfactorily. Indeed, even if we found that consumers, on the average, had always spent just 93 percent of their disposable income on consumption in the past, we still couldn't be sure they would do so in the future, because they might change their spending-saving patterns. But through intensive empirical analysis of consumer behavior in the past, combined with a theory that explains our observations, we can greatly increase our confidence in the predictions we make. And modern statistical techniques make it increasingly possible for us to use past information as a basis for predicting the future. Economics, like any other empirical science, must continually develop new theories, test them against the real world, and reformulate them in the light of empirical evidence.

Correlation and Causation

We can predict the movements of one variable if it moves consistently in relation to another variable whose movements we know. When two variables move closely together, we say they are closely correlated. For example, disposable income and consumption expenditure are highly correlated in the preceding example. This is shown graphically in Figure 2–2 (to look ahead). Each increase in disposable income is matched by about .9 as large an increase in consumption spending.[4]

---

[4]Modern statistics provide a "correlation coefficient" in such cases that gives a precise measure of the closeness of the relationship between the variables. For details, see the section on correlation and regression in any elementary statistics text.

Can we, therefore, safely infer that rising disposable income has caused the accompanying increases in consumer expenditure? The data certainly don't prove it. The close correlation between the two variables may reflect the fact that they are both determined by some third variable—for example, changes in the amount of money in the economy. Or suppose you observe a close correlation between the annual production of corn per acre in Iowa and Illinois. Does that prove that one caused the other? Obviously, not necessarily. Both may reflect changing weather conditions.[5] A high correlation between variables can help to strengthen our belief in any theory, but a high correlation alone cannot prove causation. Assuming that it can is one of the commonest fallacies in dealing with economic problems.

Facts and Fantasy in Economics: Some Examples

Robert Malthus, one of the first economists, saw economics as a dismal science. He predicted ("theorized") that population growth would persistently outrun the earth's capacity to feed it, so that man's standard of living would seldom rise much above the subsistence level. Malthus has proved to be spectacularly wrong in America and the Western world, but much more nearly right in many of the less-developed nations. Why did his theory largely square with the facts in some places, but turn out to be fantasy in others? Indeed, fantasy seems as common as fact in economics in the newspapers and everyday conversation. Consider some simple examples.

Even in rich America, between 10 and 15 percent of the population are "poor," with incomes below the government's officially established poverty level of about $6,200 (in 1978) for a four-person urban family. Clearly, it would be desirable to get rid of poverty. Fantasy: If Congress would only pass a law requiring that everybody receive a minimum wage of $3.50 an hour, poverty could be abolished in one fell swoop. Taking about 2,000 hours as a standard full-time annual job, this would provide each worker with an income of about $7,000 per year, above the poverty level. Fact: It sounds great, but it's in considerable part fantasy. Congress can pass such a law, but Congress cannot make businesses keep on hiring everyone who now has a job, much less hire others looking for jobs, at the $3.50 hourly wage, which is above the wage currently paid many workers. Indeed, we would predict quite the contrary from the theory that most businessmen are in business to try to make a profit. It would pay them to hire fewer, not more, workers at the higher wage per worker, and to substitute machinery for labor. Workers who kept their jobs at $3.50 per hour would indeed be above the poverty level, but unemployment would probably rise, other things equal. Moreover, of the approximately 24 million people living in poverty in the United States in 1978, some 60 percent were children, women with small children, elderly people, and others who could not take a job. Thus, even paying a minimum wage of $3.50 per hour to all workers looking for jobs would leave a large portion of the poverty problem unsolved.

Second example: Nowadays, just about everybody agrees that we need to clean up the environment—cleaner air and cleaner water. Fantasy: If only greedy, profit-seeking corporations would become socially minded and stop polluting the air and water, the problem would be solved. Fact: Alas, pollution is a complex problem. The government's Council on Environmental Quality estimates that for the current decade, it will take a minimum of $275 billion to clean up the environment enough to meet the minimum standards set by government requirements as of 1978. All corporation profits after taxes in 1978 were only about $100 billion, of which about half was paid out in dividends to stockholders. Total dividends paid by all businesses in the ten years ending in 1978 were only about $300 billion. Thus, it's clear that expecting "greedy" businesses to simply clean up all pollution runs up against some serious problems. For businesses to absorb all the costs would use nearly all the dividends that were paid to stockholders, and would put many firms out of business. There

---

[5]Modern statisticians use a technique called "multiple correlation analysis" to estimate how much of a change in one variable (e.g., consumer spending) is explained by each of *several* other variables (e.g., disposable income, inflation, and unemployment) that change simultaneously. But again, correlation does not prove causation; there may be still other variables implicitly being held constant that explain part of the changes in consumer spending.

is little reason to suppose that profit-seeking businesses will simply absorb pollution-control costs. On the contrary, they will mainly pass the costs on to consumers—that is, to all of us—which is where the main burden of cleaning up the environment is going to have to rest.

Moreover, businesses account for only a fraction of the total pollution in our system. Municipal sewage, primarily handled through government agencies, does more to pollute the waterways of our nation than do industrial firms. Farmers using fertilizers and pesticides on their crops, which help to produce low-cost food for all of us, did more to make Lake Erie a "dead lake" than did the businesses pouring waste into it, as the residues of the fertilizers ran off farmland into the lake. It's the old story. To get cleaner air and water, we will have more expensive food, steel, and automobiles, and we will have less of other things we would like. In economics, we are always having to choose between alternatives.

But sometimes the fact is a happy one when the fantasy is a false black cloud. Fantasy: A rising public debt means inevitable economic collapse and disaster, or at least inevitable runaway inflation. Fact: At the simple factual level, this fantasy has been persistently refuted for the last half century. The public debt has risen from less than $20 billion in the 1920s to over $800 billion today, yet the American standard of living has risen persistently over the half century. Total output is more than five times what it was in 1929, and per capita real income (that is, income adjusted for inflation) is about three times what it was in 1929. The number of Americans holding jobs has risen from 48 million to nearly 100 million over the same period. The growing national debt in the United States has been associated with rising total economic activity, and the debt today equals only one-third of total gross national product, proportionately much less than in 1929. Moreover, most of the government bonds are held by Americans, so, from the point of view of the public as a whole, the debt represents a transfer among Americans when we pay interest on it or when we pay off parts of it. In a growing economy, both private and public debt can grow at a pace with total jobs and production without causing severe economic problems. This is not to say that there are no difficulties with the rising national debt; there may be some

painful consequences. But it is to say, as in the other cases above, that the sweeping statements of doom here are fantasy, just as the sweeping statements of an easy road to a clean environment and the end of poverty are fantasy on the other side.

Conclusion: Economics is a field where it is easy to be led astray by the daily news and casual conversation. A major purpose of this book is to give you the analytical concepts and theories, as well as the facts, to see through a lot of the economic fantasies that you will encounter in the years ahead.

ECONOMICS IN A DEMOCRACY

Throughout your life, economics will play a major role in determining what you do and how happy you are doing it. If there are depressions or inflations, you will not be able to escape them. Your income will depend largely on how effectively you participate in the economic process. Thus, from a purely selfish point of view, it will pay you to understand how your economic system works.

The other main reason citizens in a democracy need to understand the economic system is that they are voters. A century ago, governments didn't interfere much in economic life, but that time has passed. Today, most people agree that the government should provide national defense, social security, education, and a score of other services not forthcoming through the private-enterprise economy; that it should regulate the supply of money; that it should protect consumers against the excesses of monopoly; that it should prevent depressions and inflations. Many people believe the government should do more—provide medical protection for the poor, support the prices of farm products, legislate minimum wages, even guarantee full employment.

This is a book on "political economy." It is concerned with using economic analysis to find answers to the problems above and to many more. The goal is to understand how our economy works now and how to make it work better. The political economist doesn't sit on the sidelines. He is interested in what to do about the big and little problems we face.

But if you expect to find the answers in this book to what you or the government should and should not do, you're in for a disappointment. The job of a course in economic analysis is to give you the tools and the background for making up your own mind on the important economic issues of the day, and to teach you *how* to think about economic problems—not to tell you *what* to think. Economics is a way of thinking, not a set of answers.

Better understanding of how the system works will go a long way toward making you a more intelligent citizen. But you should recognize from the outset that even with a thorough understanding of economics, not everyone will come out with the same answers on problems of public policy. This is because we have different ideas on where the nation ought to be headed. Some people, for example, think that avoiding inflation is the most important thing. Others believe that assuring everyone a reasonable minimum income should have first priority. Respectable economists may advise the government to do quite different things, depending on which of these objectives is placed first. Such conflicts among the goals of different individuals and groups are an inescapable part of today's economic problems.

SOME TOOLS OF ECONOMIC ANALYSIS

Theories, or models, are a main tool of economic analysis. Most theories consist of an interlinked series of functional relationships, as in the theory described above that aggregate consumer expenditure is a function of (depends on) consumer disposable income. A good theory has both a rationale, or reason, and empirical support. Since such functional relationships play such an im-

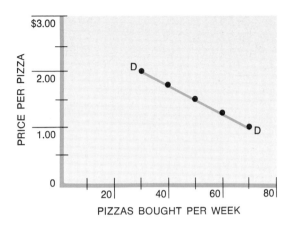

FIGURE 2–1
Weekly Demand for Pizzas
The dots and the curve connecting them show how many pizzas people will buy per week at different prices. They show the functional relationship between price and the quantity of pizzas bought.

portant role in modern economics, they bear a little further preliminary attention.

Functional Relationships and Graphs

If we want to show, or examine, a functional relationship between two variables, we customarily plot them against each other on a graph. Take a simple case first.

Suppose we want to show the functional relationship between the price of pizzas and how many will be bought in a week at your local pizza parlor; $d = f(p)$, where d is the demand for pizzas and p is the price per pizza. Other things equal (that is, incomes and prices of all other products remaining unchanged), we theorize that people will buy more pizzas at lower than at higher prices. Table 2–1 shows such a relationship. We can readily show this functional relationship on a graph, as in Figure 2–1, with price per pizza on the vertical axis and the number of pizzas bought on the horizontal one. The curve connecting the dots slopes down from northwest to southeast; we call it a demand curve, since it shows how many pizzas will be bought (demanded) at each price, *other things equal*. We can obviously read the same information in the table and the graph. The downward slope of the curve shows the functional relationship between the declining price and the increas-

TABLE 2–1
Weekly Demand for Pizzas at Local Pizza Parlor

PRICE PER PIZZA	NUMBER BOUGHT
$2.00	30
1.75	40
1.50	50
1.25	60
1.00	70

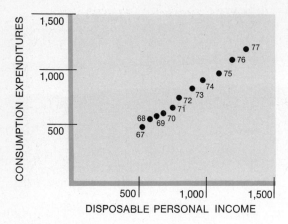

FIGURE 2–2
Relation between Disposable Income and
Consumption (billions of dollars)
The dot for each year shows the relationship between
the nation's disposable personal income and its
spending on consumption. The dots show a quite
stable functional relationship between the two during
the decade.

a satisfactory test of our theory; we cannot necessarily conclude that the rising disposable income was the cause of the rising consumer expenditure. All we know is that over these years, in fact, they rose very closely together, for whatever reason.

Note that these graphs of functional relationships are of two different sorts. Figure 2–1 is a hypothetical demand curve that shows how many pizzas *would be* bought *if* prices were as shown, other things equal. This is an analytical graph, to help us examine the relationship between the two variables. Figure 2–2, on the other hand, plots actual data that permit us to examine whether *in fact* the relationship between the two variables was as we theorized over the decade shown. Thus, we might say that Figure 2–1 is a statement of a theory, and Figure 2–2 is a test of whether the facts were consistent with the theory it states. Both purposes are perfectly legitimate, but it is important to be sure which is being used in any give instance.

Some Warnings on Historical Data and Charts

Economists use historical data and charts incessantly, as they should, for history is the basis of empirical support for, or rejection of, alternative theories. But historical data must be used with care. There is an old saying that one can prove anything with statistics, and the saying has an uncomfortable kernel of truth. By selecting the right historical series for the right sample of years, one can often seem to demonstrate results quite different from those supported by other related series for different years. For example, had we plotted the years 1929–49 in Figure 2–2 (including the Great Depression and World War II), the correlation between disposable income and consumer expenditure would have been far less close and stable. Or suppose we are interested in whether unemployment is becoming more or less volatile in recent years. Consider Figure 2–3, which shows two alternative presentations of the data for the *same* period, 1960–78. The left-hand section shows variations in the unemployment rate; it shows a substantial

ing number of pizzas bought, other things equal.

These data are hypothetical. If, however, we wanted to determine this functional relationship in the real world, we could try to get weekly sales data for our pizza parlor at different prices, other things equal, and see whether in fact the relationship is like the one shown in Figure 2–1. (Actually, such data might be hard to come by because of the difficulty of holding all other relevant things equal, so we might have to be content with a rough approximation.)

Figure 2–2 shows a different kind of functional relationship—that between the nation's disposable personal income and consumption expenditures for ten years, with disposable income on the horizontal axis and consumption expenditure on the vertical one. Each dot shows the relationship for one year, from 1967 through 1977. For example, the highest and furthest-right dot is for 1977, when DPI was $1,310 billion and consumption expenditure was $1,240 billion. The general relationship is clear; as DPI increased, consumer spending rose roughly in proportion. But note that we have not held other things equal over the ten years, so we don't have

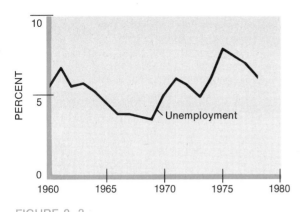
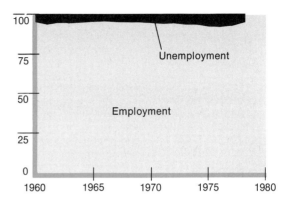

FIGURE 2–3
U.S. Employment, 1960–1978
Both halves of the figure show the same data. Note the different impression conveyed by the two ways of presenting the data; unemployment seems much larger and more volatile in the left-hand portion.

variation in the level of unemployment. But the right-hand section, which shows the percentage of the labor force employed, gives an impression of very little variation. Both halves depict the same economy during the same period. The trick comes in the vertical scale used to show the variations in unemployment; the left-hand portion shows only the unemployment data, so changes are large relative to the 0–10 scale used. The right-hand scale shows the entire labor force, so variations in unemployment look very small. And we could easily have made the unemploy-

ment variations seem even larger, by using a vertical scale for the left-hand portion that ran only from 10 percent down to 3 percent, rather than to zero. Try it for yourself and you'll see how different is the impression now given by the plotted unemployment series.

The purpose is not to warn you never to trust historical data; that would be foolish. But whenever you find historical data on charts used to demonstrate particular theories or arguments, it is a useful precaution to look carefully at the evidence to be sure it says what it seems to say.

SUMMARY AND REVIEW

1. To understand and predict the complex economy, economists use simplified models (theories), which show the main variables involved and the relationships among them.

2. In constructing and using these models to study the real world, economists, like other scientists, usually assume "other things equal" so as to isolate

the effects of the variables or changes being studied. This is analytically a substitute for studying particular changes under controlled conditions in laboratory sciences.

3. Also like other scientists, economists often study "equilibrium" conditions. Equilibrium is the position to which a system, or part of it, would move and

where it would stay if all "other things were equal." An example is a family spending its income so as to maximize the satisfaction it obtains from the expenditures.

4. Theories can be supported, or rejected, in two different ways: (a) by examining the assumptions on which the theory rests and the internal logic by which the conclusion is derived from the assumptions; (b) by examining how well the theory predicts actual behavior in the real world. Economists now tend to rely more on the second test. But unless the theory rests on plausible assumptions (for example, about the behavior of households and businessmen), it is subject to serious reservations, even though it has generally predicted well in the past. This is because the past predictions may have reflected other factors at work, and these may not recur.

5. No matter how valid it appears, no theory can give *sure* predictions of the future, because people may behave differently in the future. But the more consistently a theory has predicted well in the past, the more we can trust it for the future.

6. Close correlation between two variables does not necessarily show that one causes the other.

7. Use of well-validated theories can help you distinguish between "facts" and "fantasy" in day-to-day life.

8. Economics makes extensive use of graphs and charts. These may be very useful, but they can also be misleading if not read carefully.

New Concepts to Remember

theory (or model, or hypothesis)
empirical evidence
functional relationship

other things equal
equilibrium
correlation

For Analysis and Discussion

1. What is a "theory"? A "model"?
2. Why should we assume "other things equal" in economics when we know they aren't that way in the real world?
3. We suspect that ten-year-olds' demands for ice-cream cones depend on the temperature, their allowances, and the price of ice-cream cones. Can you write an equation showing the demand for cones (D_c) as a function of price in this case? How about demand as a function of temperature? What "other things" do you hold constant in each case? How might you go about determining the relative importance of the explanatory variables for ten-year-olds in a particular community?
4. Suppose you observe a close correlation between changes in union and non-union wages in your community. Can you safely conclude that one causes the other? Can you think of other variables that might be the cause of both?
5. According to the "laws" of probability, if you toss an unbiased penny 100 times, it will come down heads and tails about 50 times each. How does this compare with an economic "law"—for example, that, other things equal, people will buy less of any product at a higher price than at a lower price?
6. "Theory is all right for college professors, but not for me. I'm a practical man. Give me the facts and they'll speak for themselves." Do you agree or disagree with this sentiment? Why? How do facts speak for themselves?
7. *Based on the appendix to this chapter* Analyze the validity of the following statements. In each case, explain carefully why you accept or reject the statement.
   a. What goes up must come down. (True about prices?)
   b. Human beings are all different, so you can't generalize about them. Just look at any five of your friends.
   c. In the past, booms have always been followed by depressions, so we can look forward to a depression in the next few years.
   d. The way for farmers to get higher incomes is to raise larger crops. (Consider the position of the individual farmer and all farmers combined.)

APPENDIX   Some Common Fallacies

The preceding chapter has outlined the positive job of straight thinking in economics. But the buzzing, booming, confusing world of economics seems to produce controversy everywhere. This appendix is intended to suggest some of the common fallacies lying in wait for the unwary, in addition to the warnings in the chapter. Many of these fallacies, incidentally, show up everywhere you go, not merely in economics.

Wishing it were so. One of the most common of human frailties is to believe the things we want to believe. The boss believes his employee-education program is opening the worker's eyes to the necessity of large profits for continued prosperity—and he may be a surprised man the next time the wage contract comes up for renewal if he's just been wishing it were so. Remember the wishful thoughts on poverty and pollution control in the text above.

This is one of the most insidious fallacies. We tend to talk to people who agree with us, to read the newspaper that reports things the way we like, and to run away from information and conclusions that are painful to us. Confronted with two interpretations of an event, one favorable and the other unfavorable, most of us will choose the favorable one. The union members believe the company could pay lots higher wages if only it would. Top management believes that all right-thinking people see that management is right and labor wrong in most wage disputes. Just wishing it were so?

Post hoc, propter hoc. Suppose there's a bad depression. The government pays out large sums on public-works projects. Six months later, we're on the way up. Was the government spending the cause of the recovery?

Many people would say yes. The government spent, and recovery came. What could be clearer? But maybe the recovery was on its way anyhow, and the government spending did no good at all. The observed evidence tells us that government spending *may* have caused the recovery. But the mere fact that one event precedes another doesn't necessarily mean the first caused the second. They may both have been caused by some third factor. To assume that causation can be determined so simply is the fallacy of post hoc, propter hoc—"after this, therefore because of it."

Keep your ears open and notice how often people rely on this sort of reasoning, especially in discussing economic problems. (Note also that this is closely related to the correlation-causation trap warned against in the chapter.)

The fallacy of composition. Next, perhaps the most dangerous fallacy of all in economics—the fallacy of composition. Suppose one rancher increases his cattle production. He can reasonably expect that the increase will bring him more money when marketing time comes around. But suppose that *all* ranchers decide to raise more beef cattle this year. Will they get more money for the cattle in total? Quite possibly not. More cattle coming to market will, other things equal, push down the price of cattle. If prices fall a long way because of the increased production, the total revenue to all cattle farmers may be less for the larger output of cattle. Clearly, what is true for one rancher alone is not necessarily true for all ranchers taken together.

Consider another example. Saving is obviously a sensible procedure for most families. But suppose that in a depression, everyone decides to increase his savings. What this will mean, other things equal, is that everyone cuts down on his consumption expenditures. Unless someone spends more, merchants' sales will fall off. People may lose their jobs. Incomes fall, and with lower incomes, people may actually find they are able to save *less* than before.

There are examples elsewhere too. Suppose you're in a crowded hall and can't see the stage very well. So you stand on your chair and can see beautifully. But now suppose everyone else stands on his chair too. As a result, no one is better off. You can't conclude that what worked for you will work for the whole crowd.

To assume that what is true of one part will necessarily be true of the whole is the fallacy of composition. It may not seem reasonable that when we aggregate everybody together, everything may go topsy-turvy from the way it looked when we considered one person alone. But it does in economics, in a surprising number of cases. It's easy but fallacious to assume that what you know about the individual family or business is necessarily true for the whole economy.

Reasoning by analogy.   One of the most effective ways to explain something is to use an analogy. For example, in trying to explain the effect of continued repression on human behavior, you may say, "Not letting someone express his feelings is like building up steam in a boiler." This conveys a vivid impression; if those feelings aren't let out, the person is going to burst like an overheated boiler.

Is the analogy a useful means of communication, or a fallacy? It may be either, depending on how closely a human being with repressions actually corresponds to a steam boiler. It would be difficult to communicate without using analogies, but don't let them lead you farther than can be justified by careful analysis. Analogies are everywhere. For example, are big businessman in economic life robber barons?

Generalizing from small samples.   "I know that businessmen are greedy; my grocer is always trying to palm off wilted vegetables and overripe fruit, and look at the huge profits big businesses make." Or, "I know that dogs like bones, because I've seen lots of dogs and they all like bones!" Such statements are a favorite way of backing up your position that you "know for a fact."

To generalize about all businessmen or about all dogs on your personal small sample is extremely dangerous, unless you have some convincing reason to suppose that this tiny sample is representative of the whole universe of grocers or dogs. There is probably no commoner fallacy than that of generalizing unthinkingly from small samples. We are continually learning from what we see and do; this is the commonest way of extending our knowledge. Thus, we inevitably build up tentative generalizations about the world from our everyday experience. But anyone's limited experience may or may not be typical. The safest generalizations have been established by careful, systematic observation of a large number of cases. When is a fact a fact? The problem of empirical evidence again.

Black, or white, or gray.   There is another, related fallacy. If you are not wary, you can go astray by (explicitly or implicitly) assuming that there is no middle ground between two extremes. On a foggy day, someone asks, "Is it raining?" You reply, "No." "Oh," he retorts, "you mean it is sunny." But of course it may just be cloudy. Often there is a perfectly logical middle ground between what appear at first glance to be two mutually exclusive alternatives; the alternatives stated may not exhaust the possible situations. The wise observer of the economic scene is one who sees the grays in their proper shadings—not one who sees everything as black or white, true or false.

Private
Enterprise,
Government,
and the
Price System:
An Overview

CHAPTER 3

Our economic system is a mixed system, fundamentally capitalist and market-directed, but with a large amount of government intervention. The purpose of this chapter is to provide a brief overview of the way this largely private-enterprise, but mixed, system works—how its goals are set and how it uses our resources in responding to our many wants.

The chapter begins by presenting the foundations of production in any economic system and the fundamental problem of economizing. Then it briefly outlines the way our system solves four big problems that every economic system must face. It concludes with a look at the role of government in the system.

The purpose of the overview is to provide a road map for the more detailed chapters to come, so that you can see the forest while you are busy studying some of the trees of the economy.

THE FOUNDATIONS OF ECONOMIC PROGRESS

Our standard of living depends on the resources at our disposal and the effectiveness with which we use them. The United States is rich in natural resources—rich in produced resources, such as factories, houses, and machinery, and rich in human resources, the most important of all. We have the world's most advanced technology, and vast research expenditures generate a stream of new products and methods. The American businessman, continually watched over by the government and consumers, uses the economy's resources to produce an immense variety of goods and services. These resources and this technology are the foundations of the American standard of living—of our sweeping growth over the centuries.

In addition, we have developed a high degree of economic specialization and a complex exchange system. How many people do you depend on to get your everyday economic wants satisfied? You may say, not many. But think a minute. Who built the car you drove to school, or your shoes if you walked? Where did your breakfast come from? Suppose you go see a movie tonight, or watch TV. How many people

have had a hand in making this possible?

To produce all the things we want takes many people, each specializing in what he can do best. Charlie Chaplin immortalized the forlorn worker on the assembly line, day after day screwing his single bolt onto the cars as they went by. But specialization goes far deeper than this. The engineer who designs the plant is a specialist. So is the banker who lends money for its construction. So are the accountant who keeps the records and the secretary who does the typing. Only by dividing up tasks and developing highly specialized human skills and equipment can the economy obtain the benefits of "mass production."

But specialization and division of labor would be fruitless without a system for exchanging the goods and services produced by the specialists. The lawyer, the banker, the truck driver, the engineer—all would starve if the intricate system of exchange we take for granted didn't enable them to buy the food they need with the incomes they earn. Even the farmer, who may eat his own carrots and potatoes, would be in desperate straits if he were really cast on his own—without electricity, new clothing, gas for his car, mail delivery, and the thousand things he gets from other specialists. Every minute of our daily lives, we depend on the specialization and exchange all of us take for granted. None of us would dare specialize if we couldn't count on being able to exchange our services and products for the wide range of things we want.

(1) Productive resources, (2) technology, (3) specialization, and (4) exchange: These are the four foundations of the productive power of the American economy—and of every other highly developed modern economy, communist or capitalist. These basic factors make the difference between poverty and plenty. Many of the most common economic fallacies are rooted in the neglect of these simple truths.

THE NEED TO ECONOMIZE

As Chapter 1 emphasized, because resources are scarce relative to what we want from them, we must "economize" them. That is, we must choose among alternative uses of them to satisfy the largest possible share of human wants. This fact is the core of economics. It cannot be emphasized too much. The money you spend to buy a car can't buy a new stereo set too. It would be nice this afternoon to play golf, to go to the movies, to study, and to pick up some spare cash by working, but you can't do them all at the same time. If we use land for a shopping center, we can't use it for a school. The steel we use for autos, we can't use for refrigerators. If we use engineers to design missiles, they can't work on pollution-control devices. Economic life is a series of tradeoffs.

For the nation as a whole, the heavy hand of war points up vividly this fundamental dilemma of scarcity. In 1979, we spent $120 billion—about 5 percent of our total national production—on "national defense." If the government had merely left this money in the hands of taxpayers, on the average every American family would have had about $2,000 more to spend on clothes, housing, recreation, and the like.

Unemployment and Depression: An Exception?

Few deny the basic fact of economic scarcity in the world today. Yet in America and the other advanced Western capitalist economies, the newspaper headlines sometimes tell of millions unemployed, of auto factories idle because the public doesn't buy enough cars, of massive waste of men and machines because there isn't enough demand to buy the goods and services that could be produced with everyone at work. How can this be reconciled with the proposition that limited resources and scarcity are the basic economic problem?

Widespread unemployment of men and factories reflects a breakdown in our economic machinery. Resources are still limited relative to the vast unsatisfied human wants they might help to fulfill. People still want better houses, more food, more of almost everything. The unemployed want jobs. Businessmen want to increase production and give them jobs—if only they could sell their products. A million men involuntarily unemployed for a year means $10–$20 billion worth of potential output lost forever. In depression, we mistakenly and involuntarily allocate part of our scarce productive resources into unemployment and waste.

CHOOSING AMONG ALTERNATIVES

Economists are fond of illustrating the problem of economizing with an economy that must choose between guns and butter. These symbolize any competing groups of commodities for which we might use our resources. Robinson Crusoe and Friday had to choose each day whether to catch fish or search for fruits and nuts. We must choose between houses and missiles; $100 billion spent on national defense means $100 billion less of tractors, food, and education in a full-employment economy.

The Production-Possibilities Curve

Assume that our economy has a fixed stock of productive resources (land, labor, machines, and the like) and of technological knowledge about how to use these resources in producing the things we want. With these resources and this technological know-how, we can produce guns or butter—say, missiles or houses—or a combination of the two. To simplify, assume that only houses or missiles can be produced.

Table 3–1 shows the hypothetical range of possibilities open to us. If we use all our re-

TABLE 3–1
Production Possibilities for Houses and Missiles

ALTERNATIVES	HOUSES (in thousands)	MISSILES (in thousands)
1	1,000	0
2	800	15
3	600	28
4	400	38
5	200	45
6	0	50

sources to produce houses, we can build 1 million a year. Or if we use all our resources to produce missiles, we can have 50,000 missiles. In between, various combinations are possible—for example, 800,000 houses and 15,000 missiles, or 600,000 houses and 28,000 missiles, and so on. The point of this table is to show the production possibilities open to us. Of course, missiles and houses are arbitrary examples. We might have used highways and refrigerators, or any other pair of products, to illustrate the same point. The important thing to see is that there is a tradeoff between the two commodities. We can have more of one only by giving up some of the other.

It is convenient for many purposes to put the production-possibilities table in the form of a curve, or graph. This is done in Figure 3–1.

Economists use graphs a great deal, so it is important to understand how to read them. In Figure 3–1, we show thousands of houses along the horizontal axis, and thousands of missiles along the vertical axis. Each dot plots one of the production-possibility combinations from Table 3–1. For example, the top dot shows that we can

produce 50,000 missiles and no houses (alternative 6 in Table 3–1). The next dot shows we can produce 45,000 missiles and 200,000 houses, and so on for the other dots. The figure is merely a graphical representation of the table, with a curve connecting the dots.

Some Applications

The production-possibilities curve can help illuminate a variety of economic problems. Suppose that, perhaps because of a depression, the economy produces only 28,000 missiles and 400,000 houses, as shown by the dot labeled X to the left of the production-possibilities curve. This dot shows that the economy is not fully utilizing its productive capacity, as in fact happens during depressions. To operate at point X is clearly to waste productive resources. We could have had an additional 200,000 houses and the same number of missiles, or an additional 10,000 missiles and the same number of houses, if we had employed all our resources. Point X shows the economy operating inside the production-

FIGURE 3–1
Production-Possibilities Curve
The curve shows how many houses, how many missiles, or what combination of the two we could produce with our limited resources.

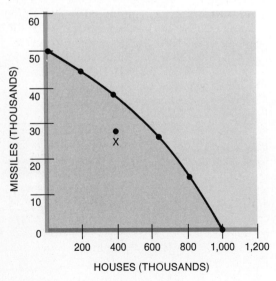

FIGURE 3–2
Economic Growth—
Production Possibilities Expand
If a nation's resources expand or its technology improves, its production-possibilities curve moves out to the right. This expansion of productive capacity is the essence of economic growth.

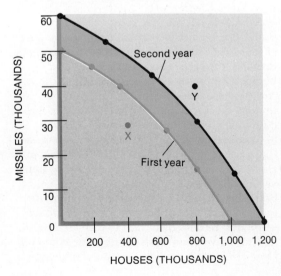

possibilities frontier. We are inside the frontier when for some reason we don't fully utilize our productive capacity.

Now suppose that immigration occurs, so that we have more workers than before, or that scientists improve technology so we can obtain more output from the same amount of resources. Then there will be a new production-possibilities curve to the right of the first-year curve. This is illustrated in Figure 3–2. The curve labeled "First year" is the same as in Figure 3–1. The curve labeled "Second year" is farther out, to the right. This new curve for the second year shows economic growth. The economy can now produce a larger total output—more houses and the same number of missiles, or vice versa, or a combination involving more of both.

Suppose the economy tries to produce 40,000 missiles and 800,000 houses (shown by point Y). Clearly, this is impossible. Production will fall short of one target or the other, or both. The economy cannot produce more than its production-possibilities curve permits.

COOPERATION AND COMPETITION IN A PRIVATE-ENTERPRISE ECONOMY

Let us focus first on the private, market-directed sector of the economy. How does it allocate our scarce production resources?

Consider New York City, teeming with 8 million people, crowded into a few square miles. As Bastiat, a famous economist, remarked about the Paris of a hundred years ago, here are millions of human beings who would all starve in a short time without a constant flow of provisions into the metropolis. One could hardly support himself for more than a few days without help from others. "Imagination is baffled," Bastiat wrote, "when it tries to appreciate the vast multiplicity of commodities which must enter tomorrow in order to preserve the inhabitants from falling prey to the convulsions of famine, rebellion, and pillage. Yet all sleep, and their slumbers are not disturbed for a single minute by the prospect of such a frightful catastrophe."

Every day, New York City gets hundreds of tons of meat, coal, oil, furniture. Every year, it gets millions of shirts, automobiles, rugs, nails, movies, and more other goods and services than you can think of. Yet no individual, business, or government agency plans it that way. The same is true, on a smaller scale, of every city and village throughout the country.

Man lives by cooperating with his fellow men. In all economics, there is no more basic truth. And in modern American economy, this cooperation is indescribably broad and complex. Yet this vast cooperative system, as a system, has not been consciously designed by man. No human director tells the 100 million workers in the United States where to work, what to do, or how to do it. On the contrary, each of the 100 million is motivated mainly by his own self-interest—to get the largest income he reasonably can and to get the most of what he wants by spending the money he earns. Yet somehow the system seems to organize itself, with a minimum of central planning or direction. Viewed from above, Adam Smith wrote 200 years ago, it is as if a beneficent invisible hand were guiding the competitive, private-enterprise system to allocate our scarce productive resources to produce the most of what we want at the lowest possible costs. Instead of chaos, somehow an extraordinary order comes from the competitive attempts of millions of citizens to look out for their own self-interests.

Man can organize, and indeed he has organized much. Tens of thousands of workers are employed in some large industrial plants. Often, many of these huge plants are joined together in a single organization. The General Motors Corporation, for example, spreads over the entire world, with more than 750,000 employees and annual sales of over $50 billion. But in spite of the immense power of such huge aggregations, each business concern plays a tiny part in the total picture of organizing economic resources to satisfy human wants in our $2-trillion economy. And in spite of the great expansion of government controls, the private-enterprise economy still does the bulk of the job in its long-established, unplanned way—in contrast to the central plans that control our biggest rival, the Soviet economy.

HOW A PRIVATE-ENTERPRISE SYSTEM SOLVES THE BASIC ECONOMIC PROBLEMS

Even though you may be swallowing hard on the "beneficent invisible hand," patience! We shall examine the problems in due course. It is useful first to summarize in a systematic although oversimplified way, continuing to disregard government intervention, how a private-enterprise system allocates resources to solve four basic economic problems.

How It Decides What to Produce

Under a private-enterprise, competitive, market-directed system, consumers determine what is produced. We register our preferences by the amount of money we spend on various goods and services. The more you want something, the more you will spend on it and the higher price you will be willing to pay for it. This is how the price system decides which are the most important goods and services to produce. You vote for more Levis each time you buy a pair. Economists call this "consumer sovereignty," since consumer demands basically determine what shall be produced.

But one point is vital. In order to count, consumer demands have to be backed up with dollars. The price mechanism is hard-boiled, impersonal. It produces Cadillacs for the affluent while many poor live in slums. Market demand reflects not necessarily how much consumers "need" goods and services, but how much they are willing and able to pay for them.

How It Gets the Goods Produced

The goods and services consumers want get produced by businessmen in search of profits. They will make the largest profits by producing things whose prices most exceed their costs of production. Profit-seeking businessmen thus have an incentive to produce more when consumer demand bids up the price of anything. They equally have an incentive to reduce their costs of production, because that too will increase their profits. In producing more, business-

men will offer more jobs in those industries, and workers will be pulled into producing the most-wanted goods because that is where they will be able to earn the largest incomes.

But alas for the businessman! If competition prevails, whenever he succeeds with a high-profit venture, those high profits will lure other profit seekers into the same industry. Thus, although he may temporarily make big profits by introducing a new product or reducing costs without cutting prices, profit-seeking rivals will soon arrive on the scene to increase output and force prices down to a level where they just cover costs and a normal profit. Why does the businessman keep trying if he knows competition will eat away his excess profits? Because many businessmen are optimists, and he may make handsome profits while he still leads his rivals.

Thus, the businessman is essentially a link between consumers and productive resources. His private goal is to make profits, but his social function is to organize productive activity in the most efficient (lowest-cost) way possible and to channel productive resources into industries where consumer demand is strongest. Profits are the mainspring of the system—the carrot in front of the profit seeker. And competition forces businessmen to produce efficiently and to sell at the lowest price that covers costs. In seeking profits within a competitive framework, the businessman performs a vital social function.

This point is so important that it merits an example. In 1945, Milton Reynolds produced the first ballpoint pen. Although it cost only 80 cents to produce, he retailed it for $12.50, presumably because he thought he'd maximize profits by doing so. Consumers loved it, and profits were large. He apparently made about $500,000 per month on an initial investment of only about $25,000. But although the new pen was patented, the huge profits led others to produce similar ballpoint pens. They found they could undercut Reynolds's price and still make a juicy profit—and they did. By the end of 1946, there were nearly 100 ballpoint-pen manufacturers, and retail prices were in the $3–$5 range. By 1948, ballpoint pens were everywhere and could be bought for less than 50 cents at most stores. Production costs had been reduced to 10–20 cents. Reynolds served an important social function in developing and introducing the ballpoint pen. He reaped a large reward—temporarily. Competition in the market soon made ballpoint pens available to everyone at a much lower price than Reynolds charged, partly because the competition eliminated much of the special profits on the new product and partly because costs were rapidly reduced under the pressure of competition. Adam Smith's "invisible hand" is easy to see in the ballpoint-pen case. No government plan was needed to get the job done.

Another example: Only a few years ago, Hewlett-Packard, a medium-sized electronics firm, developed and put the first pocket-size calculators on the market. The first market was engineers, who had previously had to do their calculations by slide rule or office-based computers; the cost was from $300 to $800 per calculator. Hewlett-Packard made a pleasing profit on its innovation. But the technological key to the small calculator was the silicon semiconductor, basically developed by Texas Instruments Company, and in a matter of months, Texas Instruments had its hand-held calculator on the market—at a lower price than Hewlett-Packard's. With basic computer technology exploding and semiconductor prices falling rapidly, small, lesser-known firms soon jumped into the market; and five years after H-P's first models, department stores were flooded with simple hand-held calculators for under $100. A few years later, $39.50 models were commonplace, slide rules had vanished from campuses, and making a profit had become a difficult task indeed for the dozens of domestic and Japanese firms pursuing the consumer's small-calculator dollars. In the meantime, H-P and Texas Instruments, the leaders, stressed quality, rapid improvements, and more complex calculators, still selling mainly in the over-$100 market. They continued to show very pleasing profits, while several of the smaller newcomers gave up the battle when red ink replaced the elusive profits. The higher-priced segment of the market is now dominated by H-P and Texas Instruments, with the lower-priced sectors increasingly Japanese and bitterly competitive. In the case of pocket calculators, the invisible hand worked again, but with more painful consequences for many profit-seeking competitors.

How It Distributes Products

Who gets the goods that are produced? The market system allocates them to consumers who have the desire and the income to buy them. There are two steps in this process.

The first is the distribution of money incomes. We earn our incomes primarily by working for businessmen, helping to produce the goods and services consumers want. The prices we get for our services depend on how much we are worth to the businesses we work for, in helping to produce what consumers will pay for. Competition forces the businessman to pay each of us about what he contributes to the sales value of what he helps produce. The incomes we receive in this way largely determine what we can afford to buy.

The second step is the distribution of goods and services to those with money income to pay for them. Each consumer will pay a price that measures how important the product is to him. The price of each commodity is bid up by competition among consumers until the buyers least able and willing to pay for it are eliminated, and the supply goes to those with the strongest demand for it. This does not necessarily mean that low-income buyers are eliminated completely. Often it means that they can afford only a few units at the price established, while higher-income groups can afford more. Poor people buy steaks, but not many. In other cases, such as mink coats and Mercedes-Benzes, most poor are eliminated from the market. Here again, prices play a vital role; they ration final products among consumers on the basis of who will pay most for each product. Those unwilling to pay at least the full cost of producing any commodity will get none in the long run.

How It Decides between the Present and Future Economic Growth

We can use our productive resources either for current consumption or for capital accumulation. By building new factories and other productive facilities (that is, by accumulating capital), we can shift the economy's production-possibilities curve out. In the same way, we can send our children to school rather than putting them directly to work, thereby investing in "human capital" and increasing the nation's future productive potential at the cost of lower present output. Here again, the private-enterprise system largely depends on the self-interest-dominated decisions of consumers and profit seekers to allocate resources between present and future.

In money terms, to grow we must save some of our incomes and invest some in building new factories and the like, rather than spending everything on consumption. In our individualistic economy, each person and each businessman decides how much of his income to save. If these savings are a large proportion of our total income, investment in factories and people (that is, capital accumulation) can be large relative to current consumption and the economy will grow rapidly. If we save only a small proportion of our total income and investment is correspondingly small, the growth in productive capacity will be slow.

Solving All the Problems Simultaneously

These four decisions are not made separately. The economic system is a huge, interconnected set of markets, each with many buyers and sellers. All four decisions are simultaneously the outcome of millions of free, individual choices by people largely concerned with their own private welfare. How all these complex decisions are simultaneously and continuously made and how they interact in our economic system is the core of the study of economics.[1]

The Organizers: Self-Interest and Competition

The essence of the private-enterprise, market-directed economy is this: In pursuing their own self-interests, individuals unintentionally do more to advance the social good than if that

---

[1]In mathematical terms, it may be helpful to think of all these interdependent markets and decisions as a large system of simultaneous equations. In fact, one of the first clear perceptions of the entire process was by Leon Walras, one of the first mathematical economists, who saw it just that way about a century ago.

had been their primary interest. Self-interest is a powerful incentive for consumers, laborers, businessmen. Indeed, it might well lead to chaos if it were not constrained and directed to the common good by the force of competition, which Adam Smith properly stressed as essential to the working of the "invisible hand." But with competition, Smith and his followers argue, in a private-enterprise economy absence of government planning and control does not mean chaos, but rather order in an economy so complex few human minds can comprehend it—and so complex that government planners, however well-intentioned, are likely to produce chaos rather than order.

Suppose, for example, that instead of relying on self-interest and the market, you were made Grand Economic Planner for the nation. How, for example, if you did not rely on Milton Reynolds and his competitors, would you decide how many ballpoint pens to produce? How many cars, in what sizes, colors, and makes? How many airplanes? Would you run a consumer poll on each, gathering some 200 million preferences per commodity? How would you decide how each good was to be produced, and who should work at what in the economy? To whom would you allocate the dirty jobs of mining coal and collecting garbage, and to whom the pleasant ones of managing and teaching in universities—and how would you assure adequate incentives and rewards for each? How many air conditioners would you produce, and who would get them? To suggest some of the more difficult problems, how would you plan for the machine tools, labor, and raw materials needed to produce the factory equipment and computers that in turn are needed to produce the right number of such final products as refrigerators, gasoline, and women's dresses? If you trace back the decisions needed to plan completely the production and assembly of all the parts that go into a modern jetliner, you quickly get up into the millions of separate decisions.

It is important to recognize that "self-interest" may include much more than just maximizing one's money income. I may prefer the air-conditioned comfort of a bank clerk's job to earning much more as a plumber. Or I may prefer to work as a Peace Corps volunteer at a low wage to earning much more as an auto salesman. Or I may prefer lots of leisure to a full-time job. If so, my self-interest is maximized by working in the bank, joining the Peace Corps, or taking only part-time jobs. If I am a businessman, I may get much satisfaction from producing only top-quality products, providing good working conditions in my plant, and eliminating polluting smoke from the factory stack. And I may feel that *in the long run,* profits will be maximized if I act as a good citizen in dealing with employees, customers, and neighbors, rather than squeezing out every dollar of profits I can get now. The self-interest argument does not necessarily imply that only money income and current profits serve to motivate us. Be careful not to construe self-interest too narrowly.

The Incredible American Economy

Understanding how a market-directed economy solves the basic economic problems is a number one task in studying economics. But this is a lesson that must not be overlearned. We can understand and admire the way the private-enterprise, market-directed system ticks on year after year, impersonally solving its millions of intertwined problems, and still not shut our eyes to its failings. For failings there are—drastic ones, some people think. The invisible hand must have slipped up, they say, to produce depressions and inflation, all that smog outside the window, filthy streets, and decaying slums.

It's easy to find things wrong with a largely private-enterprise, "unplanned" economy like ours. The preceding paragraphs present a drastically oversimplified picture of reality. Today's world is different from that of Adam Smith, and a lot of people feel that Smith was way too optimistic, that any market-type economy will fall short on many scores. In particular, they cite modern technology and the huge corporations apparently now needed to obtain low-cost production. How are these consistent with Adam Smith's competition? But thoughtful observers, even including such critics as Karl Marx, have long been impressed by its remarkable efficiency in producing the infinite variety of goods and services consumers want. And don't be too quick to write off competition, even among the giants.

Only one of the nation's ten largest corporations in 1900 is still on the list. General Motors, Ford, and IBM didn't even exist then. International Mercantile Marine and Central Leather Company, numbers 4 and 7, are long since departed. (For the data, look ahead to Table 15–2.) And even if a firm doesn't have much direct competition, potential substitutes always lurk just around the corner—aluminum for steel, semiconductors for vacuum tubes.

THE IMPORTANT ROLE OF GOVERNMENT

We have left government out of this overview so far. But it is time now to turn to the important role government plays in the modern American economy. There are a lot of doubters about that "invisible hand." A little history can help provide perspective.

The British, French, and American revolutions that gave us political democracy provided the ideological framework for economic individualism. Political democracy and modern private-enterprise economics arose in the same historical setting, part of the same broad sweep of history. Individual freedom and self-interest were at the core of this revolution of the eighteenth and nineteenth centuries: In politics, everyone should be free to vote as he pleased—to look out for his own interests at the ballot box. In economic life, everyone should be free to seek his own self-interest—to work where he wished, and to spend his money on whatever he wanted most. Self-interest and individual initiative were the driving forces for the common good. The ballot box in politics and the market in economics were the ultimate, impartial arbiters of differences of opinion.

This philosophy assigned to government only a small role. The less government interfered with individual freedom, the better. This was the "laissez-faire" philosophy of the nineteenth century. To be sure, individualism never went so far as to exclude government intervention altogether. True freedom necessarily involves some restrictions on freedom. A society that gave you freedom to murder your neighbor when you felt like it would be anarchy.

So it was in the economic sphere. Clearly, the government needed to establish and enforce a few "rules of the game." One basic rule was that no one should be deprived of life, liberty, or property without due process of law. Others were rules against fraud and against default on contracts. But the rules should be simple, and government had little business in economic life outside these rules.

As time passed, mass production and the modern corporation swept away the possibility of an economy of tiny, highly competitive firms. Powerful unions replaced the individual worker in bargaining with big business. Concentration of economic power and reliance on group activity spread. Many new products brought objectionable side effects, such as smoke from factory chimneys and polluted rivers.

Moreover, with a wealthier, more complex society, people wanted more things that couldn't be readily provided through private profit incentive in the marketplace—highways, space shots, and the like. Thus, besides setting the rules of the private-enterprise game, governments were called on to do more and more things directly. At the same time, common concern grew for the individual who couldn't take care of himself. Government "welfare" and social security largely replaced private poor relief. Willingness to abide by the impersonal income allocations of the market diminished. Desire to "do something" about booms and depressions became widespread. A subtle shift in the meaning attached to the words "individual freedom" marked the changing tenor of the times. The rules of the game have grown into an intricate mass of law and administrative controls. The government has become a major participant as well as the umpire in the economic game.

The Mixed Economy

Today, ours is a mixed economy—still basically private-enterprise, but with large areas of government control and direct participation. It's up to you to decide whether you like what's been going on—whether you want to move back toward the traditional private-enterprise system, or on toward a more administered, planned economy, or in some other direction.

This is no ivory-tower, academic issue, dreamed up for college classrooms. It is a basic issue of public economic policy today. Clearly, the government must step in to provide national defense, but how about slum clearance and public housing? How heavily should government tax upper-income families to guarantee minimum incomes for all, whether they work or not? Nearly everyone agrees that the government should act to minimize inflationary booms and depressions, but how far should it regulate private decisions on wages and prices in the process? These are big national policy issues of the 1980s. You will have to answer them if you are to vote intelligently. The issue of how much private enterprise, how much government, is everywhere.

CAPITALISM TODAY

"Capitalism" is a term often used but less often defined carefully. Words so used often generate more heat than light, and over the years, "capitalism" has become a fighting word for many who advocate or oppose it. Recourse to dictionaries and learned treatises of economists and historians unfortunately does not resolve the dilemma of just what we should mean when we say "capitalism," for these authorities don't agree.

So this book generally uses such less colorful but more descriptive terms as the "private-enterprise" and "market-directed" system in referring to the big private sector of the modern American economy. Still, a brief note on "capitalism" may be useful. Most writers agree that a capitalist economy is marked by at least these major characteristics:

1. Private ownership of property prevails.
2. Property has been accumulated by individuals and businesses, and this accumulated "capital" provides incomes to its owners.
3. Individuals and businesses are free to seek their own economic gain; the profit motive plays a central role; and resources are mainly allocated through the market.
4. Some writers add to this list a highly developed banking and credit system.

This list gives the basic flavor of such a system. But the lines are hazy. How free must individuals be to own and use property if a system is to be termed "capitalism"? Is an income tax that takes away part of your income each year, depending on how much you earn, consistent with capitalism?

We shall be concerned with all these questions and others like them. But there is little to be gained by debating just which measures are and which are not consistent with "capitalism" when the answer often hinges on just how the term is defined. Instead, we will concentrate on trying to decide whether particular policy measures are good or bad on their merits, taking into account the different social goals held by different groups in America today. Don't let your emotional attachment or antagonism toward the term "capitalism" get in the way of your thinking objectively about the issues.

ALTERNATIVE SYSTEMS

Obviously, not everyone agrees that a private-enterprise, market-directed economy is the best. Indeed, in two nations alone, China and the USSR, over 1.2 billion people live in communist economies, with government ownership of productive resources and central planning and control of economic activity. Thus, a centrally planned, "command" economy, with the major choices made by the central government, appears the main practical alternative to the private-enterprise, market-directed economies of most Western industrial democracies.

There are two other alternatives for small, nonindustrial economies. They may make their decisions and organize their activities on the basis of custom, or tradition. Many of the early American Indian tribes used this basis; some African tribes still do. Or a very small, nonindustrial economy might make its decisions in true democratic, "community" style, with everyone participating. This is the model suggested by some young people who want to opt out of our modern complex industrial society. But neither offers a feasible alternative for organizing a huge, immensely complex economy like ours.

The following chapters analyze mainly the American economy and the problems it faces. But throughout, comparisons with more centrally planned, "command" systems are suggested. And in the final chapter, we shall undertake a full-fledged comparison of the way these different systems operate as a practical matter, to place the American system, its achievements, and its shortcomings in perspective.

SUMMARY AND REVIEW

1. Productive resources, technology, specialization, and exchange are the four foundations of the productive power of every modern economy.

2. The productive capacity of even the affluent American economy is not adequate to give everyone all he wants of everything. Thus, economic life is a series of tradeoffs; to have more of something, we must take less of something else.

3. In depressions, we unintentionally allocate resources to waste and idleness rather than to producing wanted goods and services.

4. The production-possibilities curve is a convenient way of illustrating graphically the choice between different combinations of products in using our productive capacity.

5. Every economy must solve four basic economic problems:

    a. What shall it produce?

    b. How shall it use its productive resources to get maximum output of the goods and services it produces?

c. How shall it distribute those goods and services among the people?

d. How shall it decide between present and future economic growth?

6. The American basically market-directed, private-enterprise economy relies primarily on activities of individuals looking out for their own self-interests and on competitive markets to provide most of these answers.

7. In the last two centuries, government has intervened substantially in this process, and we now have a mixed economy—still mainly private-enterprise, but with large areas of government control and direct participation. How much of our economy shall be private, how much public, is a basic issue of public policy today.

8. "Capitalism" (with extensive private ownership of property and primary reliance on the market to make the big economic decisions) competes primarily with "communism" (with government ownership of property and central planning and control) as the best way to organize modern large, complex economies.

New Concepts to Remember

productive resources
technology
specialization
exchange
scarcity
economizing
production-possibilities
  curve

production-possibilities
  frontier
tradeoffs
private-enterprise economy
market-directed system
economic growth
laissez-faire
capitalism

For Analysis and Discussion

1. Does this chapter help explain the wide differences in per capita outputs shown in Table 1–1? Explain how.

2. "Man lives by cooperating with his fellow men. In all economics, there is no more fundamental truth than this." "The core of the competitive, free-market system is the driving urge of most men to get ahead, to rise above their fellow men."

   Are these two statements about the American economic system consistent or contradictory? If they are consistent, how do you reconcile their apparent contradiction?

3. The price system allocates resources where consumers spend their dollars. Thus, the rich person has more influence than the poor person. Is this consistent with the democratic presumption that "all men are equal"?

4. In a market-directed system, who decides how many jobs there will be in each industry? Who should make the decision?

5. Do you believe that most businesses are efficient in producing the goods and services they sell? Is your presumption different for large and small businesses? Why?

6. "The economics of scarcity is obsolete in our affluent society. There's plenty for everybody." True or false? Define "scarcity," "plenty," and "everybody" in answering. Do we still face the need to economize?

7. Suppose American college students were to develop a craze for pork-chop sandwiches, instead of hamburgers. Trace through as carefully as you can the impact of this craze on the allocation of the economy's productive resources. Would such a shift be good or bad?

8. Leading TV stars receive annual salaries in the millions of dollars. Many baseball players receive $50,000 to $150,000 for the eight-month season. Yet an intelligent, skilled, hardworking nurse or auto mechanic will ordinarily earn no more than $15,000 or $20,000 a year, if that.

   a. Are such differences predictable results of the free-market system, or do they reflect breakdowns in the functioning of the system?

   b. Do you approve of such inequalities in the distribution of income? Why, or why not?

CASE 2

CAMPUS PARKING

Good parking spaces on the Stanford campus, as on most campuses, are at a premium, especially on rainy days. Stanford has about 11,000 students—of whom about half live on campus—about 1,000 faculty, and perhaps 8,000 nonteaching "staff members" and other such employees. Sampling suggests that perhaps 8,000–10,000 drivers may seek parking on a rainy day.

While there is no simple way to indicate the number of desirable parking spaces available (desirability depends on where one wishes to go on the campus), there are perhaps 1,500–2,000 spaces that are very convenient to different parts of the central campus. Including all outlying areas of the campus (perhaps 3–5 blocks from classrooms and offices), there are a large number of additional parking spaces available.

For many years, by tradition the best parking spaces were exclusively set aside for faculty members (via free "A" parking stickers), and the next most desirable ones for staff members (via free "B" stickers). Other reasonably close-in spaces were allocated to students at a small charge ("C" stickers). Distant campus parking was free to all. Some special parking was provided for physically disabled persons.

Not surprisingly, students frequently complained, as indeed did faculty and staff from time to time, since on rainy days there was an excess of cars for all three reserved parking areas. (1) Some argued that reserved areas should be eliminated and that all parking should be on a first-come, first-served basis, except for the physically handicapped. (2) Others contended that the existing faculty-staff preference system was basically satisfactory, but that spaces should be allocated within each of the three reserved areas on the basis of need, so that people living close to the campus, who do not really need the spots, would not get them in preference to those who live further away and need them more. (3) Another group favored using the price system. They would maintain three classes of parking areas but eliminate all faculty-staff-student preferences. Stickers for each of the areas would be sold to anyone who wanted to buy them. Each price would roughly equate the number of stickers bought with the number of spaces available in that class. Thus, those who would pay the most would get the "A" spaces in the most desirable areas at the highest price; those who paid less would take the "B" places; those who paid still less would buy "C" stickers; and those unwilling to pay at all would use the outlying areas. There would be a liberal sprinkling of metered areas on the campus for those who wanted to buy short-term parking. (4) Still others argued that none of these approaches was obviously superior, and that in accordance with democracy, students, faculty, and staff should all elect a special parking committee to say who should get the spaces each year.

How should Stanford allocate the limited supply of desirable parking spaces?

Consumers
and Market
Demand

CHAPTER 4

y and large, businesses can make profits only by producing goods and services that people want to buy—autos, houses, dry cleaning, air travel, dog food. If there is no consumer who is willing and able to buy, the businessman is out of luck. Maybe the government will temporarily come to his rescue with a subsidy, or maybe he can keep going by using up his own invested capital. But over the long pull, it is customers who are willing and able to buy who direct production in a private-enterprise economy.

THE SOVEREIGN CONSUMER?

Consumers direct production by the way they spend their money. If consumers demand portable TVs, businesses will produce portable TVs. If consumers want to rent cars at airports, the rent-a-car agencies will prosper there. If consumers develop a taste for artichokes, enterprising farmers will soon be raising artichokes to gain a profit by meeting that demand.

Consumer demand is the mainspring of economic activity. But never forget—it is the consumer with money to spend who counts! Many of us would like to have a Porsche, and filet mignon for dinner. But unless we have the money and are willing to spend it on these objects, our desires have little significance for auto producers or the local supermarket.

Thus, your "vote" on what gets produced in a private-enterprise economy is largely determined by your income, unless you have accumulated funds to supplement your income. The factory worker has less influence than the rich person, even though the former may be a virtuous, hard-working father of five needy children and the latter a ne'er-do-well who has inherited his money through no effort of his own. This is not to imply that virtue resides in poor rather than rich souls, but merely to emphasize that the private-enterprise economy responds to what people have to spend, not to who they are. But when you're thinking who controls production most, don't forget that there are a lot more factory workers than rich people.

Incomes and Consumers Buying Power

Personal incomes in America have risen strongly and persistently since 1900. Total personal real income (that is, income after the dollar growth attributable merely to inflation has been eliminated) has soared. Per capita real income, and hence per capita buying power, is roughly five times what it was at the beginning of the century. And we have more leisure time as well. Our average workweek now is only about 60 percent of what it was in 1900, about 40 hours per week compared to nearly 60 then—the equivalent of a further big increase in real income.

A look back at Figure 1–1 will show how this real income in the United States compares with that of other nations. American consumers are, on the average, among the richest in the world.

Figure 4–1 shows who has the buying power in America. It emphasizes the huge buying power of the "middle class." Three-fifths of all families fell in the $7,000–$28,000 income group in 1978, and the average income of this group is steadily moving up.

But Figure 4–1 points up the extremes, too. Ten million families, one family out of five, had an income below $7,900. These families received only 6 percent of total personal income—far less

FIGURE 4–1
Family Incomes in 1978
The United States has a wide range of family incomes. Each bar represents one-fifth of all families. About two-thirds of all families had incomes in 1978 between $7,000 and $28,000. Half got more than $17,200, half less. (Source: U.S. Department of Commerce; preliminary estimates for 1978 by author.)

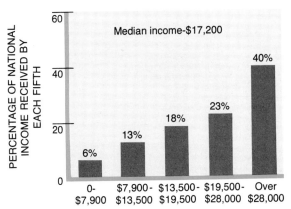

39

than their proportionate say as to what gets produced for the market. At the other extreme, about 3 percent of families received incomes over $50,000, giving them a large leverage over what the system produces.

The consumer is a powerful and sometimes capricious, sovereign. Table 4–1 shows what the typical family spends on some major categories in the American economy. It still spends the biggest chunk of its income on food, clothing, and housing. But the proportion spent on food and clothing has dropped sharply since 1929 (to only 30 percent, as against 42). Spending on services (medical care, automobiles, recreation, and the like) has grown rapidly as we have become richer and able to devote more of our incomes to "nonessentials."

Most of us are not coldly calculating "economic men." Still, most of us face a real problem of how to allocate our incomes among far more goods and services than we are able to pay for. Perhaps the Aga Khan buys everything he wants without concern for what it costs. But most of us have to calculate how to divide up our incomes among the things we want to buy. You may devote most of your income to nourishing foods, college tuition, and durable clothes; I may spend most of mine on books, stereo albums, and airplane trips; a neighbor may prefer a dissolute life of wine, women, and song. None of us is a human calculating machine, but all of us face the need to allocate our limited incomes in such a way as to maximize our satisfactions from spending them.

The economist does not pass judgment on which pattern of expenditure is the proper one.

Nor does he pretend to tell you how you should spend your income to lead a happier, healthier, or more learned life. What he does do is assume that normally, you spend your money on the things you want most. Thus, if you spent a dollar on a hamburger this noon, he takes that as evidence that you preferred that over a pizza or a paperback at the same price. If you stop and think about it, any other assumption leads to very strange results, as long as we assume freedom of individual action in spending incomes.

These rather obvious observations become important later on when we try to evaluate how well the economic system works. Unless we can assume that consumers' expenditures generally reflect what they want most, we will be at a loss for any measure of how well the system does in fact allocate its scarce productive resources to satisfying consumer wants. So we shall generally assume that people spend their money on the goods and services they want most, wisely or not.

Advertising and the Management of Demand

"Consumer sovereignty" is just establishment rhetoric, say some critics of the U.S. economy. Reality is quite different, they argue. Businesses decide what they can make the most profit producing; then they twist consumers, through advertising and other high-pressure selling, to believe that's what they really want to buy. Businesses, helped by Madison Avenue, are the sovereigns; consumers' wants are managed, manipulated—indeed, created outright.

Insofar as the critics are right, the basic argument for an individual-oriented, free-market economy is undermined, since the whole system rests on the notion that consumer wants direct use of society's resources. Does big business in fact dictate your wants?

Clearly, modern advertising influences what many people buy. In 1978, businesses spent over $40 billion on advertising—on TV and billboards, in newspapers, magazines, and stores, and by direct mail. Procter & Gamble, maker of soaps, detergents, and a myriad of household products, was the nation's largest advertiser; it spent $460 million, or 5.7 percent of its sales income, on advertising. General Motors was

TABLE 4–1 Percentage Breakdown of Consumer Spending		
SPENDING CATEGORY	1929	1978
Food and drink	28	22
Housing	14	16
Clothing	12	8
Household operations	6	15
Medical care	4	11
Recreation	3	7
Autos and operations	3	13

© 1966 United Feature Syndicate, Inc.

second, with only 0.5 percent of its sales income spent on advertising. General Foods was third, and Sears, Roebuck was fourth. Forty-one billion dollars is a very large amount, but it's less than 2 percent of the gross national product. It's hard to see how that percentage could dominate all our "wants." Moreover, a lot of the advertising is primarily informational, not merely want-manipulating; nearly a third of the total is newspaper advertising, with huge ads by supermarkets on weekend grocery prices and the like, presumably useful information for shoppers.

Obviously, advertising is a complicated problem, and there's a major section on it in Chapter 13, including both factual data and analysis of the major issues. There is surely some truth to the critics' charges, and the recent upsurge of "consumerism" shows that a lot of people are concerned. At the same time, the charges are easy to blow up into emotional overstatements; the facts just don't support some of the wilder ones. So remember that for the next few chapters, we're oversimplifying by assuming that consumers decide for themselves what they want and freely express these preferences in the market. But it's a useful first approximation, and there'll be plenty of opportunity to alter it in Part 2, when we examine household and business behavior in detail.

INDIVIDUAL DEMAND

Since consumer demand largely directs production in a private-enterprise system, it is important to define "demand" accurately at the outset. Demand is the schedule of amounts of any product that buyers will purchase at different prices during some stated time period. This definition takes some explaining, since it obviously isn't quite what the word means in everyday conversation.

What is your demand for pizzas? A little thought will tell you that this is a meaningless question until you ask, "At what price, and over how long a time?" You'll surely buy more at 50 cents a slice than at $1.00; and obviously, you'll buy more in a year than in a week. Recognizing this need to specify prices and a time period, we might construct a hypothetical "schedule" of the numbers of pizza slices you would buy at different prices during a week, as in Table 4–2. The table shows how many slices you will buy during the week at each price shown, assuming that other things (especially your income and the prices of other commodities) remain unchanged.

When we speak of your "demand" for pizza, we mean this entire schedule of amounts that you would buy at various prices, other things equal. It is meaningless to say that your demand is one or three pizza slices a week. By "demand" we mean instead your entire state of mind as to

TABLE 4–2
Individual Demand for Pizza Slices

PRICE PER PIZZA SLICE	SLICES BOUGHT PER WEEK
$1.20	0
1.00	1
.80	2
.60	3
.40	4
.20	5

how many pizzas you would buy at different prices, other things remaining unchanged. In principle, we might list every possible price from zero to infinity. Table 4–2 pictures your demand only over the price range shown.

This state of mind (your demand) can be shown graphically, as in Figure 4–2, plotted from Table 4–2. If we plot price on the vertical axis and pizza slices bought on the horizontal axis and connect the points, we can read off the resulting curve how many pizza slices you will buy during the week at any price shown, continuing the assumption of other things equal. Thus, at $1.20 you will buy none, at $1.00 you will buy one, and so on down the curve. Whether we use the schedule or the demand curve is a matter of convenience.

But watch out for one tricky point, whether you use schedules or graphs! Going back to your demand for pizzas, suppose the price is $1.00 and you are buying one slice per week. Now the local pizza parlor lowers the price to 80 cents and you step up your weekly purchases to two. This is not a change in demand. Your demand (your state of mind toward pizza) has not changed. You have merely moved to a different point on your demand schedule, or curve, as a result of the lower price, as the original demand schedule or curve says you would do. Your in-

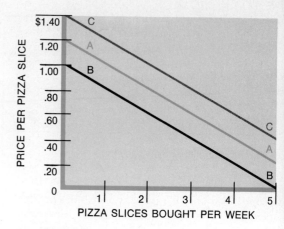

FIGURE 4–3
Changing Demand for Pizza
Curve *CC* shows an increase in demand from *AA*, curve *BB* shows a decrease. How many pizza slices would a consumer buy at $1.00 per slice in each case?

creased purchase at a lower price is merely a reflection of the downward slope of your demand curve.

Changes in Demand

Your "demand" for pizzas is your entire set of intentions about buying pizzas. These depend on how much income you have, your taste for pizza compared with other things, and the prices of alternatives. Now, suppose that you get tired of pizza and develop a taste for seafood. You will now buy fewer pizzas than before at each of the prices shown. This change in attitude is a change in demand. Your demand for pizzas has decreased.

A change in demand is easily illustrated by using demand curves. Begin with curve *AA* in Figure 4–3. Your lower demand for pizzas would be reflected in a new demand curve, *BB*, to the left of, or below, *AA*. You will now buy only one slice per week at 80 cents, and none at any higher price; only two at 60 cents; and so on. If something increases your demand for pizzas—say, a fatter paycheck to finance such delicacies—the new, higher demand might be indicated by *CC*. A change in demand is shown by a move to another demand curve.

FIGURE 4–2
Individual Demand for Pizza
The demand curve shows how many pizza slices this individual will buy in a week at different prices. He will buy more at lower than at higher prices.

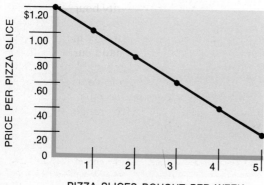

Why would your demand for pizzas, or Porsches, change? There are three major reasons. First, your tastes may change. You simply decide you don't like pizza, or that you now prefer Porsches to other cars. Second, your income may change. As a beginning office clerk, you may have to be satisfied with a secondhand Volkswagen. With a doubled paycheck, you may be in the Pontiac class. Third, changes in the availability and prices of other commodities may change your demand. If hamburger prices soar, your demand for pizzas may rise, because you'll buy more pizzas than before now that the alternatives cost more.

It is important to distinguish between movements along the same demand curve and shifts in the curve itself. Many economic fallacies are perpetrated through slippery use of the concept of "demand." Try checking your own grasp with these questions: (1) Production of sheep rises, prices fall, and consumers buy more mutton. Is there an increase in the demand for mutton? (*Hint:* Does the demand curve itself shift, or do customers merely buy more mutton on the same demand curve at lower prices?) (2) Chrysler comes out with a new engine, and Buick sales decline. Has demand for Buicks dropped? (3) Philco raises the price of its TV sets, and sales drop off. Is there a drop in demand? (4) Congress puts a new tax on movie admissions, and movie attendance drops. Is there a drop in demand?[1]

MARKET DEMANDS— SIGNALS TO PRODUCERS

Millions of consumers, each allocating his income to provide the greatest satisfaction to himself, provide the basic signals to producers telling what consumers want produced. The local department store isn't much concerned with your personal demand for shirts. But it is very much concerned with the aggregate market demand for shirts in its market territory. Aggregate, or market, demand is the sum of all the individual demands in each market. Such market demand provides the main signal to producers as to what they should supply to make the largest profits by meeting consumers' wants. Market demand tells the local retailer the relative importance its customers attach to getting more shirts, or pounds of sugar, at different prices (given their incomes and the prices of other products).

Consider the market demand for sugar at the crossroads store of an isolated village that has only three families. The demand schedules of the three families, and total demand, might look something like Table 4–3. The market demand schedule for sugar, as seen by the crossroads grocer, is the sum of the individual demands of his customers. It could be plotted on a graph just like the individual's demand schedule. The total expenditures column shows the grocer's total weekly sales of sugar at different prices. (For the moment, disregard the right-hand column.)

ELASTICITY OF DEMAND

The preceding sections say the most important things about consumer demands as signals to producers. But demands for individual products vary widely, and it is useful to be able to describe some of these differences precisely in analyzing how well the economic system responds to changing consumer demands.[2]

Consider salt. Suppose ordinary table salt sells for 10 cents a pound and you use about a pound a month. If the price goes up to 15 cents, how much less salt will you use? Probably no less at all. Unsalted beans and potatoes don't taste very good, and the fraction of a cent saved each day by not salting your food is trivial compared with the better taste of flavored cooking.

This is a case where quantity bought responds very little, or not at all, to price changes. A higher price doesn't weed out very many buyers. Plotted on a graph, the demand curve for table salt at the local grocery store would be substantially vertical over the 10- to 15-cent price range. We say that the demand for table salt is very "inelastic" over this price range. Quantity

---

[1]Answers: (1) no; (2) yes; (3) no; (4) no.

[2]Mathematical Appendix I at the end of the book provides a precise mathematical statement of demand elasticity, which may be helpful to students who know calculus.

TABLE 4–3
Crossroads Demand for Sugar

PRICE PER POUND	PURCHASES PER WEEK BY:				EXPENDITURES	DEMAND
	A	B	C	ALL THREE		
20 cents	3 lb	1 lb	2 lb	6 lb	$1.20	
15 cents	4 lb	2 lb	4 lb	10 lb	1.50	Elastic
10 cents	6 lb	3 lb	6 lb	15 lb	1.50	Unitary
5 cents	6 lb	4 lb	7 lb	17 lb	.85	Inelastic

bought changes very little in response to a change in price.

At the other extreme, take your demand for steak at the local A&P if you are substantially indifferent about whether you eat beef or pork. Suppose the price of beef jumps 10 percent. The changes are that you will cut back your steak purchases sharply and substitute pork. Here, your demand for steak would be highly "elastic." You would cut your purchases a lot in response to an increase in price.

"Elasticity" is a measure that tells how much the quantity bought will change in response to a change in price. Thus, elasticity of demand is a measure of the responsiveness of quantity bought to changes in price. (It is defined precisely on page 45.) Elasticity is one characteristic of any given demand curve or schedule. To say a given demand is elastic or inelastic is merely to describe it, just as you might describe your next-door neighbor as tall or short.[3]

Total Revenue and Elasticity of Demand

The concept of demand elasticity helps us predict what effect price changes will have on total expenditure for a commodity. Look at the last column of Table 4–3. Suppose the grocer cuts the price of sugar 25 percent, from 20 to 15 cents

---

[3]Strictly, we should call this concept "price elasticity of demand." There is a related concept, "income elasticity of demand," to be noted presently. However, throughout this book we shall use "elasticity" to mean "price elasticity," unless otherwise specified. At a more advanced level, we can also speak of "cross-elasticity" of demand. This is the percentage change in the amount of product *A* that will be bought in response to a given percentage change in the price of product *B*.

a pound. Sales jump from six to ten pounds per week, a 67 percent increase, and his total revenue from sugar goes up from $1.20 to $1.50 per week. The increase in quantity sold more than offsets the decrease in price. Looking at what happens to total expenditures (revenue) gives us a precise measure of elasticity. If demand is elastic, total expenditures will change in the opposite direction from a change in price. If demand is inelastic, total expenditures on a commodity will change in the same direction as a change in price. Examine the reasoning.

1. *Elastic demand—total revenue moves in the opposite direction from price.* This is the sugar case just described. Although the storekeeper gets 25 percent less per pound, he sells 67 percent more pounds, and total revenue increases. Demand is elastic. Reverse the process over the same price range and you will see again that total revenue moves in the opposite direction from price.

2. *Inelastic demand—total revenue moves in the same direction as price.* Now observe what happens when the grocer cuts the price from 10 to 5 cents. He gets 50 percent less for each pound of sugar, but he sells only 13 percent more pounds. The volume increase, with inelastic demand, is not great enough to offset the lower price per pound sold. Total revenue drops with a cut in price. Demand is inelastic. Now reverse the process over the same price range. Total revenue will rise if he raises the price from 5 to 10 cents.

3. *Unit elasticity—total revenue is unaffected by price changes.* The borderline case between elastic and inelastic demand is called "unit" elasticity. This occurs where an upward or

downward shift of price is just offset by a proportional change in quantity bought, so that total revenue remains unchanged. The crossroads demand for sugar between 10 and 15 cents is a case in point. Total expenditure on sugar is identical at either price, since the shift in amount bought just offsets the change in price.

A Warning: Note that the same demand curve may be elastic in some price ranges and inelastic in others. In most cases, it is not correct to speak of a demand curve as elastic or inelastic as a whole. You need to specify at what price.

The Real-World Importance of Elasticity

The elasticity of demand for his product is a prime concern of every businessman, whether or not he uses that technical term. Consider two important real-world examples that will show why.

First, the farmer. Modern studies show that the demand for most basic farm products is inelastic over the relevant price ranges. What does this mean if farmers all work hard, the weather cooperates, and a bumper crop rolls out? It means that the total revenue farmers get from selling their crops will be lower as a result of this bonanza, because the bigger crop can be sold only by cutting prices more than proportionately. This simple fact goes far to explain the continuing stream of government-sponsored crop-reduction plans, all aimed at raising total farm income. With inelastic demand, any crop restriction will induce a higher price and more total revenue from crop sales.

Contrast this with the depression-period attempts of the railroads to increase their total revenues by raising passenger fares in the 1930s. Unfortunately for the railroads, the customers stayed away in droves. Either they stayed home, or they traveled by bus or car. Demand turned out to be elastic, and total revenue moved down, not up. Only when fares were **cut** did total revenue actually rise. The impossibility of filling the coffers by raising price in an elastic-demand market is plain to see, once you understand the concept of elasticity.[4]

A Quantitative Measure of Elasticity

For some purposes, it is useful to be able to say just how elastic or inelastic demand is. A ready measure can be worked out from the previous reasoning. Elasticity depends on the relative changes in quantity and price. If the percentage change in quantity bought (Q) is more than the percentage change in price (P), total revenue moves in the opposite direction from price; demand is elastic. Thus, we can easily get a numerical value for elasticity by the formula:

$$\text{Elasticity} = \frac{\%\text{ change in } Q}{\%\text{ change in } P}$$

For example, if a cut in the price of steel ingots from $80 to $76 per ton (5 percent) leads to an increase in sales from 100 million to 101 million tons (1 percent), by inserting the 5 percent and 1 percent in the formula we get an elasticity of demand of .2. Any value less than 1 (unity) is called inelastic demand. Any value of more than 1 is called elastic demand. Unitary elasticity of demand means exactly offsetting changes in quantity and price.[5]

---

[4]What makes demand elastic or inelastic? Demand is likely to be inelastic when (1) your outlay on the object is small, (2) your want for it is urgent, (3) good substitutes are unavailable, and (4) it is wanted jointly with some complementary item. Conversely, demand is likely to be elastic where (1) the outlay involved bulks large in your total expenditures, (2) your want is not urgent, (3) close substitutes are available, (4) the commodity is durable or repairable, and (5) the commodity has multiple uses. The availability of satisfactory substitutes is crucial. For example, nobody's want for Exxon gasoline is likely to be terribly urgent as long as a similar grade of Gulf can be had for the same price across street.

[5]Since price and quantity move in opposite directions, elasticity will always be a negative figure. The minus sign is customarily dropped in using elasticity measures.

Strictly, our formula needs to be applied only to very small changes in price and quantity. Notice, for example, that the percentage change in price from 10 to 5 cents is different from that from 5 to 10 cents—50 percent compared with 100 percent. This is because the base with which we compared the 5-cent change varies with the direction in which we calculate. The difference really doesn't matter for our purposes, since the effect on total revenue will always give the right answer. (If you take the percentage change on the average of the before and after quantity figures, you can avoid this directional problem.) Obviously, the discrepancy between the two ways of figuring percentage change will gradually vanish as we take smaller and smaller price intervals—for example, a price change between 99 cents and $1.00. A more precise formula, using calculus, in the mathematical appendix, completely avoids this difficulty.

Econometric estimates have been made of the elasticity of demand for many products, although many of these are very rough. Table 4–4 gives estimates for several common products (for price variations near their then prices). The preceding footnote on what makes demand elastic or inelastic should help you explain the elasticities of the different products. Another study recently found the present demand elasticity for butter to be about 1.3, compared to a pre–World War II estimate of about .6. Can you explain the difference? (*Hint:* Consider possible substitutes then and now. Margarine came into general use in the 1940s.)

Elasticity in Graphical Presentations

A perfectly inelastic demand curve would obviously be vertical; the same quantity would be bought at every price. An example might be your demand for insulin over a wide price range if you needed the insulin to stay alive. Highly elastic demand would be a nearly horizontal demand curve. Very small changes in price would lead to very large changes in the quantity bought. But in between these extremes, trying to read elasticity by the slope of a plotted demand curve is dangerous business. Look, for

TABLE 4–4
Estimated Elasticities of Demand

Furs	2.6
Autos	1.5
Refrigerators	1.1
Local phone calls	1.0
Luggage	.8
Movie tickets	.4
Electric light bulbs	.3
Matches	.0

Source: Treasury estimates presented before House Ways and Means Committee, 1960.

example, at the two charts in Figure 4–4. Both show the demand schedule seen by our old friend the crossroads grocer, but they use different horizontal and vertical scales. Exactly the same demand is shown on both.

Because the left-hand graph uses an extended horizontal scale, the demand curve is relatively flat throughout. Yet it is exactly the same demand as in the right-hand graph, and the elasticity at every point along it is identical with the corresponding points on the right-hand graph. Both curves are marked to show the elastic and inelastic areas. This example emphasizes the danger in trying to generalize that flat demand

THE IMPORTANCE OF ELASTICITY

When the OPEC oil embargo hit the United States in 1973, there was widespread debate as to the best way to cut back domestic consumption of oil and gasoline and to allocate what was available among consumers. Some people argued for government rationing, others for letting prices rise to discourage consumption and to allocate the available supplies to those who would pay most for them; still others proposed voluntary restraints and "jawboning" by the president and federal officials. Nearly everybody disliked rationing, and few thought that voluntary restraint would do the job. Many economists lined up behind the higher-prices approach as the simplest, most efficient way of discouraging consumption and allocating available supplies.

But the air was blue with conflicting claims over how high prices would rise if left unregulated, and how effectively rising prices would reduce consumption to match the lower supplies available. Several experts produced estimates of price elasticity of demand ranging from .3 to .8 in the short run (one year), and from .5 to 1.8 in the long run. Such estimates necessarily rest on historical experience, and while we had lots of data on the effects of small price changes on gasoline consumption, we had none at all on price increases of anywhere from 10 to 100 percent, which were included in the estimates of probable necessary reduction in our consumption of gasoline.

Query: Why were the estimates of short-run elasticity of demand so much lower than those for long-run elasticity? In both the short and long run, what feasible substitutes were there for oil and gas in the United States, and what were their prices compared to gasoline? If you had been a government regulator, which plan would you have favored? Would you have hoped for a high or low price elasticity of demand for gasoline?

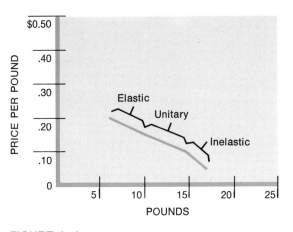
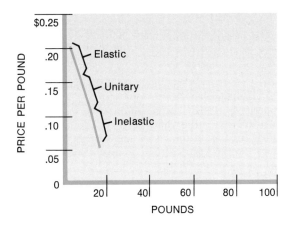

FIGURE 4–4
Demand for Sugar, Shown on Different Scales
Trying to judge elasticity of demand by looking at the slope of a demand curve is
tricky. These two curves show identical demands, plotted on different scales.

curves are elastic, whereas steep ones are inelastic. You have to remember that elasticity is a matter of *relative* (percentage) changes in price and quantity. Elasticity changes continuously along a straight, diagonal demand curve. Check it for yourself if, as is likely, this statement seems to you intuitively wrong.[6]

Income Elasticity

Economists use a closely related concept, income elasticity of demand, in a similar way. It measures the response in quantity bought to a change in the buyer's income, instead of to a change in the commodity's price. Thus, if a small increase in Joe's income, other things equal, induces a large increase in his purchases of stereo albums, his income elasticity of demand is high. If his response is very small, his income elasticity of demand is low. If a 10 percent increase in his income leads to a 10 percent increase in purchases of stereo albums, his income elasticity of demand is unity. The concept is parallel to price elasticity of demand, substituting income for price changes—though remember that income elasticity will generally be positive, not negative.

That is, an increase in income will generally lead to more purchases, whereas an increase in price will generally lead to less.

INTERACTING DEMANDS

If you buy a car, your demand for gasoline is pretty sure to increase. But, assuming that your total income stays unchanged, your demand for some other things (say, bus rides) will drop. This example illustrates the two main kinds of interrelationships among demands for different things: (1) *complementary*, or joint; and (2) substitutive, or *competitive*. When you buy a car, you take on a "complementary" demand for gasoline to run it. But now you don't need to ride the bus. Bus rides are "competitive" with cars in your demand pattern.

In the broadest sense, if your income is a given amount, every expenditure is competitive with every other. More of anything means less of something else. But in many instances, this effect is quite remote; for example, your car purchase may have little effect on your demand for potatoes. By contrast, the substitution of car rides for bus rides is very direct. Thus, in many cases it is important to recognize complementary demands, even though in the broader sense all are competitive, given the budget constraints nearly all of us face.

---

[6]For mathematicians: The curve that shows unitary elasticity at all points is a rectangular hyperbola. The equation is $xy = $ constant.

SUMMARY AND REVIEW

1. Consumers' demands, expressed through market expenditures, provide the basic signals to producers on what is to be produced in our society. Economists generally assume that consumers spend their income on the goods and services they want most, so their expenditures indicate the satisfaction they expect to obtain from the goods and services they buy.

2. For most consumers, their income determines roughly how much they can spend on consumption—that is, how many votes they have in signaling to producers.

3. "Demand" is the entire schedule of amounts of any good or service that a buyer, or buyers, will purchase at different prices during some stated time period, assuming incomes, prices of other commodities, and other things are equal. A change in demand is a change in the schedule—that is, in the amount that will be bought at any given price. An increase in the quantity purchased in response to a lower price thus is not a change in demand. It is important to understand the difference between changes in demand (a change in an entire schedule) and changes in amounts purchased at different prices within the same schedule.

4. Graphically, demand is a curve showing the amounts that will be bought at different prices, other things equal. A change in demand is a change in the curve, not a change along any given curve.

5. Elasticity of demand is a measure that tells how much the quantity purchased will change in response to a small change in price. The formula is:

$$\text{Elasticity} = \frac{\%\ \text{change in } Q}{\%\ \text{change in } P}$$

6. When demand is elastic, total expenditures on a good or service vary inversely with changes in price; when demand is inelastic, total expenditures vary directly with changes in price.

7. Elasticity of demand is important to sellers because it tells what will happen to total expenditure on their product if they raise or lower the price.

8. Income elasticity of demand measures the percentage change in quantity purchased for any small percentage change in the income of the buyer, other things equal.

9. In the broadest sense, given your income, any expenditure on each good or service is competitive with expenditure on any other good or service. But viewing only closer relationships, expenditure on any good may be either "competitive" or "complementary" with that on other goods.

New Concepts to Remember

demand
individual and aggregate
    demand
elasticity of demand
elastic demand

inelastic demand
unit elasticity
income elasticity of demand
competitive demands
complementary demands

For Analysis and Discussion

1. Do you act like the mythical "economic man" in allocating your income among alternative uses to maximize your satisfaction from it? If your answer is no, are you saying that you are irrational?

2. Calculate roughly how big a voice people in your own family's income group have in the allocation of the economy's resources. Does it seem to you to be a fair share? (Check the income data in Figure 4–1.)

3. "Every individual is different. Thus, it makes no sense for economists to lump them all together in talking about aggregate market demand." True or false?

4. "Since consumers' demand signals what is to be produced in America, it follows that consumers are responsible if our economy produces 'wasteful' products like elaborate chrome trim on automobiles." Do you agree or disagree?

5. How elastic is your demand for the following, at the present price for each?
   a. Beer
   b. Stereos
   c. Porsche roadsters
   d. Required textbooks
   e. Gasoline
   f. Airplane tickets home
   In each case, see if you can isolate the factors that make the elasticity what it is.
6. If the demand for wheat is inelastic, would a bumper crop raise or lower wheat farmers' total income?
7. Explain why you would expect price elasticity of demand to be negative, but income elasticity to be positive, using the percentage-change formula.
8. What effect would a successful advertising campaign by the Gulf Oil Company have on the elasticity of consumer demand for Gulf gas? Explain your answer.
9. Suppose unsold stocks of gasoline are piling up in the storage tanks of the major refineries. If you were regional sales director of one of the major companies, would you recommend a marked reduction in the filling-station price? How would you go about deciding?

CASE 3

THE PRICE OF PEARS

Substantially the following news story appeared in leading West Coast newspapers in August 1976:

GROWERS MAY DUMP 30,000 TONS OF PEARS

SACRAMENTO—Growers expect to dump 20,000 to 30,000 tons of pears this year because they lack a market for all the fruit, a spokesman says.

Cameron Girton, manager of the California Canning Pear Association, said Friday a big crop, a heavy carryover of canned pears from last year, the cannery strike and the high cost of labor all contribute to the bad situation.

Most processors have agreed to a price of $105 a ton for No. 1 Bartlett pears this year, Girton said. Last year's price was $125 and the 1974 price was $165.

"Unfortunately, this does not mean consumers will enjoy lower prices for canned pears this fall," Girton said. "Increased wage rates for cannery workers and other escalating costs of processing and distribution will eliminate any possibility of price reduction on retail shelves."

This year's Bartlett crop was about 345,000 tons, 17 percent more than last year, according to the state Crop and Livestock Reporting Service.

Girton said there is a carryover of 3.2 million cases of canned pears, down 500,000 from last year, but still well over the "desirable" carryover of 2.5 million cases.

In Placerville, packinghouse owner George Visman said foothill farmers face a loss of 40 percent of their crop for lack of a market.

"It's disgusting," he said. "Growers work all year to pull their crop through and then they find out a good part of it probably will have to be dumped."

Visman said about 1,500 tons, worth $165,000, will go to waste in the foothill area near Placerville.

1. What elasticity of consumer demand for pears is being assumed by the California pear growers?
2. As their consulting economist, would you advise them to destroy the 30,000 tons of pears, as stated in the news story?
3. If you (as a citizen) don't like this policy, can you suggest a better one that will be appropriate for the pear growers and also for the consumers and citizens like you?

Business Firms and Market Supply

CHAPTER 5

In a private-enterprise economy, the profit-seeking business firm is at the center of the economic process. The businessman decides what will be produced in response to market demand, and how much of it. In the process, he decides how many employees to hire, and how much he is willing to pay them. Within the rules established by society, his decisions most directly determine how effectively the private-enterprise economy utilizes its resources.

Anybody can see that many business firms in the modern economy are a long way from the myriad of small competitors envisaged by Adam Smith two centuries ago. Not only are General Motors, Ford, General Electric, AT&T, and other such well-known firms industrial giants, but hundreds of other firms like them have sales of hundreds of millions or even billions of dollars per year. They employ thousands of people and obviously have some degree of market power in setting wages and market prices. At the same time, small firms, not unlike those envisaged by Smith, number in the millions—especially in agriculture, retail trade, and the service industries (for example, dry cleaners, doctors, and lawyers). Over the last century, very large firms have accounted for an increased share of the total economy's activity. But this increase has come almost entirely in manufacturing, which now provides only about 25 percent of all the jobs in the country. In services, which are the most rapidly growing sector of the economy, small businesses have prospered, and the dominance of the giants is far less widespread. It is this potpourri of large and small businesses that has the job of responding to consumer demands and using our resources effectively to produce what consumers most want.

We concentrate here and in the following chapters on the profit-seeking businesses, large and small, that account for the bulk of our economic activity. But two other sectors of the economy also play important roles in providing wanted goods and services—governments, and not-for-profit organizations like hospitals, universities, foundations, and the like. Both produce goods and services themselves (government services like police and fire protection, national defense, and education, and not-for-profit ser-

vices like health and education), and both provide massive transfer payments in our economy (Social Security, unemployment benefits, foundation grants, and the like). Moreover, their share of the total economy has been growing rapidly over the past half century. We shall return to them later, especially in Part 4.

It is the first purpose of this chapter to describe briefly the major forms of business enterprise that supply most of the goods and services in the modern American economy, with some attention to small businesses but more to the huge corporations that dominate the news headlines. If you want to understand the role of big business in America and how much economic power it really has, you need to know something about what corporations are and how they operate. Second, the chapter introduces the concept "supply," parallel to "demand," introduced in Chapter 4.

ENTREPRENEURS, PLANTS, FIRMS, AND INDUSTRIES

Business enterprises are called "firms." John Brown and his family run a farm; the farm is a firm. U.S. Steel is also a firm, with steel mills in many cities, with iron and coal mines, with ore ships on the Great Lakes. The important characteristic of the firm is that it is owned and controlled essentially as a unit, however diverse its parts.

The function of making fundamental policy decisions in a firm is generally called entrepreneurship. The entrepreneur decides when to establish a firm, what goods to produce, how the concern will be financed, what price policies to follow, when to expand or contract, and so on. A firm is thus a business unit under one coordinated entrepreneurship.

In the independent corner grocery store, the proprietor is the entrepreneur. He decides whether to borrow funds to remodel his store, what prices to set on his merchandise. In bigger businesses, it is harder to pick out the entrepreneur. For example, who is the entrepreneur of AT&T? The 3 million stockholders? The board of directors? The president? Here, it is impossible to pick out any person or group of persons as the entrepreneur; the functions of the entrepreneur are performed in a coordinated way by the various individuals and groups concerned.

A plant is a building or a group of buildings, along with other more or less fixed physical equipment, that are used together in producing something—such as a shoe-manufacturing plant, or an auto-assembly plant. The Ford Motor Company is a firm with plants in Dearborn, St. Louis, Kansas City, and so forth. John Brown's farm, on the other hand, is a firm with only one plant.

An industry is harder to define. Usually, we use the word to mean all the producers of any "commodity." Farmer Brown is part of the wheat industry if he produces wheat, part of the corn industry if he produces corn; he may be in both simultaneously. General Motors, like most other big firms, is part of many industries; it produces a wide range of autos, trucks, diesel engines, refrigerators, and hundreds of other products. The trouble comes when we try to be precise. Shall we consider a "motor-vehicle industry," or an "auto industry," or a "low-priced auto industry"? For many purposes, how finely we divide up commodities is not a major problem. You will seldom get in trouble if you let common sense be your guide and if you stick to the same definition of "commodity" and the associated "industry" in analyzing any problem.

The Shifting Economic and Legal Organization of Firms

The economic and legal forms of business firms have changed with the times. When small-scale business was the rule, the individual proprietorship was dominant. This is a simple arrangement in which an individual puts up the money, starts his own business, runs it himself, and has the profits and losses to himself. There are still more individual proprietorships in the United States than any other form of business organization— some 9 million in all. Of these, 3 million are in agriculture, and most of the rest are small-scale retail concerns and service enterprises, such as cleaning establishments, filling stations, doctors, lawyers, and so on. Nearly all farms are still single proprietorships, but the 1 percent that are corporations do over 25 percent of all the business. In wholesale and retail trade, the 80 percent of all firms that are single proprietorships do only about 25 percent of the business; remember Sears and the big grocery chains.

As the need for larger capital funds increased, partnerships became popular. In these, two or more people become joint proprietors—usually with joint provision of funds, joint management, and joint financial responsibility. This arrangement has substantial advantages over the single proprietorship, especially in raising funds, but it still falls short of providing enough capital for really large-scale business operations. And it shares one serious drawback with the single proprietorship: The partners are personally liable for the debts of the business. Thus, in most cases, each partner is personally liable to an unlimited amount for the deeds of the other partners—a somewhat precarious position at best, and definitely not suited to drawing in funds from absentee investors. Partnerships are not very important in the United States today, although there are some 900,000 in existence. About half of them are in retailing; the rest are widely scattered.

THE MODERN CORPORATION

The modern corporation, which was conceived to meet the financial-managerial needs of large-scale business and to avoid the drawbacks of partnerships, has become the dominant form of American business enterprise. Although there are only about 1.2 million business corporations, they do the bulk of the nation's private business, employ nearly half the workers, account for about two-thirds of the nation's privately produced income, and pay out over 50 percent of the total national income. They do virtually all the business in public utilities, manufacturing, transportation, and finance; around half in trade and construction; but less than a quarter in services and agriculture.

The biggest modern corporations are Goliaths. In 1978, for example, the assets of the American Telephone and Telegraph Company (the world's largest business) were $103 billion. Those of Exxon (formerly Standard Oil of New Jersey) and of General Motors were $42 and $31 billion, respectively. Their 1978 sales of $60 and $63 billion, respectively, were larger than the entire gross national product of most of the world's nations. In all, in 1978 there were 257 nonfinancial corporations with sales of over a billion dollars.

Many financial corporations (banks and insurance companies) are as large, even though most of their assets consist of investments in corporate and government securities and of direct loans to businesses and individuals. In 1978, the total assets of the Prudential Life Insurance Company, the largest insurance company, were $50 billion. Those of the Bank of America, the biggest bank, were $95 billion. Thus, modern finance and industry are heavily concentrated in the hands of large firms. (More details on "big business" in Chapters 14–16.)

Nevertheless, only about one American worker in four works for a giant corporation. The share of the total national income produced by all private corporations is now only about 52 percent, and has declined gradually since hitting a peak of 55 percent in the 1950s, as government and other nonprofit service industries (for example, health and education) have expanded. The share of the giants in manufacturing has grown gradually since World War II, but their profits haven't grown as fast as their sales. Ours is still a very mixed economy.

What Are Corporations?

A corporation is an organization that exists as a "legal person" apart from the individuals who own and control it. A corporation may carry on business in its own name, enter into contracts, sue and be sued, own property, borrow and lend money. In general, it may as a business unit do all the things that any individual person may legally do in business.

As was indicated above, the corporate form of organization was developed mainly to facilitate financing and management of large business firms. Briefly, its advantages are the following:

1. Stockholders who invest money in corporations have no liability for the debts of the corporation; at worst, they can lose their original investment. Thus, corporations can obtain funds by selling "stocks" and "bonds" to many investors who merely want to earn a return on their investments without further financial involvement. These advantages are spelled out below.

2. In a corporation, management is delegated to a board of directors elected by the stockholders. The directors in turn supervise the salaried officials who actually run the business. Thus, the individual stockholder need not concern himself with the details of managing the concern unless he wishes to—quite another story from the continuous attention required in a single-proprietorship or partnership. Freedom to delegate power and responsibility to expert "managers" is essential to the operation of today's mammoth business enterprises.

3. Corporate securities are readily transferable. No matter how many individual stockholders die or lose interest in the corporation, the business can go on unaffected.

Financing Corporate Enterprise—Stocks and Bonds

Corporations obtain funds by selling "stocks" and "bonds" to savers. Individual investors who buy these securities may be part owners of the corporation, or they may simply lend money to the business. Stocks represent ownership in the corporation. Bonds represent money lent to the corporation by bondholders. There are many variations within each class, and at the margin they run together. The most important differences are (1) the priority of the security owner's claim on the income of the enterprise, and (2) the owner's right to vote on personnel and corporate policy, and hence his power to control the corporation.

Common stockholders are the owners of a corporation. They own the company's stock. They have the right to elect the board of directors and hence to control the policies of the corporation. They are entitled to any income remaining after prior claims of creditors have been met. If the corporation is dissolved, they get all that remains (if anything) after everyone else has been paid. The common stockholders are the "residual claimants" to the corporation's income and property. They gain the most when income is high, and they are the first to lose when things go badly.

Profits paid out to stockholders are called

"dividends." Although the profits of the business "belong" to the stockholders, often the corporation does not pay them all out, but instead reinvests part in the business. This is called "plowing back" earnings. Whether the profits are paid out or reinvested, however, they accrue to the benefit of stockholders, since reinvested earnings increase the value of the business.

Bondholders are creditors of the corporation. When corporations want to borrow large sums for long periods, they commonly issue bonds that are sold to people or institutions with funds to invest. Bonds are promises by the corporation to repay the funds to bondholders at some specified future date, with a set rate of interest.

If you own a bond, you are merely a creditor. You ordinarily have no voting power to elect directors and control the corporation's policies. You take less risk than the stockholders do, since the interest on your bonds must be paid before they get any dividends. On the other hand, you will receive only your set rate of interest no matter how big profits are. Bondholders also have a prior claim on the assets of the corporation in case of liquidation.

Preferred stockholders have a position intermediate between common stockholders and bondholders. Preferred stock sometimes carries a vote; more often it does not. Typically, it has a set rate of dividends—say, $6 per share—that must be paid before any dividends can be paid on the common stock. It also has priority over common stock in case of liquidation. But preferred stock stands behinds bonds in priority of claim on income and assets.

Who Controls the Corporations?

Suppose you own 100 shares of General Electric stock. How much control do you have over how General Electric is run?

The answer is, for practical purposes, none. Not because anyone is cheating or hoodwinking you—least of all the GE management, which makes a continuous effort to keep stockholders informed and to get them interested in company affairs. It is because of a combination of factors. In the first place, you own only a tiny fraction of 1 percent of the company's stock. Moreover, you don't and can't know much about the operations and internal policies of GE, a $20 billion

corporation producing thousands of products, most of them involving complex scientific processes and know-how. Besides, GE pays good dividends on your 100 shares, and that's what you bought them for. You have no intention of spending a lot of money and time on an obviously fruitless trip all the way to Schenectady, New York, to tell the management how to run GE, or to throw them out for a new management.

Even if you don't go to the annual stockholders' meeting, you are entitled to send a "proxy," a person of your choice whom you designate to vote for you. Before each annual meeting, you will receive from the management a proxy form, suggesting that you designate someone to vote for you in case you don't plan to be present. You may throw the proxy in the wastebasket. If you do send it back, the chances are you'll designate the person suggested, thereby giving the present management the votes to reelect themselves.

Surprisingly enough, you will be acting like the typical stockholder when you do this, even though you may assume there are many other interested "big" stockholders who are keeping a sharp eye on the operating management from a stockholder viewpoint. AT&T now has 3 million stockholders, no one of whom owns as much as 1 percent of its stock. U.S. Steel has 250,000 stockholders; Westinghouse, 200,000. Many big corporations now have more stockholders than employees. On the other hand, a few well-to-do people and large investment institutions (like pension and trust funds) own large blocks of stock in many companies.

This widespread dispersion of stock ownership, coupled with the lethargy of most stockholders, goes far to explain the substantial control over most large corporations exercised by small groups of management "insiders" who may themselves own very little stock. This divorce of active control from ownership is a major development of modern business enterprise. It is probably inevitable in the large corporation. It certainly does not provide a "democratic" government of corporation affairs in most cases, however good the intentions of the management on this score.

Of course, stockholder lethargy does not always exist. In some smaller companies, stockholders take an active interest in the conduct of the business. Even in large corporations, conflicts and sharp struggles for proxies sometimes occur, with control of the corporation at stake. But for the most part, management or other minorities retain effective control without holding more than a small fraction of the voting stock. They are on the scene; most of the stockholders are far away and little interested. Less than 10 percent of the voting stock is enough to assure working control of most major corporations.

A recent study of the 200 largest nonfinancial corporations in the United States found that in 85 percent of the companies, control was exercised by the management without material stock ownership. None of the corporations was directly controlled by a private family through ownership of over 50 percent of the stock, and in only 12 percent was direction exercised by a particular family or other special group of stockholders with a substantial share of the stock—say, 20 to 50 percent. By contrast, in 1929, 50 percent of the top 200 companies were controlled by families or other special groups through substantial blocks of stockholdings, while only 44 percent were management-controlled. Clearly, there has been a major change in the way our big corporations are controlled.[1]

What proportion of the public owns corporation stock? There are now about 25 million individual stockholders in "publicly owned" corporations, plus probably 1 to 2 million more in "privately owned" companies whose stock is held entirely by family or private control groups. This total is down from over 30 million in 1972; many small holders have sold out as stocks slid down in price over much of the 1970s. However, the comparable total for 1955 was only 6 or 7 million. Thus, perhaps 20 percent of all adults now own stock in business corporations. But most of them own only a few shares. Many more own stock indirectly, however, because part of their insurance and pension-fund reserves are invested in common stocks.

The bulk of privately owned corporate stock is held by a small number of well-to-do families. In 1971, the richest 1 percent of all families owned about 50 percent of all stock owned by individuals, and over one-third of all stock. The richest 10 percent held about 75 percent of all individually owned stock.[2] But modern antitrust laws and Securities and Exchange Commission (SEC) regulations have substantially circumscribed their power, certainly their power to abuse their positions. For example, no individual can now serve as a director of competing corporations.

Nearly 40 percent of corporate stock is held by financial institutions—pension funds, bank trust departments, mutual funds, insurance companies, and the like, and the total is growing rapidly. To date, such financial institutions have seldom intervened directly in corporate management. But as savings pile up in such institutions, their potential power becomes enormous, far exceeding that of the wealthiest families. Even corporations' and unions' own pension funds, amounting to billions of dollars, are now being invested in corporation stocks, including their own, posing intriguing problems of future corporate control. Who should watch over the managers of these vast accumulations of funds?

A Preliminary Summary

The facts of business size are reasonably clear; we shall review them in more detail in Chapters 14–15. There are many huge corporations that produce a wide variety of necessities and luxuries. There are also many markets supplied by multitudes of smaller firms. The American $2-trillion economy is so vast that even corporate giants are tiny by comparison. GM's total sales are less than 3 percent of GNP. Exxon, GM's only rival as the world's largest industrial corporation, nonetheless has only 7 percent of the U.S. gasoline market. As we shall see, absolute size confers some types of economic power, but it is the intensity of competition that matters most for getting consumer demands met efficiently. Where large firms must compete actively with others, domestically or internationally, their economic power is greatly constrained.

Corporate size per se brings other types of power. But many big business concerns are now

---

[1]The data are from R. J. Larner, "Ownership and Control in the 200 Largest Nonfinancial Corporations," *American Economic Review,* September 1966.

[2]For details, see "Stock Ownership in the United States," *Survey of Current Business,* November 1974.

managed both more efficiently and with a greater view to the social welfare than they were under the direct control of owner-operators. If you have $5,000 invested in IBM, it is doubtful that your interests would be better protected were Messrs. Frank Cary and John Opel (the top executives of IBM) larger stockholders than in fact they are, or if you could personally participate in the management of the business. Similarly, today's growing group of professional managers seems more concerned with serving the public well than was the typical captain of industry a half century ago. Nor is there much evidence that most dominant large stockholders use their positions to exploit other stockholders.

There is little likelihood that the modern corporation, with its vast accumulation of capital and its professional management divorced from most stockholders, will soon disappear from the American scene. Its advantages are too great. The problem is how to make such businesses efficient suppliers of the goods and services we as consumers want.

SUPPLY

Businesses are the main suppliers of goods and services in our economy.[3] To understand more precisely how they respond to consumer demands, we need to define "supply" carefully, as we did "demand."

Supply is a schedule of amounts that will be offered for sale at different prices during some time period, other things remaining unchanged.

Like demand, supply can also be plotted as a curve with amounts on the horizontal axis and prices on the vertical one. But it differs from demand when it is plotted, since the supply curve ordinarily slopes uphill, whereas the demand curve ordinarily slopes downhill. The upward slope of the supply curve reflects the fact that more units will usually be offered for sale at higher than at lower prices, in contrast to the reverse demand relationship.

Upward-sloping supply curves may seem obvious to you: The higher the price, the greater will be the profit inducement to produce and to sell more. Or they may seem anything but obvious: You may think of the economies of mass production and suspect that more units will be produced when demand increases, without any rise in price. This may, of course, be true under some circumstances, and sometimes—for example, in the auto industry—to a significant extent.

The relation between firms' costs and the supply curves for their products is analyzed in detail in Chapters 8–14. For the moment, take it on faith that many supply curves are flat or upward-sloping.

Individual and Market Supply

Individual suppliers are the basic decision makers underlying market supply curves. For consumer goods and services, business firms are the main suppliers; for labor and other productive resources, individuals (sometimes through unions) are the main suppliers.

Suppose there are three dairy farms. Column A in Table 5–1 shows the supply schedule for Farmer A—that is, how many quarts he will offer to sell this week at different prices. Column B shows the same information for Farmer B, and so on. By adding the three schedules horizontally, we get the market supply schedule for milk in this area, shown in the last column to the right.[4]

This supply schedule can be plotted on a graph just as the demand schedule was. Again putting price on the vertical axis and quantity on the horizontal one, we get the three individual supply curves and the market supply curve shown in Figure 5–1. Graphically, the market supply curve is obtained by adding the three individual curves horizontally.

It is important to remember some of the same warnings on supply that apply to demand: (1) Supply is a schedule, not a single amount. Thus, more output at a higher price may merely be a movement to a new point on the supply schedule, not an increase in supply. A change in

---

[3]The supply concept can also be used in analyzing the behavior of nonbusiness sellers—for example, workers selling their services to businesses, or savers selling the use of their funds to borrowers.

[4]Farmer C is what some economists call a "marginal producer." He comes into the market only if the price rises to a relatively high level.

TABLE 5–1
Supply Schedule for Milk

PRICE PER QUART	NUMBER OF QUARTS SUPPLIED PER WEEK BY:			
	A	B	C	ALL
20 cents	50	50	20	120
15 cents	50	40	20	110
10 cents	40	30	0	70
5 cents	35	30	0	65

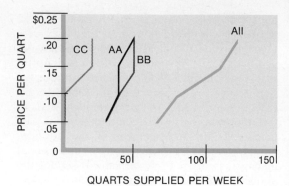

FIGURE 5–1
Market Supply Curve for Milk
The dark curves show how much milk will be supplied by individual farmers at different prices. The "All" curve shows the amounts that will be supplied by all farmers combined.

supply is a change in the schedule (a shift of the curve). (2) Supply has meaning only with reference to some time period. The period should always be specified. (3) A supply schedule or curve is always drawn on the assumption of "other things equal." Just what "other things" we hold constant will vary from case to case, depending partly on the time period involved. For a one-day period, the number of cows and the amount of mechanical equipment the farmer has must be taken as constants. If we're talking about supply per year, obviously such factors become variable. This would lead you to suspect that the supply curve per year might look quite different from the supply curve per day—and it does, as we shall see next.

Elasticity of Supply in the Short and Long Runs

Supply can be elastic or inelastic, just like demand. This is true of both individual producers' and market supplies. If the amount put on the market is highly responsive to price changes, the supply is elastic. If the amount offered is little affected by price variations, the supply is inelastic. Except that the amount supplied and the price ordinarily move in the same rather than opposite directions, the concepts of demand and supply elasticity are similar. You can calculate a precise measure of supply elasticity by using the same percentage-change formula as that given for demand, in Chapter 4.

Elasticity of supply varies with the time period involved. Take an extreme case of inelastic supply first. Suppose you have a strawberry patch and a roadside stand, but no overnight refrigeration. If you picked 20 quarts

this morning, you must sell them today at whatever price you can get or let them spoil (neglecting the possibilities that you may eat them fresh yourself or preserve them). Thus, your supply curve *for the day* may be completely inelastic—a vertical line at 20 quarts of strawberries. By the end of the day, if you have them left, you're willing to sell your 20 quarts at any price from zero up—the higher the better, of course. Figure 5–2 pictures this simple assumption, in which, incidentally, cost of production appears to play no role in determining your supply curve for the day.

Now take a case at the other extreme. Suppose some simple commodity like lead pencils can be produced almost without limit at a certain cost—say, 3 cents per pencil—merely by duplicating existing manufacturing facilities, materials, and workers. *Given enough time to build new facilities,* almost any given number of pencils will be produced for sale at a price of 3 cents or above. Thus, the long-run supply curve might be completely elastic—a horizontal line, at 3 cents per pencil, as in Figure 5–3.

This case, like that of the strawberries, is oversimplified; cost per pencil may not be quite constant in the real world, and the resulting supply curve may not be perfectly flat. Most cases and most time periods, of course, fall somewhere between these two extremes, as we shall see when we begin to look at real-world cases in Chapter 6.

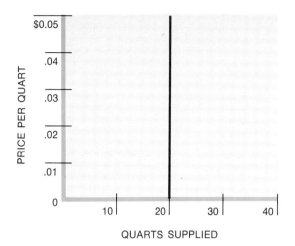

QUARTS SUPPLIED

FIGURE 5–2
Supply of Strawberries on a Given Day
The chart shows completely inelastic supply.
The same number of quarts
is offered at any price shown.

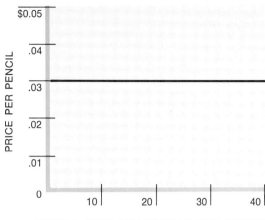

PENCILS SUPPLIED PER YEAR (THOUSANDS)

FIGURE 5–3
Supply of Pencils, Given a Long Time to Adjust
This chart shows infinitely elastic supply. Given a long
time to adjust, any number of pencils can be produced
for sale at 3 cents a pencil.

SUMMARY AND REVIEW

1. A business firm is an organization producing goods or services that is owned and controlled essentially as a unit.

2. A business firm may produce one or many products, and may therefore be in one or many industries. It may have one or more plants.

3. There are three main legal forms of business firms—individual proprietorships, partnerships, and corporations. Although there are many more individual proprietorships and partnerships than corporations, the bulk of the nation's private business is done by corporations.

4. A corporation is an organization that exists as a "legal person." It may carry on business in its own name, make contracts, sue and be sued, own property, and generally do the other things that an individual may legally do in business. It offers major advantages in obtaining large amounts of capital from absentee investors, providing for separation of ownership and management, offering limited liability to investors, and providing indefinite life, independent of the lives of individual investors.

5. Corporations are financed by selling bonds, common stock, and preferred stock. Bondholders are creditors of the corporation; stockholders are the owners of the corporation, who hold the residual claims on its income and assets.

6. Although there are some 25 million stockholders in America, the bulk of stock in private corporations is owned by a relatively small number of well-to-do investors and by financial institutions, especially pension funds, insurance companies, bank trust funds, mutual funds, and the like.

7. Most large modern corporations are controlled by "inside" managerial groups that own only a small percentage of the corporation's stock.

8. Supply is a schedule of amounts that will be offered for sale at different prices during some given time period, other things remaining unchanged.

9. The concept of supply closely parallels demand, except that supply responses to change in prices are usually in the same direction as price, rather than in the opposite direction as in the case of demand.

10. In most cases, supply is more elastic in the long run than in the short run.

11. Market supply is the summation of the supplies offered by all the individual firms, or sellers, in a market.

59

entrepreneur
plant
firm
industry
individual proprietorship
partnership
corporation

common stock
dividends
"plowed-back" earnings
preferred stock
bond
supply
elastic and inelastic supply

**For Analysis
and Discussion**

1. Explain the difference between stocks and bonds.
2. Suppose you are planning to set up a small dry-cleaning shop. Will you be better off with a single proprietorship, a partnership, or a corporation as your legal form of business? What are the main considerations involved in choosing?
3. Single proprietorships and partnerships predominate in retailing and agriculture, whereas corporations dominate the manufacturing industries. How do you account for these differences? How can you reconcile the statement above with the great success of such retail corporate giants as Sears, Roebuck and J. C. Penney?
4. Public-opinion polls repeatedly indicate that the majority of the public view common stocks as a speculative and somewhat uncertain investment. How do you account for this fact, in view of the great growth in the aggregate value and earnings of American corporations over the past century?
5. If you are a stockholder in General Motors, would you prefer to have earnings paid out to you as dividends or directly reinvested by the management? Why?
6. Should individual stockholders in business concerns take a more active part in the management of the concerns involved? Why, or why not?
7. *Based on the appendix to this chapter* Construct the profit-and-loss statement of the Amalgamated Widget Company for 1979 from the following data:

(000s OMITTED)	
Wages and salaries paid	$ 500
Interest paid on bonds	40
Materials used	500
Net sales	3,000
Selling costs	250
Dividends on common stock	50
Provision for income taxes	200
Real estate taxes	60
Dividends on preferred stock	20
Maintenance and repairs	250
Administrative costs	400
Depreciation	150

8. *Based on the appendix to this chapter* XYZ Corporation reports the following data on its position as of December 31, 1979. Construct its balance sheet. Note that the figure for surplus is missing and must be computed.

(000s OMITTED)	
Accounts payable	$300
Common stock	400
Accounts receivable	500
Buildings and equipment	500
Inventories on hand	250
Bonds outstanding	300
Cash	250
Goodwill	10
Surplus	—
U.S. Government bonds	50
Reserve for taxes	70
Loan from bank	300

APPENDIX
The Elements of Business Accounting

In order to understand the workings of modern business, you need to know something about the elements of business accounting. Although the details of accounting are complex, its fundamentals are simple. A knowledge of these fundamentals is essential for our purposes.

The balance sheet. A balance sheet is a cross-section picture of the financial position of a firm at some given point of time. It is an instantaneous snapshot. A second sort of picture, discussed below, is an "income" or "profit-and-loss" statement that summarizes the firm's operations over some period of time.

The balance sheet of any business rests on a fundamental equation. One side of the balance sheet shows what the business owns—its assets. Exactly corresponding to the value of these assets must be their ownership, which goes on the other side of the balance sheet. Obviously, the two are always equal—the balance sheet always balances.

It is not easy to say just *who* "owns" the assets of the business. At the one extreme, the common stockholders are considered the "residual owners"—that is, the ones who would receive all the cash left over if the business were liquidated and its debts (liabilities) were paid off. But this statement makes it clear that the various creditors of the business (for example, the bank that has lent it funds or the supplier from whom it has bought on credit) also have a claim on the assets. Such creditors, to whom the business owes money, are at the other extreme of the claimants on the business's assets—they get their funds first. Bondholders, whose interest is contingent on satisfactory incomes, have a less-preferred claim on the assets. Plainly, the line between "creditors" and "owners" is indistinct. The two groups shade into one another as a continuum of claimants on the business's assets.

Fundamentally, the balance sheet reflects the basic accounting equation (or identity) that Assets = Liabilities + Net worth; or, put the other way around, that Net worth = Assets − Liabilities. That is, the business is worth to the stockholders what assets they would have left over if all the liabilities were paid off.

Table A is the balance sheet of the General Electric Company, as of December 31, 1977. (A number of smaller items are omitted, to simplify the picture.) The left-hand side lists all the assets of the company—everything of value that it owns. The right-hand side lists all claims against these assets, broken down into two groups: first, its liabilities (what it owes), and second, its "capital" or "owners' equity" accounts (sometimes called its "net worth" or "proprietorship") on that date.

ASSETS. Once you see the basic equation underlying the balance sheet, most of its items are self-explanatory. Assets are usually arranged beginning with the most liquid (the most readily convertible into cash) and ending with the least liquid.

The amount shown for each asset is its estimated value as of the date of the balance sheet. Cash was obviously worth exactly the amount shown. But inventories, for example, are often carried at their cost, which may turn out to be higher or lower than their actual value on that date. Accounts receivable may include some noncollectible items, so they are not necessarily worth quite what they are listed at, and so on. The value placed on plant and equipment, as we shall see, is particularly susceptible to the vagaries of managerial and accounting judgment, because the current value shown is generally nothing but the original cost of the assets less an estimated amount of depreciation.[5]

Some companies show as an asset "patents and goodwill," which is obviously an estimated figure, a more or less arbitrary valuation determined by the company's officials and accountants. The item is so obviously intangible, even though of tremendous importance for such well-established products as Coca-Cola and Lucky Strike, that it has become accepted conservative business practice to place a very low value on it. GE carries such "intangible" assets at a nominal figure.[6]

LIABILITIES AND OWNERS' EQUITY. The liability side seems a little more tricky at first glance. "Short-term borrowings" are mainly funds borrowed

---

[5]See the discussion of "depreciation" charges in the following section.

[6]U.S. Steel and American Tobacco (Lucky Strike), for example, carry "goodwill and patents" at $1. Coca-Cola, on the other hand, carried goodwill, trademarks, formulas, and so on, at their cost—$95 million in 1977.

from banks. "Accounts payable" are debts owed to suppliers. "Accrued taxes, etc." are tax liabilities and other liabilities that have been incurred but have not yet been paid. "Bonds outstanding" are liabilities that may not come due for a much longer time.

"Owners' equity" (net worth) consists of two main items on this balance sheet. Part of the company's funds were obtained by sale of common stock. The amount shown is the amount for which the stock was originally sold (although this is not always so). GE has issued no preferred stock. "Retained earnings" are profits of the company that have not been paid out as dividends to stockholders, but instead have been reinvested in the company. Sometimes this item is called "surplus."

There is no reason to suppose that these past profits now repose in the cash account. More likely, as part of the firm's regular operations, they have been "plowed back" into inventory, plant and equipment, or some other assets. Or they may be reflected in a reduced level of the firm's liabilities. It is essential to understand that there is no direct correspondence between individual items on the two sides of the balance sheet. Any attempt to link up individual items directly will lead to fallacious conclusions.[7]

The income (profit-and-loss) statement. The income or profit-and-loss statement is the accountant's summary view of a firm's operation over some period of time—say, a year.

Table B shows General Electric's profit-and-loss statement for 1978, the year following the balance sheet shown in Table A. This is a straightforward account of the income received during the year and what was done with it. The first line shows GE's income from sales in 1978. Then the expenses of producing the goods and services sold are deducted, which gives GE's operating profit for the year.[8] GE had some other income (mainly, from its investments in other, partially owned companies and interest on consumer credit extended), and some other expenses (mainly, interest on its bonds). These figures are shown separately. This gives total profits before income taxes. Then federal income tax liability is deducted, which gives GE's net profit after taxes of $1,230 million for 1978.

The last part of the statement shows how GE allocated this profit. About half was paid out as dividends; the other half was reinvested in the company, shown as retained earnings. Thus owners' equity (net worth) is now $660 million higher

---

[7]The common argument that higher wages should be paid out of accumulated retained earnings is an example of such an inadequate understanding of the elements of accounting.

[8]The "Net sales" item corresponds to the revenue from sales shown by the "demand curves" in Chapter 4; the expenses correspond to the costs analyzed in Part 2.

TABLE B
GENERAL ELECTRIC COMPANY
Income Statement for Year Ended December 31, 1978[a]
(In Millions of Dollars)

Net sales		$19,654
Manufacturing and selling costs:		
Materials	$9,867	
Labor cost	7,401	
Depreciation	576	
Taxes (other than income taxes)	251	
Decrease in inventories	−399	17,695
Net profit from operations		$ 1,958
Other income—interest and dividends		419
Less interest charges on own bonds outstanding		−224
Net income before federal income taxes		$ 2,153
Provision for federal income taxes		−922
Net income (or profit)		$ 1,230
Allocation of net income:		
Dividends on common stock		$ 570
Increase in retained earnings		660

[a] Some minor items are combined with items listed. For more detail, see GE Annual Report for 1978.

than if all the profits had been distributed to the stockholders. Common stockholders—the corporation's "owners"—may thus be as well off one way as the other. In one case, they get cash dividends; in the other, the value of their investment accumulates. Such plowing back of earnings has long been commonplace in American industry, and some industrial giants such as Eastman Kodak and Ford have grown largely through reinvestment of earnings.

One warning about the profit-and-loss statement: The income and costs shown are not necessarily cash receipts and outlays; the profits are not necessarily cash profits. The distinction between cash transactions and accounting records is illustrated by the "Materials" item. The materials used may have been purchased long before and already have been in inventory at the year's beginning. Or materials purchased during the year might have been larger than the $9,867 million shown, if GE had chosen to build up its inventories during the year. The materials cost shown is for materials used, not for materials bought, during the year.

The same point is illustrated by the cost item "Depreciation." Every engineer and accountant knows that plant and equipment depreciate. If a truck bought in 1978 is expected to last five years, after five years it will have only scrap value if the

original estimates were accurate. The concern will not have to buy another truck until 1983, but if it does not figure the using up of the truck as a current expense, it is obviously understating its costs and overstating its profits in the intervening years. If no current depreciation is charged, in 1983 the entire cost of the new truck would have to be charged against 1983 income. Hence, accountants "charge" depreciation annually, even though no cash outlay is involved. Thus, one-fifth of the cost of the truck might be charged off as a current cost each year, or some more complicated depreciation formula might be used. There need be no cash expenditure that matches the depreciation shown.

Since cost and income items are accounting entries rather than cash transactions, obviously there is no necessary cash accumulation at the year's end equal to net profit earned during the year. The firm's cash may be higher or lower, depending on what has seemed to the managers the best use of available funds. (As we shall presently see from Table C, GE increased its cash on hand by about $275 million during 1978.) Managers need only be sure they have cash on hand to meet their obligations, one of which is dividends. Dividends may be paid in years when no profits have been made. AT&T, for example, paid its regular cash dividend of $9 per share each year

TABLE C
GENERAL ELECTRIC COMPANY   Balance Sheet   December 31, 1978 (In Millions of Dollars)

ASSETS		LIABILITIES & OWNERS' EQUITY	
Current assets:		Current liabilities:	
Cash	$1,993	Short-term borrowings	$ 960
Marketable securities	470	Accounts payable	1,217
Accounts receivable	3,289	Accrued taxes, etc.	543
Inventories on hand	3,003	Other	3,455
Total current assets	$ 8,755	Total current liabilities	$ 6,175
		Bonds outstanding & other	2,274
		Total liabilities	$ 8,299
Fixed assets:		Owners' equity:	
Investment in affiliated		Common stock	$1,065
companies	$1,411	Retained earnings	5,522
Plant and equipment	4,023	Total owners' equity	6,587
Other	848		
Total assets	$15,036	Total	$15,036[a]

[a] Does not add to exact total because minor items are omitted. Sometimes combined for simplicity.

straight through the depression of the 1930s, even though annual profits fell well below $9. Retained earnings, of course, then declined by the excess of dividend payments over net profits.

Relation between income statement and balance sheet. These observations tell us a good deal about the relation between the income statement and the balance sheet. Suppose now we draw up GE's balance sheet at the end of 1978—another spot picture, linked to the earlier one by the 1978 income statement.

During the year, assets have been continually used up in the production of current output; sales or other sources of funds have continually rebuilt the firm's assets. Since a net profit of $1,230 million after taxes was made during 1978, total owners' equity (net worth) was up by this amount at year-end before payment of dividends. As was emphasized above, the increase in assets over the year may have come in cash, inventories, accounts receivable, or any other item—or there may have been a decrease in liabilities. All we know from the income statement is that, on balance, assets less liabilities are up $1,230 million.

This $1,230 million is reduced to $660 million by the payment of dividends. On the asset side, the cash is reduced; on the other side, the reduction is in retained earnings, which would have shown a steady increase through the year if monthly balance sheets had been made. This leaves the retained earnings account up $660 million over December 31, 1977.

Together, the income statement and balance sheets provide an overall accounting of the firm's operations and changing status over the period. (The small discrepancies reflect some minor items omitted.)

Corporate profits and the stock market. Throughout this appendix, we have been primarily concerned with the mechanics of business accounting. Stop now and look for a moment at what this all means economically. During 1978, GE had a good year. It made $1,230 million in profits on its average owners' equity (investment) of $6,275 million during the year. This is a 19.6 percent return, even after paying taxes. Before taxes, the return was about twice as high. If you compare this rate of return with that of other leading American corporations, you will find that it looks very good.

How did this good year show up for the common stockholders? They collected $570 million of dividends. We can safely assume that the price of GE stock has been bid up in the market by investors to reflect this high rate of return. If you had bought one share at the end of 1978, you would have had to pay about $50 for it, nearly double the $29 "book value" per share of stock outstanding (obtained by dividing the 228 million shares outstanding into total owners' equity). Although market prices of common stock fluctuate widely, depending on many circumstances, in 1978 no "blue-chip" stocks like GE could be bought to give an earnings yield of anything like 19.6 percent. About half that was more usual, and the

$50 price to which GE stock had been bid up gave a 10.6 percent yield on the 1978 earnings of $5.29 per share.

Note that this was considerably higher than the rate of return provided by the $2.50 per-share dividend paid by GE—a cash yield of only 5 percent. But of course, the stockholders also gained from the $660 million ($2.89 per share) of profits plowed back into the business, which shows up on the December 31, 1978, balance sheet as additional retained earnings. This means that the company now has either that many more dollars' worth of assets, or that much less debt, or some combination of both, which should make it a more profitable company in the future, with larger total profit figures in the years ahead. Thus, savvy investors look at the total earnings of companies, not just at the dividends they pay. They calculate a "price–earnings ratio" in comparing stocks to buy. For example, GE's price–earnings ratio

at the end of 1978 was about 9.5 to 1; that is, you had to pay about $50 for a share of stock to get GE's earnings of $5.29 per share—about $9.50 for $1 of earnings. This was a relatively high "P–E ratio" (as financial experts call it), reflecting GE's long record of solid growth and good profits, and the presumption of more good years to come. Stocks in less stable, successful companies could be bought at much lower P–E ratios; 5:1 or 6:1 was not uncommon in 1978, which meant that your current return per dollar invested would be higher than in GE. But don't rush out to buy the lowest P–E-multiple stock you can find. Chances are that it's very risky, and that its low price relative to current earnings reflects precisely this fact. With millions of investors constantly looking for bargains, P–E ratios tend to reflect the relative prospective earnings of different companies fairly accurately, and it's hard to get rich quick by outguessing other investors.

REVIEW

New Concepts to Remember

This appendix has introduced several important new concepts. You will meet them in the newspaper as well as throughout the course:

balance sheet
assets
liabilities
owners' equity
net worth
profit-and-loss statement

income statement
dividends
depreciation
retained earnings (or surplus)
price–earnings ratio

CASE 4

GENERAL ELECTRIC COMPANY
(Based on the Appendix to Chapter 5)

Get a copy of the most recent General Electric Company annual report, or that of some other company in which you are interested. On the basis of your review of the report, what are your answers to the following questions? [On financial information, concentrate only on the profit-and-loss (or income) statement and the balance sheet (usually toward the end of the report), since the details in many corporate statements go beyond the points covered in the preceding appendix to Chapter 5.]

1. What are the main lines of business in which the company is involved?
2. Does the annual report give you a good picture of what the company does and how well it is doing it?
3. Last year, did the company do a good job for its stockholders? for its customers? How, if at all, can you tell?
4. What rate of return did the company earn on its stockholders' investment? (Use owners' equity as the measure of stockholders' invest-

ment.) What were the company's earnings as a percentage of its sales?
5. What part of its after-tax earnings did the company pay out in dividends? plow back into the company? If you had been a stockholder, would you have preferred a different allocation of the earnings? Why?
6. Was last year a good or bad year profitwise, compared to the preceding years?
7. Look up on the New York Stock Exchange page of your newspaper the current price of GE stock (or of whatever company you are using). What was the ratio of the stock price to last year's GE earnings (often called the price–earnings ratio)? For you as an investor, is this ratio or the rate of return on stockholders' investment in question 4 above a better measure of what you can earn on your money if you now invest in GE stock? Why should the price–earnings ratio for GE stock be higher than that for many other stocks (as it in fact is)? (*Hint:* Look at the growth of GE earnings over the years in the "Historical Review" section of the report, usually inside the back cover.)
8. Does GE have more stockholders or employees?

Supply,
Demand,
and Market
Prices

CHAPTER 6

Chapter 3 provided a bird's-eye view of how producers respond to consumer demands in a private-enterprise, free-market economy. Chapters 4 and 5 looked briefly at households and businesses, the main demanders and suppliers in the economy. This chapter examines in more detail the role of the market and market prices in connecting consumers and producers. If you thought economics was going to be about "supply and demand," this is it.

THE ROLE OF MARKETS AND MARKET PRICES

In a loose way, it is easy to see how consumer demands get the goods and services produced that consumers want. If consumers buy more wool sweaters, the immediate result is increased retail sales, and stores order more sweaters from wholesalers to replenish their stocks. Wholesalers in turn order more sweaters from the manufacturers; and manufacturers, with joyous hearts, produce more sweaters, because their profits depend on doing just that. The linkage may be jerky and imperfect, but each participant has an incentive—the profit incentive—to do his part.

Sometimes the linkage between consumer and producer is direct. An example is when you go to the barber for a haircut. More often, consumer demand has to pass through many links before it hits the ultimate producer. An example is consumer demand for automobiles, which goes through the local auto dealer back to GM or Ford, and through them to literally thousands of different suppliers of parts and productive equipment—steel, tires, electrical switches, machine tools, brake linings, shock absorbers, spark plugs, batteries, and so on. And behind each of these lies an array of suppliers to them, involving other raw materials and components. Moreover, at each stage, the supplier must hire the labor he needs (engineers, accountants, stenographers, janitors, salesmen, assembly workers, and others). Add on arranging transportation, storage for inventories, and financing, and you begin to get a picture of what's involved.

What ties all these decisions and operations together? What brings order out of the potential chaos in an economy that includes millions of different products demanded by millions of consumers? As Chapter 3 suggested, the answer is, an intricately interlinked net of markets and market prices. The grocer knows you want sugar when you walk into his store and buy ten pounds. Similarly, there is a market that links grocers to wholesalers; one that links wholesalers and sugar refiners; one that links sugar refiners and sugar growers; one that links each of these to the workers needed at each stage. Your purchase triggers a set of signals all the way back to producers.

In each market, price acts as the adjuster between demand and supply. When you demand more, price tends to move up. When price rises, there is an increased profit incentive to produce more. It is this interaction among demand, supply, and price that is the core of the self-adjusting mechanism of the private-enterprise system. A good understanding of the much-cited "law of supply and demand" is a powerful tool indeed for understanding how our modern economy works—how it produces order rather than chaos in allocating scarce resources.

SUPPLY, DEMAND, AND MARKET PRICE— PRICE THEORY IN ACTION

You may have visited the "wheat pit" at the Board of Trade in Chicago, which is one of the world's major wheat-trading markets. Here, millions of bushels of wheat are bought and sold daily by a relatively small number of traders, acting largely as dealers and agents for others. Suppose the supply and demand for wheat in the pit on some particular day are as shown in Table 6–1, and that these schedules are constant for the entire day.

In effect, each of these traders acts as an agent for people wanting to sell or buy wheat. Imagine that each seller tries to auction his wheat off at the highest possible price. Suppose that the first bid on this day is $1.50 a bushel for 1,000 bushels. It is readily filled, but it's clear that at this

TABLE 6–1
Supply and Demand for Wheat, Chicago, on a Given Day

BUSHELS OFFERED (IN MILLIONS)	PRICE	BUSHELS DEMANDED (IN MILLIONS)
18	$3.00	8
16	2.50	11
14	2.00	14
12	1.50	17
10	1.00	20

price there's going to be trouble, because buyers will demand 17 million bushels, whereas sellers are willing to offer only 12 million bushels. Table 6–1 shows that a lot of buyers are willing to pay more than $1.50 if they have to. And most of them soon discover they have to, because offerings are 5 million bushels short of demand at $1.50. We say there is an excess demand of 5 million bushels at $1.50. As buyers bid higher prices to get the wheat they want, the price will move up toward $2.00. As the price rises, those unwilling to pay the higher price will drop out and new sellers will come in, until at $2.00 the amount offered for sale just matches the amount demanded. There is no reason to suppose that the price will be bid higher this day, because everyone who is willing to pay $2.00 is getting his wheat and everyone who has wheat for sale at $2.00 sells it.

Try starting with a price of $3.00 to see whether that price could last long in this market. Where does the price stabilize?

This same analysis can be done graphically just as well. Figure 6–1 graphs these same demand and supply schedules. The curves intersect at a price of $2.00 with 14 million bushels traded. This is the only price at which the amount demanded just matches the amount supplied, and it is the price that will be reached through bargaining in the market. The reasoning is the same as with the schedules. Try any higher price—say, $3.00—and you can see from Figure 6–1 that it can't last. At $3.00, 18 million bushels will be offered but only 8 million bushels demanded; there is an excess supply of 10 mil-

lion bushels. Competition among sellers will push the price down. At any price higher than $2.00, there is excess supply. There will be too many sellers for the buyers, and sellers will shade their prices in order to find buyers. At any lower price, buyers won't be able to get the wheat they demand and will shade up the prices they offer.

Equilibrium Price and Market Equilibrium

When a price is established that just clears the market, economists call it an "equilibrium price." The amount offered just equals the amount demanded at that price. Price is in equilibrium when, with given demand and supply curves, it stays put at that level. At any other level, there will be excess supply or excess demand that will drive price up or down toward a level that will eliminate the excess supply or excess demand.

When an equilibrium price has been reached, with given demand and supply curves, we say the market is in equilibrium. At the prevailing price, there is neither excess supply nor excess demand. Unless either demand

FIGURE 6–1
Supply and Demand for Wheat
With these supply and demand curves, the equilibrium price will be $2.00, with 14 million bushels exchanged.

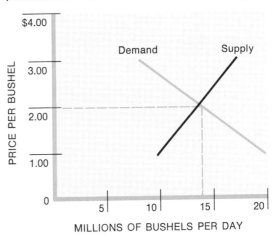

MILLIONS OF BUSHELS PER DAY

or supply changes, price and the amount bought and sold in each time period will remain unchanged.

Buyers' demands and sellers' responses to those demands are thus meshed together through market adjustments toward equilibrium. Once a market has reached equilibrium, it has impersonally and automatically accomplished the following:

1. It has reflected the wants of all buyers willing to spend their dollars in that market, weighting each want by the number of dollars that particular consumer will spend at different prices. If each buyer's demand schedule truly reflects the marginal utilities of different amounts of the product to him, the market has given him the largest utility obtainable for his dollars.

2. It has led sellers to sell as much of the product as consumers will buy.

And we can be reasonably sure this equilibrium accurately reflects the preferences of all parties concerned, buyers and sellers, because the exchanges are voluntary. If any individual saw the purchase or sale as against his best interests, he would not have bought or sold at that price.

Changes in Demand and Supply

Suppose that on the following day, the demand for wheat increases, to D^1D^1 in Figure 6–2. The supply curve remains unchanged. Common sense tells you that with constant supply and increased demand, the price will be bid up—and it is. With increased demand D^1D^1, the price is bid up to $2.50 with 16 million bushels bought. Although the supply curve is constant, more wheat is supplied at the higher price. The result of the increased demand is both a higher price and more wheat traded. Suppose now that on the third day, demand rises again, to D^2D^2. The price is then bid still higher—up to $3.00 with 18 million bushels bought. The demand curve slides up the fixed supply curve.

Now try holding the demand curve constant and increasing or decreasing supply. Figure out the effect on price and sales of each shift in supply.

Last, consider a case in which both demand and supply shift simultaneously. Suppose the price of turnips is 10 cents a pound and 2,000 pounds are being sold daily, with curves SS and DD in Figure 6–3. Now both supply and demand increase, to $S'S'$ and $D'D'$. The result is a big increase in sales, to 4,000 pounds, and a rise in price to 12 cents. Try shifting the curves to other positions, and with steeper and flatter

FIGURE 6–2
Supply and Demand for Wheat—
Changing Demand
Increases in demand D^1D^1 and D^2D^2 cause increases in both price and quantity traded. The new equilibrium with D^2D^2 involves a price of $3.00 and 18 million bushels exchanged daily.

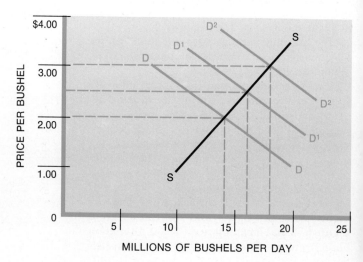

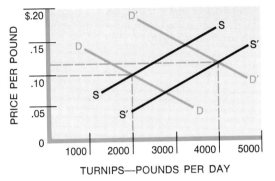

FIGURE 6–3
Changing Supply and Demand for Turnips
When both demand and supply shift simultaneously, as shown by the dashed lines, sales rise to 4,000 pounds and price rises to 12 cents. Try shifting the curves to other positions.

slopes. The market price and quantity sold will automatically adjust to reflect the preferences of both buyers and sellers.

Supply and Demand: Some Special Cases

Completely inelastic supply. Some extreme cases may help to clarify what is involved in market adjustments to different demand-and-supply relationships. First, take a case in which the amount supplied is absolutely fixed. A favorite economists' example is that there are only four corners at State and Madison Streets in Chicago, one of the busiest corners in the world. The supply curve for building space on this corner is thus completely inelastic—there's no more land available on the corner no matter how high land prices or rents may go. Suppose we graph the supply of land on this corner in square feet, and the demand (*DD*) for it on either a purchase or a rental basis. The result is Figure 6–4, with annual rents in equilibrium at $1,000 per square foot.

Now suppose the demand for space on the corner increases. The demand curve moves up to D^1D^1. Property owners can now charge $1,100 per square foot. The amount of land rented is identical before and after the increase in de-

mand. This outcome is very nice for the landowner, not so good for the consumer. But if demand falls, the full burden falls on the landowner. The price (rent) going to the supplier (landowner) is determined solely by the demand. Supply in this extreme case, and only in this case, has no active role in determining the price. Note that supply may be inelastic for many products in the short run, but long-run very inelastic supply is uncommon.

Completely elastic supply with "constant costs." Now take the other extreme—the pencil industry described in Chapter 5, where the amount supplied could be increased at a constant cost by merely duplicating productive facilities. Given a long enough time period, the supply curve would look flat, as in Figure 6–5. If *DD* is the demand, the price of pencils will be 3 cents, and 10,000 per day will be made and sold. If demand increases to D^1D^1, the price remains unchanged while production and sales rise to 12,000 daily. This is a case of constant costs. Since more pencils can be produced at the same cost per pencil, increased demand will simply call forth more pencils without bidding up the price.

FIGURE 6–4
Supply and Demand for Rental Space
(Inelastic Supply)
With completely inelastic supply, increased demand means merely a higher price.

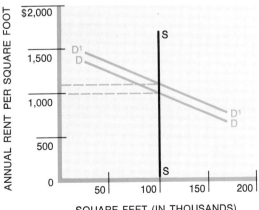

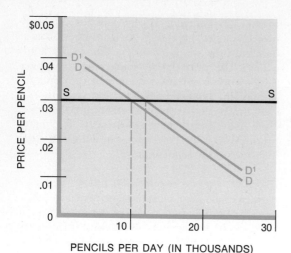

FIGURE 6–5
Supply and Demand for Pencils (Elastic Supply)
With infinitely elastic supply, increased demand
leads to more output with no increase in price.

Most real-world cases lie between the land and pencil extremes—although many commodities approximate the pencil case, given a long enough time period for adjustment. If increased output can be obtained only by constructing more expensive factories, or by paying higher prices for raw materials and labor, the supply curve will slope upward.

Try working out graphically the results of increased demand in constant- and increasing-cost cases. You will see that it makes a good deal of difference to you, the consumer, which kind of product you want more of. In the elastic-supply case, you get more at the same price; in the inelastic-supply case, you get more only at a higher price. (With falling costs and a downward-sloping supply curve, which we have tem-

porarily ruled out, you could be happier still, since then increased demand could mean more goods at a lower price.)

THE SOCIAL FUNCTIONS OF MARKET PRICES

It is easy to get bogged down in the mechanics of demand and supply curves. Stop and be sure you understand the three big social functions of market prices as they move to equilibrate demand and supply in different markets. Note that they serve these functions automatically, in response to many buyers and sellers, each intent on looking out for his own self-interest.

Suppose, to take a case recently much in the news, the demand for gasoline and other oil products grows, beginning from a market equilibrium like that for wheat in Figure 6–1. Suppose, using the figures there, the equilibrium price is $2.00 per barrel of crude oil (about what it was before the formation of the OPEC cartel and their escalation of oil prices), with 14 million barrels sold per day. Demand grows by 1 million barrels per day. What will the results be?

The demand curve moves out, or up the supply curve, by 1 million barrels at each price. In Table 6–1 and Figure 6–1, add 1 million barrels to the amount demanded at each price. Thus, the price of oil will rise to a new equilibrium level of about $2.15, with about 14.8 million barrels bought daily. (Note that the amount bought does not rise a full million barrels, because at $2.15 per barrel, the short-run supply curve says that suppliers will offer only about 14.8 million barrels, not 15 million.) Note the three functions of the rising price.

1. The higher price calls forth more production. (a) It immediately calls forth 800,000 additional barrels of oil per day in response to increased consumer demand, given the short-run supply curve indicated. (b) With more time to adjust (that is, in the long run), the higher price will also stimulate further drilling for oil, moving the entire supply curve out to the right. This is a long-run supply increase, whereas (a) was a short-run increase in output, given the short-run supply curve.

2. The higher price rations the available supply of oil to those who want it most, and induces them to economize on its use as it becomes more expensive. As Table 6–1 indicates, the public wants vastly more oil than there is to go around; the table shows a demand for 20 million barrels daily at $1.00 a barrel, and the amount would be still larger at lower prices—perhaps almost infinite if oil were very cheap. Price is the rationer of scarce supplies in a market system; it leads users to economize on the use of the increasingly expensive commodity. If, for example, the supply of oil is reduced (as it was by the OPEC cartel in 1974), rising prices will ration the less urgent demanders out of the market, determining who gets the increasingly scarce oil, and stimulating the use of substitutes.

3. Although it is not shown on our chart, the higher price for oil will increase the demand for substitute energy sources (such as coal, natural gas, and nuclear energy). This will raise their prices too and stimulate greater production of them in both the short and long runs. A higher price for any product stimulates the production of substitutes, an important effect indeed, as some natural resources are exhausted and society needs to stimulate the production of substitutes. (Note that this effect may stimulate research seeking currently unknown substitutes, as well as more output of currently known energy sources.)

To summarize, rising market prices, reflecting excess demand, serve three vitally important social purposes: (1) They increase the amount of the scarce product produced by profit-seeking suppliers; (2) they ration out less urgent demanders, leading users to economize their use of the scarce commodity; and (3) they stimulate the production of substitutes.

THE ECONOMICS OF PRICE FIXING

The law of supply and demand states that market price and quantity sold are determined by supply and demand under competitive conditions. But lots of times, people—labor unions, farmers, businessmen, congressmen—don't like the prices and quantities set by market demand and supply. And they want to do something about it. What then?

Price Ceilings and "Shortages"

Most people don't like to pay high prices. When prices rise, the pressures mount on Congress and the president to hold them down. "How can I pay $1.00 a pound for butter and $300 a month rent for a poor apartment when my income is only $8,000 a year?" asks the stenographer. So sometimes Congress passes laws to keep prices down. Suppose it slaps an 80-cent price ceiling on butter, below the equilibrium level. The demand for and supply of butter are shown in Figure 6–6. The equilibrium price would be $1.00 a pound.

At the legal price ceiling, clearly there is excess demand of about 600 pounds; people want a lot more butter than there is to buy. The amount demanded daily is 2,200 pounds; that

FIGURE 6–6
Supply and Demand for Butter (Price Fixing)
When the government sets a legal maximum price below the market equilibrium price, there's trouble. There is excess demand for butter at the artificially low price.

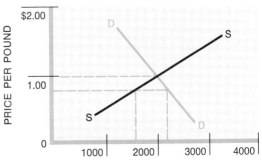

73

offered is only 1,600. There is, in short, a "shortage."

Who gets the butter? The price system is tied down—it can't ration the butter by equilibrating supply and demand through a higher price.

"First come, first served" may be the answer. Housewives get the children off to school early and head for the grocer's. They stand in lines in the grocery store. This solution is not calculated to make anyone very happy, least of all the grocer, who loses his friends fast when there isn't enough to go around, and customers who can't do their shopping till evening. We had a painful experience sitting in long gasoline lines in 1974, when the OPEC oil embargo plus a government price ceiling created a temporary gasoline "shortage," and another in 1979.

In frustration, grocers may set up informal butter-rationing systems of their own—say, only a half pound to a customer. Or they may decide to protect their regular customers, so they put away a few cases of butter for them. This is hard on people who shop around, and disastrous for families that move to new neighborhoods.

If enough people become unhappy enough, the government may have to step in with a formal rationing plan, whereby the customer has to have a government ration ticket as well as money to buy a pound of butter (or his weekly ration of gasoline). Nobody is very happy about being rationed, and everybody complains about the red tape. Unless the government officials are both skillful and lucky, the number of ration tickets issued won't exactly match the supplies available, and mixups can be counted on.

Finally, the price system may sneak in the back door again and take over part of the equilibrating job outside the law. "Black markets" may develop, whereby prices actually charged and paid slide above the legal ceiling. It's pretty hard for well-to-do consumers not to offer the corner grocer a little extra for an extra pound of butter. And it's pretty hard for the grocer, pinched between rising costs and fixed price ceilings, to refuse. Short of a regimented system like Hitler's Germany, it's very hard to enforce rigid price ceilings when excess demand is large. In World War II, such ceilings worked reasonably well in the United States, partly because of intense patriotic pressures and partly because the government gradually raised ceilings as pressures built up on various commodities. The surprising thing to most economists was not that black markets developed, but that the public's sense of fair play was so strong that the price-control system didn't blow apart faster than it did.

Whether the job is done by informal seller rationing, government rationing, or black-market price increases, someone or something has to decide who is to get the butter when a price ceiling is imposed below the equilibrium market price. A price ceiling works no magic. It just transfers the rationing job to some other channel, and it eliminates the stimulus to supply that higher prices would produce. You can't get rid of the basic supply-and-demand forces at work by passing a law.

Rent Controls and Housing Shortages

In recent years, rents on apartments and houses have risen rapidly almost everywhere. This reflects growing pressures of population in many areas, rising construction costs, higher taxes and maintenance, and many other factors. Rent is a big part of many family budgets, especially for poor families, and it is not surprising that many cities have felt strong pressures to impose rent ceilings, particularly since it is commonly believed that landlords are high-income individuals and businesses that gouge renters whenever they are able to do so.

Rent ceilings were widely used during World War II, and three large cities—New York, Stockholm, and Moscow—provide interesting case studies of the effects of retaining these ceilings over extended periods. Let us assume that the rent ceiling is set below the market equilibrium level; otherwise, there would be no point in applying it. The immediate result, our supply-and-demand analysis tells us, will depend on the supply and demand curves involved. In the short run, presumably the supply of rental apartments in, say, New York City is substantially fixed; the supply curve is almost a vertical line. If the legal rent ceiling is below the market-clearing level, there is little landlords can do (if they obey the law) other than complain and see part or all of their profits shifted to renters. What renters get the benefit of the lower rents? Presumably those who are lucky enough to be in the controlled apartments. There will be an excess demand for apartments at the controlled price (a "shortage" of apartments), and newcomers looking for places to live will have a tough time, since they can't get apartments by offering to pay higher rents. But all in all, the rent-control program seems to be providing lower rents at the expense of those well-to-do landlords. (*Query:* How would you ration the apartments among the excess demanders in such cases when present occupants moved out?)

The long-run effects are worse. The supply-increasing effects of higher prices are tied down by the rent-control laws. If you were a landlord, what would you do? As your after-costs profit on rented apartments fell, you would transfer your investment out of rental housing to some uncontrolled activity where you could make a normal profit. If you couldn't sell the property outright (and it would be difficult, because potential buyers would know about the rent controls too), you would probably transfer your investment out by skimping on maintenance and repairs. Above all, you certainly wouldn't invest in constructing new rental housing if it were also rent-controlled.

Precisely these things happened. In New York, for example, there has been wholesale undermaintenance and actual abandonment of older apartments that would have been maintained in livable condition without rent controls. In 1975, for example, 50,000 undermaintained apartments were simply abandoned as unlivable in spite of the drastic housing "shortage." New apartment construction was virtually zero, until the city began to relax the rent-control laws and exempt new housing. Families holding leases on controlled apartments went to great lengths to keep their apartments, whose rents were far below free-market levels. They were passed on within families, or sold for (often illegal) side payments where leases were transferable. Hopeful renters perused the obituary columns of the local papers, and arrived ahead of the first mourners. The subsidy was large for those who benefited; but the cost to newly marrieds, families who had to move, and all those who would have benefited from new housing construction was large. Not least, massive under-maintenance of rent-controlled apartments contributed significantly to the rapid decay of New York City slum areas.

In Stockholm, the results of long-continued rent controls were similar. World War II rent controls were maintained, with only slow rises permitted to meet rising costs. By the mid-1960s, over 40 percent of Stockholm's entire population was registered in the city government's official queue, which is supposed to govern priority as to who gets the controlled housing as it becomes available. Children are given official-queue list certificates as christening gifts, and obituary columns are a closely watched source of rental openings. The average waiting time on the official government queue has approached ten years. However, much new housing is outside the rent-control system, and most residents find their housing at higher rates through more usual market arrangements now.

Moscow (and the USSR generally) is the extreme case of controlled rents. Housing is very scarce and generally poor in quality. Since it is virtually all owned by the state, the issue is merely one of how the available supply is rationed. Rents are very low (often less than 5 percent of family income, compared to about 25 percent in the United States), so there is an enormous shortage of (excess demand for) housing, which is allocated by government fiat, with preference given to Communist party members, good workers, and others who meet special standards set by the government. Most families must share their apartments with others, and young people often wait for years after marriage before getting an apartment of their own.

Price Controls, Shortages, and Rationing

Is there a "shortage" of good apartments in New York? Was there a shortage of gasoline in 1974 when OPEC embargoed the United States and the government here applied price controls? Is there a shortage of Porsche sportscars, of filet mignon, of fine whiskies? In each case, there obviously isn't enough to go around to everybody who would like to have some. But the appropriate question in each case is, At what price? You may say there's no "shortage" of Porsche sportscars. But suppose the government fixed the price at $2,500? It is easy to predict that there would be long waiting lines of potential buyers. Or suppose Congress decreed that the price of filet mignon could be no more than 50 cents a pound. A huge "shortage" would predictably develop overnight.

You may say that, in some moral sense, there is a shortage of adequate housing for poor families, quite different from the cases of gasoline and apartments. But if we define "shortage" (as most economists do) to mean "excess demand," a shortage arises only when there is unsatisfied demand at the existing price. And this condition cannot last in a free market. An economic "shortage" will arise and continue only when the price is fixed below the equilibrium market level.

Whenever there is a shortage, with the price system tied down, some other form of rationing must be found. Many have been devised, officially and unofficially—government ration tickets; illegal black-market payments; first come, first served; friendship with the rationing officials. Price rationing rewards those with money; first come, first served rewards those with patience and lots of free time; and so on. Are long waiting lines for gas better or worse than higher prices or government ration tickets to determine who gets the scarce gas?

Troublesome as the rationing problem may be, outlawing the supply-increasing effects of rising free-market prices where supplies are scarce is likely to create even more serious economic problems. In the New York case, for example, many critics argue that the long-run supply-reduction costs far exceed the "equity" advantages to protected renters.

Farm Price Supports

Some people—usually sellers—worry because prices aren't high enough. Labor unions often try to set wages above free-market levels. Some business firms do the same thing with their prices. The government is a large-scale participant in the game of putting floors under prices above the free-market level; farm price-support programs and minimum-wage legislation are big examples.

Suppose the government decrees that wheat shall not sell for less than $3.00 a bushel when the market-clearing price would be only $2.00,

as pictured in Figure 6–7. It's clear that there will be a lot of unsold wheat around—excess supply at the $3.00 price is 30 million bushels.

Suppose the government price floor is enforced and nobody undercuts the stated $3.00 price. Are wheat farmers better or worse off as a result? First, only about 80 million bushels will be bought. Another 30 million bushels are offered, and either the government will have to buy them up or strong price-cutting pressures will develop among the farmers with the unsold wheat. Second, our old friend elasticity of demand reenters. If demand is inelastic (as in Figure 6–7), total expenditures on wheat are larger at the higher price, and total farm income is up (even though consumers get less wheat to eat). But if demand is elastic, the higher price leaves everyone worse off; then, farmers get less total income from their wheat, and consumers get less wheat.

But even if demand is inelastic over the price range involved, this simple form of government price edict won't prove very satisfactory. If you are one of the farmers with the millions of bushels of wheat that nobody bought, the higher total income of wheat farmers is small solace to you when you have no income at all. You want the government to help you, too.

So the government program will probably take one of two basic courses: (1) The government may support the legal price through buying up the extra 30 million bushels of wheat. This would in effect move the total (private plus government) demand curve to the right (to $D'D'$ in Figure 6–7), so the equilibrium price is $3.00 with 110 million bushels sold. Or (2) the government may restrict wheat production (maybe through a "soil-conservation" program) to reduce supply to a point where the new market price is $3.00 with sales of 80 million bushels. This policy would bring supply and demand into equilibrium by shifting the supply curve to the left (to $S'S'$ in Figure 6–7).

In approach 1, the government ends up buying the 30 million bushels of wheat at $3.00 a bushel—at a cost of $90 million to the taxpayers. Who gains? Farmers. Who loses? Taxpayers, and consumers who end up with less wheat and a higher price for what they buy. Moreover, unless something changes, the government will keep on piling up wheat indefinitely.

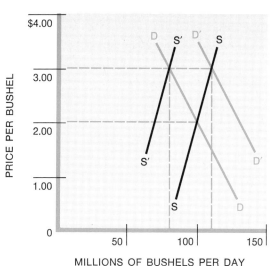

MILLIONS OF BUSHELS PER DAY

FIGURE 6–7
Supply and Demand for Wheat (Price Supports)
When the government sets a minimum price higher than the market equilibrium price, there's also trouble. At $3.00, there is excess supply of 30 million bushels. D′D′ shows the new demand curve if the government buys up the excess; S′S′ the new supply curve if the government induces farmers to restrict their output.

up or by restricting output. But laws that fix prices above or below market equilibrium levels without dealing with excess demand or supply soon face painful problems of which simple supply-and-demand analysis can give ample warning.

Minimum-Wage Laws

In conclusion, to check your grasp of supply-and-demand analysis, try the following problem. A popular remedy for poverty is getting the government to pass a minimum-wage law that will ensure all workers an above-poverty annual wage. For example, suppose Congress sets a legal minimum wage of $3.50 per hour; given an average annual workyear of 2,000 hours, this should provide an annual income of $7,000 for all workers—not magnificent, but above many incomes now, and above the federal "poverty level." Will the minimum-wage law eliminate poverty when it applies? (*Hint:* Draw a hypothetical demand curve of a typical business firm for unskilled teenagers and older workers, and a hypothetical supply curve for such workers. Suppose the market-clearing equilibrium wage for unskilled workers is now $3.00. What would you predict as the effect of the new law? Who would gain and who would lose?)

In approach 2, this continuing "surplus" situation is avoided by requiring that 30 million fewer bushels of wheat are produced. If the government merely required everybody to cut production by the required percentage, this would be the end of the matter. But the government pays farmers for not producing. Here again, taxpayers pick up the bill for the subsidy paid to farmers for not producing the 30 million bushels of wheat. And as under approach (1) consumers pay more and get fewer bushels of wheat. Strikingly, under both plans, it is the big, rich farmers who get most of the benefits. Under (1), the big farmers get most of the higher price benefits because they have more output to sell. Under (2), they get the biggest government payments for cutting back production, since they begin with the biggest production to cut back. The farm income and price-support programs have increased mainly the incomes that were already highest.

The government can keep the price up—if it's willing to eliminate excess supply by buying it

CONCLUSION: SUPPLY, DEMAND, AND MARKET PRICES

Continuous interaction among demand, supply, and prices in a myriad of interlinked markets for goods and services is the core of the private-enterprise, market-directed economic system. Supply-and-demand analysis provides a simple but powerful tool for thinking through a wide range of economic problems—in both individual markets and the economy as a whole. The preceding pages provide a variety of examples of supply-and-demand analysis at work. Over and over in the chapters ahead, we shall be asking, What determines demand and supply in this market, how do they interact, and what is the equilibrium outcome toward which they move? These questions are the core of "price theory," and of understanding the operation of our basically market-directed economy.

ANOTHER APPLICATION

Who really pays the taxes? Suppose the government imposes an additional $1 tax on each fifth of whiskey distilled for sale. Assume that the long-run supply curve before the new tax is *SS* in Figure 6–8 (same in both halves). The left-hand diagram shows a highly elastic demand curve for whiskey, the right-hand diagram a highly inelastic one. Before the new tax, the price is $5 per fifth, and 100,000 fifths are being sold weekly in both diagrams.

The new tax raises the effective cost of producing whiskey by $1 per fifth; hence the supply curve moves to the left by $1 at each level of output. Less will be produced at each price. *S'S'* represents the new supply curve (after tax) in both halves of the diagram. But as supply is restricted, the results are very different with the two demand curves.

With highly inelastic demand (right-hand diagram), as price moves up, consumers continue to buy nearly as much whiskey; the new equilibrium shows nearly as much whiskey produced and sold as before the tax, with the price to the consumer higher by nearly the full amount of the tax. Nearly the whole $1 tax has been shifted onto consumers. With highly elastic demand (left-hand diagram), the amount bought drops rapidly as price rises. The new after-tax equilibrium shows mainly a reduction in production and purchases, with the new price (including tax) only a little above the old $5 level. The main result is that consumers get less whiskey, while producers share $1 of the $5+ price with the government. Simple supply-and-demand analysis can help on a wide variety of problems.

FIGURE 6–8
Tax Effects with Elastic and Inelastic Demand
A new tax on whiskey is largely passed on to consumers with little drop in consumption if demand is inelastic (right-hand portion), but results mainly in reduced output and consumption if demand is elastic (left-hand portion).

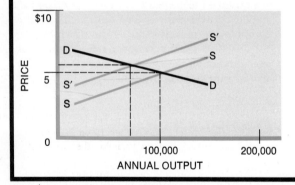

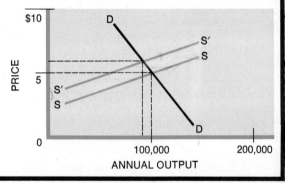

SUMMARY AND REVIEW

1. An intricate set of thousands of interconnected markets connect consumers' demands with producers' supplies in a market economy.

2. Each competitive market moves toward an equilibrium in which the amount demanded is just equal to the amount supplied at the market price. Excess supply and excess demand are both eliminated in equilibrium.

3. When a competitive market has reached equilibrium, it has reflected the wants of all consumers who are willing to spend their dollars on that product, weighting each want by the number of dollars that consumers spend on it at different prices; and it has led firms to sell as much of the product as consumers will buy at the equilibrium price.

4. In markets with perfectly inelastic supply, price is determined entirely by market demand; in markets with infinitely elastic supply, output is determined entirely by demand.

5. A rising market price in response to excess demand serves three important social functions:
   a. It stimulates more production of the good or service in question.
   b. It rations the available supply to those who want it most, and induces them to economize on its use as it becomes more expensive.
   c. It stimulates production and use of substitutes.

6. When a price is fixed above or below its equilibrium level, there is excess demand or excess supply, and some other rationing device must take over, since the price system is immobilized. "Shortages" occur when a price is fixed below its market-clearing equilibrium level. "Surpluses" appear when the price is fixed above its market-clearing equilibrium level.

New Concepts to Remember

equilibrium price
supply
supply curve
elasticity of supply
market price
market equilibrium

excess demand
excess supply
shortage
rationing
constant costs
increasing costs

For Analysis and Discussion

1. What are the social functions of rising prices when there is excess demand? If we hold down prices by law, how are these social functions carried out?

2. Is it demand or supply that primarily determines price? If your answer is, "Different in different cases," give an example in which you would expect each to be the dominant force.

3. Explain carefully what is meant by saying that an equilibrium price "clears the market."

4. When demand is large, we can be sure the price of the commodity will be high. True or false? Why?

5. Why are diamonds so high-priced, when they serve for the most part only as decoration, while air is free?

6. Are the factors determining the price of a Picasso painting the same as those determining the price of potatoes? Explain your answer.

7. Is there a shortage of T-bone steaks? Would there be if the government set a price ceiling of 50 cents a pound? How about hamburger?

8. Go back to Figure 6–6, and assume that the demand for butter increases. Explain what will happen.

9. Suppose that the demand for cigarettes is very inelastic and a new tax is imposed on cigarettes. Would the tax be passed on to consumers through higher prices? Compare this with a product for which the demand is highly elastic.

10. How does elasticity of demand help to explain why, historically, governments often imposed a salt tax when they wanted to obtain more revenue?

CASE 5

CONSUMER CREDIT AND USURY LAWS

Throughout the Middle Ages, to charge interest for the use of money was improper under Catholic church doctrines (most lending was done by Jews) and was prohibited by law in many kingdoms—with violation sometimes punishable by death. Such laws were commonly evaded by borrowers and lenders because of the obvious benefits to both of borrowing and lending, and, with the Protestant Reformation and the commercial and industrial revolutions, official antagonism to lending at interest faded rapidly. Yet, today, most states still have laws limiting the interest rates that can legally be charged on loans, presumably to safeguard borrowers against greedy lenders.

State laws have varied widely, but many have had a general ceiling (say, 10 percent or so on business and mortgage loans), with an escape provision permitting higher rates where (as on small loans to consumers) extra costs or risks of lending can be shown. In such cases, upper limits of 30–42 percent are not uncommon. The volume of such lending is large—nearly $250 billion of consumer credit was outstanding in 1979 on department-store installment credit, credit cards, bank loans, auto-purchase loans, and the like.

In response to the recent wave of "consumerism," the National Uniform Credit Act was passed to limit to 1.5 percent per month (18 percent per annum) the interest rate that department stores, credit-card companies, auto dealers, banks, and others can charge borrowers. This was well below the going rate for many borrowers, especially high-risk, low-income individuals and families. Moreover, in the 1970s, several states went still further and reduced the legal ceiling rate to 10 (Arkansas, Montana, and Tennessee) or 12 percent (Minnesota, Washington, and Wisconsin). Consumer-protection groups are pushing such legislation in other states.

Parallel pressures to impose lower interest-rate ceilings on home mortgage loans (which now total over $500 billion) arise each time money becomes "tight" and interest rates rise. The following news item is an example.

TUNNEY URGES 6% HOME LOAN INTEREST LIMIT

LOS ANGELES—"The economy needs a bang to shock it back into economic health," Senator John Tunney says, and one big help would be a mandatory six percent interest rate upper limit on home loans.

"We're really on the brink of depression," the California Senator said Saturday, at the conclusion of a three-hour conference he called with representatives of labor, business, and the League of Women Voters. Home buyers need more money at reasonable rates.[1]

Should your state lower its ceiling on consumer and mortgage loans? What do you predict will be the results of these new consumer-protection laws? Who will gain, and who will lose?

---

[1] *San Francisco Chronicle,* April 7, 1975.

Part 2

Markets, the Price System, and the Allocation of Resources

PROLOGUE TO PART 2

We turn now to microeconomics—to the study of the behavior of the individual households and business firms that make up our economy, the prices they charge and pay, and the incomes that different businesses and individuals receive. Chapter 3 sketched out the way self-interested individuals spending their incomes on what they want most, profit-seeking businessmen trying to earn large profits, and self-interested workers trying to earn a good living all mesh together through many interlinked markets so as to allocate our productive resources to yield the most of what we want at the lowest possible costs, with a maximum of individual freedom. Parts 2 and 3 now study in detail the way households and businesses behave.

It is useful to have in advance a map of the terrain we are approaching in studying the modern American economy—a brief overview of the structure of markets in the modern economy. Chapters 7–14 are devoted mainly to analyzing how these different market structures work (microeconomic analysis). Chapters 15–17 focus on policies designed to make them work better (microeconomic policy).

THE STRUCTURE OF MARKETS

There are four main types of markets:

1. Pure competition exists in markets where there are so many sellers that no one is big enough to have any appreciable influence over market price. Specifically, pure competition is characterized by:

a. Many sellers, each acting independently and each so small relative to the market as to have no appreciable effect on market price.

b. An identical product, so that the buyer is indifferent as to whom he buys from.[1]

c. Freedom of entry for new sellers who wish to enter the market. (This assumption is not necessary where characteristics 1 and 2 hold, but most economists include it in analyzing pure competition.)

---

[1] The added assumption is usually made that all buyers and sellers have full knowledge of prices being quoted over the entire market.

In a purely competitive market, the individual seller is a "price taker," not a price setter or price maker. He takes the market price as given and, considering his costs of production, decides how much to produce in order to maximize his profits. The individual wheat farmer, in the absence of government controls, is an example. But, although no one firm *acting alone* can significantly influence market price, the summation of all the individual producers' actions can and does. If each of many individual sellers is led to restrict output, for example, the summation of all these thousands of individual cutbacks will reduce market supply and, other things equal, raise the price.

2. **Pure monopoly,** at the other extreme, is characterized by:

a. Only one seller of the good or service
b. Rivalry from producers of substitutes so remote as to be insignificant

Under pure monopoly, the monopolist can set the market price himself. He is a "price maker." But even the monopolist has to face up to the realities of elasticity of demand. He can put his price where he wishes, but unless demand for his product is perfectly inelastic, the higher he puts his price, the less he will sell. In fact, there is almost no product for which there is not at least a partial substitute, however distant, and no monopolist faces a perfectly inelastic demand curve. Thus, examples of pure monopoly are scarce in the real world. The local waterworks would be a close approximation—but note that almost all the cases one can think of are now public utilities, regulated by government action.

3. **Monopolistic competition** exists when there are numerous sellers of slightly differentiated, but not identical, products. For example, different brands of ice cream are likely to be very similar, but they differ slightly. Moreover, some sellers are more conveniently located than others; have nicer surroundings, sell on credit, stay open on Sundays. The product, including conditions surrounding its sale, is "differentiated" among sellers. But the differentiated products are close enough so that no one seller can get his price very far out of line with the others without losing sales substantially. In such markets, sellers compete on price and also on the quality of the product, conditions of its sale, and the like. Although each seller is a "price maker" for his own product, unless he can differentiate that product substantially from substitutes, he is

in fact pretty much a price taker in the total market.

4. **Oligopoly** occurs when there are only a few dominant sellers of identical or closely substitutable products. Automobiles are an example: General Motors, Ford, and Chrysler dominate the American market, but there are other, smaller firms here and firms abroad that compete. The critical thing about oligopoly is that each producer must carefully weigh the effects of his behavior on the behavior of his competitors. Oligopolistic markets vary widely in the extent to which they involve price and nonprice competition. As we shall see, there are strong pressures in oligopolies for the leading companies not to become involved in price wars with each other. Moreover, some oligopolies produce substantially identical products (for example, virgin aluminum ingots), while others have substantially differentiated products (for example, automobiles).

The four kinds of markets can be summarized as follows:

1. **Pure competition**—many sellers of an identical product (wheat), with ease of entry for new competitors
2. **Monopolistic competition**—a substantial number of sellers of closely substitutable, but not identical, products:
   a. Price competition (vegetables in local grocery stores)
   b. Nonprice competition; "demand creation" through advertising (beer, men's suits)
3. **Oligopoly**—a few dominant sellers of identical or closely substitutable products[2]
   a. Competition—on prices and through nonprice competition and demand creation (aluminum, television sets, and autos)
   b. Collaboration:
      i. Formal collusion on prices and on output—"cartels" (nickel internationally)[3]
      ii. Price leadership or informal price stabilization (steel, gasoline)
4. **Pure monopoly**—one seller of a product without close substitutes (local water company and other public utilities)

---

[2] Where there are only two sellers, "duopoly" exists. This is a special case of oligopoly.

[3] Formal collusion to set prices or divide up markets is illegal under the Sherman Act in the United States, as we shall see presently.

Minimum Essentials Track Information

Some teachers and students will want to concentrate mainly on the "big picture" in microeconomics—on getting a general overview of the way the price system works and how effectively it performs in competitive compared to imperfectly competitive markets. The "price theory" sections of Part 2 are written to provide a **"Minimum Essentials Track"** for such readers. This track omits most of the technical details of the "theory of the firms" and stresses only the main allocative role of competitive markets. It includes only Section A of Chapter 8 and Section A of Chapter 10—omitting Chapter 7, Section B of Chapter 8, Chapter 9, and Section B of Chapter 10. Those who want a more complete, rigorous statement of the basic theory and its implications should read the complete chapters as written, including the Section A core materials of the Minimum Essentials Track.

THEORY

NOTE: This chapter can be omitted by those assigning only the **Minimum Essentials Track.** However, it may be helpful to review Chapter 4 before going on to Chapter 8, in that case.

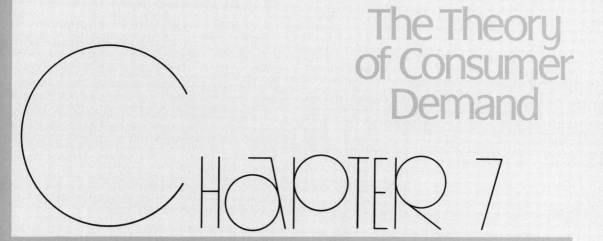

The Theory of Consumer Demand

Chapter 7

Consumers direct production by the way they spend their money. Chapters 3 and 4 provided the rudiments of consumer demand as the basis for "consumer sovereignty" in a basically private-enterprise, market-directed system. We need now to examine in more detail exactly what lies behind consumer demands and the extent to which they can be taken as evidence of what consumers most want produced. Before going further, if Chapters 3 and 4 are not fresh in your mind, it would be worth while to go back and review them.

THE LAW OF DEMAND

Chapter 4 emphasized one of the stablest relationships in economics: Consumers will buy more of any good or service at a lower price than they would at a higher price, other things being equal. That is, demand curves slope downward. Although, as we shall see in a moment, this is not uniformly true, it is almost always so, and it is so stable a relationship that it is generally called the "law of demand." This "law" shows up repeatedly in many different parts of economics. It merits some further investigation now.

Why Demand Curves Slope Downward

Most people accept downward-sloping demand curves as intuitively obvious. It is sensible that you will buy more of anything at a low price than at a higher one, other things equal. Thus, on graphs of demand as typically drawn (with price on the vertical and quantity on the horizontal axis), demand curves slope downward, from northwest to southeast.

But such an important relationship is worth further investigation. Why does it hold?

First, at a lower price for anything, you can afford to buy more of it with a given money income. Given your total money income and all other prices constant, a drop in the price of anything will increase your total real income and make it possible for you to buy more of it without buying less of other items. This is called the income effect. Second, at a lower price, you are likely to want to buy more of any item, because it becomes relatively more attractive compared

with other things you might buy, given unchanged prices of other things. At a lower price for pizzas relative to hamburger and other foods, you will want to substitute pizzas for hamburgers as pizzas become cheaper. This is called the substitution effect.[1]

The Law of Diminishing Marginal Utility

Many modern economists consider the substitution and income effects sufficient to explain the persistence of downward-sloping demand curves. However, a century ago, economists developed another explanation, based on "marginal utility," and many economists use this as the basic theoretical explanation of why demand curves slope down. It is consistent with use of the substitution and income effects, not contradictory to them.

Suppose we want to explain your downward-sloping demand for oranges per day. The first orange you purchase and consume today gives you a certain amount of satisfaction; many economists call the satisfaction "utility." (We might measure the utility in terms of "utils.") Although the util is a perfectly arbitrary unit of measurement, suppose that the first orange today gives you four utils of satisfaction. Suppose now you buy a second orange and have it for breakfast as well. This will give you some more satisfaction, but probably not as much as the first orange did—perhaps three utils worth. If you buy still a third orange, it may in turn give you some satisfaction, but by this stage you are getting pretty full of orange juice for that breakfast. And if you buy still a fourth orange and

---

[1]Three exceptions should be mentioned: (1) "Prestige goods," such as mink coats and exotic perfume, may be bought largely *because* their price is high. A decline in price might lead rich people to buy less as the goods come down into a price range open to the less wealthy. (2) Some goods, called "inferior," are bought by poor people simply because they are cheap and useful. Potatoes in Ireland were the classic example. If the price of the food staple, potatoes, went up, the Irish peasants had to buy even more potatoes, which were still the cheapest food, because they had even less left than before to buy other, more expensive foods. (3) When price drops, people may buy less because they expect the price to decline still further. But this is a dynamic effect that depends not on whether the price is high or low but on buyers' expectation of further price changes.

consume it, the *extra* or *marginal* satisfaction you get will be pretty small—perhaps one util. Thus, you might get four utils of satisfaction from the first orange, three from the second, and so on through the fourth, giving a total of ten utils from the four oranges this morning. The important thing to note is that you get less satisfaction from each additional orange.

We call the additional satisfaction we get from each orange the marginal utility it provides. Thus, the marginal utility of the first orange would be four utils, but the second provides only three additional utils, and so on for additional oranges today.

This can be shown readily in Figure 7–1. The left-hand portion shows the total utility from all four oranges, building up from the first through the second, third, and fourth as explained in the text. The right-hand side of the graph shows marginal utility. The marginal utility of the first orange is the largest, that is the second orange is smaller, and so on for additional oranges. The marginal utility of the oranges decreases as you buy additional oranges per unit of time.

This is the law of diminishing marginal utility, and it provides a logical basis for downward-sloping demand curves. You are willing to pay some amount per orange for the first orange you buy today. But you will pay only a smaller amount for the second, still less for the third, and less yet for the fourth orange. Quite possibly, the fifth orange would give you no extra satisfaction at all; total utility would not increase and marginal utility would be zero. In that case, your demand curve would hit zero; you presumably wouldn't pay anything for a fifth orange today.[2]

The law of diminishing marginal utility explains clearly why demand curves for individual products are downward sloping. Since each successive unit of a good or service obtained yields a smaller marginal utility, the customer will buy additional units of the product only if its price falls. If you are willing to pay up to 50 cents for the first orange, you won't be willing to pay as much for the second, because it will give you a smaller marginal utility than the first did. Thus, only if the price goes down to, say, 40 cents per orange will you buy two instead of one. Similarly, only if the price goes down further, say to 30 cents, will you buy three, and so on for larger numbers of oranges. Your demand curve for oranges is downward sloping because the marginal utility of oranges to you per unit of time declines.

---

[2]Could a sixth orange have a negative marginal utility? If so, show it on both halves of Figure 7–1.

FIGURE 7–1
Total and Marginal Utility
Total utility rises with the total number of oranges consumed, but each additional orange brings a smaller addition to that total.

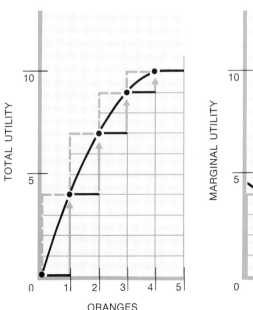

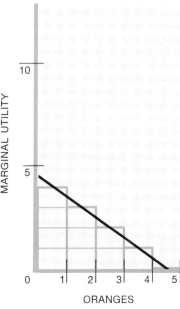

Try the law of diminishing marginal utility for other products and see if you get the same downward-sloping demand curve. For example, how about movies per week, airplane trips home per term, new suits per year?

The fact that you are willing to pay a higher price per unit for one orange than for two or three or four may trouble you, because you know that usually, the price per orange is the same whether you buy one or four at the local store. Your curiosity is right. This situation leads to a very interesting result, called consumer's surplus, which we shall consider in a moment.

THE THEORY OF CONSUMER DEMAND

It is useful to pull this all together into a general theory of consumer demand. Chapter 4 emphasized that economists do not assume that consumers are all perfectly rational and buy only the things that are best for them, but merely that they spend their money on the things they want most. That is, we assume that consumers (households) generally try to maximize the utility (or satisfaction) they get by spending their incomes. This does not mean that every person is a careful, calculating machine who weighs and balances each possible expenditure before he makes it in terms of the satisfaction he expects, compared to all other alternatives. But it does mean that, by and large, people spend their money on what they expect will give them the most satisfaction, at least as a first approximation, assuming that people are *free to spend their incomes as they wish.* Any other assumption gives very strange results. Try another for yourself.

Equilibrium of the Household

In analyzing consumer behavior, as in other parts of economics, it is often convenient to think of movements toward equilibrium positions. Each household (consumers commonly make their expenditures as household units) tries to maximize the satisfaction obtained from spending its income. Suppose a household is in equilibrium, maximizing the satisfaction obtained from all the things it can buy with its current

income. Now the prices of some commodities change. Assuming that consumers preferences have not changed, this will lead households to spend more on the commodities that have become cheaper, less on those that have become relatively more expensive. And this expenditure shift will go on until each household has reached a new equilibrium, in which it is again maximizing the satisfaction obtainable from the income it has. In the same way, if consumer income changes, this will lead to changes in the amounts of different goods and services purchased, until each household is again back in equilibrium position.

Each consumer (household) will change the pattern of goods and services he buys whenever he can get more utility by spending an extra dollar on item A than he can on item B. He will maximize his total utility when he allocates his income so that the marginal utility he receives from the last dollar spent on each item he buys is identical. When he so allocates his income, the consumer is "in equilibrium," in the sense that he is maximizing the satisfaction he can obtain by spending his income. He has no incentive to change to another spending pattern.

This is only common sense. If you get a larger marginal utility from the last dollar you spent on A than from the last dollar you spent on B, obviously you should shift that dollar from B to A. Whenever the marginal utility of the last dollar spent on different commodities is unequal, you can increase your total utility by switching from the lower to the higher marginal utility commodities. If, to simplify, we assume that the price of every commodity is the same, you should so allocate your income as to obtain the same marginal utility from every commodity you buy. We could write this in equation form as follows:

$$MU_x = MU_y = MU_z$$

and so on, where x, y, and z are the commodities bought.

If the prices of different commodities differ, the consumer in equilibrium would not expect to get the same marginal utility from each commodity, but only from the last dollar spent on each commodity. It would be nonsense to think of so allocating your income as to obtain the same marginal utility from a movie and an automobile. But if we divide the marginal utility from each by the price of each, we make them comparable, putting both on a marginal-utility-per-dollar basis. Then we can state our central proposition again: For the consumer to be in equilibrium, the marginal utility of the last dollar spent on each good or service bought must be equal. In equation form, the equilibrium condition is, therefore:

$$\frac{MU_x}{P_x} = \frac{MU_y}{P_y} = \frac{MU_z}{P_z}. \quad .$$

where P is the price of each commodity.[3]

We can extend this reasoning to other uses of households' incomes. You may save part of your disposable income rather than spending it. To be in equilibrium, you must so allocate your income between saving and spending that the marginal utility obtained from a dollar saved is equal to that obtained from a dollar spent on each item you buy. Equating marginal utilities works for all uses of the dollars we have to spend or to save.[4]

When consumers spend their incomes this way, their demand curves for different products accurately reflect the relative marginal utilities they think they will obtain from different products they might buy. If you spend $5 for a jazz album rather than for a movie ticket or anything else, we assume you prefer the album to anything else you can buy for $5. Your preferences are reflected in your demand curves for the different products, and your demands will signal to producers the relative values you place on jazz albums, movies, and other products. This is an extremely important point, since we rely largely on consumer demand to give signals to producers as to what should be produced and in what quantities. A household's (consumer's) demand curves show what it most wants.

---

[3]Wouldn't this lead the consumer to allocate all his income to x instead of y or z, if x has the highest marginal utility? No, because of the law of diminishing marginal utility. Remember that the marginal utility obtained from an additional unit of each commodity declines as the consumer gets more of it in any time period. Thus, spending more dollars on x will produce diminishing marginal utility for x, and this will keep the consumer from switching all his expenditures to x (that is, to any one commodity).

[4]Note that this is precisely parallel to balancing asset portfolios to maximize total utility from all assets held.

The Paradox of Value

How is it that air, without which we should all die, is free, whereas most other things, which are much less essential, command a price? The answer is obvious once you do a demand-and-supply analysis. What is the supply of air? It is substantially unlimited at zero cost in most locations. Since the supply of air at zero cost is practically unlimited, the demand curve cuts the supply curve at zero cost and price.

Marginal utility analysis tells us more basically what is involved on the demand side. The total utility of the air we breathe is enormously large; without air we would die. But the marginal utility of the last unit of air we breathe every day is extremely small. We could give up the last cubic foot of air and scarcely notice the difference. Thus, the marginal utility per cubic foot of air is very low (for all practical purposes, zero), even though some air is so very important to us. Since all air is substantially identical for breathing purposes (leaving aside the problems of smog and the like), we don't have to pay for

FIGURE 7-2
Consumer's Surplus
The consumer pays only 50 cents (gray rectangle) for his five bananas, but his demand curve shows he would have been willing to pay more than 10 cents for each of the first four. Thus, the light blue triangle measures how much more he would have been willing to pay to get the total utility provided by five bananas, and hence measures the "consumer surplus" he obtains free.

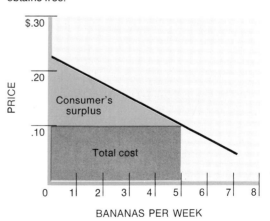

the first, high marginal utility units we consume. Since there is only one price for identical units in a competitive market, every unit must sell for what the least useful unit sells for. If the least useful unit is free, the price of all air is zero. Some economists have compared this to the case of the tail wagging the dog. If you just remember that it is *marginal* utility, not *total* utility that matters in determining the price of any commodity, you will have the main point.

Consumer Surplus

Consumers receive a "consumer surplus" on most commodities they buy. Figure 7–2 shows a typical downward-sloping demand curve—say, for bananas. The market price is 10 cents and you buy five per week. But your demand curve shows that you would have been willing to pay 20 cents for the first banana, 17 cents for the second, and so on. The price you would have paid for each

banana indicates the marginal utility you expect to receive from that banana. Thus, you get a "consumer surplus" of utility on each of the first four bananas, since you had to pay only 10 cents for each. The light blue area provides a measure of this consumer surplus in Figure 7–2.

Why don't sellers raise the price and take that consumer surplus away from you, since you would have been willing to pay more than 10 cents each for the first four bananas? The answer is, of course, that you and other consumers would not buy all the bananas now being sold if the price were placed higher. As long as there is a single price for all bananas (presuming they are all the same), the price of all is set by the marginal utility of the least valuable banana. You are very likely to have a consumer surplus in most of your purchases. This follows from the downward-sloping demand curve, together with the single price for all units of the commodity you buy.

SUMMARY AND REVIEW

This chapter further develops the rudiments of consumer demand that were presented in Chapter 4.

1. The "law of demand" states that consumers will buy more of any good or service at a lower price than at a higher one, other things being equal.

2. Three kinds of explanation are used in regard to why demand curves slope downward:

    a. The intuitive plausibility of the statement

    b. Income and substitution effects

    c. The law of diminishing marginal utility

3. The law of diminishing marginal utility states that the marginal utility (satisfaction) obtained per unit falls as you consume more units of any good or service within a stated time period.

4. Economists assume that, by and large, consumers spend their income so as to maximize the satisfaction they get from doing so. Each will maxim-

ize this satisfaction, or utility, by allocating his income so that the marginal utility received from the last dollar spent on each item bought is identical. When a household is so allocating its income, it is "in equilibrium," in the sense that it is maximizing the satisfaction it can obtain by spending its income.

5. The price a consumer is willing to pay for any product is a measure of the marginal utility expected from that product. Thus, his demand curve represents to producers what he most wants to have produced.

6. The paradox of value (that is, that air, water, and other such obviously essential things are substantially free while less important things command a price) reflects the principle of diminishing marginal utility.

7. Consumer surplus is the extra utility consumers receive because they need pay only the price set by the marginal utility of the least valuable unit bought.

New Concepts
to Remember

law of demand   law of diminishing marginal utility
income effect   equilibrium of the consumer (household)
substitution effect   consumer's surplus

For Analysis
and Discussion

1. Is price a good measure of the marginal utility of a good to each buyer? Explain.
2. Do you allocate your income among alternative uses so as to maximize your satisfaction from it? If your answer is no, are you saying that you are irrational?
3. Explain the concept of "equilibrium of the consumer." How useful does this concept seem to you in understanding consumer behavior? If you don't think it is useful, can you suggest a better model?
4. "Since consumers' demand signals what is to be produced in America, it follows that consumers are responsible if our economy produces 'wasteful' products like elaborate chrome trim on automobiles." Do you agree or disagree?
5. Explain to a visitor from Mars why you pay high prices for useless (if ornamental) things like diamonds but little or nothing for water, which is essential to life.
6. Suppose a major drought hits your area. Would you expect the price of water to stay low, or at zero? Explain.
7. Is the price you pay for anything you purchase voluntarily a good measure of its marginal utility to you? If your answer is yes, how about consumer surplus?

CASE 6

CASH OR FOOD STAMPS FOR THE POOR?

One controversial part of the government's overall program to aid the poor has been the food-stamp program. Following its introduction in the 1960s, the program was expanded rapidly, and by 1979, nearly 20 million people were receiving benefits, with a total annual cost to the federal government of about $6 billion. Under the program, the government provides participants with stamps that can be used to purchase food in most stores, and then redeems the stamps from the grocers who take them in payment for food.

Congress has raised the value of the food stamps provided, at roughly the same pace as inflation. By 1979, an eligible family of four could receive free $182 in food stamps monthly (about $2,200 annually) if its "net" annual income was under about $7,300. "Net" income was calculated by subtracting taxes, medical expenses, rent, utilities, mortgage payments, and several other items from gross money income. Thus, a $7,300 "net" income corresponded to a substantially higher gross income for some families. In extreme cases, families with gross incomes up to $15,000 could in the past qualify for food stamps, but the bulk of the stamps have gone to families and individuals with current money incomes below the federal "poverty" level ($6,200 in 1978), and there is a complex regulation disqualifying families with substantial holdings of earning assets.

The stated purpose of the program is to ensure that poor families, especially those with children, receive a reasonably adequate diet. By giving the poor food stamps instead of money, proponents argue, we ensure a minimum level of nourishment for poor families at a much lower cost than if we gave the poor money aid, because food stamps must be used for food and cannot be diverted to liquor, gasoline, drugs, paying off old debts, or other less urgent needs.

Others, including some of the poor themselves, disagree. It is insulting and inefficient, they say, to give food stamps rather than money, restricting the recipients' freedom to judge for themselves what is best for them. It is inefficient, they argue, because if the government gave the poor the same amount of money, the poor could not possibly be worse off, and would almost certainly be better off, since they would be free to allocate their incomes so as to maximize their own utilities. The poor recipient could buy all food with his money grant if food is what he wants and needs most, or he could use the funds for something else if other needs are more urgent. The plan is insulting because it implies that the poor cannot be trusted to know and to do what is best for themselves and their children. Moreover, as a practical matter, many food-stamp recipients sell their stamps (illegally) to others and spend the funds as they please.

In 1977, President Carter proposed to Congress that the food-stamp program be replaced with a cash grant program, with benefits directly paid to, and limited to, the poor. But as this is written, Congress still had not agreed.

Who is right? Should we scrap the food-stamp plan and go to a system of cash grants only for the poor? The question is an important one not only because of the size of the food-stamp program, but also because the same basic issue arises with many other types of government assistance. For example, rent supplements to provide better housing, free public education, and subsidized health benefits under Medicaid all parallel food stamps as "in-kind," rather than cash, aid to the poor.

THEORY

NOTE: Those using only the **Minimum Essentials Track** should read only Section A of this chapter, plus the brief section, "Social Costs and Private Costs," at the end of the chapter.

Business Firms and Their Costs

CHAPTER 8

We turn now to examine how, and how well, business firms respond to consumer demands. If businesses try to maximize their profits, how they respond to consumer demand will depend significantly on their costs of producing what consumers want. The bigger the spread is between their costs of production and the prices consumers will pay, the larger will be business's incentive to increase production. This is true for big firms like General Motors, producing millions of autos each year, and for small firms like truck farmers, producing only a few bushels of turnips and tomatoes annually. Although their scales of operations are very different, the principles they follow in analyzing their costs and deciding how much to produce are basically similar. We shall look first at some very simple firms, turning to big, complex firms later.

SECTION a

WHY STUDY COSTS?

Why study costs? Because a businessman's costs largely determine how much he will produce in response to different demands, and the lowest price at which he can sell and stay in business. If customers won't pay more than $1 for a widget and the minimum cost of producing widgets is $1.25, you don't need to be an economist to see it won't pay to produce widgets. How far any business will go in producing what consumers want will depend on how much that article costs to produce, relative to how much buyers will pay for it.

Business costs are important for another reason. Looked at as wages, salaries, rent, and interest payments, business costs are the incomes of workers and of resource owners. In explaining business costs, therefore, we are simultaneously explaining why most people receive the incomes they do.

Most important, the basic fact of scarcity (limited resources) means that the "real" cost of producing anything is the alternatives foregone that might have been produced with those resources. For example, the real cost of producing an auto is the other things given up that might otherwise have been produced with the same steel, glass, rubber, and labor. The real cost is an "alternative cost"—the alternative uses of the resources that are given up when the resources are used in producing autos. Sometimes, alternative cost is called "opportunity" cost, because it is a measure of the opportunities foregone.

This concept of opportunity cost can be put into money terms. Thus, the cost of producing one TV set is the amount of money necessary to get the factors of production needed for the set away from alternative uses. The TV manufacturer has to pay enough to engineers to get them away from auto and radar plants, enough for copper wire to bid it away from telephone companies. And so it is for every resource he uses. In economic terms, the cost of the TV is the amount necessary to bid all the required resources away from the strongest competing uses.

Accounting and Economic Costs

Business money costs of production include wages, materials, rent, interest, and all the other items listed in the profit-and-loss statement in the

94

appendix to Chapter 5. But the alternative-cost concept leads economists to somewhat different cost figures from the ones that businessmen and their accountants work with—primarily because the economist includes several items that the accountant ordinarily doesn't consider as costs when he draws up his profit-and-loss statements.

A simple example is the independent corner grocer, who has bought a store with his own money and runs it himself. In addition to the regular business costs in the profit-and-loss statement, the economist would say:

How about a return on your own investment and a salary for yourself? If you didn't have your money tied up in the store, you could be earning 5 percent on it in another investment. If you weren't working in the store, you could earn $10,000 a year working for Kroger's. You ought to account as costs a 5 percent return on your investment and a $10,000 salary for yourself before you compute your profit for the year, because these reflect real alternatives that you're giving up when you stay in your business.

If the grocer does not include these costs and finds he's making a $9,000 annual "profit," he may think he's doing well—but actually he's kidding himself. The $9,000 doesn't even give him the salary he could earn working for someone else, much less the return he could get by doing that and investing his money somewhere else. If his investment was, say, $20,000, his interest foregone elsewhere at 5 percent would be $1,000 annually. His accounting "profit" would have to be $11,000 on the store just to break even—that is, to cover his own $10,000 salary plus $1,000 interest on his money.

A similar, although less obvious, situation is found in business corporations. Corporations pay salaries to their officers and employees, so there's no problem there. And they pay interest to their bondholders, which is considered a cost in computing profits. But they don't consider the interest on the owners' (stockholders') investment to be a cost. Dividends to stockholders are treated as a *use* of profits, *not as a cost.* The economist, however, includes in the firm's costs a reasonable ("normal") rate of return on stockholder's investment (measuring the alternative return that is foregone elsewhere).

He therefore considers as "economic profit" only the excess income above this basic alternative cost, because this normal rate of return is part of the cost required to keep funds invested in any business. Thus, part of dividends to stockholders should be counted as costs.[1]

Throughout the rest of this book, we shall use the alternative-cost concept. Thus, costs of production will include the normal rate of return (profit) on investment necessary to keep the funds invested in that concern rather than elsewhere. Costs will include the entrepreneur's salary if he is self-employed, and dividends equal to a normal return on capital invested in stockholders. Broadly, they will include all costs required to get and keep resources in the firm being considered. Most costs will be the same as those used by the accountant, but remember that the cost data and curves used here include a "normal" return, or profit, on investment, if you want to avoid some dangerous pitfalls later on.

Costs of Production and the Rate of Output

It is important to distinguish among some different measures of cost incurred by firms, even though you don't plan to study costs in detail. They are (1) "sunk" (or committed, or fixed) costs; (2) "average" cost, or total cost per unit produced; and (3) "marginal" cost.

Suppose you run a guided fishing service on a nearby lake. You have leased five fishing boats for the summer, and you hire local college students to serve as boat operators and fishing guides for wealthy visiting fishermen. Your lease cost for the boats, plus your own time and rental on a wharf, comes to $50 per day, or $10 per boat. Your operating cost per boat per day (guide plus gas and oil), is $20, incurred only when a boat is rented out for the day. Note the following different measures of costs.

---

[1] In economics, costs that show up in the usual accounting procedures are often called "explicit" costs, and alternative costs (such as a return on stockholders' investment) that are not usually recorded in modern accounting are called "implicit" costs.

CASH VS. ECONOMIC PROFITS: A MANAGERIAL APPLICATION

A simple managerial example may help show the importance of these distinctions, as well as give you an impression of how basic economic analysis can help in day-to-day business. Suppose you're in business for yourself, doing miscellaneous repairs (carpentering, electrical wiring, and so on) at a minimum charge of $10 per call and $4 per hour additional after the first hour. Your only equipment is your family station wagon; you have converted the back to carry your working tools. You are prepared to answer calls anywhere in your general area. You've spent $20 for an ad in the local paper and for a supply of mimeographed postcards mailed at random to names from the phone book.

After a month, you've collected a large amount of experience, considerable boredom waiting for the phone to ring, and $620. Have you made a profit? Should you stay in business?

The answer to the profit question hinges on what your costs have been. If you deduct the original $20 outlay, you have $600 left. Not bad for a summer month. But look again. There is clearly gas and oil for the station wagon, and wear and tear on it, which may be appreciable from this use. Then, aside from any materials (for which you may have charged extra), there's the question of your own time.

Suppose gas and oil allocable to this work have cost $80. And you make a rough estimate of $50 a month extra depreciation on the car. That still leaves you $470. Is that more or less than a reasonable wage for your own full time and energy for the month? Here the concept of opportunity cost provides a guide to the answer. What could you make elsewhere, doing work you consider about equally interesting, difficult, and convenient? If the answer is above $470, you've made a loss, although maybe a very small one. Central concepts: the distinction between cash and income, and opportunity cost. Without them you're apt to pull a real boner.

Your *fixed,* or committed, or "sunk," *costs* for the summer are $50 per day, or $10 per boat. You are committed to these costs, whether or not you have customers for your fishing-guide service.

Average total cost is your total cost divided by the number of units produced (boat-days rented). Suppose you rent out only one boat with guide today. What is the average total cost of boat-days sold to customers today? Answer: $70. Your total cost has been $50 of sunk costs, plus $20 for one guide and gas, or $70. Since you have rented only one boat for the day, the average cost per unit (boat-days) produced is $70. But suppose you rented all five boats. Then your total cost is $50 sunk costs (same as before) plus $100 for five guides and gas, amounting to $150. If you divide this by the five boats rented, the average total cost per unit rented is obviously $30, far less than when you rented only one boat. You have spread your $50 fixed, or "sunk," or "overhead," cost over all five boats, instead of concentrating it all on one. Average total cost thus varies with the number of units produced. In this simple case, it falls steadily as the number of units produced per day rises. In more complex cases, this is also commonly true over a considerable range of output, but average cost generally turns up after a firm has reached roughly the production "capacity" for which it was designed. For example, Bethlehem Steel's huge Sparrows Point steel works, designed to produce thousands of tons per day, would run at a very high average total cost per ton if it produced only a few tons daily. The whole fixed cost ("overhead") of the huge plant would have to be allocated against those few tons of steel. Average cost per ton would fall steadily as output approached the plant's "capacity." But if Bethlehem tried to produce more daily than the plant is designed for, its average cost per ton would rise again; management would have to pay overtime rates to workers, defer maintenance, and incur other special costs. (More details in Section B of this chapter.)

Marginal cost is the additional cost incurred in producing one more unit. For your guide service, this is obviously $20 per unit, the extra outlay in putting one more boat into service for a day. Note that the $50 sunk lease cost is not involved, since it does not increase or decrease when we produce one more unit. In this simple example, marginal cost is the same ($20) whether we are renting out the first or last boat for the day. In more complex cases, this may not be true.

As we shall see, these three cost concepts are important ones for economic analysis. Looking ahead, four brief suggestions may be helpful. First, once "sunk" costs are committed, they should not affect our decisions on pricing and production for the period of that commitment— for example, in deciding how much to charge in renting out our boats.

Second, the difference between average cost and selling price per unit determines the profit per unit sold. In a competitive economy, whenever price is above average cost, other firms will have an incentive to enter the industry to obtain some of the profits.

Third, marginal cost, which is often different from average cost, provides a useful tool for deciding whether or not we will gain by producing and selling one more unit. If marginal cost is below the extra, or marginal, revenue obtained by selling the additional unit, you will increase profits by selling the additional unit. Suppose we can rent out an additional boat

today for $40. Since our marginal cost is only $20, clearly we will increase total profit, or reduce our total loss, by selling the additional unit; it adds $40 to income and only $20 to costs. But if marginal cost is higher than marginal revenue, we would reduce our total profit by renting the additional unit, since it would add more to total cost than to total revenue.

Fourth, to reemphasize, all costs except sunk costs vary with the rate of production. Thus, it is generally meaningless to say that the cost of producing anything is some fixed amount; the cost will normally vary depending on the number of units produced per day or week or year.

SECTION B

More Detailed Analysis— Costs

COSTS OF PRODUCTION AND THE RATE OF OUTPUT—ANALYSIS

Let us turn now to a more detailed and rigorous analysis of costs in relation to the rate of output.[2] Imagine a somewhat more complex company but still one that produces only a single product—the Amalgamated Widget Company (AWC). Suppose the company's only costs are raw materials, labor, rent, and management salaries. Suppose further that rent and management salaries are fixed (sunk) for the next year—they go on whether the company operates at full capacity or partial capacity, or shuts down. The other costs (wages and materials) are variable; they depend on the company's rate of output.

---

[2]The appendix to this chapter, "Physical-Production Relationships Underlying Cost Curves," provides the logical foundation for this cost analysis. It should be assigned here by those intructors who wish a complete rigorous analytical foundation for this and the following chapter, but students can grasp the central points in the text without it.

Assume that AWC's fixed costs total $1,000 per week, and that the variable costs vary with changes in output as in the first four columns of Table 8–1. Total cost is simply the sum of fixed and variable costs. Note that the $1,000 fixed costs (rent and managerial salaries) stays the same whether we produce 1,000 or 8,000 widgets, but total variable cost (wages and materials) and total cost both rise steadily as output increases.

Costs Per Unit of Output

For many purposes, managers are more interested in costs per unit of output than in total-cost figures. We can readily convert all our cost data to a per-widget basis, by dividing each total-cost figure by the number of widgets produced. For example, average fixed cost per widget when we are producing 1,000 widgets weekly is $1.00, obtained by dividing the total-fixed-cost figure of $1,000 by 1,000 widgets. Average variable cost per widget when output is 1,000 weekly is

TABLE 8–1
Amalgamated Widget Company—Costs[a]

OUTPUT	TOTAL COSTS			PER-WIDGET COSTS			MARGINAL COSTS	
(PER WEEK) (1)	TOTAL FIXED COST (2)	TOTAL VARIABLE COST (3)	TOTAL COST (4)	AVERAGE FIXED COST PER WIDGET (5)	AVERAGE VARIABLE COST PER WIDGET (6)	AVERAGE TOTAL COST PER WIDGET (7)	PER 1,000 WIDGETS (8)	PER WIDGET (9)
1,000	$1,000	$ 2,000	$ 3,000	$1.00	$2.00	$3.00		
							$ 500	$0.50
2,000	1,000	2,500	3,500	0.50	1.25	1.75		
							600	0.60
3,000	1,000	3,100	4,100	0.33	1.03	1.36		
							900	0.90
4,000	1,000	4,000	5,000	0.25	1.00	1.25		
							1,000	1.00
5,000	1,000	5,000	6,000	0.20	1.00	1.20		
							1,600	1.60
6,000	1,000	6,000	7,600	0.17	1.10	1.27		
							3,400	3.40
7,000	1,000	10,000	11,000	0.14	1.43	1.57		
							6,000	6.00
8,000	1,000	16,000	17,000	0.12	2.00	2.12		

[a]Unit costs are rounded to nearest cent.

$2.00 ($2,000 total variable cost divided by 1,000 widgets). These results, showing all costs on a per-widget basis, are calculated in columns 5–7 of Table 8–1. Since both managers and economists use these unit-cost data extensively, they are worth a further look.

Average fixed cost per unit (AFC) will always be a steadily decreasing series, because the constant total-fixed-cost figure (here, $1,000 of rent and management salaries) is divided by a rising volume of output. This is what is commonly known as "spreading the overhead." The drop in average fixed cost per unit is very rapid at first, but as volume grows, the additional cost reduction per unit steadily decreases in importance.

Average variable cost per unit (AVC) will generally fall at the outset, then flatten out, and then rise again as plant "capacity" is approached. To produce any widgets at all, the company has to have labor and materials of all the types needed. It will clearly be inefficient to try to call in each type of skilled labor just long enough to work on a few widgets. If we try to use two or three jacks-of-all-trades, we get less efficient work. Similarly, it may be cheaper to buy materials in large quantities, and so on. It's clearly not efficient for AWC to produce only one or two thousand widgets a week.

At the other extreme, once the "capacity" for which the plant was planned has been reached, average-variable and average-total costs per unit will shoot up if we try to produce still more output per month. "Capacity" is seldom an absolute limit in a plant. For example, steel plants may temporarily operate above 100 percent of capacity; rated capacity allows for an average amount of shutdown time for maintenance and repairs, which can be postponed temporarily. But expansion of output beyond plant "capacity" often means expensive overtime work, hiring of lower-skilled workers, more spoilage under pressure of speedup, and a variety of other such cost-raising factors.

Thus, with any given plant, average variable costs per unit will rise rapidly at some point beyond "capacity" output. Just where this point is reached depends, of course, on the individual firm. At Amalgamated Widget, average variable costs per unit (column 6) are approximately flat over a range of output from 3,000 to 5,000 widgets weekly. They rise substantially for larger outputs.

Average total cost per unit (ATC) can be obtained by adding average fixed and average variable costs per unit, or by dividing total cost by the number of units produced. The decreasing fixed cost per unit will always pull down on average cost as output rises. At first, as long as both average fixed and variable costs per unit are declining, clearly average total cost per unit is declining. But at some point, total unit costs will begin to rise, when variable cost per unit turns up more than enough to offset the downward pull of spreading the overhead (fixed cost). This point is at 5,000 widgets weekly at Amalgamated. The lowest average total cost figure in column 7 is $1.20, at an output of 5,000 weekly, although average total unit cost is relatively stable over the output range of 3,000 to 6,000 widgets weekly.[3]

This simple example should warn you again against the common fallacy that each firm has a cost of production for its product. In every firm, cost of production per unit varies with output. This is certain at the extremes of very low and above-capacity output. It often also occurs over the range of normal variation in operations.[4]

Graphical Analysis—Cost Curves

Figure 8–1 shows total costs at different levels of output. It uses the data in columns 1–4 of Table 8–1. Economists usually plot costs and prices in dollars on the vertical axis, output on the horizontal axis. Thus, the gray bar at the bottom shows total fixed cost from column 2—a total of $1,000 at every level of output from zero to 8,000 widgets weekly, the maximum for which we have data.

On top of this, we put total variable cost (column 3)—zero for zero output, $2,000 for 1,000 widgets, $2,500 for 2,000 widgets, and so on. The total-cost curve (top line) thus shows the sum of total fixed and total variable cost at each level of output.

It is easy to see that total cost does not rise

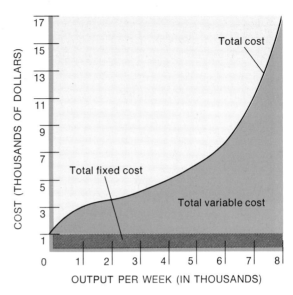

FIGURE 8–1
Amalgamated Widget Company:
Total-Cost Curves
Total fixed costs is $1,000 at all outputs. Total variable cost rises as output increases. Total cost for any output is the sum of fixed and variable costs; it rises rapidly once the "capacity" of the plant is reached.

[3]In the real world, AWC would have more detailed cost data, with estimates for smaller changes than the 1,000-widget jumps shown in column 1 of Table 8–1. Thus, AWC's lowest average total cost per unit might be a shade below $1.20, if we had data for output just above and below 5,000 units weekly.

[4]Many firms now use what they call "standard costs" in pricing their products. A "standard cost" for our widgets would be an estimate of how much it would cost to produce one widget at a normal, or typical, rate of output. If we think of 4,000 units weekly as about normal operation, our standard-cost figure would be $1.25 per widget. It is important, however, to remember that "standard cost" is only an estimate of unit cost at some selected level of output, not necessarily the minimum unit-cost level.

at an even rate. It doesn't cost much more in total to produce 2,000 widgets than 1,000, or 3,000 than 2,000, once you've set up the plant. But as AWC gets up to 6,000 or 7,000 widgets per week, total cost begins to rise much more rapidly. Total variable cost shoots up. The company was set up with a capacity of only 6,000 or 7,000 widgets a week, and to exceed this capacity involves expensive readjustments in equipment, hiring of more workers or overtime labor, and other special problems. Most firms see their variable costs soar if they try to produce much beyond their plant's planned capacity.

The per-unit cost data can also be plotted on graphs as cost curves. Figure 8–2 shows the average-cost-per-widget data for AWC, from columns 5–7 of Table 8–1. Note that average fixed cost per unit falls steadily as the constant total cost of $1,000 is spread over more and more units. Average variable cost per unit and average total cost per unit are both U-shaped, for the reasons explained in the preceding para-

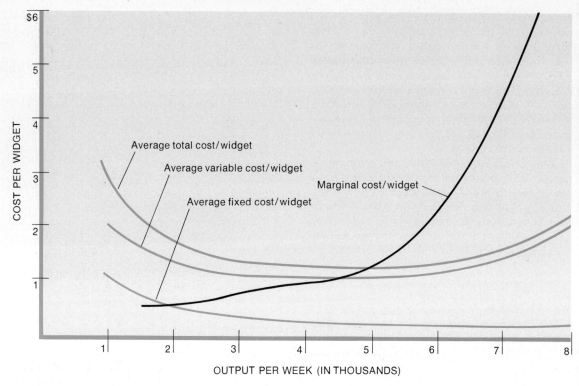

COST PER WIDGET

Average total cost/widget

Average variable cost/widget

Marginal cost/widget

Average fixed cost/widget

OUTPUT PER WEEK (IN THOUSANDS)

FIGURE 8–2
Amalgamated Widget Company: Average (Unit-Cost) Curves
Unit-cost curves are derived by dividing the corresponding total-cost curves by total output. Here, fixed unit cost slopes continuously downward as the constant total fixed cost is spread over more units of output. The variable and total average-cost curves are U-shaped, and are cut by the marginal-cost curve at their lowest points.

graphs. In most manufacturing firms, the AVC and ATC curves are probably flatter than in this hypothetical case. That is, there is a wider range of output over which average total cost per unit is substantially constant, between the low-output inefficiencies shown at the left of the graph and the above-capacity inefficiencies at the right. (Disregard the marginal cost curve for the moment.)

Be sure you know just what the graph shows. For example, at an output of 5,000 widgets weekly, the average fixed cost per widget will be 20 cents, and the average variable cost per widget $1.00, for a total of $1.20. This happens to be the lowest point on the ATC curve. It is

called the "least-cost combination." It is the lowest average cost at which AWC can make widgets, given the existing plant and the firm's other commitments.

Marginal Cost

Marginal cost, as was explained in Section A above, is the addition, or increment, to total cost involved in expanding output by one unit. Marginal costs at Amalgamated Widget are shown in columns 8 and 9 of Table 8–1 on two bases—first, when output is increased in units of 1,000 widgets (column 8), and then converted to a per-widget basis (column 9). Consider column

8 first. To increase output from 1,000 to 2,000 widgets, total cost (column 4, not column 7) increases from $3,000 to $3,500. Thus, marginal cost per 1,000-widget increase is $500; that is, how much extra, or additional, it costs AWC to increase production from 1,000 to 2,000 widgets weekly.[5] To convert this to marginal cost per widget, simply divide the $500 by 1,000 widgets, which gives the marginal cost per widget (or per unit) of $0.50 in column 9.[6]

Try it for another level of output, to be sure you have it right. Suppose AWC is considering increasing output from 3,000 to 4,000 widgets weekly. Total cost (column 4) would rise from $4,100 to $5,000, giving a marginal cost of $900 for the increase of 1,000 widgets (column 8), or of $0.90 per widget (column 9).

Note that the marginal-cost data are printed between the lines for the output levels to which they apply. Thus, the marginal cost of $500 at the top of column 8 show the extra cost involved in increasing output from 1,000 to 2,000 widgets weekly; it applies to the change from one output level to another, not to either one of the levels alone. And in plotting marginal-cost data graphically in Figure 8–1, the marginal-cost figure is plotted halfway between the two output levels to which it applies.

Marginal cost is a very important concept. Most economic decisions involve choices—comparisons of alternatives—"at the margin." Shall we increase output another unit? Shall we paint the house this year? Shall we raise the tax rate to increase Medicaid benefits for the poor?

In making such choices, the logical procedure is to compare the marginal cost of the change with the marginal income, or benefit, from it, to see whether the net result is positive or negative. Be sure you understand marginal cost and the basic process of comparing alternatives at the margin.[7]

The marginal-cost-per-widget data from column 9 of Table 8–1 are plotted in Figure 8–2. Marginal cost is the heavy black line. Reading a marginal-cost curve takes special care. The marginal-cost curve shows that total cost (not average total cost per unit) would rise by 90 cents if output is increased from 4,999 to 5,000 weekly.

One last introductory point about marginal cost. The marginal-cost curve always cuts the average-total-cost-per-unit (ATC) curve at the latter's lowest point. This is so because marginal cost is the increment to total cost in producing one more widget. Whenever this increment to total cost is less than the existing average cost per unit, its addition will lower the average cost per unit. Whenever the increment is larger than the existing cost per unit, its addition will raise the average cost per unit. The same reasoning holds for the relationship of the marginal-cost and variable unit-cost curves. For mathematically inclined readers: Marginal cost is the first derivative of total cost; for more details, see the Mathematical Appendix.

SHORT-RUN AND LONG-RUN VIEWS OF COSTS

Economists speak of the "short run" and the "long run." Time is an important variable in the analysis of economic problems, and this distinction is an attempt to clarify the assumptions being made about the time period involved in any case. We mean by the "short run" any time period in which some costs (such as rent and interest on borrowed funds) are fixed and do not vary with changes in the firm's output. We mean

---

[5]Thus, mathematically, marginal cost is the first derivative of total cost, not of average total cost per unit. Note, too, that marginal cost can equally well be stated as the derivation of total variable cost. The change in total and in total variable cost must be the same, since total fixed cost (the difference between them) is a constant.

[6]"Marginal cost" can thus be used more generally than as just the additional cost of producing one more unit of output. Economists often speak of the marginal cost of doing any particular act; marginal cost is the additional (incremental) cost of doing that act, as compared to not doing it. For example, the marginal cost of your raising the average temperature one degree in your house next winter might be $1 per day—the increment to your total heating bill daily to raise the temperature one degree.

[7]For students who study the appendix to this chapter: Marginal cost is the cost counterpart of marginal productivity. Other things equal, marginal cost will be lowest when marginal productivity is highest.

by "long run" a time period long enough for all costs to become variable. Thus, the distinction is an analytical one. In calendar time, the short run for one firm may be longer than the long run for another, depending on how long the cost commitments run in different cases.

Some examples will clarify this distinction. For Amalgamated Widget, next week is clearly a "short run." During that week, certain costs are fixed no matter how many widgets we produce—rent on the factory building, for example. Given a longer time period, the rental contract will expire; or if we own the building, it will depreciate fully, or it may be sold, so the capital tied up in the plant becomes available for other uses. Similarly, the manager's salary is a fixed cost for the next month, but over some longer time period, his contract will expire and his salary will become a variable cost. If a firm has commitments for fixed costs extending for years ahead, the "short run" for that firm will be a long time.

In the "long run," all the firm's costs become variable. The entrepreneur can decide to build a new plant of different size if he likes. He can transfer his investment to another industry. He has complete freedom to move.

The Optimum Scale of Enterprise

The "long run" is thus a planning period, free from the short-run limitations imposed by fixed plant and other commitments. The big long-run planning problem is, What is the "optimum scale of enterprise" for the firm? How big a fixed plant,

how big a labor force, how much equipment? The questions involve everything related to planning the enterprise's scale of operations in the future.

Businesses seldom find themselves in a position to make all these decisions on future scale at one time. But they are continually making changes, so that in essence they may replan their overall scale of enterprise much more frequently than would appear from a superficial glance.

A set of five possible planning curves, showing expected costs for five different scales of enterprise, is given in Figure 8–3. Each ATC curve corresponds to a given scale of enterprise—a plant of certain size, equipment of certain sorts, and so on. The scale of enterprise at the extreme left would be advantageous only for a very small market. In this figure, the scale corresponding to the fourth cost curve gives the lowest possible least-cost point. A firm of this size is the "optimum scale of enterprise," in the sense that it provides the possibility of the lowest cost per unit of output of any possible scale of enterprise. Note, however, that if total market demand is small, it may not be economical to build and operate a firm of this scale.

How Big Is "Optimal"?

The optimal scale of enterprise varies widely from industry to industry. In some (for example, autos, cigarettes, petroleum, and steel), very large plants and firms are required to obtain peak efficiency. But the evidence is also clear that

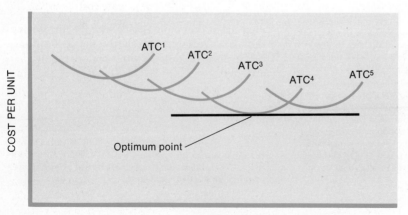

FIGURE 8–3
Average Cost Curves for Firms of Different Sizes
Larger firms have lower minimum total-unit-cost points until the optimal scale of firm is reached. Then, still larger firms face higher minimum ATCs.

in some industries, medium-large or even small firms manage to achieve costs as low as those of the giants. Rates of return on invested capital do not appear to be consistently larger for huge than for medium-large firms, although many of the giants are among the most profitable firms. An indirect test of the optimal scale of firm is provided by the size of firm that grows fastest. Here again, the evidence is mixed. For the economy as a whole, the share of market obtained by the largest firms is growing in some industries but not in others—although nearly all firms are getting bigger as the economy grows. The empirical evidence shows clearly that there is no single, pat answer to the question, How big is optimal?

But the empirical evidence shows equally that in many technologically complex manufacturing industries, the cost advantages of very large scale production are great. The least-cost point for the optimal scale of plant continues to fall for larger and larger firms. The auto industry is perhaps the clearest case, but look ahead to Figure 14–1 for a list of industries dominated by a few very large firms. For them, as we shall see, the long-run cost curve may look more like an L than like a U, for practical purposes. That is, given the demand for their products in relation to the efficiencies of largescale production, they never seem to rach the rising-cost scale of firm shown by ATC[5] in Figure 8–3. Much more on this when we come to Chapters 12–16; it leads to serious questions as to the feasibility of effective market competition to protect consumer interests.

Do Businesses Operate at Optimal Scale?

If we look at all the firms in any industry, we will probably find a wide divergence in size. Why aren't all firms the "optimal" size? There are many reasons. For example:

1. In some cases, the market isn't big enough to permit all firms to operate at optimal scale.

2. Some firms overexpand as part of a drive to attain dominance in their industry. Men with dreams of industrial empire may expand beyond optimal scale in their push for bigness and prestige. It is hard to measure this factor, but the last century of U.S. history has produced many

cases where this motive appears to have been important.

3. Sometimes, fear of government action holds firms back from profitable expansion—for example, when a firm fears that further growth may bring government antitrust action to break it up. It is often alleged that this fear is what keeps General Motors from taking a still larger share of the auto market.

4. Probably most important of all, errors and delays in adjusting to changing conditions mean that at any time, most firms will not be at optimal scale. Plans in establishing a new plant are inevitably imprecise on many factors: new technology, future wage rates and prices, scale of market available, and so on. And even if the estimates could be precise, change is inescapable in economic life. Before long, new situations will arise, new technological changes will appear. Replanning optimal scale is a continuous process for the well-managed firm.

SOCIAL COSTS AND PRIVATE COSTS

Large profits in an industry are a signal that resources can profitably be moved into that industry from elsewhere. Losses are a signal that resources can earn more elsewhere and should be moved away. Profits and losses are thus crucial signals in the working of a free-market economy.

If the signals are to be correct, costs of producing goods should reflect fully the alternatives foregone. Generally, the private costs incurred by the firm in obtaining resources (wages, rents, raw materials, and so on) are a good measure of what it takes to get resources away from other industries. But in some cases, additional costs are involved in the production of a good or service. If, for example, a steel mill produces steel for $100 per ton, but also spews out smoke and soot that cover the surrounding neighborhood, the $100 is not a complete measure of the total social cost of producing the steel. The extra costs involved in grimy window sills and curtains, discolored paint, and smoke-filled lungs are all real costs for the people in that community. They are social costs ("negative externalities," or diseconomies imposed on the community), but they are not included in the money costs that the steel company must pay to produce steel at $100 per ton.

In such a case, total social costs including the externalities exceed the private costs faced by the steelmaker. The $100-per-ton price does not cover the full cost, so, as we shall see, price is too low and steel companies produce too much steel in meeting consumer demand at $100 per ton. If consumers had to pay the full social cost (say $110 per ton), they would buy less steel and fewer resources would be devoted to steel-making.

Consumers do not pay the full social cost of the steel they buy.

There may be positive external economies as well as diseconomies; that is, production may involve side benefits to the community instead of side costs. For example, a company may build an attractive new facility that improves the appearance of the neighborhood. Possible government policies vis-à-vis both positive and negative externalities will be examined in detail in Chapter 14 and Part 4.

SUMMARY AND REVIEW

1. Costs are important, because each producer's costs determine how much he will produce in response to consumer demands, and the lowest price at which he can sell and stay in business.

2. Looked at as wages, salaries, rent, and interest payments, business costs are the incomes of workers and resource owners.

3. The basic fact of scarcity (limited resources) means that the "real" cost of producing anything is the alternatives foregone that might have been produced with those resources. In economic terms, therefore, the cost of any product is the amount necessary to bid all the required resources away from the strongest competing uses.

4. Economists include a "normal" return, or profit, on a business investment, in calculating business costs.

5. Fixed (or sunk) costs are those that must be paid for some time period ahead regardless of the firm's rate of output.

6. Variable costs are those costs that vary with changes in the rate of output.

7. Total costs are the sum of fixed and variable costs.

8. Marginal cost is the increase in total cost incurred by producing one more unit of output.

9. Fixed, variable, and total costs can be converted to a per-unit-of-output basis by dividing each by the number of units produced.

10. If the marginal cost of carrying out any activity is smaller than the resulting benefit or contribution to income, it will pay (increase profits) to carry out that activity.

11. Most average-total-cost and average-variable-cost curves are U-shaped. But in some industries with extensive economies of large-scale production, increased output involves falling average total cost per unit over a large range of output, and the cost curve is more L-shaped than U-shaped.

12. The marginal-cost curve always cuts the ATC curve and VTC at the latters' minimum points.

13. The long run is that period of time in which all costs become variable.

14. In cases of external diseconomies ("negative externalities"), production involves costs to third parties that are not included in the costs paid by the producer (for example, where a steel mill spews out smoke and soot on the surrounding neighborhood). In such cases, private costs that control output are less than the full social costs of production, price is too low, and too much of the product is made for consumers.

New Concepts
to Remember

In Section A:

alternative cost
opportunity cost
real costs
accounting costs
money costs
fixed (sunk) costs
average total cost
    per unit (ATC)
marginal cost
marginal comparisons

In Section B:

variable costs
total costs
average fixed cost per unit (AFC)
average variable cost per unit (AVC)
least-cost point
short run
long run
optimal scale of enterprise
total social cost
externalities (positive and negative)

For Analysis
and Discussion

For Sections A and B:

1. Define opportunity, or alternative, cost. Explain why the dollar cost of producing a TV set is a measure of the alternative uses of the resources foregone.
2. If you were operating a grocery store, would there be any significant difference between your cash outlays per month and your costs per month? If so, what items would account for the difference?
3. You are considering the possibility of setting up a pizza parlor near the campus. Make a list of all the costs you ought to have in mind in estimating whether the expected demand will produce a profit. Which of the costs would be fixed regardless of how many pizzas you sold, and which would vary from week to week with sales volume?
4. In the fishing-boat example in the text: (a) Explain why marginal cost is independent of (does not depend on) the level of fixed cost. (b) How many boats would it pay you to rent out today at a price of $25? $15?

For Section B only:

5. The ABC company has the following costs. From this information, prepare a table showing the following: average fixed cost per unit, average variable cost per unit, average total cost per unit, and marginal cost. Then plot your data on a graph.

Total fixed cost per month, $2,000
Total variable costs:

UNITS PRODUCED	TOTAL VARIABLE COST
10	$1,000
11	2,000
12	2,800
13	3,500
14	4,000
15	4,800

6. Why are manufacturing concerns typically bigger than dry-cleaning establishments? Can you reconcile your explanation with the observed fact that some dry-cleaning establishments are bigger than some manufacturing companies?
7. "By and large, the competitive system sees to it that every firm is near the optimal size for producing its product." Do you agree with this statement? Explain carefully why, or why not.
8. List three cases of external diseconomies of business firms. Do such diseconomies seem to you rare, or pervasive?

CASE 7

POLLY POET'S PROBLEM

Professor Polly Poet of the English Department plans to spend next year traveling, and is trying to decide whether to put her house up for rent. She has never studied economics, and indeed is rather uncomfortable with figures. She has, nevertheless, compiled the following list of monthly costs that she is using to decide whether to rent the house and what rent to charge if she does so.

Assuming that the list is complete and that no other factors affect her decision (for example, the increased probability of burglary if the house is empty), what is the lowest rent she should be willing to accept rather than leave the house unoccupied? (*Note:* It is customary in this area to include the price of gardeners in the rent.) Explain your advice so that she will fully understand your reasoning.

Property taxes	$200
Insurance	15
Mortgage payments	100
Gardener (for lawn and trees)	50
Depreciation and maintenance:	
With house empty	40
With house occupied	80
Total: House empty	$405
House occupied	$445

APPENDIX   Physical-Production Relationships Underlying Cost Curves

This appendix provides a brief statement of part of the "theory of production," which underlies the cost of production in a firm and provides a foundation for understanding the distribution of income to different factors of production. Its purpose is to examine rigorously the physical and technological relationships involved as the businessman combines the various factors of production in turning out the product. It is intended for those who want a rigorous physical-output foundation for the previous and following sections on business costs. It can be omitted by others.

The simplest case occurs when one variable factor of production (say, labor) is applied to a fixed amount of some other factor (say, land). Consider the results of applying an increasing number of units of labor to a fixed plot of land, abstracting from other factors of production, such as fertilizer and tools. Table 8–2 shows what might happen in such a case. The physical outputs obtainable from various combinations of productive factors are what economists call a "production function."

Column 1 shows the number of laborers used. Column 2 shows the total production—say, bushels of wheat—obtained as more workers are added. Total product rises until, at some point (twelve workers with 3,300 bushels of output, in this example), so many laborers are being used on this small plot of land that they get in each other's way, and thereafter there is an actual decrease in the total output of wheat. Obviously, no intelligent farmer would ever carry production of wheat beyond this point, because by hiring more laborers, he would actually decrease the total crop he obtained.

Column 3 shows the average product (bushels of wheat) per worker on the land. This average product rises at first, because total product rises faster than in proportion to the number of workers used. But the average output per worker reaches a peak (at seven workers and 2,604 bushels in this example, which gives the maximum output per worker of 372 bushels.) Thereafter, even though total product continues to rise for a while, the average output per worker falls.

Column 4 shows the marginal product as more workers are used. This column shows the additional, or marginal, output obtained by adding each extra worker. Thus, adding the first worker increases total product by 100 bushels. For the second worker, the marginal product is 250 bushels, as total product rises from 100 to 350. Marginal product reaches its peak at five workers. After this, adding workers (up to eleven)

TABLE 8–2
Variable Output with Increasing Inputs

UNITS OF INPUT (LABOR)	TOTAL OUTPUT (BUSHELS)	AVERAGE OUTPUT PER UNIT OF LABOR (BUSHELS)	MARGINAL OUTPUT OF LABOR (BUSHELS)
1	100	100	100
2	350	175	250
3	702	234	352
4	1,152	288	450
5	1,700	340	548[a]
6	2,190	365	490
7	2,604	372[a]	414
8	2,908	364	304
9	3,114	346	206
10	3,240	324	126
11	3,300[a]	300	60
12	3,300	375	0
13	3,250	250	−50
14	3,080	220	−170

[a]Denotes highest point for each output series.

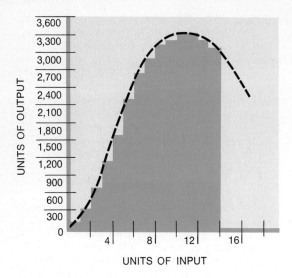

FIGURE 8-4
Total output rises fast at first as variable factors are added to a fixed factor, then levels off, and eventually turns down.

Figure 8–5 plots average product and marginal product from Table 8–2. Marginal product reaches its peak first, and then turns down as the rate of growth of total product begins to slow. Average output per worker shows a similar inverted U, but the peak is reached with more workers, as Table 8–2 shows.

Note that the marginal-product curve cuts the average-product curve at the latter's highest point. This is necessarily true because as long as marginal product is higher than average product, each additional worker is adding more to total product than the average of all workers up to that point. As soon as the marginal worker adds less to total product than the average up to that point, the marginal-product curve will be below the average-product curve. Thus, it will always cut the average-product curve at the latter's highest point.

The other significant point is the one at which marginal product becomes zero. Comparing the two figures, we see that this is at twelve workers, which is just the point where total product turns down. This clearly must be so, because marginal product is merely the amount by which total product increases as additional workers are added. Thus, when adding another worker decreases total product, marginal product becomes negative.

continues to increase total product, but not as rapidly as before; so the increment per additional worker falls.

These relationships can be seen readily in Figures 8–4 and 8–5. Figure 8–4 shows total product as additional workers are hired. It rises rapidly at first as production becomes more efficient, then gradually levels off, and finally (after twelve workers and 3,300 bushels) turns down, for there are just too many workers to avoid getting in each other's way.

The law of diminishing returns, or variable proportions. The preceding paragraphs provide a statement of Ricardo's famous "law of diminishing returns." They show just what happens when additional units of one factor of production are combined with a fixed stock of some other factor or factors.

Modern economists have come to a more general

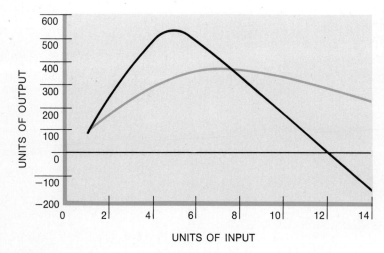

FIGURE 8-5
Marginal product shoots up rapidly as total output grows fast when the first variable factors are added. It turns down as the growth in total output slows, and becomes negative when total output turns down. Check it against Figure 8–4

statement of these relationships, which they call the "law of variable proportions." As the proportion of one variable factor of production to other fixed factors increases, the average product of the increasing factor will first rise and then fall persistently; and the marginal product of the increasing factor will also first rise and then fall, cutting the average-product curve at its highest point.

Thus, if all factors increase in proportion, there is no reason to expect Ricardo's law of diminishing returns to set in. This is a critical fact, for it says that neither an individual firm nor an economy need face diminishing returns just because it gets bigger.

Production foundations of cost curves. These production relationships underlie the cost data for the firm. Assume that the market prices of all factors of production are fixed—labor and land in our case. Then the total-fixed-cost curve (as in Figure 8–1) is obtained directly by multiplying the fixed amount of land used (fixed factor) by its rent per acre. The total-variable-cost curve is obtained by multiplying the number of workers (variable factors) by the wage per worker.

These total costs can readily be converted to the per-unit cost curves of Figure 8–2 by dividing through by the number of units produced. Thus, the average-variable-cost curve will be the inverse of the average-product-per-worker curve, because wage per worker is constant. When average product per worker is rising, average variable cost per unit of output falls (we continue to assume that workers are the only variable cost involved). When average product per worker begins to fall, average variable cost per unit of output begins to rise. Fixed cost per unit (rent on the land, in the example above) steadily falls as more bushels are produced with the same total fixed cost for land.

The combination of the persistently declining average-fixed-cost-per-unit curve with the U-shaped average-variable-cost curve gives the (flatter) U-shaped average-total-cost curve. Thus, given the prices of the factors of production, the physical-production relationships determine the shape of all three average-cost curves in any situation. The average-cost curves are the inverses of the physical-production curves in Figure 8–4. The marginal-product curve is the basis for the marginal-cost curve.

THEORY

NOTE: **This chapter should be omitted by those using only the Minimum Essentials Track.**

Section I of the Mathematical Appendix at the end of the text provides a concise mathematial statement (for students who know calculus) of the relationships of the preceding chapter and the profit-maximizing behavior of the firm in the short run, as stated in this chapter.

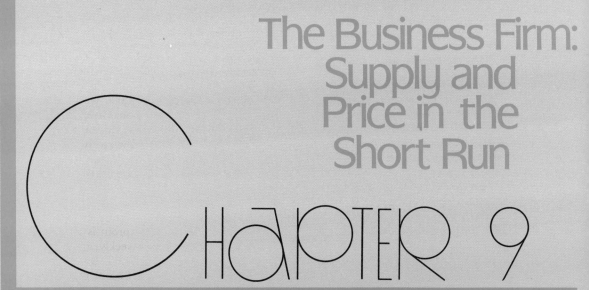

The Business Firm: Supply and Price in the Short Run

CHAPTER 9

This chapter examines how business firms, given their costs, respond to consumer demand in purely competitive markets in the short run. We postpone until later a look at the partially monopolized sectors of the economy.

THE THEORY OF THE FIRM

Let us assume, as a first approximation, that firms try to maximize their profits. Profits are the difference between total cost and total revenue. Hence, the firm does what it can (within the legal rules and mores of society) to maximize this difference. It produces profitably when the price more than covers costs, so it tries to make its costs as low as possible—that is, to produce as efficiently as possible. Whenever the firm can increase its profits by increasing its revenues or by reducing its costs, it will do so.

When it is maximizing its profits to the best of its ability, the firm will be in "equilibrium"—in the sense that it will not change its own actions unless conditions change. Actually, external conditions (e.g., consumer demand and wage rates) do change frequently, so business firms seldom reach equilibrium and stay in it for long. But we assume that the firm will always be aiming at this maximum-profit position in conducting its day-to-day affairs and in its long-run planning.

We know, of course, that not all firms behave this way. But for the moment, assume that firms in our highly competitive industry have the single goal of maximizing profit.

THE COMPETITIVE FIRM IN THE SHORT RUN

The individual firm in a highly competitive industry (for example, Amalgamated Widget, or an individual wheat farmer) is so small that it has no appreciable influence over the price of its product or the prices it pays for its inputs (labor, materials, and the like). As a practical matter, Amalgamated Widget or the wheat farmer must take the market price as given—fixed in the market by total demand-and-supply conditions over which the firm has no significant control. Under this assumption, it can't charge a higher price than the one prevailing in the market for widgets or wheat. If it does, it won't sell anything, be-

cause consumers can get all they want at the prevailing price from other sellers. In sum, our firm is a "price taker," not a "price maker."

This means that the firm sees the demand curve as a horizontal line at the market price. This assumption may seem to you extreme, and it is the limiting case of what economists call perfect competition. But it is an instructive case with which to begin. We will modify the assumption later.

Comparison of Total Costs and Total Revenue to Maximize Profits

Amalgamated Widget, with the costs shown back in Table 8–1, wants to maximize its profits. *Assume that the price of widgets is $1.80.* How many shall it produce weekly to maximize profits?

To simplify matters, assume first that AWC only changes output in units of 1,000 widgets. We have the total cost of producing different levels of output from Table 8–1; these are reproduced in the first two columns of Table 9–1 here—$3,000 to produce 1,000 widgets, $3,500 to produce 2,000, and so on. Given the market price of $1.80 per widget, we can easily construct a parallel column of revenue received from selling these widgets. Simply multiply the number of widgets produced by the price per widget, and we get column 3—$1,800 for 1,000 widgets, $3,600 for 2,000, and so on. Subtracting cost (column 2) from revenue (column 3) gives us total profit (column 4). Clearly, total profit is largest when we produce 6,000 widgets weekly, given our costs and the market price of $1.80. At that level of operations, we can make $3,200 profit weekly. We could also make a profit on any other output from 2,000 to 7,000 weekly, but it is largest at 6,000 weekly.

To check your understanding, assume that the market price drops to $1.50. What will be the new maximum-profit output level? Calculate a new total-revenue column and compare it with total costs. *Answer:* 5,000 widgets per week, with a profit of $1,500.)

Maximizing Profits—Marginal Analysis

We can make the same maximum-profit calculation by using marginal analysis, which may be

TABLE 9–1
Amalgamated Widget Company
Total Cost, Total Revenue, and Profit When
Price Is $1.80

OUTPUT (1)	TOTAL COST (2)	TOTAL REVENUE (3)	PROFIT (4)
1,000	$ 3,000	$ 1,800	− $1,200
2,000	3,500	3,600	100
3,000	4,100	5,400	1,300
4,000	5,000	7,200	2,200
5,000	6,000	9,000	3,000
6,000	7,000	10,800	3,200
7,000	11,000	12,600	1,600
8,000	17,000	14,400	− 2,600

TABLE 9–2
Amalgamated Widget Company,
Marginal Costs and Marginal Revenue

MARGINAL COSTS		OUTPUT	MARGINAL REVENUE	
PER 1,000 WIDGETS (1)	PER WIDGET (2)	(3)	PER 1,000 WIDGETS (4)	PER WIDGET (5)
$ 500	$0.50	1,000	$1,800	$1.80
600	0.60	2,000	1,800	1.80
900	0.90	3,000	1,800	1.80
1,000	1.00	4,000	1,800	1.80
1,600	1.60	5,000	1,800	1.80
3,400	3.40	6,000	1,800	1.80
6,000	6.00	7,000	1,800	1.80
		8,000		

simpler than calculating all possible profit positions. To do this, we need to introduce a new concept—*marginal revenue*. Marginal revenue is the increase in total revenue from selling one more unit (here, 1,000 widgets). Marginal revenue thus parallels marginal cost. Marginal cost shows the increment to total cost in producing one more unit; marginal revenue shows the increment to total revenue from selling that additional unit.

Table 9–2 shows marginal cost and marginal revenue for Amalgamated Widget, first using units of 1,000 widgets. Column 2 shows marginal cost, from column 8 of Table 8–1. It is simply the increase in total cost involved in producing each additional 1,000 widgets—

$100 in going from 1,000 to 2,000 widgets, $600 in going from 2,000 to 3,000 widgets, and so on. Marginal revenue (column 4) is obviously $1,800 for each additional 1,000 widgets sold, since the price per widget is $1.80. Or you could calculate marginal revenue as the change in total revenue for each 1,000 widgets sold (column 3 in Table 9–1). Now, the rule: To maximize profits, increase output as long as marginal cost is less than marginal revenue, and no further. As long as producing more widgets adds more to total revenue than to total costs, we obviously increase total profit by producing and selling more. Conversely, we will reduce total profits if we produce more when marginal cost is higher than marginal revenue.

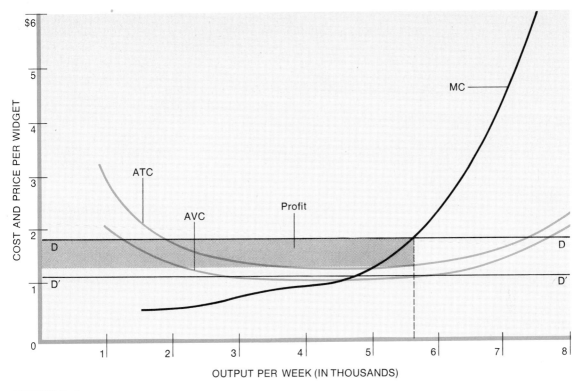

FIGURE 9–1
Amalgamated Widget Company: Maximum Profit Output Determined by
Marginal-Cost and Marginal-Revenue Curves
Profit is maximized by carrying production up to the intersection of the marginal-cost
and marginal-revenue curves—if you operate at all. Horizontal price lines (*D* and *D'*) are
also marginal-revenue curves for this producer under perfect competition.

Table 9–2 shows this clearly. Suppose we have been producing 3,000 widgets, making a weekly profit of $1,300. Could we do better by increasing output to 4,000 weekly? Table 9–2 shows that the answer is, clearly, yes. By raising output to 4,000 weekly, we add $900 to total cost and $1,800 to total revenue, increasing total profit by $900. This squares with Table 9–1, which shows total profit at $1,300 for 3,000 widgets and $2,200 for 4,000, the $900 increase indicated by the marginal method. But if we are producing 6,000 weekly now and increase to 7,100, marginal cost is $3,400 while marginal revenue is $1,800, reducing total profit by $1,600. We will maximize profits by producing 6,000 weekly. If we produce either less or more, the total-profit figure will be lower. The same maximum-profit level of output is, of course, given by following the equate-marginal-cost-

and-marginal-revenue rule if we use the per-widget data in columns 2 and 5 of Table 9–2.

Marginal Analysis Using Graphs

This analysis can readily be shown graphically. The cost curves in Figure 9–1 are the same as in Figure 8–2, except for the omission of the average-fixed-cost-per-unit curve. The marginal-cost curve shows the increment to total cost in increasing output by one unit. We have data only for changes of output in 1,000-widget units, and these points are plotted. But we can read off the *MC* curve the approximate marginal cost per widget for output levels between the plotted points. For example, the marginal cost of increasing output by one widget, from 4,200 to 4,201, is approximately $1.20.

113

We also need to add marginal revenue to Figure 9–1. Since we can sell all we produce at $1.80 per widget, the *MR* curve is simply a horizontal line at $1.80. This line, labeled *DD,* is also the demand curve Amalgamated sees for its widgets. We can sell all we produce at the market price of $1.80, none if we ask more than $1.80. The demand curve we see is infinitely elastic.

To maximize profits, we should produce up to the point where marginal cost equals marginal revenue. This is obviously about 6,000 widgets weekly on the graph. For any smaller output, *MC* is below the *MR* curve; for any higher output, *MC* is above *MR.* For example, to produce the 5,700th widget adds about $1.75 to the total cost and $1.80 to revenue, increasing profits. To produce the 6,200th widget adds about $2.20 to total cost and only $1.80 to revenue, decreasing profits. (Using graphical analysis, which permits us to read off approximate marginal-cost data for individual widgets between the 1,000-widget points in the tables, suggests that a little less than 6,000 widgets—about 5,800 weekly—may be our maximum-profit level if we can vary production between the 5,000- and 6,000-widget levels. In fact, some firms have accurate, detailed cost-of-production data; others operate on only rough estimates something like our tables.)

We can calculate AWC's profit per widget and total profit from Figure 9–1. Suppose price is $1.80 and we decide to maximize profits by producing 5,800 widgets weekly—where the marginal-cost curve equals the $1.80 demand and marginal-revenue curve. (Since we know the cost data exactly only for the 1,000-widget levels of output, this calculation may be only approximate, but the principle is unchanged.) The price per widget sold is $1.80; multiplied by 5,800 widgets, this gives total revenue of $10,440. The average total cost per widget at an output of 5,800 (reading from the ATC curve) is about $1.23, making total cost about $7,130. Subtracting total cost from total revenue gives us a total profit of $3,310, shown by the shaded area in Figure 9–1. (This is a little larger than the $3,200 maximum profit at an output of 6,000 given by Table 9–1, because there we assumed the firm could produce only in blocks of 1,000 widgets.)

Ask yourself one more question, to be sure you understand. Wouldn't we be better off to produce 7,000 instead of 6,000, getting the profit on the seventh thousand widgets, since the $1.80 price exceeds the average total unit cost of $1.57 at a 7,000 weekly output? The marginal-cost-marginal-revenue comparison gives the answer. Going from 6,000 to 7,000 adds $3,400 to total cost and only $1,800 to total revenue. The fact that price is above average total cost tells us that we can make a profit at that output level, but not that we will make our maximum profit at that level. Trying to pick up the profit on a seventh thousand widgets weekly would be a mistake, because it would involve adding more to cost than to revenue; average cost per unit would be higher on all 7,000 widgets if we increase output to 7,000. Compute the total profit at 7,000 widgets weekly and you'll see that it's only $1,600 ($12,600 revenue less cost of about $11,000), less than the $3,200 profit on 6,000 widgets.

Minimizing Losses in the Short Run

With the market price at $1.80, we're in clover. But suppose consumer demand for widgets nosedives, and the market price falls to $1.10, shown by *D'D'* on Figure 9–1. A quick look at that figure shows that we're going to lose money at this price, no matter what we do. The lowest average total cost per unit at which we can produce is $1.20, at an output of 5,000 weekly, and the price is only $1.10.

What should we do to minimize our losses? One possibility would be to shut down. This way we'd lose $1,000 a month, the amount of our sunk costs, which continue whether we operate or not. But if we operate, producing 3,000, 4,000, or 5,000 weekly, we'll be getting $1.10 per widget produced and only have to spend about $1.00 per widget in variable (out-of-pocket) costs (see Table 8–1 or the *AVC* curve of Figure 9–1 for data). This income will provide 10 cents per widget left over to apply on our $1,000 of fixed costs, which we have to pay in any case. So we'd better operate as long as we're stuck with the fixed costs whenever the price more than covers our average variable cost per unit, even though we lose money. By operating, we lose less than by shutting down.

The marginal-cost–marginal-revenue principle still tells us how many units to produce. The answer is 5,000. Producing every unit up to and including the fifth thousand adds more to revenue than it does to costs. Marginal revenue for the fifth thousand widgets is $1,100; marginal cost is only $1,000. But marginal cost for the sixth thousand is $1,600, above marginal revenue. The principle for minimizing loss is the same as for maximizing profit: If you operate at all, carry production up to the point where marginal cost equals marginal revenue, and no further.

The Decision to Shut Down in the Short Run

Would it ever pay us to shut down in the short run? Obviously, yes. If price falls below $1.00, which is the lowest average variable cost per widget we can manage at any output level, we'd better close up shop. Suppose price falls to 90 cents. No matter how many widgets we produce, our income is not even enough to cover our variable costs, much less provide anything to help cover the $1,000 of fixed costs. Suppose we produce 3,000. They will cost $4,000 but will bring in only $2,700, leaving a loss of $1,300, compared with only $1,000 if we just shut down. At any price below the lowest average-variable-cost-per-unit point, we will minimize losses by shutting down altogether. This rule does not contradict the marginal-cost–marginal-revenue principle for maximizing profits, since that principle tell us only what to do *if* we operate at all.

Short-Run Equilibrium of the Firm

When will Amalgamated Widget be in short-run equilibrium? When it is maximizing its profit or minimizing its loss, given consumer demand and given its fixed costs that it cannot alter in the short run. It will then be in short-run equilibrium when it is producing just up to the point where marginal cost is equal to marginal revenue (price).

This concept of the equilibrium of the firm parallels the concept of the equilibrium of the household (or consumer) developed in Chapter 4. Both tell us the situation toward which an economic unit will move in trying to improve its economic position. In a real world of constant change, we will seldom find firms actually in equilibrium for long. But when a household or firm is out of equilibrium, we can generally ex-

pect it to move to maximize its satisfaction or profit.

PROFIT MAXIMIZING IN THE SHORT AND LONG RUNS

A firm may be in short-run equilibrium and still be making substantial profits or losses. But such a situation will not last. If there are large profits, as with Amalgamated Widget when price is $1.80, other firms will invade the industry, increasing supply and forcing down prices. If there are losses, the losing firm must do better or ultimately go broke. Hence, short-run losses lead firms to move resources to greener pastures unless demand rises or costs can be reduced in the long run. Short-run equilibrium in such cases is clearly only a temporary equilibrium.

In the short run, managers may be inefficient; they may over- or underadjust to change; they may guess wrong about consumer wants and production costs. But not in the long run, when there is time for new competitors to enter the industry and for firms to go broke. Adam Smith's "invisible hand" will be at work, and other profit seekers will enter to produce more cheaply (efficiently) if existing firms have high costs. If losses prevail, better profit prospects elsewhere will lure resources away from the loss-ridden industry. In the long run, excess profits and losses will tend to be eliminated by competition, and prices will tend to be just high enough to cover all costs, including a normal profit. Chapter 10 examines these long-run adjustments in detail.

SHORT-RUN COST CURVES AND SUPPLY CURVES

If firms try to maximize profits in the short run, we can tell from any firm's cost curves what output it will produce at any given price. Each firm will produce up to the point when marginal cost equals price (marginal revenue). The firm's marginal-cost curve will be its short-run supply curve everywhere above the minimum point on the average-variable-cost curve. Look at Figure

9–1 or Table 9–3. At any price below $1.00, our firm will supply zero units. At prices from $1.00 to $1.59, it will supply 5,000 widgets weekly; at prices from $1.60 to $3.39, it will supply 6,000; and so on, up the marginal-cost curve. The short-run marginal-cost curve is the firm's short-run supply curve; output will be set where the demand curve (price) cuts the rising *MC* curve.

If this is true for all firms, it is easy to get a short-run market supply curve for the industry. Just add together horizontally the short-term supply curves (or schedules) of all the individual firms. Suppose there are 1,000 similar firms in the widget industry. Then the short-run industry supply schedule will be column 3 in Table 9–3, and *SS* in Figure 9–2. At each price, the supply offered will be 1,000 times the supply offered by Amalgamated Widget.

THE FIRM AS A BUYER OF PRODUCTIVE SERVICES

Before ending this chapter, it is important to look at the short-run output policies of the firm from a different angle. Whenever businesses decide to produce 1, 10, or 1,000 units of output, they simultaneously decide to buy or hire the "inputs" of productive services needed to produce those units—labor, raw materials, machinery, and so on. When Amalgamated Widget decides to produce 6,000 widgets weekly, it is deciding to hire, say, ten workers, buy raw materials, and so on.

We can, therefore, analyze the most profitable level of output in terms of units of productive inputs used, as well as in terms of units of output. For example, assume that AWC needs only labor and raw materials in addition to its rented plant

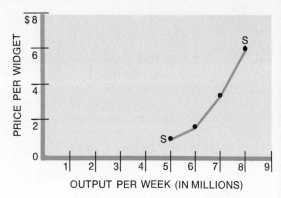

FIGURE 9–2
Short-Run Supply Curve—Widget Industry
Short-run industry supply curve is the sum of the short-run supply curves (marginal-cost curves) of the 1,000 firms in the industry.

and equipment, and that these are conveniently hired in units costing $100 per unit—perhaps one worker per week plus the material he uses. For each input, there will be some corresponding output of widgets. Thus, our cost schedules above could have been stated in terms of costs to hire different inputs rather than in terms of producing one, two, three, or more thousand widgets per week as output.

How many units of labor—materials input should we hire each month at $100 per unit? The marginal-cost—marginal-revenue principle holds here as before. Whenever adding one more unit of input adds more to revenue than to cost (that is, when marginal revenue is more than $100, in this case) it pays to increase inputs and hence output. As soon as marginal cost exceeds marginal revenue, stop expanding, because you have reached your best profit level.[1]

In explaining the firm's output decisions, we have thus explained simultaneously its demand for inputs (labor, capital, and so on). Because workers' wages depend on supply and demand forces, just like other prices, the theory of the firm here gives us half the picture of what determines wages, as we shall see when we come to explaining in Part 3 why people receive the incomes they do.

[1]The marginal revenue from hiring an additional unit of variable input is based directly on its "marginal product," as described in the appendix to Chapter 8, although, of course, the marginal product needs to be converted to dollar terms to become marginal revenue.

TABLE 9–3
Short-Run Industry Supply Schedule

PRICE	OUTPUT OF TYPICAL FIRM	INDUSTRY OUTPUT
Under $1.00	0	0
$1.00–1.59	5,000	5,000,000
$1.60–3.39	6,000	6,000,000
$3.40–5.99	7,000	7,000,000
$6.00 and over	8,000	8,000,000

SUMMARY AND REVIEW

1. The individual firm in a purely competitive market is a "price taker." It must take the market price as given, and adjust to it.

2. Given its costs and the market price of its output, the individual firm can determine its maximum-profit output by comparing total cost and total revenue at different output levels.

3. It can also determine its maximum-profit output by comparing marginal costs with marginal revenue. Profit will be maximized, or loss minimized, when it increases output up to the output where marginal cost equals marginal revenue, and no further.

4. Marginal revenue is the addition to total revenue from the sale of one more unit of output.

5. Graphically, the firm's maximum-profit output will be where the rising marginal-cost curve intersects the marginal-revenue (price, or demand) curve.

6. It will pay to continue operating in the short run as long as price is higher than the minimum point on the AVC curve, even though the price is not high enough to cover average total cost.

7. The firm is in short-run equilibrium when it is maximizing its profit or minimizing its loss, given consumer demand and given its fixed costs that it cannot alter in the short run.

8. The firm's short-run marginal-cost curve will be its short-run supply curve above the minimum point on its average-variable-cost-per-unit curve. The industry's short-run supply curve will be the summation of the individual firms' short-run supply (marginal-cost) curves.

9. When firms decide how many units of output to produce, they are simultaneously deciding how many units of input to buy or hire. Thus, the firm's output decisions determine its demands for labor, capital, and the like, and in that way they help determine the incomes received by the owners of productive services (labor and capital).

New Concepts to Remember

The essence of this chapter is the way a profit-seeking firm would try to maximize profits in the short run by carrying production up to the point where marginal cost equals marginal revenue and no further, if it operates at all. The following new concepts are important:

profit maximization   equilibrium of the firm
marginal revenue   price taker

For Analysis and Discussion

1. You are the manager of Amalgamated Widget, with the costs shown in Figure 9–1. Explain approximately how much you would produce at each of the following prices: $4.00; $1.40; $1.20; $1.05; $0.90. (Assume that you can vary production freely; you are not restricted to 1,000-widget changes.)

2. A competitive firm will always maximize profits by producing at the lowest possible total unit cost. Ture or false? Explain.

3. Fixed costs are often substantial and real. Why then do economists assert that businessmen should disregard them in short-run decisions on setting price and output?

4. Explain carefully why a firm will maximize its profits by carrying production up to the point where marginal cost just equals marginal revenue. If there are any exceptions to this rule, specify them.

5. You operate a roadside fruit stand. You have been selling raspberries at 60 cents a quart; they cost you 50 cents to produce. It is now midafternoon and raining. With customers scarce, you now estimate your demand schedule for the rest of the afternoon as follows:

PRICE	QUARTS
50¢	20
40	30
30	40
20	50
10	60

You have 60 quarts on hand and no storage facilities to avoid spoilage before tomorrow. What price should you charge to maximize profits? Explain. What is the importance of your costs in this case?

6. You are managing the plant shown in Figure 9–1 and are now producing 4,000 widgets a month. You have an order for 1,000 additional widgets a month, but the customer will pay only $1.05, per widget, less than your minimum total cost per unit. Should you accept the order? Show both graphically and through arithmetic calculations why your answer is sound.

7. Explain why the firm's short-run marginal-cost curve is its short-run supply curve. Is this always true?

CASE 8

AIRLINE TAKES THE MARGINAL ROUTE[2]

Continental Airlines, Inc., last year filled only half the available seats on its Boeing 707 jet flights, a record some 15 percentage points worse than the national average.

By eliminating just a few runs—less than 5 percent—Continental could have raised its average load considerably. Some of its flights frequently carry as few as 30 passengers on the 120-seat plane. But the improved load factor could have meant reduced profits.

For Continental bolsters its corporate profits by deliberately running extra flights that aren't expected to do more than return their out-of-pocket costs—plus a little profit. Such marginal flights are an integral part of the overall operating philosophy that has brought small, Denver-based Continental—tenth among the eleven trunk carriers—through the bumpy postwar period with only one loss year.

This philosophy leans heavily on marginal analysis. And the line leans heavily on Chris F. Whelan, vice-president in charge of economic planning, to translate marginalism into hard, dollars-and-cents decisions.

Getting management to accept and apply the marginal concept is probably the chief contribution any economist can make to his company. Put more simply, marginalists maintain that a company should undertake any activity that adds more to revenues that it does to costs—and not limit itself to those activities whose returns equal average or "fully allocated" costs. . . .

Whelan's work is a concrete example of the truth in a crack made by Prof. Sidney Alexander of MIT—formerly economist for Columbia Broadcasting System—that the economist who understands marginal analysis has a "full-time job in undoing the work of the accountant." This is so, Alexander holds, because the practices of accountants—and of most businesses—are permeated with cost allocation directed at average, rather than marginal, costs.

In any complex business, there's likely to be a big difference between the costs of each company activity as it's carried on the accounting books and the marginal or "true" costs that can determine whether or not the activity should be undertaken.

The difficulty comes in applying the simple "textbook" marginal concept to specific decisions. If the economist is unwilling to make some bold simplifications, the job of determining "true" marginal costs may be highly complex, time-wasting, and too expensive. But even a rough application of marginal principles may come closer to the right answer for business decision makers than an analysis based on precise average-cost data.

Proving that this is so demands economists who can break the crust of corporate habits and show

concretely why the typical manager's response—that nobody ever made a profit without meeting all costs—is misleading and can reduce profits. To be sure, the whole business cannot make a profit unless average costs are met; but covering average costs should not determine whether any particular activity should be undertaken. For this would unduly restrict corporate decisions and cause managements to forego opportunities for extra gains.

MARGINAL ANALYSIS IN A NUTSHELL:

Problem: Shall Continental run an extra daily from City X to City Y?

The facts: Fully-allocated costs of the
flight $4,500
Out-of-pocket costs of this
flight $2,000
Flights should gross $3,100

Decision: Run the flight. It will add $1,100 to net profit—because it will add $3,100 to revenues and only $2,000 to costs. Overhead and other costs, total $2,500 [$4,500 minus $2,000], would be incurred whether the flight is run or not. Therefore, fully allocated or "average" costs of $4,500 are not relevant to this business decision. It's the out-of-pocket or "marginal" costs that count.

Whelan's approach is this: He considers that the bulk of his scheduled flights have to return at least their fully allocated costs. Overhead, depreciation, and insurance are very real expenses and must be covered. The out-of-pocket approach comes into play, says Whelan, only after the line's basic schedule has been set.

"Then you go a step farther," he says, and see if adding more flights will contribute to the corporate net. Similarly, if he's thinking of dropping a flight with a disappointing record, he puts it under the marginal microscope: "If your revenues are going to be more than your out-of-pocket costs, you should keep the flight on."

By "out-of-pocket costs" Whelan means just that: the actual dollars that Continental has to pay out to run a flight. He gets the figure not by applying hypothetical

[2] Reprinted from *Business Week,* April 20, 1963, with permission of the publisher, © 1963, McGraw-Hill Book Company.

equations but by circulating a proposed schedule to every operating department concerned and finding out just what extra expenses it will entail. If a ground crew already on duty can service the plane, the flight isn't charged a penny of their salary expense. There may even be some costs eliminated in running the flight; they won't need men to roll the plane to a hangar, for instance, if it flies on to another stop.

Most of these extra flights, of course, are run at off-beat hours, mainly late at night. At times, though, Continental discovers that the hours aren't so unpopular after all. A pair of night coach flights on the Houston–San Antonio–El Paso–Phoenix–Los Angeles leg, added on a marginal basis, have turned out to be so successful that they are now more than covering full allocated costs. . . .

Continental's data-handling system produces weekly reports on each flight, with revenues measured against both out-of-pocket and fully allocated costs. Whelan uses these to give each flight a careful analysis at least once a quarter. But those added on a marginal basis get the fine-tooth-comb treatment monthly.

Is Continental Airlines right in using marginal analysis to decide whether to add flights? What if each flight, looked at individually, more than covers marginal cost, but added together they don't cover the firm's total costs? Would this latter case invalidate the marginal principle?

THEORY

NOTE: Those using only the **Minimum Essentials Track** should read only Section A of this chapter, plus the concluding section, "Purely Competitive Economy—Evaluation."

Long-Run Competitive Equilibrium and Economic Efficiency

CHAPTER 10

Building on our detailed analysis of individual households, firms, and markets in the short run, we need now to see how they all fit together in the long run. The main purpose of this chapter is to analyze how a purely competitive economy would work in the long run—how well the long-run competitive pressures of Adam Smith's "invisible hand" would guide the economy, and how efficiently it would allocate society's scarce productive resources to satisfy consumers' demands. On the basis of this examination, you can judge for yourself whether Smith set economists off on the right track with his talk about the "invisible hand," or whether he gave us a bad steer.

First, we need to be clear on two important points that have been glossed over so far. Precisely what do we mean by "pure competition" and by "long-run equilibrium"—two key analytical concepts?

SECTION a

The Competitive
Market System—
Overview

COMPETITION IN THE MODERN ECONOMY

No business firm is free from competition. Even AT&T, which you may have thought of as a monopoly in the field of telephone communication, faces lively competition from other forms of communication. Until 1946, Alcoa was the only firm producing aluminum in the United States, but six major firms produce aluminum today, and steel, copper, and other metals are potential substitutes for aluminum. Alcoa and the other aluminum companies are acutely aware of this fact. Competition is inescapable in business.

But it is obvious that competition is a lot more active in some industries than in others. At the competitive extreme, we find the individual farmer producing such standardized products as wheat, corn, and hogs. He has thousands of competitors, and his product is so standardized that the buyer has no interest in who the producer is. If Farmer Jones prices his No. 2 hard nothern wheat at 1 cent a bushel more than other farmers do, he just won't sell any.

There is a whole spectrum of market positions between the protected monopoly position of the public utility and the extreme competition of farmers. Most of the real world lies somewhere between these two extremes, and we will look at the less competitive sectors later. Here we want to examine how the economy would function under "pure competition"—roughly, the situation of Amalgamated Widget, or the wheat farmer without government intervention.

Pure Competition

As the Prologue to Part 2 emphasized, the essence of pure competition is that (1) no single seller is big enough to have any appreciable influence over market price, and (2) the product produced by all is identical, so buyers are indifferent as to what seller they buy from.

But although no one firm alone can significantly influence market price, the summation of all the individual producers' actions can and does. If prevailing costs and market price lead each individual firm to restrict output, the summation of all the thousands of individual cutbacks will reduce market supply and, other things equal, raise the price. Thus, quantity produced and the market price are "automatically" determined by the impersonal mechanism of the competitive market as it responds to consumer demand. No one has to plan how much cabbage should be produced. The profit motive, harnessed by the competitive market, determines how much, as farmers respond to consumers, demands.

Why Study Pure Competition?

There aren't many purely competitive industries in the modern American economy. Even agriculture, which has long been the standard example, doesn't quite represent pure competition any more, since the government has frequently intervened to control prices and output levels. Why study pure competition, then? There are two main reasons:

1. Economics is concerned with the overall performance of the economic system, and with how well it allocates society's scarce resources among alternative uses. To get at these problems, we must have an overall picture of the way the various parts of the economy fit together. The purely competitive model, with all markets competitive, has the great virtue of providing a reasonably simple picture of the way markets signal consumer demands to producers and producers respond to those demands. Many economists believe that this picture also provides a rough approximation of the "ideal" way a private-enterprise system ought to work. They thus use the model as a standard of comparison to ferret out those areas of the actual economy that aren't operating as well as they ought to.

2. Pure competition, although limited, does provide a rough approximation to the behavior of major sectors of the modern economy. Most of agriculture, broad areas of retailing, wholesaling, and service establishments, and some sectors of manufacturing where a moderate scale of plant is big enough for efficient production—all come reasonably close to the pure-competition model. To be sure, their products are not quite identical, and each producer has some control over the price at which he sells his product. But the pressures of competition are strong, and if he gets far out of competitive line on costs or prices, the individual producer finds himself steadily losing out in the market.

Long-Run Equilibrium

Long-run equilibrium is a situation (level of output and prices) that would be reached and maintained indefinitely unless some external force came along to disturb it. In long-run equilibrium, everyone (consumers and producers) is content to keep on doing what he is doing. He has no alternative that would improve his position.

Suppose we want to know how a purely competitive system, beginning from an equilibrium position, would respond to an increased consumer demand for strawberries in moving to a new long-run equilibrium position. Assume, for purposes of analysis, that all other economic variables remain unchanged, except as they may change in response to the increased demand for strawberries.[1]

We will certainly want to examine the reactions of grocers and strawberry farmers to the increased demand. For a complete analysis, we should also consider all the millions of interrelated effects throughout the economic system. However, once we get far from the strawberry industry, the effects are likely to be negligible. When the demand for strawberries rises, people may also buy more cream to put on their desserts, and fewer paperback books because they have less disposable income left for other products. If we took all such effects into account, we would be looking at the general equilibrium of the whole economy. But most of these effects are small, and we shall generally concentrate our analysis on the strawberry industry and others closely related to it, such as the raspberry industry. Thus, we shall look mainly at the long-run equilibrium of firms involved and the long-run equilibrium of the industry they constitute (here, the strawberry industry).

When we talk about long-run equilibrium, therefore, we are talking about the new situation toward which the industry moves and would ultimately reach if no other forces interfered. Long-run analysis provides guides to the ultimate effects of particular changes. Long-run equilibrium tells us the new levels of produc-

[1] If the increased demand represents a switch from, say, demand for raspberries, we could trace through the resulting reduction in prices and output of raspberries, comparable to the increase for strawberries.

123

tion and prices that would result from the shift in demand. It gives a picture of how efficiently such a system would use our scarce productive resources in producing what consumers demand.

LONG-RUN EQUILIBRIUM: THE CONTINUOUS SEARCH FOR PROFITS

The mainspring of the private-enterprise economy is the businessman's continuous search for profits. It is this search for profits that largely drives the economic system to a new equilibrium following a shift in demand. This does not imply that the proprietor of the local grocery spends every waking hour worrying about how to squeeze the last nickel out of his business, or that the farmer doesn't decide to visit his friends some afternoons when he could be working. But it does imply that, by and large, the desire to earn profits is a dominant one among businessmen, and that business concerns generally adopt those policies, consistent with prevailing law and mores, that they will produce the largest profits for the company.[2]

In the long run, all costs become variable. Existing plant and equipment wear out. Wage and salary contracts come up for renewal. Long-term contracts for supplies and materials expire. With all costs variable, the entrepreneur is completely free in making his output decisions. He can expand, contract, change the nature of his productive processes, or go out of business altogether, moving his resources to a more promising industry.

Thus, in the long run, firms will expand or contract, move into or drop out of any purely competitive industry, until expectations of prof-

its or losses have been eliminated—until it is no longer possible for anyone to better his position by moving into or out of the industry.[3] Thus, as long as the expected market price is above the expected minimum average total cost of producing a commodity, firms will move into the industry and present firms may expand. Output will increase, and the price will gradually be forced down to the minimum-average-cost point. But if the expected market price is below the minimum expected average total cost of production, firms will drop out of the industry, output will decline, and price will gradually rise toward the minimum-cost level. Under pure competition, with firms free to enter and leave the industry, market price cannot in the long run stay higher or lower than the minimum average total cost per unit of producing the commodity. This is the long-run equilibrium price and output level toward which the industry will move.

Each firm and the industry will be in long-run equilibrium when there is no advantage to any firm in increasing or decreasing its output, either by varying utilization of existing plant or by changing the scale of plant. This equilibrium will be reached when (1) each firm is producing in the most efficient way available (otherwise there would be an advantage in shifting to more efficient operations), and (2) market price is just equal to the least-cost point on the average total cost curve for that scale of enterprise. In this equilibrium position, profits have been eliminated by competition (remember that costs include a "normal" return on investment), and each firm will continue using just the same amount of all productive resources that it now uses.

Survival of the Fittest and Pressures toward Cost Minimization

The competitive market is an impersonal arbiter of who survives and who vanishes from the business scene. With a standard product, such as oats, the buyer is indifferent to who the producer is. Any farmer whose production cost is above the

---

[2] To assert that most businesses try to maximize profits each day, or month, or even each year, would be naïve indeed. Any alert businessman will tell you that it is the long pull that matters. The businesses that last and pay good dividends to their shareholders year after year are seldom out to "turn a fast buck." They are the ones that hold back new products until they have worked out the bugs, even though short-run profits are foregone. They are the ones that say that the customer is right, even when they're burned up at his unreasonable demands on return privileges. But this is not to say that the search for profits is not pervasive in the long run.

[3] Remember that a "normal," or "going," rate of return (or profit) on investment is included in the costs of each firm.

market price simply makes a loss, and in due course will vanish from the scene unless he improves his efficiency or receives a subsidy from someone. In long-run equilibrium, only those who produce at a cost as low as market price will survive, and this price will be no higher than the least-cost point on the average-cost curve of firms using the most efficient methods.

LONG-RUN EQUILIBRIUM: THE RESULTS

A brief summary now of the results of the competitive process. Would a purely competitive economy do a good job? In purely competitive equilibrium:

1. Each consumer would be getting as much of every product as could be produced at the cost he was willing to pay for it.
2. Each productive resource (labor, capital, etc.) would be used in that industry and occupation where it would contribute most to satisfying consumers' demands; and (as we shall see presently) in so doing, it would be earning the largest income consistent with its ability and willingness to help produce what consumers want to buy. The cost of each product would thus reflect the occupational and industry preferences of workers and other resource owners.
3. Each business would be producing in the most efficient way possible, so consumers would be getting their products with the smallest feasible use of resources in producing each; and each business would be earning just a normal rate of return on its investment.

Any system that achieved these results in allocating society's scarce productive resources would deserve a high mark indeed for economic efficiency. But, as you no doubt suspected, there are some problems we have glossed over so far, which may make a highly competitive, market-directed economy less attractive than this summary suggests. They are summarized in the final section of this chapter, and will be examined in detail in the chapters to come.

SECTION B

Long-Run Competitive Adjustment— More Detailed Analysis

Let us turn now to a more detailed and rigorous analysis of the operation of a purely competitive economy. A careful look at how such an economy would adjust to a change in consumer demand can provide useful insights.

ILLUSTRATION OF RESPONSE TO AN INCREASE IN DEMAND

Suppose that the purely competitive lead-pencil industry of 125 firms is in long-run equilibrium and that consumer demand for pencils increases. How will the industry respond?

The immediate effect will be (1) a higher price for pencils, with improved profits. (2) Then each firm will increase its output, because with a higher price, it is now profitable to produce more pencils. (This is a move upward along the industry short-run supply curve, before there is time for new firms to move in.) (3) In the new short-run equilibrium, price will be higher, output larger, and profits in the industry greater than before the increase in demand.

This short-run adjustment is pictured in Figure 10–1. The left-hand portion shows the short-run industry supply of pencils (S^1S^1). D^1D^1 is the original demand for pencils, and D^2D^2 shows the increased demand. The result of the increased demand is to raise the price from 6 to 8 cents. At

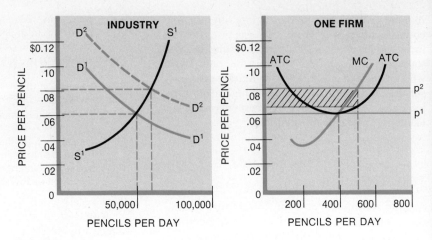

FIGURE 10–1
Increased Demand: Adjustment before Entry of New Firms
New increased demand (D^2D^2) raises the market price and makes increased output profitable for the individual firms.

this higher price, each firm can increase its profits by increasing its output from 400 to 500 units, as indicated on the right-hand portion of the graph. That is, each firm increases output to the point at which marginal cost (its short-run supply curve) equals the new higher price of 8 cents.

The right-hand portion shows the happy result for each firm; it is now producing more and making the profit indicated by the shaded area. The summation of all these increases by the 125 firms is shown in S^1S^1 on the left, which indicates the total increase in pencils supplied at the higher price of 8 cents. Consumers are now getting 62,500 pencils instead of the original 50,000, but they have to pay 8 instead of 6 cents per pencil. This increase results automatically from the independent actions of hundreds of purely competitive firms producing pencils, each acting to maximize its profits.

But this situation is obviously unstable. New resources will be attracted to the industry by the generous profits. As new firms enter and productive capacity is expanded, the industry supply curve (S^1S^1) will gradually move to the right; more will be produced as more resources move into the pencil industry in the long run.

With more pencils produced, the price will gradually fall back toward its original level. If unlimited productive resources can be attracted to the pencil industry without the necessity to pay more for them (that is, if new firms can enter without bidding up costs in the pencil industry), the new long-run equilibrium will be back at the original price but with more pencils being produced. This would be a case of long-run "constant costs" for the industry. If, however, the entrance of new firms raises costs for all firms because higher payments are necessary to attract labor, materials, and other resources from other industries, we have a case of "increasing costs." Either way, as the price of the product falls back and costs rise, profits are gradually squeezed out. When the price is again equal to the lowest average total cost, there will be no further inducement for new firms to enter and a new long-run equilibrium has been reached. It will probably be at somewhat higher costs and price than originally, with the larger industry output, because most industries probably face long-run increasing costs.

These long-run adjustments are shown in Figure 10–2. S^1S^1 is the new short-run aggregate-supply curve after new firms have had time to come into the industry; it has shifted to the

126

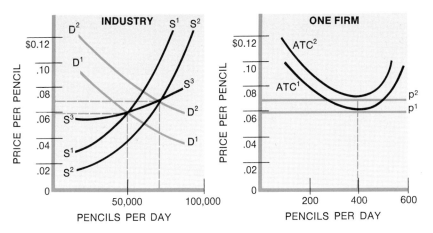

FIGURE 10–2
Increased Demand: Adjustment after Entry of New Firms
Increased demand draws new firms into the industry and produces new equilibrium for
the firms and the industry at a price of 7 cents. S^3S^3 is the long-run industry supply
curve.

right. Under these new conditions, supply and demand are equal at a price of 7 cents per pencil, with an output of 70,000 pencils in the industry as a whole. This is the new long-run industry equilibrium; price is now just equal to the new higher ATC curve at its minimum point, shown in the right-hand portion of Figure 10–2. Thus, there is no longer any incentive for resources to move into or out of the industry. Note that the cost curves of the typical firm have risen, because the increased production of pencils has bid up the price of labor and raw materials. As demand increased, price first rose from 6 to 8 cents, and then fell back to 7 cents, the lowest point on the ATC curve. In the new long-run equilibrium, the typical firm is again producing about the same amount as before, again at just its lowest average total-cost point.[4] But since there are 50 more

firms than before, the aggregate output of the industry is greater than it was initially. In response to their increased demand, consumers are getting 20,000 more pencils, and are getting them at the lowest price that will cover costs. But they have to pay 1 cent more per pencil, because that much more was necessary to attract more productive resources from other uses into pencil making.

Long-Run Industry Supply Curves

S^3S^3 in Figure 10–2 is the long-run supply curve for the pencil industry. It joins the points at which the demand and supply curves intersect before and after the increase in demand. More fundamentally, it joins the lowest points on the typical firm's average-total-unit-cost curves as more firms enter the industry.[5]

This is shown in Figure 10–3, patterned after Figure 8–3, which considered the optimal scale of enterprise for firms. The little ATC curves show the average-total-cost-per-unit curves for the

---

[4]Figure 10–2 shows the new equilibrium output of the firm identical with the old—that is, the new average-cost curve is merely raised by 1 cent for each level of output. This will be the result if the costs of all factors of production rise in the same proportion. This need not, of course, be the case, and the particular type of cost increase shown is not important for the basic analysis of the industry's response to an increase in demand.

---

[5]This is not quite accurate, since the envelope to the small ATC curves cannot just join their minimum points, but it is a close enough approximation for our purposes here.

127

typical firm as more firms enter the industry. The *SS* curve in this figure corresponds to the S^3S^3 curve in Figure 10–2. The industry shown is one of constant costs between 15,000 and 30,000 pencils, and of gradually increasing costs above 30,000 pencils.

THE DEMAND FOR PRODUCTIVE SERVICES: WAGES AND OTHER INCOMES

When a business expands output to meet consumer demand, it hires more workers, rents more land, and uses more capital as long as marginal cost is less than marginal revenue. Thus, the business hires more workers, for example, as long as the marginal cost of labor (its wage) is less than its marginal revenue (the contribution one additional worker makes to increasing the sale value of the firm's production—often called its marginal revenue product).[6]

Competition among businessmen for productive resources will bid up the return (wage, rent, and so on) on each productive resource to roughly its marginal revenue product, and no higher. Whenever the price of any productive service (say, the wage of a particular grade of labor) is lower than its marginal product, businessmen can increase their profits by hiring more of that factor, and this competition will bid the wage up. Whenever the price of a productive service is higher than its marginal product, businessmen will cut back on hiring that factor, and its price will fall until it just equals its marginal product. In long-run equilibrium, each worker's wage will thus be just equal to his marginal revenue product.

Moreover, each productive resource will have its highest marginal product when it is in the industry where its contribution is greatest in producing the products consumers want. Thus, each productive factor will earn the most when it

---

[6]Marginal product is the addition to total output made by using one more unit of labor or capital. A slightly more precise statement of this paragraph will be presented in Chapter 17.

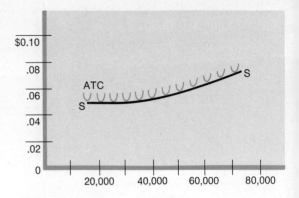

FIGURE 10–3
Long-Run Industry Supply Curve
This figure shows the relationship between typical individual-firm average-cost curves and long-run industry supply curves over a wide range of outputs. *SS* corresponds to S^3S^3 on Figure 10–2.

is contributing most to satisfying consumer demands. And each resource (worker) will be drawn to the use where its marginal product is highest if it wishes to maximize its income. The invisible hand again! A more detailed look at this in Part 3.

GENERAL EQUILIBRIUM OF A COMPETITIVE ECONOMY

The concluding segment of Section A above, "Long-Run Equilibrium—The Results," provided a summary view of the results of the competitive process. We want now to provide a more complete and vigorous analysis of the results of a purely competitive economy, to see just how well such an economy would allocate society's scarce resources. Suppose the entire pattern of consumer demands for the economy is frozen, and a full "general-equilibrium" adjustment to these demands has worked itself out in a purely competitive economy. Would the resulting long-run general equilibrium represent an efficient allocation of our scarce resources to best satisfy consumers' demands? In long-run equilibrium:

COMPETITIVE ADJUSTMENTS—SOME FINER POINTS

What to maximize—profits, or present value of the firm? This chapter assumes that businessmen try to maximize profits, and this is a satisfactory approximation for our elementary purposes. But if you take more advanced courses in economics or finance, you will find that we are sliding by some more sophisticated points that real-world managers and investors must take into account.

First, we have not specified exactly what we mean by profits. Is it total profits of the firm? Profits per share of common stock? Rate of return on stockholders' investment? And over what time period? For our elementary analysis, we need not distinguish. But the goals are all somewhat different, and if you become a corporation manager or investor, you will need to be more precise.

Second, profit maximization as a goal will not help us choose between alternative actions whose profits accrue at different times. For example, is an investment that yields $500 annually beginning this year more or less profitable than one that yields nothing now but $600 annually beginning in five years? Which would you prefer?

Third, profit maximization as a goal ignores the "quality" of different investments. Some are riskier than others.

Many economists and financial analysts therefore now substitute for profit maximization the goal of maximizing the present value of stockholders' investment in the firm. This involves discounting back to the present the value of all expected earnings in the future. The longer one has to wait for future profits and the riskier they are, the less will be their present value. All these factors are presumably taken into account by investors buying and selling the firm's stock, so the market value of all the comon stock outstanding can be used as an approximation of the present value of the firm at any given time. Issues like these are what make the lives of business managers and investors lively and challenging. But we can safely leave them to more advanced courses.

Do all firms minimize costs under pure competition? At any time, every industry includes firms of varying efficiency, with different levels of profits and losses. This is partly because in the dynamic economic world, some firms are on the way up, some on the way down. Partly it is because many industries are far from purely competitive; some markets are not open to new firms. But in purely competitive long-run equilibrium all firms in any industry would be driven to produce at the same minimum average (total per-unit) cost. This must be true, since any firm with a higher cost would have been driven out of business, and any firm with a lower cost would be luring business away from others.

It is easy to see that in the long run, inefficient firms will be eliminated by competition. But we need not assume that all remaining firms would become identical. Some entrepreneurs are more efficient than others. Some firms are located near good markets and pay high rents, whereas others are more distant but pay lower rents. Some firms are small and obtain efficiency through close personal supervision; others are large and count on mass-production methods to provide low costs. It is not necessary that all firms be identical, only that each be able to produce an average total unit cost as low as that of its competitors.

For example, suppose that one manager of a textile firm is more effective in organizing production than anyone else in the industry is. Won't his firm continue to make a juicy profit even in the long run? The answer is no. When the manager is hired, his firm will have to pay him a higher salary than other managers receive in order to keep him away from other firms. Assuming active competition among firms, his salary will be bid up until it is higher than that of a less efficient manager by the differential advantage of his service. If the entrepreneur himself is the efficient manager, he should charge a salary for himself equal to what he could get in alternative opportunities.

1. There is no excess (unsold) supply or excess (unsatisfied) demand at the existing price in any market.

2. Each consumer is getting as much of every good demanded as can be produced at the price that consumers are willing to pay for it, given the costs of producing the good. Since each price paid is a measure of the marginal utility provided by that product, consumers' market demands are accurate signals as to how much of different products consumers want produced at different prices.

3. Each business is producing each good in the most efficient (lowest-cost) way possible, so consumers' demands are satisfied with the smallest feasible use of resources. Each firm, to achieve this result, has carried production up to the point where marginal cost just equals price. Remember that MC always cuts the ATC curve at ATC's minimum point, so in equilibrium, Price = Marginal cost = Minimum average cost.

4. Profits have served as an incentive to produce desired goods in the most efficient way, but no firm is earning more than a "normal" return ("profit").

5. Each productive resource (labor, capital, etc.) is used in that industry and occupation where it contributes most to satisfying consumers' demands, consistent with the occupational and industry preferences of its owner. Thus, the costs of producing each good reflect both the resources used and the income demands and occupational and industry preferences of workers and other resource owners.

6. Each productive resource is receiving an income equal to its marginal contribution to producing the goods and services consumers demand—the largest income consistent with its ability and willingness to help produce what consumers demand.[7]

How can we be sure that each resource is being used most efficiently in satisfying consumers' demands? *The critical point is that in equilibrium, output of each product will be carried up to just the point where price equals marginal cost.* Remember that price is a measure of the marginal utility received by consumers from the last unit of each product bought. Price is also equal to the marginal cost of the last unit each good produced, where mar-

ginal cost reflects the resources used in producing the last unit, and the income, occupational, and industrial preferences of all resources owners. Additional resources have been used in each industry up to the point where the marginal utility obtained by consumers from the last unit produced is just equal to the marginal cost to society of making that additional output. To produce more of any good A, so its marginal cost exceeded price, would mean incurring a marginal cost in other goods foregone greater than the marginal utility provided by more of A. Conversely, restricting the output of A by raising its price above marginal cost would reduce society's welfare because the marginal cost of producing another unit of A would be less than the marginal utility attainable from it. (For a more complete, rigorous proof, see the appendix at the end of this chapter.)

PURELY COMPETITIVE ECONOMY—EVALUATION

Such is the case for an individual-initiative, market-directed, purely-competitive economy. It is an impressive one, especially if we want to avoid authoritarian control over what gets produced and where we work. The purely competitive private-enterprise system offers a nonpolitical, individualistic way of making the millions of interrelated compromises required among the different interests involved. Each individual, as consumer, laborer, or business manager, looks out for his own self-interest. No individual consumer or resource owner has any appreciable influence over what gets produced and how much of it, but in the mass, they efficiently direct the allocation of society's resources among all possible alternative uses. The result is an organization of our scarce resources that looks amazingly as if it had indeed been guided by some invisible hand for the welfare of society as a whole. And the Western, democratic, largely market-directed economies, although they differ substantially from the purely competitive ideal, have in fact done very well in raising the standards of living of their people over the last two centuries. Only two (the USSR and East Germany) of the top twenty nations as measured by per capita income are not mainly "capitalist,"

---

[7]Some economists describe such general-equilibrium conditions in mathematical terms. Because general equilibrium involves considering a vast number of demands, costs, markets, prices, and productive factors simultaneously, we can view the system as a large set of simultaneous equations and investigate the effects of different changes mathematically. Leon Walras, a French economist, was one of the first, a century ago, to use mathematics in analyzing economic problems, and apparently the first to state precisely the essential general-equilibrium conditions for such a competitive economy.

market-directed economies, and they are both far down the list. (See Table 29–1 for the data.)

But even a purely competitive economy, for all its virtues, would fall short of satisfying some people's personal and social goals on three major fronts—three main "market failures" to attain a theoretically ideal result. The following paragraphs list these market failures, to round out this evaluative overview of an individualistic, market-directed, purely competitive economy. Each possible failure is analyzed in detail in one of the following chapters (15–17, 24, and 25); so you can decide for yourself how serious such failures are and what ought to be done about them.

Problems in Making Competitive Markets Work Effectively

Resource allocation when total social costs exceed private costs. To get the optimal allocation of resources among different products, the price of each product to the consumer should cover both the marginal and average total unit cost of producing it. In some cases, there are hidden costs ("externalities") that are not paid by the producer and hence do not enter into the commodity's price but nevertheless are borne involuntarily by others. Pollution is a leading example. Factories may impose costly side effects on swimmers, fishermen, and downstream users of the water by dumping wastes in a river, but these costs are not included by its accountants as a basis for pricing its products, since the company does not pay them. In such cases, the price charged by the company is lower than it should be and output is larger than is socially justifiable; the market system fails to produce an "ideal" pattern of resource allocation. Most economists believe that in such cases of negative externalities, we should take collective (government) action to bring results nearer to the competitive ideal. (Details in Chapter 17.)

Imperfect information, immobility, and demand manipulation. For a competitive system to work well, consumers must be informed about the goods and services available at different prices, and resource owners must be well informed about employment opportunities that are open to them. If consumers don't know about a new product, they can't buy it. If farm workers in Montana know nothing of available jobs in Detroit's auto-assembly plants, or secretaries in Chicago don't know about better jobs in St. Louis, the optimal allocation of resources is blocked. Perhaps the Montana worker would prefer to stay out on the range even if he knew about the higher-paying Detroit jobs, but we can't be sure unless he knows about them.

A similar misallocation may result if resources are immobile, even though information is available. If our farmer has a big family and no savings, he may be unable to take the better Detroit job, no matter how badly he wants it. Both the farmer and society would be better off if he could somehow get over the hump into the new industrial job.

Another problem is perhaps even more serious, if we temporarily drop the assumption of a perfectly competitive economy. In the modern world, advertising influences, and sometimes even determines, what consumers want. Some people say that big business tells us what we *should* want, rather than responding to our own wants. If so, the basic assumption of free consumer choice is unacceptable. But advertising also plays a vital positive role of providing information on prices and product availability. (Details in Chapters 13 and 16.)

The problem of minimum size for efficient production and dynamic progress. Pure competition requires that no one seller be large enough to have appreciable influence over market price. If one gets very big, there is a danger that he may respond to increased consumer demand by raising price and trying to shut out new competitors, rather than by expanding output. For pure competition, there have to be lots of firms in every industry.

But in many industries—for example, autos and steel—firms have to be big in order to produce efficiently. Moreover, much of the research and development underlying our new products and methods is done in big businesses. In such industries, we face a difficult choice. We can insist on many small firms to assure competition, but this will mean higher production costs, and possibly less research and development spending, than a smaller number of large firms would involve. Or we can tolerate some degree of monopoly, but lose some of the pressures of competition obtainable with large numbers of producers. (More on this dilemma in Chapters 14 and 15.) We certainly don't need *pure* competition to get the benefits outlined above, but just how many firms are needed in each industry for workable competition is a debatable issue.

Public Goods and the Public Sector

There are some public, or collective, wants that cannot be satisfactorily provided through the marketplace. National defense and the court system are examples. We agree that they are essential and, through the political process, legislate taxes (compulsory payments) to hire resources to provide them. There is no practical way to leave it up to each individual to buy in the marketplace the amount and kind of national defense or general law and order he wants. The special characteristics of public goods are that they are widely agreed to be essential and, if provided, cannot practically be withheld from any citizen just because he doesn't pay.

What we do directly through government action, we often call the "public sector" of the economy. This now totals over $700 billion annually, nearly a third of the total GNP. Just how far we should go in using compulsory taxes to "buy" public goods and services is another highly debatable issue. The lines defining public goods are sometimes far from clear. Is slum clearance a "public good," not salable through the market? For true public goods, there is no practical alternative to turning to the political process for making decisions, but lots of cases are marginal. (Details on the public sector in Part 4.)

Equity in the Distribution of Income

In a purely competitive economy, every individual's income would rest on his own and his property's economic contribution. And this would mean an unequal distribution of incomes. In a competitive race, some win and some lose. Moreover, we don't all start equal in the race. Some individuals inherit large fortunes, from which they obtain large incomes in the form of interest and dividends. Some people have higher intellectual abilities than others. Some are born into higher-income families, which means they get better educations and broader opportunities. Minority youngsters in the slums start with a big handicap.

Many Americans believe that we should reduce these inequalities through government action. Others argue that an income distribution based on "economic contribution" through the market would be both just and efficient—that it would provide both incentives and a fair income for all. Still others stress the need to give everyone a more equal start.

Whichever test of equity you prefer, it is clear that the distribution of income produced by a highly competitive market system need not meet your test, however efficiently the system may allocate resources to meeting consumer demands.

Both the United States and all the Western European democratic nations use taxes and government expenditures to redistribute incomes substantially through "transfer payments." Such transfers to reduce inequality may be combined with reliance on market prices to obtain efficient resource allocation, once incomes are redistributed. (Details in Chapters 25 and 26.)

SUMMARY AND REVIEW

1. A purely competitive market is characterized by many sellers of one product, with no seller large enough to influence appreciably the price of the product. Although there are few purely competitive industries, the purely competitive model provides a reasonably simple picture of the way markets channel consumer demands to producers and producers respond to those demands. The competitive model also provides a rough approximation of the "ideal" way in which a private enterprise system ought to work. Moreover, much of the actual economy roughly approximates the condition of pure competition.

2. Long-run competitive equilibrium is a situation that would be reached and maintained indefinitely in a market, with all costs variable, unless some external force came along to disturb it.

3. Their persistent search for profits will lead firms to move into or out of each purely competitive industry until expectations of profits or losses have been eliminated.

4. Under long-run purely competitive equilibrium:

   a. There will be no excess supply or excess demand in any market.

   b. Each consumer will obtain as much of every good demanded as can be produced at the price he is willing to pay for it, given the costs of producing the good.

   c. Each business is producing at the most efficient (lowest-cost) way possible, so consumers' demands are satisfied with the smallest feasible use of resources.

   d. Profit has served as an incentive to produce desired goods in the most efficient way, but no firm is earning more than a "normal" return.

   e. Each productive resource is drawn to that industry and occupation where it contributes most to satisfying consumers' demands; and in that occupation, each resource receives an income equal to its marginal contribution in producing the goods and services consumers demand.

5. A purely competitive economy would avoid authoritarian control over what gets produced, where we work, and the incomes we get. Power in the economy would be widely dispersed, and "efficient" allocation of resources would be achieved. However, in such a purely competitive economy, three important "market failures" might occur:

   a. Some markets cannot be made purely competitive without forgoing the economies of large-scale production. Others may produce undesirable side effects (externalities) that are not reflected in producers' costs of production and hence in prices.

   b. There are some public, or collective, goods that cannot be provided satisfactorily through the marketplace; for example, national defense.

   c. While purely competitive markets would provide an efficient distribution of income, giving each resource an income equal to its marginal productivity, this distribution might not be considered equitable by many people.

New Concepts to Remember

pure competition
long-run equilibrium
equilibrium of the firm
equilibrium of the industry
general equilibrium

economic efficiency
constant-cost industry
increasing-cost industry
long-run supply curve
public goods

For Analysis and Discussion

1. Explain briefly but concisely how individuals and businesses, each pursuing its own self-interest, interact to produce a widely beneficial outcome under competitive market conditions.

2. "Under pure competition, the consumer is king. The price of what he wants to buy can never stay for long above the minimum cost of producing any article." Is this quotation sound?

3. Under a purely competitive system, what incentive, if any, would remain for businessmen to do an efficient job, since competition would eliminate profits?

4. Pure competition, strictly speaking, does not prevail in any part of the economy. Then why study it?

5. "A purely competitive economic system would be ideal." Do you agree? Why, or why not?

6. (*Section B only*) Suppose a tax of 1 cent per pencil has been included in the costs of all pencil producers. Now the tax is removed. Beginning from the situation in Figure 10–1 with the price at 6 cents and demand D^1D^1, trace through the adjustment to a new equilibrium.

7. (*Section B only*) As a consumer of widgets, would you prefer that the industry be one of constant or increasing long-run costs? Why?

8. Chapter 10 demonstrates that under pure competition, price will be set equal to the minimum cost of production. How, if so, do you explain the cost of a Picasso or Rembrandt painting? (*Hint:* Is there pure competition among sellers?)

9. "Most people would agree that a dollar means more to a poor than to a rich person. Since this is so, an economic system that merely reacts to the number of dollars spent is grossly unfair in the way it allocates resources." Do you agree or disagree? Why? If you agree, how should we modify the system to get around the problem?

10. What would be the main weaknesses, if any, of a purely competitive system? Should we use public policies to move further toward such a system?

CASE 9 SHOULD BUSINESS SERVE THE PUBLIC INTEREST RATHER THAN ATTEMPT TO MAXIMIZE PROFITS?

Americans have long had a kind of love-hate attitude toward business, especially big business. We admire big business for its efficiency, the huge flow of goods it produces, and the good jobs it provides. But we mistrust the power that seems concentrated in the hands of big-business owners and managers, and are quick to blame big business when things go wrong.

The pollsters have consistently found one overriding public attitude: Although the "man in the street" thinks there is a lot that is good about big business, he feels that it is "too concerned with making profits" and not enough with serving the public. This picture recurs in study after study, almost without exception. Moreover, this criticism of big business seems to have grown much stronger in the last decade or two. The proportion of respondents who are strongly critical of business on this score has gone up in recent decades from 20–25 percent on many polls to as high as 80 or 90 percent now.

On the other hand, Professor Milton Friedman, one of the most influential proponents of the private-enterprise system, has written, "Business has one and only one social responsibility—to make profits (so long as it stays within legal and moral rules of the game established by society). Few trends could so thoroughly undermine the very foundations of our free society as acceptance by corporate officials of a social responsibility other than to make as much money for their stockholders as possible."

Friedman argues that if businesses try to maximize profits, they will draw society's scarce resources into those industries where consumer demand is strongest, away from those where demand is weak. Thus, in attempting to maximize their profits, businesses will use resources just as the public wants, as indicated by its market demands for all different products. What more socially responsible behavior to serve the public can be imagined? By contrast, if business managers decide to "serve the public" and use the business's resources for "socially responsible" ventures like rebuilding the slums or helping the hardcore unemployed, how will they know whether their ventures comprise the socially most advantageous use of the resources? Substituting their decisions for those of millions of consumers in the market is hard to justify unless you believe that businessmen have special wisdom or a private pipeline to the Deity.

1. Is the criticism that businesses try to make profits rather than "advancing the public interest" justified? Should business "serve the public interest" *rather than* attempting to make profits?

2. Is there a conflict between attempting to maximize profits and serving the public interest?

3. If you were a businessman, how would you reply to the public's widespread criticism of excessive business concern with profits?

4. If businessmen decide to "serve the public interest" rather than maximize profits, what criteria should they use in deciding what specific public interests to undertake and how much money to spend on each?

APPENDIX   General Equilibrium and Economic Efficiency: Pareto Optimality

A purely competitive system of the sort described in this chapter would provide the most efficient possible allocation of resources in the sense described in the text of the chapter (abstracting temporarily from the "market failures" described in the last section). More precisely, we can show that such a purely competitive system would allocate resources most efficiently, in the sense that no possible reallocation would increase the welfare of anyone in the system without harming someone else. This condition, which economists call "Pareto optimality" (after the famous French economist who first stated it precisely), seems to some observers a weak claim for an optimal system. But it is a major claim indeed, if you stop to think about it. For if Pareto optimality does not prevail, we could make someone better off without harming anyone else, thus unambiguously increasing the public's total utility. Any system that does not provide Pareto optimality is producing a socially inefficient allocation of resources that holds total utility for the economy below what it could otherwise be.

It is possible to demonstrate precisely that Pareto optimality will prevail under competitive general equilibrium (that is, no one can be made better off without injuring someone else); while under other market arrangements (for example, with some degree of monopoly), it is generally possible to increase the welfare of someone without injuring anyone else. For simplicity, consider only two goods, x and y, although the argument can be generalized to many goods.

Assume that competitive general equilibrium prevails. We know then (from Chapter 7) that when a consumer is in equilibrium, maximizing his utility, he spends his income so that the marginal utility obtained from the last dollar spent on x is the same as that obtained from the last dollar spent on y. Alternatively, we can say that the marginal utilities of the two products must be proportional to their prices. In equation form:

$$\frac{MU_x}{MU_y} = \frac{P_x}{P_y} \qquad (1)$$

We also know (from Chapters 9 and 10) that in long-run competitive equilibrium, each producer in each industry maximizes profits by producing up to the point where marginal cost equals price. Thus:

$$P_x = MC_x \text{(for industry } x) \qquad (2a)$$
$$P_y = MC_y \text{(for industry } y) \qquad (2b)$$

Combining equations (1) and (2), we can then write:

$$\frac{MU_x}{MU_y} = \frac{P_x}{P_y} = \frac{MC_x}{MC_y} \qquad (3)$$

Equations (1), (2), and (3) state the conditions under which, with the competitive prices P_x and P_y, every consumer and business firm is in the best position it can achieve. No one can increase his utility or profits by changing his behavior. Equation (3) also emphasizes that prices provide the basic equilibrating link between consumers (expressing their preferences through expenditures) and businesses (maximizing their profits by hiring resources up to the point where marginal cost equals price).

Now, consider any situation where perfect competition does not prevail—for example, where a monopolist is restricting output and raising price to enlarge profits so that he holds his selling price above marginal cost. (We will demonstrate rigorously in Chapter 12 why he will do so in order to maximize his profits. once he is free from competitive pressure.) Suppose, for example, that monopoly prevails in industry y, so marginal cost in y is less than price. Then equation (2b) will not hold, and hence neither will equation (3).

Suppose, for example, that

$$\frac{MU_x}{MU_y} = 2$$

but that

$$\frac{MC_x}{MC_y} = 3$$

because marginal cost is below price in industry y, while MC equals price in industry x. Thus, the marginal utility of one unit of x is twice that of one unit of y, but the marginal cost of producing one more y is only one-third that for x. This means that in terms of costs, producers could make three additional units of y by giving up one of x. By so shifting resources to produce one less x and three more y, we can make consumers better off, by giving them more than the two units of y they view as equivalent to one unit of x in their utility functions. Similarly, for any other condition than the (competitive) one specified in equation (3), it will be possible to make someone better off without injuring anyone else. When equation (3) is satisfied, Pareto optimality will prevail.

Competitive equilibrium provides Pareto optimality, and monopolistic equilibrium does not, except in some unlikely hypothetical cases that need not concern us here. Thus, economists presume that a monopolistic situation that holds price above marginal cost will generally lead to a less efficient allocation of resources than would a competitive system.

But remember that a Pareto optimal competitive system would not necessarily be the best system, even though it provided the most "efficient" allocation of resources in response to consumer demands. You might still object to its failure to take into account externalities, to provide enough public goods, or to produce an "equitable" distribution of income. The substantial benefits from purely competitive markets do not necessarily imply that, economically, no government is the best government.

THEORY

Agriculture:
A Case Study
in Competition

Chapter 11

$\mathcal{A}$griculture is the area of the American economy that comes closest to the model of pure competition. For most major farm products—wheat, cotton, hogs, and many others—the conditions of pure competition substantially prevail except insofar as the government has stepped in to alter them.

This chapter has three main parts. First, it asks, How well has substantially pure competition worked in agriculture? How close have the results come to the picture painted by Chapter 10? Second, what have been the causes and consequences of government intervention in agriculture over the past half century? Government has intervened repeatedly, and these government policies provide excellent opportunities to apply the supply-and-demand analysis that you have learned thus far in predicting their consequences. Third, after over a half century of repeated government attempts to raise farm prices and incomes by restricting farm output, people have increasingly come to recognize the danger of world food shortage affecting many of the less-developed nations while we pay farmers to produce less. Somehow, it all has a Catch-22 flavor. American agriculture provides a fascinating case study of competition at work, and of the political economy of a major industry in our democratic society.

RESPONSES TO CHANGING DEMANDS

Table 11–1 presents data on spending for, and production of, food in the United States since 1929. How well has agriculture responded to changing consumer demands over the past half century? Using Table 11–1 and what you have learned about competitive markets thus far from Chapter 10, try to answer this question for yourself before reading on.

Suggestions for Analysis

Although Table 11–1 provides only a small subset of the data for a complete answer, it has the crucial information on most of the important points.

First, what has happened to consumer demand for food since 1929? Line 1 shows that consumers bought nearly five times as much food in 1978 as in 1929. (Total spending on food rose even more, but a part of the increase was merely higher prices, and this inflation has been eliminated by converting all years to the same [1967] prices. Thus, the line shows both growing consumer demand [mainly more people] and farmers' increased production in response to that demand.) But line 2 shows an equally important fact about demand. Demand for food grew much less rapidly than demand for other goods and services: Food's share of total consumer spending fell from 29 to 20 percent as the American people became more affluent.

How did agriculture respond? We know from line 1 that production grew to meet growing demand. Lines 3 through 8 tell us more, that people have persistently moved out of farming to the rest of the economy where consumer demand has grown more rapidly, as the competitive model predicts—but that fewer and fewer farms and farmers nonetheless managed to produce the big increase in food demanded. Lines 3 through 5 show the big exodus from farming to the rest of the economy, and line 9 suggests why. Average incomes from farming have persistently been far below those in nonfarm occupations. Millions of farm proprietors and workers have moved out of low-profit and low-income farming to other industries where income prospects are higher, just as economic theory says they will. A half century ago, a quarter of the labor force was in farming. Now it is only 3.5 percent.

Lines 6 through 8 tell how the farm industry managed the big increase in food production. Land devoted to farming remained virtually unchanged, but farmers invested large sums in tractors, chemicals, and other modern capital equipment that dramatically raised output per worker and per acre. Investment per worker in farming is more than double that in manufacturing. And modern technology has been spectacular on the farm. New fertilizers, hybrid seeds, plant-disease control, and modern farm machinery have revolutionized food production. A century ago, one farmer fed five people; today he feeds nearly 60. Output per man has grown about 6 percent per year, about twice as fast as in manufacturing. As part of this revolution, the average farm has tripled in size; increasingly,

TABLE 11–1
Food in the United States, 1929–78

	1929	1947	1978
1. Consumer expenditures on food (billions of 1967 dollars)	$ 38	$ 72	$190
2. Food as percentage of total consumption	29	28	20
3. Number of farms (millions)	6.2	5.5	2.6
4. Number of farm workers (millions)	13	10	4.1
5. Farmers as percentage of total population	25	16	3.5
6. Output per farm worker (1967 = 100)	17	33	156
7. Investment per farm worker (1967 = 100)	34	71	118
8. Acres devoted to farming (millions)	974	1,055	995
9. Per capita farm income as percentage of nonfarm[a]	29	37	35

[a] Farm income excludes payments and nonfarm earnings. 1978 data are preliminary.

only very large farms can produce at the lowest costs per unit. Today, nearly 40 percent of all farm products come from the largest 2 percent of farms, with over $200,000 each of annual sales and utilizing advanced modern machinery and technology. But although farm experts estimate that it is a rare farmer selling $10,000 or less annually who can cover his costs in basic crops, over 30 percent of all farms still have total sales (not profits) of less than $2,500 annually—clearly far too small to produce efficiently with modern methods. (Part of the reason for this is that many "farms" are small plots farmed by people who have full- or part-time jobs elsewhere.)

Line 9 is perhaps the most striking of all. In spite of a large, continuing exodus of young people from farming, per capita income from farming (excluding government subsidies and nonfarm earnings) remains only about one-third of nonfarm incomes. Figure 11–1 shows the picture in more detail. The bottom line shows per capita incomes from farming. The middle line adds government subsidies and nonfarm income of farmers (dividends, interest, wages earned elsewhere, and so on), but even that brings farm incomes up to only about 80 percent of nonfarm. Farm incomes rose dramatically during the world food "shortage" of 1973–74; inclusion of capital gains from rapidly rising farm land prices nearly doubles reported incomes during the 1970s; and there are some very rich farmers. But most farmers are small and many are poor.

So, all things considered, how well would you say agriculture has responded to changing consumer demands?

ARGUMENTS FOR AID TO AGRICULTURE

For many years, farmers have argued that, as the producers of society's food, they deserve higher incomes than their highly competitive markets give them. And much of the public has agreed. What are the main arguments supporting special government aid to farmers, over and above what they can earn in the market?

1. *Low-income status.* Low farm incomes are a major argument. Farmers say they deserve a reasonable living and a fair return for a hard day's work, just as high as anyone else's. If you believe that everyone should have at least some minimum income, this plea is understandable. But remember that while many farmers are poor, many others are not.

2. *Special susceptibility to instability and business cycles.* Farmers are hard hit by depressions; their incomes drop sharply as food prices fall in highly competitive markets where demand is generally inelastic. (It's not so often mentioned, but they also prosper especially in booms.) This argument, you should note, is easy to confuse with the general low-income argument above. Don't count the same thing twice.

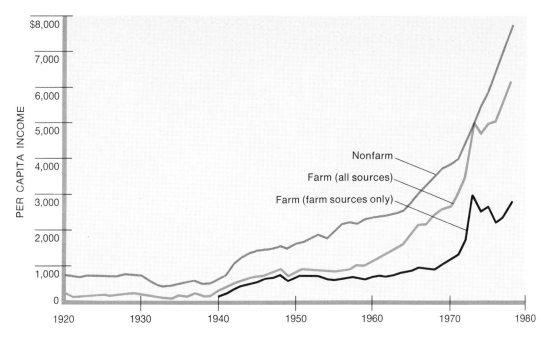

FIGURE 11–1
Per Capita Farm and Nonfarm Incomes
Per capita farmers' incomes from farm sources have long been far under nonfarm incomes, but many "farmers" receive substantial incomes from nonfarm occupations and government payments. (Source: U.S. Department of Agriculture.)

3. The weather. Farming is especially exposed to the vagaries of nature, to droughts and floods.

4. Special aid to offset advantages of other groups. Farmers claim that they are injured by special privileges for other groups and that they deserve offsetting special assistance. American tariffs on industrial products force farmers to pay higher domestic prices. Monopolistic conditions in business and labor have been tolerated by government officials in many industries. These raise the prices paid by farmers and restrict movement from farms to urban occupations.

5. Soil conservation. Much of the farm-aid program has been justified as soil conservation (for example, conserving soil by not planting part of the land each year).

6. Agriculture as a way of life. Some people look on agriculture as a stable, sound way of life, harking back to the ways of our fathers—an anchor to windward in a hectic world of assembly lines, tenements, skyscrapers, and neuroses. The farmer is still an individual, not just a cog in

a huge economic machine. This, they feel, is a way of life worth preserving.

This case raises some economic dilemmas, because the very traits of the farmer and his life that are admired most in this view are the ones associated with small-scale, often inefficient, family farming. A closely related argument hinges on large farm families. There is no provision in the price system, some say, for paying farmers for the outlays of money and effort they make in bearing, rearing, and educating a large number of children who later move into other economic areas. Economically, the argument runs, human beings are capital resources of the nation just as much as are buildings and machines. (Note that on closer examination, this, like the low-income argument, is logically a personal, not an industry, argument. If we want to encourage and pay for large families, presumably the aid should be based on size of family, not on where they live.)

All these claims face substantial counterarguments. But they have convinced enough congressmen to produce a large farm-aid program

141

from the 1930s to today, involving widespread government intervention in farm markets. How well has it worked?

THE ECONOMICS OF FARM AID— PRICE THEORY IN ACTION

Parity

Since the New Deal, "parity" between farm incomes and prices and those in the rest of the economy has been a foundation of the farm-aid program. To be fair, it is argued, farm prices and incomes should rise at least as fast as nonfarm.

As it was developed in the New Deal legislation, farm parity meant that prices paid and received by farmers should be in the same ratio as in the "normal" years 1909–14. If farm prices drop *relative* to other prices (or don't rise as fast as other prices), government action should push the farm prices back up to parity.

If you're a skeptic, you will recall that 1909–14 was the golden age of agriculture. You may ask, why not a parity program for buggies and women's high-buttoned shoes, based on the years 1905–06, which saw the peak for the buggy and high-button-shoe industries? But the goal of parity was the foundation of most farm-aid programs.

Output-Restriction Programs

One major approach to raising farm prices and incomes has been government restriction of farm output. The demand for most farm products is inelastic, so reducing output will, other things equal, raise both price and total consumer expenditure on farm products.

Suppose that *SS* in Figure 11–2 is the supply curve and *DD* the demand curve for beans. Given these curves, the equilibrium price will clearly be 20 cents per pound, with 20,000 bushels of beans produced each year. All farmers producing beans will be doing so at a cost of no more than 20 cents per pound, because at any lower price, their incomes would not cover their costs. Everyone who is willing to pay 20 cents per pound for beans is getting all he wants to buy at that price.

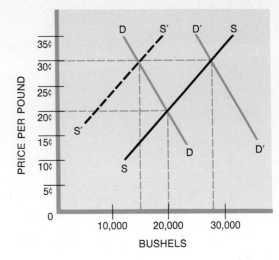

FIGURE 11–2
Supply and Demand for Beans
The market-clearing price for beans is 20 cents, given the original demand and supply curves *DD* and *SS*. If price is fixed at 30 cents, there are 13,000 bushels of unsold beans, which the government must either buy up (*D'D'*) or keep from being produced (*S'S'*) to maintain the price.

Suppose, however, that bean farmers protest that the price is too low, below parity, and they are not making a decent living at that price. They lobby for a price-support program for beans, and they get it—at a price of 30 cents per pound, which they allege will give them a decent living. What is the result?

The first result is that there is a large excess supply in the market. At 30 cents per pound, roughly 28,000 bushels of beans will be produced, but buyers will only take about 15,000 bushels. Those farmers who sell at 30 cents per pound may be very happy, but there are a lot of unhappy farmers holding the unsold 13,000 bushels of beans.

The government, considerate of the bean farmers' plight, offers to pay them to cut back production to 15,000 bushels. It might, for example, provide a "soil-conservation" payment of 10 cents per bushel for beans, to reduce bean acreage so that no more than 15,000 bushels are produced by the industry as a whole. This, in effect, moves the supply curve back to the left, so that the total amount supplied at 30 cents per pound is just the 15,000 bushels that the private market will take. This movement of the supply curve is shown by $S'S'$.

How do the various parties fare? The bean farmers should be happy. They are getting 30 cents a pound for their beans, and they are permitted to either produce, or be paid for not producing, a total of 28,000 bushels. But taxpayers end up spending 10 cents per pound on subsidies for 13,000 bushels of beans not produced under the output-restriction plan. And consumers must pay 30 cents per pound for beans, getting only 15,000 bushels at that price—they are now paying more for 15,000 bushels than they were for 20,000 bushels before the farm-aid program, since demand is inelastic. Clearly, there are too many bean farms and farmers in the industry, but they are paid to stay there by the "soil-conservation" subsidy paid by the government to reduce supply.

Government Purchase or Loan Programs

Alternatively, the government could maintain the bean price at 30 cents by buying up the excess supply (13,000 bushels) left by private buyers at that price. This would move the total private-plus-government demand curve to the right by 13,000 bushels at the 30-cent price in Figure 11–2 (as shown by $D'D'$), clearing the market and ensuring bean farmers their desired prices and incomes. This is fine for bean producers, but bad for consumers, who are again paying more for fewer beans, and for taxpayers, who have to pick up the bill for 13,000 bushels of beans. The government could not sell the beans on the open market, because to do so would undercut the price it is trying to support. Thus, in all probability it will store them, at least temporarily.

Sometimes the government, instead of buying up the overhang, merely lent the farmers the parity price on the excess crops, with the beans as security—say, 30 cents a pound on unsold beans. Then the farmer could pay off the loan and sell the beans if the price later rose above 30 cents, or default on the loan and turn the beans over to the government if the price stayed below 30 cents. It was a heads-I-win, tails-you-lose deal for the farmer, much like the outright purchase plan for consumers and taxpayers.

If, under such a plan, the government ended up with lots of beans in storage, which it couldn't

sell here without depressing the market price, it could recoup part of its investment by selling them abroad at the competitive world-market price, well below the 30-cent supported domestic price. But if it did so, it would encounter cries of "dumping" by foreign bean producers who found themselves in competition with a government-subsidized price from the United States. If the government couldn't sell the beans abroad, it could give them away to hungry countries or to the hungry poor at home (under the food-stamp program). This should make the cost of the gifts clear, with the full amount of the subsidy seen as a cost to taxpayers.

Some observers say that the give-aways are costless, since the government was going to support the price anyhow. But don't forget that even then, domestic consumers are only getting 15,000 bushels in the market, and have to pay 30 cents per pound for them.

Direct Income-Support Subsidies

More than 2 billion people in the less-developed nations live with inadequate diets, millions of them literally on the brink of starvation. Even in the United States, there are millions of ill-nourished poor people. In such a world, U.S. farm programs that pay farmers not to produce food have long seemed anomalous to many observers. Years ago, Secretaries of Agriculture Brannan (under Truman) and Benson (under Eisenhower), frustrated by the expensive and ineffective farm policies they administered, proposed a modification that would substitute direct cash subsidies to farmers for the elaborate crop-reduction plans. The Johnson, Nixon, and Carter administrations more recently have urged Congress to move in this direction, and the Food and Farm Act of 1973 marked a big step toward direct income subsidies. Worldwide crop failures in 1972 and 1973, record prosperity in the industrial nations, massive U.S. grain sales to Russia, nationwide food hoarding by U.S. consumers, and international speculation in grains—all combined to shoot farm prices up to unprecedented levels. Wheat, which for years had averaged below \$2 a bushel, soared to over \$5 a bushel. Soybeans rose even more. Beef and pork prices doubled.

In such an environment, it was obviously

foolish to reduce production. Crop restrictions were dropped, and Congress, after long debate, enacted a new farm program that combined direct cash subsidies to farmers with traditional price supports. The core of the new program was to free production and prices from controls and to provide direct cash subsidies to farmers if needed to keep their incomes up to desired levels. But Congress retained parts of the old production-restriction plan for use if needed, and part of the old crop-loan price-support programs.

The new program was a desirable step away from the old, inefficient programs that tied farm benefits to crop prices rather than to need, and that kept farm prices to consumers high by restricting output. Prices are now somewhat freer to fall if market forces push them down—but only to a limited degree. If farm prosperity continues, taxpayers will now have lower bills for farm subsidies. But if farm prices fall below target levels, farmers will have an unlimited claim on the federal Treasury for cash subsidies to keep incomes up.

The 1972–73 peak prosperity days for farmers lasted only a couple of years. Meat and grain prices slid back down to pre-boom prices by 1976, and, with no crop restrictions, government-financed surpluses piled up rapidly. In 1977, the Carter administration and Congress devised a new modified loan program, using the accumulating surpluses to form food and feed-grain "reserves" of up to 35 million tons to meet domestic and international needs in the event of another food "shortage." By 1978, the United States held 38 percent of the world's wheat reserves and 58 percent of its feed grains. Under this program, most of the reserves are held by the farmers under government-subsidy arrangements that hold them off the market when prices are low and bring them out of reserve when prices go above specified trigger levels. With these huge reserves, the government in 1978 reestablished land set-asides for producers, thus combining the new cash income subsidies with crop-restriction plans.[1]

Programs to Promote Agricultural Efficiency

Long before the government set out to raise farm incomes by restricting production, the Department of Agriculture was busy telling farmers how to increase production. A broad program of scientific research, on-the-ground help for farmers through nationwide agricultural experiment stations, advice on soil-conservation practices, and a variety of other measures have played a

---

[1]For a brief summary of the current farm-aid program, see *Economic Report of the President,* January 1978, pp. 203–6.

FIGURE 11–3

Percent of Major Crops Loaned On by Government

A big proportion of the cotton, wheat, and corn crops has been brought up or loaned on by the government in many years. (Source: U.S. Department of Agriculture.)

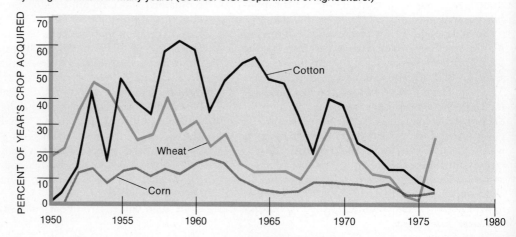

major role in raising the efficiency of American agriculture to a level unparalleled in most other nations.

But by carrying out this eminently sensible program, the Department of Agriculture has persistently sabotaged its own crop-restriction programs. The American farmer is nobody's fool, and he took full advantage of modern methods to increase yields and diversify crops even while he was cutting back acreage under the income-support programs. Would you do differently if you were a farmer?

The Farm-Aid Program in Action

The core of the farm-aid program over the past half century has been the effort to keep up prices and incomes by preventing crop "surpluses" or buying them up if they occurred. Figure 11–3 shows the percentage of the annual crop bought up or loaned on by the government each year for wheat, cotton, and corn. Some twenty crops were covered by the price-support program in the 1970s.[2]

Table 11–2 summarizes the cost of these programs to the government and the beneficiaries. Note that this does not include the costs to consumers in the form of higher prices.

Nor does the table convey the concentration of federal aid payments to a relatively small number of large farmers. Most poor small farm-

[2]The average loss was about 25 percent of the C.C.C. (government) investment.

ers, who needed help most, got tiny subsidy payments because benefit payments were based on the acreage or crop cutback, usually some proportion of previous output levels. In 1975, the smallest 50 percent of all farms received only 9 percent of total government benefits. In 1977, Congress limited payments per crop to each farmer to $40,000, although many large farmers had earlier avoided such limits by breaking up farms into smaller legal units and by diversifying crops.

The effects of nearly a half century of price support and production-control plans are hard to assess precisely. It is not clear, for example, that farm output was in fact reduced by all these payments; farmers greatly increased output per acre when their acreage was reduced, and they substituted noncontrolled crops for the forbidden ones in many cases. But two results are clear.

First, in the two decades following 1950, federal agricultural expenditures, mainly through price- and income-support programs, amounted to more than the entire increase in farm income over the period, although even this support was insufficient to raise average farm incomes to equal nonfarm ones. Second, the huge farm surpluses piled up by the government have been expensive evidence of the difficulties of trying to maintain prices above market levels through government action, even when billions were spent paying farmers not to produce. To a man from Mars, the American farm program would have seemed a strange phenomenon. It would be hard to explain to him why we should

TABLE 11–2 Federal Government Aid to Agriculture			
	FEDERAL AID (IN BILLIONS)	PERCENT OF TOTAL FEDERAL BUDGET	FARM POPULATION (IN MILLIONS)
1950	$3.0	6.9%	23.1
1960	3.7	4.0	15.6
1970	6.2	3.2	9.7
1972	5.3	2.3	9.6
1974	2.3	0.9	9.3
1976	2.0	0.6	8.7
1978	9.1	2.0	7.4

Source: U.S. Budget and *Economic Report of the President.*
Figures are for fiscal years.

pay farmers not to produce food, and buy up available food to hold prices so high that people can't consume it, when so many people are hungry.

U.S. AGRICULTURE AND THE WORLD FOOD PROBLEM

U.S. Food Power and the World Economy

U.S. agriculture, with its labor, capital, land, and modern technology, can produce vastly more food and fibers than the U.S. public will buy at prices high enough to provide anything like a competitive return on the labor and other resources involved. We export annually nearly two-thirds of our total production of wheat and about half our oilseeds, rice, and cotton. Perhaps more important, our grain exports in 1977, a typical year, totaled over 80 million tons, about two-thirds of total world grain exports. Canada, the second largest exporter, shipped only about 18 million tons. By contrast, the USSR, Japan, Great Britain, Italy, and the other major industrialized nations imported significant parts of their total food, ranging from about 30 million tons for the USSR downward for the other nations (see Figure 11–4). U.S. farm exports rose from $7 billion in 1970 to $25 billion in 1978, paying for a huge volume of U.S. imports (see Figure 27–1). Although we usually think of America as an industrial power, it is now the one great source of grain exports to feed the rest of the world.

While the highly competitive farm sector has apparently responded very effectively to U.S. and other Western industrialized nations' demand for food and fibers, should we fault it for not meeting the needs of 2 billion undernourished people in the "third world"? Why hasn't it met their demands as well? Why should the United States not produce all the food it can and sell or give the "surplus" above our needs to

FIGURE 11–4
Haves and Have-Nots in the World Grain Trade
The United States is the one massive grain exporter in today's world. Many poor countries not listed would like to import more grain if they could afford to pay for it. (Source: U.S. Department of Agriculture.)

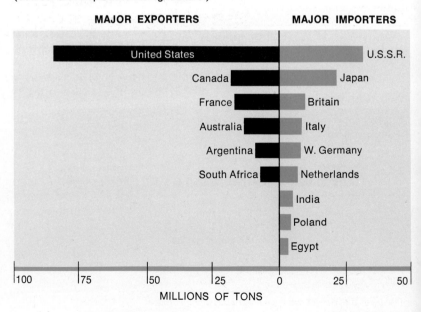

MAJOR EXPORTERS   MAJOR IMPORTERS

Exporters	Importers
United States	U.S.S.R.
Canada	Japan
France	Britain
Australia	Italy
Argentina	W. Germany
South Africa	Netherlands
	India
	Poland
	Egypt

100   75   50   25   0   25   50
MILLIONS OF TONS

the hungry less-developed nations? A thorough analysis must wait for Part 5, on the international economy. But the main answer is that the less-developed nations can't pay for it at anything like world prices. American farmers haven't volunteered to produce the extra food free, and neither Congress nor most American citizens appear willing to pay American farmers to produce the food and then give it to the less-developed nations. Poor people abroad are in much the same position as poor people in the United States, except that Congress hasn't enacted as many special programs (like "welfare" and food stamps) to help them get food.

In fact, the United States has given away every year during the past two decades a large amount of "surplus" food, accumulated under the U.S. farm-price-support program. During the 1960s, for example, food aid to the less-developed nations averaged between $1.0 billion and $1.5 billion annually. More recently, the total has declined gradually, reflecting partly a reduced congressional willingness to provide foreign aid, and partly the smaller surpluses accumulated by the U.S. farm program during the early and mid-1970s. Still more recently, U.S. economic aid to the less-developed countries has increased again, to over $5 billion, including contributions to the World Bank and other multinational aid institutions. The United States' position as the bread basket for the world gives us a powerful international position.

Agriculture in the Political Economy

In 1978, the federal government spent $9 billion on aid for agriculture. In the same year, total farm income from farming (excluding income from investments and other nonfarm sources) was about $19 billion. Thus, nearly half of total income from farming was provided by federal government aid. Yet in 1978, there were fewer than 3 million farm families in the United States, out of a total of 60 million family units.

In perspective, three big facts stand out about the farm legislation of the past half century. One is the farmers' success in getting what they want. As one Washington correspondent put it, "As long as they act together, the farmers can get anything out of the government short of good growing weather—and Washington is working

on that through cloud seeding." Some observers believe the political force of agriculture is weakening, and recent reductions in annual farm-aid budgets support this analysis. But it is not clear that much has changed politically.

Second, forty years of massive federal aid hasn't solved the basic farm-income problem. The worldwide boom of the early 1970s swept both farm product and land prices upward, reflecting the highly unusual set of circumstances outlined above. But even then, small farmers' incomes remained at poverty levels. It was the big, efficient farmers who prospered. Moreover, the productive capacity of U.S. agriculture, once unleashed from government production restrictions, is huge indeed, and there is little reason to suppose that the farm dilemmas of the past half century have vanished permanently. There are still too many resources in American agriculture to earn competitive returns without either strong boom conditions, government aid, or new ways of channeling food to the less-developed nations.

Third, there has been widespread failure to distinguish between the economic problem of efficiency in resource allocation and the ethical problem of ensuring minimum income levels. Fundamentally, the American farm problem is rural poverty. The underlying purpose of farm-aid programs is presumably not higher farm prices per se, but higher farm incomes. Yet farm-aid legislation has by and large required farmers to stay in farming as a condition of receiving aid. They have been paid for not raising crops and have been guaranteed prices that include government subsidies. If they leave agriculture, they lose the subsidies. What could be less efficient?

Thus, tying benefit payments to products, not to people, has failed to channel aid to poor families, and it has produced a domestically inefficient allocation of resources. By raising farm prices, the program has given the biggest benefits to the biggest farmers, because they have the most to sell. By paying farmers for cutting back production in proportion to acres farmed, the program has handed the biggest benefit checks to the highest-income farmers, now including many corporate farms. This adds up to the anomalous result of passing out benefits in inverse relation to need. The program has fallen short on both efficiency and equity criteria.

SUMMARY AND REVIEW

1. Agriculture is one sector of the modern American economy that approximates perfect competition, except where the government intervenes to control prices and output. By and large, it has responded effectively to growing consumer demand for food. Rapidly increasing productivity, reflecting large capital investment and increasing efficiency, has rapidly reduced the number of farmers required to meet these growing demands, and many farmers have moved to other parts of the economy where demand has grown faster. But this exodus from farming has not been fast enough to raise farm incomes parallel to those of the rest of the economy.

2. Farmers have advanced a number of arguments as to why government should help raise their incomes and prices above competitive levels, and since the 1930s, the government has continuously intervened for this purpose.

3. Farm-aid programs have stressed reductions in farm output and government support of farm prices as means to aid farmers, looking toward raising farm incomes to parity with nonfarm incomes. But these programs have been both inefficient and inequitable. They have raised prices to consumers, increased costs to taxpayers, been generally ineffective in raising farm incomes, and primarily aided well-to-do rather than low-income farmers.

4. Recently, direct income-support cash payments have been added to the farm-aid program. Most economists consider direct income-support subsidies both more efficient and more equitable than the older farm programs, which generally provided the largest benefits to the largest and richest farmers and failed to restrict output effectively.

5. American agriculture can produce vastly more food and fibers than the U.S. public will buy at free-market prices. Thus, we are the main source of grain exports to the rest of the world, especially to the less-developed countries where starvation is always near. U.S. food aid to the less-developed countries has varied substantially from year to year, but it has been only a small fraction of potential U.S. farm surpluses in the absence of crop restrictions.

6. Government intervention in agriculture has been a limited success over the past half century, especially because it has failed to distinguish between the goals of efficiency in allocating resources and equity in aiding low-income farmers. Benefit payments tied to products, not to people, have failed to channel aid to poor families, and have wasted potentially productive resources.

For Analysis and Discussion

1. Has pure competition in agriculture worked as Chapter 10 says it should?
2. In a competitive economy, resources are supposed to move where consumer demand is strongest, as individuals seek higher incomes. In the light of the comparative incomes shown by Figure 11–1, how do you explain the fact that so many families stay in agriculture?
3. In agriculture, output per man has recently grown at the rate of 6 percent per annum, twice that for the rest of the economy. Since we apparently face a situation of continuing farm "surpluses," would decreased productivity in agriculture be a desirable solution to the farm problem?
4. Are there too many farmers?
5. Who will gain and who will lose the most from Congress's shift to more use of direct cash-income supplements in the farm-aid program?
6. Does agriculture's failure to provide food for the third-world countries represent a failure of Adam Smith's "invisible hand"?
7. There are fewer than 3 million farm families in the United States. Yet Congress has repeatedly voted to grant large subsidies to agriculture. How do you explain this fact?
8. If you were a congressman, what legislation would you support on the "farm problem"?

CASE 10

EGGS, COPPER, AND COFFEE

On January 8, 1975, substantially the following story appeared in West Coast newspapers:

California egg producers decided yesterday to continue diverting 5 percent of the state's weekly egg production from the consumer market to keep egg prices up.

The 16-member State Egg Advisory Board, on a 9–5 vote with two abstentions, turned down a motion from consumer representatives to quit diverting 10,000 cases of eggs a week—30 dozen eggs to the case—from the consumer marketplace for later sale abroad at lower prices. The policy, in effect since November, helps hold prices up to about 72 cents a dozen in San Francisco.

Inflation-squeezed egg farmers, hurt by soaring grain and feed prices, said that ending the diversion policy would depress prices, probably as much as 5 to 8 cents a dozen, and would force smaller egg producers out of business.

A few days earlier, substantially the following two stories had appeared:

The government of Chile announced today the closing of one of its major copper mines for six months, in order to help halt the downward slide of copper prices. Three other major copper-producing countries—Peru, Zaire, and Zambia—recently announced plans to cut their copper exports by 10 percent, with the same goal.

Latin America's coffee-exporting countries met together in Caracas last week, they announced today, to discuss plans for withholding 20 percent of the new coffee crop from world markets. The announcement stressed rising costs of production and rising prices of other products which coffee-producing countries must pay in world markets with continuing inflation. While coffee prices have risen sharply in the past two years, the spokesman said that many coffee producers are losing money, and that coffee-producing countries face serious problems in paying for their imports.

1. Should the state of California legalize and support agreements of egg farmers to restrict supply in order to keep prices up? If not, should the state take any other steps to ensure the farmers reasonable prices and incomes? Would consumers be better off if "cutthroat competition" prevailed?

2. Assuming that the state gives permission through the Egg Advisory Board, if you were an egg farmer, would you favor diverting eggs from the domestic to the overseas market, as described in the news story?

3. Do you see any significant differences between the case of eggs in California and those of copper and coffee in the other stories?

4. Suppose hi-fi stereo manufacturers applied to the government for exemption from antitrust laws to arrange together to limit production so as to avoid the surpluses that periodically led to price wars in the hi-fi field, with losses for many companies. Would you favor granting the request, with a Hi-Fi Advisory Board (comparable to the Egg Advisory Board), with government-appointed members, to pass on industry plans? What, if any, difference do you see between the egg and hi-fi cases?

THEORY

Monopoly
and
Public Utilities

Chapter 12

$\mathcal{M}$onopoly is something like sin. Everyone says he's against it, but a lot of people aren't very clear just what it is they're against. Like sin, monopoly has to be defined before one can talk much sense about it, or decide what, if anything, ought to be done about it.[1]

THE SPECTRUM FROM COMPETITION TO MONOPOLY

Monopoly is generally defined as a market in which there is only one seller. But this is deceptively simple. There is no commodity that doesn't have some substitute, more or less close, and we have no sharp criterion of how close the substitute can be before we no longer have a monopoly. The Aluminum Company of America, until World War II, was often called a monopoly; there was no other American producer of basic aluminum. But steel, wood, copper, and other materials are possible substitutes, if the price of aluminum gets too high. Or consider General Motors: It has a monopoly in producing Chevrolets, but there is Ford next door producing close substitutes. In one sense, every producer who isn't in a purely competitive market has a monopoly in selling his own product. But the closer the substitutes produced by others, the less of a "monopoly" he has as a practical matter.

Pure Monopoly

In spite of this problem, economists have defined a situation they call "pure" monopoly. As the Prologue to Part 2 pointed out, a pure monopoly is characterized by:

1. Only one seller of the good or service
2. Rivalry from producers of substitutes so remote as to be insignificant

Under these circumstances, the pure monopolist can set the market price himself. He is a "price maker," unlike the wheat farmer who is a "price taker." But even the monopolist has to face up to the realities of elasticity of demand. He can put

his price where he wishes; but unless demand is perfectly inelastic, the higher he puts his price, the less he will sell. In large part, the elasticity of demand for any product reflects the presence of potential substitutes, and there is no monopoly so pure that it can escape completely the possibility of partial substitutes. Thus, pure monopoly in the textbook sense is never quite found in the real world, and pure monopoly shades into competition, just as pure competition shades into lesser degrees of competition. But many public utilities come close to the pure-monopoly case.[2]

THE BASES OF MONOPOLY AND PARTIAL MONOPOLY

The basic test of an effective monopoly is its power to exclude competitors from the market. If a firm can keep out potential competitors, it can raise prices with relative impunity. The nearer the substitutes that competitors can put on the market, the weaker is the firm's monopoly position. The ideal monopoly (from the monopolist's viewpoint) would cover an absolutely essential product with no substitutes.

Government Action as a Basis for Monopoly

The strongest monopolies are the public utilities. An exclusive government franchise is about as airtight protection as any monopoly can hope for. This arrangement is found in most localities for water, electricity, gas, and telephone companies. Having granted this enviable monopoly position, however, governments invariably regulate the prices the monopoly can charge. Otherwise, the stockholders of the local water or gas company would be in a happy position indeed. Less exclusive franchises are common—the rail-

---

[1]A review of the Prologue to Part 2 will be useful here if you don't have it in mind.

[2]The analogy to pure monopoly on the buyer's side is sometimes called "pure monopsony," which means one buyer. This case might prevail where there is only one buyer for labor services—say, the mill in an isolated mill town. But like pure monopoly, pure monopsony is hard to find. For instance, workers are free to move to another town if the monopsonist exploits his position too much.

Where there are two sellers or buyers, "duopoly" or "duopsony" exists.

roads, taxi medallions in many cities, TV stations.

Governments intervene in other ways to provide bases for partial monopolies. The farm-aid programs of the past four decades have supported prices and induced farmers to behave like cooperating monopolists (a cartel) in restricting output. Government licensing of doctors and other professionals is manifestly intended to protect the public against such things as incompetent medical service, but in fact also provides a basis for monopolistic practices by the doctors and others where supply is restricted by licensing. The entire federal patent system, discussed below, protects the monopoly position of the inventor. Federal legislation establishes the right of workers to combine in unions that in essence act as monopolies in selling their labor to employers.

Patents and Research

The patent law gives the inventor exclusive control over his invention for 17 years, to stimulate and reward inventions. Key patents underlie the industrial position of many major American concerns. Research has become part of the American industrial scene, and the "blue chips" of American industry come automatically to mind when we think of technological advance— IBM, General Electric, du Pont. These firms maintain their leading positions in oligopolistic industries in no small part by being first with the best in research. Over the past 20 years, almost two-thirds of all patents have gone to corporations. General Electric alone, for example, received about 13,000; AT&T about 10,000. Research is an expensive and cumulative process. It's hard for the little firm to compete, quite aside from the patent laws.

Control of Raw Materials

If you can get exclusive control over the raw materials needed to make your product, you're sitting pretty—at least until someone figures out a substitute material. For example, the International Nickel Company of Canada for years owned more than nine-tenths of the world's known reserves of nickel, and produced more than 90 percent of the world's output of nickel.

Financial Resources and the Capital Market

The money needed to set up an efficient firm in many industries today is tens and even hundreds of millions of dollars. Not many people have this much money, and it's hard to borrow $10 million unless you're already a very well established firm, no matter how engaging a picture you paint of your prospects.

In a "perfect" capital market, funds would be available whenever the prospective borrower was willing and able to pay the going rate of interest on loans of comparable risk. In fact, however, it is hard for newcomers to raise funds in the market. Lenders are skeptical of unknown faces. Moreover, borrowing is more expensive for small, new borrowers, even when they can get the funds. These facts give an important advantage to established monopolists, who are likely to have a well-established credit position.

Advertising

Advertising by itself would have a hard time establishing or even maintaining a monopoly on any product. But the entrenched positions of names like IBM and du Pont in the mind of the American consumer are a cause of dismay to prospective competitors. Modern advertising has become increasingly "institutionalized." That is, ads aim primarily at building up the company's name and prestige, rather than at selling a particular product. Large-scale prestige advertising (for example, national TV advertising) costs big money, and only big and successful companies can afford it. On the other hand, advertising offers potential competitors a way of luring customers away from established firms; advertising works both ways on the monopoly problem.

Unfair Competition

Running the little fellow out of business by unfair price cutting, after which price is raised to a monopolistic level, is one of the charges commonly brought against big business. If Safeway prices groceries very low, it is accused of a devious intent to run the independents out and then to boost its own prices when competition is gone.

Some observers say that the Standard Oil Company of the 1800s provided spectacular cases of such behavior.

Such predatory price competition is now illegal. But the line between legitimate and unfair price cutting merely to eliminate competition is often hard to draw. The more efficient producers always tend to eliminate the inefficient.

Large-Scale Production and Decreasing Costs

Low-cost mass production is the pride of American industry. In many industries (steel, electrical equipment, autos, chemicals, and so on), maximum efficiency can be obtained only by large firms, each producing a substantial share of the market. In local areas, taking advantage of the economies of large-scale production may mean one or a few monopolistic firms—for example, the one grocery store a small town can reasonably support. In such cases, until a firm reaches this optimal scale, it is operating in its range of "decreasing costs," or "increasing returns to scale." That is, by increasing output, it can cut its average total cost per unit produced.

Figure 12–1 represents such an industry. The ATC curves are simply average-total-unit-cost curves for different scales of enterprise for a firm in the industry—say, a local gas company. Scale ATC^3 is the most efficient scale in this case; its least-cost point is the lowest of any possible scale of enterprise. This is a decreasing-cost industry if demand is small relative to the first three scales of enterprise—for example, if demand is D^1D^1 or D^2D^2. It is a "decreasing-cost," or "increasing returns to scale," industry because the economies of scale within the single firm have not yet been fully exploited at any output less than OM, the least-cost point on ATC^3. Up to output OM, it has an obvious cost advantage from increasing its sales.

Clearly, competition with many firms is not going to work in this industry. It is what is often called a "natural monopoly." If there are several firms and demand is, say, D^2D^2, each firm will cut price to increase its share of the market, reduce its unit costs, and increase its profit. This price competition will persist until one firm has driven out the others and has a monopoly, or until the firms (illegally) get together and agree to divide up the market.

The social advantage of limiting such an industry to one firm is obvious; this is the basis for most exclusive public utility franchises. To insist on several firms would obviously mean higher costs, and higher prices to cover those costs, if they all stayed in business. But it would be foolish to expect the one firm not to try to exploit its monopoly position to obtain high profits unless it is regulated.

PURE MONOPOLY[3]

In the American economy, except for the public utilities, we seldom find only one firm in a market, no available substitutes for the commodity produced, and no possibility that other firms may invade the market. Yet looking at such an extreme case is useful, because it gives some insight into what the world might be like if pure monopolies were tolerated without regulation. It

FIGURE 12–1
Increasing Returns to Scale
The industry has decreasing unit costs up to output M. For any demand short of that amount, competition is unlikely to work effectively.

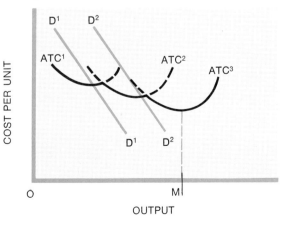

---

[3]Since this section rests directly on the marginal-cost–marginal-revenue analysis of Chapter 9 instructors who assigned only the Minimum Essentials Track in micro theory should skip the remainder of this chapter.

suggests rules for controlling public utilities. And it may be a quite realistic description of the temporary monopoly position in which firms sometimes find themselves because of special advantages of location, development of new products ahead of competitors, patents, or other such circumstances.

Imagine a single electric-power company in an isolated community, free to charge whatever rates it pleases. Suppose you are the owner-manager of this hypothetical concern. You are a price maker; you can set your price where you wish. Waiving the fear that the local government will begin to regulate your rates, how would you maximize your profits?

The answer, as you have probably predicted, is: Increase output up to the point where marginal cost equals marginal revenue and set the price to sell that amount. The profit-maximizing principle is the same as for the competitive firm in Chapter 9. Consider the answer in more detail.

Total and Marginal Revenue

Suppose your market-research people estimate demand as shown in columns 1 and 2 of Table 12–1. Column 3 shows the total revenue obtained at different prices. But as a monopolist, you need to face a new fact. You are a price maker, and you can sell more electricity only by lowering your price, unlike the infinitely large (perfectly elastic) demand faced by Amalgamated Widget under pure competition. Under pure competition, price and marginal revenue were identical; if you sold one more stereo set for $1,000, you increased your total revenue by $1,000. But not here.

Now you face a downward-sloping demand curve. To sell more, you must cut price, not only on the extra sales but on all the electricity you sell. For the monopolist, marginal revenue is always less than price. This is because he must lower his price to sell more units, and he must lower it not just on the marginal unit but on all units sold.[4]

For example, Table 12–1 says you can sell 1,000,000 kilowatts at 8 cents per kilowatt. (To simplify the language, we will use the word *kilowatt* for *kilowatt hours*.) To increase sales to 1,100,000, you must reduce the price to 7.6 cents on all 1,100,000 kilowatts. Thus, your marginal revenue is your income from selling the extra 100,000 kilowatts (100,000 × 7.6 cents = $7,600) minus the .4 cent price cut you must take on each of the other 1,000,000 kilowatts (1,000,000 × .4 cents = $4,000). The marginal revenue from the extra 100,000 kilowatts is thus only $3,600 (not $7,600), as shown by column 4. To convert to marginal revenue per kilowatt, we simply divide the figures by 100,000, getting a marginal revenue per additional kilowatt of 3.6 cents (in column 5). And so it is all along the

---

[4]This assumes that you sell at the same price to everyone, not discriminating between residential and commercial users, or others. Many utilities do discriminate in price, but this does not change the principles stated here.

TABLE 12–1
Hometown Electric Company—Customer-Demand Schedule

| | | | MARGINAL REVENUE | |
KILOWATTS (1)	PRICE (2)	TOTAL REVENUE (3)	PER 100,000 KILOWATTS (4)	PER KILOWATT (5)
1,000,000	8.0¢	$80,000		
1,100,000	7.6	83,600	$3,600	3.6¢
1,200,000	7.25	87,000	3,400	3.4
1,300,000	6.9	89,700	2,700	2.7
1,400,000	6.5	91,000	1,300	1.3
1,500,000	6.1	91,500	500	.5
1,600,000	5.7	91,200	−300	−.3

demand schedule. Marginal revenue is always less than price, and it even becomes negative when you must cut price to 5.7 cents in order to increase sales to 1,600,000 kilowatts.[5]

Graphically, this means that the marginal revenue curve will always be beneath the demand curve from which it is derived. Look ahead to the demand and marginal revenue data for Hometown Electric, plotted as curves DD and MR in Figure 12–2. MR lies below DD throughout.

This relationship between price and marginal revenue is fundamental for every seller who is not in a perfectly competitive market. Whenever he faces a downward-sloping demand curve, to sell more he must cut price both for the extra units he hopes to sell and for the units he could otherwise sell at a higher price. His gain from cutting prices is never as big as it appears at first glance.

Maximizing Monopoly Profits

Suppose your costs are as shown in Table 12–2; total cost for the outputs shown is in column 2 and marginal cost, converted to a per-kilowatt basis, in column 5. Consumer demand is given in columns 4 and 6. What price should you set to maximize your profits?

One answer is: Compare total cost and total revenue at each different level of output to find where the difference is biggest. As columns 2, 4, and 7 show, you should set price at 6.9 cents per kilowatt, which gives the maximum profit of $32,500.

Another way is: Equate marginal cost and marginal revenue. MC and MR are shown in columns 5 and 6. As long as the marginal revenue from selling an additional unit of output is greater than the marginal cost of producing the unit, obviously profit is increased by producing the extra unit. Up through 1,300,000 kilowatts, this is so; MC is below MR. But moving to 1,400,000 kilowatts adds more to cost than to

<hr/>

[5]Marginal revenue is always zero when elasticity of demand is unity, positive when demand is elastic, and negative when demand is inelastic. Why? From this proposition it obviously follows that no perceptive monopolist will ever increase his output into the range where demand is inelastic, because in this range cutting price to increase output would *reduce* his total revenue from sales.

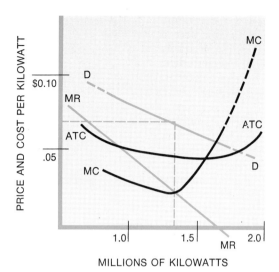

FIGURE 12–2
Hometown Electric Company:
Monopoly Output and Price Setting
The monopolist maximizes profit by equating marginal cost and marginal revenue—here, at an output about 1.32 million kilowatts to be sold at a price just under 7 cents.

revenue. The maximum-profit output rate is 1,300,000 kilowatts, which can be sold at a price of 6.9 cents per kilowatt.

Still a third way would be by comparing marginal cost and marginal revenue per 100,000 units, instead of on a per-kilowatt basis.

Which way is better? Take your pick. All three give the same result.

Graphical Analysis of Profit Maximization

The same calculation can be shown graphically. Figure 12–3 shows the relevant per-unit data. DD is the estimated market-demand curve. MR is the associated marginal-revenue-per-unit curve. ATC is the estimated average-total-unit-cost curve. And MC is the associated marginal-unit-cost curve. The solid part of each curve represents the data from Table 12–2; the dotted lines extend the curves hypothetically beyond the range of data we have. Note that, as was emphasized above, the MR curve is always below the downward-sloping demand curve.

155

TABLE 12–2
Hometown Electric Company—Profit Calculations

KILOWATTS (1)	TOTAL COST (2)	PRICE (3)	TOTAL REVENUE (4)	MARGINAL UNIT COST (5)	MARGINAL UNIT REVENUE (6)	TOTAL PROFIT (7)
1,000,000	$50,000	8.0¢	$80,000			$30,000
				2.8¢	3.6¢	
1,100,000	52,800	7.6	83,600			30,800
				2.4	3.4	
1,200,000	55,200	7.25	87,000			31,800
				2.0	2.7	
1,300,000	57,200	6.9	89,700			32,500[a]
				3.0	1.3	
1,400,000	60,200	6.5	91,000			30,800
				4.3	.5	
1,500,000	64,500	6.1	91,500			27,000
				5.9	−.3	
1,600,000	70,400	5.7	91,200			20,800

[a] Maximum total profit.

Using the *MC* and *MR* curves, you can easily determine the maximum-profit position. It will be the output where marginal cost just equals marginal revenue. This is a little above 1,300,000 kilowatts, which you could sell at a price of about 6.8 cents, reading off the demand curve at that output. If you want to compute your total profit from this graph, first take the distance between the selling price and the *ATC* curve, and then multiply this profit per unit by the total number of units sold. This would give a profit of roughly 2.5 cents per kilowatt on

1,320,000 kilowatts—about $33,000 at the best level.

Note that this is a slightly higher profit than the peak shown by Table 12–2. The graph, which gives you estimated data for **all** levels of output rather than just figures for each 100,000 kilowatts, tells you to produce an extra 20,000 kilowatts beyond the prescription of the table. The continuous curves on the graph give you a quick guide to the maximum-profit level of output and prices, which includes all levels of output, not just the ones shown in the table.

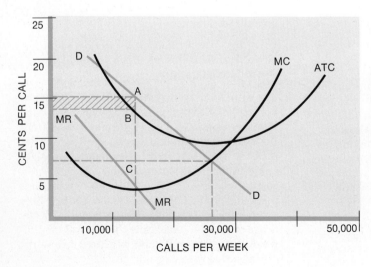

FIGURE 12–3
Talkalot Telephone Company: Public Utility Regulation
Talkalot will maximize profits by pricing calls at 15 cents (where *MC* = *MR*). But the socially optimum price would be 7 cents (where *MC* = price), 3 cents per call below *ATC*. As a member of the Public Utilities Commission, where would you set the price?

PURE MONOPOLY— EVALUATION

Monopoly leads to an inefficient allocation of resources from the consumers' point of view. The monopolist restricts output and raises price to maximize his profits, holding price above marginal cost. But Chapter 10 told us that $MC =$ Price is the condition for achieving the socially most efficient allocation of productive resources to satisfy consumers' demands. Thus, monopoly price is too high, and too few resources are hired into the monopolized industry. Consumers get too little of the monopolized product. Conversely, too many resources are used in other sectors of the economy, since resources shut out from the monopolized industry must seek employment elsewhere. Thus, prices are too low and output is too large elsewhere.[6]

Are there limits, other than legal regulation, to how much the monopolist can exploit consumers? The answer is yes. He faces two limiting factors. First, even a monopolist faces a downward-sloping demand curve, reflecting basically the fact that every product has some substitutes if its price becomes high enough. Second, if the monopolist does not have a government-bestowed, airtight franchise, the larger his profits become, the greater will be the incentive for new firms to enter, even though the cost may be high and the risks great. Thus, while an unregulated pure monopolist would be in a strong position to bleed the public through high prices, even he would face the increasing likelihood of competition and substitutes the further he exploited his position.

Monopolies are also likely to be inefficient in reducing costs and slow to introduce technological improvements. This is called "X-inefficiency." Pure competition forces each firm to be efficient or perish. If new production techniques that reduce the minimum average cost of production are developed, the laggard who fails to

keep up with the leaders soon loses out in the market. Under monopoly, this pressure is weak. It does not necessarily follow that monopolies are inefficient or uninterested in progress. But absence of strong competitive pressures does often lead to X-inefficiency and lessened interest in meeting consumer needs. We hear a flood of complaints that AT&T doesn't provide the newest telephone equipment as fast as it should, that the local utility is full of bureaucrats and red tape. But the evidence is mixed (compare the ease of making a long-distance phone call here and in other nations), and utility prices have risen much more slowly than the cost of living over the past century. For some interesting evidence, see the concluding section of this chapter.

PUBLIC UTILITY REGULATION— PRICE THEORY IN ACTION

"Natural monopolies"—cases where the economies of large-scale production are so great that consumer demand doesn't require even one firm of the maximum-efficiency size—obviously can't be left to competitive market pressures for regulation. Without government regulation, price wars will recur between profit-seeking firms until one firm wins out with a monopoly position. Most economists agree that government regulation is the answer in such cases, although some would leave the market unregulated. So government gives one firm an exclusive right to operate in the area, and prescribes the maximum price and minimum service that must be provided. These are the public utilities—water, gas, electricity, telephones.

Price theory warns us that competitive market pressures probably won't work to protect consumers in such cases. What does it tell us about what price and output the regulatory authorities ought to prescribe?

Suppose demand and costs are as shown in Figure 12–3 for the Talkalot Telephone Company. DD and MR are the demand and marginal revenue curves; ATC and MC are the average-total-cost and marginal-cost curves per phone call. The management is out to maximize profits for the stockholders. If we don't regulate the company, it will presumably maximize profits by

---

[6]The difficulty in making a precise comparison with competitive price and output in such a case should be clear. Because the market is not large enough to support a large number of producers, each with a least-cost point as low as the large monopolist's, we cannot demonstrate rigorously that monopoly price is higher than competitive price would be.

equating marginal cost and marginal revenue—that is, by setting rates to sell about 12,000 calls weekly at 15 cents per call. Their profit then would be about $240 a week, as shown by the shaded rectangle. It is the profit of 2 cents per call (the excess of the price over the *ATC* curve at that output) times 12,000 calls. It's not a very big profit, but the best the company can do given the demand and costs shown. But marginal cost is only about 4 cents a call at that output, so price would be far above marginal cost, the condition for a socially optimum allocation of resources. Thus, consumers would be getting too little phone service and paying too much for it.

Suppose that we, as regulators, follow the social optimum rule from Chapter 10, that price should be equal to marginal cost—where *MC* intersects *DD*. This would call for a price of about 7 cents with customers making about 26,000 calls weekly, clearly a lot better deal for the town's citizens. But alas, at 7 cents per call, Talkalot Telephone makes a loss. The price would be about 3 cents below the *ATC* curve at that output, for a loss of $780 weekly on the 26,000 calls. It's clear that Talkalot isn't going to keep providing telephone service long with that loss rate, nor would it seem fair to ask its stockholders to do so.

This is the dilemma often faced by public utility regulatory commissions. How can we get the socially optimum price and output without a long-run outflow of resources from the regulated industry. One answer, preferred by many price theorists, is to have the government (for all consumers) set the price at 7 cents but pay a lump-sum benefit to the Talkalot Company to bring its rate of return up to the market rate. This would be ideal economics, but few governments have yet faced up to the political problems of explaining to the voters and the taxpayers the case for such a tax-financed subsidy to public utilities, especially when the underlying consumer-demand data would only be roughly estimated.

As a practical matter, most regulatory commissions have substituted a second-best rule. They say to the utility: We'll give you an exclusive franchise; you produce as efficiently as possible, and charge the lowest price that will give you a fair return on your investment. Of course, this price may or may not be near marginal cost; in industries where demand is small relative to the most efficient scales of production, price may be far above *MC* although approximately the same as average total cost for that output. Moreover, this approach runs into three knotty problems:

1. *How shall we measure the company's investment?* For example, the investment figure varies greatly during inflations; depending on whether we use the original cost of the investment less depreciation or the higher replacement cost (because of the inflation). Most economists consider replacement cost the more meaningful and flexible figure, but many commissions drag their feet because replacement cost implies higher rates in inflationary times like now.

2. *What is a "fair" rate of return?* On this issue, commissions and courts vary, often arbitrarily setting 6, 7, or 8 percent. Many lawyers and economists make a fine living arguing the proper investment base and rate of return in these cases.

3. *How shall we keep the company efficient and on its toes to minimize costs without the pressure of competition?* X-inefficiency is one of the greatest dangers for regulated monopolies. The danger is compounded by the fact that by increasing its scale of investment wastefully, a regulated utility can increase the size of the "rate base" on which its "fair return" is calculated, if the regulators don't catch on to what it is doing.

What at first looks like a simple, straightforward answer to the question of how to deal with natural monopolies—"regulate them"—turns out in practice to be a complex, difficult problem. This leads some economists to warn against much reliance on regulation. More on this in the following chapters.

For one last check on your grasp of the monopoly problem, turn back to the Hometown Electric Company, as shown in Figure 12–2. If you were the Hometown Public Utility Commission, what price and output would you approve for the company? The analysis is identical to that for Talkalot, but you will find, happily, that Hometown Electric makes a profit when price is set equal to marginal cost, with price about 5 cents and output about 1,650,000 kilowatts. Two questions: (1) Who should get the profit if you set price at 5 cents? (2) Wouldn't you be wiser to lower the price even further, to about 4.5 cents, where it would just cover *ATC* for an even larger output of about 1,800,000 kilowatts? Suggested answers: (1) Pass the profit back to the government (for all consumers), just as you took the subsidy for Talkalot from the government. (2) No.

A Concluding Note

Recently, many economists have become increasingly skeptical concerning the effectiveness of government regulation of business. Even in cases of "natural monopoly," they suggest that as a practical matter, regulation often will not approach socially optimum allocation of resources, and that any allocative gains from regulation will often be more than offset by X-inefficiency resulting from the absence of competitive pressures to reduce costs. A recent study by Professor Walter Primeaux compared actual price and output levels for pure monopoly and duopoly (two-firm) municipally owned electric companies in middle-sized cities. Matching otherwise substantially identical pairs of companies, one a regulated monopoly and the other facing direct competition from one competitor, Primeaux found a mixed picture. In some cases, the regulated monopoly price was lower, but in a number of others, the X-efficiency gain from competitive pressures appeared to produce lower duopoly costs and prices than did regulation with a single firm.[7] On balance, Primeaux opts for an exploratory use of more competition in what appear to be natural monopolies, but most monopoly and public utility experts appear still to pick the regulated-utility option in such cases.

---

[7]W.J. Primeaux, "A Reexamination of the Monopoly Market Structure for Electrical Utilities," in A. Phillips, ed., *Promoting Competition in Regulated Markets* (Washington, D.C.: The Brookings Institution, 1975).

SUMMARY AND REVIEW

1. Pure monopoly occurs when there is only one seller and rivalry from producers of substitutes is so remote as to be insignificant. But virtually every good and service has some possible substitutes if its price becomes high enough. Thus, pure monopoly is a limiting case, and it shades into imperfect competition in many forms.

2. The main bases of monopoly and partial-monopoly positions are government action, patents and research, control of raw materials, advantages in capital markets, advertising, and the economies of large-scale production. It is unclear how important unfair competition is as a basis for monopoly power.

3. An unregulated monopoly can maximize its profits by comparing total cost and total revenue for different outputs, or by equating marginal cost and marginal revenue and setting the price to sell that output.

4. When a monopolist faces a downward-sloping demand curve, his marginal revenue curve lies underneath the demand curve and slopes down even faster. This is because in cutting price, the monopolist must reduce price on the goods he was previously selling as well as on the additional sales he hopes to stimulate.

5. Under a pure monopoly, price is set above marginal cost to maximize profits. Thus, price is too high, too few resources are used in the industry, and output is too low, compared to a socially optimum allocation of resources. This is called allocative inefficiency.

6. Absence of competitive pressures often also leads monopolists to X-inefficiency.

7. "Natural monopoly" (cases where the economies of large-scale production are so great that consumer demand does not require even one firm of maximum-efficiency size) cannot be effectively regu-

lated by competition. Such companies are often designated public utilities, given an exclusive franchise, and regulated as to price and output. To set price equal to marginal cost (the social optimum) for natural monopolies would often produce losses for the company, because price would be below *ATC* at that level of output. In such cases, price theory suggests setting price equal to marginal cost *and* paying a government subsidy to the natural monopoly to bring its rate of return up to the market rate; but politically, this is very difficult to achieve.

8. As a practical matter, public utility commissions commonly set price at the lowest level consistent with the firm's earning a "fair return" on its "investment rate base," although this may not be near the social optimum. Even with this second-best approach, serious practical difficulties are encountered in determining the properly allowable investment rate base and a fair rate of return; and without competitive pressures, it is difficult to assure maximum X-efficiency—to avoid X-inefficiency.

New Concepts to Remember

Most of the major concepts used in this chapter were introduced in earlier chapters. But there are a few important new ones:

pure (simple) monopoly	decreasing-cost industry
price makers	increasing returns to scale
"natural monopoly"	X-efficiency

For Analysis and Discussion

1. Explain the difference between allocative efficiency and X-efficiency.
2. Why do economists say that the basic *economic* criticism of monopolies is that they hold price above marginal cost?
3. If a monopoly is not making excessive (above-normal) profits, it is doing no serious harm to the public. True or false? Explain.
4. The post office and your local water company are cases that are close to pure monopolies. How would you go about deciding whether they are doing an efficient job of serving the consumer at reasonable prices? Do you have a better way of evaluating the performance of such big partial monopolies as General Motors and Alcoa?
5. Chicago's George Stigler has argued that without government support, there would be few serious monopoly problems in America today. He cites public utilities, government support of unions, government-sponsored cartelization in agriculture, and local building codes that hold up construction costs. How sound is this argument? Can you cite counterexamples?

CASE 11

U.S. v. ALUMINUM COMPANY OF AMERICA

Before World War II, the Aluminum Company of America was commonly considered a substantially complete monopoly, producing and selling virtually 100 percent of the virgin aluminum ingot in the United States. As early as 1912, the federal government had obtained a consent decree, with which Alcoa complied, that required Alcoa to desist from entering into any agreements fixing prices on finished aluminum products. It was not until 1937, however, that a major antitrust suit was brought, seeking to have Alcoa dissolved on the ground that it violated Section II of the Sherman Act. Excerpts from the court's decision, declaring Alcoa guilty, follow:[8]

. . . It is undisputed that throughout this period Alcoa continued to be the single producer of virgin ingot in the United States; and the plaintiff [government] argues that this without more was enough to make it an unlawful monopoly.

. . . The judge found that, over the whole half century of its existence, Alcoa's profits upon capital invested, after payment of income taxes, had been only about ten percent. . . . A profit of ten percent in such an industry, . . . subject to the vicissitudes of new demands, to the obsolescence of plant and process—which can never be accurately gauged in advance—to the change that substitutes may at any moment be discovered which will reduce the demand, and to the other hazards which attend all industry: a profit of ten percent, so conditioned, could hardly be considered extortionate.

. . . Having proved that Alcoa had a monopoly of the domestic ingot market, the plaintiff had gone far enough; if it was an excuse, that Alcoa had not abused its power, it lay upon Alcoa to prove that it had not. But the whole issue is irrelevant anyway, for it is no excuse for monopolizing a market that the monopoly has not been used to extract from the consumer more than a fair profit. The Act has wider purposes. Indeed, even though we disregarded all but economic consideration, it would by no means follow that such concentration of producing power is to be desired, when it has not been used extortionately. Many people believe that possession of unchallenged economic power deadens initiative, discourages thrift and depresses energy; that immunity from competition is a narcotic, and rivalry is a

stimulant, to industrial progress; that the spur of constant stress is necessary to counteract an inevitable disposition to let well enough alone. Such people believe that competitors, versed in the craft as no consumer can be, will be quick to detect opportunities for saving and new shifts in production, and be eager to profit by them. . . . Be that as it may, that was not the way that Congress chose; it did not condone good trusts and condemn bad ones; it forbade all. Moreover, in so doing it was not necessarily actuated by economic motives alone. It is possible, because of its indirect social or moral effect, to prefer a system of small producers, each dependent for his success upon his own skill and character, to one in which the great mass of those engaged must accept the direction of a few. . . .

. . . Persons may unwittingly find themselves in possession of a monopoly, automatically so to say: that is, without having intended either to put an end to existing competition or to prevent competition from arising when none had existed; they may become monopolists by force of accident. Since the Act makes monopolizing a crime, as well as a civil wrong, it would be not only unfair, but presumably contrary to the intent of Congress, to include such instances. A market may, for example, be so limited that is impossible to produce at all and meet the cost of production except by a plant large enough to supply the whole demand. Or there may be changes in taste or in cost which drive out all but one purveyor. A single producer may be the survivor out of a group of active competitors, merely by virtue of his superior skill, foresight and industry. In such cases a strong argument can be made that, although the result may expose the public to the evils of monopoly, the Act does not mean to condemn the resultant of those very forces which it is its prime object to foster. . . . The successful competitor, having been urged to compete, must not be turned upon when he wins.

. . . There were at least one or two abortive attempts to enter the industry, but Alcoa effectively anticipated and forestalled all competition, and succeeded in holding the field alone. True, it stimulated demand and opened new uses for the metal, but not without making sure that it could supply what it had evoked. There is no dispute as to this; Alcoa avows it as evidence of the skill, energy and initiative with which it has always conducted its business; as a reason why, having won its way by fair means, it could be commended, and not dismembered. We need charge it with no moral derelictions; we may assume that all it claims for itself is true. The only question is whether it

[8] 148 F. 2d 416 (1945). The relevant language of the Sherman Act is (Sec. 2): ''Every person who shall monopolize, or attempt to monopolize . . . any part of the trade or commerce among the several states, or with foreign nations, shall be deemed guilty. . . . ''

falls within the exception established in favor of those who do not seek, but cannot avoid, the control of a market. It seems to us that that question scarcely survives its statement. It was not inevitable that it should always anticipate increases in the demand for ingot and be prepared to supply them. Nothing compelled it to keep doubling and redoubling its capacity before others entered the field. It insists that it never excluded competitors; but we can think of no more effective exclusion than progressively to embrace each new opportunity as it opened, and to face every newcomer with new capacity already geared into a great organization, having the advantage of experience, trade connections and the elite of personnel. . . .

In your judgment, should Alcoa have been found guilty of violating the Sherman Act? In answering, the following questions may help focus the issues:

1. What is bad about monopoly?
2. What did Alcoa do that was wrong? How could it have avoided violating the Sherman Act?
3. Who, if anyone, was harmed by Alcoa's behavior? Who benefited?
4. Was the Court's decision, leading to more firms in the aluminum industry, in the public interest, whatever you think about the legality of Alcoa's behavior?

THEORY

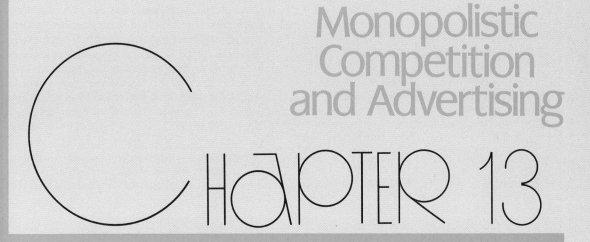

Monopolistic
Competition
and Advertising

CHAPTER 13

lmost no one has a pure monopoly. But many firms have partial monopolies. The corner druggist has a partial monopoly in his neighborhood. He can charge several cents more a tube for Colgate toothpaste than the big drugstores downtown do. And he can get it from many people, because he is so conveniently located for people in that neighborhood.

Coca-Cola has a partial monopoly. No one else can make a drink exactly like Coca-Cola without infringing the law, and for years "a Coke" has been the habitual drink of millions. But Pepsi-Cola, Royal Crown Cola, and a good many others look and taste enough like Coca-Cola to have shrunk Coca-Cola's share of the soft-drink market greatly in the last two decades. The Coca-Cola people will tell you they're in a highly competitive field.

As was emphasized in the Prologue to Part 2 and also the last few chapters, most of the American economy is in the range between competition and monopoly, an area often called "imperfect competition." Nearest to pure competition are cases with a substantial number of firms, each partly protected from competitors by trade names, location, tradition, advertising, and product quality, but far from perfectly protected; exposed to new competitors, but less exposed than the wheat farmer is. This is the area of "monopolistic competition." In it, each firm's product is "differentiated" from its competitors', but not enough to forestall active competition— on prices, selling costs, quality, or all three.

Toward the monopoly end of the spectrum is oligopoly—markets dominated by a few large firms, although there may be other, smaller firms that largely follow the leaders. Some oligopolies sell virtually identical products, like cement and basic aluminum. Most, however, involve substantial product differentiation, like autos and cigarettes.

How much of the economy is in the monopolistic-competition category? The lines are hazy, but a fair, although very crude, answer would be, perhaps a third to a half of the private sector. This would include most wholesale and retail trade, real estate, and personal services (legal,

medical, and the like);[1] a substantial sector of manufacturing (for example, apparel, lumber, and printing); and most of construction and trucking. By contrast, a large part of finance and manufacturing (for example, autos, steel, heavy electrical equipment, glass, and tobacco products) is oligopolistic.

PRICES AND OUTPUT UNDER MONOPOLISTIC COMPETITION

The Bases for Product Differentiation

The essence of monopolistic competition is a substantial number of firms, so none is dominant, with each firm's product a little different from those of its competitors, but not very different. Each producer tries to differentiate his product and to increase the demand for it. To the extent that he succeeds, he can get away with charging a little more for his product and selling more of it.

Sometimes product differentiation involves actual physical differentiation. For example, Schlitz beer tastes different from Pabst; a Frigidaire is different from a GE refrigerator. But often, the differentiation hinges on the things that go along with the product—convenience of location, thick carpets on the floors, well-groomed waitresses, easy credit terms. Sometimes the differentiation is largely illusory—it exists in the mind of the customer but not in fact. If you can really tell the difference between the various high-test gasolines in your car on the road, you're better than most of the experts.

Whatever the reason, whenever one seller is differentiated from others in the customer's mind, that seller is able to charge a price higher than his competitors' without losing all his market. His demand curve slopes downward; it is not horizontal as under perfect competition.

---

[1]Insofar as lawyers and doctors agree (collude) to set minimum fees, they are also behaving like oligopolists, in "cartels" (see Chapter 14).

Short-Run Output and Prices

The monopolistic competitor's problem is to set his price to maximize his profits. He has some freedom to raise price above what his competitors charge for similar products, but if he goes too far, his share of the market will drop sharply. The more successful he is in differentiating his product, the less elastic his demand curve will be. With an inelastic demand curve, he can boost his price without a corresponding drop in sales. But it's hard to convince customers that no substitute will do.

The firm's optimal price–output decision in the short run is hard to specify under these conditions. Any one firm's demand curve depends both on what this firm does through selling expenses to change consumer demand and on what competitors do that also affects the demand for our firm's product. The demand curve we face will depend on consumers' total demand for the whole group of slightly differentiated products, and on our share of the total. Palmolive can increase and steepen the consumer demand curve for its soap either by getting customers away from Lux, Sweetheart, and the rest, or by somehow increasing total consumer demand for soap. If Palmolive succeeds in convincing people they should wash their faces more often, this may increase the demand for other soaps as much as for Palmolive. The trick is to be sure you get the big share of the benefit if you go in for this kind of advertising. Conversely, increased advertising by Lux may leave Palmolive with a lower, flatter demand curve, even though Palmolive soap is just as good as before. And if Palmolive's advertising steals Lux's customers, retaliation is almost certain. Thus, it should be clear that under monopolistic competition (and oligopoly), the level and elasticity of any firm's demand curve depend both on what it does and on what the other firms in the industry do. It is not possible to draw a stable, unambiguous demand curve for the individual firm's product.[2]

Presumably, any monopolistic competitor will increase his expenditures on advertising and other demand-creating activities as long as he estimates that this will add more to his income than to his costs. But under monopolistic competition, uncertainty about what competitors will do makes output and price behavior hard to predict.

Long-Run Adjustments under Monopolistic Competition

In the long run, new firms enter industries and old firms leave. The search for profits goes on, with productive resources transferable throughout the economy. Monopolistic competition is like pure competition in that new firms can enter the industry. It is different in that new firms cannot exactly duplicate the product of existing firms. A new drugstore across the street from an established one might provide very close substitutes. But a new women's-wear store that sets up in competition with Saks Fifth Avenue will have a tougher time. For one thing, drugs and ice-cream are relatively standardized as compared with women's clothes. For another, few drugstores have the prestige of Saks.

But even though newcomers face problems, high profits in any monopolistically competitive field will draw new competitors. As more firms enter, the total market is divided up more ways

---

[2]Given the firm's cost and demand curves, the technical conditions for maximizing profit in the short run are identical with those for the monopolist described in Chapter 12. Thus, in the figure below, to maximize profits the firm will set price and output where marginal cost equals marginal revenue. This gives output O to be sold at price P as the optimal position. But when we say, "given the demand curve," we are assuming away a big piece of the problem, as is explained in the text.

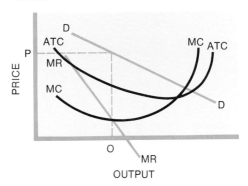

(temporarily disregard the added costs of advertising). The demand curve for each established firm is moved downward (to the left) as it loses market share to newcomers. Profits per firm are reduced by this sharing of the market. Gradually, as more firms enter, profits tend to be eliminated, just as under pure competition. A new (unstable) equilibrium with excess profits eliminated may be achieved.

This sounds like pure competition. But in this temporary equilibrium, under monopolistic competition each firm is restricting output a little to take advantage of its product differentiation. The demand curve is tangent to the cost curve to the left of the minimum point, and marginal cost is less than price. Each firm is thus operating below its optimal capacity and producing at a cost above the least-cost point on its optimal-cost curve. From a social point of view, too little of the product is being produced and sold, since price is being held above marginal cost, while $MC =$ Price is the socially optimum condition.

This process is illustrated in Figure 13–1. Case A pictures a typical firm making a profit. Its demand curve is above its total-unit-cost curve over a substantial range. The demand curve is downward-sloping, because this product is differentiated from its competitors.[3]

---

[3]The precise short-run profit-maximizing output can be found by adding the marginal cost and marginal revenue curves, as in the graph in the preceding footnote.

What will happen? Competition will pick up. As new firms enter the market, the demand curve for each old firm moves downward as its share of the market falls. Eventually, the demand curve for a typical firm will be pushed down far enough to be just tangent to the cost curve. All profit will be eliminated, and there will be no further incentive for new firms and new resources to enter the industry. Neither will there be any incentive for existing firms to leave, unless some especially attractive opportunity opens up elsewhere in the economy. This is case C in Figure 13–1.

Case B shows a typical firm making a loss. Here, firms will gradually drop out of the industry, and the demand for the products of each remaining firm will gradually rise. This process will continue until a no-loss situation has been reached, when there is no further incentive for resources to move out of the industry. Again, the firm will be in a case C equilibrium position.

Equilibrium Unstable under Competitive Demand Creation

But this is not the end of the story; the equilibrium is almost surely unstable. If you were running a drugstore and were in position C in Figure 13–1, what would you do? Maybe you'd just sit, but probably you'd try to figure a way to get more business. You might try improving your

FIGURE 13–1
Individual Firm under Monopolistic Competition
This figure shows a firm making money on left, losing money in middle, and in no-profit, temporary equilibrium on right.

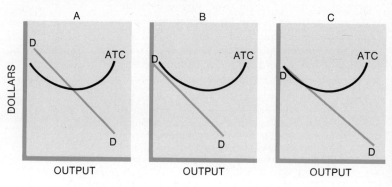

service to customers. Or putting in air conditioning. Or advertising more. All these attempts would cost you money. They might bring you more customers—that is, they might raise your demand curve—probably by drawing customers away from competitors. And they would upset the equilibrium situation shown in *C*. Such attempts to increase demand are apparent everywhere, keeping equilibrium (with the demand curve tangent to the cost curve) from being achieved or maintained. Moreover, advertising or other selling costs cost money, and we need to introduce this fact into the picture.

Imagine a monopolistically competitive milk industry in a large city, with fifteen milk companies of about equal size and no advertising. Company *A* begins an advertising campaign. It gets more customers by luring a few away from each competitor. *A*'s costs are now higher, but its profits are up with the increased volume. Graphically, its *ATC* curve is higher throughout; its *DD* is higher and above the new *ATC* curve, so it can be making a profit.

It doesn't take a business genius to predict the reaction of the other companies. After expressing a few well-chosen words about the manager of Company *A*, they will get busy on their own advertising campaigns, designed to get their customers back and to lure new customers into the fold. If every company just matched *A*'s advertising, we might think of a new equilibrium situation, with each producer getting back just his original customers, but with every company's profit eliminated, and cost and price higher by the amount of the advertising.

But having tasted success, *A* is not likely to sit quietly at the restored higher-price equilibrium. Nor are *B, C,* and *D.* Each will be busy contriving a new and better advertising campaign. If another round of advertising starts, or trading stamps with each gallon of milk are introduced, the result is likely to be similar. Everybody's costs go up. Nobody ends up with many more customers, or with any more profits. And consumers end up with higher prices. Now they're buying advertising and trading stamps along with their milk—without having anything to say about whether they really want to buy them or not. And nobody can tell where the whole process will stop.

Even in the happy event that the advertising campaign increases total spending on milk, a similar problem remains. Where do the additional funds for milk come from? Maybe the milk advertising stimulates total spending and raises total spending and GNP, but this is unlikely. If total spending is unchanged, more spending on milk must mean less spending on something else. Producers in these other industries will fight back to regain sales. This will cause another reshuffling of demand, with still other industries (possibly including milk) losing customers to the newest advertisers.

QUALITY COMPETITION

Every shopper knows about quality competition—who has the freshest vegetables, and where there are enough clerks to provide quick service. When you buy a suit, you go to a store you know will stand behind it if something goes wrong. These are examples of quality competition.

Alert businessmen are very much interested in knowing how much quality consumers want. They spend thousands of dollars on market research to find out whether consumers want softer seats in autos, cellophone around fresh vegetables, more carbonation in ginger ale, a new look on auto models each year. A shrewd businessman will improve the quality of his product whenever he believes customers will want the improvement enough to pay the extra cost—and something more. He will reduce product quality—for example, by putting his store on a cash-and-carry basis—whenever he believes that most customers would prefer to pay less and go without some service.

Some observers believe that quality competition is the pervasive form of competition in modern America, and that price competition is of secondary importance. There is evidence to support this point of view. Filling stations long ago learned that a clean rest room is more important to a touring family than a half cent off the price of gas. The first air-conditioned movie had an enormous quality advantage; now they're all air-conditioned.

Such is often the case in quality competition. Once one firm pioneers, others feel they must follow—or risk losing their customers as a consequence of holding out. If GM comes out with new auto models each year, Ford and Chrysler can't stick with last year's look without losing their share of the market. The result is higher "quality" all around, and higher prices to cover the higher costs involved in providing it, whether or not all consumers want to pay for the changes. Then every manager starts scratching his head to figure out a new change that will give him at least a temporary jump on the field again.

Quality competition can be a perfectly valid type of competition, just as much as price competition. Sometimes people don't want the extra "quality" built into new products. But if there is active competition, there's always a competitor to provide a cheaper, "lower-quality" product— witness the success of discount stores and of compact cars.

Graphically, new costs in improving product quality raise the *ATC* curve, just like advertising. And if successful, they will also raise the firm's

DD curve, and its profits. The countering quality improvements by competitors have the same effects as counteradvertising.

ADVERTISING— PRICE THEORY IN ACTION

Recently, social critics have leveled their big guns on advertising as big business's and Madison Avenue's main device for manipulating consumer demand. Certainly advertising plays a major role in many markets, and it deserves a further look.

In 1978, American business spent about $43 billion on advertising, and the total has risen persistently over the last two decades. In 1940, it was only $2 billion. Figure 13–2 summarizes these facts, and shows the composition of the total each year.

Forty-three billion dollars is a lot of money, and it represents a lot of persuasion. It would

FIGURE 13–2
Advertising, 1960–1978
Advertising has grown rapidly and persistently. Newspapers get the biggest share, followed by TV and direct mail. (Source: *Advertising Age.*)

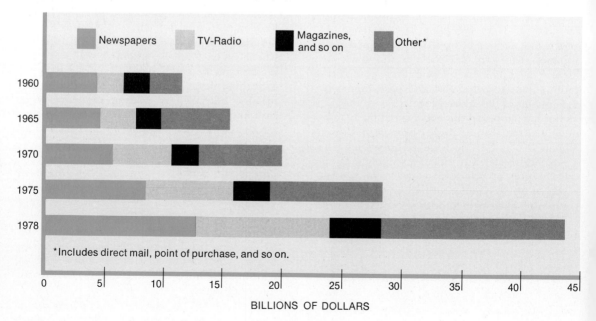

have bought a lot of other goods and services, had consumers had the cash to spend instead. On the other hand, it was only about 2 percent of the total gross national product.

Who were the big advertisers? Table 13–1 shows the top eight for 1977, plus a few others that may be of special interest. Strikingly, it was not the companies making big-ticket items like autos and appliances that spent a large proportion of their sales dollars on advertising; autos averaged only half of 1 percent, electrical appliances about the same. Firms making drugs, cosmetics, soap, packaged foods, and other such small consumer items spent the highest percentages; drugs and cosmetics averaged nearly 20 percent. Procter & Gamble is by far the world's largest advertiser; AT&T, Exxon, and General Motors, the world's largest companies, lag far behind in their use of the sales dollar to persuade customers away from their competitors. Seven of the top 100 advertisers spent more than 10 percent of their sales dollars on ads; all seven were drug and cosmetics, or soap, companies. But three of the four individual products getting the most advertising dollars were cigarettes—Winston ($31.6 million), Marlboro ($30.5 million), and Salem ($25 million).

Advertising and Information

The most important positive product of advertising is information, and useful information is worth paying for. Each household maximizes its utility from the income it receives when it allocates that income among all the things it buys so as to equate the utility received from the last dollar spent on each good and service. To make this allocation most effectively, the household needs the best possible information on the alternatives available to it. Thus, insofar as advertising provides information on prices and qualities of the alternative goods and services available, it helps buyers maximize the utility obtainable from their incomes.

Advertising can play an especially valuable role in a dynamic, rapidly changing economy of many new and improved products. It is the main means we have of spreading such information. Presumably, rational consumers would be willing to pay for such information through other channels if there were no advertising. Insofar as advertising provides misleading information, of course, it has the opposite effect. If advertising simply alters consumer wants (for example, if it convinces people to prefer wine to beer), it is hard

TABLE 13–1
Advertising Expenditures[a]

RANK	COMPANY AND PRODUCT	AMOUNT IN MILLIONS	PERCENT OF SALES
1	Procter & Gamble (soaps, etc.)	$460	5.7
2	General Motors (autos)	312	0.5
3	General Foods (packaged foods)	300	5.6
4	Sears, Roebuck (general retail)	290	1.7
5	K Mart (general retail)	210	2.1
6	Bristol-Myers (soaps and cosmetics)	203	9.3
7	Warner-Lambert (drugs and cosmetics)	201	7.9
8	Ford Motor Company (autos)	184	0.4
25	General Electric (electrical products)	112	0.6
82	Exxon (petroleum products)	35	0.06
83	Noxell Corp. (drugs and cosmetics)	33	24.2

[a] Data for 1977, from *Advertising Age,* August 28, 1978. Does not include local newspaper advertising.

to say whether that advertising increases or decreases consumer satisfaction.

The information content of advertising varies widely. Many advertisers are more concerned with attracting consumers away from competitors and with building a "corporate image" than with providing information on which consumers can make more intelligent choices. Watch TV for a whole evening and record all the information you get that is of value in helping you decide among the products advertised. Read a copy of one of the big-selling magazines. Try the morning newspaper. How much useful information does each provide?

Figure 13–2 showed the relative importance of different kinds of advertising. Newspaper advertising, which contains a lot of useful information (grocery and clothing ads, want ads, and so on) makes up about 30 percent of the total. TV and magazine advertising, which are more commonly aimed at brand emphasis and prestige building, account for another third. The remainder is a wide variety of types, some of which (for example, in trade magazines) include significant customer information, while others have limited informational value.

While brand-loyalty advertising may make entry by new firms more difficult and hence support monopoly positions, advertising can also serve as an important weapon for competitors who want to enter a market by stressing lower prices. For example, for many years, professional societies of opticians, optometrists, and others concerned with eye examinations and eyeglasses forbade their members to advertise, and in many states this prohibition was written into law. In 1972, a much-quoted study by Chicago's Lee Benham found that the prices of eye examinations and glasses were much lower in states that permitted advertising by optometrists—$29.27 in Texas and the District of Columbia, against $49.87 in North Carolina and California.[4] Similar findings were reported by Federal Trade Commission studies, and in 1978 such restrictions on advertising were ruled illegal by the FTC. The result was a widespread drop in many eyeglass prices (of as much as 50 percent) with

advertising. Information on prices is essential to effective competition and consumer sovereignty. Without advertising, how can competitors wishing to tell about lower prices or new products get the information to potential consumers? The eyeglasses case suggests that livelier competition may well more than offset the cost of informative advertising, and some information economists argue that most advertising of goods that the consumer can evaluate easily (for instance, simple consumer products) does provide useful and cost-effective information.

Most professional societies (in medicine, dentistry, law, accounting, and the like) have long forbidden their members to advertise, often obtaining state laws supporting this prohibition, on grounds that such advertising would be unprofessional, harmful, and misleading to customers. But in 1977, the U.S. Supreme Court struck down such restrictions, and tentative use of advertising by the professions is beginning to appear. Do you predict that the results will be harmful or beneficial to consumers?

The Use of Resources in "Demand Creation"

As the preceding pages have emphasized, in a fully employed economy, we must choose between alternative uses of resources. For our advertising dollar (paid in the price of the product), we get information on products, TV soap operas, professional sports, billboards, CBS News, Johnny Carson, and a wide variety of other services, the worth of some of which might be disputed. Advertising expenditures make possible 25-cent daily papers, and a $1.25 *Newsweek* magazine. But with these services mainly financed through advertising, little effective choice is left to the consumer as to how much of each he buys. The beer drinker pays for TV westerns even though he never watches TV. Still, almost everyone buys many advertised products and enjoys some of the fruits of advertising. Most people benefit from cheap newspapers and other news sources largely financed by advertising. Perhaps aside from cases of misleading advertising, everything pretty much evens out and consumers get just about the information and "entertainment" with their advertising dollars they would

---

[4]"The Effects of Advertising on the Price of Eyeglasses," *Journal of Law and Economics,* October 1972.

have bought anyway. But you may—understandably—have your doubts.

How much does advertising actually increase demand for advertised products? As was emphasized above, a large part of the total is counteradvertising, where the companies involved largely just offset each other's advertising. When TWA takes full-page newspaper ads to extol the virtues of its 747 wide-bodied planes, it is trying to increase the demand for its product by convincing (1) more people to fly, and (2) those who do fly to fly TWA instead of United or American. But United's and American's full-page ads about their 747s appear in the same papers. A 747 is pretty much the same airplane, whichever of the three big companies flies it. It gets there as fast with one as the other; prices are about the same; and it's hard to make your 747 sound more comfortable than your competitors'. Demand may not be changed much, but in the long run, air fares have to be enough higher to pay for the advertising. Do the ads increase total air travel? Possibly so, especially if they provide useful information on fares and service to possible customers. (For example, they clearly did in 1978–79, when the major airlines began serious price competition.)

Last, does advertising help everyone by increasing *total* spending and thereby providing more jobs and more total gross national product? The answer, if the economy's resources are already fully employed, is obviously no. If there are unemployed resources (for example, in a recession), more advertising might increase aggregate demand and consequently the amount of goods produced. But even if it could, monetary and fiscal policy are probably more powerful ways to increase demand, and they do not use up resources in the process.[5]

Do Advertisers Manipulate Consumer Wants?

Radical critics of today's scene, and some not so radical, argue that the American consumer has little real freedom of choice—that his "wants" are created and manipulated by big business and Madison Avenue, mainly through advertising. Businesses decide what will make the largest profits, and convince consumers to "want" that. To some extent, the problem is dishonest and misleading advertising; there has always been a fair amount of this, although such advertising is specifically forbidden by law, and the Federal Trade Commission and state agencies try to check it. But more fundamentally, advertising and TV mold our very style of life—we learn to want what the TV dangles before us. The best-known critic along these lines is Harvard's J. K. Galbraith, in his best-selling *The New Industrial State.*

This attack challenges the foundation of private-enterprise economics. If consumers merely respond to what businesses tell them to want, the whole intellectual case for an individualistic consumer-directed economy falls. Free consumer choice does not direct the allocation of resources.

Stated in the extreme form above, this argument is obviously unacceptable. Two percent of the total gross national product hardly seems adequate to govern the entire pattern of "wants" of every consumer in America. Moreover, there is a long history of business firms gone broke trying to convince consumers through advertising and other selling campaigns to buy products that the consumers stubbornly refuse to purchase. The classic case is Ford's Edsel in the 1950s, which flopped colossally in spite of an enormous advertising campaign. Less than a dozen of the 50 best-known automobile brands of the past half century are still with us, in spite of the best advertising assistance Detroit and Madison Avenue have been able to provide over the years. Much-advertised Camel, Chesterfield, and Lucky Strike held 42 percent of the cigarette market in 1956, only 18 percent in 1966, and even less in 1979. The history of American business is littered with well-advertised products that just didn't sell.

On the other hand, it would be ridiculous to argue that advertising has no effect on how consumers spend their incomes. TV is indeed pervasive in American life, and it is full of "beautiful people" and beautiful things to want. Just how far advertising does influence the expenditure pattern of the American public is a

---

[5]It is doubtful that advertising has much influence on total consumer spending in the economy, but the evidence is not conclusive.

much-argued issue. Alas, there is no evidence that can give a simple, clear-cut answer. Look back at Table 4–1, which summarized what consumers buy, and make your own judgment on how much of it is dominated by the kinds of advertising you see around you.

Finally, whatever your answer, there's a basic issue involved as to the meaning of truly "independent" consumer wants. Galbraith's argument suggests that we have a basic set of wants that are good, while wants influenced by advertising are suspect and incompatible with maximization of consumer satisfaction. But beyond the most basic wants for food and shelter, all our wants are heavily conditioned by our environments. Suppose I prefer Chopin and champagne, while you choose beer and baseball. Does the fact that my tastes were developed largely independent of advertising while yours were heavily influenced by advertising make yours somehow less valid than mine?

Conclusion

With advertising, as with almost everything else, the principle of marginalism applies. It would be surprising indeed if we were to conclude that advertising is all bad or all good, that we should completely eliminate advertising or increase it to some very large amount. From a social point of view, the decision as to whether we want more or less advertising is a marginal one. We need to weigh the gains from the last dollar spent on advertising against alternative possibilities for that dollar devoted to other uses. Is advertising socially cost-effective? Clearly, some advertising has high social value—for example, if it tells consumers about a new, highly desirable product. Conversely, misleading advertising has a negative marginal value. As to how much advertising we ought to have in our society, marginalism is the principle to follow. The biggest question is how to implement the principle effectively.

SUMMARY AND REVIEW

1. Most of the American economy lies between the limiting cases of pure competition and pure monopoly. "Monopolistic competition" lies nearer the pure-competition end of the spectrum, with a *substantial* number of firms so no one is dominant, and with products somewhat differentiated from those of other firms, but not very different. Toward the monopoly end of the spectrum is oligopoly, with a *few* dominant firms selling either identical or differentiated products.

2. At any given time, a monopolistically competitive firm will maximize its profits by equating marginal cost and marginal revenue. It will usually have an incentive to differentiate its product further and increase demand for the product, by advertising or improving "quality." This raises both its *ATC* and demand curves; if successful, it will increase profits by raising *DD* above *ATC*.

3. Such product differentiation and demand creation generally lure customers from competing firms, and they retaliate.

4. Such competitive advertising and product differentiation among competing firms will continue until a (temporary) long-run equilibrium is reached, with all cost curves higher and all demand curves just tangent to those cost curves so that all above-normal profits have been eliminated.

5. This equilibrium will be unstable, because there will still be incentives for each firm to increase its demand further by advertising or improving product quality.

6. The social results of such monopolistic competition are that (a) price is higher than marginal cost, since the demand curve is tangent to the cost curve to the left of its minimum point; and (b) costs and prices are generally higher than they would have been without advertising and other product differentiation, although no above-normal profits remain.

7. The main benefit of advertising is to provide useful information for consumers on products, prices, and the like; this information is especially important in introducing new and better products. But much

advertising has little useful informational content for consumers, and is devoted instead mainly to institutional image building by sellers. Advertising also helps pay for TV programs, low-priced newspapers, magazines, and the like. Whether the cost of such advertising (paid in the price of the product) is justified by the benefits it provides is widely debated. Advertising should be assessed in terms of cost-benefit analysis, differentiating between different types of advertising.

8. Some critics argue that "big business" and "Madison Avenue" essentially dictate consumer wants, so that the notion of consumer sovereignty is irrelevant in modern society. Although this is clearly an overstatement, there is some element of truth in the argument.

New Concepts to Remember	product differentiation quality competition	demand creation unstable equilibrium

For Analysis and Discussion

1. Explain why equilibrium in a monopolistically competitive industry is likely to be unstable.
2. Is the absence of high profits in an industry satisfactory evidence that monopolistic competition is not injuring consumers of the product concerned? Explain your answer to a noneconomist.
3. "As long as there is relatively free entry to an industry, I can't get worried about the dangers of monopoly in that industry." Do you agree or disagree? Explain.
4. Some critics argue that we now have "producer sovereignty" rather than "consumer sovereignty," because advertising determines what we think we want. Marshal the evidence for and against this argument.
5. "If we had adequate 'Truth-in-Advertising' legislation, I wouldn't worry about excessive advertising or manipulation of consumer wants by Madison Avenue." Do you agree or disagree?
6. As a consumer, would you like to see aggressive price competition among sellers of all the products you buy? Under such competition, would you get the same breadth of display, return privileges, and charge-account arrangements now provided by major department stores?
7. Do you get your money's worth out of the advertising for which you pay? If not, what specific steps would you propose to improve the situation?

CASE 12

SHOULD LAWYERS, DOCTORS, AND DENTISTS ADVERTISE?

Advertising by lawyers, doctors, and dentists has long been considered unethical by the American Bar Association, the American Medical Association, the American Dental Association, and their local associations. In 1977, however, after long litigation, the U.S. Supreme Court struck down an Arizona regulation barring advertising by lawyers. The decision apparently also set aside other regulations and laws forbidding advertising by members of the professions.

Today, the professions are deeply and often bitterly divided on advertising. There are two main arguments on each side of the issue. The traditional position, apparently still held by most professional men and women, holds that, although advertising cannot now be forbidden, it should be voluntarily foregone, because advertising, especially on prices, is unprofessional and degrading for professional people, and because quality of service will be sacrificed for quantity if price competition develops. Those in favor of advertising argue that advertising will help make services available to people who didn't understand them before, and that price competition in the professions will develop to the benefit of consumers.

Although advertising is spreading, particularly among dentists, the spread has been slow among lawyers and, especially, physicians, who have traditionally limited their advertising to listings in the Yellow Pages of telephone directories. A statement by Lawrence Walsh, president of the American Bar Association for 1976, sums up many of the arguments against advertising by professionals: "Unrestricted advertising would be a disservice to the public. It would mean that some people would retain an attorney on the basis of who mounted the best advertising campaign or who charged the lowest fees, factors which are not relevant to professional performance." But the opposition counters that "it should be up to the public to decide whether price is relevant in choosing a lawyer or a doctor and in deciding what services to buy; and surely the customer should know what he is getting into on price before he chooses the doctor or lawyer he wants to retain. Open information on pricing will help consumers make intelligent choices, and competent doctors and lawyers should not be afraid of this open choice."

To date, there has been some open price advertising by dentists, especially those engaging in group practice, and by lawyers, mainly for routine services such as simple divorces, drawing up of wills, real estate purchases, and the like. Most major firms, medical clinics, and leading practitioners among lawyers, doctors, and dentists have so far continued their practice of not advertising beyond simple listing in telephone directories. They point out that information on specialists can be obtained from the local offices of the American Bar Association or the American Medical Association.

---

1. If you were a young doctor, dentist, or lawyer, would you advertise the prices you charge for your services?

2. Do you believe the professional associations in law, medicine, and dentistry (and other professional associations) should encourage their members to advertise, or to continue their avoidance of advertising? Why?

3. Will the public be better served by extension of advertising to most professionals in law, medicine, and dentistry, or by continuation of the traditional avoidance of such advertising?

CASE 13 ADVERTISING AND CONSUMERISM

Ralph Nader and other consumer advocates urge a wide range of new measures to protect consumers in the marketplace. Some advocate direct government regulation of product quality. Others favor stronger laws controlling advertising. Still others believe that present legislation is generally adequate but that we need a more strongly consumer-oriented government agency to enforce the laws protecting consumers.

Present law, reaching back to the Federal Trade Commission Act of 1914 and broadened several times since, specifically forbids "dishonest or misleading" advertising and directs the FTC to enforce the law, both to protect consumers and to protect other sellers from unfair competition. "Truth in Lending," "Truth in Packaging," and several Food and Drug Acts have extended consumer protection beyond the original FTC Act. Over the years, the FTC has undertaken many thousands of investigations to halt deceptive advertising, most of which have ended in informal agreements that the advertiser will halt the challenged behavior.

Recently, one consumer-protection group proposed that Congress and/or all state legislatures pass legislation providing that:

1. No advertising be permitted that does not provide information useful to consumers.
2. No firm be permitted to spend on advertising more than 10 percent of its income from sales in the preceding year.
3. No firm be permitted to engage in dishonest or misleading advertising, and that any firm doing so be liable to triple damages to all injured consumers through class-action suits, brought by either consumers or the government.
4. The Federal Trade Commission, or appropriate state agencies, be empowered to enforce these rules.

Do you recommend that your senator and representative vote for the proposed legislation?

THEORY

Oligopoly,
Collusion, and
Market Power

CHAPTER 14

hree companies—General Motors, Ford, and Chrysler—make nearly all the automobiles produced in the United States. Over 90 percent of all flat glass and electric light bulbs are produced by the top four companies in those industries. In dozens of industries, from half to three-fourths of the total business is done by only a few firms. These are the oligopolies—industries in which a few firms dominate, even though there may be many small firms that generally follow the leaders, or take what is left over. Figure 14–1 summarizes the domination by the leading four firms in a number of major industries.

These examples are on a national scale. The number of oligopolists in local markets is far larger. Building materials (such as cement and bricks) are produced by hundreds of different firms scattered all over the country; but in any one local market, production is usually concentrated in one or a few firms. The more important

transportation costs are and the harder it is for customers to shop around, the more likely local oligopolies are to be found. On the other hand, international firms abroad (for example, Japanese and German cars) in many cases produce much more competition than the domestic production data alone suggest.

Many economists consider "concentration ratios" (the percentage of total sales concentrated in the largest four, or sometimes eight, firms) an important indication of likely market performance. But it is important to recognize that this is only one measure of the degree of monopoly power held by the leading firms. Probable price–output behavior may be quite different, for example, in two industries with the same concentration ratio of 80 percent, if in one case the biggest firm has 60 percent of the market while in the other it has only 25. Similarly, the total number of firms in the industry aside from the

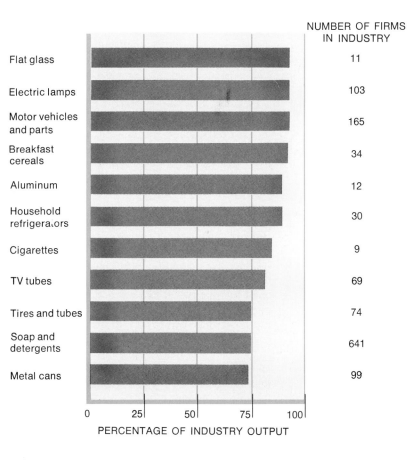

NUMBER OF FIRMS
IN INDUSTRY

Flat glass	11
Electric lamps	103
Motor vehicles and parts	165
Breakfast cereals	34
Aluminum	12
Household refrigerators	30
Cigarettes	9
TV tubes	69
Tires and tubes	74
Soap and detergents	641
Metal cans	99

0   25   50   75   100

PERCENTAGE OF INDUSTRY OUTPUT

FIGURE 14–1
Market Domination by Four Leading Firms
The largest four firms dominate the industry's output in some leading industries, but the total number of firms varies greatly from industry to industry. (Source: *1972 Census of Manufacturers*.)

177

leaders may make a difference. The soap and match industries have similar four-firm concentration ratios, with the additional industry characteristics shown in the following table. Which would you say is more concentrated? In general, economists suspect that monopoly-like results are more likely in highly concentrated markets. But this measure provides only a rough presumption.

	SOAP	MATCHES
Total number of firms	267	14
Percentage of total industry sales by:		
Largest 4 firms	85	74
Largest 8 firms	89	93
Largest 20 firms	95	100

Some industries, with the characteristics noted below, have been dominated persistently by a few large firms. Moreover, concentration ratios are similar for major industries in leading industrial nations. Table 14–1 compares concentration ratios for leading industries in five industrialized nations. The strikingly similar patterns suggest common underlying factors in the industries concerned. But here again, there are numerous cases that don't fit the general pattern. And remember that the spectacular growth of large multinational firms, doing business across many national borders, has substantially eroded the domestic market power of many domestic oligopolies. In the non-communist world, multinationals accounted for 8 percent of total GNP in 1950, for 24 percent by 1976.

These observations stress the size of firms relative to their markets. But some observers are more concerned with absolute size. Exxon is the biggest industrial corporation in the world, with $37 billion of assets and $52 billion of sales in 1978. But the gasoline industry is not highly concentrated in the United States, and Exxon has only a modest 7 percent of the retail gasoline market; the biggest four firms accounted for only 30 percent of total sales. Yet Exxon's sales and assets made it bigger than many of the world's nations. In fact, it, like such other corporate giants as GM and GE, produces many products, in many different industries. Vast economic and

political power must go with such size, many critics contend—power over jobs, wages, products, prices, and governments at home and abroad.

Clearly, power over market output and prices depends primarily on size relative to that market; a small firm may have great monopoly power in a tiny market, while Exxon's is limited by competition. And as economists, we shall be mainly concerned with market power in this chapter. But in the following chapter, we shall also turn to nonmarket powers of giant corporations, which are of greater concern to many Americans than is the danger of monopoly prices.

THE FOUNDATIONS OF OLIGOPOLY

At bottom, most oligopolies rest on one or both of two factors: (1) the necessity of large-scale production (relative to the size of the market) for low-cost output, and (2) barriers against the entry of new firms into the industry.

If total market demand will support only a few firms of optimum size, clearly the competitive struggle will tend to make a few big firms the winners. This situation rests fundamentally on the economies of large-scale production—on modern technology and efficient organizational arrangements. In each of the industries in Figure 14–1, large-scale production is essential to obtain low unit costs.

How do these big firms maintain their positions, once attained? As we shall see presently, seldom through aggressive price competition. Instead, the oligopolist often tries to increase his market share and his profits by improving his product, by demand-creating activities, and by setting up barriers against new competitors. Patents, an established marketing organization, the high capital costs of entry, or control over raw materials may be the key to keeping out newcomers. The bases for oligopoly power are similar to those for other monopolies indicated in Chapter 12. But dominant firms in an oligopoly are seldom safe from potential competition. It is the rare oligopoly that escapes for long the pressures of competition from new firms and new products. Even patents, large size, and technological dominance provide only partial and temporary insulation.

TABLE 14–1
Concentration Ratios in Five Nations[a]

	U.S.	U.K.	CANADA	FRANCE	JAPAN
Primary aluminum	98	43	100	100	100
Autos	98	74	100	79	76
Cigarettes	82	74	85	100	
Trucks	77	86	100	78	
Matches	74	86	98	100	74
Steel ingots	64	32	81	40	52
Flour	40	46	35	12	53
Petroleum refining	32	93	79	72	41
Beer	27	11	49	25	98
Cement	31	89	100	52	48
Cotton textiles	18	4	60		7

[a] Ratios are for four firms in the United States, three firms in other nations. Figures show percent of total sales accounted for by leading firms. Data vary between 1950 and 1960 for different nations, but have apparently changed little since then.

Source: J. Bain, *International Differences in Industrial Structure* (New Haven, Conn.: Yale University Press, 1966), pp. 67–106.

OLIGOPOLY PRICES AND OUTPUT

Analytically, the crucial thing about an oligopoly is the small number of sellers, which gives each one substantial market power and makes it imperative for each to weigh carefully the reactions of the others to its own price, production, and sales policy. Given the wide range of possible reactions of competitors in most oligopolistic markets, it is difficult to predict precisely what these reactions will be, and therefore difficult for the oligopolist to determine what price–production levels will give him the largest profits. We have, therefore, no simple oligopoly theory to tell us reliably just what prices and output will be in equilibrium. The outcome will be different depending on how each business assesses the likely reactions of competitors to its policies.

While many reaction patterns are possible, history suggests some central tendencies in oligopoly price–production decisions. In oligopoly, one attractive alternative for the rivals is collectively to establish the profit-maximizing price for the industry as a whole, and then divide up the market and profits among themselves. This is called a "cartel." But the law strictly forbids collusion of this sort, so oligopolists who agree to fix prices and divide up markets must make secret agreements or rely on unwritten understandings to "go along" with avoiding price competition. But in such a situation, it will also generally be to the self-interest of each individual producer to get a bigger share of the market for himself, which he might hope to do by cutting prices and luring away some of his competitors' customers. But if he cuts price, there is always the danger that competitors will meet the price cut, and the only result will be a lower price and lower profits for all the oligopolists.

Oligopoly Theory: Avoidance of Aggressive Price Competition

Suppose that you are the manager of a local brick factory, and that you have two competitors in the area. You are making a reasonable profit, and so are your competitors. Each of you sets the price at which he sells. You are price makers. Each of you knows he could make a larger profit if he could manage to increase his share of the market, because each of you is operating below capacity. Will you cut your price to lure customers away from your competition?

Maybe you will. But you'd better think twice before you try it. Your competitors will almost surely retaliate by meeting your price cut. Maybe they'll undercut you if you stir them up by

179

disturbing the stability of the market. Your price advantage can't last more than a day or two before they know about it, and you can't get very rich in that length of time. Heaven only knows just what will happen if you start a local price war, but three things look reasonably sure: All three of you will end up with lower prices; none of you will have lured many customers away from the others; and everyone's profits will have taken a beating.

This is only a small-scale, hypothetical example. But the questions are the same ones that the presidents of huge corporations ask when they consider cutting prices in oligopolistic markets in steel, automobiles, cigarettes. With only a few firms in the industry, the forces toward letting well enough alone are strong. Price reductions are likely to come only to meet a competitor's cut or under severe pressures—in recessions, for example. When firms do cut, they usually do so in the expectation that their cut will be met by rivals. Thus, the cut is made with the intention of moving the whole industry price scale to a lower level, in the hope of stimulating overall demand for the industry's product. In many cases, one major firm in an oligopolistic industry acts as a "price leader" in this way, although there may be no formal agreement and others don't always follow. For years, U.S. Steel was the price leader in basic steel. Alcoa is said to be in basic aluminum, GE in light bulbs.

Such a "live-and-let-live" policy makes sense to most producers. It leaves room for each firm to try quality and advertising competition to increase its share of the market. It leaves room for some price shading when times are hard or when one firm is losing out badly in the market. But aggressive price competition will probably blow the situation wide open. Cigarettes are a good example: The leading firms almost never compete on prices, but spend huge sums on demand-creating activities.

Oligopoly Theory: The Kinked Demand Curve

Economic theory helps present the price problem that faces the oligopolists. Go back to the brickworks case above. The current price is 20 cents a brick, and you are selling 10,000 bricks per week.

As you sit in your office, you try to imagine what your demand curve looks like, as a basis for deciding whether to change your price. Chances are you will decide it is something like Figure 14–2, a "kinked" demand curve.

It says that if you raise your price and the others don't follow, your sales will fall off sharply because your customers will desert you; your demand curve looks highly elastic if you raise your price above 20 cents. On the other hand, if you cut the price, you can be almost sure your rivals will follow to avoid losing customers to you. Thus, a lower price may increase sales a little, because the market will take some more bricks at a lower price; but there's little reason to suppose you'll get a bigger share of the market away from your competitors. Your demand curve looks very inelastic if you cut your price below 20 cents. This situation puts a high premium on keeping the price where it is, just as the commonsense reasoning above suggested.

Note now the critical assumptions. The first is that if you raise price, your rivals will not follow. It is this assumption that underlies the highly elastic curve to the left of the "corner" *P*. If, by contrast, you are a price leader and your rivals will follow your increase, the *DP* section of the

FIGURE 14–2
Kinked Demand Curve
Kinked demand curve suggests that you will lose total revenue if you either raise or lower price. Demand is elastic above 20 cents, inelastic below it.

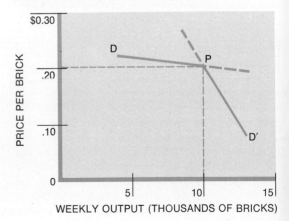

curve will be much less elastic and will probably just extend directly on up from $D'P$, as in the dashed line. This is because you won't lose share of the market to the others; the only loss in sales volume comes because fewer bricks will be bought at the higher price.

The second crucial assumption is that if you cut price, the others will also cut. If they do not, then $D'P$ of your demand curve will probably be highly elastic, as your rivals' customers switch to you. Then the "corner" in the demand curve would again vanish, and your demand curve will just be an extension of DP. This would be a wonderful situation for you, but it is not very likely unless you can hide your price cuts from your rivals. And that's difficult in an oligopoly.[1]

In summary, then, the kinked demand curve exists because you assume a different reaction from your competitors when you raise and when you lower your price. If you are the recognized price leader, there will be no kink, and you are merely moving price up or down along the

demand curve for the whole industry. If you are so little that nobody reacts to your price changes, there is also no kink—but this case is really a violation of the oligopoly situation, because the essence of oligopoly is so few competitors that each must be concerned with the others' reactions. Last, your freedom to move price without immediately risking rivals' reactions is larger the more differentiated your product is.

Many economists find the kinked-demand theory useful in understanding and predicting oligopoly behavior. But others doubt its usefulness. So some, led by Chicago's George Stigler, have tested it empirically (as explained in Chapter 2 on the methodology of economics) to see how well it predicts, and have found that actual behavior is inconsistent with the predictions of the theory a substantial part of the time. Observed oligopoly prices were not as sticky as predicted, and often competitors did not respond to price changes as predicted; but the theory predicted well some of the time. The kinked-demand-curve theory is a good example of a theory under test and reformulation. At the moment it should clearly be considered a hypothesis, yet to be verified.[2]

---

[1]Where the demand curve is kinked, the corresponding marginal revenue curve has a break, or discontinuity. The following graph shows the demand and marginal revenue curves form Figure 14–2. Note that given this marginal revenue curve, a marginal-cost curve (MC) could move up or down considerably without logically leading the firm to change its price. This fact may further explain the observed oligopoly tendency toward price stability, even when costs change substantially. (The lower half of the MR curve need not be negative, although of course it will be if $D'P$ shows inelastic demand.)

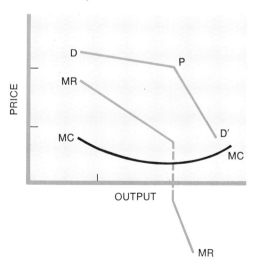

Oligopoly Theory: Cartels

Cartels, with price fixing and market sharing, are illegal under American antitrust law. But they are legal in some other nations, and some observers believe they exist surreptitiously even in the United States. Actually, U.S. farm policy in effect supports cartel action there.

What does a profit-maximizing theory of business behavior predict will be the results of a formal cartel—or of informal cartel-like price-stabilization arrangements? The line between not competing aggressively and formally agreeing to stabilize prices is nebulous. In the brickworks example above, there was no open collusion on prices, but the result was much the same as if there had been.

Assume a hypothetical furnace industry, in which there are only five firms. What are the

---

[2]For a summary and references, see W. Primeaux and M. Smith, "Pricing Patterns and the Kinky Demand Curve," *Journal of Law and Economics,* April 1976.

long-run results of a cartel in the industry, if the five firms agree to "stabilize" prices and to share the market equally?

To maximize their profits, the firms will act like one pure monopoly in setting price and then divide up the business and profits.[3] This will raise price above, and reduce output below, the competitive level. Assume that the competitive price for furnaces would be $400, the lowest point on the average-total-unit-cost curve of each producer, shown in Figure 14–3. At $400, consumers would buy 15,000 furnaces monthly (3,000 per firm), but profits would be eliminated. But by raising the price, the five firms can make substantial profits. So they raise the price to $500, at which level 10,000 furnaces can be sold monthly, this price being estimated to maximize profits for the group as a whole. Then each firm sells only 2,000 furnaces monthly but, at the higher price, reaps a profit of about $75 per furnace (the difference between the $500 price and the $425 total unit cost at the 2,000 output level). The situation is pictured in Figure 14–3.

Price is now higher than the competitive level; output is lower; use of labor and raw materials is lower; and production is less "efficient," with unused (excess) capacity in each firm. Consumers pay more; price is well above marginal cost. If the furnace makers can keep new competitors out, they're sitting pretty.

But suppose new firms can't be kept out. Oligopoly profits lure them in. To keep prices up, the cartel must allocate a share of the 10,000 furnaces monthly to each newcomer; otherwise, the newcomer will cut prices to get customers. The entry of new firms will thus divide up the same total sales among more firms. Profits are eliminated as new firms enter, not by price reduction but by rising unit costs as each firm reduces its output to a less and less efficient level. New firms will continue to enter in search of profits, cutting down the market available to each, until finally profits are eliminated when the cost per unit has risen to equal the cartel price of $500 at an output of 1,250 for each of eight firms.

---

[3]Logically, the cartel would set price and output where marginal cost equals marginal revenue for the industry as a whole. See Figure 14–2 above for an example.

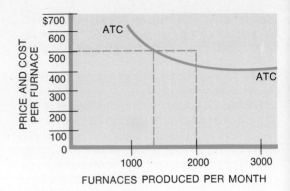

FIGURE 14–3
Typical Furnace Producer in a Cartel
At the cartel price of $500, a firm first makes $75 per furnace, selling 2,000 monthly. As more firms enter, each firm's market share and profit diminish.

This is shown in Figure 14–3. The original cartel members agreed to stabilize the price at $500, so each producer could sell 2,000 furnaces monthly and make $75 per furnace. But as more firms enter, building similar plants, the sales allotted to each producer fall until with eight producers, each can sell only 1,250 furnaces monthly and rising costs have eliminated profits.

Consider the results. Producers are no better off than under competition; consumers suffer all the results of monopoly, with price still up at $500 and total output restricted to 20,000 furnaces; and society bears the loss of extensive "overinvestment" in the industry, because far more productive facilities have been built than are required. Such a cartel arrangement with free entry, it might thus be argued, is not a halfway point between competition and monopoly, but rather an arrangement that combines the worst characteristics of each and the benefits of neither.

Obviously, this eight-firm "equilibrium" would be highly unstable. Each producer sees a big potential gain from cutting his price, and he has little inducement to remain in the agreement, since profits have been eliminated. Cartels without effective restrictions on entry seldom last long.

Nations, as well as private sellers, may form cartels. In 1973, the OPEC (Organization of Petroleum Exporting Countries) oil cartel, made up of the major Middle East and other oil exporters, shocked the world by raising the price of oil from about $2.50 to over $10 per barrel. OPEC included most of the world's major oil producers except for the United States, Canada, and the USSR. The short-run elasticity of demand for oil was, as the cartel hoped, inelastic. Consumption dropped somewhat as nations and private users tried to economize on the use of oil and shift to alternative energy sources, but these responses to higher prices took time, and OPEC profits soared. By 1975, however, the rate of growth in world oil consumption had dropped sharply, from about 4 percent annually to near zero, and output of both oil and other energy sources increased in other nations. To keep prices from falling, the OPEC countries had to reduce their production sharply, and strains began to develop among the cartel nations as to how these cutbacks were to be shared.

On the basis of the cartel theory above, how long would you expect the OPEC cartel to be able to maintain very high oil prices? On what factors does your answer depend? (*Hints:* Will demand be more or less elastic in the long run? How fast will new oil sources be developed—in Alaska, Mexico, the North Sea fields, Indonesia, U.S. offshore waters? What alternative energy sources—coal, shale, natural gas, nuclear power, solar power, and so on—become economically and technologically feasible at the new higher price for oil? What is the long-run elasticity of the demand for oil?)[4]

Oligopoly Theory: Restrictions on Entry

The preceding section points up the importance of restrictions on entry of new firms in determining the price—output performance of an oligopolistic industry. If the original five furnace producers above had had some effective way of keeping new firms out of the industry, their cartel would have worked out very nicely for them in terms of continuing profits—although there would always be the danger that one firm would become dissatisfied and cut prices to increase its

share of market and profits. If OPEC had controlled all the world's energy sources, it would have had a secure position. But if outsiders are free to enter, profits are eroded for everyone as more firms enter, and the pressure toward price cutting becomes almost irresistible.

Recent research confirms that barriers to entry do protect above-average profits, at least temporarily. When industries are classified by the barriers they have against new entrants, the average rate of return is highest for those with the highest entry barriers.[5] The drug industry's continued success in marketing brand-name prescription drugs at prices two to ten times as high as the same drugs sold under their generic names is a notable case in point. For example, Pfizer Terramycin in 1973 sold at wholesale for $20.48 per 100 capsules, while as oxytetracycline (its generic name), the same drug sold for $1.95 per 100 capsules; Squibb's Pentids sold for $10.04 per 100 tablets, but as penicillin G for only $1.45. The rate of return on investment in the ethical-drug industry has persistently been among the highest.[6]

Oligopoly—Price Theory in Action

Try one last check on oligopoly theory. Suppose the six barbers in Hometown are pricing haircuts at $4 and making what seems to them a very bad living. So they get together and agree to raise the price of haircuts to $6. Predict the results of this cartel-type agreement—for barbers and for customers. (*Hints:* What is the elasticity of demand for haircuts? What will happen to the number of barbers in Hometown? How, if at all, will barbers compete if they agree not to cut prices?)

Research, Development, and Innovation

Oligopoly gets poor marks on the criterion of efficiency in the allocation of resources. But there is another important kind of efficiency—effi-

---

[4]This states only part of the complex issues involved in the OPEC cartel.

[5]See H. M. Mann, "Barriers to Entry and Long-Run Profitability," *Antitrust Bulletin,* Winter 1969; and J. Bain, *Barriers to New Competition* (Cambridge, Mass.: Harvard University Press, 1956).

[6]See "Hearings before the U.S. Senate Subcommittee on Monopoly," 1973.

DO PARTIAL MONOPOLISTS MAXIMIZE PROFITS?

Do partial monopolists, operating with various degrees of protection from market competition under monopolistic competition and oligopoly, produce efficiently and maximize their profits? If businessmen in highly competitive industries don't make a good stab at this behavior, competition will remove them from the scene in due time. With the monopolist and partial monopolist, we can't count so fully on competition to exert this pressure.

There are several reasons why a businessman may not be maximizing profits at any time:

1. It's the long run that matters, and he may be willing to absorb a short-run loss for long-run gain.
2. It takes time to adjust to changes in demand, costs, and the like.
3. Businessmen never know what costs and demand in the future will be. They can only estimate, and often they're wrong.
4. Sometimes managers just aren't very efficient. They don't do a very good job of either minimizing costs or increasing revenues.
5. Unusually large profits may be an invitation to new competitors, lured by the hope of winning some customers away. Thus, the partial monopolist may think twice before reaching for more profits that may invite more competition.
6. Unusually large profits may bring unwanted scrutiny from the government's antitrust officials.
7. Historians point to many firms that have grown big as a result of the promoters' and managers' desire for bigness per se. They focus on growth in total sales and share of market, rather than on profits per se.
8. Some managements engage in "business statesmanship." They concentrate on improving the community and on social responsibilities. These things cost money and may or may not help long-run profits.
9. Last, the modern hired manager (as distinct from the owner-operator) may have important objectives in addition to profits—the desire to get along well with others in the company; to avoid ulcer-producing arguments with the union; to avoid looking foolish by being wrong when he takes risks. Management has more freedom to follow these other motives if it is sheltered from vigorous competition. (There is some evidence that owner-controlled firms do achieve a higher rate of return on investment than do similar management-controlled firms. Between 1952 and 1963, owner-controlled firms earned a 12.3 percent rate of return on investment as against 7.3 percent for management-controlled firms.)*

There are clearly wide differences among firms on all these scores. We assume in this chapter that, by and large, making profits is a dominant goal for partial monopolists. But in using profit-maximizing models, don't forget these other possible motives and problems.

*R. J. Monsen, J. Chin, and D. Cooley, "The Effect of Separation of Ownership and Control of the Performance of Large Firms," *Quarterly Journal of Economics,* August 1968, p. 441.

---

ciency in using resources to promote economic progress and in lowering the minimum point on firms' *ATC* curves. This is often called X-efficiency.

The general presumption of economic theory is against monopoly on this score as well. The pressure of competition is the greatest prod to progress, Adam Smith and his successors tell us. The more protected from competition any business is, the less likely it is to work hard at producing new and better products.

But there is another side to the issue. Progress in the modern economy depends heavily on research and development spending. And only big firms have the resources to afford large R&D expenditures. Thus, as a practical matter, it is mainly in oligopolistic market structures that we are likely to get the heavy R&D spending on which modern industrial progress depends.

What do the facts show? Table 14–2 details R&D spending in industry in 1976, financed by both federal and industrial funds. Of all industrial R&D expenditures, less than 5 percent was in industries dominated by small firms—for example, textiles and construction. Conversely, the great bulk of R&D is done by big firms, and by the same token in oligopolistic industries—for example, aerospace, chemicals, and electrical equipment, although much of this research is ultimately financed by government funds. Only in agriculture among the industries approaching pure competition is there large R&D spending,

TABLE 14–2
Industrial Research and Development Spending[a]

INDUSTRY	R&D SPENDING (IN BILLIONS)	FEDERAL FUNDS AS PERCENTAGE OF TOTAL
Aircraft and missiles	$ 6.1	77%
Electrical equipment	5.6	45
Machinery	3.5	15
Chemicals	3.0	9
Autos, transport equipment	2.8	12
Instruments	1.3	12
Petroleum and extraction	.8	N.A.
Rubber products	.5	10
Food products	.4	N.A.
All other[b]	2.6	N.A.
Total	$26.6	35%

[a] Estimates by National Science Foundation for 1976. This series excludes certain commercial-product-development activities sometimes included in R&D estimates.

[b] Includes mining, construction, transportation, public utilities, agriculture, and others.

and this is financed almost entirely by the government and conducted largely in the universities, not shown in Table 14–2.

The research and development picture is complex. Very large firms clearly do the bulk of research in industry, but in some industries, medium-large firms spend a larger proportion of their sales dollars on research than do the giants. And the most important question is, Whose research contributes the most to innovation and economic progress? We have few clear measures of success. Researchers have looked especially at three measures—patents received, important innovations achieved, and the rate of increase in productivity.

A few giants dominate the total number of patents awarded (Bell Labs, GE, and du Pont). However, most big firms receive patents only in proportion to their larger expenditures on research.

A more important, but more difficult, measure is the number of important innovations actually produced by different-sized companies. A growing number of studies suggest that generally, the larger the firm and the bigger its R&D effort, the more useful are its results. But, there are numerous exceptions. For example, while bigger seems clearly to be more effective in the energy field, chemicals, and aircraft development, in

steel the results of some medium-large firms appear to be larger per dollar than in some of the giants. But the evidence must be recognized as mixed. Firm conclusions lie in the future. Many major advances have originated outside the big business labs, in universities and smaller firms.

Which industries show the highest rates of growth in productivity? Broadly speaking, the oligopolies—chemicals, aerospace, and communications. Productivity has apparently grown more slowly in industries dominated by small firms—the services, construction, and textiles. Agriculture is a major counterexample, with a very high growth rate in productivity, but, as mentioned above, its research is mainly financed by the government and disseminated through state agricultural extension services.

How about the influence of entry barriers on the rate of innovation? As was indicated above, profits on invested capital tend to be higher where barriers to entry are high, which might suggest that oligopolists have been progressive in reducing costs. However, numerous well-protected oligopolists have failed to introduce major innovations until the way has been charted by others—for example, the development of jet engines outside the established aircraft-engine manufacturers. But there are numerous counterexamples.

SOME PRACTICAL ASPECTS OF BUSINESS PRICING

Businessmen frequently have inadequate information on future costs and revenues. Yet decisions have to be made, day in and day out. Many managers thus look for some reasonable rules of thumb to avoid the necessity of starting from scratch on each price problem.

Standard costing. Cost per unit of output varies at different output levels. Yet you can't quote everybody a different price and be jiggling your price up and down all the time. So a lot of businessmen ask their accountants and engineers to estimate the total cost of one unit of output at near-capacity operations. They call this estimate the "standard cost" and use it for price setting, even though actual output may vary markedly from day to day and month to month.

"Standard costing" may not be very precise, and many economists explain that it may lead the firm to less than maximum profits on some orders. But standard costing is a rule-of-thumb shortcut for getting the day's business done when there are thousands of different customers and orders. The alternative might well be utter confusion rather than a more perfect approach to profit maximization.

Cost-plus pricing. Using standard costs as a basis, many firms engage in "cost-plus," or "full-cost," or "markup" pricing. They price their product by taking their standard-cost estimate and adding on some standard markup—10, 50, or 100 percent—to provide a reasonable profit. They are likely to use this same markup to quote prices on all orders, regardless of substantial variations in the actual cost of filling the orders. This approach leads to reasonable simplicity in business operations, but it is easy to see how it may also lead to less-than-maximum profits on individual orders.

Actually, businessmen are often better economists than this would suggest. When standard-cost pricing gets them too far out of line with the results they would get through maximum-profit pricing, they often modify their standard-cost pricing. For example, in booming markets where standard-cost pricing clearly undershoots what the market will bear, larger markups are common. In depression, price cutting under "full-cost" prices is widespread. And big buyers often get price concessions on large orders.

Return on investment. Increasingly in recent years, big corporations use some "target" return on capital investment as a rough guide to pricing policy (and to capital investment in new ventures as well). General Motors, for example, shoots for 20 percent on invested capital after taxes. This, of course, doesn't give any automatic guide to setting prices, but it provides some guidelines. Thus, current pricing and plans for expansion are all wrapped up in the same general process, in which the test of effective performance is whether it meets this profit-rate standard.

Why does GM choose 20 percent as the target rate? U.S. Steel is reported to use 8 percent after taxes; Alcoa, 20 percent before taxes. Maybe each is out to maximize profits, and their target rates are merely about the peak they think they can earn. Certainly we need to know more about how the targets are set to evaluate their impact on pricing. But for better or worse, lots of big businesses use this approach as one major guide in pricing and investment planning.*

*There is a large literature on business pricing practices. For easy-to-read accounts, see A. D. H. Kaplan, J. Dirlam, and R. F. Lanzillotti, *Pricing in Big Business* (Washington, D.C.: The Brookings Institution, 1958); and G. Burck, "The Realities of Corporate Pricing," *Fortune*, April 1972.

What is the conclusion on oligopoly and economic progress? Clearly, firms of substantial size are needed in most industries to undertake substantial R&D activities, if we expect the research to be done by private firms.[7] But just how big firms should be for optimal progress remains an unsettled issue.[8]

[7]Some observers suggest introduction of government-financed research and dissemination for the business sector, to parallel the arrangements that have worked so well in the small-firm agricultural sector.

[8]For a detailed survey of the evidence, see M. Kamien and N. Schwartz, "Market Structure and Innovation: A Survey," *Journal of Economic Literature*, March 1975.

The Dynamics of Oligopoly

Many rapidly growing industries are dominated (led) by one or a few firms. Rapid growth tends to come with the introduction of new products or new methods, and understandably, the firms that innovate achieve a leadership position. Figure 14–4 shows a typical life-cycle curve for a new product. After introduction, sales grow slowly as it becomes better known on the market. Then, as it catches on, it grows rapidly, often reaching rates of 10–30 percent per year, or even higher. Profits soar, both because new products are often priced to "skim the cream" off the market and because of the rapidly rising sales volume.

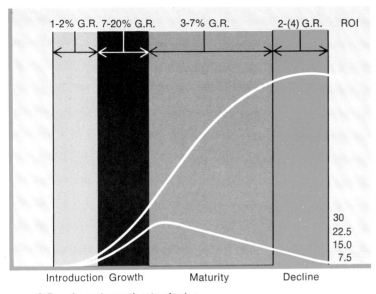

G.R. = Annual growth rate of sales
ROI = Percent return on investment, after taxes (right-hand scale)

FIGURE 14–4
Typical Produce Life-Cycle Pattern
Typically, sales of successful products grow rapidly at first, then gradually level off, and ultimately turn down. Profits peak earlier. (Source: "Economic Concentration," Hearings before the Senate Subcommittee on Antitrust and Monopoly, 1964, p. 138.)

As the product matures and other producers come into the market, the growth rate tends to slow. Profit margins for the innovating firm tend to level off. As the product reaches "maturity," the sales growth rate slows and finally turns down, as new products and new methods tend to replace this one.

Figure 14–4 is, of course, only illustrative. Many products never catch on in the market at all; others have short lives and are soon outpaced by competitive products. But the success stories usually look something like Figure 14–4, and in such cases, one or a few firms very often dominate the market.

Table 14–3 shows some of the success stories of modern times. These are firms that pioneered new product lines and then stayed ahead of competitors during the rapid growth of their industries. Each firm was dominant in its industry during this rapid-growth period.

The fact that each industry grew around one pioneering firm is not a coincidence. Competi-

tion developed only as the successes became apparent. Oligopoly thus often comes with rapid growth, but oligopolies, of course, do not guarantee rapid growth.

One last observation on the dynamics of oligopoly. Alert firms know that spectacular growth rates for individual products must end. Thus, most large firms try to diversify with many products. They try always to have a new growth product in the wings as established lines reach maturity. Otherwise, they may fade as competitors' new products make them obsolete. The most successful oligopolists are those that manage to keep a step ahead of their competition with new products.

GROWTH THROUGH MERGER

Many of the big oligopolies of today have grown through competition—by producing goods and services that large numbers of consumers are

187

TABLE 14–3
Growth Rates of Innovative Industries, 1945–75

COMPANY	PRODUCT LINE	AVERAGE ANNUAL GROWTH RATE	
		SALES	JOBS
Texas Instruments	Transistors, integrated circuits	29%	11%
Xerox	Photocopiers	28	19
IBM	Computers, office systems	18	13
3M	Tapes	15	8
Polaroid	Instant photography	15	8
Total economy		3.6 (GNP)	1.6

Source: U.S. Department of Commerce, *Technological Innovation: Its Environment and Management;* and *Fortune.*

willing to buy at profitable prices. All the rapid-growth firms in Table 14–3 fall in this category. So do the leading firms in such older industries as autos, aluminum, and flat glass. But others, especially the big new "conglomerates" (firms that produce several or many products in different industries), have grown mainly by buying up (merging with) smaller firms. The oil, whiskey, cordage, and other "trusts" of the 1800s were the predecessors in growth through accumulating smaller firms in single industries. More recently, market pressures to diversify and the antitrust laws against "horizontal" and "vertical" mergers that threaten competition have pushed firms toward conglomerate mergers. (Horizontal mergers involve acquiring competing firms in the same industry; vertical mergers involve acquiring suppliers or customers.)

The number of mergers has surged since World War II. From only four large mergers in manufacturing (firms with assets over $10 million) in 1948, the number rose to 174 with assets totaling over $12 billion in 1968; followed by a sharp decline and then another surge to about the same level in the late 1970s. Pure conglomerate mergers (no discernible relationship between the merging firms) rose from 12 percent of the total in 1960 to over 40 percent in 1977. Product- and market-extension mergers (where the products are different but related—for example, refrigerators and room air conditioners) in the 1970s were about 50 percent of the total, leaving

only about 10 percent for horizontal and vertical mergers.

Why do firms merge? One answer is, to increase their efficiency and profits, especially when they are operating with decreasing unit costs so larger market shares mean lower unit costs. Vertical mergers may also produce efficiencies, for example by guaranteeing sources of supply. Conglomerate mergers may facilitate the mobility of capital among the various products, or to spread central managerial, financial, and research services over a wider range of activities and so reduce unit costs. But critics argue that another big reason is to reduce competition and increase the dominant firm's market power. The Celler Antimerger Act of 1950 forbids all mergers where the effect "may be to substantially lessen competition or tend to create a monopoly," and the courts' application of this act has virtually eliminated the possibility of horizontal mergers except for small firms or cases where one firm is on the verge of failing. But the case against vertical and conglomerate mergers is much weaker. Strictly speaking, conglomerate mergers do not reduce competition, because they merge firms producing different (noncompeting) products. How far the courts will go in applying the Celler Act in those cases remains to be seen. Thus far, they have permitted most such mergers.

Thus, growth by merger instead of by winning the competitive race has played an important, but still relatively minor, role in the development of the big oligopolies. ITT, Litton Industries, Textron, and LTV are large conglomerates put together largely through mergers. But most of the giants, like General Motors, Exxon, GE, and IBM, have attained their dominant positions mainly through successful market performance.

THE GROWING ROLE OF INTERNATIONAL COMPETITION

The period since World War II has seen a vast growth in international competition. Except for a few products that are so heavy or bulky as to make international transportation very expensive, most major products have been increasingly exposed to competition from abroad, both in the United States and in other leading Western countries. In 1950, for example, nearly all motorcars in America were made by the big three American firms. By the 1970s, Japanese and European cars were everywhere in America, accounting for over 10 percent of annual U.S. purchases. Nearly all television tubes are imported from Japan. Many of our shoes come from Southern Europe or the developing nations. So it is for many other commodities. Thus, to look at the domestic market structure alone for

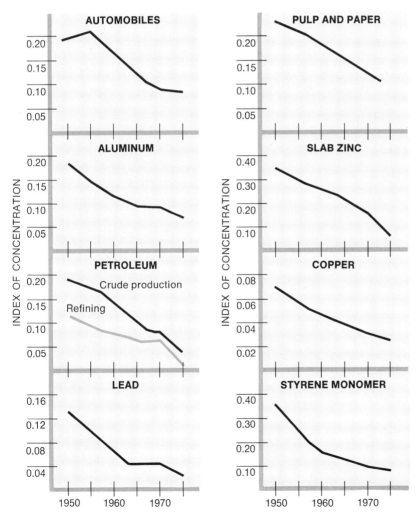

FIGURE 14–5
Decreasing Concentration in World Commodity Markets, 1950–1975
Charts show persistently decreasing indexes of concentration among leading sellers in world markets for major commodities, largely reflecting growth of international trade. Index of concentration shows how concentrated the power of leading sellers is in each market. Perfect concentration (monopoly) would give an index of 1; pure competition, and index of 0. (Source: R. Vernon, *Storm Over the Multinationals.* Cambridge, Mass.: Harvard University Press, 1977, p. 81.)

any commodity is to see only part of the picture.

Figure 14–5 shows the declining concentration of world production in the hands of a few firms for eight major commodities over the period 1950 to 1975 as international competition spread. The lower the index of concentration, the less concentrated is world production of the commodity. Although there is a wide variation among commodities, these charts provide typical examples of what is happening when domestic markets open up to producers from all over the world.

We shall postpone most discussion of international trade until Part 5. But remember the great importance of such trade in opening up markets to competition and reducing the power of monopolists and oligopolists in domestic markets.

CONCLUSION

It is a complex picture of the big oligopolies that emerges from the preceding pages. Giant corporations have great power; yet on all sides, they face actual and potential competition. They are said to restrict output and raise prices; yet most evidence suggests that growth in sales and share of market is a dominant goal of most big firms.

Some oligopolies have managed to avoid open price competition for many years without illegal collusion; cigarettes are an example, with lots of "quality" competition and advertising. But the pressures toward illegal collusion are great. A spectacular case was the heavy-electrical-equipment industry in the 1950s, where executives of GE, Westinghouse, Allis-Chalmers, and others were found guilty of elaborate price fixing and market-sharing arrangements.[9] Price leadership, go-along attitudes, and heavy demand-creation outlays appear now to be the rule of the day in most modern oligopolies—although sometimes with more price competition than many of them like. Unfortunately, oligopoly theory gives us no consistently reliable prediction of price and output behavior, even though it suggests some highly probable lines of behavior in particular cases.

Beyond the price and output issues considered here, many observers argue that the biggest objection to the giant oligopolies is their non-market power—the sheer economic and political power of billions of dollars over the lives of the people they deal with. We turn to these issues in the next chapters.

---

[9]For a vivid account, see "The Incredible Electrical Conspiracy," *Fortune*, April and May 1961.

SUMMARY AND REVIEW

1. Much of manufacturing, mining, and finance are dominated by oligopolies—cases where a few firms dominate the market. There are many local oligopolies. International competition tends to weaken domestic oligopolies.

2. Most oligopolies rest on (a) the necessity of large-scale production (relative to the size of the market) for low-cost output, and (b) barriers against entry of new firms into the industry.

3. Where not forbidden by law, oligopolies often act as cartels. In combination, they set price and output to maximize profits and divide up the market among members of the cartel. If they can exclude new entrants to the industry, special profits may continue indefinitely, and the result may be like that of a pure monopoly. If new entrants cannot be excluded, they will be attracted by the special oligopoly profits, and the market will be divided up among the increasing number of firms until unit costs rise to eliminate special monopoly profits, although price stays high. Oligopolies without restriction on entry are seldom long lasting.

4. In oligopolies, there are strong pressures against price cutting and starting price wars, but competition on quality, advertising, and the like is pervasive.

5. Since competitive pressures are limited in oligopoly, oligopolists may not reduce their costs as far as they would with more competition. However, effective research and development spending requires large firms in many cases, and many oligopolies are leaders in R&D spending and innovation in new products and methods.

6. Some large oligopolies have been built up by mergers. Recently, most mergers have been conglomerates, combining noncompeting firms.

7. International competition has developed rapidly since World War II. This reduces substantially the market power exerted by oligopolists in each country.

New Concepts
to Remember

administered prices
cartel
concentration ratio
standard costs
kinked demand curve

cost-plus pricing
price leader
price stabilization
conglomerate, horizontal,
   and vertical mergers

For Analysis
and Discussion

1. "The big oligopolies like General Motors, General Electric, and Alcoa have been primarily responsible for making better goods available to consumers. Breaking them up into smaller units to obtain more active price competition would be counterproductive." Do you agree or disagree? Support your position against a critic.

2. Is the rate of profit earned on invested capital a good indication of whether an oligopoly is abusing its position?

3. Suppose you were manager of one of the furnace firms orginally forming the cartel described in Chapter 14. What would you do to promote your own best interests as additional new firms entered the industry?

4. Consider the international coffee-producers' cartel described in Case 31 (Chapter 29). What would you predict would be the crucial factors determining how successful the cartel would be?

5. What are the main forces that determine whether there will be few or many firms in any given industry?

6. In many of the major oligopolistic industries, entry is difficult for new firms because of both the technical know-how and the large financial investment required for effective competition. Can you suggest desirable ways to overcome these difficulties?

7. Suppose that you are president of the largest firm in an industry in which the great bulk of the business is done by the largest five firms. As the industry leader, your firm ordinarily initiates any price changes in the industry.
   a. How would you go about deciding what price to charge for your product?
   b. Is there a conflict or community between your interests and those of the other four firms in the industry?
   c. Would consumers be better off, by and large, if active price competition were enforced rather than price leadership in the industry?

CASE 14 THE BATTLE OF THE SUPERMARKETS

In early 1972, there were 288,000 retail food stores in the United States, down from 313,000 five years earlier. In 1971, sales of the top four supermarket chains totaled about $17 billion, somewhat under 20 percent of total retail food sales (excluding tobacco and liquor) of about $90 billion. A total of fourteen supermarket chains reported sales of over a billion dollars each, and their combined sales of about $30 billion were about one-third of total national sales.

	SALES (IN BILLIONS)
A&P	$ 5.5
Safeway	5.4
Kroger's	3.7
Food Fair	2.1
	$16.7

Very small stores have accounted for almost all the dropouts from the industry; some have merged together.

At the national level, food retailing was thus a highly competitive industry as measured by the number of firms, but in some areas, a few big supermarkets dominate, with local oligopolies. As judged by profits as a percentage of sales, the industry is highly competitive. Average profit per dollar of sales has recently been less than 1 percent.

For half a century, the Great Atlantic and Pacific Tea Company (A&P) had been the world's largest food retailer. But late in 1971, culminating a long, rapid growth, Safeway edged past A&P in total sales. A&P, which markets largely in the eastern half of the country, had steadily slipped in market share and profitability over the preceding decade, while its chief competitors, marketing more heavily in the West and South, gained. Some of the regional chains (Albertsons, Jewel, Winn-Dixie, and Safeway itself) have done especially well, although, as the table shows, none except Safeway and Kroger's approach A&P in total size.

In 1971, the A&P management took a dramatic step. In what some competitors labeled a desperate move to regain market leadership, they converted most of their stores to a new "Where Economy Originates" (WEO) "discount-store" format. Prices were slashed by 10–20 percent on thousands of products to lure the customers back.

The results were dramatic. By 1972, A&P sales had jumped 15 percent, but profits nosedived. The company lost $41 million during the first half of 1972. Between 1968 and 1972, the price of A&P stock fell from 40 to 15. With the market leader cutting prices, smaller stores had to cut too or lose customers, and most cut. Customers smiled happily at the price cuts in the middle of inflation, but in October 1972, the *New York Times* reported:

Five of the 10 largest supermarket chains in the country are in "bad financial shape" while half a dozen food chains in the metropolitan New York area are on the brink of insolvency, Clarence Adamy, president of the National Association of Food Chains, declared yesterday. He attributed the situation to:
One of the most dramatic and widespread price competitions that we have had in the retail food field since the 1930s. . . .
Inflation, which is particularly difficult for such a tightly-competitive industry. Stores are being forced to absorb rising costs. . . .
Earnings in the supermarket industry will probably fall to less than 0.50 percent of sales by the year's end, he added, down from 0.86 percent during the summer and 1.41 percent in 1965.

As the price war spread in 1972 with more stores converting to "discount" pricing, profits turned to losses for many of the leading supermarket chains—and apparently for many small retail stores, although accurate published data are not available for such small retailers. Nearly all supermarket stocks nosedived on the security markets. Accusations and counteraccusations of unfair price cutting filled the air. Joseph Binder, president of Bohack, a large New York supermarket chain, charged "The truth of the matter is this: The Great Atlantic and Pacific Tea Co. didn't know how to run its own business, so it decided to run everybody else out of business." But A&P shrugged off the complaints. William Kane, A&P's chairman, said the charges leveled by competitors "seem a little strange in an economic system that prides itself on being based on competition."

1. Why did cutthroat competition break out in this oligopolized industry in a period of generally rising prices and inflation?
2. Did A&P management act wisely in its own self-interest in adopting its new policy?

3. If you were head of one of the competing supermarkets, would you have met the A&P price cuts?

4. If you ran a small corner grocery near a supermarket, what would you do?

5. How long would you expect this war of the supermarkets to last, and how would you expect it to end?

6. If you were a supermarket-chain head, what would you do to restore reasonable stability and profits to your firm? to the industry?

7. Are customers (at A&P and elsewhere) likely to be better or worse off as a result of A&P's policy change? In the short run? In the long run?

8. If price cutting continues, would you expect more or less investment in food retail stores in the future?

9. What, if anything, should the government do?

CASE 15 SOME MANAGERIAL APPLICATIONS[10]

Elasticity of demand and product pricing. Demand is often elastic. And when it is, a price policy that doesn't recognize this fact can mean disaster. But a price policy founded on full knowledge of demand elasticity can make life pleasant for the stockholders, and unpleasant for competitors.

The record industry is a classic case. For decades, classical records were high-priced luxury items, aimed at a small market. In 1938, Columbia broke the oligopoly price pattern, cutting the price per record (on the old shellac 78-rpm records) from $2 to $1. The response was overwhelming. Total expenditure on classical records, to the amazement of almost everyone else, rose drastically. Demand turned out to be highly elastic, and the competition was left behind. Soon other companies had to meet the cut.

About the same time, the railroads, desperate for revenue, raised their fares. The result was equally impressive. The customers switched to cars and buses, or just stayed home in droves; total revenue dropped as the railroads learned about elastic demand the hard way.

Of course, individual product demand is sometimes inelastic. But over and over again, businessmen have underestimated the gain to be had from reducing prices and expanding markets in which elastic demand prevails. Economists sometimes describe this as "elasticity pessimism." Mass markets based on low costs and low prices have been the foundation of the growing American economy.

New-product decisions—marginal cost versus average cost. Suppose you manage a filling station. You have handled only gasoline, oil, and a few miscellaneous supplies like auto polish, windshield-wiper blades, and so on. The local wholesaler approaches you to put in a line of batteries and tires. He argues that there will be very little extra expense because you're not pressed for space, and that you have a small but ready-made market in your regular customers, who don't want to go to the inconvenience of shopping around for these items.

You've had a course in economics and you know about costs. So you calculate carefully what the marginal (extra) cost of putting in these lines would be, compared to the likely increase in revenue. The answer looks good. The only marginal cost you can see is the money tied up in keeping an inventory on hand, and it looks as if you might sell $200 to $300 a month worth of tires and batteries. At a markup over wholesale that will keep the final price roughly competitive with other retailers, this should yield an extra $50 to $75 a month even after allowing for interest cost on the money tied up in inventory. On the other hand, if you allocate against the tires and batteries their proportionate share of other costs (space, your time and that of the help, taxes, electricity, and so on), the line would probably show a small loss. Should you put in the tires and batteries?

The answer clearly hinges on whether you use marginal or average costs, assuming your estimates are reasonable. Adding the line will clearly increase revenue more than cost for the enterprise as a whole, unless you've overlooked some new costs associated with the tires and batteries. Following the principles of Chapter 9, you'll increase your total profit by expanding, even though when you compare the average total

[10] For more detailed analyses of the use of economic analysis in managerial decision making, see C. J. Christenson and others, *Managerial Economics* (Homewood, Ill.: Richard D. Irwin, 1973); and D. S. Watson, *Price Theory in Action* (New York: Houghton Mifflin Company, 1973).

cost of the batteries and tires against their selling prices, they wouldn't appear to provide a profit. If it's total profit that matters to you, the comparison based on marginal cost and marginal revenue will point to the best answer.

But this is a rule to be used with care. It depends on being sure of what is truly marginal and what is not. Suppose you add the tires and they seem a great success, selling better than you'd expected and taking up more and more space and time. You have to add a new man and expand your building. Where do you allocate the cost—to the gasoline, the tires, where? You can look at any one part of your output first, and then the rest looks marginal.

Many businessmen use this kind of marginal (or incremental) analysis in adding products, but only when the addition is small relative to their total activity, and understandably so. When any product line becomes relatively large, they expect it to carry its regular share of the "overhead," or the "burden," as indirect costs of running the business are sometimes called. In principle, comparing marginal cost with marginal revenue always gives the right answer in deciding whether or not to take on a new product to expand output. The trick lies in applying the principle carefully, and being sure which costs are really marginal in both the short and long runs. Remember Continental Airlines in Case 8.

Sunk costs and operating decisions. Try another case—similar but different. You manufacture men's suits. Your costs fall roughly into two groups—variable (mainly labor and materials) and fixed (rent, management salaries, and so on). You know that for the range of output in which you usually operate, you must add about 30 percent to your variable costs to get a price that permits you to break even; you normally price by adding 40 percent to variable costs, with the prices of individual suits varying largely with differences in cloth and the amount of hand labor.

This season, demand has been slow and you are operating well under your normal rate. It has been a bad year, and you probably will not even break even. You have a chance to make 1,000 suits on a special order from a wholesaler who is not a regular customer. However, he will only pay a price that would cover variable costs plus 20 percent. Should you take the order?

Your fixed costs are "sunk." That is, they go on and must be paid, at least for the short run, whether you operate or not. Because they are sunk, economic analysis says they should have no effect on your decision to accept or reject the order. By taking the order, you will cover all your variable costs and will have the 20 percent addition to apply on your fixed costs. You may not make a profit on your total operations, but your loss will be smaller than without the order, as was explained in Chapter 9.

The logic is right. But many businessmen would think a long time before taking the order. They worry about the long run, and properly so. Suppose you cut the price on this order and your regular customers hear about it. Might this break your whole price line, with dire results for profits over the longer run? Or might it lead your competitors to cut their prices? If the answer is yes, looking only at the particular gain from taking this order would be wearing blinders to the long-run result. *In the short run,* you may minimize losses by taking orders at less than total cost, but both economic analysis and managerial common sense say that *in the long run,* your price has to cover all costs or you'll end up in bankruptcy.

The nature of costs: depreciation. You operate a fleet of taxicabs. With the hard use the cabs receive, you estimate that after three years they will have depreciated to the point where it is no longer economical to operate them. At that time, you anticipate, you will be able to sell or trade them for about 10 percent of the original cost of $3,000 each. Thus, you account as a cost an annual depreciation charge of 30 percent ($900) per cab, in addition to regular operating and maintenance costs.

At the end of three years, you have fully depreciated the cabs, except for the small turn-in value. Yet they seem to be still in reasonably good condition. Should you turn them in on new cabs, using the accumulated depreciation reserve to finance the new cabs, or continue to use the old ones?

The forward-looking nature of economics, and the principle above that "sunk costs are sunk," suggest the answer. The fact that you estimated a three-year life and have now accumulated a 90 percent depreciation reserve does not give you an answer to when you should replace these particular cabs. Don't be overimpressed by the bookkeeping. The optimal choice depends on analyzing the cost and performance of new cabs against the cost and performance of continued use of the old cabs. If the total profit by continuing to use the old cabs exceeds the profit with new cabs,[11] then keep the old ones. If not, buy new ones. The crucial point is the importance of the forward-looking decision, not the fact that three years is the end of your estimated depreciation period. If you made a mistake in estimating the cabs' useful life, it may pay you to replace long before the cabs are fully depreciated or to wait until long after. Depreciation charges represent only an estimate of the proper cost to be currently charged for the use of durable assets, not a determinant of when assets should be replaced.[12]

---

[11] Remembering possible consumer preferences for new models and all such relevant considerations, and recognizing that the money can temporarily be used another way if it is not used to buy new cabs.

[12] For a precise analysis of how to decide the best time to replace durable plant and equipment, a more advanced text is needed. See, for example, E. L. Grant and W. Ireson, *Principles of Engineering Economy* (New York: Ronald Press, 1970), Part II.

POLICY

Big Business, Antitrust, and Workable Competition

CHAPTER 15

Business plays a central role in converting our resources into the goods and services consumers want and in providing the jobs by which we earn our livings. And historically, America has provided a friendly environment for business. We have admired initiative and success in economic life, and have widely supported rewards for those who win the economic races.

But business, especially big business, has also long been a favorite target of critics of American capitalism. Early "Populists" pressed for legislation to control the "trusts." More recently, "radical" critics (especially the "New Left" and Marxists) blame just about everything on big corporations and corporate executives—high prices, pollution, concentration of economic and political power, poor products, manipulation of consumers, racism, sexism, international imperialism. Many others see much virtue in the American economic system, but still raise serious questions about big business's power and support more extensive government regulation. Still others argue that individual self-interest and the profit motive are the most powerful incentives of all—the driving forces that have made the American standard of living one of the highest in the world—and that more regulation and government controls risk killing the goose that lays the golden eggs.

Communism or a massive government takeover of the businesses that now produce our goods and services seems very unlikely in America. But continuing criticism and government regulation of businesses are very likely indeed. Chapter 10 summarized both the case for private enterprise and the probable "market failures," or problem areas, that may be faced in a market-directed economy—and each "market failure" has led to widespread demands for government action to correct it. The next three chapters explore the three big problems in making competitive markets work effectively: how to assure workable competition, especially where large firms are required to obtain the economies of large-scale production (Chapter 15); problems of imperfect buyer information, demand manipulations, and consumer protection (Chapter 16); and what to do where social costs exceed private costs because of externalities, as with pollution (Chapter 17). The other two probable big shortcomings of a competitive system noted in Chapter 10 (failure to produce desired "public goods," and undesirable inequality of incomes) are considered in Part 4, which focuses on the government's own direct economic activities in the "public sector."

MONOPOLY, BIGNESS, AND PUBLIC OPINION

Why should government intervene at all in business affairs? Adam Smith suggested one answer: because self-seeking will be channeled to the common good only if *competition* prevails. Seldom do merchants gather together, he wrote, that their talk does not turn to means of obtaining higher prices for their products. It is the job of government, representing all the people, to see to it that competition prevails.

Everyone agrees, moreover, that in an individualistic society there have to be some rules of fair play in economic life, just as in personal behavior. Without common consent to eliminate fraud, to respect property ownership, and to honor legal contracts, economic dealings would be carried on under a great handicap. By general agreement, it is the job of the government to establish and enforce these basic rules to enable men to work effectively together. Among Adam Smith's nineteenth-century followers, "laissez faire" never meant that the government should do nothing, but rather that it should leave economic affairs alone *within* a framework of basic moral and governmental rules of the game.

But economic theory gives no clear answer as to just how much competition is optimal—just how the public interest is best served where the economies of large-scale production require bigger firms than are consistent with Adam Smith's pure competition. This poses difficult problems for modern antitrust, aimed at assuring "workable," although not "pure," competition.

Second, many Americans are concerned about the sheer power of bigness that goes with the billions of dollars of assets and sales of the giant corporations. The issue of monopoly power shades into the problems of bigness and corporate power per se. Consider the following comparison between General Electric and an isolated country grocery.

In 1978, the General Electric Company had assets of $7 billion, and reported profits after taxes of $570 million on sales of $15 billion. It had about 400,000 employees. Although no exact figures are available, GE apparently accounted for about half the total sales in the country of heavy electrical machinery, light bulbs, and other major categories of electrical equipment. It was rivaled only by Westinghouse, another giant about one-third the size of GE. Allis-Chalmers in heavy equipment and Sylvania in bulbs and lighter equipment absorbed another sizable chunk of the market, but they were far short of the two leaders in overall size and market power. GE did business all around the world. Does GE have too much monopoly power? Should it be broken up into several smaller concerns in the public interest?

Now consider Jones's Grocery Store, at the crossroads corner of an isolated village in northern Minnesota—population 150. Jones's total sales in 1978 were about $30,000, on which he realized a return after paying all costs (except his own salary) of about $7,000, as near as he could figure it. Jones had one employee—himself. His service was so-so. There is no other grocery store within 35 miles. Is Jones's Grocery Store a monopoly? Should it be broken up into several smaller concerns in the public interest?

No reasonable person would answer that Jones's store ought to be broken up to provide more competition in the village. The market can't support one respectable grocery, let alone two or three. Yet Jones's monopoly power over the customers in that village may far exceed GE's power over its customers. If Jones takes advantage of Widow Smith down the street and slips a bad potato into every peck, she's pretty much out of luck. Let GE treat one of its customers that way, and Westinghouse will get a phone call the next day from the outraged purchasing agent.

How about GE? If you think it should be broken up or subjected to more government control, why? Because GE clearly has a dominant position in its major products, with around half

the market for many of them? Or just because GE seems too big—because you feel that no one business ought to control so much wealth, with the far-reaching economic and political power that goes with it?

Analytically, it is important to distinguish between these two reasons, even though they are closely intertwined. The degree of monopoly power depends largely on the size of the seller *relative to* the market in which he sells. Broader economic and political power depends more on *absolute size,* which bears no necessary relationship to the degree of monopoly the firm possesses. Jones's Grocery has a pretty effective monopoly in its market, according to the economist's definition, but it's a tiny concern. GE clearly holds some monopoly powers too—it's an oligopolist. But the striking difference is GE's absolute size. Its managers exert economic power—the power of $20 billion—over the lives of 400,000 workers, over the communities in which they live, over millions of consumers. And, some would add, political power over what happens in Washington and in state capitals.

This difference between absolute and relative size is illustrated vividly by the oil industry. Six of the ten largest industrial corporations in the United States are oil companies—Exxon, Mobil, Texaco, and so on—and together they had assets of nearly $175 billion in 1978, some ten times those of GE. Yet no one of them had more than 8 percent of the domestic gasoline market, and together they accounted for only 39 percent of total sales.

IS ECONOMIC CONCENTRATION GROWING?

Is economic concentration growing? The answer is mixed, and it's possible to cite figures that seem to prove the answer either way. Ask the question three ways.

Are the big firms getting bigger? The answer to this is yes. General Motors employs more people than live in San Francisco or Boston. Both GM and Exxon, the world's two largest industrial firms, have sales of over $50 billion annually, more than the gross national product of over 100 nations. The combined sales of the top

TABLE 15–1
Concentration in Manufacturing

	SHARE OF TOTAL ASSETS IN:	
	1948	1977
Largest 5 firms	10%	14%
Largest 20 firms	21	32
Largest 100 firms	39	59
Largest 200 firms	48	76

Sources: Federal Trade Commission and *Fortune.*

500 industrial companies exceed $1.2 trillion, more than twice those of five years ago and triple those of 1970. But everything is getting bigger fast in the modern world, especially with inflation, and we need to ask another quesiton.

Do the giant firms have a bigger share of the assets and sales of the total economy? Again the answer is yes, at least in manufacturing, where we have the most complete, accurate data. Table 28–1 provides the data. There is no doubt that economic concentration is growing in manufacturing. If we use sales instead of assets, the picture is similar.[1]

However, even in manufacturing, the picture is complicated. The profit share of the giants has fallen relative to the rest of the top 100, even though the 100 have increased their share of total manufacturing profits. Similarly, the top five have fallen relative to the rest of the top 20 and 100, in both profits and sales. And the makeup of the top 20 or 100 has changed considerably over the years. The top is a slippery pinnacle. Table 15–2 shows the largest ten industrial firms in 1909, and what happened to them by 1978. Only one was still in the top ten, and eight had vanished from the list of the largest 100. General Motors, Ford, and IBM, three of the top five now, didn't even exist in 1909.

If we look at the whole economy, not just manufacturing, there is much less evidence of

[1]Concentration statistics are tricky, and it is possible to convey significantly different pictures by changing the groupings of products and measures used (assets, sales, value added, and so on). When reading such statistics, it is generally wise to probe for possible biases of the writer.

increasing market concentration. In the rapidly growing services area, markets are widely divided among large and small sellers. Construction continues to be dominated by relatively small firms. There are still millions of farmers, even though the market share of big commercial farms has been rising steadily. But the biggest development has been the explosive growth of the government (see Part 4) and nonprofit sectors especially in the service areas—hospitals and medical insurance, private education, research institutes, and the like. The share of the national income produced by profit-seeking corporations apparently reached a peak of 55 percent in the mid-1950s. By the 1970s, it was back down to 53 percent, its level of twenty years earlier. The problem of growing economic concentration, if we eliminate the already highly regulated public utilities, appears to be centered in the manufacturing sector, if it exists anywhere.

Is monopoly growing? Big corporations in manufacturing are growing, both absolutely and relative to total manufacturing, but it is far from clear that monopoly and oligopoly market power over individual products are growing in the same sector. After all, most of the giants now produce many products, not just one, and much of their

TABLE 15–2
Ten Largest Industrial Firms, 1909–1978

RANK		
1909	1978	
1	13	U.S. Steel Corporation
2	1	Standard Oil Co. (New Jersey) (now Exxon)
3	a	American Tobacco Co.
4	a	International Mercantile Marine Company
5	a	Anaconda Co.
6	33	International Harvester Co.
7	a	Central Leather Company
8	a	Pullman Inc.
9	a	Armour & Co.
10	a	American Sugar Refining Co.

a No longer in top 100 firms.

Source: A. D. H. Kaplan, *Big Enterprise in a Competitive System* (Washington, D.C.: The Brookings Institution, 1964), and *Fortune.* Rankings based on total assets.

growth has come through diversification and production of new products. Thus the firm-concentration figures don't necessarily tell us the degree of monopoly exercised by that firm in the different industries in which it competes. GM, for example, has over half the automobile market, but it is far behind GE in home appliances, which it also produces. Exxon is the leading petroleum company but lags far behind several of the chemical firms in chemical sales, which also make up a substantial part of its business. The big conglomerates, like ITT and Litton Industries, operate in dozens of different industries, in some of which they play only a minor role.

Further, as Figure 14–5 showed, international competition, which has been growing rapidly in the last two decades, has substantially eroded the market power exercised in domestic markets by American firms. Volkswagen, Toyota, Datsun, and Mercedes have assumed leading roles in America. Most TV tubes are made in Japan. American steelmakers complain bitterly of competition from both Europe and Japan. In 1977–78, merchandise imports exceeded $150 billion annually, about 7–8 percent of our GNP. Domestic-firm concentration ratios substantially overstate the effective concentration of market power in many industries.

All things considered, most of the experts conclude that the degree of monopoly market power has been roughly stable in the United States over the last decade or two. But the evidence is ambiguous and the facts differ from industry to industry.

THE WELFARE COSTS OF MONOPOLY

Leaving aside the broader issue of corporate power because of absolute size, what is the cost to the public of the inefficiencies induced by monopolies? How much could we hope to gain by reducing the amount of monopoly in the system? Unfortunately, there are no precise estimates of these costs, but some approximations have been attempted. They suggest that the costs arising purely from misallocation of resources (allocative inefficiency) are probably quite small, not more

than a few billion dollars. But the costs arising from internal technological and bureaucratic inefficiency (X-inefficiency), because monopolists aren't forced to reduce costs as much as under competition, may be much larger.

Many economists are skeptical of the small estimates of allocative inefficiency, but the possible gain from competition on this score is the difference between the productivity of the resources employed in two different businesses producing what consumers want. By contrast, X-inefficiency has no such obvious limits; more competitive pressure might force partial monopolists to lower costs substantially (to operate more efficiently) and thereby reduce unit costs and prices substantially.

More reliable estimates of the welfare costs of monopoly would provide a better basis for judging how hard we ought to try to reduce monopoly. Most estimates of allocative inefficiency find that these costs are probably largely concentrated in mining and manufacturing industries—metal mining and fabricating, petroleum extraction and refining, plastics, drugs, tobacco manufacturing, office machinery, photographic equipment, and, perhaps most important, autos. This suggests focus of antitrust activities on these areas. But as to the potentially more important savings in technological efficiency, we have few systematic comparisons but many studies of particular firms and industries. As we shall see, application of antitrust laws has not been guided primarily by such estimates of the probable relative efficiency gains in different industries.[2]

THE LAW, COMPETITION, AND MONOPOLY

The law is what is written down in the statute books, and more. It is what the courts say it is, what the long rows of past court decisions suggest, altered as the judge thinks proper in any particular case. It is what the Justice Department

---

[2]On the probable size and locations of allocative inefficiency, see J. Siegfried and T. Tiemann, "The Welfare Cost of Monopoly," *Economic Inquiry,* June 1974; for a broader review, see H. Liebenstein, "Allocative Efficiency versus X-Efficiency," *American Economic Review,* June 1966.

thinks it is; most law is enforced without ever coming near a courtroom. It is what the president and his advisors think it is, through the way they instruct the government's law-enforcement branches. Above all, it is what the people will obey and support. In our democratic system, no law that does not command widespread public support can long be enforced. Sometimes the law is changed when it loses support, but equally often, its enforcement varies to mirror the times.

This description is especially accurate in the field of government–business relations. Here, much of the law is in the mass of court decisions and in the policies of the government's administrative agencies. Both reflect (with lags) what the public wants—often more accurately than we realize. Our antitrust laws seldom change by formal congressional action. But in fact, they alter constantly—with changing congressional appropriations for enforcement, changing personnel in the antitrust agencies, and changing judicial attitudes.

The Common Law

Until 1890, there was no federal legislation that declared monopoly illegal. Nor did the states have any antimonopoly laws of consequence. Under the common (unwritten) law inherited from England, contracts to restrain trade unreasonably or to raise prices were unenforceable. But the common law did not hold monopoly practices to be criminal, nor did it even provide for damages to those harmed by the restraint of trade. The contracts were merely unenforceable. Thus, the common law provided little protection to the consumer or to the little competitor who was squeezed out by combinations in restraint of trade.

Legislation

The last half of the nineteenth century saw the development of the great trusts. Standard Oil, American Sugar, American Tobacco, and dozens of others amassed huge empires that held almost complete monopolies over the products concerned. Standard Oil at its peak controlled over 90 percent of the country's oil-refining capacity,

and the bulk of the pipelines. American Sugar controlled 98 percent of the country's sugar-refining capacity. American Tobacco had virtually complete control of tobacco manufacturing.

Moreover, the means used to build up these monopolies aroused widespread ire and fear. Standard Oil, for example, is said (although historians differ) to have driven small competitors to the wall by cutthroat competition, bought them up cheap, and then raised prices. Competitors who resisted found themselves up against ruthless force.

The Sherman and Interstate Commerce Commission Acts. With half a hundred trust giants on the American scene, popular resentment was reflected in two major acts—the Interstate Commerce Commission Act (1887) and the Sherman Antitrust Act (1890)—which established the pattern of U.S. regulation of monopoly for the century to come. The I.C.C. Act established federal control over railroad rates and services for the first time, making them a public utility, since effective competition was unfeasible. The Sherman Antitrust Act was aimed at preventing monopoly and enforcing competition in the great bulk of the economy, where effective competition seemed feasible.

The Sherman Act outlawed restraints of trade and attempts to monopolize, as follows:

Section 1. Every contract, combination in the form of a trust or otherwise, or conspiracy, in restraint of trade or commerce among the several states, or with foreign nations, is hereby declared to be illegal. . . .

Section 2. Every person who shall monopolize, or attempt to monopolize, or combine or conspire with any other person or persons to monopolize any part of the trade or commerce among the several states, or with foreign nations, shall be deemed guilty. . . .

This was broad and sweeping language. Inevitably, a wide range of questions arose over the years as to just what was actually outlawed. As with all such legislation, such questions have been answered primarily through a long series of court rulings interpreting the law. No legislation regulating the complex modern economy can hope to specify in detail every case and situation that is to be covered.

The Clayton and Federal Trade Commission Acts. In 1914, two new acts were passed—the Clayton Act and the Federal Trade Commission Act—to clarify the Sherman Act by specifically prohibiting certain practices, and by setting up new enforcement procedures.

The Clayton Act listed specifically as illegal (1) discriminatory price cutting; (2) tying contracts, which require buyers to purchase other items as a condition of getting the item they want; (3) acquisition of stock in competing companies to obtain monopoly powers; and (4) interlocking directorates in competing corporations. But each of these was prohibited only "where the effect may be to substantially lessen competition or tend to create a monopoly. . . ."

The Federal Trade Commission Act created a commission to act as a watchdog against unfair competitive practices aimed at creating monopoly or injuring competitors—for example, through predatory pricing or misleading advertising. The commission was given power to hold hearings and to issue "cease and desist" orders that require offending firms to discontinue illegal practices.

New Deal legislation of the 1930s. During the Great Depression of the 1930s, the New Deal was mainly concerned with recovery, greater economic security, and helping the little fellow. It sought to halt falling prices and cutthroat competition. The Agricultural Adjustment Administration (AAA) was designed to raise farm prices and incomes by government-sponsored cartel-like agreements to restrict production. The Bituminous Coal Act did the same thing for soft coal. In labor markets, the Wagner Act threw the full force of the government behind workers' right to unionize and bargain collectively.

This desire to help the small competitor and avoid "destructive" competition was reflected in two other new pieces of legislation. The Robinson-Patman Act of 1936 strengthened the prohibition against price discrimination that might help such large buyers as chain stores to undersell small retailers. In 1937, the Miller-Tydings Act guaranteed protection from Sherman Act prosecution to manufacturers and retailers who participated in "fair-trading" arrangements, whereby the manufacturer specifies that no retailer may sell his product below a specified price. Too much competition was feared more than too little.

The Celler Antimerger Act of 1950. After World War II, many corporations found that acquiring other companies outright was a profitable way to expand. Such extension of market power through merger was not limited by earlier antitrust legislation. To close this loophole, in 1950 the Celler Antimerger Act was passed forbidding the acquisition of, or merger with, other companies where the effect "may be substantially to lessen competition, or tend to create a monopoly."

The Law in Operation

Antitrust law is what its administrators and the courts make it. And they, by and large, make it what the public wants, albeit often very roughly and with a considerable lag. The first big enforcement campaign under the Sherman Act was President Theodore Roosevelt's, conducted with a total staff of seven lawyers and four stenographers. With this tiny staff, but with the big stick of aroused public opinion, the government tackled the biggest trusts. In 1911, the Supreme Court required both Standard Oil and American Tobacco to divest themselves of a large share of their holdings and to desist from numerous specific unfair competitive practices. But there, too, for the first time, the Court enunciated the now-famous "rule of reason." Only trusts that "unreasonably" restrained trade were illegal. In a series of earlier cases, the Court had given a broad interpretation to the interstate-commerce clause, permitting federal regulation to apply to all firms that had any direct dealing across state lines or (later) in products or materials crossing state lines; this interpretation brought most big businesses within the purview of federal antitrust legislation.

By 1920, the attitude toward big business had altered, with the checking of the flagrant abuses of the 1800s. In the *U.S. Steel* case of 1920, the Supreme Court refused to dissolve the company. It held that neither mere bigness nor unexerted monopoly power was illegal as such; that actual unreasonable restraint of trade must be proved under the Sherman Act. The tenor of the 1920s was one of prosperity and "leave well enough alone." The total budget allocated the Antitrust Division averaged only $250,000 annually for the decade. Big business was popular.

With the strong antibusiness sweep of the New Deal, the last major change in the application and interpretation of the antitrust laws began in the late 1930s. Under Thurman Arnold, Antitrust began an aggressive drive in the late 1930s against several of the industrial giants. Its budget was upped to $1 million (to police the entire economy). Succeeding administrations have continued active prosecution under antitrust legislation. Appropriations to both the Federal Trade Commission and the Antitrust Division of the Department of Justice have been greatly increased. The Antimerger Act has become a powerful barrier to business growth through acquisition of competitors. The government does not win all the antitrust cases it initiates, but under the Warren Court it won most of them. The new, more conservative Burger Court appears to be less certain to support antitrust action.

Not all economists, understanding the theoretical presumption against monopoly, agree that antitrust always serves the public interest. Some economists, for example, argue that the courts' strong interpretation of the Antimerger Act can give topsy-turvy results. To prevent mergers among relatively small firms may hinder useful, cost-saving combinations and protect small, inefficient competitors more than it protects consumers. In the 1966 *Von's Groceries* case, the court forbade a merger between two Los Angeles grocery chains that together held less than 8 percent of the Los Angeles market. (See Case 16, at the end of this chapter.)

Where does antitrust law stand now, as a practical matter? First, all price-fixing agreements are illegal per se. Second, oligopolies in which a few firms dominate the market are probably legal as long as no leading firm tries to expand its market share by merger or by aggressive competition that endangers small firms.[3]

Third, growth through merger in the same industry is virtually forbidden, except among small or failing firms—although growth without merger is generally permissible. The IBM case now in the courts raises this issue squarely, as to how big a market share can be won by legal means. How far the law prohibits conglomerate mergers remains to be determined by the courts. Fourth, many specific practices (price discrimination, tying clauses in contracts, misleading advertising, and the like) are illegal when they may tend to create a monopoly or substantially reduce competition. Fifth, a growing number of consumer-protection laws have been passed recently, regulating sellers' behavior; these, which are not primarily antimonopoly acts, are considered in Chapter 16. But the Miller-Tydings "Fair Trade" Act was repealed in 1975.

Why has antitrust again become a potent force since the 1930s? First, the budget given the Antitrust Division by Congress is now about $20 million, larger than ever before; Antitrust now has some 300 lawyers to police the economy. Looked at another way, however, this is still a tiny sum compared with the vast resources of the billion-dollar corporations it has to police. The budget reflects America's ambivalent attitude toward antitrust. We want the advantages of big business, but we also want to be sure that big business doesn't abuse its powers.

One last point on the law in action: The main impact of the antitrust law is preventive, not punitive. Since 1890, only about 1,600 suits have been brought under the Sherman Act. Of these, the government has won about three-fourths, with a large proportion settled out of court through "consent decrees." Total fines paid by defendants over the eight decades were only $40 million dollars—very little compared to the billions of dollars of assets in the companies concerned. But a company convicted of antitrust violation is also liable for triple damages if customers or competitors can show they were injured by the illegal acts. GE and Westinghouse were sued for hundreds of millions of dollars by customers after they were found guilty of price fixing in 1961. And suits charging antitrust violations can be brought by customers or competitors, as well as by the government. Moreover, no business likes to be called criminal. It does not like to have its affairs dragged into open court even though it thinks it may win out in the end.

---

[3] J. K. Galbraith has argued vigorously that the effect of present antitrust is to let the big, established oligopolies go untouched while applying the Antimerger Act to smaller firms trying to grow through mergers.

"It so happens, Gregory, that your Grandfather Sloan was detained by an agency of our government over an honest misunderstanding concerning certain antitrust matters! He was not 'busted by the Feds'!" (Drawing by W. Miller; © 1971. The New Yorker Magazine, Inc.

WHERE TO FROM HERE FOR ANTITRUST?

Nobody thinks the modern American economy can look like the economist's perfectly competitive model. It never has, even back in the pre–Civil War days, and it certainly doesn't now. We're in for a mixed economy of some sort. How shall we ensure that business performance is efficient and in the public interest?

Antitrust and Economic Efficiency

Would stronger antitrust action really produce a more "efficient" economy, in the sense of giving consumers the largest possible amount of what they want at the lowest feasible prices? The presence of more firms creates a general presumption of more active competition. But no magic number of firms is needed to ensure effective competition. Sometimes (for example, in the auto industry) there is aggressive competition with only three or four big firms. But most observers agree that the presence of more firms generally increases the likelihood of strong price and quality competition.

If more firms are generally good for competition, we need to face the issue of whether this is consistent with having firms big enough to take advantage of modern technology. It is important to remember that most technological economies of scale come at the plant level, so no more production efficiency is gained by combining similar-sized plants in one firm. Some critics argue that U.S. Steel, for example, is little more than a number of Inland Steels put together in one firm, although Inland is big enough to be technologically efficient. But bigger firms may yield marketing, financial, and managerial efficiencies. Nothing but a detailed analysis of each industry is likely to provide clear answers on such issues.

Professor Frederick Scherer has estimated the size of plant and firm needed to obtain the full economies of large-scale production, relative to the size of the U.S. market, for a sample of companies. Table 15–3 gives the results. These estimates should be taken as very rough at best. But it is clear that in some industries (such as autos, cigarettes, and oil refining), the cost of an efficient plant is so high that there is little point in pretending the competition can be readily open to new producers. This means that relying on competition to regulate output and prices in these industries is risky, but that government action to break up the oligopolies would also risk insisting on inefficiently small firms.

Professors George Stigler and Thomas Saving suggest that the market will settle the issue for us if we just let firms battle it out.[4] They postulate that, by and large, the most efficient sizes of plant and firm will win out in the competitive race. During the postwar period, medium-large plants survived most effectively in most industries. This test therefore suggests that in many industries, plants small enough to permit effective competition can produce efficiently. But in some industries—for example, computers—the biggest firm is clearly the most efficient by this test.

Many economists are critical of antitrust actions that tend to protect small competitors, not competition. From the economist's and the consumer's point of view, it's not clear why price cutting isn't just what competition is supposed to produce, as long as it isn't used as a device for driving out competitors by temporarily selling below cost just to gain a monopoly position.

---

[4]See, for example, T. R. Saving, "Estimation of Optimum Size of Plant by the Survivor Technique," *Quarterly Journal of Economics,* November 1961.

TABLE 15–3
Estimates of Scale Economies in U.S. Manufacturing Industries

INDUSTRY	OUTPUT OF ONE EFFICIENT PLANT AS PERCENTAGE OF NATIONAL MARKET	NUMBER OF EFFICIENT PLANTS NEEDED FOR EFFICIENT MULTIPLANT FIRM	SHARE OF U.S. MARKET NEEDED FOR EFFICIENT FIRM
Beer brewing	3.4%	3–4	10–14%
Cigarettes	6.6	1–2	6–12
Paints	1.4	1	1.4
Petroleum products	1.9	2–3	4–6
Shoes	0.2	3–6	1
Glass bottles	1.5	3–4	4–6
Cement	1.7	1	2
Steel mill products	2.6	1	3
Ball and roller bearings	1.4	3–5	4–7
Refrigerators	14.1	4–8	14–20[a]
Automobile batteries	1.9	1	2

[a] If refrigerators are manufactured along with other appliances; for an efficient firm specialized in refrigerators, the national market share would be higher, as the first column shows.

Source: F. M. Scherer et al., *The Economics of Multi-Plant Operation: An International Comparisons Study* (Cambridge, Mass.: Harvard University Press, 1975).

Antitrust and Economic Progress

The other big question about monopoly and partial monopoly is what they do to the rate of economic progress—whether they contribute to or impede a dynamically growing economy. The issues and some of the facts were presented in the concluding sections of Chapter 14. Broadly speaking, those industries with the highest growth rates tend to be oligopolies—big firms with large R&D expenditures. Most research and development spending is done by large firms. Productivity has grown more slowly in industries dominated by small firms (except agriculture, with its government financing and distribution of research). But the picture is far from uniform; there are numerous exceptions, and industries protected against entry by new competitors clearly have the power to suppress innovations that might otherwise have been forced by competition.

What is the implication for antitrust? Not clear. It seems certain that we can generally not expect much R&D spending from small firms in industries that approach perfect competition, however aggressively they may compete for the consumer's favor. If we want R&D in such industries, the pattern of government financing and dissemination of results in agriculture may be the best way. But remember that firms short of giant size can spend heavily on research and obtain results that compete with the giants' in many industries. Even on the score of economic progress, few industries require such large firms for efficient R&D that they cannot support numerous sellers and substantial price competition.

The Dilemma of Modern Antitrust Policy

The dilemma of antitrust policy in the modern economy is a painful one. How can we have both the efficiencies of size and the benefits of active competition among many sellers? Two contrasting alternatives have been suggested.

The Federal Trade Commission recently brought suit against the four major breakfast cereal producers (General Mills, General Foods, Kellogg, and Quaker Oats), which have 91 percent of the ready-to-eat cereals market, on grounds that they constitute a "shared monopoly" in violation of the antitrust laws. Although the FTC admits there is no evidence of collusion to fix prices or allocate markets, it charges that the four firms act *as if* they were colluding by not competing actively on prices (just as oligopoly theory from Chapter 14 suggests they would do). The FTC proposes to require more active price competition and to break off parts of the companies into new competitive units. The FTC has brought a similar suit against major oil companies, and would be ready to expand the charges to many other oligopolistic industries if it wins the cereals case when it is eventually appealed to the Supreme Court, as it probably will be.

By contrast, *Fortune* magazine has urged a major revolution in our antitrust laws and philosophy, as follows:

Congress should amend the antitrust statutes to make it clear that the national policy is to foster competition by punishing restraint of trade, including conspiracies to fix prices, limit production, allocate markets, and suppress innovation; but that it is not the national policy to prefer any particular size, shape, or number of firms to any other size, shape, or number; and that mergers—horizontal, vertical, or conglomerate—are entirely legal unless they spring from a manifest attempt to restrain trade.[5]

Should either the FTC's or *Fortune*'s proposal be made a key part of national antitrust policy?

BIGNESS AND CORPORATE POWER

Beyond monopoly, do we face a major national problem because of the sheer power of corporate bigness? Should we break up the giant corporations or regulate them more just because they're too big, whether or not they violate the Sherman Act? This is the most basic question of all for some people. Political power, economic power, power over other people's lives, just the power that goes with a billion dollars—these are the things that worry many people about big business. And it is power without accountability, they say, since most corporate managements have virtually unchallenged power to make corporate

decisions (remember Chapter 5 on insider management).

A. A. Berle, a long-time observer of the business corporation, pointed up this problem. Only 500 corporations control nearly two-thirds of the entire manufacturing sector of the American economy, he wrote, and within each of those 500, a relatively small group holds the ultimate decision-making power. "Since the United States carries on not quite half of the manufacturing production of the entire world today, these 500 groupings—each with its own little dominating pyramid within—represents a concentration of power over economies which makes the medieval feudal system look like a Sunday School party. In sheer economic power, this has gone far beyond anything we have yet seen."[6]

Corporate Power—For Good or Ill?

Gallup, Harris, and the other pollsters have repeatedly asked the public what they think of big business, how much confidence they have in it, how good a job they think it does. The results have been surprisingly consistent over the years. The American public believes in the private-enterprise system. It feels that big business has played a major role in producing the goods and services that support our high standard of living and in providing good jobs at high pay. But people equally consistently report that they don't trust big business—it has too much power and is "too ready to put profits ahead of serving the public interest and of helping to solve the nation's big problems." The public wants somebody to check up on big business and to regulate its use of that power, and that somebody is usually the government.

Some 80 to 90 percent of the public consistently believe that big business should put more emphasis on helping to solve the problems of pollution, rebuilding the cities, eliminating discrimination, wiping out poverty, and the like, instead of just seeking profits. Most believe that monopoly is still a major problem and that businesses charge too high prices. The American public thus seems to have a kind of love–hate

---

[5]Max Ways, "Antitrust in an Era of Radical Change," *Fortune*, March 1966.

[6]A. A. Berle, *Economic Power and the Free Society* (New York: Fund for the Republic, 1958), p. 14.

affair with big business. Clearly, it is not convinced that business will serve the public best by trying to maximize its profits. If the "man in the street" has read Adam Smith, the message hasn't registered very firmly, and it's no wonder he has a mixed assessment of big businesscs' achievements when his goals are significantly different from the managers' and investors'. And it's no wonder the public clamors for more regulation of big businesses that seem to use their economic power to achieve the wrong goals.

Is Big Business Socially Responsible?

How much, if any, of its resources should the corporation devote to helping solve the big social problems of society? Milton Friedman, perhaps the outstanding spokesman for Adam Smith, private-enterprise economics today, has a direct answer: none, unless it contributes to earning more profit in the long run. "The manager's first and only social responsibility is to maximize profits," he says. Corporate managers have no expertise or society-bestowed mantle to make them proper judges of what is good for the general public. If they devote the firm's wealth and energy to being "socially responsible," they will probably do a worse job of meeting consumer demand to maximize profits, their proper social function.

But most others say this goes too far. Business, like any other citizen, must be a good citizen and help solve society's problems. Singleminded focus on maximizing profits will not only undercut our chances of achieving a better society but also will turn the public against big business as selfish and uninterested in the public welfare. NYU's Irving Kristol has written in a much-quoted piece, "The Corporation and the Dinosaur": "Every day, in every way, the large corporation looks more and more like a species of dinosaur on its lumbering way to extinction,"[7] because managers fail to see that the big corporations must meet the public's goals if they are to avoid being regulated to extinction or taken over by government. Ralph Nader has been even more critical.[8]

[7] *Wall Street Journal,* February 14, 1974.

[8] *Taming the Giant Corporation* (New York: Norton, 1976). For a policy statement by the heads of 200 of the largest corporations, see Committee for Economic Development, *Social Responsibilities of Business Corporations,* June 1971.

Today, it is a rare member of *Fortune*'s annual list of 500 largest corporations that does not at least pay lip service to social responsibility. For many, critics argue, it is indeed lip service. After a few appropriate paragraphs in the company annual report, managers spend as little as possible of "the stockholders' money" on such activities. But "socially responsible" behavior has increasingly been required by law (for example, pollution control and affirmative action for minorities). And a substantial number of big companies (for example, IBM, AT&T, Bank of America, Levi Strauss, and Cummins Engine) spend millions of dollars annually on major programs to help renovate the central cities, assist minority groups, clean up the environment, and support universities and the United Fund.

It is hard to know how pervasive such corporate activities are, and how they compare with abuses of corporate power. The newspapers and Nader's Raiders report all-too-frequent cases of corporation bribery abroad and unsavory political activities at home, violations of Clean Air and Clean Water Acts, shoddy products and safety violations, business's admissions of guilt in discrimination cases. And one abuse of corporate power may outweigh hundreds of cases of good corporate citizenship and superior market performance that go unreported on the evening news broadcasts.

Policies to Control Corporate Power

Observers of the modern corporate scene have suggested many measures to control abuses of corporate power. Probably the commonest is more vigorous enforcement of the antitrust laws, especially against oligopolies. Others call for increasing regulation of business behavior—on product quality and safety, on pollution, on hiring practices, and the like—although, as we shall see in the next chapter, such regulations have a very mixed performance record. Still others say that corporations' political power is the key to the situation, and would further restrict business lobbying and other political activities. Another approach is through revolutionizing the internal governance of corporations, especially by requiring more "outside" directors who would be charged more directly with monitoring the legal and ethical performance of corporate management. In 1979, Senator Edward Kennedy introduced a bill specifically aimed at bigness, whether or not monopoly was involved. No firm over $2 billion in assets or sales would be permitted to grow through merger, and no firm over $350 million in assets or sales would be permitted to grow through merger unless it could show that the result would increase competition or improve efficiency. The bill did not pass, but it achieved considerable support. Galbraith, impressed with the technological efficiency of large corporations, concludes that nationalization (socialization) of big business is the only way to get these efficiencies without allowing excessive private corporate power.

Most of these proposals call, directly, or indirectly, for more government action to check the improper use of corporate power. But this raises a further problem. For the public repeatedly reports that it doesn't trust "big government" either. The last two decades have seen a major erosion of public trust in all big, impersonal institutions.

There are no easy answers, either as to whether we need more controls to limit business's power or as to the best steps if we do need more restraints. An uneasy, shifting balance of powers, with lots of uncertainty, may be the most accurate description of the total situation.

SUMMARY AND REVIEW

1. To permit the benefits of a market-directed economy, government must ensure workable competition.

2. Large corporations are growing larger—both absolutely and relative to total economic activity—in manufacturing, which they dominate. There is less evidence of such growing dominance in other areas of the economy, or of growing monopoly power over individual products. Many of the largest firms now produce many different products.

3. The welfare costs of monopoly because of inefficient allocation of resources are relatively small. The costs of X-inefficiency may be much larger.

4. The main antitrust laws in the United States are the Sherman Act, the Clayton and Federal Trade Commission Acts, the Robinson-Patman Act, and the Celler Antimerger Act. These are all intended to increase competition and restrain monopoly. In addition, "natural monopolies" are generally treated as public utilities and are regulated by regulatory commissions, like the ICC.

5. The effectiveness of this antitrust legislation depends on the enforcement activities of the government and attitudes of the courts, which change from time to time.

6. Perhaps the biggest issue facing antitrust now is how to obtain the benefits of large-scale production methods and modern R&D spending while having enough firms in each industry to ensure workable competition.

7. Very large corporations may have substantial economic and political power in addition to their market power over prices and output of particular products. Although the public generally approves of the private-enterprise economic system, it mistrusts big businesses and fears their abuse of power. Many believe that big business is too concerned with making profits and not enough with helping to solve society's major problems.

8. There is little agreement on what, if any, further steps should be taken to control corporate power. Policies ranging from more vigorous application of antitrust laws and more detailed regulation of large firms to nationalization of them have been suggested.

For Analysis and Discussion

1. Does big business have too much power? (Define "power" carefully in your answer.) If so, who should do something about it, and what should they do?
2. How should we decide whether it is in the public interest for any industry to consist of a large or a small number of firms?
3. Many businessmen argue that vigorous government prosecution under the antitrust laws is a sign of government antagonism toward business and profits. Is

this a proper criticism? If you think it isn't, how would you convince such a critic?

4. Critics of big business often argue that the majority of large modern corporations could be broken up into several competing units without loss of productive efficiency, because as a rule they control many plants, each of which could just as well operate as a separate, competitive business. Is this argument a sound one? If so, how should we go about implementing the proposal?

5. Should conglomerate mergers be challenged under the antitrust laws, even though the merging firms handle noncompeting products?

6. Would you favor direct government conduct or support of all basic research, with the results freely available to all? List the advantages and disadvantages. Who should pay for the research?

7. Would you favor doubling the congressional appropriation to the Department of Justice for antitrust enforcement?

8. Is Milton Friedman or Irving Kristol right in their dispute over whether corporations should do more than try to maximize profits?

9. Is there a conflict between trying to maximize profits and serving the public interest?

CASE 16

U.S. v. VON'S GROCERIES⁹

In 1966, the Supreme Court, by a 6–2 decision, found that a merger of Von's Grocery Company and Shopping Bag Food Stores in Los Angeles violated Section 7 of the Clayton Act (often called the Celler Antimerger Act). The following excerpts summarize the majority and minority decisions. Which do you think was right? (See the questions at the end of the case.)

The majority decision. On March 25, 1960, the United States brought this action charging that the acquisition by Von's Grocery Company of its direct competitor Shopping Bag Food Stores, both large retail grocery companies in Los Angeles, California, violated #7 of the Clayton Act which, as amended in 1950 by the Celler-Kefauver Anti-Merger Bill, provides:

No corporation engaged in commerce shall acquire the whole or any part of the assets of another corporation engaged also in commerce, where in any line of commerce in any section of the country the effect of such acquisition may be substantially to lessen competition or to create a monopoly.

The market involved here is the retail grocery market in the Los Angeles area. In 1958 Von's retail sales ranked third in the area and Shopping Bag's ranked sixth. In 1960 their sales together were 7.5 percent of the total two and one half billion dollars of retail groceries sold in the Los Angeles market each year. For many years before the merger both companies had enjoyed great success as rapidly growing companies. From 1948 to 1958 the number of Von's stores in the Los Angeles area practically doubled from 14 to 27, while at the same time the number of Shopping Bag's stores jumped from 15 to 34. During that same decade, Von's sales increased fourfold and its share of the market almost doubled while Shopping Bag's sales multiplied seven times and its share of the market tripled. The merger of these two highly successful, expanding and aggressive competitors created the second largest grocery chain in Los Angeles with sales of almost $172,488,000 annually.

In addition, the findings of the District Court show that the number of owners operating a single store in the Los Angeles retail grocery market decreased from 5,365 in 1950 to 3,818 in 1961. By 1963, three years after the merger, the number of single-store owners had dropped still further to 3,590. During roughly the same period from 1953 to 1962 the number of chains with two or more grocery stores increased from 96 to 150. While the grocery business was being concentrated into the hands of fewer and fewer owners, the small companies were continually being absorbed by

the larger firms through mergers. According to an exhibit prepared by one of the Government's expert witnesses, in the period from 1949 to 1958 nine of the top 20 chains acquired 126 stores from their smaller competitors. . . . These facts alone are enough to cause us to conclude contrary to the District Court that the Von's Shopping Bag merger did violate #7. . . .

From this country's beginning there has been an abiding and widespread fear of the evils which flow from monopoly—that is, the concentration of economic power in the hands of the few. On the basis of this fear, in 1890, when many of the nation's industries were already concentrated into what Congress deemed too few hands, it passed the Sherman Act in an attempt to prevent further concentration and to preserve competition among a large number of sellers. . . .

Like the Sherman Act in 1890 and the Clayton Act in 1914, the basic purpose of the 1950 Celler-Kefauver Bill was to prevent economic concentration in the American economy by keeping a large number of small competitors in business. In stating the purpose of the bill, both of its sponsors, Representative Celler and Senator Kefauver, emphasized their fear, widely shared by other members of Congress, that this concentration was rapidly driving the small businessman out of the market. As we said in *Brown Shoe Co.* v. *United States,* 370 U.S. 294,315, "The dominant theme pervading congressional consideration of the 1950 amendments was a fear of what was considered to be a rising tide of economic concentration in the American economy." By using terms in #7 which look not merely to the actual present effect of a merger but instead to its effect upon future competition, Congress sought to preserve competition among many small businesses by arresting a trend toward concentration in its incipiency before that trend developed to the point that a market was left in the grip of a few big companies. Thus, where concentration is gaining momentum in a market, we must be alert to carry out Congress' intent to protect competition against ever-increasing concentration through mergers. . . .

The facts of this case present exactly the threatening trend toward concentration which Congress wanted to halt. The number of small grocery companies in the Los Angeles retail grocery market had been declining rapidly before the merger and continued to decline rapidly afterwards. This rapid decline in the number of grocery store owners moved hand in hand

⁹ 384 U.S. 270. Case 21, *U.S.* v. *Aluminum Co. of America;* Case 19, Should Business Serve the Public Interest or Maximize Profits?; or Case 27, TV Advertising and Children's Teeth, can equally well be used here.

with a large number of significant absorptions of the small companies by the larger ones. In the midst of this steadfast trend toward concentration, Von's and Shopping Bag, two of the most successful and largest companies in the area, jointly owning 66 grocery stores, merged to become the second largest chain in Los Angeles. . . .

Appellee's primary argument is that the merger betwen Von's and Shopping Bag is not prohibited by #7 because the Los Angeles grocery market was competitive before the merger, has been since, and may continue to be in the future. Even so, #7 "requires not merely an appraisal of the immediate impact of the merger upon competition, but a prediction of its impact upon competitive conditions in the future; this is what is meant when it is said that the amended #7 was intended to arrest anticompetitive tendencies in their 'incipiency.'" (*United States* v. *Philadelphia Nat. Bank,* 374 U.S., p. 362.) It is enough for us that Congress feared that a market marked at the same time by both a continuous decline in the number of small businesses and a large number of mergers would, slowly but inevitably, gravitate from a market of many small competitors to one dominated by one or a few giants, and competition would thereby be destroyed. . . .

The minority dissent. First, the standards of #7 require that every corporate acquisition be judged in the light of the contemporary economic context of its industry. Second, the purpose of #7 is to protect competition, not to protect competitors, and every #7 case must be decided in the light of that clear statutory purpose. Today the Court turns its back on these two basic principles and on all the decisions that have followed them.

The Court makes no effort to appraise the competitive effects of this acquisition in terms of the contemporary economy of the retail food industry in the Los Angeles area. Instead, through a simple exercise in sums, it finds that the number of individual competitors in the market has decreased over the years, and, apparently on the theory that the degree of competition is invariably proportional to the number of competitors, it holds that this historic reduction in the number of competing units is enough under #7 to invalidate a merger within the market, with no need to examine the economic concentration of the market, the level of competition in the market, or the potential adverse effect of the merger on that competition. This startling per se rule is contrary not only to our previous decisions, but contrary to the language of #7, contrary to the legislative history of the 1950 amendment, and contrary to economic reality. . . .

The concept of arresting restraints of trade in their "incipiency" was not an innovation of the 1950 amendment. The notion of incipiency was part of the report on the original Clayton Act by the Senate Committee on the Judiciary in 1914, and it was reiterated in the Senate report in 1950. That notion was not left undefined. The legislative history leaves no doubt that the applicable standard for measuring the substantiality of the effect of a merger on competition was that of a "reasonable probability" of lessening competition. The standard was thus more stringent than that of a "mere possibility" on the one hand and more lenient than that of a "certainty" on the other. I cannot agree that the retail grocery business in Los Angeles is in an incipient or any other stage of a trend toward lessening of competition, or that the effective level of concentration in the industry has increased. Moreover, there is no indication that the present merger, or the trend in this industry as a whole, augers any danger whatsoever for the small businessman. The Court has substituted bare conjecture for the statutory standard of a reasonable probability that competition may be lessened. . . .

I believe that even the most superficial analysis of the record makes plain the fallacy of the Court's syllogism that competition is necessarily reduced when the bare number of competitors has declined. In any meaningful sense, the structure of the Los Angeles grocery market remains unthreatened by concentration. Local competition is vigorous to a fault, not only among chain stores themselves but also between chain stores and single-store operators. . . . The record simply cries out that the numerical decline in the number of single-store owners is the result of transcending social and technological changes that positively preclude the inference that competition has suffered because of the attrition of competitors. . . .

Section 7 was never intended by Congress for use by the Court as a charter to roll back the supermarket revolution. Yet the Court's opinion is hardly more than a requiem for the so-called "Mom and Pop" grocery stores—the bakery and butcher shops, the vegetable and fish markets—that are now economically and technologically obsolete in many part of the country. No action by this Court can restore the old single-line Los Angeles food stores that have been run over by the automobile or obliterated by the freeway.

The District Court found that Von's stores were located in the southern and western portions of the Los Angeles metropolitan area, and that the Shopping Bag stores were located in the northern and eastern portions. In each of the areas in which Von's and Shopping Bag stores competed directly, there were also at least six other chain stores and several smaller stores competing for the patronage of customers. . . . The actual market share foreclosed by the elimination of Shopping Bag as an independent competitor was thus slightly less than 1 percent of the total grocery store sales in the area. . . .

Moreover, it is clear that there are no substantial barriers to market entry. . . .

In your judgment, should this merger have been allowed—under Section 7 of the Clayton Act? Was forbidding the merger in the public interest, whatever you think about its legality?

POLICY

Consumer
Protection
and Government
Regulation

CHAPTER 16

Where there is active competition among sellers, that competition for consumers' dollars protects consumers. If Safeway doesn't give consumers the quality of vegetables they want, Krogers will be happy to do so, assuming that consumers are willing to pay the cost of producing the desired vegetables. The consumer is king, and competition guards his interests. Well-meaning attempts to protect consumers through government regulation are both unnecessary and often harmful. So say many economists, reminding you of Adam Smith's "invisible hand." If people want more safety features on cars, GM will see that they're available if Ford doesn't.

But lots of consumer advocates, led by Ralph Nader in recent years, say, "No way!" First, they say, effective competition doesn't exist in many markets, including autos. Second, even where it does, consumers aren't able to protect themselves adequately from the greed and wiles of sellers, especially big corporations. Most of the goods consumers buy, they argue, come from giant businesses that hold all the cards in dealing with individual consumers. They twist consumers' wants through advertising, often misleading or downright dishonest. They offer only the goods on which they can make big profits, not the ones consumers would like to have. Many products are complicated, and there's no effective way for consumers to detect the poor ones until after they've spent their money. The giant firms produce cars that are "unsafe at any speed," as Nader's first book was titled; toys that endanger children who play with them; drugs and pesticides that threaten the health of all of us; shoddy products that wear out too fast and don't do what they're supposed to. As the final section of Chapter 10 stressed, "market failures" occur even in highly competitive markets when consumers lack accurate information on products available, where advertising distorts their wants, or where there are important externalities. The invisible hand falters, the critics argue.

Since the turn of the century, new legislation has intermittently been passed to protect both consumers and small competitors against unfair competition through misrepresentation, misleading advertising, and the like. The Food and Drug and the Federal Meat Inspection Acts of 1906 and 1909, and the Federal Trade Commission Act of 1914, were early examples. The New Deal spawned a whole set of new regulatory agencies—for example, the Securities and Exchange Commission (SEC), Federal Aviation Administration and Civil Aeronautics Board (FAA and CAB), Federal Communications Commission (FCC), and Federal Power Commission (FPC)—and gave new power to others. With the advent of modern "consumerism," the past decade has seen a flood of new consumer-protection measures, ranging from auto safety to honest packaging, product safety, truth in lending, and occupational licensing. This has produced a new alphabet jungle—EPA, NEFP, OSHA, ERISA, and many others. The American instinct seems to be, if you don't like it, regulate it.

In 1970, 20,036 pages were required in the *Federal Register* to print the regulations passed by Congress; by 1977, this total had risen to 65,603. In addition, in 1977, 75,000 pages were needed to print the regulations issued by federal agencies to implement Congress's laws. There are now over 400 regulations (on safety, pollution control, gasoline mileage, and the like) governing the production of autos in the United States.

THE ECONOMIC THEORY OF CONSUMER PROTECTION

The preceding introductory comments suggest the economic theory of consumer protection. In a market-directed system with effective competition, consumers will indicate what they want by the way they spend their incomes, and the market will produce the quality of various products that consumers are willing to pay for. No special government regulations to protect consumers will be needed except where there are "market failures." These market failures may arise primarily where there are important externalities (for example, pollution), where adequate information does not exist to permit consumers to make well-informed choices (for example, the energy efficiencies of different refrigerators), or where consumers are unable to understand adequately the information available (for example, the effects of medicinal drugs). In such cases, government intervention to "protect" consumers can help provide a better allocation of resources in response to consumer wants.

Economic theory can warn us, too, of probable dangers when government intervenes to protect consumers. If, for example, government requires that all plumbing be done by licensed plumbers, presumably to protect the public against shoddy, unsafe plumbing, licensed plumbers are likely to push for strict licensing requirements that will "protect" consumers against poor plumbing but will also help plumbers maintain a legal cartel (monopoly) by keeping down the number of licensed plumbers in the town. Thus, the result may be "higher-grade," more expensive plumbing than consumers want to buy, since the consumer cannot use nonlicensed plumbers and competition to drive down licensed plumbers' wages is limited.

Consider a sample of government regulations designed to protect consumers: (1) direct product-quality protection, (2) occupational licensing, and (3) the practical politics of the regulatory process.

CONSUMER PROTECTION

Auto Safety

Purchasers of new cars produced in the United States in 1978 paid perhaps $2 to $3 billion extra for the equipment and modifications necessary to meet federal safety requirements—mandatory buzzers and harnesses, padded dashboards, safety glass, impact-absorbing bumpers, and the like. The stated goal was to protect consumers. Nader's Raiders were pleased, although unhappy that so many lives had been lost before the measures were passed. Many consumers were also pleased. A lot of others complained bitterly at having to pay the extra bill, and the mandatory buzzer-harness interlock that kept the car from starting until the driver was fastened in lasted only about six months. Most car passengers, especially drivers, while potentially safer than before against serious injury, continued not to fasten their seat belts.

As an economist, how would you evaluate the consumer-protection legislation? Your economics should lead you to a familiar question: Did the marginal gains exceed the marginal costs?

This is a difficult question to answer, partly because we don't have all the relevant information, and partly because the people paying and those benefiting are not the same and we have no satisfactory way of comparing costs and benefits as between different people. If you say that a life is priceless and the new legislation saves lives, you will presumably rate it high. But if, as seems more reasonable, safety is something each of us considers very important but hardly of infinite value when the chance we will be involved in an auto accident is quite small, we face a cost–benefit tradeoff. Is the extra safety we get from each safety component worth what we have to pay for it?

As Case 1 emphasized, moreover, your economics should lead you to ask another question: Why should the government require each individual to buy this set of safety devices rather than leave to each the option of deciding for himself whether it's worth the price? We (the government) don't require everyone to buy warm woolies for winter, or gloves and scarves, even though those would presumably help keep us healthier. Why auto safety equipment?

One answer might be that the government knows better than each of us what is good for him—but that line doesn't read very well. Another answer might be that auto safety equipment has important externalities. It may protect others against my bad driving; hence, I should have to pay for it whether or not I want to buy it for my own protection. If we consider safety equipment to include headlights, good brakes, and the like, this is a compelling argument. I shouldn't be free to endanger the lives of others by driving without good brakes. But for seat belts, air bags, padded dashes, shock-absorbing bumpers, and the like, the case is different. These mainly, or entirely, protect the occupants of the car, not an innocent third party.[1]

But some stretch the externalities argument to cover the safety-equipment case. Without the equipment, the car's occupants would be more likely to be injured, and society would have to take care of them if they could not pay for their

---

[1]Indeed, some economists argue that the added protection for the driver makes him more likely to take risks and hence to injure others, so the safety equipment probably leads to no reduction at all in total injuries and deaths. See S. Peltzman, "The Effects of Automobile Safety Regulation," *Journal of Political Economy*, August 1975.

own medical attention; also, insurance rates will be higher for all without the safety equipment. Judge for yourself whether this externalities argument is convincing.

Unless there are clearly positive externalities from adding the safety equipment that exceed the costs of correcting the negative externalities, the presumption of the free-market economy is that each individual is the best judge of whether the extra benefits are worth the extra cost to him. This has the further advantage that we don't need to balance out marginal cost against marginal benefit for society as a whole—a very difficult task—since we can leave the choice up to each individual to decide for himself, which he is presumably competent to do.

Mandatory auto safety equipment is an interesting example of government regulation designed to protect consumers. The problem is more complex than it may seem. For example, suppose that without legislation, most consumers would not buy today's safety equipment, but some would like it. Would auto manufacturers offer the option to those who want to buy? If so, at what price?

Drugs

The worst horror stories supporting the case for government protection of consumers have been those of untested, unsafe drugs. Consumers have little competence to protect themselves in such cases; they must rely on doctors' recommendations, hearsay, or hunch, and may be easy prey to unscrupulous drug manufacturers and panacea salesmen. Modern drugs have revolutionized the practice of medicine, but they have also brought dangers.

The best-known example is thalidomide. During the late 1950s, this new sedative was widely used in Europe, where it seemed highly effective and free of unwanted side effects. Dr. Frances Kelsey, of the U.S. Food and Drug Administration, in considering thalidomide for use in the United States, noted German reports of nerve inflammations where the drug had been heavily used and held up U.S. approval to check the facts further. Within a year, major birth defects began to appear everywhere that thalidomide had been used by pregnant women, although the connection was not recognized for

some time—with the poignant results that became worldwide news as thousands of deformed babies were born. Dr. Kelsey was a heroine in the United States. The Food and Drug Administration's regulations on approval of new drugs, the most stringent in the world, seemed clearly validated. Helpless consumers certainly need protection against dangerous drugs. They do not have the information to make their own judgments, and often could not assess the information adequately even if they had it.

But consider another case: High blood pressure (hypertension) afflicts millions of people in the United States, bringing disability or death to many. A powerful new drug, guanoxan, has been widely used in England since 1964 to reduce high blood pressure, but it has serious side effects on the functioning of the liver in a substantial fraction of people who take it, although these side effects can be reversed if the drug's use is stopped. Many British doctors believe the liver risk is worth taking for hypertension patients who don't respond to other treatment. In the United States, however, guanoxan is illegal; the FDA decided it was too dangerous to use. Although an estimated 25 million Americans suffer from hypertension, the FDA approved none of six new drugs that have come into wide European use in treating the disease over the past decade.

Has the FDA protected consumers, or condemned an unknown number of hypertension sufferers to pain and earlier death than they might otherwise have faced with use of the new European drugs? Economics cannot answer the question. But it does suggest that drugs, like almost everything else, involve tradeoffs between costs and benefits. To look at only the "protection" provided Americans against liver dysfunction from taking guanoxan is to look at only one side of the problem. The possible gains to hypertension sufferers that are lost by the FDA's prohibition need to be measured against the possible costs. Clearly, one alternative would be a more permissive approach by the FDA, which would permit individual doctors and patients more choice in such cases as guanoxan.

The FDA has a long history of stricter barriers to the introduction of new drugs until they have been proved "both safe and effective" than comparable agencies have in West European nations. Most estimates put the U.S. approval lag behind European nations at two to five years. Before 1962, when FDA rules were tightened substantially after the thalidomide episode, some 40 to 50 major new drugs were approved each year. In the following decade, the number fell to 15, even though U.S. drug manufacturers greatly increased their spending on research. American drug manufacturers complain that FDA approval requires extremely long, expensive test procedures, which hold health-giving drugs off the market for years and seriously underrate the costs to potential patients. They argue for quicker provisional approval with continued close surveillance during early years of use.

On the other hand, other legislators and consumer advocates argue for more, not less, stringent procedures to protect American people from unsafe, inadequately tested new drugs. They accuse the drug companies of being interested only in profits, not patients' welfare.

Economic analysis suggests an approach to weighing such arguments. Again, comparing marginal costs and benefits is the key, but be sure you've included *all* the relevant costs and benefits. Clearly, the consumer needs protection in the drug case, but equally clearly, too much protection may involve a higher cost than he may want to pay if he considers all the costs and benefits. In any event, it is important to remember that in the United States, it is fundamentally Congress, not the FDA, that sets the basic directives.[2]

Building Codes

Nearly every city has building codes that specify minimum standards for plumbing, electrical wiring, building materials, and the like in all newly constructed or renovated houses. The stated purpose is usually to protect buyers against shoddy construction and unsafe buildings. Often the codes specify that major plumbing and wiring must be done by contractors or workmen licensed by the city, to ensure that the work will meet code standards.

To many consumers, government protection against shoddy, unsafe construction makes sense.

They don't know enough about construction to be sure otherwise that they are getting good-quality construction, and safe plumbing and wiring. Is this a consumer-protection regulation that everyone can support?

Alas, not necessarily. The situation should bring the auto safety case above to mind. Unless there are important externalities involved, why should the government tell you that you must buy grade A, expensive plumbing, wiring, and other materials, when grade B might meet your standards adequately? Why should the government tell you that you must have an expensive licensed plumber or electrical contractor, using expensive union labor, do your work rather than permitting you to hire less expensive workers or do it yourself? You're the one who is going to live in the house, and who will pay the cost if you have to replace the plumbing in five years, or suffer the damage if faulty wiring leads to a fire.

Perhaps there are positive externalities for the rest of the community from your using the code-specified, high-cost materials and labor, but it's not apparent what they would be in most cases, beyond meeting minimum fire-protection standards. Or one might argue that the code will protect future buyers of your house, who otherwise might innocently buy a house with inferior wiring and plumbing. But this gives little credit to the intelligence of the future buyer. If he has any sense at all, unless he's competent to judge for himself, he'll surely want to get an expert appraiser to come in and look over the house before he buys it, which will readily disclose the state of the plumbing and wiring.

While many codes have been passed by city councils with the best of intentions, often they have become effective means of protecting the quasi-monopoly positions of materials suppliers, licensed contractors, and union labor in the city. Attempts to relax codes to permit use of new, cheaper materials and methods have often met bitter resistance from entrenched suppliers and labor unions. Thus, not surprisingly, the "protection" the code gives consumers costs something, because it prescribes high standards. No less, it costs because it effectively shuts out cheaper materials, contractors, and labor that might have done the work for less. Whether the extra "quality" is worth the extra cost to each home buyer or renovator will depend on his

[2]For a popular analysis of the drug-regulation problem, see W. S. Ross, "The Medicines We Need But Can't Have," *Reader's Digest*, October 1973.

comparison of marginal costs and benefits. But unless he violates the law (a risky practice, since the city building inspector may require any "substandard" work to be torn out and replaced according to the code), the buyer has no option. He must buy the code-approved, expensive materials and construction, whether or not he thinks they're worth to him what they cost.

Conclusion: Should city building codes be eliminated? Not necessarily, of course. Some may provide minimal standards necessary to the public health and safety, and no more. But economics suggests comparing marginal costs and marginal benefits again—a careful look at just how much of the prescribed standards are unnecessary or outdated, how much can safely be left to individual choice, and how much the code has in effect been taken over by local suppliers, contractors, and unions to protect an otherwise illegal cartel.

OCCUPATIONAL LICENSING

Nearly every state licenses architects, barbers, beauticians, chiropractors, dentists, embalmers, lawyers, pharmacists, physicians, registered nurses, and veterinarians. Without a state license, practice of any of these occupations is illegal. Many states also license a wide variety of other occupations—bail bondsmen, garage operators, pest controllers, plumbers, tree surgeons, junk dealers, and others. The stated purpose is generally to protect the public against incompetent, shoddy, or unsafe work. Before the turn of the century, the number of licensed occupations was far smaller. What accounts for their rapid increase, and what have been their main effects?

Although consumer protection is commonly advanced as the main goal, most of the arguments for more and stricter licensing have, strikingly, come from the occupations themselves, not from consumers. And little wonder, if you stop to think about it. Government licensing is a powerful way indeed to restrict entry into an occupation, and the higher the "consumer protection" standards, the harder it will be for new practitioners to enter and drive down prices and incomes. Chicago's George Stigler has compared incomes in a list of licensed occupations with those in

nonlicensed occupations requiring roughly comparable education and skills, and he finds, to no economists' surprise, that median incomes in the former are about 50 percent higher.[3] Restrictions on entry are an effective way of maintaining a cartel, for individuals as well as for businesses.

This is not to suggest that all members of licensed occupations are greedy, self-seeking souls who merely want to pad their pockets. On the contrary, many of them honestly believe that the public needs protection from untrained incompetents and quacks in their fields. And such may indeed be the case. But the same questions as in the preceding section recur: Should consumers have the option to decide for themselves whether the extra "protection" is worth the extra cost? Remember that the extra cost may be not only the cost of higher-quality services but also the monopoly cost of higher prices because of restricted supply. If we don't permit individual consumers to make this choice, is the social marginal benefit of the "consumer protection" provided larger than the social marginal cost?[4]

THE PRACTICAL POLITICS AND COSTS OF REGULATION

When Americans are unhappy with the behavior of business, especially big business, they cry for government regulation. The man in the street's faith in more competition to provide consumer protection against big business is limited. When he thinks business is unreasonable, he wants the government to do something about it.

This attitude has spawned a large group of government regulatory agencies, big and small. From two agencies and a few thousand dollars in 1890, federal government regulation of business has grown to 41 agencies today and nearly $5 billion annually in direct federal costs. Over half this growth has come in the last five years, as shown by Table 16–1. But the $4.8 billion federal

---

[3]Stigler, "The Theory of Regulation," *Bell Journal of Economics and Management Science,* Spring 1971.

[4]Some economists argue that the social costs of government regulation (largely aimed to protect consumers) are substantially larger than the social costs of monopoly per se. See Richard Posner, "The Social Costs of Monopoly and Regulation," *Journal of Political Economy,* August 1975.

TABLE 16–1
Federal Expenditures on Regulation of Business (Billions of dollars)

	1974	1979
Consumer safety and health	$1.3	$2.7
Job safety and working conditions	.3	.6
Environment and energy	.3	1.1
Financial reporting	a	.1
Specific industry regulation	.2	.3
	$2.2	$4.8

a Less than $50 million.

Source: The Costs of Government Regulation of Business, U.S. Congress, Joint Economic Committee, April 10, 1978, pp. 12–13.

expenditures shown there is only a tiny fraction of the major cost—the cost of compliance with the regulations by businesses in every part of the economy. These compliance costs were estimated at about $100 billion in 1979, some twenty times the federal government outlay. The $100 billion estimate is very rough, but it suggests the order of magnitude involved. Government regulations reach into every part of modern business. And the costs are mainly borne by the public—the direct federal costs by taxpayers, and the bulk of the compliance costs by consumers of the products concerned. Unless the regulated firms have monopoly positions with barriers to entry, little or none of the costs will be borne by stockholders; competition will force them onto consumers or back to suppliers of productive services to the firms involved.

Early regulation was mainly in the form of broad rules on what firms could and could not do—the ICC and Sherman Acts are examples. By contrast, the new wave of regulation goes into great detail on the operations of the firm. Environmental-protection legislation and regulations include thousands of pages of detailed provisions by Congress and the EPA; the OSHA legislation and regulations specify safety rules and practices in minute detail. The new regulation deals with a broad range of socioeconomic problems (discrimination, pollution, safety, and consumer protection) that touch every phase of business operations. It is no accident that Ameri-

can businesses have complained increasingly in recent years of growing government interference and controls, whichever way they turn.[5]

How well has all this regulation worked? Sometimes pretty well; sometimes badly. Many of the new commissions have moved with vigor to carry out their duties during their early years. The legislation is new, the mission seems clear, strong appointments are made to the commissions, and there is enthusiasm for getting the job done. Often the businesses being regulated have protested that the regulators are overenergetic, even antagonistic. In a few cases, this attitude of vigorous enforcement and protection of the public interest has persisted; the SEC is sometimes cited as an example, although many disagree. But in most cases, after a decade or two, the inaugural enthusiasm wears off, new appointments to the regulatory commission are often less than distinguished (frequently made as payment of political debts by the administration in power), and gradually the agency develops more "understanding" of the problems of the regulated industry, to the point that it serves as much to protect the industry itself as it does the public interest. At the extreme, the regulatory agency is essentially taken over by the industry and used as government legitimization of cartelization of the industry.

Who Regulates Whom?
The Iron Triangle

The Interstate Commerce Commission is an example. During the early decades of its existence, the ICC developed an enviable reputation for honesty, expertness, and impartiality. It

---

[5]Not surprisingly, conflicts and contradictions are plentiful in such a mass of regulations. One food processor complained plaintively to the Joint Economic Committee: "The Department of Agriculture requires that our kitchen floors be washed repeatedly for sanitary purposes; yet the Occupational Safety and Health Administration rules that floors must be dry. What shall I do?" A construction firm wrote "There is a federal regulation that vehicles moving on a construction site have bells to warn of their approach. Sensible. But! There is another regulation requiring workers at the same site to wear ear muffs against noise pollution. This means, of course, that the workers cannot hear the warning bells."

moved strongly to eliminate railroad-rate discrimination against farmers, other small shippers, and short-haul traffic. Down to World War I, support for the commission came largely from those responsible for its establishment, dissatisfied farmers and commercial shippers. But with the 1920s, this gradually changed. The worst discriminatory practices were gone, "normalcy" was the tone of the times, the railroads had been convinced that they must live with the commission, and their enthusiasm for rampant rate competition had faded. They and the commissioners came to understand each others' problems. New commissioners were appointed from the industry, and retiring commissioners predominantly moved to positions in the industry. The railroads and the commission have both praised their harmonious relations. And the railroads increasingly looked to the commission for support and defense against new forms of competition.

Since World War II, as rail transport has gradually lost business to trucks, buses, airlines, and pipelines, the ICC has increasingly worked with the railroads to avoid active price competition among themselves and with other carriers. Procedures have become more and more complex and cumbersome, a veritable sea of red tape. The commission must approve each rail-and truck-rate change, and each year, thousands of miniscule changes of rates on particular products between particular points clog ICC dockets. The commission has shown little ability to deal with the major problems of transport policy that confront the nation. In recent years, it has increasingly moved toward a more understanding relationship with the trucking industry, similar to that with the railroads. It has been widely criticized for its red tape, its failure to represent the interests of shippers (including, not least, those families at the mercy of truckers in moving their household goods), and its general support of the status quo. Truck rates are much higher on regulated routes than on nonregulated ones. Many trucks are prohibited from carrying cargo on return trips, and must follow long, roundabout routes with certain cargoes, to avoid "excess competition" with established lines. Safety rules are loosely enforced. Unauthorized price competition is forbidden.

Increasingly, economists argue that competition among different carriers (trucks, buses, airlines, railroads, and pipelines) would now be substantial if they were freed from ICC and other government restrictions, and that the ICC should be abolished. Its current social product is negative, they say. It stifles innovation and mainly protects the cartel practices of the common carriers, which can continue only with the legal support given by supportive commission rules on rates and practices. And in 1979 the Carter administration announced its support of deregulating trucking, and possibly railroads.[6]

Similar criticisms have been levied at other major regulatory commissions. Consumer interests often fall by the wayside as the regulated firms and the commissions work together over the years. Generally, the firms have found it more rewarding to cooperate with the commissions than to fight them. The firms have a strong interest in bringing all the political pressure they possess to bear on getting regulations and rulings that are workable for themselves. History records a long list of generous political contributions from the regulated industries to key state and national legislators who oversee the regulatory commissions. By contrast, individual consumers seldom have enough at stake to mount major attacks on commissions that fail to support their interests aggressively.

Critics have dubbed this kind of cooperative arrangement between the regulatory agency, the regulated industry, and the overseeing congressional subcommittee the "iron triangle." Working together, they can provide a highly effective cartel from which each benefits. The industry avoids the stress of price competition and of new competitors. The regulatory agency bureaucrats lead a comfortable life, and one in which rewards from the industry may be substantial—sometimes actual payments, more often good jobs for the commissioners and top staff when they leave the agency for careers in the regulated industry or as lobbyists or consultants. The controlling

---

[6]For a highly critical, detailed study of the ICC, see the Ralph Nader Study Group Report, *The Interstate Commerce Omission* (New York: Grossman, 1970). A shorter, more balanced criticism is L. M. Kohlmeier, *The Regulators* (New York: Harper & Row, 1969), Chap. 7.

subcommittees in Congress exert great power over the regulated industries and their practices, but exercise it cooperatively, to the mutual advantage of all three groups concerned.[7]

But there are many exceptions to industry control. Especially in inflationary periods, public utility commissions have usually lagged in permitting higher prices to cover rising costs. In all periods, the rate of return to investors has generally been low in regulated compared to unregulated firms. The Federal Power Commission for many years held the price of natural gas sold in interstate commerce far below free-market competitive levels, resulting in massive consumption of gas because it was such a cheap fuel. Today, as a result, the nation faces a severe gas "shortage," and the federal government has at last moved to deregulate natural-gas prices in order to discourage consumption and encourage production. It is hard for regulators to set prices and output at just the right levels to assure optimal use of productive resources.

Moreover, the "new regulation" of the past decade appears to mark a major change from the iron-triangle pattern. At least thus far, there is little evidence of friendly cooperation between regulators and regulatees; on the contrary, many of the new regulators are social reformers, out to beat down the power of big businesses. Nor are the congressmen who pass and administer the new laws generally friendly to the businesses they regulate. Indeed, some observers see the new regulation as a kind of class warfare, with the intellectuals and other critics of big business in full pursuit, led by Ralph Nader and other ardent consumerists.[8]

---

[7]Scholars have adduced at least four different explanations of this pattern of behavior. The "life-cycle" theory stresses the gradual loss of vigor and growing cooperation with the industry as regulatory agencies age. The "capture" theory stresses the direct takeover by the regulated industry, with only secondary attention to the life-cycle factors. The "protected cartel" theory says that such regulatory agencies are set up at the outset to establish cartels for the benefit of the "regulated" industries. The "regulatory process" theory, mainly from political scientists, stresses the bureaucratic interests of the many participants in the regulatory process in protecting and expanding their jobs—bureaucrats, lawyers, lobbyists, consultants, congressmen.

[8]For this argument, see P. Weaver, "Regulation, Social Policy, and Class Conflict," *The Public Interest,* Winter 1978.

Submerged in a Sea of Trivia?

It seems very hard to run government regulation of business efficiently and with common sense. For example, Congress established the Federal Trade Commission in 1914 to mount a major attack on the antitrust front, with sweeping powers of investigation. It also gave the commission a secondary task of protecting both competitors and consumers against unfair competitive practices, deceptive advertising, and the like.

Over the years, the FTC has often seemed submerged in a sea of trivia. Each year it has issued hundreds of rulings dealing with such matters as how manufacturers of aluminum storm windows can advertise their product, that lace made elsewhere can't be called Irish lace, that Ipana toothpaste can't claim to prevent pink toothbrush, and the like. In the course of a year, its Bureau of Deceptive Practices examines more than 250,000 printed advertisements and 500,000 radio and TV commercials.

Perhaps its most famous defense of consumers was the Rapid Shave case. Rapid Shave shaving cream produced a TV commercial showing a New York Giants football star, "a man with a problem just like yours . . . a beard as tough as sandpaper," and then a separate picture showing a razor shaving clean a piece of sandpaper lathered with Rapid Shave. But, the FTC found, it wasn't real sandpaper at all. Real sandpaper, it turned out, looks just like plain colored paper on TV, so the advertiser substituted Plexiglass sprinkled with sand. Real sandpaper, like what the Plexiglas seemed to be, could be shaved as Rapid Shave claimed, but only after prolonged prior soaking. Colgate-Palmolive, the manufacturer, argued that it hadn't committed any material sin, and the FTC examiner agreed that the case should be dismissed. But the FTC overruled the examiner, and two years later the Supreme Court finally upheld the conviction of guilt.

The commission and the courts spent an incredible sixteen years deciding that the word "liver" had to come out of Carter's Little Liver Pills because there was nothing of therapeutic value to the liver in the pills. But in spite of the commission's preoccupation with relatively minor consumer-protection matters, Congress has continued to load still more such responsibilities on it. The FTC, with the FDA, is responsible for enforcing the Fair Packaging and Labeling Act, the Wool Products Labeling Act, and a variety of other new consumer-protection laws. Intermittently, the commission has attempted to emerge from this sea of detail to deal with larger issues. But it has had limited success, partly because of a long-lived, status-quo-oriented staff. The practical politics of maintaining a vital, responsive government regulatory agency are difficult indeed to manage.

The Move to Deregulation?

In 1976, Jimmy Carter ran for the presidency on a plank of less regulation, fewer bureaucrats in Washington, less government in business. While the public wanted government to regulate many business practices, there was a backlash against too much government regulation. OSHA's 20-page regulation defining a stepladder; highly technical, elaborate language in regulations; and regulatory conflicts of the sort noted above were standard cocktail-party jokes. Even though most of these were of minor importance, they reflected a deeper resentment against too much government interference and power. President Carter found it much harder than he expected to pare down the Washington bureaucracy, but he pressed the regulatory agencies to simplify, to cut back staffs, and to concentrate on the essentials, not the trivia (but note the overall results in Table 16–1).

In 1978, the first big step toward deregulation was taken by the CAB and Congress—almost complete deregulation of airline fares. Price cutting was encouraged; only minimal constraints were retained on service to different areas. As air

fares dropped, air travel rose by leaps and bounds. Special coach fares were only about half their pre-deregulation levels. Many travelers loved it. Some others, especially full-fare business travellers who couldn't take advantage of the special fares, weren't so sure, as they found themselves crowded in with the bargain-rate customers. Many smaller cities worried that they might lose their air service. One horrible week, thousands of reduced-fare travelers trying to return to the United States were stranded in the London airports when almost all available seats were used by regular-fare passengers. But the main result was cheaper, more plentiful air travel.

What will happen if deregulation goes farther, and customers and workers find themselves without the "protections" they both used and criticized, remains to be seen. By the time you read this, there should be a good deal more evidence on both the costs and the benefits, if the Carter administration lives up to its promises. Deregulation of trucking will apparently be next. But the probability that we face a massive deregulation of American business seems low, even though we take considerable steps in that direction. How far would you go in abolishing safety regulations in the nation's factories, even given the obvious inefficiencies and even sometimes foolishness of OSHA?[9]

---

[9]For a more detailed, lively examination of six consumer protection problems, see the series of articles in *Fortune* on phosphates, toys, food additives, auto safety, appliances, and packaging, during the first half of 1972, reprinted in *Consumerism: Things Ralph Nader Never Told You* (New York: Harper & Row, 1972). For a more scholarly analysis, see Roger Noll, *Reforming Regulation* (Washington, D.C.: The Brookings Institution, 1971).

SUMMARY AND REVIEW

1. Theoretically, in a highly competitive, market-directed economy, competition among producers ensures "consumer protection"—that consumers will obtain the goods and services they want if they are willing to pay for them.

2. Critics disagree, arguing that effective competition does not exist in many markets, that consumers are unable to protect themselves adequately against big business, and that there would be important "market failures" in even highly competitive systems.

3. Economic theory suggests that the market failures that may call for "consumer protection" through government regulation are (a) externalities; (b) inadequate information on available goods and services to permit consumers to make wise decisions; and (c) cases where consumers are unable to understand adequately the information available. Economic theory also warns of probable conversion of attempts to protect consumers to government-sponsored cartelization of the industries concerned, especially when occupational licensing or "quality standards" are imposed.

4. Auto safety equipment, drugs, building codes, and occupational licensing are examples of "consumer-protection" measures; each should be examined using the criteria above to see whether or not government regulation to protect consumers is justified.

5. Government regulation of business has grown steadily over the last century, but has surged very rapidly in the last decade. Regulations aimed at providing consumer safety and health account for nearly half of all federal spending on business regulations. The new regulations tend to be more detailed and to go more deeply into business operations than did earlier regulations, which primarily specified prices and competitive practices that were not permitted. Total compliance costs now are apparently about $100 billion per year.

6. The results of government regulation of business have been mixed. In several important cases (for example, the ICC), regulation has turned into government-sponsored cartelization of the industry, with the industry, the regulatory agency, and responsible congressional subcommittees cooperating together more for their own benefit than to protect consumers. But there are many counterexamples.

7. The new wave of regulations appears to be significantly different—interfering more deeply in day-to-day business operations, and lacking the cooperative behavior between regulators and regulated industries that was common in past regulation. Some observers see the new regulation as almost class warfare by ardent consumerists against big business.

8. Managing government regulation of business effectively, especially when detailed specifications are involved, appears to be very difficult. Many regulatory agencies become excessively concerned with trivia.

9. We may be approaching a period of experimentation with deregulation, or at least less regulation than now prevails in some industries. The CAB's deregulation of air fares is an interesting example.

For Analysis and Discussion

1. Some free-market advocates argue that government should restrict itself to ensuring that consumers receive honest information on products offered for sale, leaving each consumer free to decide for himself what he is willing to pay for. How much information should the government require sellers to provide on each product, to make it possible for each consumer to protect himself?

2. Many consumerists argue that much more government protection is needed for consumers. If you accept this position, what criterion would you use in deciding how safe manufacturers should be required to make power lawn mowers? Try drafting the legislation you would favor.

3. The president of the American Bar Association was recently quoted by news reporters as objecting to advertising by lawyers: "Unrestricted advertising would be a disservice to the public. It would mean that some people would retain an attorney on the basis of who mounted the best advertising campaign or who charged the lowest fees, factors which are not relevant to performance." Should the ABA support advertising by lawyers in its Code of Professional Ethics?

4. Do consumers need more protection from advertisers? If so, how would you advocate providing it?

5. Trucks, buses, pipelines, and airlines are now at least as important as railroads in freight and passenger transportation in most areas. Has the time come to abolish the Interstate Commerce Commission and turn the transportation field back to open competition, to provide more effective incentives to efficiency and progress?

6. Should the FDA license production and sale of more potentially dangerous drugs, as long as full information on the danger is provided to each purchaser? How about saccharin, which may be cancer-causing but whose probable danger is still hotly disputed and which offers real advantages to diabetes sufferers?

7. Should your city require the use of city-licensed electricians on all major electrical jobs in homes and business establishments? Who would gain, and who would lose?

CASE 17 TV ADVERTISING AND CHILDREN'S TEETH[10]

Section 5 of the Federal Trade Commission Act forbids the use of unfair or deceptive advertising. In 1978, the staff of the Federal Trade Commission, following an extensive investigation, recommended to the Commission that it (1) forbid all television advertising aimed at small children (aged 8 or less) who are "too young to understand the selling purpose or otherwise comprehend or evaluate the advertising"; (2) also ban television adds for sugar-coated breakfast cereals and other sugar products whose consumption is dangerous to children's teeth, which are aimed at "older children" (perhaps to age 12) who are too young to understand the health or nutritional consequences of sugar consumption; and (3) require that television advertising for children under 12 for any sugar products be balanced by nutritional and health messages, funded by the advertisers, which point out the dangers involved.

In support of their recommendations, the staff pointed out that in 1977, the average American child aged 2 through 11 watched television more than 25 hours per week, or more than 3 2/3 hours per day. This works out to over 1,300 hours per year, more time than schoolchildren spend in the classroom. Each year, such children view an average of 20,000 television commercials, about 60 percent of which are for sugar-coated cereals, candy, other sweets, and eating establishments. They found, moreover, that children are more influenced than adults are by what they see on television. In some instances, they reported, children actually believe that little people are inside the TV set, standing beside a box of cereal. The staff argued that children under 8 have no ability to separate commercial messages from the rest of what they see on TV; children are highly vulnerable to this kind of advertising, and the $660 million spent on television advertising aimed at young children each year is evidence that advertisers are convinced that the undertaking is worthwhile. Moreover, children's teeth are particularly susceptible to damage from excessive consumption of sugar, which is heavily advertised on the programs aimed at children. Thus, small children who cannot protect themselves have a right to be protected against deceptive and unfair advertising.

After a study of the staff's report, the Federal Trade Commission issued tentative rules on advertising aimed at children, for comments and reactions by all concerned parties over the next 16 months. The proposed rules would:

1. Ban as deceptive or unfair all television advertising addressed to children aged 8 or less, who are too young to understand its selling purposes;
2. Ban as deceptive or unfair television advertising of sugar products most likely to cause tooth decay, when addressed to children under the age of 12, who are too young to understand the health or nutritional consequences of sugar consumption; and
3. Require that television advertising for sugar products to children under 12 be balanced with nutritional and health messages funded by the advertisers.

Outraged protests have come from advertisers, especially the major cereal firms (General Mills, General Foods, and Kellogg's). They argue that (1) cereals are not particularly dangerous to children's teeth—children add sugar to unsugared cereals if the cereals are not already treated; (2) the proposed rules violate the advertisers' rights of free speech under the Constitution; (3) the rules attempt to replace by FTC regulations the responsibilities of parents as to what their children should watch and eat; and (4) without advertising, children's programs on television would deteriorate or disappear completely.

Should the FTC adopt the proposed rules?

---

[10]This case can equally well be used with Chapters 26 or 28.

CASE 18

Americans love consumer appliances. And the American economy has responded spectacularly with mechanisms that wash, dry, spray, fan, shave, stitch, warn, pop, grind, mow, warm, cool, fan, and entertain. No other nation has such a mass of appliances aimed at making the life of the consumer happier and easier.

Yet a lot of people don't seem very happy about it all—consumers, manufacturers, retailers, even repairmen. It is a close race between automobiles and consumer appliances as to which generates more complaints to offices of consumer affairs around the nation. With so many hundreds of millions of consumer appliances in use, it is no wonder a lot of them break down and develop problems, causing consumer complaints. But somehow, these new handmaidens to consumer happiness and economic progress seem to generate more than their share.

To begin with, it's hard to know which one to buy. Shopping for appliances is confusing for most people. Those long rows of refrigerators all look about alike; it's hard to tell one air conditioner from another; who knows which is the best electric toothbrush to buy? Unlike an automobile, you can't take out and drive most consumer appliances to try them out. Neither can you try them on and look in the mirror to see how well they fit. Understandably, consumers in such circumstances are often suckers for fast-talking salesmen and for cut-price tags.

Warranties might seem to help, and they do to some extent. But the well-hedged warranty is another source of complaints. Many leading manufacturers stand behind their products commendably. But a lot of the warranties in fact say less than is guaranteed to the consumer by the general law protecting him against fraud and misrepresentation, once you read them carefully. Many of them take a lawyer to decipher.

But that's only the beginning. When you have the appliance home and it breaks down, that is the really unhappy time. The typical consumer may tinker with it and try to fix it, but almost invariably with limited success. Then he calls the repairman, and the complaints really begin to accumulate—ranging from their casual habits in keeping appointments and their frequent "need to go back to the office" to get missing parts, to their so-so record on really fixing what needs fixing without doing a lot of other things as well. The cost of having the refrigerator repaired has in most communities reached the proportions of the cost of a specialized medical expert, and somehow that doesn't seem right.

There are other problems to consider. Consumers complain bitterly about unsafe products. Each summer brings hordes of stories about consumers who have managed to cut off their toes or fingers as well as the lawns they are manicuring with their new power mowers. Should the mowers be made safer (and more expensive), or is it the consumers themselves who are at fault?

It is easy to overdo the problems with consumer appliances, given the hundreds of millions of them that work well on the whole. But there's not much doubt, there is a problem there. . . .

What, if anything, should the federal or state government do to protect buyers and users of consumer appliances? Among the actions suggested have been these:

1. Require that detailed information be attached to all appliances, covering their cost of operation, performance specifications, and likely life.

2. Establish minimum standards of performance and durability for all consumer appliances.

3. Establish a Consumer Appliance Protection Agency to develop and enforce standards for all major appliances and for service work on them. (Alternatively, assign this responsibility to some existing agency).

4. Make all appliance manufacturers and sellers responsible for triple damages to all consumers if any of their products is shown to be unsafe.

5. License all appliance service firms, approving only those that meet established standards of reliability, satisfactory service, fair prices, and guarantee of work done.

POLICY

Externalities,
Pollution, and
the Environment

CHAPTER 17

Chapters 15 and 16 considered government intervention to prevent or alleviate market failures—antitrust laws to limit monopolies, and a variety of regulations to protect consumers from misleading information and other producer distortions. This chapter considers another possible market failure—the existence of "externalities"—which may require government intervention if the market system is to serve us effectively. These three make up the first big class of "market failures" listed at the end of Chapter 10. The other two—failures to produce "public goods" and an acceptable distribution of income—are considered in Part 4, on the public sector.

In the United States, we have a strong tradition of trying private enterprise first and calling on government or government regulation only when private enterprise falls short. As long as trade takes place voluntarily between a buyer and a seller and affects only those two, we can be confident that their satisfactions and the general welfare are increased by each trade. Both buyer and seller must believe they are better off from the trade; otherwise they would not have traded. And no one else is harmed, so total satisfaction must be increased. This is summarized by Adam Smith's famous argument that it is not from his benevolence that we get our meat from the butcher, but out of his regard for his own self-interest. He buys beef and sells it to you because he feels he will be better off by doing this. You buy the meat because you would rather have it than the money you give him in exchange.

Unless you believe that superwisdom resides in dictators or elected leaders, it is hard to imagine a system that will guard the interests of both you and the butcher better. One of the system's most important advantages is the freedom it provides for individual choices, and the way it disperses economic power among many buyers and sellers. However, when the world becomes complex and your bargain affects the interests of others, the answer is less clear.

EXTERNALITIES AND PROPERTY RIGHTS

If I sell you cement made in a plant that pollutes the air for miles around, we can be reasonably sure that you and I both gain from the trade; otherwise we would not have traded. But our transaction, in effect, worsens the lot of people who live near the cement mill, and they have had no say in our transaction. Thus, we can no longer be sure that the general welfare is increased by the transaction. This is the case of "externalities," noted in Chapter 10 as a possibly important market failure. An external effect, or externality, occurs when your behavior affects the well-being of someone else without his agreement. Externalities can be either positive or negative; your action can either improve or worsen the lot of others without their assent. The cement case produces negative external effects; but if I hire a landscaper to beautify my lot, this produces positive external effects for my neighbors.

Consider the cement-plant case more thoroughly. What are the crucial variables? First, this is a case of complex exchange where third parties are affected by the exchange. There are externalities. Second, one of the important goods, or resources, is not privately owned. The air over the land surrounding the plant is publicly owned; private rights to its use are ill-defined. For the most part, it is treated as if it were a free good, available for anyone to use (pollute) as he wishes without payment. Third, since there are numerous landowners and residents affected by the dust from the cement plant, there would be substantial "transactions costs" involved in their all getting together to work out some voluntary group solution to the problem.

Note that if the air over the surrounding land were privately owned, the externalities problem would probably not arise. Private owners would not permit the cement plant to violate their air space without payment for the dirt it imposed. Thus, the cost of using the surrounding air to discharge cement dust would be a cost of production, just like raw materials and labor, and it would enter into the price charged for cement produced by the plant. The price would cover total costs, and the market system would provide the optimal level of cement output. The division between private and additional social costs noted in Chapter 10 would simply not arise.

Since the air is treated as a free good, it is not surprising that the cement plant uses it for dumping its dust; disposing of the dust in some other way would cost more. Any resource, good, or service that is free, or underpriced, will be overused. One major function of prices, as earlier chapters have repeatedly emphasized, is to ration, or limit the use of, the priced resource or good. Similarly, suppose the Ohio River, a heavily polluted stream, were privately owned—say, by General Motors, or by the thousands of people whose property lines the river. You can safely predict that polluters would be charged for using the river as a dumping ground for their effluents.

This case raises the third point noted above, the problem of "transactions costs." If GM owned the river, a price would promptly be set. But if thousands of river-rights owners and possible dumpers were involved in working out a charge for using the river to dump effluents, we can safely bet it would be a long and complex process; indeed, there is a good probability that they would never all be able to agree on an acceptable price and set of controls. Where only two or a few parties are involved, usually transactions costs are relatively small, and the parties are more likely to reach a voluntary agreement.

To summarize: Where externalities exist, private property rights are ill-defined, and transactions costs are large, a socially satisfactory solution to the pollution problem is almost certain to require collective (government) intervention. The same is true for other cases of both positive and negative externalities. For example, we will get the socially optimal amounts of education and noise (which have substantial positive and negative externalities, respectively) only with government intervention.

POLLUTION AND ENVIRONMENT

Pollution provides the most prominent, but by no means the only, example of externalities and the problems we face in dealing with them. Indeed, some observers argue that externalities are everywhere; that they are a pervasive market failure that requires equally pervasive government intervention in the market system. Whether or not this is true, pollution provides a major, timely case study.

National concern for the deteriorating quality of the environment has snowballed in recent years. Air and water pollution are pervasive by-products (externalities) of modern industrial society. On every side there are cries for the government to do more to halt pollution.

Water, air, solid wastes, noise, and the ecological system per se are the main elements of the pollution problem. Many of our rivers and lakes are contaminated and dangerous from sewage, industrial wastes, farm chemicals, and other pollutants. Each year America's industries, cars, and homes spew over 200 million tons of smoke and fumes into the air. Each year we throw away 60 billion metal cans, 20 billion bottles, 150 million tons of garbage, and 3 billion tons of mine tailings and debris. Especially in big cities, noise is reaching ever-higher levels of intensity. A typical subway train produces 95 decibels, a power mower 110 decibels, and a jet aircraft at takeoff 140 decibels. Electronically magnified rock-and-roll music reaches well above 100 decibels. Most broadly, ecologists, who study the interactions of entire systems of living things, go far beyond the problems above. They suggest that population growth and modern technology have gone so far so fast that they threaten man's very existence on this globe.

Deterioration in the quality of the environment is not confined to the United States, although our massive increases in real GNP and modern technology make the problem especially vivid for us. Nor is the problem confined to capitalist systems. Soviet newspapers complain of the same conditions in the USSR, and Soviet cartoonists are equally caustic in their drawings of pollution as it envelopes the Russian man in the street. Their rivers vie with ours for the title of dirtiest.[1] Japan's environmental problems are already worse than ours. And the Rhine, fabled in song and verse, is possibly the dirtiest of the world's major rivers. Open sewers and polluted water are daily threats to health and life itself in the world's less-developed nations, many of which are neither rich nor capitalist.

Pollution in the United States is largely a problem of high levels of consumption coupled

---

[1] For example, see K. Iosifob, "The Vokhna River Flows," and O. Volkov, "A Writer's Notes: A Trip to Baikal," reprinted in M. Goldman, ed., *Controlling Pollution* (Englewood Cliffs, N.J.: Prentice-Hall, Spectrum Books, 1967).

with externalities, although governments themselves are often major polluters, especially through inadequate sewer systems. In responding to market demands, businessmen do not charge the full social cost of their operations in their prices to consumers. The result is that the price of these products is too low; consumers buy too much paper and steel produced by the polluting plants. In effect, we make those harmed by pollution subsidize users of steel and paper. In the same way, the price of autos does not reflect their full cost to society; car users do not have to pay for the air pollution they create.

In principle, to provide an optimal allocation of society's resources in response to the public's wishes, costs should include both private and by-product social costs. If the price system doesn't do the job, we must turn to collective action if we want pollution reduced.

Put another way, manufacturers and auto drivers treat clean water, clean air, and quiet as if they were free goods, when in fact they are increasingly scarce and are overconsumed at a price of zero. We should be able to charge users of clean air and clean water for the privilege of making them dirty.

SOLUTIONS TO POLLUTION

Pollution, Population, and Economic Growth

Pollution, population growth, and economic growth are intimately related. But this does not mean that the way to reduce pollution is to stop economic growth. Economic growth means growth in total economic output per capita—it is growth in generalized productive capacity. We may use the increased capacity to produce things that pollute (for example, leaded gasoline), things that involve no pollution (art museums), or things that reduce pollution (smoke filters on chimneys). Even though output of some goods inescapably involves pollution (solid waste from many products), in general we can use our productive capacity to produce the combination of goods, services, and cleanliness we are willing to pay for. The choice of more clean air will mean

less steel and auto transportation from the resources available, but more steel and autos need not mean dirtier air if we are willing to pay for "clean" methods of production. GNP in total and per capita will not then be as large as with pollution, because cleaner air (less pollution) doesn't get included as we measure GNP; but this does not change the fact that we can allocate our productive resources as we wish to maximize our satisfaction from them. Indeed, the more we grow (increase productive capacity), the greater will be our ability to have *both* cleaner air and water *and* more of the other goods and services we want. To oppose economic growth because that seems the only way to lessen pollution is short-sighted indeed.

Population growth is different. More population, other things equal, means *less* output *per capita*—a lower standard of living. It also inescapably means more crowding of the environment, because the total amount of space to be shared is substantially fixed.

As a practical matter, combined population and economic growth have brought a devastating amount of environmental pollution over the last half century. But this does not mean that zero economic growth (ZEG), or even zero population growth (ZPG), is the best way to clean up the environment. On the contrary, we need to be careful not to throw the baby out with the bathwater.

Controlling Water Pollution—An Example

There are, broadly, four approaches to pollution control—voluntary action, direct government regulation, effluent charges, and subsidies. Let us consider briefly how each would work in controlling water pollution.

Voluntary action. To many environmentalists, pollution is a moral issue. Those who pollute are immoral, especially if they are large corporations. They ought to stop. Economics cannot pass judgment on people's moral and ethical values. But it must warn such moralists that their approach is not likely to get very far in cleaning up the nation's lakes and streams. First, the notion that big corporations are the devil in the piece is a half-truth. Much of the worst water pollution comes from public sewer systems, from private homes. Much comes from use of chemical fertilizers, pesticides, and the like on farms. And, although a lot does come from big corporations, much comes from little firms as well. Second, and still more important, elimination of pollution from industrial and agricultural production will be very expensive for many firms and farms. Thus, if only one paper mill along a river, voluntarily or under social pressure from its critics, spends the money to treat or recycle its effluents that have been polluting the river, it will find that its costs are higher than those of its competitors, and that it is pricing itself out of the market. Alone, it can do little good in reducing the overall level of water pollution, and it is likely to go broke trying. Only if other paper mills are required to meet similar effluent standards is any one firm economically safe in spending the money to reduce its pollution.[2]

To rely on voluntary action by businessmen to eliminate pollution, therefore, is to misconstrue the nature of the competitive process. Effective action to alleviate pollution (to internalize the externality) must, in most cases, be collective action. Moral pressure and persuasion may help, but by themselves they are unlikely to produce major changes against the pressures of market competition.

Direct regulation.   To reduce water pollution, the government may simply order all industries to reduce the amount of effluents they discharge into the lakes and rivers concerned. First, it must decide how clean it wants the lake or river to be—say, 90 percent cleaner than now. Then it orders each firm to reduce its untreated discharges by 90 percent. This would appear to be the simplest approach.

In fact, however, direct regulation faces many problems, even if a law is passed ordering a cleanup of the waterways. Under the 1956 and 1965 Amendments to the Water Pollution Con-

trol Act, first, the government was to determine the standard of cleanliness needed in each lake or stream to meet the overall goal; then it was to determine how much each polluter contributed to the excess pollution, and order each to cut back its pollution to meet the prescribed standard. But there are some 40,000 individual industrial sources of water pollution. Some firms have previously dumped few effluents, some many. The former understandably argue that they pollute little, that they should not have to reduce their effluents by a further 90 percent; and they are likely to go to court against the Environmental Pollution Agency if it applies the 90 percent rule to them. Moreover, it is obvious that the most efficient way to achieve the 90 percent overall reduction goal would be to concentrate cleanup action where the cost of reducing effluents is the least, not across the board. But either way, individual firms will protest that they are not in fact responsible for the pollution observed, and long court battles have ensued over the reasonableness of the regulatory actions.

Effluent charges.   Increasingly, economists and conservationists favor special taxes, or effluent charges, per unit of effluent discharged, to limit water and air pollution. As with direct regulation, the first step is to decide how much pollution is to be reduced. Then an across-the-board tax per unit of effluent discharged is levied (for example, 2 cents per pound of solid waste dumped into the stream). The level of the tax is set to reduce pollution to the desired level; by reducing their effluents, firms can avoid the tax. The higher the tax, the more it will pay the firm to avoid discharging effluent into the stream.

This approach has three big advantages over direct regulation: (1) It avoids the necessity of making a special administrative decision as to the limit to be placed on each separate firm; each firm pays the tax in proportion to its own polluting. (2) It achieves the desired reduction in total pollution at a lower cost. The incentive to reduce effluents will be greatest for those who can reduce their pollution at the lowest cost. Those firms that face a very high cost of reducing pollution may prefer to pay the tax, although since all firms face rising costs per unit as they eliminate more and more pollution, we can be

---

[2]Similarly, it would be unreasonable to expect the individual consumer to invest voluntarily in an expensive smog-control device for his car when other car users were not required to do so. Alone, he could do no measurable good in reducing smog. Only if all, or most, car users are required to add smog-control devices can the individual be sure that cleaner air will in fact result.

sure that the effluent charge will lead virtually all polluters to reduce their effluents to some extent. The result will be that the cost (price) of goods produced by the polluters will rise as little as is consistent with reducing pollution to the desired level.[3] (3) With direct regulation, once a firm meets the legal standard, it has no incentive to reduce pollution further. But with an effluent charge, it always has an incentive to reduce pollution further—for example, if technological advance reduces the cost of cutting back on effluents, it will pay the firm to reduce its pollution further to reduce its effluent tax. Conversely, with direct regulation, the firm has no incentive to reduce effluents further, even if it becomes cheaper to do so.

Some critics have called effluent charges "licenses to pollute," because a firm may choose to pay the tax and continue polluting. But the same charge can be levied against a regulatory limit; then all firms have a free license to pollute up to that limit. Precisely the same pollution reduction can be obtained under either approach, but more cheaply with effluent charges. Effluent charges can be set high enough to discourage any amount of pollution we want to eliminate. The only way to eliminate completely any license to pollute would be to forbid pollution completely, by either regulation or a prohibitively high effluent tax.

Subsidies. The fourth way to deal with pollution is to subsidize polluters to stop polluting. The government might pay polluters to install the equipment to clean up discharges before they enter the stream. In that case, taxpayers rather than customers pay the bill.

Economists are generally unenthusiastic about such subsidies, because they have the wrong incentive effects. If the government pays for the antipollution devices, the private firm incurs no costs and has no incentive to minimize the cost of cleaning up the effluent. More impor-

tant, since costs and therefore prices are not raised, the consumer of the product involved has no incentive to consume less of the more costly product. Thus, more is produced, and the total cost of resources devoted to pollution control will be larger with subsidies than with either direct regulation or effluent charges. In both the latter cases, the cost of cleaning up the effluent is included in the higher price the consumer must pay when he buys the product, and less will be produced and sold.

Who Should Pay?

The preceding sections generally presume that consumers should pay the full cost of the products they buy, including any related cost of pollution control. Most experts feel this is ethically desirable as well as economically sound. But suppose city *A* decides it wants exceptionally clean air or water, well above the standards of other cities. If it imposes either effluent charges or direct regulations on local industries to attain this goal, those firms will have higher costs than competing firms in other cities, and hence will lose sales. If *A* wants cleaner air than its neighbors, it will have to subsidize the local firms to meet these standards, or see those firms lose sales and ultimately be driven out of business by competitors elsewhere. Local taxpayers, rather than consumers elsewhere, will end up paying for the exceptionally clean air in *A*. See if you can devise a way to make the local firms and their customers bear the costs of extra cleanliness in the long run. Will it make a difference whether the firms involved sell in highly competitive or quasi-monopoly markets?

Marginalism—How Clean Is Clean Enough?

It should be clear by now that the cost of clean water depends substantially on how clean we want the water to be. If we want all our streams and lakes to meet distilled-water standards, the cost will be astronomical.

Urban sewage disposal, an unglamorous but central part of the water-pollution problem, illustrates this point. In many communities, raw

---

[3]If the effluent tax *rate* is the same for every firm and each firm reduces its effluent discharge to the point where the marginal cost of reducing discharge is equal to the effluent fee per unit of discharge, the marginal cost of reducing discharge is the same for all firms, and the total cost of obtaining the desired reduction in pollution is minimized. The marginalist principle gives the right answer again!

sewage is dumped directly into flowing streams. In about 35 percent of the cases, sewage is passed through a one-stage treatment; in another 25 percent, through a two-stage treatment, which removes perhaps 90 percent of the pollutant qualities of the sewage before it is dumped into streams. In virtually all cases, common sewers are used for rainwater runoff and sewage waste. Thus, heavy rainstorms may produce such flooding that the combined sewage plus rain runoff must be bypassed around the treatment plants, pouring directly into streams or lakes without any sewage treatment at all.

Use of sewers for both waste and rain runoff works well most of the time; both sewage and rainwater are funneled through the sewage-treatment plants. To protect against infrequent overloads would require either a new, dual sewer system or new sewage-treatment plants so large that they would handle even the massive runoffs in large storms. These would be extremely expensive. For industrial wastes, costs soar similarly as firms try to clean up their effluents to higher and higher standards of cleanliness. Cost estimates vary, but a total additional annual cost of $40–$50 billion would possibly suffice to provide two-stage sewage treatment for all major municipalities. This would, of course, fall substantially short of 100 percent water purification. In virtually all cases, the cost of additional cleanliness rises far more than proportionately as absolute cleanliness is approached.

How clean is clean? Clean water is not an all-or-nothing proposition. As almost everywhere in economics, the question is one of degree, a tradeoff between cleaner water and higher costs. Sensible policy involves comparing the marginal cost of each additional unit of cleanliness against the marginal benefits of that unit. And, to repeat, in most cases marginal costs rise sharply as cleanliness standards go up.

A simple example may emphasize this point. Johnny's mother tells him to wash his hands before he comes to dinner. When she sees the result, she says he has not *really* washed his hands. Johnny protests that he has; he has passed his hands through a stream of cold water before coming to the table. His mother sends him back, to use hot water, soap, and a towel, and then his hands pass inspection. Yet Johnny's hands, even

after a two-stage treatment, are far from clean enough to meet a surgeon's hospital-operating-room standards. The surgeon would demand a third-stage process. To insist on this third level of cleanliness in day-to-day life for most of us would be incredibly expensive in terms of time, energy, and money—and pointless. So it may be with many pollution issues.

THE ECONOMICS AND POLITICS OF POLLUTION

Reducing pollution, we have learned painfully over the past few years, is a complex, expensive job. The economic analysis involved is simple in principle, but complicated in its application to individual situations. Much of the difficulty arises from the fundamental fact of conflicts of interest that can be compromised only through the political process.

Balancing Costs and Benefits

How much should we spend on cleaning up pollution, at the local or national level? How clean is clean enough? The answer in principle is simple—spend more to clean up the air and water as long as the marginal cost is less than the marginal benefit. But it is often very difficult to measure these costs and benefits, especially when those paying the costs may not be the ones getting the benefits. So the marginal principle suggests a fundamental, useful approach, and cost–benefit studies to help decide what projects to undertake are based on it. But as a practical matter, most antipollution decisions are made on a cruder basis, without formal cost–benefit studies.

In 1975, Doctors Allen Kneese and Charles Schultze of Brookings estimated it would cost at least $500 billion to achieve by 1983 the goals for air and water already written into legislation. Since that time, Congress has raised some standards further and prices have risen sharply, so the figure is now much larger, amounting to perhaps $75 billion annually. Of this, perhaps a third would be spent by governments at all levels, the rest by private firms. Brookings's Edward Denison has estimated that by the mid-1970s, this huge annual expenditure had already reduced the nation's annual growth rate in per capita output by about 20–25 percent, by diverting funds that would otherwise have gone into private and public investment to increase output. The steel industry alone will have to invest $5–$6 billion annually on pollution-control measures to meet the present legal standards by 1983.

Emotions run deep on environmental matters. In 1973, Congress passed a new Water Pollution Act, over President Nixon's veto, decreeing that by 1977 all companies must install the "best practicable" pollution-control technology, by 1983 the "best available" technology, and must by 1985 have reached "zero discharge," complete elimination of water pollution—with heavy fines for violators. Experts question whether the new legislation will work: What does "best practicable" or "best available" mean in any particular case?; "zero discharge" may be more than we really want to pay for; the advantages of a flexible effluent-charge approach still look impressive.[4]

The battle against air pollution has also been a shifting one. Congress has passed stringent bills requiring all communities to meet much higher standards, and auto manufacturers to improve dramatically their emission-control performances. But difficulties in meeting these standards at acceptable costs (ultimately to consumers and taxpayers) have led to repeated extensions of time deadlines. Public enthusiasm for pollution control, not surprisingly, moves inversely with the cost of achieving the desired results.[5]

---

[4]Effluent-charge systems have proved workable in action. For example, water pollution in the Ruhr River valley in Germany, one of the world's most concentrated industrial complexes, has for over 40 years been controlled by such a set of charges—and very effectively, in the eyes of most observers.

For a brief description, see L. E. Ruff, "The Economic Common Sense of Pollution," *The Public Interest,* Spring 1970, pp. 84–85. More detailed treatments of the pollution problem are presented in E. G. Dolan, *TANSTAAFL* ("There Ain't No Such Thing as a Free Lunch") (New York: Holt, Rinehart & Winston, 1971); and A. Kneese and C. Schultze, *Pollution, Prices, and Public Policy* (Washington, D.C.: The Brookings Institution, 1975).

[5]This is especially true when the cost of a cleaner environment is jobs. In 1977, for example, the Dow Chemical Company, after two frustrating years and $20 million of expense trying to get all the environmental clearances required to build a huge new chemical complex near San Francisco, gave up the entire project, which would have provided some 2,000 construction jobs and another 2,000 long-term jobs when the plant went into operation. In such cases, the tradeoff between cleaner air and more jobs is painfully clear, especially for unemployed workers and the governments trying to get them jobs.

SUMMARY AND REVIEW

1. Externalities occur when behavior affects the well-being of a third party without his agreement. Externalities can be either positive or negative.

2. Externalities occur when property rights involved are not privately owned, or where the ownership is ill-defined.

3. Where externalities exist, private property rights are ill-defined, and transaction costs are large, a socially satisfactory solution to the pollution problem is almost certain to require collective (governmental) intervention.

4. Pollution, population growth, and economic growth are intimately related. But this does not mean that the best way to reduce pollution is to reduce economic growth.

5. There are four major approaches to pollution control—voluntary action, direct government regulation, effluent charges, and subsidies.

6. Voluntary action to eliminate pollution by private firms is unlikely to work, because the firm will be unable to compete effectively if it alone incurs the extra cost of eliminating pollution.

7. Effluent charges are generally more efficient than direct regulation in reducing pollution to any desired level. Effluent charges avoid the necessity of

making special administrative decisions concerning each separate firm; they achieve the desired reduction completion at a lower cost; and they provide incentives to firms to reduce pollution further.

8. Subsidies generally have the wrong incentive effects, and are not usually an efficient means of reducing pollution.

9. Generally, it seems both equitable and economically efficient for consumers to pay the full cost of the products they buy, including related costs of pollution control. However, if any locality wants less pollution then others, it will have to subsidize local firms to meet its especially high standards, or see those

firms eliminated by competition from lower-cost producers elsewhere.

10. Most antipollution measures involve a tradeoff between costs and benefits. Often the costs rise more than proportionately as higher standards of cleanliness are achieved.

11. In principle, the decision on how much to spend on antipollution measures should be made by equating marginal cost and marginal benefits. While this principle is helpful in suggesting cost—benefit comparisons, it is often not feasible as a practical matter, especially since costs and benefits often affect different persons. Decisions are thus usually made primarily on a political basis.

New Concepts to Remember	externalities	ill-defined property rights
	transaction costs	effluent charges

For Analysis and Discussion

1. Explain why you would expect "market failure" in cases of externalities.
2. Explain why effluent charges will generally be the most efficient way to achieve any pollution-control goals.
3. Should the Ohio River be cleaned up so that it is again attractive for swimming, boating, and fishing? If so, how, and who should pay for the reclamation?
4. Many critics argue that the auto manufacturers are responsible for smog and air pollution in the cities. They argue that the auto companies should be required to bear the cost of eliminating the auto-exhaust contribution to smog.
   a. Is this a correct analysis of responsibility?
   b. If you believe the cost of eliminating auto air pollution should be placed on the auto manufacturers, how would you accomplish this? (Remember your price theory from Chapters 10–14.)
5. Your city has an air-pollution problem, primarily from autos, private furnaces, and industry. Devise an acceptable program to clean up the air to acceptable standards. Will direct effluent limits or effluent charges work better?
6. Should the federal government pay for upgrading the sewage systems of cities that do not meet the new federal water-cleanliness standards? Why?
7. Should the federal government spend more to improve the environment? How do you decide how much is the right amount, and who should pay?
8. Should students picket corporations that cause air or water pollution

CASE 19

THE $66-BILLION MISTAKE

On February 21, 1973, the Mobil Oil Company placed the following full-page advertisement in major newspapers throughout the country. Although the figures are a little out of date now, the ad still presents the basic problem very effectively.

In 1970, Congress passed a series of amendments to the Clean Air Act. One of them said that all cars sold in the United States after 1974 must be near-zero polluters.

It sounded fine. Near-perfect emission control seemed not only desirable, but imperative. At that time, people widely assumed that the air was getting steadily dirtier because of the automobile. Most people also assumed that industry could solve any technical problems that might be encountered—and at a reasonable cost.

The goal has proved elusive. Despite the expenditure of hundreds of millions of dollars and uncounted hours of research and development time, no control system that meets all the requirements of the federal standards has yet been proved.

Bad news? Not necessarily. Today both industry and government have the benefit of research results and other information that were simply not available when Congress passed its amendment in 1970. Today we know that:

1. Total air pollution from cars has already been rolled back to the level of about 1960, and is continuing to drop.
2. Cars that met the federal standards would probably be poor performers and gasoline-guzzlers. They also could need costlier maintenance than today's cars.
3. A less restrictive level of controls on automotive emissions would do very nearly as much for air quality as the federal standards would.
4. Meeting the federal standards could cost $100 billion over ten years starting in 1976; meeting the less-restrictive standards could cost $34 billion. The difference could be a $66 billion mistake.

If not perfection, what? The only way to completely eliminate auto pollution would be to do away with the auto itself. Since this would be neither practical nor desirable, what percentage reduction of emissions should we aim at? By what date? And at what cost?

The goal should be to make the auto as small a contributor to air pollution as technology allows—but without incurring exorbitant costs for dubious results. Since technology does not stand still, this would be a moving goal. Today's impractical dream often can be tomorrow's reality.

Today's reality in automotive-pollution control is, in fact, yesterday's dream: As Chart 1 indicates, emissions of hydrocarbons, carbon monoxide, and nitrogen oxides have been drastically reduced from the days (not long ago) when exhaust emissions were uncontrolled. Changes in engine design plus pollution-control devices have reduced emissions by 1973-model cars an average of 66 percent.

This is quite an achievement. And as a result, total air pollution from automobiles has been declining in the United States since 1968, and is now down to the levels of about 1960. It would continue to decline for several more years even if no further controls were imposed, as old cars with few if any controls are scrapped.

So, how much further should we go? And by when?

California has a better way. The Air Resources Board of the State of California has proposed automotive emission-control levels based on air-quality standards calculated to restore the atmosphere of Los Angeles to its quality of the early 1940s. California

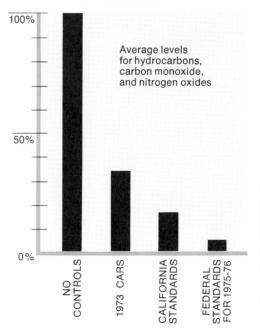

CHART 1
Emission Levels of U.S. Cars

Average levels for hydrocarbons, carbon monoxide, and nitrogen oxides

100%

50%

0%

NO CONTROLS

1973 CARS

CALIFORNIA STANDARDS

FEDERAL STANDARDS FOR 1975-76

proposes to cut the three principal auto emissions by an average of 83 percent. . . .

The California standards are similar to those proposed by the federal government's own Department of Health, Education and Welfare in 1970.

The HEW standards were not accepted. Instead, Congress voted for the last bar on Chart 1. The Clean Air Act now mandates that the three emissions be reduced by 97, 96, and 93 percent—for an average of 95 percent. These levels must be reached by 1975 for hydrocarbons and carbon monoxide, and by 1976 for oxides of nitrogen, unless the federal government grants an extension.

A 95 percent reduction in emissions may not seem much more difficult to achieve than an 83 percent reduction. But did you ever try to wring the last drop of water out of a wet towel? One good twist and most of the water flows out. Another hard twist and a little more dribbles out. But now the law of diminishing returns sets in. It's just plain impossible to wring the towel dry, and not worth the effort.

Similarly, the last few percentage points of automotive emission control are far costlier and far more difficult to achieve than the first 80 to 85 points.

Mobil sells gasoline, but we have no desire to see our products wasted. Cars built to the federal standards could consume as much as 15 percent more gasoline per mile than cars built to the California standards. That 15 percent would require refining an extra 30 million barrels of crude oil in 1976, and an extra 150 million barrels a year by 1980. All that crude oil would have to be imported, with a substantial drain on our country's balance of payments.

Up the Matterhorn. Which brings us to Chart 2. The one with a curve that looks like the southeastern slope of the Matterhorn.

Control equipment to meet the 1973 standards adds about $65 to $100 to the cost of a new car. Not

Auto Emission Reductions below Pre-Control Levels

	HYDRO-CARBONS	CARBON MONOXIDE	OXIDES OF NITROGEN
1973 Cars	80%	69%	50%
California	94	81	75
Federal	97	96	93

excessive, considering how far the cars have come in reducing harmful emission.

The price curve turns up to meet the California standards—to a range of $175 to $300 per car for the control equipment. Perhaps still not too expensive, considering the extra gains in pollution reduction. But to reach the federal standards that are now the law for 1975 and 1976 models, the cost curve heads almost straight up. These systems could cost $500 to $600 a car—and maybe more. We can't determine the exact costs, since systems to meet the 1976 standards have not been proved.

These are just the initial costs of the emission-control systems. Add the extra maintenance, and throw in the additional gasoline, and the grand total for meeting the federal standards comes to $100 billion over the decade starting in 1976.

CHART 2
Extra Cost of Cars with Emission Controls

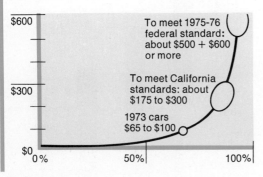

234

Add the same expenses for the California standards, and the grand total is $34 billion. (All these figures are Mobil engineers' estimates, expressed in today's dollars.)

Our calculations do not include a cost for the special kind of gasoline that would be needed to meet the federal standards.

Clean air and public transportation. Is there a better way to spend all or part of $66 billion to reduce total automotive air pollution?

There is indeed. Public transportation. Public transportation clean enough, safe enough, fast enough, and priced attractively enough to induce Americans to use their automobiles less and public transportation more.

More and better public transportation can go a long way toward several desirable objectives: Less air pollution. Less waste of gasoline. Less pressure on the U.S. balance of payments as our imports of oil inevitably rise. And maybe less emotional strain on motorists and fewer accidents.

Under such a program, motorists could drive better-performing, less expensive, and safer cars. A substantial drain on the U.S. balance of payments, for crude oil and platinum, would be avoided. A vital and scarce natural resource—petroleum—would be conserved. And the advance of technology would enable automakers to meet even stricter control standards—if they were found necessary at some future date—with durable, trouble-free, and reasonable economic systems.

Not to mention avoiding a $66 billion mistake.

Do you agree with Mobil's analysis and recommendations? If not, what is your program for handling the auto air-pollution problem? Under Mobil's proposal and yours, who are the main beneficiaries, and who would pay most of the costs of cleaner air?

The Distribution
of Factor and
Personal Incomes

Part 3

Incomes:
The Pricing
of Productive
Services

CHAPTER 18

One of the hottest issues in economics has long been the distribution of the national income—between wages and profits, rich and poor, "haves" and "have-nots." Governments have risen and fallen on the struggle for income shares. The revolutionary doctrines of Karl Marx centered around the "exploitation of the worker" by the "rich, greedy capitalist." In a different setting, this same struggle over income shares is the issue when the United Steelworkers fight the steel companies for wage increases. It is the issue behind the race riots in the cities. History tells a recurrent story of the "have-nots" fighting for more and the "haves" struggling to protect their share.

Thoughtful observers of the private-enterprise economy point out that we're all in the same boat. If everyone pulls together—labor, capital, management—total output will grow and everyone can have more. No one who understands the basic interdependence inherent in the modern economy would deny this. There is an enormous community of interest in making the private-enterprise economy work effectively, and the spectacular growth of U.S. total output, with rising income for every group, is one of the great success stories of economic history.

But part and parcel of that community of interest is a basic conflict, rooted deep in our traditions of self-interest and competition. This is the struggle of each individual to get more for himself and his family. It is the struggle over who gets how much of the economic pie. However rich the nation is, we're all interested in our own shares—relative and absolute. Nothing is gained by refusing to face this fact.

This chapter has two major sections. First, the facts—who gets how much income in the United States today? Second, the theory of income distribution—why do people receive the incomes they do? Then the following chapters apply this theory to explaining wages and salaries, rents and interest, and profits.

WHO GETS HOW MUCH?

The Income Revolution

American incomes have risen persistently and rapidly for over two centuries, and nearly every

TABLE 18–1
Family Incomes in 1947 and 1978

ANNUAL INCOME (In 1978 dollars)	PERCENT OF FAMILIES	
	1947	1978
Under $3,000	19	3
3,000–5,000	24	4
5,000–10,000	37	20
Over $10,000	20	73
Median family income	$8,400	$17,200
Total income—all families	$550 billion	$1,700 billion

Source: U.S. Census Bureau. Preliminary estimates of distribution for 1978 by author.

group has participated. Our standard of living is one of the highest in the world.

Table 18–1 summarizes the facts since World War II. Total real national income (that is, the sum of all incomes adjusted to eliminate rises due only to higher prices) has tripled—from $550 billion to $1,700 billion (in 1978 prices). In 1947, median family income was $8,400 in 1978 dollars; in 1978, it was about $17,200.[1] In 1978, nearly 75 percent of all families received over $10,000, compared to only 20 percent 30 years earlier. The other big element of the U.S. income revolution was the rise of the huge middle class. In 1978, about 50 percent of all families received incomes between $10,000 and $25,000, and another 20 percent between $25,000 and $50,000. Only about 2 percent received over $50,000.

Figure 18–1 poses an interesting question about the distribution of incomes in America. The regular, bell-shaped curve shows what statisticians call a "normal" distribution. Intelligence, physical traits, and many other phenomena seem to approximate this type of normal distribution, when large numbers are considered. More people are at the midpoint of the curve than at any other level, and those above and below the average shade off about equally either way.

---

[1] The median is the figure that divides the total number of families in half. Thus, in 1978, half of all families received more than $17,200, half less.

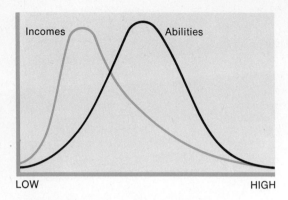

FIGURE 18–1
Human Abilities and Income
Ability and most other human characteristics seem to be "normally" distributed through the population at birth, as shown by the regular bell-shaped curve. Incomes are much more equally distributed. Why?

We might assume that general ability is normally distributed among the total population at birth. But incomes received, shown by the blue line, are "skewed." That is, there are many more relatively poor than rich people. These account for the big hump in the curve toward the lower-income end of the scale. There are a few very rich, who give the curve a long "tail" out to the right. Why are incomes less "normally" distributed than human abilities at birth?

Is income becoming more or less equally distributed? Since the 1920s, more equally. (Before that, the data are highly unreliable, although apparently the same conclusion would apply.) The facts are shown in Table 18–2.

Another way of measuring changes in income distribution is shown by the "Lorenz curve" in Figure 18–2. The income of all families is cumulated along the horizontal axis, beginning with the lowest-income family; the percentage of total income received by those families is cumulated along the vertical axis. For example, in 1929, the bottom 40 percent of all families received about 12 percent of the total national income, the lower 90 percent received about 60 percent. By comparison, in 1978, the bottom 40 percent of families received about 18 percent, and the bottom 90 percent received about 75 percent.

If all family incomes were equal, the points plotted would all fall on the diagonal. That is, the lowest 10 percent would receive 10 percent of the total income, and so on up the line. Thus, the more bowed out the Lorenz curve is, the more unequal the distribution of income is; the nearer it is to the diagonal, the more equally incomes are distributed.

Figure 18–2 thus shows that incomes are somewhat more equally distributed now than either in 1929 (the peak of the boom) or in 1935–36, the Great Depression years. It also shows that the distribution has changed only moderately over that tumultuous period.

One last historical observation: Are the very rich—the millionaires—being squeezed out by high income and inheritance tax rates? Apparently not. Invested capital continues to be a major source of very high incomes. In 1969 (the last reliable study), the bottom 80 percent of all families held only 22 percent of the wealth. At the other extreme, the richest 1 percent held 24 percent of all wealth, but this share had declined persistently from 36 percent in 1929. In 1970, there were some 50,000 millionaires in the nation in terms of wealth, compared to only a few hundred in the 1920s; and in 1970, about 1,000 people had annual incomes exceeding $1 million. Still, the richest 1 percent (families with incomes over $50,000) received only 6 percent of the total

TABLE 18–2
Family Income Shares, 1929–78

	PERCENT OF TOTAL INCOME RECEIVED			
	1929	1950	1960	1978
Bottom fifth	3.5	4.5	4.8	5.5
Second fifth	9.0	12.0	11.7	12.0
Middle fifth	13.8	17.4	17.4	17.5
Fourth fifth	19.3	23.5	23.6	24.2
Top fifth	54.4	42.6	42.6	40.8
All families	100.0	100.0	100.0	100.0
Top 5 percent	30.0	17.0	16.8	15.2

Source: U.S. Census Bureau. Preliminary estimates for 1978 by author.

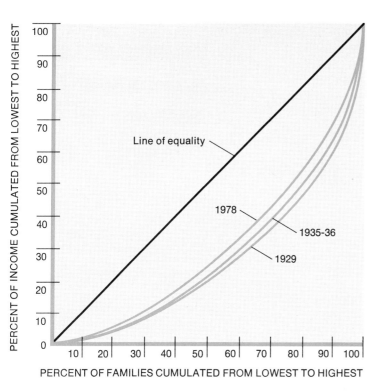

PERCENT OF INCOME CUMULATED FROM LOWEST TO HIGHEST

Line of equality

1978
1935-36
1929

PERCENT OF FAMILIES CUMULATED FROM LOWEST TO HIGHEST

FIGURE 18–2
Distribution of U.S. Incomes, 1929–1978
Incomes are somewhat more equally distributed now than in 1929 or 1935–36. The more bowed the curve is, the less equal the distribution of income was in that year. (Source: U.S. Census Bureau.)

national income. Roughly, double the income figures in this paragraph to convert the 1969–70 data to 1980, reflecting both growth in real income and inflation.[2]

Money and In-Kind Incomes

All the income data in the preceding paragraphs are for *money* income—wages, salaries, rents, interest, profits, Social Security and unemployment benefits, and the like. But, as we shall see in Part 4, the government takes a big chunk of our incomes in taxes and provides us a lot of useful goods and services—education, food stamps,

public housing, highways, and the like. The net result of these taxes and expenditures is some transfer of real income from the more wealthy to the poor, although a lot of the transfers occur within the big middle-income classes.

If we take the in-kind services provided by the government into account, the money-plus-in-kind income is more equally distributed than is money income alone. For example, the experts estimate that although about 11 percent of the population is "poor" (four-person urban family income under $6,600 in 1978) in money-income terms, the figure falls to about 5 percent when in-kind income received from the government (food stamps, Medicaid, public housing, and the like) is included. More details in Chapters 23 and 25, but remember that the money-income figures commonly cited are only part of real income received, and government-provided services have grown rapidly since the 1920s.

[2]For details on the distribution of income and wealth, see D. Radner and J. Hinrich, "Size Distribution of Income in 1964, 1970, and 1971," *Survey of Current Business*, October 1974, especially pp. 21–23; and J. Smith and S. Franklin, "The Concentration of Personal Wealth," *American Economic Review*, May 1974, pp. 162–67.

Occupational and Educational Differences

What jobs provide the best incomes? At the peak, a few TV, rock, and movie stars get astronomical salaries. Elton John, the rock star, reported taxable income (after all expenses) of $8 million in 1978. Paul Newman collected $1 million for three weeks' work on a film. Johnny Carson gets $3 million per year for three nights a week on TV. Top athletes are down with the peak-pay business executives. Jimmy Connors collected $825,000 in tennis tournament and exhibition winnings; O. J. Simpson is said to be the highest-paid football star at an $800,000 annual salary.

Table 18–3 gives rough estimates of median incomes for a sample of less exotic occupations in 1978. Physicians, lawyers, and other highly trained professionals top the list. The median figures for managers and proprietors don't look like the huge salaries you read about for corporation presidents. *Answer:* There are a few huge salaries, but most managers earn lots less. Nor do

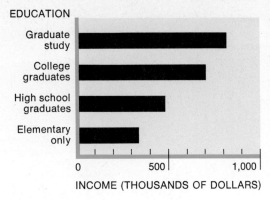

EDUCATION

INCOME (THOUSANDS OF DOLLARS)

FIGURE 18–3
Estimated Lifetime Earnings and Educational Achievement
The biggest earned incomes go to physicians, dentists, lawyers, and other professionals with postgraduate schooling; the smallest to unskilled and low-skilled workers with high school educations or less. (Estimates based on 1970 census data.)

TABLE 18–3
Median Incomes in Different Occupations, 1978[a]

Physicians and surgeons	$70,000
Dentists	41,000
Lawyers	34,000
Engineers	25,000
Economists	24,000
Managers and proprietors	20,000
Auto workers	19,900
College and university teachers	19,500
Accountants	18,000
Postal clerks	14,500
Librarians	12,500
Secretaries, typists	9,100
Retail salesclerks	8,700
Waiters	5,900
Unskilled workers, farm	5,800

[a] Based on U.S. Census and Department of Labor data (except for physicians, based on special studies), assuming that interoccupation differences remained substantially stable following 1970 census. Figures are only rough approximations. Some figures are averages of diverse groups (for example, managers and proprietors). Figures do not include "fringe benefits."

many people who are in business for themselves get rich quick; some succeed, many don't. At the bottom of the list, low-skilled and unskilled laborers in business or agriculture don't do very well. Women's incomes in the same occupations were lower throughout.

Table 18–3 suggests a high correlation between incomes earned and the amount of education workers have. Eight of the ten top occupations in the Census Bureau's detailed list of income receivers involved schooling beyond a college degree, averaging 17+ years of school. Figure 18–3 shows this clearly. The estimated lifetime earnings (as of 1972, in 1972 prices) for males with only an elementary school education was only $390,000. They were $540,000 for high school graduates, $710,000 for college graduates, and $820,000 for holders of advanced degrees.

Women and Minority Groups

The average income of working women is about 60 percent that of working men. Women generally get paid less than men do for similar jobs, even though by law they must receive equal pay for equal work. Mainly, the difference in incomes reflects the heavy concentration of women in low-paying jobs—especially clerical and service work, and unskilled labor. Women are now increasingly showing up in higher-paid occupations—the professions, skilled labor, and middle management—but there are still relatively few in peak-income jobs.

Similar income differentials prevail for minority groups, of which blacks are the largest. The median black family income in 1977 was only about $9,600, compared to about $16,700 for white families. But the relative position of blacks and other minority groups has improved since the early 1900s; in 1950, the black-to-white income ratio was only .54, compared to about .60 in 1977. Incomes of Hispanic-origin families (mainly from Mexico, Puerto Rico, and South and Central America) averaged slightly higher than those of blacks but still well below white incomes.[3]

The overall minority-group figures mask dramatic differential movements for men and women, and for different education levels. Since 1939, black male full-time earnings have risen from 45 to 65 percent of their white counterparts, mainly during the tight labor market of World War II. But black full-time female workers' incomes rose from 38 to 94 percent of their white counterparts over the same period, including a big advance in the 1960s and 1970s. By 1980, blacks with college and postgraduate educations had achieved nearly full income parity with whites. But massive unemployment and low incomes still characterized young black school dropouts and other minorities with less than high school educations.

Why do these differences exist, and why are they changing? To answer these questions, we need a theory of income distribution, to which the last half of this chapter is largely devoted.

---

[3]Although apparently some 12 million people of Spanish origin live in the United States, the Census Bureau has only recently begun to collect separate data on them, and we have little reliable information on their economic status.

WAGES, INTEREST, AND PROFITS— FUNCTIONAL SHARES

Most very rich people get a big part of their incomes from invested capital—from interest and profits. Most low- and middle-income families receive little or nothing from such investments, except for the use of the houses some own. Thus, the wide spread in incomes reflects big differences in the income received from capital even more than the wage and salary differentials above.

Yet the American economy today doesn't look much like Karl Marx's picture of capitalism in its death throes, with the workers poised to seize ownership of the means of production. American labor and management do exchange some violent words, and strikes are sometimes long and bitter. But in the showdown, management and labor get together; production goes on, with the worker's rights still intact and the capitalist's control over his investment substantially maintained. When the workers in America go to the polls, they vote Republican or Democratic, not Communist. The radicals who want to destroy the capitalist system usually find themselves lined up against management and workers who are defending the basically private-enterprise economic system.

But within this framework, labor and management wrestle constantly over the division of the consumer's dollar betwen wages and profits. Figure 18–4 gives an overall picture of the outcome of the wage–profit bargaining during the last four decades. The left-hand section plots the actual dollar shares of national income that go to wages and salaries, corporate profits, unincorporated business incomes (a mixture of salaries and profits), rents, and interest, all before payment of income taxes. The right-hand portion shows the percentage shares that go to these various groups.

The first lesson comes from the left-hand chart. Everyone's income has grown rapidly, and in a serious depression we're also all in the same boat—everyone takes a beating. The second lesson, from the right-hand chart, is the dominance of wage–salary incomes and the

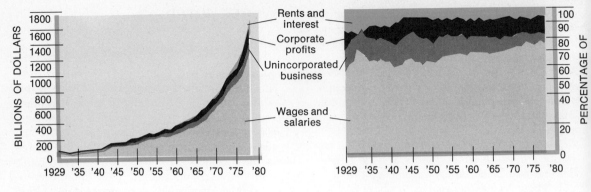

FIGURE 18–4
National Income Shares, 1929–1978
Everyone's income has grown since 1929, but wages and salaries by much the biggest amount. They have also gradually increased their share of the total. Note that profits vanished in the Great Depression. (Source: U.S. Department of Commerce.)

general stability in the major income shares, except during big business fluctuations. The wage and salary share has trended upward, from the 65 to the 75 percent range. Partly, the rising wage share reflects the steady population shift from farms to urban jobs, but beyond this, there has apparently been some tendency for the profit-plus-interest share to be squeezed.

A different picture of the outcome of the labor–capital struggle for income shares is given if we compare the return *per unit* of labor and capital used in the economy. Real wages per hour are more than four times as high as they were in 1900, while the real long-term interest rate (a crude measure of the return per dollar of capital invested in the economy) is still about the same. The real (inflation-adjusted) profit rate appears to be about what it was a half century ago, or somewhat lower.

Looked at this way, it appears that virtually all the fruits of increased output have gone to labor and virtually none to capital.[4]

---

[4]The amount of capital has grown much faster than the number of workers, so the total return to capital keeps up with the total wages even though the return per dollar invested falls far behind the growing annual wage per worker.

INTERNATIONAL COMPARISONS

How does the U.S. distribution of income compare with other countries? Table 18–4 gives a partial answer, for the Western industrialized nations. The columns show the percent of total

TABLE 18–4
Distribution of Personal Income

	PERCENT OF INCOME RECEIVED BY:		
	BOTTOM 10%	MIDDLE 80%	TOP 10%
Australia	2.1	74.1	23.8
Canada	1.2	71.7	27.1
France	1.5	67.5	31.0
Germany	2.5	66.4	31.1
Japan	2.9	68.5	28.6
Netherlands	2.3	66.6	31.1
Sweden	2.0	73.6	24.4
United Kingdom	2.1	73.2	24.7
United States	1.2	70.4	28.4
Average, all countries	2.0	70.7	27.3

Source: Data from Organization for Economic Corporation and Development, *Economic Outlook—Occasional Studies,* July 1976. Data are for the early 1970s.

income received by different deciles (tenths) of the population. For example, in Australia, the bottom tenth received 2.1 percent of total income, the top tenth 23.8 percent. The United States is, roughly, in the middle of the income distributions shown. Although the bottom tenth here is *relatively* poorer, the top tenth gets a smaller share than in several other countries. France, Germany, and the Netherlands have the largest share going to the top tenth; Japan has

the largest share going to the bottom tenth.

Remember that these are all relative figures; the bottom tenth in Japan, for example, is absolutely much poorer than the bottom tenth in the United States. Note, too, that these are money-income figures. Several of the European countries have large government social service programs that provide free or cheap health care, housing, employment training, and other real income to lower-income or all families, in addi-

---

INEQUALITY, OPPORTUNITY, AND UPWARD MOBILITY

Have industrialization, big business, and modern technology increased economic and social stratification in America? Does today's inequality of income and wealth mean that only the children of the rich have a chance to become rich and powerful in their generation?

The answers are complex and the evidence is mixed. The poor face a tough path in trying to rise from poverty. But it has always been tough to rise from the lower-income classes, and today's concentration of income and wealth is less than it was a century ago. Overall, the evidence suggests that economic stratification is less rigid today than it was 50 or 100 years ago.

A recent study of the sources of top business executives found:

*Only 10.5 percent of the current generation of big business executives . . . [are] sons of wealthy families; as recently as 1950 the corresponding figure was 36.1 percent, and at the turn of the century, 45.6 percent. . . . Two thirds of the 1900 generation had fathers who were heads of the same corporations or who were independent businessmen; less than half of the current generation had fathers so placed in American society. On the other hand, less than 10 percent of the 1900 generation had fathers who were employees; by 1964 this percentage had increased to nearly 30 percent.** *

The post–World War II period brought the greatest increase in the proportion of those from economically poor backgrounds (from 12.1 percent in 1950 to 23.3 percent in 1964) who entered the top echelons of American business; and there was a corresponding decline in the percentage from wealthy families. The replacement of family-owned enterprise by the public corporation, the bureaucratization of American corporate life, the recruitment of management personnel from the ranks of college graduates, and an increasingly competitive promotion process were all important factors. Because of the spread of higher education to the children of the working classes (almost one-third now attend college), the ladder of bureaucratic success is increasingly open to those from poorer circumstances. Business and professional families are still the largest sources of business leaders. Privileged family and class backgrounds continue to be a big help in the quest for corporate success, but training and talent can increasingly make up for their lack.†

Other recent sociological studies reach the same conclusion, although with some vigorous dissenters from the communist–socialist wing. But to say that apparently more opportunity now exists for upward mobility than a half century ago is not enough. Particularly, members of minority groups, such as blacks, Spanish-speaking Americans, and American Indians, have made very little progress in reaching top economic positions, even though their incomes have risen relative to those of whites.

*See S. M. Lipset, "Social Mobility and Equal Opportunity," *The Public Interest*, Fall 1972, for a summary and references to a number of studies.

†See G. Burck, "A Group Profile of the Fortune 500 Chief Executive," *Fortune*, May 1976.

tion to the money incomes they receive. But taxes are higher in those countries too. Comparing income distributions in different countries is a complex task.

THE THEORY OF INCOME DISTRIBUTION

Why do people receive the incomes they do—some large, some small; some stable, some insecure? The answer is complex, as with most other important issues in economics. But the core of the answer is summarized in the remainder of this chapter; then it is applied specifically to wages, interest, rent, and profits in the following chapters. You will find that you already have the central analysis from Part 2.

The income you get (leaving aside gifts, Social Security benefits, and other transfer payments) depends on the productive services you have to sell—your labor and your capital, if you have any. Most people get nearly all their income as wages or salaries, but owners of capital also get income from rent, interest, and profits.

The price of each productive service (for example, the wage of a worker) is set through supply and demand, roughly equal to the marginal productivity of that productive resource—that is, equal to the contribution that that worker makes toward producing what consumers demand. Whenever the price of, say, labor is below its marginal product (what one more worker would add to the firm's salable output), businessmen can increase their profits by hiring more labor. Competition among businesses for workers will bid up the wage rate toward the marginal productivity of that type of labor. Conversely, if the wage rate is more than labor's marginal product, it will pay businessmen to hire fewer workers, and the wage rate will fall. Only when the wage rate just equals labor's marginal product will business firms and the labor market be in equilibrium.

Each person's earned income, therefore, will depend on his marginal productivity and on how much he works, plus the marginal productivity of capital multiplied by the amount of capital he owns. His education and training, his IQ, his family background, how hard he works, his race and sex, the match of his interests with what consumers will buy, and luck—all these and more will determine his wage or salary. Add how wealthy his parents were, how much he saves, his skill in investing or in running a business, and again luck, for his income from capital. Some of these factors are clearly under the individual's own control; others, he can't do much about. In the simplest language, he has to have something to sell that consumers (or businesses catering to consumers) want to buy. The consumer is sovereign in determining factor incomes as well as in determining what gets produced.

"Distribution theory," explaining why different productive resources earn the incomes they do, is thus merely price theory from Part 2, viewed from the reverse side. There, we focused on the pricing of final products, like autos; here, we focus on the pricing of productive services, like labor and capital used to produce autos. When the businessman decides to produce 10,000 autos this week, he is, ipso facto, deciding to hire the labor and to rent or buy the machines he needs to do the job. When we compare this demand with the supply of labor or machines offered, we can determine the prices set for productive services through the same supply-and-demand mechanism as in Part 2. Obviously, the degree of competition or monopoly in the market will affect the outcome in both.

The Supply Side

To determine the price of any productive service, first we need a supply curve, or schedule. Consider the supply of some type of labor in your town—say, carpenters—as an example. The supply this month may be highly inelastic—fixed by the number of carpenters there and by their preference to work about 40 hours a week. Or the supply may be elastic, if carpenters can readily be drawn in from neighboring areas by higher wages. Or overtime work may be feasible. All these things together produce a labor-supply curve for the market for the time period under study, probably an upward-sloping supply curve indicating that more labor hours will be supplied at higher than at lower wage rates. In general, the more unattractive the job and the lower the promise of advancement, the less will be the labor supplied at any given wage rate.

Labor-supply conditions vary widely for different jobs, and over different periods of time. The supply of neurosurgeons is highly inelastic in the short run and only moderately elastic in the long run. That of waitresses or store clerks is highly elastic, because their jobs require little training, and workers can be drawn quickly from other jobs by higher pay. In general, the elasticity of supply goes up as more time is allowed for training, education, and movement of workers from other areas.

The supply of labor for any occupation can be increased by investment in "human capital" through education and training, just as the supply of machinery, factories, and other forms of nonhuman capital can be increased by investment. Thus, as we shall see in Chapter 19, the value of an individual's services over his lifetime and his wage at any time will reflect how much investment he has made in himself or others have made in him through education, training, experience, and the like.

The Demand Side

The demand for productive services is primarily a derived demand.[5] The local drugstore hires clerks because customers want to be waited on—not because the druggist wants clerks in the same way that he wants consumer goods. Businesses' demands for productive services are thus derived from ultimate consumer demands. If consumers want lots of prescriptions filled, the demand for prescription clerks will be strong. But if the customers stay healthy, the druggist doesn't need many clerks.

How many workers (or other productive resources) will a firm demand at any given wage rate? The familiar marginal-cost-equals-marginal-revenue rule gives the answer. If it is to maximize profits, the firm will hire additional workers as long as each additional worker adds more to the firm's income (marginal revenue) than he adds to its costs (marginal cost). If the wage of another worker is more than that worker adds to revenue, to hire him would lower the firm's profits. If the wage is less than the worker's marginal product, hiring him will increase profits. Profits will be maximized by hiring additional productive resources until the marginal cost just equals marginal revenue.

The marginal revenue obtained from hiring productive resources is often called "marginal revenue product." To understand the determinants of marginal revenue product of any productive resource (and hence business firms' demand for it), we need to separate two components. Additional physical output ("marginal physical product") is what the worker adds to total output. But from management's point of view, it is the increase in sales dollars that matters. Hence, it is the marginal revenue product in which we are most interested, so multiply the marginal physical product by its price.[6]

Be sure you understand that this is merely a repetition of the central profit-maximizing propositions from Part 2. There, we thought of the firm's planning in terms of units of output; here, the firm plans in terms of units of inputs of productive services used. But the rule of $MC = MR$ to obtain maximum profit applies either way, and the equilibrium position is the same either way you go at it.[7]

---

[5]The appendix to Chapter 8, "Physical-Production Relationships Underlying Cost Curves," provides a rigorous logical foundation for this section. If you studied that appendix, it may be useful to review it before proceeding. The "marginal product" of that appendix is identical with the "marginal physical product" of this chapter.

[6]The existence of monopoly raises some special problems, which will be considered in the next chapter.

[7]Although the statements above indicate only how much of a single resource it will pay the business to hire, this approach can readily be generalized to cover *all* the productive resources the firm hires. It will pay to hire more of *each* resource as long as its marginal cost is less than its marginal revenue product. In equilibrium, therefore, each resource will be hired up to the point where its marginal cost just equals its marginal revenue product, which is the same as saying that marginal cost equals marginal revenue for the firm as a whole, the profit-maximizing condition stated in Chapter 9. (For a more complete statement, see the appendix to this chapter.)

The Interaction of Supply and Demand

We now have the outlines of the market for productive services—a supply curve and a demand curve for each type of productive service in each market area, local or national. Employers will compete for more workers as long as their wage is below their marginal revenue product, but no employer will pay more than labor's marginal revenue product. Thus, competition will bid wages up to about the level of labor's marginal productivity, and no higher. And so the wage will be set.

Figure 18–5 pictures a simple supply-and-demand market equilibrium for one type of labor (say, electrical engineers) in a local market this week. The supply curve is inelastic; in this period, not many more labor hours will be supplied at moderately higher wage rates. The demand curve slopes down for the reasons suggested above. A weekly wage of $200 just clears the market, at 400 engineers per week demanded and supplied. At a higher wage, more would be supplied but less demanded; at a lower wage, the reverse.

Give your theory a workout to explore some implications of this analysis. Suppose Figure 18-5 pictured the market for heart surgeons. (Make the prices per day or per hour rather than per week.) The total supply is highly inelastic (substantially fixed in amount) in the short run. Now suppose Congress greatly increases appropriations to support research in this area and to finance heart operations for needy patients. What will happen to the incomes of heart surgeons in the short and in the long run? (*Hint:* The median income of physicians in 1978 was about $75,000, up from $24,000 in 1960; total expenditures on health services rose from $13 billion to $180 billion over the period, while the number of physicians per 100,000 population increased only moderately.)

Competition and Monopoly in Factor Markets

In factor as in product markets, an optimal (most efficient) allocation of resources depends on the existence of competitive markets. If there is monopoly in a product market, firms will restrict output to obtain higher prices and profits, and too few productive resources will be used in the industry. Moreover, this restricted demand will reduce the price (wage) obtained by workers in the industry. Similarly, if there is monopoly in factor markets (say, because a union holds the price of labor above the competitive market level), firms will hire less labor, and displaced workers will have to seek jobs elsewhere, reducing wages there. And as with product markets, effective restrictions on entry (say, because a strong union limits entry) may permit union members to continue to hold their wages above the level obtained by comparable laborers in nonunion markets. More detail on these various combinations of monopoly and competition in the next chapter. Remember that many factor markets are far from perfectly competitive.

THE INTEGRATION OF PRICE AND DISTRIBUTION THEORY

The preceding section emphasized that price theory and distribution theory (Parts 2 and 3) are substantially the same. They both look at the pricing process and at the allocation of resources and incomes in response to consumer demands. To see how the total general equilibrium system fits together, go back and reread the section "General Equilibrium of a Competitive Economy," in Chapter 10. It is the analytical core of this section as well. The pricing of productive services is part and parcel of the general equilibrium pricing process. The costs paid out by business firms are the incomes received by the factors of production. Thus, the profit-maximizing decisions of businessmen simultaneously provide the goods most desired by consumers at the lowest feasible prices and provide to resource owners the largest incomes consistent with their abilities and willingness to contribute to producing what consumers demand. The whole system relies on each individual (worker, consumer, businessman, capitalist) to look out for his own self-interest; it relies on

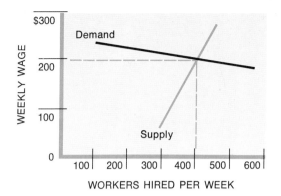

FIGURE 18–5
Supply and Demand for Labor
Wages, like other prices, are determined by supply and demand forces. Here, the equilibrium wage is $200 per week, with 400 workers hired.

competition to see that the end result is in the best interests of all.

Wages, Rents, Profits, and Prices Simultaneously Determined

Wages, interest, rents, profits, and product prices are all *simultaneously* determined in the competitive market system.[8] Economists are fond of quoting the following little rhyme by H. J. Davenport, a famous economist, to point up the interdependent determination of all product and factor prices:

The price of pig is something big;
Because its corn, you'll understand,
Is high-priced, too; because it grew
Upon the high-priced farming land.

If you'd know why that land is high,
Consider this: Its price is big

---

[8]The appendix to this chapter provides a more rigorous statement of the marginal-productivity relationships involved. Mathematically inclined readers are referred to Mathematical Appendix III at the end of the book, where the preceding theory of income distribution (factor pricing) is stated rigorously and some of its interconnections with the macro explanations of relative income shares are explored.

Because it pays thereon to raise
The costly corn, the high-priced pig.

Consider the jingle. It tells an important truth.

TOTAL INCOMES: EARNINGS AND TRANSFER PAYMENTS

This chapter has emphasized that people's earned incomes depend on the services that they and their capital provide. This accounts for most of most people's incomes. But many people also receive substantial transfer payments from the government—Social Security benefits, unemployment payments, "welfare," veterans' benefits, food stamps, Medicare, Medicaid, and a variety of others. In 1978, these transfer payments to individuals from the federal government totaled $180 billion, about 12 percent of all personal incomes. By 1980, such transfer payments were scheduled to rise to over $200 billion. For the last decade, they have been the fastest-rising share of the federal budget.

Who gets these transfer payments? Mainly members of the big middle class; Social Security benefits are by far the biggest single item. But as a percentage of total income received, they bulk largest for poor families, for some of whom such payments constitute most of their incomes. Look ahead to Figure 23–5 for estimates of the shares of income received from government transfer payments at different income levels.

Thus, the preceding pages have been right in stressing marginal productivity as the main factor explaining the incomes we receive. But this explanation needs to be supplemented by a look at the massive transfer payments that now go to many individuals and families. These transfer payments will be a major focus of attention in Part 5, on the public (government) sector of the economy.[9]

---

[9]In terms of the GNP accounts, the major portion of this chapter has been concerned with the *national income* (how the national income is earned), while this final section focuses on *personal incomes* (how much income people have for paying taxes, spending, or saving).

SUMMARY AND REVIEW

1. The first half of Chapter 18 provides mainly information on the distribution of incomes in the United States. Don't try to memorize all this detail, but get a general impression of the nature of the U.S. income distribution.

2. The incomes people receive (leaving aside Social Security benefits and other transfer payments) depend largely on the productive services (labor and capital) they have to sell.

3. The price of each productive service (for example, the wage of a worker) is set through supply and demand in competitive markets, roughly equal to the marginal productivity of that productive resource—that is, equal to the contribution that the worker makes toward producing what consumers demand.

4. The supply of any productive service (e.g., type of labor) depends on the education, training, ability, desire to work, and other qualities of the laborers concerned. The supply of labor can be increased by "investment in human capital," through education and training, just as the supply of machinery, factories, and other forms of nonhuman capital can be increased by investment.

5. The demand for productive services is primarily derived from consumers' demand for final goods and services. Any firm, to maximize its profits, will demand additional productive resources until the marginal cost just equals the marginal revenue for each.

6. The interaction of supply and demand in any competitive labor (or other productive service) market will push wages up to labor's marginal productivity, and no higher. An excess supply of labor will drive wages down in any competitive market when the wage is above that labor's marginal productivity. Thus, the wage is basically set by that labor's marginal productivity, which in turn reflects the labor's ability to contribute to producing goods and services that consumers want to buy.

7. As in product markets, the degree of monopoly must be taken into account in assessing the effectiveness of markets for productive services in allocating resources efficiently and providing maximum income to workers and other owners of productive resources.

8. "Distribution theory," explaining why different productive resources earn the incomes they do, is thus merely price theory (from Part 2), viewed from the side of pricing inputs of productive services rather than outputs of final products.

9. Transfer payments (mainly from the government) must be added to earnings from labor and nonhuman capital to obtain the total distribution of income in our society. Transfer payments are Social Security benefits, unemployment payments, "welfare," and the like. They make up about 10–15 percent of total U.S. personal income and are determined basically by political decisions, not by market forces.

New Concepts to Remember

derived demand	distribution theory	
marginal physical product	Lorenz curve	
marginal revenue product	human capital	

For Analysis and Discussion

1. Are most people's incomes a good measure of what they are worth?
2. Does marginal-productivity analysis explain the high earnings of modern rock and TV stars? of surgeons?
3. The two biggest shares of the national income are wages and profits. Are the basic interests of wage earners and of their employers competitive or complementary?
4. Explain carefully how incomes are distributed in a highly competitive, market-type economy.
5. Would a distribution of income based purely on marginal productivity give everyone about what he is worth? Explain. If you don't think the market properly measures people's worth, how would you measure it?
6. Would the equalization of incomes in the United States, as is proposed by some socialists, solve the problem of poverty? Use the figures on national income and those on income distribution (in this chapter), insofar as you think they are relevant, to support your answer.

7. According to Table 18–3, farm and other unskilled laborers receive substantially lower incomes than the other groups shown. If this is so, why do people continue to be farmers and unskilled laborers?

8. "The distribution of incomes to factors of production is no problem to one who has studied the behavior of business firms. In determining what prices to charge and what output to produce, the firm simultaneously determines how many workers to hire and what wages to pay out, what rents and interest charges to incur, and so on for the other income shares." Can you show how your analysis of Part 2 has in effect explained the distribution of incomes?

APPENDIX   Production Theory, Price Theory, and Distribution Theory

This optional appendix provides (for those who studied Chapters 8 and 9) a more rigorous statement of what economists call the theory of production and the foundation it provides for price theory and distribution theory.

The theory of production. The theory of production is concerned with the physical relationship between the factors of production used (input) and the product produced (output). The central principle is the law of diminishing returns, or of variable proportions. This law states (appendix to Chapter 8) that as the proportion of one input to other inputs rises, the additional units of output per unit of that input may rise at first, but will sooner or later begin to fall, and will fall persistently thereafter (other things, such as technology, being unchanged).

Because the law of diminishing returns applies to each productive factor as more of it is used relative to others, it constitutes a powerful analytical tool for deciding the optimal proportions among factors of production if we want to obtain the most efficient (least-cost) production of any commodity. As more of each factor is added relative to the others, its marginal physical product will decline. To obtain the minimum cost of production for any given output, we should add more of each productive factor until the last (marginal) dollar spent on each provides the same addition to total output—that is, the same marginal physical product. This is so because under any other condition, more physical product could be obtained for the same cost by switching a dollar from a lesser-contributing factor of production to a higher-contributing factor. Thus, in equilibrium:

$$\frac{\text{Marginal physical product of } A}{\text{Price of } A} =$$
$$\frac{\text{Marginal physical product of } B}{\text{Price of } B}, \text{ etc.}$$

Another (equivalent) way of saying the same thing is that in the least-cost condition, the marginal physical products of the factors of production must be proportional to their prices. That is:

$$\frac{\text{Marginal physical product of } A}{\text{Marginal physical product of } B} =$$
$$\frac{\text{Price of } A}{\text{Price of } B}, \text{ etc.}$$

This proposition implicitly underlies the discussion of the unit-cost curves in Chapters 8 and 9. The U-shape of the firm's cost curve derives in part from the physical relationships described by the law of variable proportions. Most important, assuming the prices of factors of productions to be given, the minimum-cost point on the firm's unit-cost curve can be achieved only when the factors of production are used in the proportions indicated above.

This theory of production also provides the answer to how a change in the price of any factor will affect its use. If the price of one resource (say, labor) falls, its use will be increased until its marginal physical product falls to the same proportion with other marginal physical products as the new proportion among the factor prices concerned. In other words, more labor will be hired until the marginal dollar spent on labor again produces the same marginal product as when spent on any other factor of production. Hiring more labor becomes desirable even though this reduces labor's marginal physical product under the law of diminishing returns.

Maximum-profit positions in price theory and distribution theory. The statement of the least-cost conditions above does not necessarily specify the maximum-profit position of the firm. It only specifies the conditions for obtaining the least-cost production for any given production level. The condition for maximum-profit (or minimum-loss) production is to increase production as long as marginal cost is less than marginal revenue (up to $MC = MR$). This is identical with the proposition that maximum profit (or minimum loss) will be obtained by adding units of each factor of production as long as its marginal cost (price, under competitive conditions) is less than its marginal revenue product. The statement in terms of individual factors of production merely specifies in more detail the mix of productive factors that must be used in arriving at the maximum-profit position. The

$MC = MR$ proposition of earlier chapters is silent on the optimal factor combination; it implicitly takes the optimal combinations for granted. We can now add the proposition that for maximum profit, the marginal cost of each factor used must be equal to its marginal revenue product and that the marginal costs of all the factors used must be proportional to their marginal-revenue products:

$$\frac{\text{Marginal cost of factor } A}{\text{Marginal cost of factor } B} = \frac{\text{Marginal revenue productivity of } A}{\text{Marginal revenue productivity of } B}$$

Or, to put it another way, that:

$$\frac{\dfrac{\text{Marginal cost of } A}{\text{Marginal revenue productivity of } A}}{\dfrac{\text{Marginal cost of } B}{\text{Marginal revenue productivity of } B}} =$$

Wages
and Salaries:
Applying
the Theory

CHAPTER 19

Wages and salaries account for nearly three-fourths of the total national income, and for nearly all of most people's incomes. By the same token, they constitute over two-thirds of total business costs. So it is not surprising that people have long been spinning out theories to explain why wages and salaries are what they are.

Economists' theories mirror the times in which they live, and several different theories have been widely accepted over the last two centuries. Today, we do not yet have a fully satisfactory theory of wages. Yet most economists agree that the simple marginal-productivity, supply-and-demand theory stated in the last half of Chapter 18 provides a fruitful way to examine why individual wages are what they are. This chapter is primarily an application of that theory—to explain why different people get the wages and salaries they do.

SOME DUBIOUS THEORIES

But first let us consider briefly three theories of wages that attained widespread acceptance during the last century, and that still have considerable influence in lay thinking, even though most economists today consider them to be largely fallacious, or at least of dubious value.

The subsistence theory. Nearly two centuries ago, Thomas Malthus argued that wages for the masses would never long remain above the subsistence level—the so-called "Iron Law of Wages." Malthus said that population will tend to grow geometrically—2, 4, 8, 16 . . .—while the food it can produce is limited. Thus, the growing supply of labor will always tend to force wages down toward the subsistence level. Wages cannot permanently stay below the subsistence level, for obvious reasons. But they will not for long stay above it in the absence of artificial means to limit population growth. Marx accepted much of the theory and predicted the downfall of capitalism, as workers become increasingly unwilling to accept their menial existences while capitalists appropriate the "surplus value" created by the workers whose wages fall increasingly short of the total value they create.

But history has shown an escape from this bitter prospect. In most Western industrialized nations, technological advance and capital accumulation have saved us from Malthus and Marx. In fact, real wages have risen rapidly and (except for cyclical fluctuations) steadily over the past century. Moreover, in the nations with the highest living standards, birthrates have fallen far below the rates in less-developed countries.

But don't write off Malthus too fast. For many less-developed nations, Malthus's predictions on wages look perilously close to right. Total output has grown in most nations, but, for over half the world's population, little faster than the number of mouths to feed, and starvation looms on the horizon each bad crop year.

The "lump-of-labor" theory. Another widely held, but almost completely fallacious, theory is that there is some fixed amount of work to be done in the short run, so more people seeking work will take jobs from those already at work. This theory, often unarticulated, lies behind widespread opposition to letting new workers into the labor market—foreigners, women, apprentices, and so on. It lies behind union restrictions on entry to many occupations, and behind widespread resistance to "automation"—to the introduction of machines that appear to replace human beings.

What is the fallacy in this "lump-of-labor" theory? We can—through government monetary and fiscal policy—ensure enough demand to provide jobs for as many workers as enter the labor market. At the level of the individual industry, the demand for labor is a function of the marginal productivity of that labor. Workers willing to work for a wage at or below their marginal productivity can always be employed profitably if we ensure the right amount of total national demand. The total amount of labor that will be hired is thus a function of both ultimate demand and the price (wage) of the labor. There **is no fixed amount of work to be divided up; the** number of jobs depends on aggregate demand and the real wage that workers demand.

The bargaining theory. A third theory, one with an important element of truth, is that wages depend on the relative bargaining power of employers and employees. Clearly, relative bargaining strength does matter sometimes—for example, when the United Auto Workers sit down to bargain with General Motors. But the bargaining theory leaves one big question unanswered: What are the limits within which the bargaining can vary the wage, and what sets those limits? If the union is very strong, does that mean there is no upper limit as to how high it can push its members' wages? Obviously not. At some level, the employer would have a strong economic incentive to substitute nonunion labor or machinery for the high-cost union members, or eventually go broke. If there is no union, does that mean the employer can drive down the wage virtually to zero? Obviously not. If his wages go far below prevailing levels, his employees will look for jobs elsewhere. Thus, to say that wages depend on relative bargaining strength is an obvious half-truth. The following pages should go a long way toward defining the limits within which bargaining power may dominate under different conditions.

But to point out the inadequacies of these theories does not provide a satisfactory explanation of what does set wages. We need a theory that will encompass the cases where Malthus appears to be right, where "automation" occurs, where bargaining power varies, and where new workers enter the labor market.

WAGES IN COMPETITIVE MARKETS

Supply and demand for labor, with marginal productivity determining the demand, goes a long way toward explaining all the cases in market-type economies. The wage earned by each class of labor will tend to equal its marginal revenue productivity, for the reason outlined in Chapter 18.

Figure 19–1 shows the close correspondence between output per man-hour and real wages in the American economy since 1900. It emphasizes a basic fact: It is rising productivity that has made possible the steadily rising wages of American workers. Even though there are many more workers seeking jobs now than in 1900, their productivity is so much higher now that businesses demand the larger number—even at much higher wages.

But before applying the theory in detail, two preliminary warnings: First, there are 100 million people in the American labor force, no two exactly alike. Thus, we cannot talk of "labor" and "wages" as if they were homogeneous. We need to look separately at many different types of

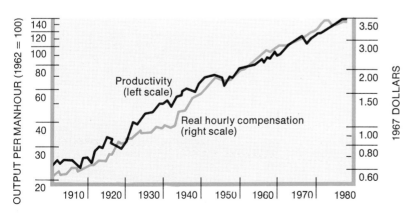

FIGURE 19–1
Real Wages and Productivity since 1900
Rising productivity has made possible the steadily rising real wages of American workers. (Source: Council of Economic Advisers.)

labor, at people with different capacities, different education and training, different attitudes, living in different places.

Second, we shall be looking at the determinants of individual wages, or wages of particular groups of workers, in contrast to the "macro" issues of wage–profit shares in the total national income. Thus, this is a chapter mainly at the "micro" level. It takes the level of aggregate demand (GNP) as given.

Begin with a simple case. What determines the wage received by William (Bill) Welder, a hypothetical laborer who works for the Acme Plumbing Company, a small plumbing-fixtures manufacturer. There is no welders' union in the area. Bill's abilities are substantially undifferentiated from those of other welders. There are many companies in the area that hire welders. And there are many plumbing-supplies manufacturers in the United States who compete actively with each other in the product market. So there is active competition at three levels—among welders for jobs, among businesses for the services of welders, and among businesses for the consumer's sales dollar.

What determines Bill's wage? He gets the going hourly rate for welders–say, $12 an hour. Acme Plumbing doesn't haggle over wage rates with each man it hires. It pays the going rate.

Something beyond Acme determines the "going wage" for welders in the area. By now, the answer "supply and demand" ought to come easily to you as the framework for looking at this price—the price of labor.

The Supply Side

What determines the supply of welders in the area? In the short run, it depends largely on the number of welders in the area, the availability of additional welders from nearby areas, and the willingness of welders to work longer hours. In the long run, supply will be more elastic. Welders may be drawn from long distances; workers may shift from other occupations; new labor-force entrants may learn welding. Plumbing manufacturers, the government, or workers themselves may invest in human capital by training nonwelders to become welders.

Figure 19–2 pictures the general relationship

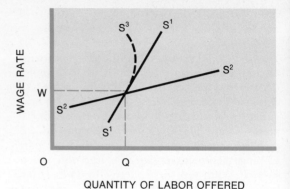

FIGURE 19–2
Short- and Long-Term Labor Supply Curves
The short-run supply curve for labor (S^1S^1) is typically much less elastic than the long-run curve (S^2S^2). If OQ labor is offered now at wage OW, a higher wage will increase the labor offered only slightly in the short run, much more in the long run. The dashed portion (S^3) of the short-run supply curve shows the special case where a higher wage calls forth less, not more, labor.

between short-run and long-run labor-supply curves. Short-run supply is usually inelastic. Except for overtime and the possibility of getting workers away from other areas or occupations, higher wages won't greatly increase the amount of labor offered. See curve S^1S^1. But in the long run, there are many new sources of supply; the curve is more likely to look like S^2S^2.[1]

The nature of the supply curve in each industry depends in part on the kind of work involved, working conditions, promise of ad-

---

[1]Sometimes labor-supply curves are "backward bending," as indicated by the dashed extension of S^1 to S^3 in Figure 19–2. This is fairly common in the less-developed countries. Workers, accustomed to low standards of living, simply stop working after they have earned enough in, say, a week to meet their minimal needs. They prefer leisure to more money with the additional work required to get it. Thus, raising the hourly wage offered will get less work, not more, because workers will earn their desired minimum income by working *fewer* hours.

Backward-bending labor-supply curves are less common in countries like the United States. But you may know people who simply prefer leisure to work once they have the current income they need to buy what they most want. At a high enough wage rate, they will feel able to afford to work less, not more, even though the money opportunity cost of each extra hour of leisure is higher.

vancement, and the like. The less attractive, pleasant, and promising the job, the higher the wage will have to be to bribe workers to accept that package of wages, working conditions, and promise for the future. Many people are surprised that even in periods of widespread unemployment, city newspapers are full of ads for dishwashers, household help, messengers, and the like. But a common reaction to such jobs is that they're low-pay, unattractive, and dead-end— why take them? "Job attachment" in such occupations is low. People, especially young people, often quit after only a brief stay. Try applying this kind of supply analysis to the job of "sandhogs"—men who drill tunnels under rivers. The work is dangerous, unpleasant, and difficult; the pay is high. Or to lifeguards at your local beach in summer.

The Demand Side

The demand for welders' services is a derived demand—derived from the ultimate consumer demand for the plumbing fixtures Acme produces. Acme (and other businesses) will demand more welders whenever it has unfulfilled demand for its product at profitable prices. More precisely, Acme will demand more welders as long as the wage is below welders' marginal revenue productivity. Other firms will do likewise. By aggregating the demands of all firms, we could draw a market-demand curve for welders' services. The lower the wage (marginal cost), the more welders the market will demand.

Marginal revenue productivity for most workers is compounded of marginal physical productivity and a product-price factor. Bill Welder's marginal *physical* product is the additional physical product Acme Plumbing turns out by having Bill on the job, compared with the output without him, all other productive factors being unchanged. This marginal physical product depends on Bill's own mental and physical abilities, training, morale, and so on—on his human capital, built up through education, training, and experience. It also depends, probably even more, on the capital (other productive agents) with which he works. The average U.S. worker in manufacturing is supported now by a capital investment of over $40,000, which goes

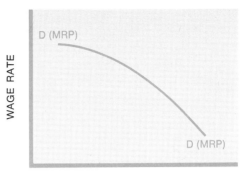

FIGURE 19–3
Firm's Downward-Sloping
Demand Curve for Labor

The competitive firm's demand curve for labor is downward-sloping. The demand curve is labor's marginal revenue product in the firm, since it will pay to hire more workers as long as marginal revenue product is more than wage.

far to explain his higher marginal productivity.[2]

The production manager is mainly interested in the number of sinks turned out per day. But the president and the stockholders are more interested in profit figures—in dollars and cents, rather than in numbers of sinks and faucets. For them, productivity figures have to be converted into marginal revenue (sales-dollars).

Bill's marginal revenue productivity is the additional sales dollars brought in by employing him. If his marginal physical product is two sinks per day, and the wholesale price of sinks is $50, then his marginal revenue productivity at Acme

---

[2] A worker's marginal physical product depends on the *proportion* of workers to other productive agents, as well as on the quality of the machinery and tools he works with. For example, if welding is one operation on a metal-sink production line, the addition of the first welder to that line means a big increase in the firm's output. But once the line is roughly balanced between welders and other workmen, adding more welders may increase output somewhat but the additional (marginal) product is much lower than it was when the first few welders were added. This is the law of diminishing returns again.

Generations of economists have worried about all the angles. Suppose we have five ditchdiggers and five shovels. What is the marginal product of a sixth shovel? *Answer:* Small, but positive. It has some value as a spare. How about a sixth ditchdigger with only five shovels? Same answer. He can fill in during rest periods, or he can go for beer.

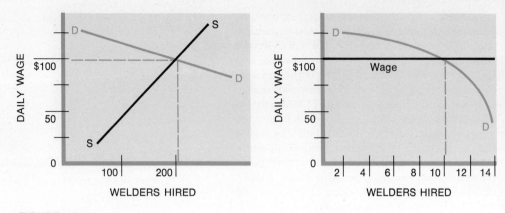

FIGURE 19-4
Equilibrium Wages: Market and Individual Firm
Welders' wages are set in the market (left-hand side). At a market wage of $100, Acme maximizes profits by hiring ten welders, at which point their wage equals their marginal revenue productivity (*DD* curve, right-hand side). A total of 200 welders is hired.

Plumbing is $100. Marginal revenue productivity is found by multiplying the marginal physical product by marginal-unit revenue (price under pure competition). Consumer demand for the ultimate product is just as important as the worker's physical output in determining his value to the business.

The marginal revenue productivity of welders will eventually decrease as more welders are put to work producing sinks—because of the law of diminishing returns and because, as more sinks are produced by this and competing firms, their price will fall, consumer demand remaining unchanged, although Acme alone is too small to influence market price. Thus, the demand curve for workers will generally be downward-sloping, as in Figure 19–3. Starting from any equilibrium position, firms will hire more labor only as wage rates fall, given an unchanged demand for sinks. The marginal revenue product curve for welders in the firm is that particular firm's demand curve for welders.[3]

---

[3]Note that if firms are prepared to increase the capital with which welders work (for example, by increasing the scale of plant), the effect of diminishing physical productivity can be avoided. But the declining-price effect will nevertheless pull down marginal revenue productivity.

SUPPLY, DEMAND, AND PURELY COMPETITIVE WAGES

To demonstrate rigorously that the wage will equal marginal productivity, assume temporarily (1) that perfect competition prevails (no union), (2) that welders are all identical, (3) that employment conditions are similar at different plants in the area, and (4) that information on wages at different plants is circulated freely. Then all plants will have to pay about the same wage to get welders, just as there tends to be a single price for any identical commodity within any given market area.

Figure 19–4 shows an equilibrium position for welders and their wages. The left-hand side shows an equilibrium wage of $100 per day with 200 welders hired. There is neither excess demand nor excess supply of welders. The right-hand side shows Acme Plumbing; given the market wage of $100 per day, it is maximizing profits by hiring ten welders, where the wage just equals marginal revenue productivity (shown by the *DD* curve). Each welder is earning just what he is "worth"—that is, just his marginal productivity.

Now suppose consumer demand for metal sinks increases. We have no diagram of the final-product market, but the increased consumer demand will raise the marginal revenue productivity curve for welders; their physical marginal product is now worth more in the market. So the *DD* curve at Acme Plumbing will rise, say by $10 a day. (Draw the new Acme *DD* curve in Figure 19–4.) Since the same increase in demand for welders will occur at other firms, the total industry demand curve for welders (*DD* in the left-hand part of the figure) will also rise by the same $10, since it is the summation of the individual-firm demands. (Draw the new *DD* curve on the left side of Figure 19–4.) This increased market demand will lead to both a higher wage for welders and the hiring of more welders. You can see that the wage will rise about $8 per day and about ten more welders will be hired, given the supply curve of welders, *SS.*

This is a new market-equilibrium situation, with welders getting $108 per day and ten more welders hired. The wage that Acme, a wage taker, must pay is now $108, but it will pay Acme to hire perhaps one more welder, since the $108 wage is still just under the new higher *DD* at eleven workers. Note that, although the immediate effect of the increased demand would be to raise the wage offered to welders by $10, that will not be maintained—because as more welders are hired in different firms, their marginal physical product will fall, and as output grows, the price of sinks will fall back from its original response to increased consumer demand (that is, the *DD* curve for each firm is downward-sloping). But in the new equilibrium, we would again expect to find the following:

1. The wage rate is equal to welders' marginal revenue productivity in the plants where they are hired.
2. Welders' wages are identical at all plants in the area.
3. Each firm is hiring as many welders as it "can afford" at that wage; each firm continues to hire welders as long as the wage is lower than welders' marginal revenue productivity.
4. All welders in the area who are seeking work at $108 or less are employed. If any were still looking for work at that wage or less, the market wage rate would be driven down by their willingness to work for less than the rate being paid to the employed workers.

Thus, each worker earns what his labor is "worth," as measured by its marginal contribution to producing the goods and services consumers demand. But remember: Each individual's marginal revenue productivity, and hence his wage, depends on a lot of forces outside his own control—on shifts in consumer demand, changing technology, the efficiency of management, the state of the business cycle.

Now try applying the same analysis to a related question. What will your starting salary be when you are graduated from college? How about five years later?

WAGE DETERMINATION IN MONOPOLIZED INDUSTRIES

What difference does it make if either labor or final-product markets are partly or completely monopolized? First, suppose the plumbing-supplies industry is monopolized by one or a few major producers? Continue the assumptions that each firm does the best it can to maximize profits, that firms in this and other industries compete actively for welders, and that there are no unions.

As under competition, each firm will continue to hire more welders as long as the wage is lower than welders' estimated marginal worth to the concern. But the total number of welders hired in this industry will be lower than under competition, because the monopolist restricts output to get higher prices and higher profits.

Thus, fewer welders will have jobs making plumbing supplies. If welders could work only there, clearly wages would be forced down by their competition for the reduced number of jobs. But since (we assume) welders are mobile, those unemployed will compete for jobs elsewhere, forcing down welders' wages there. Welders' wages will again be identical everywhere in the new equilibrium, but at a lower level than without the monopoly. By restricting output below the competitive "ideal," the monopolist forces an inefficient allocation of labor, and this produces a lower wage for welders than under competition, both in the plumbing-supplies industry and elsewhere. Too few workers are employed in making plumbing supplies, too many in the rest of the economy. They are not efficiently allocated.[4]

---

[4]The argument can be stated rigorously, as follows: Since the monopolist always faces a downward-sloping demand curve, marginal revenue is always less than price. The marginal revenue product obtained by hiring more labor is therefore always less than marginal physical product times the product price; instead, it is marginal physical product times marginal revenue. Since the marginal revenue product curve is the firm's demand-for-labor curve, the firm's demand for labor under monopoly will always be less than in a comparable competitive case.

WAGE DETERMINATION UNDER EMPLOYER MONOPSONY

Now assume a different situation, where there is no competition among employers for labor. An example might be an isolated company mining town, where there is no significant alternative to working in the mine. The mine operator has a substantially complete "monopsony"—that is, a monopoly in hiring workers. Such a business is a wage maker, not a wage taker. There is no competition to make it pay a wage as high as the

---

DOES DEMAND REALLY DEPEND ON MARGINAL REVENUE PRODUCTIVITY?

In a purely competitive labor market, the individual employer is a wage taker, not a wage maker. He has to pay the going wage; his problem is how many men to hire at that wage. This depends on the marginal product an additional worker will provide. But how can businessmen estimate anything as complex as a worker's marginal revenue productivity?

In a small firm like Acme Plumbing, the boss will have a good idea of how much his daily output will go up if he puts on an extra man. And he knows the price of sinks. This was the kind of situation economists had in mind when they developed the marginal-productivity approach to explaining the demand for labor.

But what about the marginal revenue productivity of a welder at U.S. Steel? It has nearly 300,000 employees scattered over the U.S., with hundreds of welders among them. Welders work on jobs many steps removed from the ultimate products sold to customers. For example, one welder may do repair work on the company's railway cars that shuttle materials around the mills. What is his marginal productivity?

Obviously, no one knows precisely. It would be impossible to isolate the effect on the ultimate production of steel of laying off that one welder. And there are millions of workers in American industry who present similar problems in estimating marginal productivity.

Still, U.S. Steel has to decide how many welders it will hire. Company officials might tell you that they simply hire enough welders to get the steel produced for which they have orders. But this answer drives us back to the question of the price at which U.S. Steel will book orders. Clearly, this decision depends in large part on the costs estimated by the steel people for producing steel sheets. All these interrelated variables have to be put together, and somehow the managers at the plant level have to decide when it will pay to hire another welder.

Where does all this leave us on the demand for labor? First, it's clear that no very precise estimate of marginal productivity is possible in many cases. Second, hard as the estimating job is, businessmen have to make some such calculation (consciously or subconsciously) in their hiring and pricing decisions if they are intelligently trying to maximize profits. Third, often several types of labor must be hired as a group to operate as a production unit. You either have the people it takes to run a modern assembly line, or you just shut the line down. In such cases, it is very difficult to separate out the marginal product of each kind of laborer.

Out of all this emerges a rough notion that businessmen are willing to pay workers only what they are "worth," viewing them sometimes as individuals but often as groups required for an integrated operation. What workers are worth **logically** boils down to a notion of marginal revenue productivity. Although this figure can't be estimated precisely in most cases, many businesses use their cost-accounting systems to get working ideas of when it pays to take new orders and to hire more workers. Behind these money-cost estimates are time-and-motion studies of how much labor time should turn out how much product. Using such studies, the businessman can get a rough estimate of the "productivity" of different types of workers.

workers' marginal revenue productivity. If the workers are immobile, the manager may "exploit" them—that is, he may pay them a wage below their marginal revenue productivity to him.

How much can the monopsonist exploit his workers? It depends mainly on their mobility. If his wages get too far below rates elsewhere, workers may move away to other areas where they can earn more. If he has to go outside his monopsony area to hire more workers, competition with other employers is likely to eliminate his ability to exploit the workers.

Most economists define exploitation as a wage below a worker's marginal revenue productivity. Although such cases may seem unethical or improper to you, "exploitation" in economics is an analytical, not a moral, term. Johnny Carson or a corporate executive may be exploited in this sense, just as may a secretary or an itinerant fruit picker, if there is not effective competition for his services. (Note that this is quite different from Marx's definition of the term.)

To hear workers tell it, monopsony is a com-

"Leave it to good old GM to break the monotony of the assembly line!" (Drawing by Alan Dunn; © 1972 The New Yorker Magazine, Inc.)

mon case, often because employers agree not to compete for labor. Thus, the worker needs a union to protect himself against exploitation. According to employers, this is a rare case. The evidence suggests a mixed world. But everywhere, the strength of monopsony positions diminishes as job-information channels improve, and as workers' mobility increases. For example, even though waiters' wages are low in most cities, it is very difficult for employers to exploit them. There are hundreds of restaurants, so collusion is difficult, and any waiter will soon move elsewhere if his boss pays wages below the going competitive rate.

UNIONS AND WAGES

Let us turn now to the effects of unions on wages. From one point of view, a union is merely a monopoly that sells the labor services of its members. Neglecting for the moment all the other things that unions do, how effective are they in raising wages for their members under different market conditions? And how do employers and consumers fare?

Let us first assume that the union is an effective organization (monopoly) in controlling its workers. It speaks for them all, and it need not worry about defections from the ranks. Assume also, for the moment, that aggregate demand in the economy is constant, unaffected by the behavior of individual unions and employers.

Competition

First, consider the case where employers are highly competitive with one another both in selling products and in hiring workers—for example, retail clerks in a large city. Here, in the long run, all economic profits will tend to be eliminated. Price will be forced down to about the minimum average cost at which each product can be produced. Wages will be roughly equal to the marginal revenue productivity of the clerks hired.

Suppose now that a union comes in and organizes all the salespeople in the area. It demands a wage increase and gets it. This raises costs, and forces up merchandise prices. At the higher prices, consumers will buy less at these stores. There will be fewer jobs for salesclerks here; how many less will depend on the elasticity of demand for the stores' products. Thus, with a higher wage but the same marginal product, it will pay employers to hire fewer clerks. Union wage demands lead to higher wages for members who keep their jobs, but fewer jobs. In a highly competitive industry, unions can't push up wages without reducing employment in the long run (unless aggregate spending is somehow increased). The workers who keep their jobs are better off, but those laid off bear the brunt. And it becomes harder for new job-seekers to find work as salespeople, and this depresses wages elsewhere and in other occupations as more people look for jobs there. Last but not least, consumers pay higher prices for their purchases at the stores.

Monopoly and Partial Monopoly

Second, consider the case where there is monopoly or monopolistic competition in selling products, but still active competition among firms for workers. Suppose, for example, there are only a few stores in the area, or at the extreme, only one. Can the new union now force the stores to pay higher wages without reducing the number of jobs? Our theory tells us, probably not. If the firms are maximizing profits before the union, they will be hiring clerks up to the point where the wages equals the clerks' marginal product. If the union raises wages, it will, logically, pay employers to cut back on the number of clerks hired and to raise prices; the new maximum-profit will be smaller than before because costs are higher. And it will pay employers to substitute labor-saving machinery (for example, electronic check-out equipment) for workers. Again, logically, the union can obtain higher wages only at the cost of less employment.

But partial monopolists—especially oligopolists—may not be maximizing profits in the precise sense above. Oligopoly is the world of live and let live, of price leadership, of partially protected markets. Under these conditions, the effect of a wage increase on prices and employment is harder to predict. If firms have a protected profit position, this special profit provides a melon over which the union and management can bargain, and higher wages need have no effect on either product price or output and employment. In oligopolies where firms behave as if they faced kinked demand curves, the union may have a considerable range over which it can force up wages without inducing higher prices and reduced employment. But wherever the union makes substantially the same bargain for all major firms in the industry, it faces much the same likely result on employment and prices as with a single monopoly firm; higher wages for union workers will generally mean fewer available jobs, and higher prices for consumers.

Bilateral Monopoly or Oligopoly

Where workers are being exploited through a wage less than their marginal revenue productivity, a union can push the wage up without decreasing employment.[5] The employer is making a special profit by exploiting the workers, and theoretically the union can grab this sum back for the workers. But the employer isn't going to be enthusiastic about turning his profits over to the workers. He'll fight to keep wages down. Where this struggle comes out is indeterminate so far as economic theory is concerned. To guess who will win, look at the relative bargaining power of employer and union. How big is the union strike fund? How adept are both parties around the bargaining table? How badly does the employer want to get his customers' orders out on time? This is a case of bilateral monopoly,

where the union (a monopolist in selling labor) meets a single employer (a monopsonist in buying labor). A simple example might be the isolated mining town mentioned above.

Real-world examples often combine parts of the cases above. For example, wage bargaining in the steel industry pits a union monopoly against combined steel firms, which, however, compete as oligopolists in the steel-product markets. Such a situation has elements of the bilateral monopsony-monopoly case. But if excess profits are eliminated by competition in selling steel, there are no excess profits left for the unions to seize. Then higher wages mean higher prices and less employment, as in the partial-monopoly case above.

Impact of Unions on Nonunion Wages

If unions reduce the number of jobs in unionized industries, they force wages down elsewhere by increasing the number of workers who must seek work in nonunionized industries. A substantial part of union gains thus comes at the expense of nonunion workers. But in some cases, unions may also indirectly raise nonunion wages. If nonunion employers want to keep unions out (perhaps to protect other managerial prerogatives), they may, and often do, raise their wages at roughly the same pace as union increases. This is known as the "union-threat effect." It works most strongly where employers are exposed to possible union organizing drives, and in prosperity when labor is scarce.

Union Wages and Capital Substitution

The short-run effect of union wage pressures on the number of jobs in an industry is often hard to predict accurately. But one longer-range effect is highly predictable. Higher labor costs will lead businessmen to invest in labor-saving machinery more rapidly than they otherwise would. It will pay to shift to coal-mining machinery to replace miners as hourly wages rise, to install mechanical dishwashers in restaurants, to replace farm laborers by automatic vegetable pickers. Higher union wages clearly speed automation.

---

[5]In fact, the union theoretically might *increase* employment by eliminating exploitation. Without the union, the employer bargains wages down and gets as many workers as possible at his low wage. With a union, he must pay the going wage and he can get as many workers as he wants at that wage. Thus, he hires workers up to the point where the wage equals their marginal revenue productivity; there is no longer any incentive to restrict output and employment to get the advantage of low wages.

Do Unions Really Raise Wages?

This may sound like a silly question. Everyone has read of many cases where union demands for higher wages have finally been granted by employers. But such instances don't really answer the question. Maybe supply and demand would have produced the same raises in the market without any union. Don't forget the fallacy of *post hoc, propter hoc.*

Although any union man and most employers will tell you that *of course* unions raise wages, the dispassionate, objective evidence is less clear. One careful study estimates that unions raised the wages of their members by about 25 percent relative to nonunion workers in 1933 at the bottom of the depression (reflecting temporary union resistance to wage cuts), by about 5 percent in the inflationary boom of the late 1940s when all wages were bid up rapidly in tight labor markets, and by 10–15 percent during the 1950s.[6] Another concludes that in perhaps one-third of all cases, unions have raised wages by 15–20 percent; in another third by perhaps 5–10 percent; in the other third not at all.[7] The unions' effects are greatest during recessions when union contracts hold up wages, least in inflationary booms when strong employer demand bids up all wages rapidly. In the latter case, nonunion wages often rise faster, because union wage increases are slowed by three-year contracts made earlier. (Note that in this section, we have dropped the assumption of constant aggregate demand.)

Unions have raised unskilled wages relative to skilled wages. Economic theory doesn't explain this completely. In part, it seems to reflect industrial union pressures to raise low wages relative to high ones. They have also pressed to eliminate interfirm and regional differentials by leveling up the lower rates.[8]

---

[6]H. G. Lewis, *Unionism and Relative Wages in the United States* (Chicago: University of Chicago Press, 1963), p. 193.

[7]A. Rees, *Wage Inflation* (New York: National Industrial Conference Board, 1967), p. 27.

[8]G. E. Johnson, "Economic Analysis of Trade Unionism," *American Economic Review,* May 1975, provides a balanced summary of the evidence on all types of union effects since World War II.

Note a commonly cited but unconvincing bit of evidence, that union wages are nearly always higher than nonunion ones. This is true, but many unionized industries were high-wage industries before they were unionized—big companies with lots of highly skilled labor.

WAGE AND SALARY DIFFERENTIALS— THE RICH AND THE POOR

Now turn to another application of the marginal-productivity theory—the explanation of wage and salary differentials. Why should rock and TV stars, corporation presidents, and professional athletes make literally millions of dollars a year, when most of us have to be content with a small fraction of that? And especially, why should they get it when their work, by and large, looks so pleasant compared with ditchdigging or typing, which pays only a few dollars an hour?

Supply and Demand Again

The most fundamental things about wage and salary differentials can be seen by using the same supply-and-demand, marginal-productivity model again. Give your theory a workout.

Salaries are extremely high where the supply is tiny and the demand is large. Wages are low where there are lots of workers relative to the demand. How hard, how unpleasant, how tedious the job is—such considerations aren't very important except as they influence the supply of workers to the job. But sometimes, such supply differentials have a big impact on the "wage structure." The wage structure must be a set of relative wages in different occupations and industries that equalizes supply and demand conditions for all different workers in all different occupations in equilibrium.

How can a surgeon get away with charging hundreds of dollars an hour? Because his skills are very scarce, and the demand for them is relatively very large. His marginal productivity is very high; it reflects a very large investment in human capital. In contrast, it's easy to be a delivery boy or a retail clerk, and lots of people try these jobs. Their marginal productivity is low. So are their wages and job attachment.[9]

The biggest factor accounting for wage differentials thus lies in the ability and willingness of the individual to do something that few others can do—something that is demanded by consumers with money to pay for it. There are big differences in the capabilities of different people. Some reflect innate physical and mental differences, others the amount of investment in human capital through education, training, and experience. Psychologists tell us that our basic intelligence apparently changes little over the years, no matter how hard we study. But our capabilities also depend on family environments, the amount and quality of education, hard work, and other things that are, to at least some extent, controllable. Not least, luck often plays a big role—certainly as to what kind of family environment you are born into. To understand the incomes different people earn, we therefore need to analyze their basic abilities, how these abilities have been modified by environment, education, and training, and the markets for the particular workers.

Psychologists dispute bitterly the relative importance of heredity and environment in making people what they are. Here, we can look only at the economic factors involved in determining marginal productivities.

Education and Investment in Human Capital

Clearly, most of the highest-paying occupations have high educational requirements. Look back at Table 18–3. The best-paid occupations are professional or managerial, averaging over 17 years of schooling. Most salary studies show a

high rate of return on investment in education—over 10 percent in many cases. In other words, every year of additional schooling beyond the eighth grade seems to be worth an extra $500 or so a year over one's working lifetime; college may be worth $100,000 or more in extra earnings, a tidy return. There is some trickery in these figures, of course, since we know that those who go on to college are generally more able and would presumably earn above-average salaries even without the extra schooling. It is very difficult to separate returns to education from returns to higher ability of those who go on for more education, and some economists estimate a lower return to education per se.[10]

Figure 18–3 showed the relationship between education and earning power clearly. There is a consistent rise in income with increased education, for both whites and nonwhites. Despite a lot of individual variation, low-education families are concentrated at the lower-income levels; very few reach the higher levels. Interestingly, however, the rate of return declines steadily with each year of additional education, other things equal. It is extremely important to get through grade and high school, a little less important for each additional year of schooling. Education is an income equalizer. The income gap between whites and nonwhites has almost vanished at high-education levels.

Don't fall into the trap, however, of thinking that formal education is the only important form of investment in human capital, or that education alone determines the incomes people receive. On the contrary, we learn basic habits and skills in everyday life, in childhood, at home, and on the job, and recent sociological studies suggest that for most people, especially in the below-median-income groups, early nonschool forces dominate the learning process. Moreover, most highly skilled jobs (medicine, law, management, engineering, and so forth) require continued learning after formal education has been completed. Some of this further investment in human

---

[9]Anomalously, TV superstars and the like may be more susceptible to wage "exploitation" than most common laborers. This is because there are only a few potential buyers of the TV star's services, and without competition we can't be sure the wage will be bid up to the star's full marginal productivity—although we can be reasonably sure it won't go higher, because presumably no buyer will be willing to pay more. Does Walter Cronkite get his full marginal product, with only three major chains to compete for his services?

[10]See, for example, P. Taubman, *Income Distribution and Redistribution* (Reading, Mass.: Addison-Wesley, 1978), Chap. 4.

capital is financed by employers; a lot is the result of drive and hard work by those who win out in the highly competitive race for the best-paying jobs. The importance of continued buildup of human capital is confirmed by the lifetime-earnings patterns of different occupations. The annual earnings of doctors, lawyers, managers, and others with extensive education and continued learning by experience peak in their fifties and sixties, whereas the annual earnings of low-education, unskilled workers who depend largely on simple physical labor peak in their twenties or thirties and slide downhill thereafter. Figure 19–5 shows the combined importance of age and investment in human capital on lifetime-earnings patterns. Each curve shows the lifetime pattern of earnings for a different education level. For example, the bottom curve shows the lifetime-income pattern for people with four or less years of education, the top line the same information for people with over 17 years of formal education.

Many modern economists see investment in human capital as part of the rational utility-maximizing behavior of individuals. Each person decides what to do with his income, time, and energy, allocating each to maximize the utility received over his lifetime to come. It is rational to invest in his own human capital through education and training when that seems likely to provide the highest return over his life-span per dollar spent. In investing in human capital, as with any other investment, one must look ahead over the entire life of the investment, and compare the expected lifetime returns with the shorter-run satisfaction received from spending on consumption now. Investment in human capital thus becomes part of the entire rational process of allocating each individual's money and other resources to maximize his satisfaction (utility) over his life.[11] Other economists doubt that most people make their economic decisions so rationally.

Four concluding questions for discussion: (1) How much education should each individual invest in, assuming he wants to maximize his lifetime income? (Remember that education has costs as well as benefits, including the earnings foregone during years spent in college and graduate school.) (2) If education pays off so well, should we count on people to finance their own education, by borrowing if need be? (3) How much should the government spend on education, who should get the subsidized education, and who should pay the bill?[12] (We shall return to these questions in Part 4, on government policy and the provision of public services.) (4) Do existing differentials (for TV stars, surgeons, corporation presidents, schoolteachers, nurses, factory workers, farm laborers) reward most highly those who make the greatest contribution to human welfare? If your answer is no, how do you explain why we pay some people those enormous incomes?

FIGURE 19–5
Annual Earnings, by Age and Education
Annual earnings vary widely with age and education. Numbers on curve show years of schooling. Data for white males, 1959. (Source: J. Mincer, *Schooling, Experience and Earnings.* New York: National Bureau of Economic Research, 1974, p. 68.)

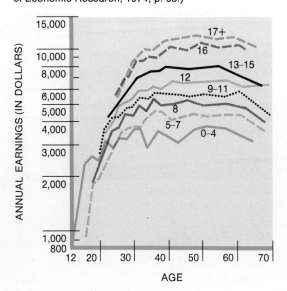

[11]How to compare income streams received at different times in the future is explained in Chapter 21.

[12]For example, the average family-income level of students at the University of California at Berkeley is substantially larger than the average family-income level of California taxpayers.

TABLE 19-1
Family and Individual Incomes

	MEDIAN INCOME	INCOME AS % OF WHITE MALES
Families:		
White	$16,740	—
Black	9,560	58%
Hispanic	10,420	68
Individual Workers:[a]		
White—male	15,400	—
—female	8,870	58
Black—male	10,600	69
—female	8,300	54
Hispanic—male	10,900	71
—female	7,600	49

[a] Includes only workers with full-time, year-round jobs. Difference between whites and others is larger when all workers are included, because of more unemployment among minority groups.

Source: U.S. Census Bureau. Data for 1977.

Discrimination and Inequality

Table 19–1 summarizes the income differences between white and nonwhite families, and between male and female workers. Black family incomes averaged about 60 percent of whites, families of Hispanic origin about 66 percent. Wage and salary earnings of individual workers showed similar racial differences. Female full-time, year-round workers earned from 60 to 75 percent as much as males. Nonwhite female earnings were considerably higher relative to nonwhite males than was the case with female and male whites.

Table 19–2 provides some historical perspective on these differences. Nonwhite workers' earnings have risen substantially relative to whites' since World War II. This has been true for nearly all minority groups, but especially for nonwhite females. Average earnings for white and black female full-time, year-round workers are now virtually identical. Similarly, the spread between white and nonwhite incomes has narrowed rapidly since the early 1960s for people with college and postgraduate study. But nonwhite males with little formal schooling, although they improved their relative incomes in the 1950s and early 1960s, have shown a much slower relative advance since then. Indeed, for minority high school dropouts, unemployment rates have remained very high, and relative incomes have apparently actually worsened in some years.

For economic analysis, we need to define discrimination precisely. If an employer can hire a black or a woman for wage W, but he in fact acts as if the effective wage were $W + D$, then D can be called a coefficient or measure of discrim-

TABLE 19-2
Black Workers' Earnings as Percentage of Whites—Full-Time, Full-Year Workers

YEAR	MALES	FEMALES
1950	.52	.40
1955	.56	.56
1960	.59	.68
1965	.60	.80
1970	.65	.83
1974	.67	.89
1977	.70	.97

Source: U.S. Census Bureau.

ination. For an employer who completely refused to hire blacks at any wage, however low, D would be infinitely large. If the employer discriminates in favor of blacks or women, his D is negative.

Let us analyze the *economic* effects of discrimination. Discrimination clearly harms the group discriminated against—say, black workers. They are partly or completely shut out of some jobs, which means they are forced to compete elsewhere for less-attractive jobs, forcing down the wage for those jobs. White workers in the jobs from which blacks are excluded clearly gain, since fewer workers compete for the jobs, and white wages are therefore higher. But discriminating employers lose, rather than gain, economically from their discrimination. They presumably feel better by not having blacks in the jobs, but they are foregoing profits by not hiring blacks up to the point where their wages are equal to their marginal products. They are paying higher wages to the whites than they could have paid blacks for the same work. This conclusion is in striking contradiction to the standard Marxist argument that employers discriminate in order to increase their profits.

In effect, discrimination shutting minority workers out of some jobs sets up "dual labor markets"—with the best jobs reserved for whites. Then each market must be analyzed separately, although there is clearly some spillover between them. Note, for example, that any white workers who must compete for jobs in the lower (minority) job areas will suffer, with the blacks, from the antiminority discrimination, because wages are forced down in those areas by the larger number of blacks.

Employers may discriminate not because of their own prejudices, but because they believe customers or other workers would object to being served by, or working with, minority groups or women. If this belief is correct, it is less clear that discriminating employers forego maximum profits by discriminating; the result then depends on the particular circumstances, mainly on how strong the prejudices of customers or other workers are.

Discrimination in the United States now seldom takes the form of paying lower wages to minority groups or women than to white males for the same job in the same place, because this is a clear violation of the law. Instead, discrimination usually involves refusing to employ minorities or women in jobs for which they are qualified, or insisting on higher qualifications than for white males for the same job. But the overall economic result is similar in either case. Nor does the economic analysis of discrimination against women differ in essentials from that against minority groups.

A substantial part of the lower earnings of minorities and women reflects not current discrimination but their lower productivity. Employers argue, often correctly, that few blacks and few women are currently qualified for many of the highest-paying jobs. But in substantial part, this is because past discrimination kept them out of the education and experience required for the top jobs. Measuring how much of the existing income differentials is due to current discrimination is very difficult, but the combination of past and current discrimination surely accounts for a lot. And a lot more goes back to the poor social and economic backgrounds in which many minority younsters are raised.[13]

AUTOMATION AND WAGES

Technological advance is a dominant force in the American economy. New methods, new machines, new products are the lifeblood of a dynamic, growing economy. Without the linotype, we'd still be setting type by hand, and books and newspapers would still be for the elite few. Without the electric light bulb, we'd still be lighting our houses with candles, oil, and gas.

But "automation" (as technological advance is sometimes called when new automatic machines replace men) is often blamed for wide-

---

[13]For more details, see R. Freeman, "Black Economic Progress since 1964," *The Public Interest*, Summer 1978; M. Blaxall and B. Reagan, *Women and the Workplace* (Chicago: University of Chicago Press, 1976); and the references cited there.

spread unemployment. Computers replace thousands of clerks in processing checks and keeping records in banks and businesses. Modern chemical plants are almost fully automated. On a humbler level, spray guns and rollers get work done a lot faster than the old-fashioned paintbrush. Everywhere, new factories produce more goods with fewer workers.

Technological progress increases output per unit of input—output per worker, output per unit of capital, or both. Thus, we might expect it to raise both wages and the rate of return on capital—and so it generally will, other things equal. But how much of the gain goes to each under what circumstances is a more complex question.

Some Facts

Figure 19–1 showed the steady parallel growth in output per man-hour and wages in the American economy. Moreover, the growth in total output has been much greater than the total input of labor and capital combined. The total incomes of both capital and labor have risen greatly over the past century, but the return per unit of labor (the real wage rate) has gone up much more than the return per unit of capital (the real interest rate). The average real wage now is about 500 percent of what it was in 1900, while the real interest rate is substantially unchanged. Labor has apparently been the great gainer from technological advance as measured this way. However, as Figure 18–3 showed, the percentage share of the total national income going to labor has grown only gradually, because the quantity of capital has grown much faster than the quantity of labor.

Analysis

Against this factual backdrop, let us examine the impact of automation on wages in a particular industry and occupation. Look back at Bill Welder. Suppose a new machine is invented that stamps out metal sinks, eliminating the need for welding. Trace through the results, assuming that all markets are perfectly competitive and all prices flexible both upward and downward.

1. Sink producers will adopt the new method if it's cheaper per unit produced than the old one, and competition will force sink prices down to the lower-cost level.

2. Some welders will lose their jobs in plumbing-supply companies. Welders' wages will fall as they compete for jobs elsewhere.

3. Employment will increase in plants that manufacture the new stamping machine, in industries producing raw materials and parts, and in plumbing-supply companies that need men to install, service, and operate the new machines. Wages will rise for those workers.

4. At the lower price of sinks, more sinks will be produced and sold, and consumers will be better off, with more sinks and more other goods, since sinks are now cheaper (note, though, the importance of elasticity of demand). More goods in total can be produced, because technical advance has made it possible to produce the same number of sinks with fewer welders, so these workers can help make something else instead.

In all this, what has happened to the wages of different labor groups and to the wage share in the national income?

First, welders' wages drop. Welders thrown out of work look for other jobs. If they stay unemployed, average wages of all welders are clearly down. Even if they get jobs as welders elsewhere, welders' wage rates and incomes will be pulled down as more welders seek jobs there.

Second, the demand for other types of labor rises—for workers to make the new machines and to service and operate them. Wages will rise in those other industries and occupations.

Third, if we assume constant aggregate demand in the economy, no long-run unemployment need result. Welders thrown out of jobs will get work elsewhere or at different jobs in the plumbing industry, as consumers buy more sinks and other products. Consumers will spend more on other products if they spend less on sinks, and more jobs will open up in other industries. This pleasant conclusion, however, depends on two critical assumptions: that workers are mobile in moving to new jobs, and that individual wages are flexible, so that the displaced workers can be absorbed elsewhere. Thus, it skips lightly over the big short-run retraining and readjustment problems facing individual workers. Probably the biggest help in providing jobs and incomes elsewhere in the face of "automation" is government assurance of prosperity and continued high aggregate demand.

Fourth, what happens to the total wage share in the national income will depend largely on the elasticity of demand for the product concerned and on the ratio of labor to capital used in the innovating industry, relative to the rest of the economy. This gets pretty complicated. But since labor clearly benefits along with all of us in its role as consumer, in the real world it's reasonably clear that labor's aggregate real income is raised by technological advance, whatever happens to its relative share of the national income. The real wage per worker has grown rapidly. And the gradual rising share of wages and salaries in the national income over many years of rapid technological advance suggests that wage earners have benefited greatly from such advance.

MARX AND THE RESERVE ARMY OF THE UNEMPLOYED

One last application of the theory: Marx put great emphasis on the "reserve army of the unemployed" as a force inevitably driving wages down to a minimum subsistence level—his "iron law of wages." The final result would be revolt and the overthrow of capitalism. How about it?

Suppose the demand for and supply of labor are as shown in Figure 19–6. Suppose the wage rate is W^1; then there is indeed unemployment (excess supply of labor), as shown on the chart. This unemployment, presuming competitive markets, will indeed push wages down, inciden-

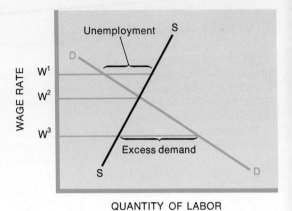

FIGURE 19–6
Marx and the Reserve Army of the Unemployed
Marx argued that unemployment would always force wages down to the minimum subsistence level (W^3). But if we assume unemployment shown at some wage rate (W^1), competition for workers will keep wages from falling below W^2.

tally providing jobs for some of the unemployed workers at the lower wage rate. But will wages fall to W^3, assumed to be the minimum level of subsistence? Clearly not. They will fall to W^2, the level at which the amounts of labor demanded and supplied are just equal; there is nothing to make them fall further. Quite possibly, employers would like to pay still lower wages, but competition among them will prevent this outcome. Workers, on the other hand, might like to have wages higher than W^2, but at a higher wage, fewer men will be hired and competition among the unemployed will push the wage rate back down to W^2.

Suppose, to examine Marx's argument, wages were somehow depressed to W^3, the subsistence level. Would they stay there? They would not. At wage W^3 there would be a large employer excess demand for labor, and competition among employers would bid wages up. Only if competition among either employers or laborers is eliminated by collusion or government action can the wage rate stay far below or above W^2 in the economy shown in Figure 19–6.

SUMMARY AND REVIEW

1. Three partially or largely fallacious theories of wages are the subsistance, lump-of-labor, and bargaining theories.

2. While we have no completely satisfactory theory of wages, most American economists agree that supply-and-demand analysis, with demand determined largely by marginal productivity, provides a useful basic framework for analyzing wages. In competitive markets, wages will be bid up to labor's marginal productivity, and employers will not be willing to pay more than that amount. The demand for labor is mainly derived from ultimate consumer demands for goods and services. Thus consumer demand and labor's ability to help produce goods and services that consumers want are parallel determinants of marginal productivity.

3. Wages will be lowered by employer monopoly in product markets, because the employer reduces his output (and his demand for labor) in seeking monopoly profits.

4. In cases of employer monopsony, the wage may not be bid up to the worker's full marginal productivity, because there is no competition for labor among employers.

5. Unions act as monopolies in selling the labor of their members. Unions may raise wages above competitive levels for members, but in doing so they raise product prices and reduce the number of workers employed in the companies involved, unless the employer has a protected profit position of some sort (monopsony vis-à-vis labor, or barriers to entry against other producers of the final product). In cases of employer protected-profit positions, unions may be able to raise wages without raising product prices or reducing the demand for labor in that industry.

6. Wage and salary differentials can be explained in considerable part by the same theory. Higher wages and salary incomes by and large reflect higher marginal products. To explain wage differentials, therefore, one needs to explain variations in consumers' demand for products and in laborers' abilities to provide goods and services that consumers demand.

7. Investment in human capital is one major way in which some individuals raise their incomes relative to others.

8. Current discrimination accounts for some of the inequality between incomes received by white males, white females, and minorities. However, much of the lower productivity of minorities and women today reflects past discrimination. Wage differentials based on discrimination are narrowing, but substantial discrimination remains in many markets.

9. The impact of "automation" (investment in labor-saving machinery and methods) is complex. The constant-lump-of-labor theory (constant number of jobs) is, however, clearly incorrect, and laborers as well as investors gain from most investment in automation. However, automation may reduce the incomes of those workers directly substituted for, while raising the incomes of other workers and consumers generally.

10. Marx's theory of the reserve army of the unemployed is incorrect theoretically and has not been substantiated by U.S. history. It fails to recognize that employer competition for workers will bid the wage above the minimum subsistence level whenever marginal productivity is higher than that level, as it is generally in the United States.

New Concepts to Remember

monopsony	wage structure
exploitation	discrimination
investment in human capital	dual labor markets
wage taker	"automation"
wage maker	job attachment

For Analysis and Discussion

1. Suppose you want to maximize your lifetime income. What factors should you take into account in selecting your occupation and in timing your entry into it? How much should you invest in your own human capital?

2. "Labor is just another commodity, and wages are its price. All we need to explain wages is a basic understanding of supply and demand." Do you agree with this quotation from an economics textbook? Is it immoral? Explain.
3. The average salary of professional basketball players in 1978 was about $150,000. Can you explain this large salary by the marginal-productivity theory of Chapter 19?
4. Look at Tables 19–1 and 19–2. Are the income differentials between whites and nonwhites shown there a measure of discrimination? What other factors may help explain the differences?
5. Is "automation" good or bad for workers in the industries in which it occurs? for workers elsewhere? for consumers? Explain.
6. Malthus argued that population would tend to outrun the world's food supply, and that wages would tend to be forced back down toward a bare subsistence level.
   a. Is this an acceptable theory of wages?
   b. How would you differentiate between its usefulness in explaining wages in America and in India?
7. One theory holds that wages are the result of bargaining between workers and employers, and that the only important determinant of the outcome is the relative bargaining power of the two parties. Is this theory correct?
8. Is inequality of economic opportunity a major factor in the present unequal distribution of personal incomes in the United States? If it is important, what, if anything, should be done to reduce such inequality of opportunity?
9. Define "exploitation" as it is used by economists. What are the factors that determine whether or not any worker is likely to be exploited?
10. Can you explain to a confirmed Marxist why greedy employers will not be able to force workers' wages down to subsistence levels in America?

CASE 20

ECONOMICS OF THE DRAFT

Should we fill the needs of the armed services by a "draft," or by paying wages high enough to induce the required number of men and women to volunteer? The draft was highly unpopular during the Vietnam War. Yet the idea of a volunteer army also faced strong opposition. After much dispute, the nation shifted to an entirely volunteer armed force in the early 1970s.

In many respects, the volunteer armed services have been a great success. The hated draft, and the uncertainty it brought to all young men, is gone. Many volunteers see a tour of duty in the armed services as a good way to learn a trade, to travel and see the world, and to have a reasonably well-paying job. Nobody has to enter if he doesn't think it's better than the alternative of staying out. But by the late 1970s, substantial criticism had arisen, that the ratio of blacks and other minority groups to whites was higher in the armed forces than in the general population, and that the armed services were not getting enough intelligent, well-educated, high-capability individuals. The issue is still in dispute.

The prodraft forces argue that a draft, based entirely on chance, is the only fair way to decide who must serve in the armed forces. Moreover, it is the cheapest way to maintain the national defense. One may argue about the proper size of the army, navy, and air force, but however big they must be, the draft is the way to fill them.

On the other side, the antidraft forces argue that fully volunteer armed forces are both more efficient and more equitable. The government has to offer a salary big enough to get the troops needed, but every individual can decide for himself whether he prefers the armed services to other employment opportunities at going salary rates, taking all factors into account as he sees them. And the evidence is clear that we can get the men and women needed for the armed forces without paying exorbitantly high salary rates.

But the prodraft forces counter that this is producing an army of poor and minority people who have few other employment opportunities, while well-to-do whites are much less likely to volunteer, even at the present higher military salaries. Moreover, the cost of military pay is going to rise rapidly as people find the armed services to be less attractive compared to private-sector occupations.

Which is economically preferable and a more equitable way to maintain the armed forces? What should our national policy be? (*Hint:* Draw the demand and supply curves for the two alternatives and remember the importance of the concept of opportunity costs. Some help is provided by the suggestions for analysis at the end of the text.)

Unions,
Collective
Bargaining, and
Public Policy

CHAPTER 20

Labor unions loom large on the current American scene. On the economic front, they exercise great pressures on wages, hours, and working conditions. They are behind the worker in his differences with the foreman, the day-to-day arguments that seldom reach the public's eye. Their votes are felt in elections—usually on the Democratic side. Their lobbyists are among the most effective in Washington and the state capitals, and it is a secure congressman who can afford to disregard what organized labor thinks.

Important as unions are, don't overrate their power. Unions do influence wages and hours. But supply and demand still set a confining framework for labor–management negotiations. Although the combined AFL-CIO loosely joins together many unions, the member unions are still separate, often disputing among themselves. Less than one-fourth of all workers are unionized, and union membership has grown little in recent years outside the public sector, although the labor force has expanded rapidly. Throughout the services, agriculture, and clerical and professional areas, unions have little hold, although in recent years they have grown rapidly among government workers and teachers. Politically, the divisions within organized labor weaken the power it can exercise, and since World War II, labor has gone down to defeat on some of its most bitterly fought issues.

HISTORY OF AMERICAN UNIONISM[1]

The foundations of labor unionism in America lay in the skilled crafts during the early 1800s. But it was not until the 1870s that the first loose nationwide labor association appeared. This was the Knights of Labor, founded as a secret society to avoid public antagonism and employers' reprisals against members. A decade later, the American Federation of Labor (AFL) became the first effective national union organization. Under the leadership (1886–1924) of Samuel

Gompers, a remarkable figure in American labor history, the Federation became a significant force, with an outspoken philosophy of "practical" unionism. Gompers reflected the spirit of the times in organized labor—"Get more, now." Only this pragmatic, typically American attitude began to win a little grudging acceptance for unionism from employers and the public at large.

But it was Franklin Roosevelt and the New Deal that gave unions their place in modern industrial society. Depression was everywhere—massive unemployment, low wages, low purchasing power. Higher wages and higher prices to promote recovery were cornerstones of the New Deal. The National Industrial Recovery Act for the first time gave workers the right to organize and bargain collectively with employers. Although the NIRA was soon declared unconstitutional, the Wagner Act was passed in 1935, to become the foundation of modern union powers. It spelled out workers' rights vis-à-vis employers, put teeth in the unions' powers to bargain collectively, and forbade the employer antiunion practices then prevalent. Unions were guaranteed recognition if they won a majority vote among the workers.

The labor history of the middle 1930s was stormy. The newly formed Congress of Industrial Organizations (CIO), with the fiery John L. Lewis as its first president, opened big organizing drives—violent, spectacular, and successful. Open defiance of management rather than workers' traditional subservience was the tone. The famous sit-down strikes, when the unions seized possession of the major auto plants, rocked the companies and the public. But in the bloodshed and bitterness that ensued, the unions won recognition time after time—with the open support of the Roosevelt administration and local Democratic government officials. The Who's Who of American industry fell to CIO organizing drives one by one—U.S. and Bethlehem Steel, General Motors, General Electric, Goodyear, and so on down the list. By 1940, union membership had more than doubled, to about 10 million. By 1945, it was nearly 15 million, about one-third of the nonagricultural labor force.

Public sympathy during the 1930s was by and large prolabor, although many friends were lost by the sit-down strikes. But inflationary union

---

[1]For a good account, see U.S. Labor Department, *Brief History of the American Labor Movement* (Washington, D.C.: U.S. Government Printing Office, 1964). This is updated by John Dunlop, "American Labor Organizations," *Daedalus,* Winter 1978.

wage demands during World War II, interunion jurisdictional quarrels and strikes, and open defiance of the federal government by a few leaders convinced the bulk of the public that organized labor's power had gone too far. In 1947, Congress passed the Taft-Hartley Act, restricting the powers of unions and restoring some rights that employers had lost during the preceding decade. And the years since World War II have seen a definite leveling off of union power.

Figure 20–1 shows the picture. Union membership (excluding Canada) rose above 17 million in the mid-1950s, but then leveled off. Unions have made slow headway since, especially with white-collar workers and employees of the rapidly growing service industries. Including Canada, American unions now have about 21–22 million members, and unionlike employee associations of teachers, nurses, police, and the like have another 3 million. The bottom half of the chart shows the union problem more strongly. Union membership as a percentage of the total civilian labor force hit a peak of 28 percent in the 1950s, and has declined since then.

In 1955, the merger of the AFL and the CIO into one loose organization (the AFL-CIO)

marked a major step toward a united labor movement. But interunion rivalries have limited the new organization's powers, economically and politically. Neither the United Auto Workers, the Teamsters, nor the United Mine Workers now participate. Jurisdictional disputes have been a persistent source of quarrels.

Moreover, the unions face a new problem. The average union member has a good job, and often a house in the suburbs. He belongs to the big middle-income class, well above the insecurity and poverty that threatened during the 1930s. He wants more pay, longer vacations, better fringe benefits. But the old class solidarity that once united workers against employers is gone. There is an increasing gap between the goals of young union members and the militancy that motivated the now-aging leaders. Many younger members feel little tie to the union. And unions can hope for big gains only among white-collar workers in the services, education, government, and the like. Total employment in manufacturing has been slowly declining over the last decade.

Where is union power concentrated today? In transportation, contract construction, autos, metals, paper, electrical machinery, and mining,

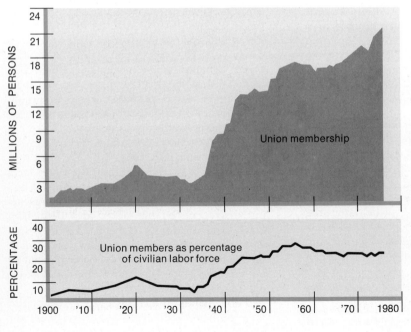

FIGURE 20–1
Union Membership
since 1900
The big growth period for unions was during the 1930s and 1950s. Since then, union membership has declined somewhat as a percentage of the civilian labor force. (Source: National Bureau of Economic Research and U.S. Department of Labor.)

if we judge by the percentage of workers unionized. The Teamsters, Air Line Pilots, Longshoremen, Carpenters, Plumbers, Painters, Steelworkers, Papermakers, Electrical Workers, and United Mineworkers all have unionized 75 percent or more of the workers in their industries and possess a large degree of monopoly power. Most of the other big, well-known unions are in manufacturing, with membership varying between 25 and 75 percent of the workers involved. The degree of unionization in the service industries is generally less than 25 percent—retail clerks, hotel workers, teachers, local government employees, secretarial-clerical workers. Their market power is a lot less.

WAGES, COLLECTIVE BARGAINING, AND LABOR–MANAGEMENT RELATIONS

Unions' powers to raise wages and their impact on employment and consumer prices were analyzed in Chapter 19. Here we want to examine the labor–management bargaining process.

The big wage negotiations and strikes make the headlines. But the great bulk of union–management collective bargaining and negotiation goes on unheralded behind the scenes. After a union contract is signed, the day-to-day relations of the foreman and his workers take over. Wage rates have to be set for individual jobs; broad contract wage provisions must be translated into elaborate wage structures in large firms. Decisions must be made as to which jobs are on a flat-hourly-pay basis and which "on incentive," where the pay depends on the number of units turned out. Arrangements have to be agreed on for handling the introduction of new machinery and new methods. Wrangles between foremen and individual workers have to be adjudicated. A thousand and one problems arise in a big plant that involve disputes between labor and management.

Some union–management agreements provide elaborate machinery for handling worker–management disputes that can't be settled by the foreman and the worker. These often culminate in calling on an impartial arbitrator, paid jointly by union and management, whose decision is final on disputed issues under contract. Such agreements usually try to set up a body of rules under which workers and management can minimize friction and disagreement. The contract is something like the laws under which we operate our democratic system. This procedure has gone far toward creating stability and order in employee–management relations in thousands of industrial plants. But in industrial as in political democracy, the rules alone can't make the system work. They only provide a framework within which people of reasonable goodwill can work peaceably together.[2]

Union and Management Motivation in Bargaining

You don't need a course in economics to tell you the main reason why unions fight for higher wages. They want more pay! But some other things aren't so easy to explain.

Why will unions strike for an extra few cents an hour in pay, when third-grade arithmetic will show that it would take months or even years at the extra rate to make up for the pay lost in a long strike. Why are the union leaders willing to keep the men out over a few dollars? The same question can be asked the other way around, too. Why doesn't the company give in and end the divisive strike?

Try putting yourself in the workers' shoes. You'd probably think, "That so-and-so who runs the company! He gets a big salary and has everything. His plushy stockholders are getting

---

[2]"Union-shop" and "right-to-work" laws cause much controversy. Under a union-shop agreement, everyone who works in the firm covered must join the union. The union's big argument for this arrangement is that if workers get the benefits of union activities (higher wages, better working conditions, and so on), they should have to pay dues and bear their share of the union costs. Otherwise they get a "free ride," which makes no more sense than permitting a citizen to benefit from government but decide for himself that he won't pay taxes.

The counterargument says that union shops take away the individual worker's right to work without joining a union, and that this abrogates an important individual freedom. Make up your own mind. The union shop is legal under federal law, but prohibited in a number of southern and western states that have enacted state "right-to-work" laws. Such right-to-work laws are fought bitterly by the unions.

big dividends. Yet we have to scrape along on pay that just keeps the wolf away from the door. He won't even give us a few cents extra when he could save himself profits by doing it instead of trying to break this strike. We'll fight it out and lick him yet!"

Now turn around and see how you'd feel as the employer. You see the wages your company is already paying as generous. You see the workers stubbornly holding out for "unreasonable" demands. You may see the union leaders as self-seeking hypocrites, out to protect their own jobs. The whole business is just one more step in the union's attempt to dictate to the management. Would you give in if you were the employer?

Now put yourself in the union president's shoes. You know that your best bet in the long run lies in getting along with management. But you also know that there's never enough money to go around, and that you're going to have to push hard to get the wages to which your members are (in your eyes) clearly entitled. You know a strike is costly to everyone, but you know too that a threat often repeated but never carried out loses its force.

You know that unless you produce for your members, you're likely to be just another ex-president. If other unions have been getting a dollar an hour plus fringe benefits, you'd better get that much too. You know that your chances of rising in the union ranks, say, to a position in the international, depend on your success in getting more than other unions do. As you sit across the bargaining table from management, with tempers frayed by a long strike, would you give in?

The issues at stake in a labor negotiation are seldom simple. The quarrel that the public sees in the newspapers is often only part of the real issue. To look at the problem in terms of a simple dollars-and-cents comparison is naïve. The issues are real, and no purpose is served by pretending that nothing but a common interest is involved.

The Changing Role of Strikes

Collective bargaining is a process of challenge and response. For the most part, it settles the disputes between employers and unions. But sometimes they can't, or won't, reach agreement. Tempers fray. Bitterness grows. Finally the union goes out on strike.

Strikes are rare events. With over 150,000 collective-bargaining contracts in force, strikes over the last five years have caused a loss of only one-fifth of 1 percent of the total working time involved. Table 20–1 shows the record since 1935. Time lost exceeded 1 percent in only one year—1946.[3]

Moreover, most of today's strikes are orderly and nonviolent, in sharp contrast to the bitter, bloody battles of thirty years ago. Strikes now arise largely over renewal of contracts and most often involve wage and work-rule arguments, far less explosive issues than the life-or-death organizing conflicts of the 1930s. Arbitration is now widely used to settle disputes that arise during the life of the contract. International officers generally try to help avoid or settle "wildcat" strikes, in which local unions strike in contravention of contract arrangements.

Thus, conflict resolution between labor and management has been moved increasingly to an orderly, peaceful procedural basis. But conflicts do persist, and the strike remains labor's weapon of last resort to enforce its views. Sometimes big strikes are enormously disruptive—for example, a long steel or public utility strike. But many labor observers feel that an occasional strike in most industries does no great harm and indeed may be a useful incident in the continuing bargaining relationship between labor and management. A strike is a device for letting off steam, for reasserting bargaining powers. It is not necessarily a symbol of the failure of collective bargaining. Thus, few labor experts favor laws to outlaw strikes, except possibly strikes that clearly threaten the public interest. For to outlaw strikes would not resolve conflicts but merely force them into other channels. But public tolerance of

---

[3] A Department of Labor study shows that higher wages were the main issue behind 44 percent of all strikes between 1964 and 1974; work rules or conditions, 15 percent; union recognition or union shop, 13 percent; and union jurisdictional differences, 11 percent.

TABLE 20–1
Time Lost in Strikes, 1935–78

PERIOD	NUMBER OF STRIKES (ANNUAL AVERAGE)	WORKERS INVOLVED (ANNUAL AVERAGE) (IN THOUSANDS)	PERCENTAGE OF WORKING TIME LOST
1935–39	2,862	1,130	0.27
1940–44	3,754	1,386	.16
1945–50	4,210	2,940	.61
1951–55	4,540	2,510	.31
1956–60	3,602	1,620	.29
1961–65	3,560	1,365	.14
1966–70	5,032	2,653	.27
1971–75	5,735	2,485	.20
1976–78	5,160	2,210	.17

Source: U.S. Department of Labor.

disruptive strikes has been strained in recent years, and better devices are needed to settle labor disputes within less costly, more orderly channels. (More on this subject in the next section.)

GOVERNMENT AND LABOR

Many labor–management disputes are now a test of strength between equals—sometimes equals of prodigious strength. When Douglas Fraser sits down to bargain for the United Auto Workers, he speaks for a million men. Literally billions of dollars are at stake in these bargains; not only wages, but also the pensions of tomorrow's retired families, workers' health and disability insurance, their working hours, their vacations—and the prices consumers will have to pay for cars. A nationwide Teamsters strike could bring the economy to a grinding halt in a matter of days. In local areas, small groups of union workers can achieve comparable results; a mere dozen bridge-tenders nearly shut down New York City in 1971.

Is union power excessive? Many say yes; they stress that antitrust laws do not limit union power. Most union members say no. Do we need more stringent laws to limit union powers? Should government intervene when disruptive strikes occur, or when wage settlements threaten the government's antiinflation programs? Labor–management relations have many unanswered questions.

Major Legislation

The *Norris-LaGuardia Act of 1932* was the first major national prolabor legislation. Employers had long been able to get court injunctions against labor groups to prohibit just about anything—for example, striking or picketing. Once the injunction was obtained, labor was the wrongdoer in the eyes of the law. Norris-LaGuardia outlawed the injunction in federal courts as an employer weapon against a wide variety of union activities—strikes, joining a union, peaceful picketing, or giving financial aid to unions. The intent of the law was clear. It was to give unions support in achieving a more equal bargaining status with employers, and to eliminate one of the most powerful employer weapons.

The New Deal, a year later, was frankly and aggressively prolabor. The *Wagner Act of 1935* is the cornerstone of modern prolabor legislation. The act:

1. Affirmed the legal right of employees to organize and bargain collectively, free from employer interference or coercion.
2. Required employers to bargain with unions of the workers' own free choosing.

279

3. Specifically prohibited a list of "unfair" employer practices.

4. Set up the National Labor Relations Board to provide a mechanism through which workers could gain recognition for unions of their own choosing, and to act as a quasi court to protect workers against unfair labor practices. (The NLRB does not act directly to mediate or settle labor–management disputes.) Employer intimidation, antiunion discrimination in hiring and firing, company attempts to influence union elections, and a variety of other employer practices were soon outlawed as unfair practices as NLRB and court decisions interpreted the new law.

By the early 1940s, the bitterest union organizing struggles were over, and industrial unionism in the mass-production industries was firmly entrenched. In the courts, labor also fared better. The Supreme Court, reflecting the changing temper of the times and the presence of several Roosevelt-appointed judges, in the *Apex* and *Hutcheson* cases (1940 and 1941) reversed a long line of judicial precedent and granted unions virtual immunity from the Sherman Act, although in the *Allen Bradley* case of 1945, an exception was made where they conspired with employers to fix prices or divide markets.

The federal *Fair Labor Standards Act of 1938* established minimum wages, maximum basic hours, and other fair labor standards for all labor in interstate commerce. The FLSA has been periodically amended since 1938, both to widen its coverage and to raise the minimum wage.

All through the 1930s and during World War II, labor rode high. But the pendulum had swung too far. More and more middle-of-the-roaders began to feel that labor had overstepped its bounds, first in the sit-down strikes of the 1930s; then in the spreading jurisdictional disputes and strikes that the public and employers seemed powerless to halt; in its persistent wage demands during the World War II fight again inflation; and last, in its outright defiance of the federal government itself in disputes of critical importance to the national economy. The Taft-Hartley Act of 1947 was passed to redress the balance of power between management and labor.

Taft-Hartley defined unfair labor practices of unions to parallel those of employers. It clarified the powers of employers to speak against unions; it prohibited the closed shop; it contained provisions to protect individual workers against the union; it empowered the president under conditions of national emergency to obtain an 80-day cooling-off period before a strike, and required a secret union ballot on the last company offer before the end of that period.

By 1950, labor racketeering had become a national scandal, and Congress passed the *Landrum-Griffin Act,* again over the violent objections of union leaders. Landrum-Griffin included a new "bill of rights" for individual union members, requirements for more detailed financial reporting by unions, and a requirement for secret-ballot elections.[4]

Labor and the Antitrust Laws

Unions are substantially exempt from the antitrust laws, except as they may collude *with employers* to restrict output or to fix prices. The Wagner Act put the National Labor Relations Board in the position of granting official patents of monopoly to the unions it certified as exclusive bargaining agents. Many businessmen and economists who believe in the efficacy of competitive markets believe that the antitrust laws should, at least in part, be applied to unions as well as businesses.

One proposal is to forbid industrywide bargaining, just as firms may not collude to fix prices and output. Union suporters retort that this would *de facto* emasculate unions, moving back to the old relationships where all the power was on the employer's side. Another proposal would forbid union pressures on employers to restrict output and union "featherbedding" (for example, work rules that prohibit use of paint sprays in place of brushes). But such distinctions have proved very hard to enforce. Only legal reforms that command widespread public support have much chance of enactment and enforcement on such emotionally charged issues. And such widespread public support is hard to mobilize when

---

[4]For a fuller account of the changing legal foundations of unions and collective bargaining, see L. G. Reynolds, *Labor Economics and Labor Relations,* 7th ed. (Englewood Cliffs, N.J.: Prentice-Hall, 1978), Chap. 5.

the issue seems to be the working man against business, even where the consumer ultimately pays the bill.

The Government as Watchdog and Wage Setter

Congress has long been concerned with labor–management affairs. The biggest issues arise around disruptions of the national economy through strikes. But with persistent inflation seen as the number one economic problem in recent years, government intervention in wage setting seems never far from the headlines. The detailed analysis of incomes policies in Chapter 19 laid out the difficulties in making wage–price controls or national incomes policies work in our society. Every president in recent times has bumped up against this problem in trying to fight inflation.

UNIONS AND STRIKES IN THE PUBLIC SECTOR

Strikes have long been illegal in the public sector—at the federal level and in most states. Only recently has the right of public employees to join unions been widely recognized. Yet today, collective bargaining between public employees and governments (or quasi-government agencies like school boards) poses the most difficult problems in labor relations.

A few public workers—for example, postal employees—have long had unions. But membership in public-service unions and "associations" (for example, the National Education Association of over a million teachers) has soared in recent years. Today, probably 40 percent of the nation's 12 million public employees belong to either unions or associations that are increasingly acting like unions in collective-bargaining relationships, and membership is growing faster than anywhere in the private sector. Public-sector salaries have risen much faster in the last decade than those in the private sector.

Until the 1950s, strikes by public employees were virtually unheard of. But as resort to power tactics spread in society, especially during the 1960s, public employees began increasingly to use strikes to achieve their wage goals, just like other unionized workers, albeit illegally. The New York subway workers, then bus drivers, airport traffic controllers, postmen, garbage collectors, teachers, and even firemen went out, and often achieved their demands when important services were crippled and public attitudes were divided. Government employees elsewhere followed suit. Antistrike laws were discreetly disregarded by public officials, or quickly amended in some cases. Sometimes, nonstrike actions are used to get the same results. If airport traffic controllers just work "according to the rule book," the result can be to slow down air traffic dramatically without their violating any antistrike

provision. If teachers report in sick, it is very difficult to teach the schoolchildren.

Should public employees have the same rights to strike and to bargain collectively as private workers have? Most people apparently still say no, although attitudes toward public unions are far more permissive than they were two decades ago. Clearly, this issue goes beyond economic analysis, into ethics and politics. Shutting down the schools, or subway service, or fire protection imposes a cost many people are unwilling to tolerate. But if we deny these powers to public workers, how are they to be sure of getting a fair deal, comparable to private employees? Indeed, as a practical matter, how are we to keep them from striking, law or no law, if they just go ahead and strike? Bringing in the army to teach school, run the subways, or collect garbage is not a very promising alternative.

Some would tie public-employee salaries to comparable private salaries. Many urge compulsory arbitration if disagreement persists. Increasingly, when penalties are levied by the government, they are in the form of heavy fines against unions, not widespread punishments against individual employees. Fining or firing many individual public workers is generally neither realistic nor popular.

How do *you* believe we should handle the snowballing problem of public-employee demands and strikes? What should the law say? Perhaps even more important, what should the relevant public officials do if and when the public employees strike anyhow?*

---

*For a survey of the issues, see J. Stieber, *Public Employee Unionism: Structure, Growth, Policy* (Washington, D.C.: The Brookings Institution, 1973); and *Collective Bargaining in American Government* (New York: The American Assembly, 1971).

Suppose the government's antiinflation policy calls for holding wage increases below 10 percent. But suppose the Steelworkers, after long and bitter bargaining with the big steel companies, insist on 12 percent as their absolute minimum, and have gone out on strike to back up their demands, in spite of the White House's pleas for a moderate settlement and continued production. The union points to a soaring cost of living, high industry profits, and rising productivity. Management in the steel industry's Big Six say they won't offer a penny over 8 percent. They say that real (inflation-corrected) profits are down, foreign competition is murderous, and steelworkers are already among the best-paid workers in the nation. The strike has gone on now for two long months, and the steel shortage is shutting down not only civilian production but also national defense projects. Unemployment is rising weekly. If you were president, what would you do?

You might say, let the strike go on; it's none of the government's business. But with the economy grinding to a halt and the nation's antiinflation program at stake, you probably wouldn't.

You might invoke the national-emergency provision of the Taft-Hartley Act. This probably would get the union back to work and would give you 80 days to bring all the pressure you could on both sides to settle their differences. You'd focus as much public pressure as you could on the negotiators. If you felt strongly that right was mainly on the steel companies' side, you might tell the American people so and build up pressure on the union to settle.

The power of the federal government is great, and this kind of pressure might well bring some kind of settlement. But suppose neither the companies nor the union will give in. So the workers go out on strike again at the end of 80 days, more bitter than ever. What then?

Then is the tough time. By now, tempers are really frayed. Labor, management, and government officials have been over the issues *ad nauseam*. Each has been provoked into saying a lot of things better left unsaid. Everybody's dirty linen has been thoroughly aired before 200 million Americans.

You might decide to seize the steel industry and ask the workers to stay on the job. But this means seizing a vast, privately owned industry, against all the traditions of American freedom and probably against the Constitution. Or you might order the workers to stay on the job, in the interests of the public welfare. But you know perfectly well you can't make men make steel, either under the law or any other way, if they just won't go back to work and do it.

Well, what would *you* do?

Compulsory Arbitration?

Often a skillful third party can soothe hot tempers and help get labor and management together when they are negotiating a contract or settling a grievance. The federal government and most state governments provide "mediators" and "conciliators" who serve as impartial go-betweens in trying to get disputes settled without resort to strikes. Sometimes these men enter at the request of labor and management; sometimes they are sent by public officials who want to avoid work stoppages. Their work is generally unheralded and unspectacular, but they are successful in a great number of cases.

With the exception of a few cases (for example, railway labor disputes), the government has no legal power to enforce a settlement on the parties. Many observers believe it should have some such power, or that Congress should prescribe "compulsory arbitration," at least in disputes vitally affecting the public interest. Under compulsory arbitration, both management and labor would be bound to accept the decision of a third party, the arbitrator, if they could not resolve their own differences. No strike or employer lockout would be permitted.

Most unions and many employers oppose such a law. They want to be left alone to settle their own disputes. But should society tolerate the costly, disruptive strikes we frequently face, or the inflationary wage settlements that often come out of long strikes? These doubts are especially strong against public-sector strikes—by police, teachers, postmen, transit workers, and the like. But the case for compulsory arbitration is much weaker for smaller, run-of-the-mill labor disputes. How to define "big disputes where the public interest would require compulsory arbitration" is a tough problem, if you want to use compulsory arbitration only in those cases. And a substantial number of strikers have simply refused to go back to work even when ordered to do so by the courts.

SHOULD THE GOVERNMENT GET OUT?

Ours is an economy of power groups. The unions and their leaders have great power. So have big employers. Wage setting has moved from the competitive marketplace to the industrywide bargaining table in many leading industries. The wage bargains in steel, autos, electrical equipment, and coal go far to set a pattern for the rest of the economy. How can the government stand aside and see its antiinflation program split open, the operation of the whole economy periled by disputes in these industries? Less than 1 percent of the nation's labor force is employed in trucking. Yet that 1 percent could probably bring the economy almost to a dead stop in a few weeks.

But if it is drawn in, what can government really do? Many observers think that government intervention, especially when it becomes habitual, does more harm than good. They argue that when both sides know the government will eventually step in, there is little chance of settling the dispute beforehand. This is particularly true,

they say, in inflationary periods when both labor and management know they will ultimately get much of what they want, and the main question is how much prices will be pushed up for the consumer. One side or the other will nearly always feel it can get a better bargain by waiting to get government involved in the settlement. Thus, excessive government intervention in bargaining may hide the need for management and labor to accept basic responsibility in a free society, and may end up with more inflationary settlements too—although there is no way the government can stay out if it goes the incomes-policy route against inflation.

The American economy has come a long way from the highly competitive, individualistic system described by the classical economists. Concentrated economic power is here, like it or not. The problem is somehow to develop a framework within which economic power is responsibly channeled to the public good. The hard fact is that we cannot order huge groups of workers around in a peacetime democratic society. Wage setting must be by consensus when two powerful groups face each other across the bargaining table. And it must be by political as well as economic consensus once the government steps into the scene as a major participant in setting wages.

SUMMARY AND REVIEW

1. Labor unions play an important role in the American economy, but they include only about one-fourth of all civilian workers. Union membership has grown slowly in recent years, except in the public sector, and it is a declining percentage of all civilian employees.

2. Union motivation in bargaining vis-à-vis management is complex, with increased wages only one of the goals of union members and leaders.

3. Strikes play an important part in union–management relationships, and are the ultimate union weapon. However, they have become rarer and less violent as the years have gone by.

4. Government has stepped in to strengthen the hand of labor in dealing with management in important ways since the New Deal decade of the 1930s. While there is much criticism of excessive union power, there has been no major move to substantially reduce that power vis-à-vis management since the Taft-Hartley Act in 1947.

5. There is disagreement as to how far government should intervene in labor–management bargaining on wages and other issues. This issue has become especially important with the prevalence of inflation and the attempts of government to restrain wage–price increases through national (incomes-type) poli-

cies. Experience in the United States and abroad suggests that such government restraint will work only when there is consensus as to its desirability on the part of unions, management, and the general public.

6. Rapidly developing unions in the public sector pose difficult problems. Compulsory arbitration provides one possible "solution" to the problem of settling disputes in the public sector, but neither workers nor governments find this completely satisfactory, for either public-sector disputes or other disputes seriously affecting the "public interest."

New Concepts to Remember

collective bargaining   compulsory arbitration
mediation   union shop

For Analysis and Discussion

1. If you were a factory worker, and union members in the plant put pressure on you to join the union, would you join? Would you consider such pressures an infringement of your personal freedom of choice?
2. Should public-service unions (for example, teachers, firemen, and postal workers) have the same rights to strike as other unions? If not, what rights do they have to enforce their demands?
3. "Unions are justified where employers would otherwise be able to exploit employees, but nowhere else." Do you agree? Explain.
4. Would it be better to give employees the extra money rather than all the retirement, health, and other fringe benefits commonly included in union contracts, so that each person could decide for himself how to spend the money?
5. When the government intervenes in wage negotiations—for example, in autos or steel—what criteria should it use in deciding what wage settlement to urge?
6. Should compulsory arbitration be required by law in order to avoid strikes that involve government employees or otherwise affect the public interest? How would you define the public interest for this purpose?
7. Should labor unions be subject to the antitrust laws?
8. The Taft-Hartley Act requires unions and management to bargain "in good faith." Suppose an employer decides to make his best offer at the outset and thereafter refuses to improve the offer. Is he bargaining in good faith?

CASE 21 THE ECONOMICS OF MINIMUM-WAGE LAWS

In 1978, the federal government defined as in "poverty" any four-person urban family receiving less than $6,600 per year. By this test, about 25 million Americans were poor.

If we figure that a full-time job involves about 2,000 hours of work per year, an hourly wage of $3 would provide a $6,000 annual income, just below the poverty level. An hourly wage of $3.50 would provide a $7,000 annual income, modestly above the poverty level. The minimum wage prescribed by federal law in 1978 was $2.90 per hour. The law prescribed that this would rise to $3.35 per hour in 1981, just about enough to meet the poverty-level standard in 1978 prices. But everyone expected that inflation would continue and poverty-level annual income would be well above $6,600 by 1981.

Many have proposed, therefore, that Congress raise the minimum legal wage substantially to ensure at least a bare minimum above-poverty income for all American workers. For example, a minimum-wage law of about $3.50 in 1979 would provide a poverty-level income for all with a little margin of safety. Less than that would soon leave recipients below the poverty level, and would hardly provide a decent standard of living for American workers. American businesses and consumers should be required to pay workers at least a decent living standard wage, the argument runs. Moreover, higher-paid workers argue that employers should not be permitted to displace them with cheap labor.

This issue has been hotly debated in Congress many times. Critics of the minimum wage argue that it is especially hard on the young, inexperienced, unskilled, and presently poor workers. It is they who have low marginal productivities, and who will be shut out from jobs if employers must pay minimum wages above their marginal products. Thus, the minimum wage intended especially to help the poor will hurt most precisely those it is intended to help (although the present law prescribes that employers may get special Labor Department permission to hire student workers up to 20 hours per week—more in the summer—at 85 percent of the minimum wage, provided that their work hours don't exceed 10 percent of the company's total). The present law was hardly passed in 1977 before some people advocated postponing the rises in minimum wages prescribed by the law for 1979 and 1980, because, they argued, the higher minimum wages would cause unemployment among low-income workers whose marginal productivity was below the minimum-wage levels in the new law. Moreover, it was argued that a rise in the minimum wage was highly inflationary in the late 1970s when restraining inflation was a major government goal.

Do you favor the proposal to raise the minimum-wage law, say, to $3.50 per hour? What would be the main effects of such legislation? Who would gain, and who would lose? (For simplicity, assume that total national expenditure is constant.)

Property Incomes: Interest, Rent, and Capital

CHAPTER 21

ost people obtain virtually all their money income from wages, salaries, and transfer payments. But nearly all the wealthy, and an increasing share of the moderately well-to-do, get a lot of income from rent, interest, and profits—from property they own. In 1978, wages and salaries were $920 billion (76 percent) of the $1,210-billion total national income, while rents were $21 billion (2 percent), interest was $82 billion (7 percent), and corporation profits were $102 billion (8 percent).[1] The highest corporation salary reported was $776,000 for the head of International Telephone and Telegraph, but several hundred individuals reported taxable incomes of over $1 million, especially television, sport, and movie stars. Johnny Carson is said to get $5 million a year from NBC. But most of the very rich get much of their income from capital.

Ours is a "capitalist" economy. One of its central tenets is the right of each individual to accumulate property (capital) of his own—a house, a factory, land, stocks, bonds. And most capital produces income for its owner—rent on land, interest on bonds, dividends on stocks. Some of the income may be consumed directly by the owner—such as housing services received by living in one's own house instead of renting. Thus, every homeowner is to that extent a capitalist, just as is a bondholder or stockholder. Indeed, if we think of ourselves as owning our own productive capacities (human capital), we are all capitalists, with our incomes depending substantially on how much we have invested in human capital.

This chapter deals with two types of income from nonhuman capital (rent and interest), leaving profits until Chapter 22. Substantially the same marginal-productivity, supply-and-demand theory explains the return on both human and nonhuman capital.

RENT

In everyday usage, "rent" is the price paid for the use of land, buildings, machinery, or other durable goods. This is the way we shall use the term,

except in one later section where a special meaning is given to the term "economic rent."

What determines the rental income received by owners of land and other such durable productive resources? Although there are important institutional differences (we don't have a slave society in which we buy and sell human beings as we do land), the answer is much the same as what determines the wage income of labor—supply and demand, with demand based largely on the marginal productivity of the land or other asset. Whether the landlord is a greedy fellow or not is generally far less important than the powerful impersonal forces of supply and demand.

The *supply* of nonhuman productive resources, and hence of their services, varies widely from case to case. At one extreme, the supply of land at the corner of Fifth Avenue and 50th Street in New York City, where Saks Fifth Avenue and Rockefeller Center sit, is completely inelastic—there's just so much, and no more can be manufactured. At the other extreme, garden tools, a simple productive resource, can be reproduced readily, and their supply is highly elastic. Most cases lie somewhere in between. The supply of most productive resources is likely to be reasonably elastic *in the long run*—that is, given a long period for adjustment. Even farm land can readily be improved through the use of fertilizer, drainage, and so forth, if it pays to do so. For practical purposes, this is similar to making more land—you still have the same number of acres, but the acres have increased productivity.

The *demand* for the services of property depends basically on how much the service rendered is worth to the user, and ultimately to consumers. The property's marginal productivity underlies the business demand for its services, as for labor. Competitive bidding by businesses tends to draw each resource into its most productive use. Thus, each piece of land is rented to the highest bidder, and the high bidder must use the land where its marginal productivity is greatest to justify paying the high rent. Under competition, the rent will just equal the marginal productivity of the land. As with labor, monopsony or monopoly may lead to "exploitation" of resource owners, to inefficient allocation of resources, or to unemployment of some of the resources.

[1]The rest of the national income goes to unincorporated businesses (farmers, lawyers, small shopkeepers, and the like) as a mixture of wages and profits.

An Example

Take a simple example. What will the rent be on a ten-acre site on a highway near the outskirts of a city. Look at the demand side first.

One demand may be for use in truck farming. How much renters will pay for this use will depend on the fertility of the soil, the water supply, and other such factors. Another demand may be for use as small individual business properties, such as restaurants, garden-supply stores, and the like. Here, the amount of traffic passing by, the convenience of the location for potential customers, and other such factors will be especially important. Still another demand might be for use by a single supermarket, with surrounding parking area. Here again, the amount of traffic passing by, the convenience of location, the availability of adequate parking space, and the desirability of nearby neighbors might be especially important.

Each potential renter would make some estimate of how much he could afford to pay in rent for the site—logically, up to its estimated marginal revenue productivity for him.

Who will get the site, and at what rent? If there is active competition among the potential renters, the rent will be bid up until only the highest bidder is left. This will be the renter who estimates the marginal productivity of the site as being the highest.

Thus, the site will be drawn into the use that promises the highest return to the renter, and through this mechanism into the use where consumers value it most highly. The rent will equal its marginal productivity in this most valuable use.

Can we be sure the rent will be bid up all the way to the estimated marginal productivity of the highest bidder? Not if the value to one user is substantially higher than to others. Suppose the site is ideal for a supermarket. Then the local Kroger's manager needs only to bid higher than the truck farmers and small shop operators, to whom the land is potentially worth less. Kroger's may get the site at a rent below its estimated marginal productivity as a supermarket site. But Kroger's won't if there's a local A&P or Safeway also in the market for sites.

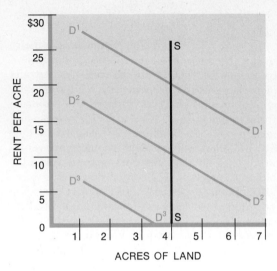

FIGURE 21–1
Economic Rent
When the supply is a fixed amount, price (rent) is determined solely by demand.

"Economic Rent"— a Price-Determined Cost

Economists have one special definition of "rent" that differs from ordinary usage: "Economic rent" is the payment for the use of a scarce, nonreproducible resource. For example, the rent paid for one corner of Fifth Avenue and 50th Street in New York covers a mixture of "site value" and use of the building on the space, with all the improvements. If we isolate the site value of that corner—the land itself, exclusive of any improvements on it—we have a resource that is scarce and completely fixed in supply; the supply is perfectly inelastic.

The rent on such nonreproducible productive agents is determined exclusively by the demand for them. The supply curve is a vertical line. If there is no demand, there is no rent; the rent rises directly as demand rises, without relation to the original costs of producing the resource. Figure 21–1 illustrates the point. Since the supply is a fixed amount, SS is a vertical line. If the demand is D^1D^1, the rent will be $20 an acre. If demand is D^2D^2, rent is only $10 an acre. If demand is only D^3D^3, the land commands no rent at all.[2]

Outside the site value of land, few cases of pure economic rent exist. But there are many cases with some element of economic rent, especially in the short run. For example, the great Wagnerian soprano, Birgit Nilsson, is unique today, and nonreproducible in the short run. The high fees she charges the Met and other opera houses can be considered a partial economic rent for the use of her great voice. Similarly, if a firm patents a new productive process, for the life of the patent the process is much like the site value of land; it cannot be reproduced (except by consent of the patent holder). Indeed, if a firm has a temporarily protected monopoly position, part of the monopoly profits may better be considered a temporary economic rent, or *quasi rent*, on the monopoly position.[3]

INTEREST

Most of us put our savings into financial assets, instead of buying real property directly. We buy bonds, or deposit the money in a bank or a savings and loan association. Our property is then a financial asset, and we collect the income from our capital in the form of interest. Interest is the price paid for the use of money or credit, and indirectly for the capital or consumer goods that can be obtained with that money or credit.

Why are interest rates what they are? Fundamentally, they depend on the marginal productivity of the real capital goods obtainable with the funds involved. Temporarily they may be heavily influenced by monetary policy and other special factors.) The same marginal-productivity, supply-and-demand framework

is again the right one to use in answering the question.

Three special points about interest need to be made:

1. Interest is paid for the use of money, or credit, rather than directly for the use of productive resources. Money itself doesn't build buildings or dig ditches. But money does give its owner purchasing power to obtain men and machines that will build buildings and dig ditches, and demand for loan funds traces back in considerable part to their power to buy or rent real productive resources. Thus, fundamentally the marginal productivity of real capital goods determines the interest rate, as it does rents.

2. Interest is stated as a *rate* of return (4 percent) rather than as an absolute sum. To say that the interest rate is 4 percent is merely to say that the borrower pays $4 interest per year for each $100 borrowed. The statement in percentage terms as a rate permits ready comparison between the payments of different amounts for widely differing resources. You can easily compare the return on money invested in an office building, in a turret lathe, and in your own education, by converting all three returns into a percentage on the funds invested. For example, if the office building cost $1 million and provides an annual net return of $50,000 after depreciation and other expenses, the rate is 5 percent. If the lathe cost $1,000 and provides an annual net return of $40, the rate is 4 percent. If a $1,000 investment in an electronics course will increase your annual income by $45, the rate of return is 4½ percent. According to these figures, funds invested in the office building provide a better return than funds invested in turret lathes or the electronics course.

3. There are hundreds of different interest rates. In 1978, for example, the government paid about 8.5 percent on long-term bonds. Short-term bank loans were about 9 percent for well-established concerns; mortgage loans to buy houses cost 10 percent or more, and small loans to individual borrowers 18 percent or more. Some consumer loan agencies charged up to 40 percent per annum. You got no interest on demand

---

[2]Years ago, Henry George argued that all rents should be confiscated through a "single tax," because they reflect a bonanza to landowners that arises as society's demand for the God-given, not man-made, land grows. Some cities—for example, Pittsburgh—still tax land more heavily than buildings, on the remnants of single-tax reasoning. A few disciples still advocate this as the basis for our entire tax system.

[3]Economists sometimes use the term "quasi rent" to describe the return on *temporarily* nonreproducible resources.

deposits, but most banks and savings and loan institutions paid 5–8 percent on savings deposits. These different rates reflect differences in risk, locality, length of loan, cost of handling the loan, and a variety of other factors, as well as the "pure" interest rate that is included in each. To simplify matters, economists often talk about "the" interest rate. They mean the interest rate on a long-term, essentially riskless loan. The rate on long-term U.S. government bonds is often considered a close approximation. At mid-1978, therefore, we might have said "the interest rate" was about 8.5 percent. But don't make the mistake of assuming you could borrow money at this rate.

Nominal and Real Rates of Interest in Inflation

During inflation, the nominal (market) rate of interest exceeds the "real" rate. If you borrow $100 for one year at 6 percent and prices rise by 4 percent, in real purchasing power you pay only 2 percent interest, because the money you pay back will buy 4 percent less than when you borrowed it. Thus, economists say, the nominal interest rate is 6 percent but the real rate is only 2 percent. Conversely, if prices fall, the real rate will be higher than the money rate.

Presumably, if borrowers and lenders correctly anticipate inflation (say, 4 percent per annum), both will take this into account in making their contracts. If the real productivity of capital is 3 percent, they will add on the 4 percent inflation allowance, making a 7 percent market rate. If their anticipation of inflation is perfect, the 7 percent nominal rate will be just high enough to produce the 3 percent real rate justified by the real productivity of capital. But we can never foresee inflation accurately, and the inflation allowance is correspondingly imperfect. Nonetheless, it is important to think of the real rate of interest if we want to make correct analyses of saving and investment decisions, in business or private affairs.

Interest and the Stock of Real Capital

Fundamentally, interest is paid for the use (productivity) of real capital—machinery, factories,

airplanes, houses. Assume for the moment that there is no technical advance to increase the productivity of capital; growth in the capital stock means merely adding more units of the same capital goods—say, through saving and investing in more factories. Thus, in Figure 21–2 S^1 is the stock of capital now, S^2 next year. DD is the demand for real capital, dependent on its marginal productivity. Thus, as the capital stock grows, we would expect the interest rate to fall from i^1 to i^2, other things being equal. The demand is fixed and the supply increases.

Figure 21–2 can also show the effect of technical advance. Suppose that inventions occur that increase the productivity of capital—say, a new computer, or improved programs (software) for computer use. With higher marginal productivity, more capital will be demanded than before at the same price (interest rate). The DD curve will move to the right—say, to D^1D^1. Thus, with **both** more capital and technical progress, the interest rate here falls slightly, to i^3, but much less than without technical progress. Of course, if

FIGURE 21–2
Interest Rates, Capital Stock, and Technical Progress

Given some level of technology and demand for capital DD, growth in the capital stock will reduce the interest rate from i^1 to i^2. Advancing technology partially offsets the growth in capital stock by increasing the demand for capital, and the resulting interest rate in the second year is i^3.

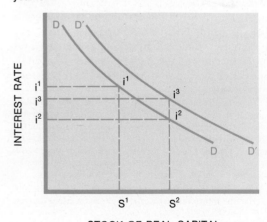

STOCK OF REAL CAPITAL

the technical progress is very large, it may dominate the growth in capital, so the interest rate would rise in spite of the increased stock of capital. In fact, over the past century, the two effects have been roughly offsetting; the real interest rate has fluctuated cyclically but without showing any clear long-term trend.

The Interest Rate, Resource Allocation, and Capital Accumulation

The interest rate helps potential business and individual investors allocate their funds among the millions of potential investment opportunities in the economy. When credit is allocated where the expected rate of return is highest, risk and other factors taken into account, it is optimally allocated from the consumer's viewpoint as well as from the investor's, because the highest returns will be found where consumer demand is relatively strongest. Unless an investment promises a return high enough to pay the going rate of interest under a private-enterprise economy, it does not justify exploitation, by the test of the market. Money capital is the fluid embodiment of real productive resources. Thus, the credit market, by channeling funds into those investments where the potential return exceeds the interest rate, provides a most valuable service to private investors and to society as a whole.

The interest rate plays another, more subtle, role. It provides a rough measure of the relative advantages of current consumption and saving—of the present against the future. By saving, the individual or business can get a continuing return of, say, 6 percent annually. If that return is enough to justify foregoing consumption now, it is advantageous to save. Without the interest rate to indicate the return on saved funds, savers would have no standard by which to measure the relative advantages of current consumption and saving.

Similarly, the interest rate helps businessmen and government planners decide among projects of different capital intensity. Suppose we can produce product *A* either with lots of labor and a simple plant, or with little labor working with long-lived, expensive machinery. Which is better? Only by calculating the "capital cost" (the interest rate times the dollar investment

discounted back to the present—see the following section) of each and comparing the expected total labor-plus-capital cost of the two alternatives can we accurately choose between the two methods.

Perhaps most important of all, the interest rate exerts a powerful influence on the rate of economic growth in a capitalist economy like ours. A low interest rate encourages investment and faster growth, because it is cheap for businessmen to borrow to expand their productive capacity. A high interest rate slows growth.

Government Policy and Interest Rates

Since the 1930s, the federal government has exerted substantial influence on interest rates, through both Treasury borrowing and Federal Reserve monetary policy. The monetary authorities influence interest rates directly through purchase and sale of government securities, and indirectly through regulating bank reserves.

Remember that Federal Reserve activities influence *money,* or nominal, interest rates more than *real* rates. Real interest rates are determined by the demand for and supply of real capital. If the Fed increases *M* but there is no change in the real forces at work, the result is likely to be inflation. Temporarily, more *M* will reduce short-term interest rates. But if substantial inflation develops, borrowers and lenders are likely to agree on adding an inflation allowance to the real interest rate. Nominal interest rates will then rise by the inflation allowance, but real rates are unchanged. In the late 1970s, for example, the long-term nominal interest rate was about 9–10 percent on industrial bonds, but with 6–7 percent annual inflation, the real rate was near its long-term historical level of 3–4 percent.

VALUATION OF INCOME-PRODUCING PROPERTY

Income distribution is primarily concerned with the pricing of productive *services,* not with the prices of the productive agents themselves—land, machinery, buildings, and the stocks and bonds representing their ownership. But nonhuman income-producing assets are bought and sold daily in our economy, and the interest rate plays an important part in setting the prices at which they sell.

To estimate the price of an income-producing asset, we need to know (1) its net annual return, and (2) the going rate of interest.

Valuation of Perpetual Fixed Income ("Capitalization")

Take a simple hypothetical case. Suppose we have a mine that will *forever* produce ore worth $100 annually, net after all expenses are met. Suppose further that the going rate of interest on substantially riskless investments is 4 percent. What will the mine be worth?

To get the answer, we simply "capitalize" $100 at 4 percent. That is, we find that sum on which 4 percent interest would amount to $100 annually. The arithmetic is simple. Four percent of x (the unknown value) is $100. In equation form, this is $.04 \cdot x = 100$. Dividing the .04 into 100, we get $2,500 as the present value of the mine (or any other riskless asset that provides a $100 annual net return). Put another way, the formula is:

$$PV = \frac{\$ \text{ Return}}{\text{Interest rate}}$$

Can we be sure the mine will really sell for $2,500? No, but we can be sure it will sell for something near that. No one will be willing to pay a much higher price, because by investing $2,500 anywhere else at equal risk, he can get $100 annually. On the other hand, if the mine's price is much less than $2,500, people will find it a very attractive investment and the price will be bid up toward $2,500.

Valuation of Depreciating Assets

The principle involved in valuing nonperpetual assets is the same. Consider a machine that will last 20 years and whose marginal revenue productivity (rent) per year is $60. The going rate of interest on comparable investments is 6 percent. Using the same approach as before, we might capitalize $60 at 6 percent, and find that $60 is 6 percent on $1,000.

But there's a catch. The $60 annual income lasts for only 20 years, because the machine wears out. Our problem then is, What is the present, or capitalized, value of an income stream of $60 at 6 percent over 20 years, rather than in perpetuity? Mathematicians and industrial engineers have worked out a series of tables giving the answer for all combinations of interest rates and time periods for such problems. The answer here is $688.

The basic reasoning is this: At the end of the first year, we get $60. At the end of the second year, we get another $60. And so on for the 20 years. Sixty dollars today is obviously worth $60, but $60 to be received, say, one year from today is clearly worth less than $60 today, since we do not have the use of it until a year hence. How much money today is equivalent to $60 a year from today? If the interest rate is 6 percent, $56.60 invested today at 6 percent will amount to just $60 a year from now. And we can make a similar calculation to get the amount equal to $60 two years hence, and so on up to 20 years. If now we add together all these "present values" of $60 to be received at the end of each of the next 20 years, we will get how much we ought to be willing to pay now for the series of 20 annual $60 net returns anticipated from the machine. Adding these 20 present values together gives the $688 above, the present value of the income stream promised if we buy the machine.

So you'd better not pay more than about $688 for the machine if you don't want to get stung. It's easy to see why this amount is less than the $1,000 the machine would be worth if it provided the $60 annually in perpetuity. If you have to pay more than about $688, you could earn more on your money by investing it elsewhere at 6 percent for the 20 years.

One other point is needed to complete this example. Unless this is a patented machine, others like it can be produced. If the current cost of producing such machines, for example, is only $500, you can be pretty sure that even the $688 price won't last. At a price of $688, it will pay to produce more machines like this one. As more are produced, the price will gradually fall. Not until the price falls to $500 will a new equilibrium be established, where the price of the machine just covers its minimum cost of production. With a lot more machines, moreover, the marginal revenue productivity of each will be lower, both because of the law of diminishing returns and because the product of the machine will have fallen in price, so that the net annual yield per machine will be less than $60.

To summarize: (1) At any time, the capitalized present value of an income-producing asset will be based on its net yield and on the going rate of interest on investments of comparable risk. (2) In the long run, the value of any asset will tend to be equal to its cost of reproduction, although it may vary widely from this figure at any given time.

Valuation of Corporate Stocks: The Stock Market

The same general principle holds in valuing corporate stocks and bonds, which represent claims on income earned by the issuing companies. But don't take your nest egg and rush for the stock market with this new knowledge. Corporate securities are interesting illustrations of the capitalization principle especially because they point up so many of the pitfalls. So far, we've assumed that we knew the yield of each asset, its life, and the appropriate going rate of interest. But in the real world, all three of these are uncertain, especially on corporate stocks. The earnings of most companies and hence the yield on their stocks, fluctuate from year to year. There is no sure way of telling what they will be for any extended period in the future. Moreover, what rate of interest should we use in capitalizing? The appropriate one is the rate that prevails on other investments of comparable risk and other characteristics. But you pick it out.

Last, and most important, the market price of stocks is determined by thousands of other people who are all looking at the same imponderables as you. Many of them are in the market as speculators, looking for a quick dollar on the price rise rather than for a long-pull investment. There is no clear reproduction cost to set a stable base level that anyone can count on. The actual market price will reflect what all those people think is going to happen. So you're betting on what other people will bet on, and they in turn are betting on what you and others will bet on.

The stock market is no place for neophytes. The capitalization principle can give you a rough steer and it can help you in comparing different securities. But the much-quoted statement of Bernard Baruch is relevant here:

If you are ready to give up everything else—to study the whole history and background of the market and all the principal companies whose stocks are on the board as carefully as a medical student studies anatomy—if you can do all that, and, in addition, you have the cool nerves of a great gambler, the sixth sense of a kind of clairvoyant, and the courage of a lion, you have a ghost of a chance.

The point of this section is not to warn you against investing in common stocks. On the contrary, overall, stocks have been a good investment over the long pull. Rather, the point is to stress the wide range of special factors at work in determining the actual market price of different income-producing assets. The analytical framework outlined above can help, but like all such models, it provides only a framework for analyzing any particular situation.

SUMMARY AND REVIEW

1. Rent is the price paid for the services of land, buildings, machinery, and other nonhuman productive resources. It is determined by supply and demand, with demand determined largely by marginal productivity, closely parallel to the determination of wages for the services of human beings. Competition will force the rent on each productive resource up to its marginal product; businesses will be unwilling to pay more than that marginal productivity.

2. "Economic rent" is the payment for the use of scarce (temporarily or permanently) nonreproducible resources. Rent on nonreproducible resources is determined exclusively by the demand for them.

3. Interest is the price paid for the use of money or credit, and indirectly for the capital or consumer goods that can be obtained with that money or credit. Thus, fundamentally, interest depends on the marginal productivity of the real capital goods obtainable with the funds involved.

4. Interest is stated as a *rate* of return (4 percent) rather than as an absolute sum. This makes it easy to compare the rates of return on different amounts of capital invested in different projects. There are many different interest rates for loans of different risk, maturity, locality, and the like. "The" interest rate is usually defined as the rate on a long-term, essentially riskless loan, usually U.S. government bonds.

5. During inflation, the nominal (market) rate of interest usually exceeds the "real" rate by roughly the rate of inflation.

6. The interest rate plays a number of important roles in a capitalist society. It provides a measure of the relative advantages of current consumption against saving; helps businessmen and planners decide among projects of different capital intensities; helps decide the most profitable place to allocate savings among all possible investment alternatives; and exerts a powerful influence on the rate of economic growth in a capitalist economy.

7. Income-producing property is valued by capitalizing its net return at the going rate of interest. Thus:

$$PV = \frac{\$ \text{ Return}}{\text{Interest rate}}$$

However, in the long run, the price of any reproducible capital asset will roughly equal its cost of reproduction.

8. While the principle in 7 is correct, the value of many investments (especially common stocks) varies widely because of uncertainty about the return on the securities, the degree of risk, and the interest rate to use in capitalizing the rate of return.

<table>
<tr><td>New Concepts
to Remember</td><td>rent
economic rent
quasi rent
interest
"the interest rate"</td><td>"real" and "nominal" interest rates
rate of return
capitalization
"present value" of an income
   stream</td></tr>
</table>

For Analysis and Discussion

1. How would you compare the rate of return on investment in yourself (human capital) through going to graduate school with the rate on investment in stocks or bonds (nonhuman capital)?

2. "Rent and wages are determined by substantially the same set of supply-and-demand forces, even though people are human and land is not." Do you agree? If not, what are the main differences?

3. "Rent is an unearned increment for any landowner, since he does not have to do any work for the rent he receives. Therefore, the government should confiscate land rents through special taxes for the general welfare." Do you agree? Explain.

4. "The profits made by a company on the basis of an exclusive patent are essentially rents, not profits." Do you agree or disagree?

5. Some economists predict persistent inflation over the years ahead. If they are correct, how would you expect this inflation to affect money and real rates of interest? Explain.

6. Other things equal, would you expect rapid technological advance to raise or lower the long-term rate of interest? Why?

7. Suppose the Federal Reserve tightens bank reserves and raises interest rates. Would this increase or decrease real investment, other things equal?

8. Find out the "carrying charge" on some article you are considering buying. Then calculate the interest rate you would be paying on the funds you in effect borrow from the seller. Would you be better off to borrow the money at a bank and pay cash? (see Case 22.)

9. Suppose you inherit an 80-acre tract of farmland. You are uncertain whether to sell it or to retain it and rent it out. How would you go about comparing the advantages of the two courses of action?

CASE 22 NOMINAL AND ACTUAL INTEREST RATES

Interest rates aren't always what they seem to be. The following three cases may help you to protect yourself against some common mistakes, by looking at some situations that frequently arise in everyday life.

Installment charges. You buy a $120 rug at the local furniture store. The store offers to let you pay over a full year, at $10 per month plus $1 per month additional carrying charge. (1) What is the actual interest rate the store is charging on the money it lends you over the year? (2) A local finance company will lend you the money at 15 percent on your unpaid balance. Should you borrow from them and pay cash for the rug, or buy on the installment plan?

ANALYSIS. The store's offer looks like a 10 percent interest rate, a reasonable rate for such a loan, especially since it has to include something extra for the nuisance of keeping the books and maybe having to dun you for the money. But look again. The actual rate is far higher. You pay a dollar carrying charge each month, but the total amount you have on loan from the store goes down $10 each month. The last month, you owe them only $10; yet you are still paying interest at the rate of $1 a month, or $12 per year. The actual rate on your unpaid balance during the last month is 120 percent per annum. The average for the year is about 20 percent, twice the apparent rate, because the average loan to you is about half the purchase price of the rug. The actual rate for each month is calculated in the accompanying table. If you want to pay the smallest amount of interest, in this case go to the finance company at 15 percent.

General lesson: Compare carefully the actual interest rate included in installment carrying charges with what the money would cost you if you borrowed it directly elsewhere. This is not to suggest that installment sellers are crooked; they have to cover their costs of foregoing interest on the money they lend you, plus their operating expenses. But actual interest rates are often higher than they seem.

Bond yields. You have about $1,000 to invest. You are considering an 8 percent corporation bond. It is a $1,000-face-value bond, so the annual interest is $80. Its current market price is $1,100, and it is due in ten years. Your main alternative is putting the money into U.S. government bonds, which pay 6 percent, can be bought at face value ($1,000), and are also due in ten years. Assume that the two investments are equally safe and attractive on all other grounds. Which one should you choose?

ANALYSIS. At first glance, the corporate bond seems to win hands down. But look again. You pay $1,100 for the bond, but you'll only get back $1,000 at the end of ten years. To get the true net yield, you need to "write off" $10 of the value of the bond each of the ten years, so your actual net annual yield would be only $70, rather than $80. Now you can calculate the exact yield on the corporate bond. It's $70 per year on $1,100 invested. This figures out to be about 6.4 percent per annum, barely above the 6 percent offered on the government bond. If the risk on the two bonds is really identical, the corporate bond is the better buy. But if (as is likely in the real world) the corporate bond is

	UNPAID BALANCE	INTEREST ($1 MONTHLY; $12 PER YEAR)	INTEREST RATE ON UNPAID BALANCE
1st month	$120	$12	10.0%
2nd month	110	12	10.9
3rd month	100	12	12.0
4th month	90	12	13.3
5th month	80	12	15.0
6th month	70	12	17.1
7th month	60	12	20.0
8th month	50	12	24.0
9th month	40	12	30.0
10th month	30	12	40.0
11th month	20	12	60.0
12th month	10	12	120.0

riskier, the choice is not clear. Which you should prefer will depend on your attitude toward risk.

Inflation, risk, and growth. Suppose again that you have $1,000 to invest. You can put it in a bank or a savings and loan account at 6 percent, buy 7 percent government bonds due in ten years, or buy IBM common stock at 75 to yield about 5 percent in dividends (8 percent in total earnings). Of course you are not sure, but you judge that we face inflation of about 4 percent annually over the decade ahead. Which investment should you make?

ANALYSIS. This is a trickier problem still, because it involves not only your risk aversion (as in the preceding case), but also probable inflation and the historically persistent growth in IBM's profitability. Inflation first: If prices rise 4 percent per year, the real rate of interest on the bank account is only 2 percent, on the government bond 3 percent, and the IBM dividend has a zero yield in real terms. Better face it that your real return will be a good deal less than the nominal rates. Second, risk: There is virtually none on the bank or savings and loan account; their deposits are government-insured up to $40,000 per person, and you can withdraw your money whenever you want. On the government bond, there's no risk on repayment when the bond comes due, but the price may fluctuate in the meantime, so you might have to sell at a loss if you want your money before ten years. Of course, there's also a possibility that the bond's price will rise in the meantime (for example, if market interest rates on comparable bonds fall), in which case you'd make a gain on your sale. On IBM, there's real risk. You have no guarantee at all that IBM will keep on earning its present $3 a share, or that the price–earnings ratio will stay as high as it is now. Everyone knows that IBM's earnings and dividends have risen persistently over the last three decades, and investors' present willingness to pay so much for a currently small dividend reflects their belief that IBM's earnings, dividends, and stock price will continue to grow in the future. Moreover, many investors figure that if inflation comes, IBM can pass along rising costs through higher prices, so money earnings will rise with the inflation rather than be eroded. If investors' expectations turn out to be seriously wrong on any of these points, IBM's high price–earnings multiple of about 14 to 1 is likely to fall, and you'll find that you can only sell your stock at a loss. But if the optimistic forecasts turn out to be right, IBM's earnings, dividends, and stock price will rise substantially; and it will be the most profitable investment.

What should you do with your money? Economic analysis can point up the issues and some consequences of various possible developments. But the best investment for you will depend on your assessment of the probability of these various developments and your attitude toward risk—and note that risk here is a far more complicated issue than just whether you will receive some stated number of dollars at a given time.

Note: Because some of the necessary analysis is not included in this chapter, the suggestions for analysis are included here for this case.

Profits:
Theory, Facts,
and Fantasy

CHAPTER 22

n 1976–78, corporation profits before taxes averaged about $177 billion annually, about 11 percent of the national income. After payment of corporation income taxes, the comparable figures were $103 billion and 7 percent. If we add in unincorporated businesses (farmers, lawyers, doctors, small shopkeepers, and the like), the pretax profit figure is probably increased by $10–$20 billion; the amount can only be estimated roughly because we have no clear separation between profits on the one hand, and implicit wages, interest, and rent on the unincorporated businessmen's own labor and investments on the other. Indeed, a substantial part of reported corporate profits is also actually implicit interest on invested capital owned by the stockholders. Implicit interest is probably between a quarter and a half of total corporation pretax profits. Thus pure "economic" profits, after taxes and allowance for implicit interest, were small in 1976–78.

About $100 billion in reported after-tax profits is enough to provide a lot of income to stockholders and unincorporated businessmen, but it's also only a small fraction of the total income received by the public. Whether profits are too big—an unconscionable exploitation of the workers, as Marxists claim—or too low—an inadequate return to induce capitalists and other risk takers to perform their proper social functions—is one of today's most debated issues.

Our look at the market system thus far has stressed two big roles for profits. They're the incentive to produce what consumers demand—the carrot that entices businessmen to perform their social function. And they're a major source of funds for the investment that makes the economy grow.

PROFITS ON THE MODERN SCENE

Potential profit indicates where society wants more resources used. Thus, the individual businessman who predicts most successfully what the consumer will want, who meets consumer demand most effectively, who handles his production most efficiently, and who buys his labor and materials most adroitly, will end up with the biggest profit. The inefficient producer who fails to respond to consumers' demands is likely to end

FIGURE 22–1
Corporate Profits since 1929
Corporate profits have risen sharply but irregularly since the 1930s. Corporate income taxes now take somewhat less than half the total. Profits shown after inventory valuation adjustment. (Source: U.S. Department of Commerce.)

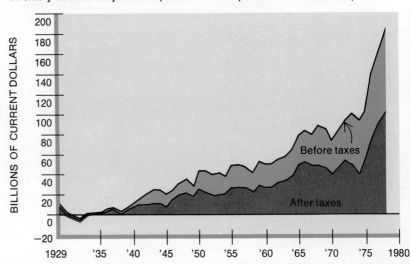

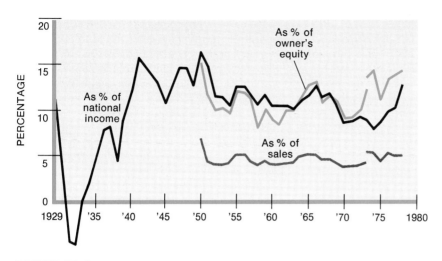

FIGURE 22–2
Are Profits Excessive?
Corporate profits reached peaks during and after World War II. Since then, they have generally been lower and have fluctuated irregularly relative to national income, sales, and owners' equity. (Source: U.S. Department of Commerce. Profits as percentage of national income are before taxes for all manufacturing corporations; those relative to sales and equity are after taxes.)

up with red ink on his books. If a seller has a partial or complete monopoly, he may be able to maintain positive economic profits without innovations, real productive efficiency, or close response to consumer demands. But wherever other firms are free to enter the market, competition will tend to eliminate economic profits.[1] The pursuit of profits plays a central organizing role for the entire economy.

If you ask the man in the street, he probably won't be very sure just what profit is, but he'll probably have a somewhat unfriendly attitude. Public-opinion polls show this time after time; most people think profits are too big. And it's highly likely he will have only a vague idea about how big profits actually are. So a further look at the facts may be in order.

The Facts

Figure 22–1 summarizes the course of *corporate* profits before and after income taxes, since 1929. About half the total now goes to the government

---

[1]Remember that elimination of *economic* profits by competition does not eliminate all accounting profits, since a substantial share of reported accounting profits is implicit interest on stockholders' investment in the firm.

in corporation income taxes, before payment of dividends or reinvestment in the firm. Clearly, the size of profits looks a lot different before and after taxes. Remember too that over two-thirds of the huge growth since 1929 is inflation—prices have more than tripled.

The aggregate dollar figures don't mean much. They're too big. Everything in the economy has grown immensely since 1929. Have profits risen or fallen compared to other income shares? Are businesses making more or less profit these days per dollar of sales, or per dollar of investment? Figure 22–2 gives some of the answers.

The profit share in the national income has jumped all over the place in business cycles. Corporate profits were actually negative in 1931–32 (negative by a far larger amount if we consider *economic* profits, eliminating implicit interest on stockholders' investment), and hit a peak of 17 percent of national income in 1950. Over the last quarter century, profits have declined substantially on all three bases shown. Lesson in statistics: Note how you can make the profit share look sharply rising or sharply falling, depending on whether you take the early 1930s or 1940s as your starting point.

Public-opinion surveys have repeatedly shown that the public holds wildly erroneous ideas about the size of corporate profits. Public estimates of after-tax profits as a proportion of sales have ranged all over the map, but have generally concentrated in the 25–35 percent range. This is some five to eight times the actual return of 4–5 percent over the last decade. If actual profit margins on sales had reached publicly guessed levels, total corporate profits before taxes in 1978 would have been nearly a trillion dollars, or nearly half the total GNP. Little wonder that many people believe that corporate profits could absorb the cost of almost any social reforms if only corporations were less greedy! And equally little wonder that many corporate executives are frustrated at how little the public understands business.

THE TWO ROLES OF PROFITS

Part 2 stressed profits as the carrot that lures businessmen and investors into meeting consumer demands, reducing costs, and innovating with new products. And losses are the stick that beats those who fail in their attempts. Let us now look more intensively at these critical roles of profits in our society, and at the theory of profits, preparatory to asking the final question: How big should profits be in the modern American economy?

Profits as an Incentive

The primary social function of profits is to give businessmen an incentive to produce what consumers want, when and where they want it, at the lowest feasible cost. This includes innovation of new products and new methods. The profit motive is at the center of a private-enterprise economy.

But a lot of questions are raised about just how the profit motive works as a practical matter. For example, most after-tax profits go to stockholders who have little to do with managing the businesses they own. Clearly, profits give them an incentive to invest, but professional managers (rather than owner-operators) now run most big businesses. Thus, some critics ask whether profit is still the most effective incentive to innovation and efficiency. The modern corporation president gets a salary plus a bonus dependent on profits, but the latter is often small. We rely on top management's urge to excel and to make large profits for the stockholders to produce the desired results, as well as on their personal enrichment from profits. We rely heavily on profits per se to draw investors' funds into the businesses where profit prospects are highest. The functions of management, entrepreneurship, and providing capital are thoroughly entangled in today's big firms.

Second, remember that it's the *expectation* of profits that must be there to make the system tick, not the achievement of profits. Never forget that this is a *profit-and-loss*, not just a profit, system. Every year, the big stick of losses pounds a large number of businesses that don't succeed in meeting the test of the market. Many a firm has gone broke.

In the 1970s failures (bankruptcies) of incorporated businesses averaged nearly 1,000 per month. Total liabilities of these failures averaged over $2 billion annually. Fewer than 25 percent of the businesses established during the immediate postwar years were still operating a decade later. Yet each year, new thousands rush in, confident that they have the knack to succeed where others have failed. Big-business failures are less common than failures among small firms. People who have $50 million or $100 million to venture are rare, and profitability calculations on such investments are made with a great deal of care. And failing big firms are often merged into other firms to avoid massive disasters. But even for big business, the story is far from one of unbroken success. Think of the auto industry, with its spectacular growth over the present century. The Oakland, Stanley Steamer, Maxwell, Hupmobile, and dozens of others were once as much household words as Ford and Pontiac are today. Yet only a few decades later, they are as extinct as the dodo. More recently, Douglas Aircraft, a multi-billion-dollar giant, was saved only by merger with McDonnell Aircraft; Lockheed Aircraft had to be bailed out by a quarter-billion-dollar government loan guarantee. The Penn Central Railroad and W. T. Grant stores were spectacular failures of big, nationally known firms.

Hope springs eternal in American businessmen's and investors' breasts. Their mistakes lead to a good deal of waste in resources devoted to ventures that don't succeed. But their optimism gives the economy much of the dynamic vigor that has pushed the American standard of living above its competitors. It is doubtful that dynamic progress in a private-enterprise system is possible without widespread losses from bad business guesses as well as profits from good ones. But without the *expectation* of profits, the system will grind to a halt.

Profits as a Source of Investment and Growth

Profits have a second major social function. Undistributed corporate profits (profits not paid out as dividends) are one important source of funds for business investment. In 1978, for example, they totaled $68 billion, and almost all were plowed back into new plant, equipment, and other such business uses. Depreciation allowances are also considered by many businessmen as sources of funds for business investments (but remember that a depreciation allowance is merely a bookkeeping charge, not actual money set aside). Because businesses seldom replace worn-out assets with identical assets, it is often hard to identify what is replacement and what is net new investment. Thus, business investment is often viewed gross (including replacement), as in the national income accounts. In 1978, depreciation charges totaled $18 billion, so net "internal" sources for corporate investment spending totaled about $50 billion; 1978 was a profitable year.

Nominal and Real Profits in Inflation

All the profit figures cited above are in nominal, or current, dollars, not adjusted for inflation. But in inflation, nominal profits overstate real profits. First, a dollar of profits, like any other income, has less purchasing power in inflation. But inflation leads to a further overstatement of real profits, more than for other income shares like wages. First of all, firms hold many fixed assets, like buildings and machinery. Depreciation on these assets is a cost. But the tax law says firms can only charge depreciation totaling 100 percent of the cost of each asset. However, in inflation, such a depreciation reserve is insufficient to replace the asset; the cost of replacement has gone up so the real cost of producing the firm's product is higher than the accounting costs show. This means that the real costs are more than the accounting costs, and the real profits are less than the nominal profits. Income taxes are levied on nominal profits, so the firm is taxed on nominal profits it does not really earn.

Second, investments lead to a similar overstatement of real earnings in inflation. Suppose the firm pays $1 million for raw materials, which it temporarily holds as inventory. With inflation, final-product prices rise, and the firm makes a special inventory profit because of the low-cost materials inventory it can use. But this is only a nominal profit; when it has to replace its materials inventory, the materials price has also risen, which uses up the special inventory profit that the accounting figures showed. The inventory profits were not real, only nominal; yet the firm must pay taxes on them.[2]

In 1978, a typical recent inflation year, the understatement of depreciation charges for all corporations was estimated at about $20 billion; the overstatement of inventory profits at $25 billion. Many corporations are also long-term debtors (mainly because they have borrowed by issuing bonds), and they will gain by being able to pay off these debts in cheaper dollars. This may partly or completely offset the depreciation and inventory losses, but the long-term debt gains affect the corporation's flow of cash only in the future and are not considered an adequate offset by many investors and businessmen. Thus, in inflation, the real rate of return earned by most corporations is less than the rate they report in their regular financial statements.

---

[2]By using LIFO (last-in, first-out) accounting, many business firms now substantially avoid this overstatement of inventory profits in inflation. They charge as costs the cost of the last raw materials bought, which are likely to be near the actual replacement cost of the materials used. But many firms still have not adopted this special method, and use FIFO (first-in, first-out) inventory accounting, which gives rise to overstated inventory profits.

THE THEORY OF PROFITS

Profits in a Static Economy

In a *static* economy, without technological advance, population change, capital accumulation, and changing consumer wants, only monopoly profits would continue in long-run equilibrium. Competition would gradually eliminate all other *economic* profits as resources were shifted into high-profit industries. Capitalization would bid up the prices and rents of especially productive resources. Economic (although not accounting) profits would be eliminated when equilibrium was achieved, except for those industries where new businesses were prevented from entering. There, and there only, monopoly and oligopoly profits would continue indefinitely. In effect, monopoly and oligopoly profits would then be a kind of rent, or quasi-rent, on monopoly position.

Profits in a Dynamic Economy

However, continuous, unpredictable change is everywhere in the real world. Uncertainty confronts the entrepreneur or manager daily. He must somehow "guesstimate" the future demand for his product, his future costs, future changes in technology, future behavior of his competitors. Then he must keep an eagle eye out for how the government is going to behave—on taxes, spending, antitrust policy, labor relations, and international affairs. In the midst of all this, he needs to worry about keeping his costs below those of competitors, keeping the union tolerably happy, being sure that his sales organization is on its toes, and so on.

If he does all these things better than his competitors, and especially if he has a partial-monopoly position to help him, he'll end up with a good profit. If he misses on many of the important decisions, the red ink will appear. The biggest job of the modern entrepreneur is to live with and to make the best of uncertainty. If he doesn't thrive on this kind of life, he'd better save himself a big doctor bill for ulcers and go to work for someone else.

Insurable risk, uncertainty, and dynamic change. Many kinds of risk can be insured against. In this way, the uncertainty can be eliminated by incurring a known dollar cost. The best-known example is the risk of loss from fire. Without insurance, this uncertainty would be a major problem for any business concern. But the likelihood of fire loss is reasonably predictable for a large number of buildings of any given type. By pooling together the moderate insurance premiums on a large number of buildings, the insurance company has enough funds to pay off the fire losses on those few buildings that do burn each year. Long experience has reduced the likelihood of such occurrences to a scientific, statistical basis. Businesses can now convert this type of risk into a known cost through insurance.[3]

Professor Frank H. Knight has pointed out that insurable risks are thus really only another business cost to be included with other business costs, and that economic profits arise only from bona fide cases of *uninsurable* uncertainty. Alas, the businessman can't go to his insurance agent and say, "I'm bringing out a new-style dishwasher; insure me against its being a flop." Economic profits beyond profits on monopoly position, Knight argues, are thus analytically linked solely to a world of dynamic change and uninsurable uncertainty.

Since profits arise largely out of dynamic change and uncertainty, much of what happens to profits is outside the control of any individual manager or entrepreneur. The biggest profits arise in booms, the biggest losses in depressions. "Windfall profits" are widespread in a lusty boom; in a bad depression, the best management in the world has a tough time making ends meet. The manager who can forsee business fluctuations and adjust successfully to them is worth his weight in gold.

Shifting consumer demand for individual products is a second big area of change largely outside the control of the individual businessman. Even General Motors is going to have a tough time making profits on automobiles if consumers decide to ride in helicopters instead. But the alert entrepreneur is far from helpless. He can change his product to keep in step with the times, and through his advertising he can influence what consumers want to buy.

---

[3]Very large firms may "self-insure." If a firm has hundreds of buildings itself, it may figure that the predictable likelihood of fire loss in any given year is less than the cost of buying commercial insurance on them.

Changes in costs are a third big area of uncontrollable uncertainty. What happens to the price of copper is outside the control of Westinghouse; yet copper represents one of the major costs in making electrical equipment. The same thing is true of many other costs. The businessman can bargain with his local union, but he isn't going to get much labor with a wage rate much below the rates that prevail elsewhere for similar work. Technological changes continually change costs. Basically, its the manager who does a good job of prediction under conditions of dynamic uncertainty, and who adjusts effectively to unforeseen conditions, who is likely to turn in good profits.

The profits of innovation. One noted economist, Joseph Schumpeter, argued that profits boil down largely to payments for keeping a jump ahead of your competitors through innovation in new products, production technology, and managerial methods. The big profits come from big, successful innovations—the motor car, color TV, and so on.

Unfortunately, no one has yet figured out a sure way of telling in advance whether a new mousetrap or a new auto engine will prove a success. First, there is the technological problem of developing the idea into a usable process or product. When this is licked, there is still that capricious monarch of all he surveys—the consumer. Business history tells a fascinating story of the sure things that flopped, and of the thousand-to-one shots that have become the industrial giants of today.

Successful innovation in effect gives a temporary monopoly to the innovator, and often big profits. Like other monopoly profits, the economic profits of innovation persist only until competitors catch up and bring profits in the industry down to competitive levels. But innovations are often protected by 17-year patents. And a running start on your competitor is often more important than the legal protection of patents. The firm with the know-how and experience that go with a new product or new method is likely to have a new innovation at hand by the time competitors catch up on the last one. The continuing success of the industrial giants of today—General Electric, IBM, du Pont—rests as much on this kind of continuing innovation as on any other single factor.

HOW BIG SHOULD PROFITS BE?

Are profits too big? Is business too concerned with making profits, and not enough with social responsibilities, as a majority of the public believe, according to repeated public opinion polls? How big do profits need to be to give the incentives they need to managers and investors to provide a dynamic, progressive, basically private-enterprise economy?

In principle, the answer is clear. Profits are big enough when businessmen and investors act as if they were big enough—when we get a satisfactory response to consumer demands in a dynamic economy, and the rate of economic growth we want. This answer puts the focus on the social functions of profits, not on the equity of the incomes received by profit makers, in contrast to much popular discussion about whether coupon clippers and dividend receivers are too rich.

The facts on profits were summarized above. In the past five years, corporate profits after taxes averaged about $90 billion, or about 5 percent of GNP. This is the amount society might consider taking away from profit receivers, if it considers profits too big. To judge the effects of such a profit transfer, we need first to remember, from above, that the total is made up of three quite different parts: (1) monopoly and quasi-monopoly profits, (2) returns (implicit interest) on stockholders' investments, and (3) true economic profits in a dynamic economy. Few economists would defend the first, but most evidence suggests it is a relatively small part of the total. If we oppose the second, we are essentially saying that savers should receive no interest on their investments. This is a position that Marx held and that we shall examine in the appendix to this chapter; this opposition would presumably apply equally to interest on bonds, bank deposits, and other savings. If we reduce the third part of profits, we question the need for profits as an incentive to businesses in both meeting consumer demands and investing for economic growth and higher living standards.

To assess these issues, we need to ask, Who gets the profits? Whose incentives are the crucial ones? The $10–$15 billion of profits in unincorporated businesses go to millions of individuals—doctors, lawyers, small shopkeepers, some poor, some rich. These are not the profits most critics challenge. Corporate profits go to some 25 million stockholders. On these, first remember that nearly half those profits are plowed back into the business involved, and hence do not show up in the current income of stockholders. Dividends actually paid out to stockholders averaged about $36 billion annually over the past five years—about 2 percent of GNP. Second, although there are over 25 million stockholders, most own only small amounts of stock, and their dividend incomes are a tiny proportion of their wages and salaries. Third, a large and growing proportion of all stock is held by financial institutions (trust companies, banks, insurance companies, and pension funds), which in turn reflect the investments of millions of people, rich and poor, in addition to the 25 million direct stock owners. Fourth, the big incomes of corporate executives are primarily salaries, not profits, although many also receive bonuses based on the profits earned and own stock on which they receive dividends.

How big profits must be to get these diverse groups and individuals to perform their social functions of investing and entrepreneurship is obviously a complex question. Some fear that we have already so weakened the incentives to save and invest by taxes, regulations, and inflation that America faces a major "capital shortage" over the next decade. They estimate that we will need perhaps $5 trillion of new investment by the mid-1980s, and that present incentives will fall far short of providing this investment, especially if government borrowing to finance deficits soaks up much of the available savings. The result, they predict, will be slower growth, weak recoveries, and a persistent tendency toward inflation as the government creates new money to finance its own spending needs when private savings and taxes are not available.

The controversy is a complex one, and there is no way of predicting accurately whether the present system will produce the huge voluntary saving and investment needed to keep the economy growing at the desired rate with reasonably full employment and without inflation. Nearly everyone agrees that inadequate capital investment is at least conceivable, given present returns on business investment, tax rates, and probable levels of government spending. Estimates that the average *real* (inflation-adjusted) after-tax rate of return to private capital investment has de-

clined from about 10 to 5 percent over the past decade strengthen the concern of the worriers.

Traditional Marxist doctrine and some modern radicals say the answer is easy. Profits and interest serve no social function; they should be zero. All property, except personal belongings, should be owned by the state, and state planners should decide what is to be produced, and how much of it. Only labor is productive, and there should be no return to property.

This answer obviously looks toward a system completely different from ours, and one with which few Americans agree. (We shall look at it briefly in the following appendix and in the final chapter.) Thus, it doesn't help much as a practical matter in answering our question on how big profits should be. The operationally important questions in America are whether we should tax away more (or less) corporation profits to provide money grants or subsidized services to other groups, and whether we should attempt to make stockholders and other investors pay for social improvements like cleaner air and water, jobs for the hard-core unemployed, and the like.

One may argue that investors would still invest as much if profit rates were lower; what else can they do with their money? Moreover, the cost of abstaining from consumption to save must be low for rich investors; they have all they want and deserve no substantial reward for saving. Similarly, actual corporation decisions in responding to consumer demands are made by paid managers, whose incomes are mainly salaries, not profits; they would do just as well if profits were lower.

These arguments seem plausible to some, but experience suggests that they should be viewed with doubts. Even if you believe profit receivers *should* be content with less, try the case, "Profits for the Picking?" at the end of this chapter. It suggests that making profits pay for good causes may be much harder than it seems. And it seems unlikely that the system would function as well with substantially lower profits. Investors do have other places to put their savings than in corporate equities; savers have a long history of searching out the investments that provide the best returns for them, shifting frequently from one to another as relative rates of return change. Perhaps they would feel they should readily give up part of their dividends to others less fortunate, without lessening their enthusiasm for risky, uncertain investments—but the stock market hasn't looked that way. Perhaps managers would do as well without a strong profit incentive, and certainly they have other important motives as well, but the drive for profits still looks like a powerful spur to getting goods and services produced efficiently in respone to consumer dollars laid on the counter.

All this doesn't say that the present level of profits is just right. No one knows what is just right. But the U.S. economy, relying heavily on profits as the carrot and losses as the stick, has been very successful in giving the masses the goods and services they seem to want—one of the world's highest standards of living. Every major high-per-capita-income nation in the world relies heavily on the profit motive in a market system.

Human motivation is a complex affair, and it varies widely from person to person. There are many incentives to good management and entrepreneurship—pride in achievement, the social acclaim for success, the development of professional standards, the pure joy of risk taking. Money is far from everything. Profits are just big enough when they induce entrepreneurs and investors to provide the social functions we want from them.

SUMMARY AND REVIEW

1. Corporate profits have grown rapidly but irregularly in dollar terms since the 1930s. They now are about 10 percent of the national income before taxes, about half that after taxes. They have declined gradually as a percentage of equity, sales, and national income since World War II. In inflation periods, nominal (current) profits substantially overstate real profits.

2. Profits have two major roles. They act as an incentive to businesses to produce most efficiently the goods and services that consumers want, and as a source of funds for investment and growth.

3. Modern theoretical analysis of profits states that profits in a *static* economy will be eliminated in the long run except for monopoly profits where there are restrictions on entry into the industry. Most of modern profits, however, arise because of the *dynamic* behavior of the economy, as returns to entrepreneurs and managers who make the best adjustments to change and uncertainty, and who manage the most effective innovations.

4. There is much controversy over how big profits should be. They need to be large enough to provide an effective incentive to businesses to produce most efficiently the goods and services consumers want, and to facilitate the rate of growth that society desires. Many economists argue that with a falling rate of real profit, America may face a major "capital shortage" over the decade ahead, which would produce slower growth, weak recoveries, and a persistent tendency toward inflation as the government creates new money to finance its own spending when private savings and taxes are not available.

For Analysis and Discussion

1. Are current profits excessive? (See Figure 22-2.) What are the best criteria to judge whether profits are too large or too small?
2. What are the main functions of profits in the modern American economy? Should businessmen be proud, or apologetic, when they make record profits?
3. "By and large, continuing profits for any firm demonstrate it is doing a good job in satisfying consumer demand." Do you agree or disagree? Explain.
4. Go back to Case 1. Suppose that you and other consumer advocates want to be sure the cost of new auto safety features is borne by the manufacturers and not passed on to consumers. How would you accomplish this?
5. "So long as we let businessmen think they have a chance to make profits, it doesn't matter whether they actually make any profits or not." Is this a sound analysis of the incentive role of business profits?

6. Who actually gets the profits made by the American corporations? (Refer back to Chapter 5 for some of the relevant information.) If it is not primarily managers, how do profits serve their presumed incentive function?

7. Many economists say that Marxist criticism of capitalist profits as creating big incomes for stockholders is misplaced—that the main function of profits is as an incentive to get businesses to do what we (the consumers) want done, and that we should expect successful businesses to earn substantial profits for serving this social function. Who is right?

8. How much should a business firm spend on "social responsibilities" like reducing pollution, supporting universities, and hiring hard-core unemployed workers, rather than concentrating on maximizing profits? Who should (will) ultimately pay for such corporate activities—stockholders or customers?

CASE 23

PROFITS FOR THE PICKING?

In 1978, corporate profits after taxes were about $118 billion, dividends $49 billion. This total demonstrated to many the ability of corporations to absorb the costs of producing better products, providing better services, and paying higher wages without raising prices to consumers. Suppose we agree (although many stockholders would not) that profits are bigger than they need be, and we propose to make corporations more responsive to consumer and social needs, which we argue they can perfectly well afford to be with their huge profits. Using the theory of the preceding chapters, analyze the likely consequences of the following.

Consumerism—who pays? Ralph Nader and many others have recently complained vigorously that many drug manufacturers release inadequately tested drugs for public consumption. Although the Food and Drug Administration sets minimum safety standards (see Chapter 6), these standards should be still higher. Drug producers should be made to do more thorough testing of new drugs before releasing them, since, as a practical matter, consumers have no way of judging for themselves which drugs are safe and which are not.

Another product recently subjected to widespread criticism as unsafe is the power lawn mower, which can be very efficient at mowing toes and fingers as well as grass, and which can hurl stones and other small objects out with the grass clippings at very dangerous velocities unless protective equipment is added. Require manufacturers to build more safety factors into mowers, insist the consumerists.

Should we pass new laws requiring manufacturers to do more extensive testing of drugs and to build safer power mowers? It looks like a good idea—safer products for consumers, and the manufacturer can well afford to do it out of those big profits. So we pass the law. Your economic theory should suggest what happens next: Costs are increased, manufacturers raise prices, and consumers have to pay more for drugs and power mowers. Maybe businesses *should* absorb the higher costs out of profits, but it's unlikely that they will. They feel they need all the profits they are making, whether or not you agree, and if costs go up for everyone in the drug and mower industries, you can be pretty sure prices will too. Consumers get safer products, and pay for them. Whether they're better or worse off as a result depends on how much you think that extra safety is worth.

But suppose consumers are outraged at the greed of business in raising prices for such obviously needed consumer safety, and get Congress to pass a law forbidding drug and mower manufacturers to raise prices. Assuming the law is strictly enforced, what does your economic theory tell you will happen then?

Right! Manufacturers will stop making the drugs and mowers on which they would now make a loss or smaller profit than on other products. Maybe they'll keep on for a while, but in the long run, capital will be transferred to other industries where the potential profit rate is higher. If consumers want safer drugs and power mowers, they can get them, but in the long run only by paying their higher costs—unless the producer has a monopoly position protected against new entrants.

Consider another case. Recently, courts and juries have been holding sellers strictly responsible for damages to consumers from products that are in any way faulty. Juries have awarded large settlements to people injured in accidents presumably due to product defect. A Wisconsin man recently received $500,000 for the loss of a leg when a safety guard on a chain saw slipped after he thought he had fastened it firmly. The average award rose from $12,000 to $67,000 over the past five years in seller-liability household chemical cases, from $38,000 to $98,000 in automobile cases. And the total number of such cases litigated rose from about 100,000 to 500,000 annually over the same period.

Fair enough! you may say. Consumers deserve safe, reliable products, and if businesses don't make them, let them pay. But get out your economic theory again. Where is all that money coming from? If the culprit is just one firm in an industry, its profits may indeed have to absorb the costs of coming up to industry standards. But if what consumers demand is higher safety and reliability standards for all, the result is probably higher costs, and if so, almost certainly they'll be passed along in higher prices, in the long if not the short run. Same reasoning as above.

Some consumers say the insurance companies will have to pay the damages, so businesses won't have to charge consumers more. But that again is shortsighted. Insurance companies must also cover their costs to stay in business, and they push up rates quickly for any class of customers who show unusually large claims. Unless you can find an industry with a protected-monopoly-profit pool, it's unlikely that consumerism will get its better products and big consumer awards out of profits for very long; they'll be paid for in prices that cover full costs in the long run.

Last, try the same reasoning on the auto industry, now one of our most regulated non-public-utility industries. In 1978, the Ford Motor Company projected that it would have to invest $20 billion in the 1978–85 period to meet U.S. government-mandated standards for exhaust emissions, fuel economy, safety, noise, and other performance criteria.[4] This compared with

---

[4] Published letter to White House from Phillip Caldwell, president of Ford, dated June 13, 1978.

its entire net worth of about $9 billion in 1978, and an average annual profit of $840 million over the preceding five years. How much of the cost would you predict will be paid for in lower profits, how much by consumers?

Wages and the profit pool. Similar reasoning throws a sobering light on the perhaps ethically attractive argument that workers getting very low wages should have more and wealthy dividend receivers less. Why not form a union or pass a law to raise their wages and let profits be squeezed? Go back to Chapters 18 and 19 for the answers. If profits rest on exploitation of workers, unions or minimum-wage laws can shift income from profits to wages. And in high-profit oligopoly industries, perhaps some profits-to-wages shift may work. But wherever competitive pressures are strong, well-meaning attempts to get higher wages for workers out of profits will not succeed in the long run. Higher wage rates will mean not lower profits but higher prices and fewer jobs in the industry concerned.

All this does not mean that consumers shouldn't insist on safer, better products, or that workers shouldn't press for higher wages. Both may be worth what they cost. But economic analysis should help you avoid using fantasy rather than fact on how far society can solve its problems by drawing on a huge pool of profits just waiting to be tapped, however strongly you may feel that profits *should* bear the cost.

Note that this problem parallels closely the corporate "social responsibility" arguments that businesses should reduce pollution and the like, instead of just trying to make profits. Should corporations concentrate on doing social good instead of meeting consumer demands? If one company spends heavily on "social responsibilities" while others don't, what happens to its competitive position? If we pass a law requiring all companies to reduce pollution or help clean up the slums, who will pay?

APPENDIX   Marx, "Radical Economics," Interest, and Profits

Karl Marx, writing a century ago, developed an elaborate theory of the workings and ultimate downfall of capitalism. The central points were the following:

1. All history can be interpreted in terms of economic issues and a class struggle between capitalists and workers.
2. All value is created by labor, and the labor time necessary for production of any commodity will determine its value (price).
3. Capitalists (employers) seize a part of what workers produce each year in the form of profits, interest, and rents. This "surplus value" really belongs to the workers.
4. The capitalists also dominate the government.
5. The class struggle will develop "basic contradictions" in a capitalist system that will bring about the downfall of capitalism. Capital will be increasingly monopolized by a few huge corporations. As capitalists seize more and more surplus value, wages of workers will be ground down to subsistence levels, and the workers will be unable to buy all the goods produced in the capitalist society. This will generate depressions and mass unemployment, and sooner or later the workers will rise and throw off the capitalist rule.
6. To keep the capitalist economy going, capitalists have increasingly turned to international imperialism in order to find and exploit abroad the cheap labor and raw materials they need in order to meet capitalism's imperative of growth if it is to survive. (This is primarily a post-Marx argument.)

Modern Marxists and radicals make many modifications on the argument, but this is the core.

Profits, interest, and wages. Marx declared profits and interest to be immoral—without social function, and obtained entirely by expropriating the surplus value produced by the workers. But modern economists point to crucial flaws in his "labor theory of value" on which the argument rests. The labor theory of value says that only labor is productive and that all prices will be proportional to labor inputs. Clearly, this is wrong; prices are basically determined by the forces of supply and demand in markets, as was explained in the preceding chapter. How will the labor theory of value explain the high price of a perfect pearl picked up with little labor by a passing beach walker? Or $11/barrel OPEC oil, brought out of the ground at a labor cost of only a few cents? The argument that capital is not itself productive is equally fallacious, or a play on words. Without the capital they work with, total output with the same workers would clearly be less.

Similarly, most modern economists, including many in the USSR and Eastern Europe, agree that without the interest rate to help guide the choice between more- and less-roundabout means of production (for example, how much expensive machinery to use, compared to labor-intensive production), it is impossible to plan efficiently. For this reason, until recently, communist planners made major errors in production processes. Similarly, without profits as a guide and an incentive to efficient production, the communist nations have faced increasingly serious difficulties in getting central plans carried out. Recently, both interest and profits have been openly introduced into the USSR's and other communist countries' economic planning.

Marx and history. Marxists have for a century persistently proclaimed the death throes of capitalism. Capitalism has been uncooperative. Indeed, income and growth statistics (see Tables 1–1 and 30–1) show the Western capitalist economies dominating the list; East Germany, well down the per capita income list, is the richest communist state. The USSR, several countries further down, reports a per capita income only about 35–40 percent of the United States'. In the capitalist nations, the poor have not become poorer and more numerous; on the contrary, the bottom-quarter income recipients in most Western capitalist nations are notably better off economically than even the middle classes in the communist nations. Capitalist economies' income distributions have remained remarkably stable. Property income, depending on precisely how it is defined, has hovered around 20–25 percent of GNP in the United States (see Figure 18–4), and not far from that in other major Western capitalist nations. Profits have neither eroded from lack of mass purchasing power nor ballooned to sweep control over spendable income into capitalist hands. Aided by persistent technical progress, they have remained roughly constant as a rate of return on investment over most of the past century (although the rate has declined somewhat recently).

Modern monetary and fiscal policy appears to have tamed the worst excesses of the business cycle and massive depressions. Wealth is concentrated in the Western, democratic, capitalist nations, but the concentration is gradually diminishing. Although monopoly is a serious problem for some capitalist countries, it is not clear in America, for example, that the degree of monopoly has changed significantly in this century. The great middle classes look more stable and conservative, not increasingly ground down into an ever-hungrier proletariat. The clank of the chains that Marx said bind the workers to poverty and subservience is faint indeed. "The people" persistently refuse to vote to tax either profits and interest, or the rich per se, out of existence. The income tax and the "welfare state" have proved more attractive to the masses than the sword in dealing with the rich.

What went wrong with the Marxist predictions? Today, many Marxists and other radicals say, "Just wait!" They say that capitalist statistics mask a growing sickness and economic instability, that modern capitalism with its profit motive is only temporarily shored up by wars and imperialism.[5]

No one can know the future, but the Marxist arguments find limited support thus far in the data of Western history. Marx flatly denied any useful role for profits or interest in the operations of an economic system. But, as was indicated above, both have recently been introduced into Soviet and satellite economic planning and management of the econ-

omy.[6] Strikingly, to most modern "radicals," the problem of economic incentives is easily manageable. If everyone, especially the rich, would only be less greedy and share what they produce, economists' persistent concern with "scarcity" and more efficient use of resources would be seen to be fatuous. In any event, others say, government planning can do whatever needs to be done.

But all-powerful government planning has yet to demonstrate superiority over profits and individual initiative. The optimal mix of planning and private economic incentives remains unsettled. But wants are far in excess of the resources available to meet them all over the world, and economic incentives lie inescapably at the heart of the problems faced by every society.[7]

---

[5]For some data on the "imperialism" issue.

[6]Although Marx was quite explicit about the death throes of capitalism, his writings are devoid of any picture of how a true "Marxist" economy should function after the revolution. Thus, it is hard to compare actual capitalist and communist developments with what Marx might have considered optimal. He predicted the gradual withering away of government after the workers' revolt, but failed to specify who would then run what parts of the economy and how. Clearly, the USSR, Communist China, and Cuba today are far from the governmentless economy Marx forecast.

[7]For a lively authoritative modern Marxist statement, see P. Baran and P. Sweezy, *Monopoly Capital* (New York: Modern Reader Paperbacks, 1966).

Part 4

Public Goods,
Income
Redistribution,
and the
Public Sector

The Public
Sector

CHAPTER 23

What should the government do in economic affairs? How much should it tax, and how much should it spend? How much should it regulate? The influential nineteenth-century English liberals argued that the primary function of the state was merely to set up and enforce certain "rules of the game" under which private enterprise could then be counted on to get goods efficiently produced and distributed. At the other extreme, the communists argue that all productive resources should be owned by the state, and that production and distribution should be directed in detail by the government.

The present attitude in America is somewhere in between, but much closer to the private-enterprise position. Most Americans believe in capitalism and a free, individual-initiative economy—but in having the government do a lot too. In 1900, total federal government expenditures were about 3.5 percent of GNP. By the 1930s this had grown to 10 percent, and by 1978 to 22.6 percent. And government regulation of economic life grew as fast, or faster.

By the 1970s, many Americans began to question whether more government was the answer to everything—economic stabilization, poverty, pollution, unsafe products, you name it. In a 1978 "taxpayers' revolt" in California, voters passed a constitutional amendment, dramatically limiting property taxes. Public-opinion polls reported public preferences of 6 to 1 for a federal constitutional amendment requiring that the federal budget be balanced each year, and that constitutional limits be placed on growth in federal spending. Keynesian expansionary policies, led by discretionary fiscal policy, were widely termed obsolete, by economists as well as politicians and the general public. Government regulation of airline fares and routes was slashed. Government suddenly seemed too big, too expensive, too intrusive. This is the biggest issue in federal economic policy today.

THE FOUR BIG FUNCTIONS OF GOVERNMENT

Modern government has four big economic functions. People may disagree widely on how far government should go on each front, but nearly everyone agrees that government needs to play all four roles.

Government as Stabilizer: Stably Growing Aggregate Demand

Two centuries ago, Adam Smith didn't worry about booms and depressions, because they didn't exist. But with the emergence of our modern industrial society, economic instability became a major problem. There is no reason why aggregate spending (consumer plus business plus government) will automatically just match the growing output potential of the system at stable prices. Clearly, no private agency can assure the needed stable growth in aggregate demand. Government has to help if we are to avoid the massive depressions and inflations that have marred the past. But traditional discretionary monetary and fiscal policies seem of limited effectiveness in controlling inflation without causing substantial unemployment.

Government as Policeman: The Rules of the Game

Even Adam Smith said that government has to act as policeman—to spell out some rules of the economic game and to see that people obey them. To live effectively together in a complex world, we have to agree that contracts will be respected. Equally important, competition must prevail in the marketplace to ensure the benefits of private enterprise, and only government can undertake this kind of regulation. The role of government in setting up and enforcing the rules of the competitive game was a main theme of Part 2. It's a vital role if a system like ours is to work effectively.

As indicated earlier, it's a complex question as to just how far government rules should go. Some people, for ethical as well as economic reasons, would regulate minimum wages and working hours, the fares airlines can charge, wage bargains, and many other economic actions. Others demur. But nearly everyone agrees that where externalities bulk large, the marketplace will fail to produce the optimal output. If a paper mill produces dirty water and an objectionable odor as well as paper, government action is needed to see that paper buyers, in addition to paying the

313

private costs of producing paper, pay for keeping the water and air clean. One way of doing this is for the government to forbid the pollution of water and air. Then the manufacturer's total cost will include pollution-control measures as well as labor, raw materials, and the like. Another approach is to impose a special tax on polluters and to use the funds to clean up the water or air. The line between the government's setting the rules of the game and its active intervention is often very fuzzy.

Government as Provider of Services: The Public Sector

There are some things a private-enterprise, profit-motivated system clearly will not provide adequately—national defense, highways, moon shots, police protection. Partly, these are instances of large externalities—social costs or benefits in addition to private costs and benefits. At the extreme are pure "public goods," such as the court system, where we clearly want the "product" but where there is no practical way of producing and selling it through the market. The critical point is the inability to withhold the benefits of the expenditure from anyone who wouldn't pay for them voluntarily. National defense is a public good.

In such cases, the government needs to act as a public store, providing the public good and collecting for it through taxes. Instead of relying on the private store to produce everything we want, we thus set up a public store alongside to handle what the private store can't or won't stock under the profit incentive. The public store is the "public sector," where we rely on political votes rather than the market to decide what to produce. The public sector allocates over 20 percent of all resources in the United States today, through taxes and government purchase of goods and services, although most of the actual production (say, of highways) is contracted out to the private sector. The taxes are the price we agree, through the political process, to pay.

Government as Income Redistributor: Transfer Payments

The fourth major economic function of government is to redistribute income—mainly by taxing some people and making transfer payments to others. If we want some people to have more and some less than the market provides, government taxes and transfer payments are one way to do something about it. The aged, the poor, farmers, the unemployed, and the vast middle-income classes—all receive large government transfer payments. Because the payments go mainly to middle- and lower-income groups, and our tax system is "progressive" (that is, the rich pay a higher percentage of their incomes than the poor do), this redistribution shifts income from upper- to middle- and lower-income groups. But, contrary to common belief, the great bulk of the redistribution is within the middle-income classes, who make up the bulk of the population. They pay most of the taxes, and they get most of the government transfer payments—Social Security, housing subsidies, and the like. Government redistribution of money income is the fourth big activity of the public sector. It currently shifts about 15 percent of the total national income this way. Thus, the public store and income transfers together account for nearly a third of total economic activity. The public sector is a big part of the modern American economy (and of most other industrialized Western economies as well).

THE PUBLIC SECTOR TODAY

First, a look at the facts. In 1978, federal, state, and local governments spent over $700 billion, and their expenditures are rising by billions of dollars every year. These expenditures have been roughly matched by growing tax collections. Thus, taxes, including Social Security payroll taxes, are now over $3,000 a year for every man, woman, and child in the United States. Total annual tax collections will cross the $1 trillion mark in the 1980s. Excluding military personnel, some 15 million workers—one out of every six—are on government payrolls today.

The Growing Role of Government

It is useful to begin with some historical perspective. Look at Figure 23–1. Four big developments deserve comment.

1. Partly, the increase in spending is due to more people and higher prices. Since 1914,

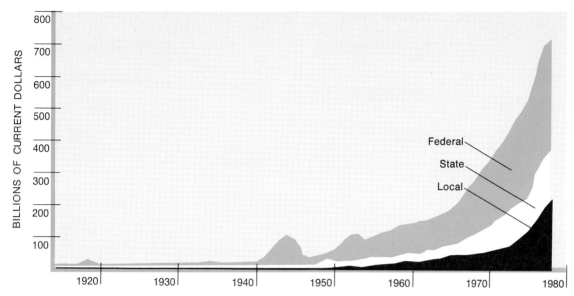

FIGURE 23–1
Government Expenditures since 1914
Federal spending has shot up during wars and again in recent peacetime years. State and local spending has grown rapidly since World War II. (Source: U.S. Treasury Department. Figures include Social Security.)

population has more than doubled and prices have more than quadrupled, so real government spending per capita has risen only about twentyfold, rather than the huge increase suggested by Figure 23–1—but twentyfold is a lot.

2. The prime reason for the big real increase per capita is that we have wanted our governments to do more for us—education, Social Security, welfare, sewers, moon shots, health, highways. The nation's shift from a rural to an urban economy accounts for a big share of the state–local increase; we need the government to do more when we're crowded together in cities. But there's a lot more than just the cities involved. Most important recently has been the enormous growth in spending on "human resources" and income security—health, Social Security, welfare, education, and the like. In earlier editions of this book, national defense dominated the total government spending picture. But no more! In 1973, federal income-security payments alone (mainly federal Social Security, welfare, and unemployment benefits)

surpassed national defense, and when other human-resources spending is lumped in, the total is now nearly double that for national defense. Social Security benefits alone are over $100 billion annually. The big increase has been in transfer payments—direct transfers of funds from taxpayers to beneficiaries, rather than government purchases of goods and services. Thus, the fourth of the big functions of government—redistribution of incomes—is increasingly dominating government budgets.

3. National defense, although it declined absolutely in real terms and from 44 to 23 percent of the federal budget between 1968 and 1978, continues to be a huge cost, especially when veterans' benefits and other defense-related costs are included. Moreover, the total began to rise again after 1976, as military spending grew all over the world. Modern war is fabulously expensive. A new nuclear aircraft carrier in 1978 was estimated to cost $2 billion, compared to only $6 million for a World War II carrier. Partly, this reflects inflation, but it mainly reflects the in-

315

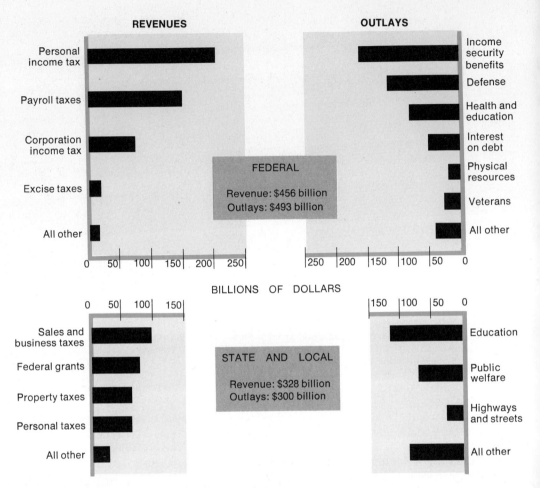

REVENUES

Personal income tax
Payroll taxes
Corporation income tax
Excise taxes
All other

OUTLAYS

Income security benefits
Defense
Health and education
Interest on debt
Physical resources
Veterans
All other

FEDERAL

Revenue: $456 billion
Outlays: $493 billion

0 50 100 150 200 250

250 200 150 100 50 0

BILLINGS OF DOLLARS

0 50 100 150

150 100 50 0

Sales and business taxes
Federal grants
Property taxes
Personal taxes
All other

STATE AND LOCAL

Revenue: $328 billion
Outlays: $300 billion

Education
Public welfare
Highways and streets
All other

FIGURE 23–2

Government Revenues and Outlays, 1978

Federal, state, and local governments collected about $700 billion in taxes and spent about $790 billion (excluding intergovernmental grants) in 1978, including transfer payments. Chart does not include government-operated businesses, such as public utilities, but it does overstate net government outlays by including state–local spending of federal grants totaling $77 billion. (Source: U.S. Budget and Department of Commerce; preliminary estimates.)

creasingly complex nature of modern war and defense.[1]

[1]For the whole world, military budgets exceed $300 billion, roughly equal to the total income of the poorest half of all mankind. In the last twenty years, the world has spent over $3 trillion on military manpower and weapons. The United States and the USSR are the biggest spenders, but military outlays in 1978 totaled $40 billion in the poverty-ridden less-developed nations.

4. The other big development of recent years has been the rapid growth of state and local governments. Between 1960 and 1978, state and local spending rose from about $20 billion to nearly $300 billion, a 15-fold increase. Today, state and local governments spend twice as much on goods and services as the federal government does. About 12 million people now work for state and local governments, only 3 million for the

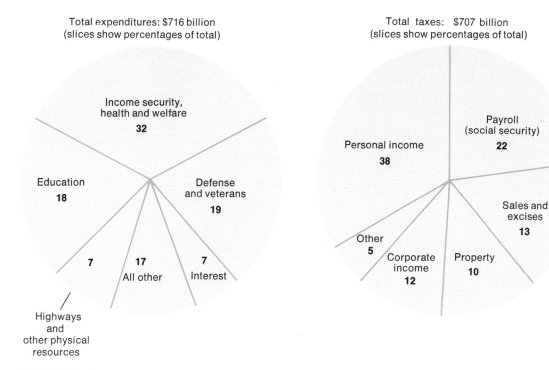

Total expenditures: $716 billion
(slices show percentages of total)

Income security,
health and welfare
32

Education
18

Defense
and veterans
19

7

17
All other

7
Interest

Highways
and
other physical
resources

Total taxes: $707 billion
(slices show percentages of total)

Personal income
38

Payroll
(social security)
22

Sales and
excises
13

Other
5

Corporate
income
12

Property
10

FIGURE 23–3
Total Government Spending and Taxes, 1978
Income security, education, and national defense are the biggest government
expenditures. Personal income and social-security payroll taxes provide 60 percent of
the nation's tax revenues, corporation, sales, and property taxes most of the rest.
(Source: U.S. Commerce and Treasury Departments; preliminary estimates.)

federal government. This distribution reflects the fact that the bulk of federal spending is on transfer payments (which require relatively few employees) and on goods and services contracted out to private industries (health research, aircraft, and so on), whereas state and local governments primarily provide services themselves (education, police protection, and the like). But a big chunk of state–local spending is financed by grants from the federal government. They totaled $77 billion in 1978.

The desperate plight of the central cities is one of the biggest unsolved government finance problems today. They face spiraling costs of providing vital services (education, law and order, welfare, sanitation, and the like) at the same time that well-to-do businesses and individual taxpayers are moving to the suburbs,

leaving a population that needs increasingly costly services but has little ability to pay taxes.

Figures 23–2 and 23–3 summarize taxes and expenditures in 1978 for federal, state, local, and all governments combined.

Taxes

Figure 23–3 also shows what taxes provided the revenue in 1978, combining federal, state, and local governments. Ours is increasingly a personal tax system. Nearly two-thirds of all taxes are raised that way—38 percent through personal income taxes, and 22 percent through payroll taxes used to finance Social Security. At the federal level, personal income and payroll taxes now provide nearly 80 percent of all revenue. Corporate income, sales, excise, and property taxes account for most of the rest; property taxes still produce nearly all local-government revenue. If you feel you're taxed wherever you turn, you're right. We can't collect over a half-trillion dollars annually for our governments without making nearly everyone pay.

Who pays these taxes? Chapter 26 is devoted to this question, but Figure 23–4 provides some very rough estimates of the burden of different taxes on families at different income levels. The burdens shown are for those who ultimately paid the taxes (for example, consumers when the cigarette tax or sales tax is passed on to them by retailers), rather than the person who turns the money over to the government. For several taxes, we can only roughly estimate who bears the final burden, especially for the corporate income and property taxes. It is also important to recognize that the tax burdens are percentages of money income only; the poor, especially, get substantial additional transfer income in kind—for example, food stamps, subsidized housing, and Medicaid—so the real burden of their taxes is less heavy than the picture suggests.

The estimates of Figure 23–4 suggest that the percentage tax burden was surprisingly similar in

FIGURE 23–4

Tax Burden by Family Income Levels, 1968

Most families pay about the same percentage of their incomes in taxes. Burden on the very wealthy ($100,000 income and up) is subject to dispute, depending on whether taxes on corporations, dividends, and property are paid by the wealthy or shifted to consumers. Last two bars show results of alternative assumptions. (Source: R. and P. Musgrave, *Public Finance in Theory and Practice.* New York: McGraw-Hill, 1977, Chap. 16; and U.S. Census Bureau.)

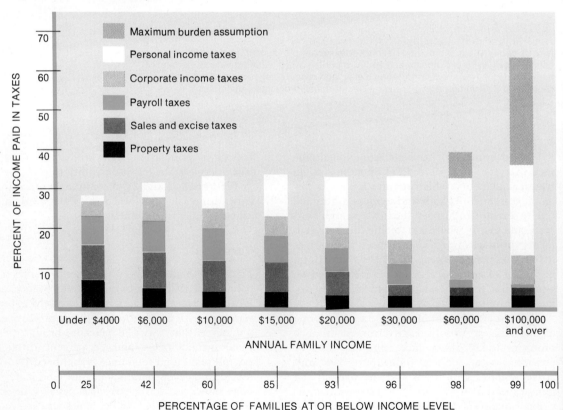

1968 for the great bulk of American families, from very low incomes up to the few very wealthy. Only the high-income receivers in fact faced sharply progressive total tax bills (that is, a a higher percentage on large than on small incomes). Note especially the double scale at the bottom of Figure 23–4. In 1968, 85 percent of all families received incomes of less than $15,000, so nearly all families were included in the first four bars of the chart. Today, well over half of all families have incomes over $15,000.

The federal corporation and personal income taxes account for most of the system's progressivity. The top 10 percent of families paid 50 percent of all personal income taxes; the lowest 25 percent paid virtually none—less than 1 percent of the total. Conversely, sales, excise, and payroll taxes are regressive; they take a larger proportion of low and middle than of high incomes.

Do these estimates still apply? Probably they are still roughly applicable, but, as suggested above, you should shift all family incomes upward. Inflation alone has doubled family dollar incomes over the past decade, moving families up into higher tax brackets for the personal income tax, where rates are sharply progressive at high income levels. Congress has reduced personal income tax rates three times since 1966, mainly for lower- and middle-income taxpayers, and the rate structure now is probably substantially more progressive than shown in Figure 23–4. In any event, the estimates should be viewed as only rough approximations. The problems of making such estimates are examined in more detail in Chapter 26.

FIGURE 23–5
Taxes Paid and Benefits Received from Governments
at Different Income Levels
Low-income groups receive much more in government services and transfer payments than they pay in taxes. The reverse is true for high-income families. Estimates for 1978 are very rough. (Source: R. and P. Musgrave, *Public Finance in Theory and Practice.* New York: McGraw-Hill, 1977, Chap. 16; and U.S. Census Bureau.)

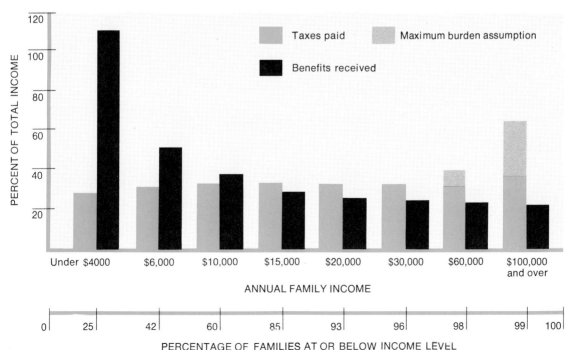

REDISTRIBUTION OF INCOME THROUGH THE PUBLIC SECTOR

What is the net redistributional effect of these massive tax collections and public expenditures? Figure 23–5 provides a very rough set of estimates. The dark bars show the benefits received from all government expenditures at different income levels, and the blue bars (reproduced from Figure 23–4) the taxes paid. Although the tax system becomes sharply progressive only for high incomes, government benefits are a large percent of income for the poor but only a small percent for the rich. Thus, overall, the government redistributes income substantially from the rich to the poor. But the bulk of both tax payments and benefits are transfers within the big middle-income classes, as will be explained more fully in Chapter 24. The big redistribution is not from rich to poor, but from some to other middle- and upper-income groups.

It is important to recognize just what these rough estimates show. The tax burden estimates are the totals from Figure 23–4. The benefit estimates attempt to measure who gets the ultimate benefit from each government expenditure, including transfer payments. (That, incidentally, explains how government benefits can be more than total income for the poor, since the family-income data exclude substantial non-money benefits like food stamps and Medicaid, which are included in the government benefits in Figure 23–5.) Estimating the final beneficiaries of old-age pensions, for example, is relatively easy. But for services such as national defense, education, police protection, and the like, only an arbitrary allocation is possible. The general picture shown by Figure 23–5 is almost certainly correct (remembering that all families over $100,000 are lumped together here), but don't take the details too seriously.

THE PUBLIC SECTOR IN THE UNITED STATES AND ABROAD

How big is the public sector in the United States compared to that of other leading Western nations? Table 23–1 answers the question, including India, a less-developed nation, for comparative purposes. These figures show tax collections as a percentage of GNP in 1977, including taxes used to finance both real and transfer expenditures.

Taxes may seem heavy in the United States, but we are one of the lighter-taxed of the major developed nations. This reflects especially the broader range of social (especially health and housing) services provided by most West European governments. Note also the low figure for Japan, which maintains virtually no military establishment. Governments of poor, less-developed countries nearly all have relatively low taxes and expenditures.

TABLE 23–1
The Public Sector in Different Nations

COUNTRY	TAXES AS PERCENTAGE OF GNP
Sweden	51
Netherlands	47
Belgium	40
France	39
United Kingdom	37
West Germany	36
Canada	34
Switzerland	32
United States	30
Japan	23
India	12

Source: Data for 1977, from Organization for Economic Cooperation and Development, except for India.

SUMMARY AND REVIEW

1. Although most Americans believe in capitalism and a free, individual-initiative economic system, they want the government to do a lot too. Many economists specify four main economic functions for government, even in a basically market-directed, capitalist economy. Government should:
   a. Help stabilize the economy through stabilizing the growth in aggregate demand.

b. Specify the basic rules for a private-enterprise economy and enforce them to attain the full benefits of such an economy.

c. Provide some services directly, especially "public goods" and services involving large externalities.

d. Redistribute incomes where the public wants to alter the distribution provided by the market.

But how far the government should go in each of these activities is vigorously disputed. Recent years have seen widespread feelings that governments have become too big and too intrusive.

2. Government tax collections and expenditures have grown rapidly and persistently during the past century, and will reach $1 trillion annually in the early 1980s. Over the century, wars and national defense have accounted for much of this growth. More recently, mushrooming expenditures on income security and human resources, mainly involving transfer payments, have far exceeded national-defense costs. America's shift from a rural to an urban economy also accounts for much of the increase.

3. Total taxes are now about $15,000 per typical four-person family. While the dollar tax burden is low for poor families and high for wealthy families, taxes as a percentage of total income are apparently quite similar, at around 30 percent for typical families except at very low and very high income levels. The mix of taxes paid varies substantially by income level, with personal and corporation income taxes providing most of the progressivity on high incomes. (See Figure 23–4.)

4. Government expenditures provide much of the income received by poor families but a very small part of the income of wealthy families (see Figure 23–5). Thus, overall, governments transfer income from high- to low-income families. But the bulk of income transfers are from politically less-effective to politically more-effective parts of the vast middle-income levels, which receive most of the nation's income.

5. In spite of the huge volume of taxes and government expenditures, the United States is one of the lighter-taxed of the major industrial nations.

For Analysis and Discussion

1. What are the main economic functions of government?

2. Do governments spend too much? What are your criteria for deciding? Is the recent "taxpayers' revolt" justified?

3. If a copy is available (for instance, in the *New York Times* about the third week of each January, or in *The Federal Budget in Brief*), read the president's most recent budget message to Congress. What are the major increases and decreases proposed from the preceding year? Do these changes seem desirable to you? What criteria have you used, implicitly or explicitly, in making these judgments?

4. Should the government do more to equalize the distribution of income? If you say yes, how do you justify your position to a doctor or businessman who is earning a large income and says he doesn't see why he should work hard to support others?

5. Locate your family income level on Figure 23–5. Assuming that these estimates are roughly accurate, do you feel that your income level is being treated fairly in the government's overall redistribution of income? Should you be taxed more heavily? Get more benefits from the government?

6. Recently, much concern has been expressed that in many areas, our educational facilities are inadequate, especially in the rural South. Should the federal government spend more money to improve these educational facilities—say, by building new schoolhouses, or making grants to raise teachers' salaries? If your answer is yes, who should pay? How much would you be willing to see your taxes raised to help pay for such new expenditures?

Markets or the
Political Process:
How Big Should
Government Be?

CHAPTER 24

s government too big? What should the public sector do? How much government will best serve the public interest in economic affairs? To answer these questions, we need a theory of the public sector—a theory that will tell us when to turn to the public sector rather than relying on the private marketplace. This chapter provides such a theory, building on the four main economic functions of government suggested in Chapter 23. Part 3 dealt with the roles of the government as stabilizer and policeman. We turn now to the government as provider of services and as income redistributor.

Where public goods or large externalities are involved, or where we want to alter the distribution of income, we should turn to the public sector—to direct government participation in allocating resources and distributing incomes.

This involves substitution of the political process for markets, and raises difficult questions of how far government should go. For, as a practical matter, in using the public sector to achieve our goals, we face possible important "public-sector failures," just as we saw important "market failures" in the private sector. Most important, we shall see that the market and the political process work best in achieving different goals. Very roughly, and with important exceptions to come, markets best provide incentives and efficiency, whereas we turn to the political process when such values as "fairness" and "equity' are dominant.

WHAT SHOULD GOVERNMENT DO?

Public Goods and Major Externalities

In the United States we have a strong tradition of trying private enterprise first, and turning to direct government operations only when private initiative clearly won't work. One major example is "public goods," which shades over into the case of major externalities of broad social concern.

Most "public goods" have four main characteristics: (1) They are widely considered to be important, but there is no practical way of providing them through the market. (2) They cannot practically be withheld from some if provided to others. (3) They have to be consumed by many people whether or not people want to pay for them. (4) Their use by some does not make them less useful to others. Some marginal cases may not have all four characteristics.

Consider the example of national defense, or of the judicial system. Nearly everyone agrees that both are essential. Yet it is impractical to rely on the private market to provide them; there is no feasible way to divide them up into salable units so that those who want to buy them can do so, while those who won't can be excluded from their use. If national defense is provided, Joe Nopay will get the benefit just as much as will those citizens who pay the bill. This is known as the "free-rider" problem. Where there is no way of keeping free riders from benefiting free, collective action to provide the "public good," with compulsory payment of the costs through taxes, seems the only practical way of providing the wanted good or service. But if national defense is provided, it must be consumed by all; some may be protected even though they did not want to buy the protection. Note, moreover, that the fact that A benefits does not lessen the possibility of B's doing so, whereas in a private-good case, if a unit of the good is sold to A, it will be unavailable to B. A lighthouse is another favorite economists' example. Once in place, the lighthouse rays are visible to all; there is no way of keeping free riders from benefiting; and the fact that A sees the light makes it no less useful to B.

Similar examples can be found at local levels. Suppose a community is threatened by floods, which can be prevented by building a dam above the city. It may be clearly advantageous to all citizens to have the dam. Yet, without government intervention and taxation to pay the bills, the dam is unlikely to be built. The free-rider possibility will lead many citizens not to pay voluntarily, because once the dam is built, all are protected whether or not they paid. The dam, like national defense, is a public good, and should be provided by the government if its prospective benefits exceed its cost.

Public financing and construction of facilities are sometimes rationalized on public-goods reasoning when they don't really meet the crucial tests above. For example, most big cities have sports arenas, often constructed partially or completely with public funds. The argument runs that big arenas are essential to draw major-league athletic teams, and such teams are a great benefit to the whole city. But in fact, only a small portion of the population of most cities attends such sporting events, and it is quite possible to keep the major benefits away from those who wouldn't pay enough for tickets to cover the full cost of the stadium; the stadium is not a true public good. Or take the case of public golf courses that operate on public subsidies. Citizens who enjoy athletics and exercise are clearly being subsidized by the general taxpayers, with a public-good rationalization that is, at best, only partially valid. Pseudopublic goods are not limited to athletics. Many cities also maintain publicly subsidized halls for symphony orchestras and ballets, which are attended by only a small fraction of the population, and an upper-income portion at that. Do the cultural gains benefit the city at large, so that they could not be withheld from nonpayers, or do they benefit mainly those who attend the subsidized concerts and ballet performances?

The line between public goods and private goods with major externalities is often hazy. For example, are highways a public good? In principle, no. Their use can be limited to those who pay; toll roads are an example. But some of the indirect benefits accrue to those who seldom drive on the road—landowners, businesses, farmers, and others nearby who gain from the increased accessibility of their activities to others—and there is no practical way of shutting off these benefits once the road is built. We can say the highway is a quasi-public good, or we can call it a private good with major externalities. Education is a similar case. Think through the extent to which its public financing and operation depend on its being a public good or just a private good with major externalities. (See Case 24 at the end of the chapter for a further exploration of the education case.)

For pure public goods and quasi-public goods where the product is very important and the externalities are both widespread and important, the common solution is for the government to take over production and distribution—national defense, education, streets, and space exploration are examples. Such services are generally financed by taxes and provided free (but not always—remember toll bridges, city transit systems, and partial tuition at state universities).[1] But how much the government should spend on any of these goods is less clear. In principle, government ought to increase production of each good up to the point where full marginal cost just equals full marginal benefit to society; but alas, there is no simple way of measuring either marginal cost or marginal benefits. Another alternative is simply to rely on a majority vote of the electorate, but as a practical matter, this is seldom feasible and, as we shall see, it would often give dubious results even if it were feasible. What actually happens in the public sector in most cases, we shall examine presently.

Redistribution of Income

The second big activity of the public sector is redistributing income, through taxes and transfer payments. Many people believe that the distribution of income produced by our largely individualistic, market-directed economy is too unequal. Even though the market may produce the most efficient use of our resources and the maximum total output consistent with our social and economic mores, the income-distribution result is ethically unacceptable. The spread between rich and poor is, they say, too wide.

This proposition is an ethical, or value, judgment, not one that follows from economic reasoning. But if one accepts it, direct government redistribution of money income from rich to poor is probably the simplest and most efficient way of attaining the ethically desired result. The desired redistribution is unlikely to occur voluntarily without collective action. Welfare payments to the poor, financed by taxes on higher-income groups, are an example of such an income transfer. Alternatively, government may intervene more directly with real transfers, especially

---

[1] For a pure public good, the proper economic charge is given unambiguously by the analysis of Part 2. Since the marginal cost of adding another user for national defense or our lighthouse is zero, the price should be set at zero; to exclude any users would be wasteful.

where some additional ethical standard is involved. For example, we aid the poor partly in the form of food stamps and cheap public housing, in part because we want to be sure they use their aid for these purposes rather than for automobiles, liquor, or other presumably less acceptable purposes. Figure 23–5 showed the substantial government redistribution of income from the rich to the poor.

But the striking thing about government redistribution of income is that it is not primarily from the rich to the poor, but from some groups to others within the great mass of middle-income families—those in roughly the $10,000–$30,000 range, which includes most American families and most of the national income. Look back at Figures 36–4 and 36–5. The federal government alone now lists its cash "income-security" transfer payments at over $175 billion annually, enough to give the bottom fifth of the income distribution nearly $15,000 per family, even if they received no other income. Obviously, most of that money doesn't go to the poor; if it did, they would no longer be poor. The big middle-income classes pay most of the taxes and receive most of the benefits from the government expenditures. Social Security transfers are mainly from some middle-income groups to other middle-income groups, basically from workers to the elderly and other nonworkers. Similarly, federal government noncash housing subsidies mainly benefit middle-income home buyers and home-owners.

Income-redistribution and resource-allocation goals are often combined in the same government transfer programs. Universal free education is provided by government largely because education is considered a quasi-public good with large, widespread externalities. But it also involves a large income redistribution. We want to be sure that poor children get a better education than their parents are able or willing to pay for. Hence, we use taxes on higher-income-level families to help finance poor youngsters' education. Often, unfortunately, trying to combine multiple objectives in the same program has led to perverse results. The farm-aid, food-stamp, and public-housing programs have been classic examples (scc Chapter 11).

THE POLITICAL PROCESS AND ECONOMIC DECISIONS

Government budgets have soared since World War II. How effectively does government—the political process—respond to the wishes of the public on economic issues? This is not a book on political science, but we must consider this question briefly in order to decide whether markets or the political process better reflects the wishes of the public under different circumstances.

One-man-one-vote, majority-rule democracy appeals to many Americans as the fairest, most effective way of making collective decisions. But with 225 million people, it is obviously impossible to take simple, national votes on many specific issues. Instead we use representative government, and that may fall far short of reflecting all individual wishes equally.

First, when you vote for A or B as your senator, you vote for a complex, ill-defined combination of positions on different issues. Once you have voted, you must take the package of virtues and failings rolled up in that senator, whether he or she is your choice or not.

Second, although in formal elections each individual has one vote in the American political system, as a practical matter some individuals and groups have far more influence than others in elections and the day-to-day operations of government. Not least, dollars can exert influence in elections. Moreover, properly reflecting many diverse voters' interests is very difficult even in theory; and in operating politics, the legislative and administrative processes of government favor some groups over others. Our governments are more responsive to the folks back home than we often give them credit for. Representatives are elected from fairly small areas, which gives local minorities a chance to be heard. In legislatures, business is largely done by committees and in informal discussion, which work out compromises that can command majorities among legislators representing widely diverse interests. But the interest groups that are well organized generally fare well at the expense of the "little man," the consumer, the great unorganized masses. Such interest groups often have a lot at stake, and it pays them to work hard to influence legislation and government practices. Conversely, individual consumers and taxpayers often have too little at stake to justify a major investment of time and money to fight each special-interest group.

Third, some political scientists argue that "the government" is actually itself an entity, which makes its own choices rather than merely serving as a quasi market for reflecting voter preferences. Any viable democratic government is *de facto* a coalition of representatives of different socioeconomic interests, this analysis runs. Government officials never know, and sometimes don't even care, just how their constituents feel on every issue. They make and carry out decisions, subject only to the constraint that no important group be treated so badly that it withdraws its support from the coalition. Thus, the common practice of viewing "the government" as a bureaucratic organization, separate from the voters it formally represents, may be in large part correct. Whether such a process meaningfully reflects voters' wishes or the "public interest" is open to argument.

Many observers argue that elected representatives and bureaucrats are motivated by their own self-interests, especially getting reelected and improving their power and status in the government. Thus, their behavior can be explained primarily by this motivation, which may or may not provide legislation and its administration in keeping with what the public wants.

Private Preferences and Collective Government Decisions

In analyzing the effectiveness of the political process in mirroring individual preferences, it is useful to consider some simple examples. First, assume that in fact all voters have an equal voice; there are no pressure groups or lobbies. In this "ideal" case, will individual voting reflect individual choices effectively? The answer is—not at all sure.

The Arrow impossibility theorem. Consider an illustration. Suppose that society must choose among alternatives A, B, and C. Take the following three individuals, each of whom prefers A, B, and C in the different orders shown. What would be proper social choice?

INDIVIDUAL	INDIVIDUAL'S PREFERENCE ORDERING		
I	A	C	B
II	C	B	A
III	B	A	C

In this case, there is no clear collective preference. Two-thirds prefer A to C, two-thirds prefer C to B, and two-thirds prefer B to A. If they first choose between B and C and then between A and C, A will command a majority. But two-thirds prefer B to A. If they first choose between A and B, then C will command a majority. But two-thirds prefer A to C. A different order of choosing can produce any one of the three as the "democratic" choice. Clearly, even if every voter knows just what he wants and has an equal vote, a democratic voting process may not produce satisfactory decisions.[2]

Voting and "political failures." Turn now to a more complex practical example of the problem of reflecting individual preferences in collective (government) decisions. Imagine a publicly owned, polluted lake surrounded by ten homes. The cost of cleaning up the lake is $10,000, and the potential benefit in improved fishing, swimming, and boating is calculated at $1,500 by each of the surrounding ten families. Clearly, collective action to eliminate the pollution is in the public interest. Perhaps informal negotiation will do the job, but the free-rider problem is likely to rear its ugly head. Certainly, with a larger number of families, transactions costs will be large and formal government action is likely to be the only feasible way of achieving the obviously desirable social result. Presumably, in a town meeting of the lakeside residents, a motion to levy an equally distributed tax of $1,000 per family to finance the cleanup would pass unanimously. Democratic government action looks impressive in solving the problem.

---

[2] The theorem demonstrated is that transitivity in all individual ordering is not sufficient to assure a collectively transitive set of choices. This is sometimes called the Arrow impossibility theorem, after Professor Kenneth Arrow who first stated it sharply.

TABLE 24-1			
FAMILY	TAX COST	BENEFIT	NET GAIN
1	$ 1,000	$ 2,000	$1,000
2	1,000	2,000	1,000
3	1,000	2,000	1,000
4	1,000	2,000	1,000
5	1,000	2,000	1,000
6	1,000	2,000	1,000
7	1,000	500	−500
8	1,000	500	−500
9	1,000	500	−500
10	1,000	500	−500
	$10,000	$14,000	$4,000

TABLE 24-2			
FAMILY	TAX COST	BENEFIT	NET GAIN
1	$ 1,000	$1,100	$ 100
2	1,000	1,100	100
3	1,000	1,100	100
4	1,000	1,100	100
5	1,000	1,100	100
6	1,000	1,100	100
7	1,000	500	−500
8	1,000	400	−600
9	1,000	300	−700
10	1,000	200	−800
	$10,000	$8,000	−$2,000

But now assume, probably more realistically, that different families attach different values to a cleaner lake, as in Table 24-1. Should the local government clean up the lake?

If we look only at the aggregate benefit, the government clearly ought to levy the tax and clean up the lake. And it is easy to predict that the vote will be 6 to 4 in favor of precisely that action. Has democratic government produced an efficient allocation of the community's resources? In one sense, yes. But the result doesn't look very good to families 7 through 10. Now consider a more complex case. The cost of cleaning up the lake is the same, but the benefits are shown in Table 24-2. Here, the net village benefit is negative. Yet a clear majority stands to gain from the action. Should the lakeside government levy the tax and clean up the lake? Will it? How would you vote if you were family 1? family 10?

If you believe in simple majority-rule democracy (or perhaps if you're an ardent ecologist), you will approve of the proposed government action here. But if you worry about protecting the "rights" of minorities, you will be uncomfortable. In a real sense, the majorities in both Tables 24-1 and 24-2 are imposing externalities on their neighbors, much as the dirty steel mill did back in the earlier section. Although the voting process is technically efficient, the minority will see the result as a political failure.

Interest groups and the "rational-ignorance effect." Suppose a small group wants the city council to spend $100,000 on a new park that will benefit them especially. The cost to the typical taxpayer will be, say $10. We can be sure the special-interest group will push hard for the park. But most voters, to whom the cost will be only $10 each if the measure passes, will pay little attention. For $10 it would scarcely be worth the cost of digging out information on the matter and taking time to urge council members to vote against it. (This is sometimes called the "rational-ignorance effect.") Thus, it is not surprising that the council may vote the subsidy to the special-interest group, even though it may be unjustifiable on grounds of the "public interest." It often simply doesn't pay the individual voter to eliminate his ignorance on many issues.

The politics of income redistribution. Last, turn to the question of how effectively political action meets the wishes of the public in redistributing income. As we saw above, government does redistribute some income from the rich to the poor. But many income transfers are from less to more politically effective middle-class groups.

Organized groups in the political process are usually farmers, the elderly, homeowners, college students, owners of oil wells, and the like—not the poor or the rich per se. The poor are not only relatively small in number, but also generally not well organized politically. The farm-aid program was sold in the 1930s as a way to help destitute farmers, but the benefits were channeled largely to large, well-to-do farmers. So it is for the federal housing program, which has helped mainly home buyers, primarily middle-income families—not the poor, who can seldom afford to buy a house at all. Social Security, by far the biggest transfer program, has been open to some of the same criticism (it has provided substantial benefits mainly to those who have had good jobs). But benefits have been widened, and the present by-and-large successful program reflects a complex mixture of self-interest, altruism, forced saving, desire to get the elderly out of children's homes, the elderly's desire to be self-sufficient, and political pressures—democracy successfully at work.

Thus, as a practical matter, democratic government operates to a considerable extent through coalitions and organized interest groups. Only on major national issues does anything approaching a simple majority view of the public dominate. The same is true to a lesser extent at state and local levels. Ours is a pluralistic society, and nowhere is this evidenced more clearly than in the political process. In a huge, complex society, it is difficult to see how anything like the old New England town-meeting ideal of democracy can operate. Add to this the realistic fact of large bureaucracies as a way of running big government, and political failures in the public sector look at least as pervasive as market failures in the private sector. But the political process can also perform very well.

MARKETS VS. THE POLITICAL PROCESS

With these observations on the political process, let us now briefly compare markets and the political process as ways of allocating resources and distributing incomes.

Balancing Costs and Benefits in the Public Economy

The principle of maximizing utility by equating returns at the margin suggests a rough guide to how big the public sector should be, and what should be left to the private sector and markets. Government expenditures should be increased up to the point where the marginal loss in giving up resources in the private sector just equals the marginal benefit from public expenditures. As long as the marginal gain is greater than the marginal loss, there is a net gain in overall welfare.

If society were a single unity, and if government were the all-comprehending brain of the unity, application of this principle would be feasible. The government could then weigh satisfaction lost against those gained, and decide what to do. But in fact, there is no such all-comprehending brain. At best, we can make only the roughest sort of approximation. Yet, however rough its application, the marginal principle of economizing the use of scarce resources poses the question to ask in thinking about the right size for the public sector. And some progress has been made toward making such comparisons (see box, "Cost–Benefit Analysis").

Note that the chances of getting good political decision making on such issues go up as the size of the government unit goes down. At the local level, there is some chance that voters can weigh tax costs directly against potential benefits of proposed projects. And there is a better chance locally than at state and national levels that legislators and administrators will be directly responsive to citizens' preferences.

Consumers' Sovereignty and Citizens' Sovereignty

The choice between markets and the political process can be summed up in "consumers' sovereignty" versus "citizens' sovereignty." Allocation of resources through the private economy occurs primarily in response to consumers' money demands for goods and services. This is "consumers' sovereignty." In the public sector, we as citizens express our preferences for roads, rockets, and zoos by voting for representatives who in turn will, we hope, levy taxes and provide the government services we want. Thus, in the public sector, there is a "citizens' sovereignty," somewhat analogous to consumers' sovereignty in the private economy. But there are some very significant differences. Five, especially, deserve attention.

1. In the marketplace, voting for resource allocation is on a one-dollar-one-vote basis. In the public sector, in a democratic country, it is on a one-person-one-vote basis. Thus, in the private sector, the wealthy person has more votes than the poor person. In the public sector, a democratic system attempts—although not always successfully—to give each citizen, rich or poor, equal voting power. Which way provides the better machinery for determining what to produce with our productive resources is a very fundamental question. Your answer will presumably depend heavily on how equitably you think spendable incomes are distributed.

2. In the public sector, it is difficult for people to weigh specific benefits and costs, as we do daily in the private economy. In private life, you can consider carefully whether you prefer to spend $20 on football tickets, an electric razor, a new pair of shoes, or nothing at all. But when you vote to elect a representative, you have little opportunity to distinguish in detail between the things of which you approve and disapprove—you must accept the decisions your representative makes and pay the taxes levied whether you think you're getting your money's worth or not. Only when a specific decision is put to the voters is there an exception—for example, when a special bond issue to finance a new school must be approved by the voters. And even then, the individual has to accept the majority verdict. Consumers' sovereignty clearly gives him greater power both to indicate what he wants for his dollars, and to get it.

3. The public sector thus involves a big element of compulsion. Even with democratic processes, once our elected representatives decide we're going to put a man on Mars, you and I must pay the taxes to support the project, however foolish we may think it is. Not so in the private sector. There, I'm not forced to pay for something I don't want.

Admirers of the market process thus stress the ability of the market to give effective representation to majority votes while protecting minority interests. The market has a built-in protection for every interest. The rich person gets the most votes, but the little fellow has his say too, in proportion to how much he has to spend. One dollar counts one vote, and no one needs to spend a dollar on any product unless he personally decides it's worth a dollar to him.

COST–BENEFIT ANALYSIS
PLANNING–PROGRAMMING–BUDGETING

In recent years, economists have begun to tackle the problem of public-sector costs and benefits empirically through "cost–benefit analysis," an approach pioneered under Defense Secretary Robert McNamara in the 1960s but now applied widely. Should the government build a series of dams in the High Sierras to provide water for the cities and farms of California? To make a sound economic judgment, costs of alternative dams and water-distribution systems must be calculated, including possible ecological damage. Benefits must be estimated—for irrigation, for industrial use, for household use in cities, for electricity generated at the dam. For a multi-billion-dollar water system, the job of fully estimating the complex intermesh of costs and benefits is a difficult one. Massive changes in property values will result, and the calculations must cover many decades ahead. Effective cost–benefit analysis is one of the most difficult, but also potentially most valuable, branches of modern economics.

To extend cost–benefit analysis of proposed government programs, President Johnson instructed the Budget Bureau in the mid-1960s to push the spread of "Planning–Programming–Budgeting" (PPB) through the civilian agencies of the federal government. Should the post office automate its handling of mail? Should the Antipoverty Program spend more on retraining programs for the poor? PPB, utilizing cost–benefit analysis to help make government program decisions, is, in principle, the right move. But getting it used effectively in the political bureaucracy has proved a difficult undertaking.

At least, this kind of marginal cost–benefit analysis helps to avoid the nonsense often heard in public discussion of such issues. (1) The assertion is often made that we "need" more police protection, or more classrooms; hence we should spend more for them. But such statements give no basis for intelligent economic judgment about whether the goverment should meet these "needs." To make that decision, the additional costs must be compared with the anticipated benefits. (2) Equally foolish is the common assertion that "we can afford" better schools and urban renewal; therefore we should have them. There are many things we "can afford." Their limit is set by our total productive resources. What and how resources should be used in the public sector can be decided rationally only by comparing expected marginal costs on each venture with expected marginal benefits.

4. As a practical matter, even in a democratic government like ours, few issues are decided on a simple town-meeting, majority rule basis. As we saw above, effectively representing many diverse voters' interests is very difficult even in theory, and in operating politics, the legislative and administrative processes of government favor some groups over others.

5. The market system imposes an inescapable, objective test of the performance of each business in responding to consumers' wants—the test of profit or loss. Unless the business makes a profit, it will fall by the wayside, and in the long run it can remain profitable only by meeting consumer demands. There is no equally clear litmus test in the public sector. Without the test of the market, there is no assurance that any public service will actually render benefits greater than its cost, or that it will be dropped when the need for it is past. But here again, the case can be overstated. At least in the federal government, a new budget is enacted each year, with widespread publicity and chances for interested groups to be heard.[3]

Incentives, Efficiency, Equity, and the Quality of Life

Economists are much concerned with the efficiency with which the economic system uses the nation's limited resources in satisfying consumers' wants, and with the incentives it provides for individuals and institutions to provide that efficiency. The basic case they make for the market system is that it seems most likely to provide that efficiency with the related incentives, while the political process appears likely to fall short on a number of scores. Moreover, history provides impressive support for the economists' presumptions, in the dominance of basically capitalist, market-directed economies among the high-per-capita-income nations. Countries that have relied primarily on government planning and operations (mainly the Communist nations) have all fallen short of the market-economy performances on these tests.

[3]See, for example, *Economic Analysis and the Efficiency of Government,* Report of the Joint Economic Committee, U.S. Congress, 1970.

Inefficiency and waste are easy to find in the public sector, where activities do not have to face the test of a market.

with the economists' tests of efficiency and "more GNP." Professor Kenneth Galbraith has made this argument forcefully in his bestseller, *The Affluent Society.* He argues that general distrust of government has led to a serious underallocation of resources to the public sector (leaving national defense aside). In the world's richest economy, we allocate less than 20 percent of GNP to satisfying all nondefense collective wants through public goods and services. Galbraith argues that we are so rich that we can readily afford more and better public services, that we need them badly, and that the alternative is generally wasteful civilian consumption just to keep our economic machinery going.

America can clearly "afford" more public services and reduction in such negative externalities as pollution if we want them. The test of Galbraith's position lies in whether we collectively want them badly enough to pay for them. By that test, it is far from clear that government should be bigger. On the contrary, the nationwide "taxpayers' revolt" of the 1970s shouted that many, perhaps most, Americans are fed up with ever-higher taxes and ever-bigger government. The fact that nearly all the growth in GNP per capita during the middle and late 1970s went into expansion of government (mainly larger transfer payments) probably fueled these fires of dissatisfaction. Whatever the reason, there was no doubt about the prevailing attitude against further expansion in government taxes, spending, and regulation of the private sector.

But the real test is yet to come. What will the public say if in fact the government does cut back on the services and transfer payments it has been making? It will be surprising if enthusiasm for smaller government does not weaken, at least among those whose living standards are reduced by the government cutbacks. Pleas for "fairness" and help for "injured" groups generally dominate economists' arguments on efficiency in the

But many critics of the market retort that efficiency is the wrong test—that we should be more concerned with fairness, justice, and producing the things that people really need than showdown in government policy making. We can count on our elected representatives to be responsive to such "fairness" pleas from the active voters back home. Responsiveness to such cries has proven, over many years, to be effective in getting reelected, a very important goal for most representatives.

Social cost—benefit analysis, program by program, is the basic foundation for rational decision making in the public sector. Fundamentally, in our individualistic society, the public interest is what 225 million Americans say it is. But how best to get their diverse preferences registered and compromised is a very difficult problem.

SUMMARY AND REVIEW

1. Direct government participation in allocating resources and distributing incomes is desirable where public goods or large externalities are involved, or where we want to alter the distribution of income.

2. A public good (a) is widely considered to be important, but there is no practical way of providing it through the market; (b) cannot practically be withheld from some if it is provided to others; and (c) does not become less useful to some because it is used by others. National defense is an example.

3. The line between pure public goods and private goods with large externalities is often hazy, and for both, the common solution is government production and distribution.

4. The public sector redistributes large amounts of money and real income through taxes and transfer payments. Such redistribution has become the biggest economic activity of government.

5. The case for such redistribution rests largely on value judgments that incomes should be more equally distributed, rather than on improving the efficiency with which consumer demands are met. However, the bulk of such transfers are in fact within the large middle- and upper-income groups, not from rich to poor.

6. The political process makes little use of simple majority-rule voting processes on economic issues. Instead, voters elect representatives whose positions they must accept without being able to specify voter preferences on individual issues between elections.

7. Even when voters can specify their individual preferences, in most cases it is very difficult to reflect

these preferences accurately through democratic voting processes, giving due weight to majority and minority interests. As a practical matter, the preferences of well-organized special-interest groups receive much more than proportionate weight in political and bureaucratic processes. This is partly because it is not worthwhile for many voters to become well-informed, active participants in government decision making (the "rational-ignorance effect").

8. There are thus four main differences between markets and the political process: (a) In markets, voting is on a one-dollar-one-vote basis; in a democratic political process it is on a one-person-one-vote basis; (b) the market permits each voter (consumer) to obtain whatever mix of goods he prefers in spending his funds, whereas the political process requires that he accept the mix of positions preferred by his elected representatives, so there is little protection for minority interests; (c) the political process thus involves a large element of compulsion through imposition of taxes to finance the expenditures voted by representatives; and (d) markets continuously confront producers with the need to make a profit by satisfying consumer wants or else go out of business, whereas there is no such objective test as to whether government activities are worthwhile.

9. By the tests of efficiency and incentives to produce the goods and services consumers want, markets rate relatively high; but critics argue that fairness, justice, and producing a better "quality of life" should be the tests applied, and that government action is required to achieve these goals.

public goods
free riders
citizens' sovereignty
balancing alternatives at the margin

cost—benefit analysis
"political failures"
"rational-ignorance
    effect"

1. Does consumers' sovereignty or citizens' sovereignty provide a better process for allocating society's productive resources?

2. As a practical matter, are the "market failures" of the private economy or the "political failures" of the public economy more serious barriers to having individuals' preferences carried out effectively?

3. Chapter 24 suggests that we should rely on the public sector only where important externalities or public goods are involved, or where we want to alter the distribution of income. Is this the proper guiding principle? Can you list cases where it should not be followed?

4. How effectively do you expect democratic political processes to take care of minority interests? Would markets do better or worse?

5. Many argue that our national priorities should place a higher value on better public services—education, slum clearance, public health, and so on—than on more consumer goods. Analyze this argument.

6. What is cost—benefit analysis? How can it help in deciding what projects government should undertake?

7. a. Many people believe that there is always a presumption in favor of reducing government expenditures. Do you agree?

   b. Why, if at all, is the presumption above more defensible than a presumption that government spending to provide public services should be increased?

8. Is government too big? What tests do you use in deciding?

CASE 24 THE VOUCHER EDUCATION PLAN

Nearly everyone agrees on the importance of ensuring all youngsters a good education, at least through the high school level. But many parents, and professional educators too, are dissatisfied with the education provided by our public schools, which all children must attend unless they happen to be among the very few with parents rich enough to afford a private school. All the rest of us face a monopoly seller of public education, and many parents find school officials and teachers impervious to suggestions for change.

The "voucher education plan," with both conservative and liberal supporters, has gained considerable attention in recent years as a possible means of improving the situation. Its most extreme form shows the central issues most clearly, although less drastic alternatives are also feasible. Its essence is this: Abolish the public schools. Then let each state or community continue to collect in taxes the same amount it is now spending on public education, determined in the usual democratic political fashion. Instead of spending this sum on public schools, let it divide the total up and give a voucher of equal value (say, $1,000 annually, if that is what is now being spent) to the parents of each child, this voucher to be spent on education at any school of the parent's choice as long as the school meets minimum state standards.

A wide range of private, profit-seeking schools would spring up, trying to obtain the business of different parents with different educational objectives for their children. While state standards would presumably require some subjects like reading and arithmetic for all beginners, high school curricula might range widely from college-preparatory to vocational focus. Instead of being faced with a monopoly school as now, consumers would be free to buy the education they want where they think they get the most for their voucher. Just as government decides how much national defense and how many highways we should have, but contracts out laying the concrete and building the bombers on a competitive basis, so the voucher plan would count on private enterprise to provide more varied, responsive education for children in response to the vouchers given to all parents.

This plan attempts to combine the best of the public and the private sectors. (1) Only the public sector can ensure that every child gets his minimum guaranteed level of education; this is essential on grounds of equity and attaining the positive externalities from widespread education. It is ensured by the government voucher for each child. (2) But most evidence suggests that profit-seeking competitors (the private sector) do the best job of actually producing what consumers want to buy; so we should take advantage of this fact in education, one of the most important services we buy. Use the profit incentive to produce most efficiently the kinds of education we consumers want for our children. Who, the private-enterprise advocates ask, will try harder to educate our youngsters better—the local public-school principal and teachers, who are responsible only to the school board, or their counterparts who must satisfy you to get the dollars to stay in business?[4]

Are you in favor of the proposed voucher education plan to supplant the present public-education system? Does the plan offer a way to obtain the best of both the public and private sectors in providing education for our children?

---

[4]Introduction of any such plan would, of course, need to be spread out over a number of years, but disregard the transitional problems here to focus on the main issues.

Poverty,
Inequality, and
Government
Income
Redistribution

CHAPTER 25

he richest fifth of the population receives about 40 percent of the national income, the poorest fifth about 5 percent. The opening section of Chapter 18 described the distribution of income in some detail, a surprisingly stable distribution over the past half century for which we have usable data. Look back and refresh your memory.

Recently, the public sector's biggest activity has increasingly been the redistribution of income through taxes and transfer payments, not the production or purchase of goods and services. In 1980, the federal budget included $240 billion, 45 percent of the total of $532 billion, of direct benefit payments to individuals—Social Security, welfare, Medicare and Medicaid, veterans' benefits, unemployment compensation, and the like. Figure 23–5 suggested that part of this represents transfers from the wealthy to the poor—but that the bulk of the total is transfers among the middle- and upper-income-level families who receive most of the national income and pay most of the taxes.

Table 25–1 summarizes the major benefit payments, in cash and in kind, made to individuals by the federal government in 1980. Only national defense, $128 billion in 1980, approached these transfer payments in size. This transfer total compared with $60 billion in 1970, and only $23 billion in 1960. A big share of the total increase in national income over the past decade has gone into taxes and government spending, mainly transfer payments.

Worldwide movement toward the "welfare state," with ever-expanding government to help the poor and needy, and a lot of others as well, went far to explain the massive growth in government spending after World War II. But recently, as taxes have passed 50 percent of GNP in such nations as Sweden, and 30 percent in the United States, and as inflation has eroded the buying power of after-tax incomes, resentment against growing taxes and government spending has swelled. Taxpayers' revolts are everywhere.

How equal, or unequal, should incomes be? How far should government go to change the income distribution produced by the market? The first part of this chapter looks at poverty and government action to abolish it, as a case study focused on those at the bottom of the income

TABLE 25–1
Federal Benefit Payments to Individuals, 1980

	AMOUNT (IN BILLIONS)
Cash benefits:	
Social Security (OASDI)	$115.8
Unemployment compensation	12.4
Federal-employee benefits	14.1
Veterans' benefits	20.5
Public assistance (AFDC, etc.)	14.7
Subtotal, cash benefits	$178.0
In-kind benefits:	
Food and nutrition	11.1
Medicare and Medicaid	46.0
Housing	5.3
Subtotal, in-kind benefits	$ 61.4
Total benefits	$239.4

Source: *Budget of the U.S. for Fiscal Year 1980.*

structure. The second part considers more broadly the question of the optimal distribution of income, and what, if anything, the government can or ought to do about it.

POVERTY—THE PROBLEM

Poverty is as old as history. America is rich, and by the standards of most of the world, poverty has been virtually eliminated here. Most of our "poor" in New York live as well as the average worker in Moscow or Mexico City, vastly better than the Indian peasant. Even by our own standards, only 12 percent of our people live in poverty. But even in our affluent society, there is an economic underworld of poverty, and most Americans agree on the need for some collective (government) measures to level up these very low incomes at least somewhat. Partly, these measures involve redistributing income directly from the middle and upper classes to the poor; partly, they involve improving poor people's chances of earning higher incomes in the market economy.

There is no one accepted definition of poverty. The most widely used definition is that suggested by the Social Security Administration and used by the government in compiling its statistics. This definition says that, as of 1978, any urban four-person family receiving less than $6,600 in

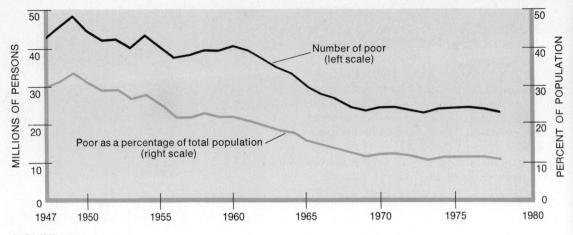

FIGURE 25–1
Poverty in the United States
Rapid economic growth persistently reduced the number of poor people in the United States after World War II until 1970. Since then, progress has been slower. (Source: U.S. Census Bureau.)

money income was considered "poor." For rural families, this figure is reduced by 30 percent. For larger or smaller families, the figure is adjusted appropriately.

These poverty-line figures were based on an extensive analysis of the living standards of lower-income families in the 1960s. They were arrived at by taking three times the cost of a reasonable but very moderate diet. Each year, the figure is adjusted to take inflation into account; thus, the "real" level defined as poverty remains unchanged.[1]

What is considered poverty, however, changes with the times. Some people argue that there is a poverty problem only in the eyes of the do-gooders. Twenty-five years ago, the median money income of all families was about $4,600 (in 1975 prices). Then, $2,000 was widely considered the poverty level, and nearly half of all families then fell below what we now call the poverty level. As Figure 25–1 shows, economic growth has steadily pushed most families above the minimal levels that seemed reasonable a generation or two ago. But progress was slow in the 1970s, and our aspirations have risen with

rising incomes. In 1978, there were about 24 million "poor" Americans, using the SSA definition—about 11 percent of the population. If we add income in kind (food stamps, health care, and the like) to money income, the number of poor is reduced by nearly half (see Figure 23–5).[2]

Who Are the Poor?

In 1962, Michael Harrington wrote a book, *The Other America*, that touched the conscience of many Americans. The other America, Harrington wrote, is the world of the poor in the midst of plenty—a world of desolation, of hopelessness, of bitterness and resentment, of slums, of discrimination. It is the world of blacks and Puerto Ricans living in the great city slums; of old men and women living alone in rented tenement rooms; of poor Southern farmers living in ram-

---

[1]For a full description of Social Security Administration procedures and historical data, see U.S. Department of Commerce, *Poverty in the United States* (*Current Population Reports,* Series P-60, 1969).

[2]Using money income as a test can overstate the problem on other scores, as well. The poor Southern farmer with an annual income of $3,000 and six children eats better off the land than the arithmetic suggests. Many elderly poor have accumulated assets, and draw on them to supplement their current incomes; thus, their actual consumption is well above the incomes they report. As a college student, you may be another example. In many ways, consumption would be a better measure of poverty than is current money income, and such a measure would show an appreciable number of the "poor" families better off than they seem.

shackle huts without plumbing; of fatherless families whose mothers struggle to support their children; of failures and rejects for a dozen other reasons.

The poor, Harrington wrote, live in a subculture of their own. Most of them feel—with apathy or resentment—that no one cares. It is a world whose inhabitants are isolated from the mainstream of American life and alienated from its values. It is a world whose occupants are sometimes concerned with day-to-day survival, where minor illness is a tragedy. Last, it is a world turned in on itself in its values and its habits, a world in which the poverty of the parents is visited upon the children.

Each year, many families move up from the ranks of the poor, and some families slide down below the imaginary line. But the bulk of the poor stay poor.

Harrington's picture of the poor is overdrawn for today. Government benefits, especially food stamps and other in-kind aid to the poor, have expanded greatly since he wrote, and nearly all (but not all) the poor are now eligible for some kind of help that wards off complete destitution. But poverty can still be very real and very bitter.

To understand the problem of poverty, you must recognize that the poor differ widely. Five groups loom large.

Blacks. Although only 7 million of the 24 million poor in 1978 were nonwhite, over 30 percent of all black families are poor. Blacks with jobs have substantially improved their incomes relative to whites since the 1960s. But unemployment is very high for minority teenagers; their unemployment rate is over 30 percent, and many more neither have nor seek work. Over half of all poor blacks live in family units headed by females. Other minority groups are also poor (25 percent of all persons of Spanish origin were poor in 1978), but their numbers are far less than the blacks involved.

Farmers. About 17 percent of all farm families are poor, much higher than the urban rate. Rural poverty is concentrated in the South. A substantial portion of poor Southern farmers are the blacks mentioned above. Government aids to agriculture provide little help to poor farmers;

the money goes largely to the big, well-capitalized farmers.

Old people. Old age often brings poverty rather than adequate retirement. About 1.3 million families in which the husband is over 65 are poor; this is about 15 percent of all such families, and the elderly account for nearly 20 percent of all the poor.

Fatherless families. Nearly half of all poor people live in families with a female head, and 35 percent of all women left alone to provide for their children are poor; for nonwhites, the figure is 55 percent. The woman who has to earn her family's living faces many lost workdays and consequently job instability. The breakdown of the family is near the core of the difficult social problems of the city slums. Probably not one out of three black children in poor families who now reaches age 18 has lived all his life with both his parents. Nationwide, the number of children on public "welfare" has risen from less than 1 million to 8 million since 1950, with most of the increase during the 1960s, a decade of growing prosperity and falling unemployment. In New York City alone, nearly a million mothers and children were on welfare in 1978, out of a total population of under 8 million.

Others. About a quarter of all poor people do not fit into any of the groups above. They live in depressed areas; they have poor motivation; they have low intelligence; most have had little education; there is little demand for the jobs they can do. By the test of the market, they are failures, the rejects of our modern economy.

One generalization applies to all these groups. Most come from poor families and have been poor all their lives.

Why Are the Poor Poor?

To decide what, if anything, to do about this poverty, we must ask, Why are the poor poor?

Inadequate aggregate demand and slow growth. When there is a recession, unemployment increases the proportion of the population below the poverty line. Conversely, prosperity brings more jobs, especially for marginal members of the labor force who are last to be taken on. A major depression is a catastrophe for the poor.

But only a small fraction (perhaps 10–20 percent) of the poor even in the recession year of 1975 were "unemployed," as measured by the unemployment statistics. Most unemployed (except for inexperienced minority youths) are only temporarily out of work and find other jobs in a few weeks, or months at most. Thus, their annual incomes stay above the poverty level. Over half the poor are simply out of the labor market; children are the largest group. Many of the poor are elderly people, past their working years. Many in the slums have given up looking for work.

A closely related fact is that poverty piles up in periods of slow economic growth. Conversely, fast economic growth erodes poverty. This is shown dramatically by Figure 25–1.

Low productivity. The message of Chapter 19 was that people's incomes depend primarily on the marginal productivity of their labor and the capital they own. If this is correct, given a reasonable level of aggregate demand, poor people in the labor market are by and large poor because their marginal-revenue productivity is low. They are poor because they are not worth more to employers in a profit-motivated economy. This is especially true of many inexperienced teenagers, especially school dropouts. Or, if they are elderly, they are poor now because they did not adequately plan ahead or did not have an adequate life income to provide a reasonable retirement income through savings.

This is a harsh conclusion, and one that is only partially correct. But it has a strong core of truth. Over 50 percent of all poor families are headed by a person with less than an eighth-grade education, only 20 percent by a person who completed high school. Many older people, although seeking work, can offer only limited services in the market. Women attempting to support their children inescapably lose more time than others. Many of the adult poor have no skills, or have obsolete ones.

Market imperfections and discrimination. If there is effective competition among employers, this competition will bid the wage of each worker up to the value of his marginal product. And the value of his marginal product will be highest where he makes the greatest contribution to producing goods and services that consumers want to buy. Conversely, if there are market imperfections that prevent workers from finding employment where their productivity is highest, or that prevent effective competition from forcing wages up to that level, society's resources are not most efficiently allocated. Workers do not earn incomes as high as they could obtain in a competitive economy.

A major market imperfection, and a major cause of poverty for nonwhites, is discrimination—in education, jobs, access to medical care, on nearly every score. If employers, rationally or irrationally, refuse to bid for black workers on the same basis as they bid for white workers, black incomes will be lower. Black incomes average only about 60 percent of whites, although since the 1960s black incomes have moved up dramatically relative to whites for the same jobs, especially for women. Average black incomes are held down by the inability of blacks, especially teenagers, to get jobs.

Many economists blame unions and the government itself for important job barriers. Many craft unions have *de facto* barriers against nonwhites for apprenticeships and union membership, thus in effect blocking them from higher-paying jobs. And the federal minimum wage of $2.90 per hour as of 1979, however admirable its purpose, shuts many low-productivity workers out of jobs that might be there at lower wage rates, especially for poorly educated, poverty-group teenagers. But on the whole, government has helped to reduce job discrimination, and union policies have apparently on balance helped as well.

Absence from the labor force and the vicious circle of poverty. Nearly 60 percent of all poor families are headed by people who are not in the labor force. Many of these are elderly people; others are discouraged youths and mothers of fatherless families who have given up looking for work. Over 40 percent of all poor people are children. Thus, the problems of poverty, family instability, and insecurity in old age are inseparably intertwined. Others are out of the labor force for a variety of reasons—ill health, lack of motivation, family circumstances, or simply because they have given up hope of finding a job. "Welfare" has helped to break up poor families, because in many states no aid can be given to a family headed by a male of working age, so fathers leave in order to make their families eligible for welfare.

Beyond these economic causes, most observers add a socioeconomic analysis. Poverty breeds poverty, in a vicious circle. A poor individual or family has a high probability of staying poor. The poor live largely in slums or in backward rural areas. Their children do not learn to read, to write, to speak well. They grow up to apathy or resentment; they go to poor schools with other poor children. They lag behind other children in middle-class schools, and their dropout rate is high—not surprisingly, for there is little in their culture to make them care about education. They find it harder to keep jobs. Broken homes are common. Often there is little motivation or hope to rise from the vicious circle of poverty, either for the young or for the adults.

ANTIPOVERTY POLICIES: LEVELING UP THE BOTTOM

The preceding analysis, together with the macro and micro theory of earlier chapters, suggests two broad lines of attack on the poverty problem. One involves raising the demand for the services of the poor and their marginal productivity in the market. The other, facing the fact that many of the poor are inevitably out of the labor market, involves direct redistribution of income from the better-off to the poor. The former is obviously preferable, since it increases the real output of society, while the latter merely redistributes the existing level of output. History suggests that progress in reducing poverty comes mainly through increasing the size of the national GNP pie, not through slicing up a fixed pie so as to give the poor more and the rich less. One basic problem, as the data of Chapter 19 suggested, is that the incomes of the rich don't go very far when divided up among the masses; another is that most Americans show little enthusiasm for really radical surgery on high and middle incomes to raise the incomes of the poor.

Our main interest here is in government redistribution of income, but since raising poor people's productivity and giving them jobs is clearly a more fundamental solution to the poverty problem than just redistributing income from rich to poor, consider briefly some promising fundamental measures.

Measures to Increase Total Output and Worker Productivity

Increased aggregate demand and falling unemployment can help to lessen poverty, although they give jobs and higher incomes only to those who have a service to sell. The best estimates suggest that reduction of the overall unemployment rate from 4 percent to 3 percent would reduce the population below the poverty line by only about one percentage point. Nonetheless, a prosperous economy is a big help toward alleviating poverty, and it makes sense on other grounds as well. Prosperity helps reduce barriers against minority groups as labor markets tighten, provides more on-the-job training for marginal workers, and opens partial employment for the elderly. Much poverty due to unemployment is a preventable waste.

As a closely related measure, accelerating economic growth over the long run (that is, faster growth in output per capita) provides a fundamental approach to eroding poverty. Over the 1950s and 1960s, economic growth reduced poverty by about 1 percent a year. If that rate could be maintained (remember that the 1960s included a cyclical upswing), poverty as it is now defined would be entirely eliminated in ten years. But the nearer poverty approaches zero, the harder it will be to make further gains. The remaining poor will be increasingly those insulated from labor markets—the aged, the disabled, what some have called the "hard-core poor."

Investment in human beings increases their productivity, just as does investment in nonhuman wealth. For many reasons, society's investment in the poor falls far short of its investment in most individuals who rise above poverty. The poor live in slums, in squalor. They receive short and poor education. They get little job training in schools—or on the job, because they so often find no employment. They receive inadequate medical care. If we want to raise the productivity of many of the poor, more investment in education and training is the first prescription of the preceding economic analysis. But remember that investment is desirable only if the resulting increase in productivity exceeds the cost of the investment, which has often not been true of special training programs for the poor.

Improving labor markets. Many of the poor are effectively isolated from jobs by lack of information, immobility, and inertia. This is especially true of the rural poor in the South. But it is also true in the slums of the great cities, where for thousands of unskilled and poorly educated teenagers and adults there is no practical channel into the jobs that are opening up elsewhere in the economy, even in the same city.

Better job-training programs, employment exchanges, guidance and counseling services, and the like could help those who suffer merely from inadequate information or are immobile because of financial difficulties. Better information, better education, and better training programs for both youths and adults make sense both to fight poverty and to improve the efficiency of our economic system. More subsidized day-care nurseries for poor working mothers could both improve their economic productivity and get underprivileged youngsters off to a better educational start.

Reduction of discrimination is essential to reducing poverty in minority groups. Substantial progress has been made. For Northern black families headed by a male aged 25 to 34, incomes in 1974 were 95 percent those of comparable whites; and black adult females have been even better. But the black unemployment rate remains over twice that for whites. The number of black "professional and technical" employees more than doubled during the 1960s, compared to a 40 percent increase for whites. But the discrimination problem is still a massive one. Debate over how to eliminate racial discrimination in jobs, housing, education, everywhere, far transcends issues of how best to reduce poverty. The answers are at least as much political and social as they are economic.

Redistribution of Money Incomes

Direct money-income transfers (grants to the poor, financed by taxes on the nonpoor) are the other line of attack on the poverty problem. It recognizes that many poor people are out of the labor force. It has the virtue of letting us see the actual cost of the program. And it gives recipients of aid freedom to spend their incomes as they wish, in contrast to programs that force them to take aid through food stamps, housing subsidies, medical assistance, education, and the like. (Remember Case 6 on the food-stamp program, in comparing money grants with grants-in-kind; there are important arguments on both sides.) To raise the incomes of all today's "poor" to the SSA poverty level would require grants of about $12 billion, less than 1 percent of the GNP, other things equal.

Fighting poverty by this approach does not raise society's total real income; it merely redistributes what we now produce without using the productive potential of many poor. Moreover, such direct cash grants to all the poor might pose serious incentive problems, because individuals now working might prefer to take direct subsidies and stop work. Thus, the actual cost of such a direct-subsidy approach to the poverty problem would probably be substantially larger than the $12 billion indicated.

Welfare. "Welfare," or "relief," is the name first applied to cash transfer payments by the government to the poor. Aid to Families with Dependent Children (AFDC) has long been the main form of direct government aid to the poor. AFDC is now supplemented by food stamps, which go to nearly all the poor, by Medicaid (medical aid to most poor), and by over a dozen other smaller aid-to-the-poor programs. For a summary, look ahead to Table 25–3. These programs are often called the "welfare system."

The current welfare system, just about everyone agrees, is a mess. It has four big failings:

1. It excludes a lot of poor people, especially the working poor, because in many states, if there is an adult male in the family, even though he earns nothing or less than the poverty level, the family is not eligible for AFDC and related programs. This also tends to break up families, because in those states, fathers often leave their families so the families can get welfare payments. Thus, only about half the poor receive any welfare payments other than food stamps.

2. The welfare system creates strong disincentives to work. It in effect imposes at least a 67

percent marginal tax rate on any welfare-family earnings, because AFDC payments are reduced by two-thirds of any earnings from work. Worse, if work raises its income above the eligibility level for AFDC, the family may also lose its eligibility for Medicaid, food stamps, and housing allowances. Thus the effective marginal tax rate on earnings may actually exceed 100 percent.

3. AFDC benefits are very unequal, because they are set by the individual states. They varied in the late 1970s from $720 a year in Mississippi for a family of four to $6,400 in Hawaii. Uneven application of other programs worsened these inequalities.

4. Administration of the complex, overlapping welfare system is inefficient and expensive. Administrative costs have used up a substantial part of the funds allocated to help the poor, and the administrative red tape has confused many poor people and kept them from receiving needed benefits.[3]

The "negative income tax." In the 1960s, a novel proposal to reform the welfare system was advanced simultaneously by Milton Friedman, an advisor to Barry Goldwater and President Nixon, and James Tobin, an advisor to President Kennedy. It is to substitute a "negative income tax" for part or all of the present welfare system—to combine compassion with incentives; by (1) guaranteeing every family or individual a basic minimum income (a negative income tax for the poor instead of the positive income tax we now pay if we have taxable incomes); and (2) increasing the incentive to work by permitting everyone to keep, say, half of all his earnings in addition, up to some moderate income level where he would slide over to a regular taxpayer status.

It should be easy to see how the NIT flows directly from the economic analysis of the present chapter. It would be simple to administer in

---

[3]Authoritative analyses of the welfare system, with detailed recommendations for changes, are provided by *Income Security for Americans*, Report of the Subcommittee on Fiscal Policy, Joint Economic Committee, December 5, 1974, based on a three-year study of the problem (see especially Chaps. 1, 8, and 9); and by L. Lynn in R. Haveman, ed., *A Decade of Federal Antipoverty Programs* (New York: Academic Press, 1977), Chap. 3. For a vivid, perceptive picture of welfare in operation, see Susan Sheehan, "Welfare Mother," *The New Yorker*, Sept. 29, 1975.

place of the present chaos of overlapping programs, would reduce disincentives to work, and would assure a basic income transfer to all whose incomes are otherwise below the agreed minimum level. It is widely favored by economists of a variety of political persuasions. In 1969 and 1971, President Nixon proposed a modified version of the NIT, and President Carter sent Congress a similar proposal in 1977, substituting a modified NIT for AFDC, food stamps, and SSI.

Table 25-2 shows how the plan might work, assuming a guaranteed minimum income of $3,200 for a family of four and a marginal negative income tax rate of 50 percent, combined with the regular 1977 federal income tax.

If a family has no private income, it would receive from the government a $3,200 annual income (negative income tax), possibly in weekly or monthly checks—see columns 4 and 5. If the family earns $1,000, it keeps the $1,000, but its payment from the government drops by half that amount. Net result: Its after-tax income is $3,700, up $500. Since each family can keep 50 percent of all earned income, its dollar aid from the government will not fall to zero until its earned income is $6,400. Moreover, since its marginal tax rate is not to exceed 50 percent, exact after-tax equality with the present tax system would not be reached until an income of $7,920, when it is back on the regular tax system, with a tax of $760.

How much would it cost? The minimum cost of the plan in Table 25-2 would be around $8 billion annually, assuming that no one stopped working because of the new NIT benefits. Probably some who now work would work less, and estimates well above $8 billion look more realistic to some experts. Note that if we want the maximum work-incentive effect from the NIT, the cost will be still higher, since the marginal tax rate on earned income must be reduced for both the poor and the large numbers just above the poverty line. If we reduce the marginal tax rate to 25 percent to increase the work incentive, the total cost skyrockets—probably to $30 billion or more annually for the Table 25-2 plan. Obviously, the cost would also vary for different minimum-income levels. President Carter's 1977 proposal, with a $4,200 family income flow and a 50 percent marginal tax rate, was estimated to cost $19 billion, roughly equal to the AFDC, food stamps, and SSI programs to be replaced.

TABLE 25-2
Negative Income Tax Example[a] (family of four)

| PRIVATE INCOME | UNDER 1979 TAX LAW | | | WITH NIT ADDED | |
	TAX (−)	AFTER-TAX INCOME		NET BENEFIT (+) OR TAX (−)	INCOME AFTER NIT AND TAX
$ 0	$ 0	$ 0		$ +3,200	$3,200
1,000	0	1,000		+2,700	3,700
2,000	0	2,000		+2,200	4,200
3,000	0	3,000		+1,700	4,700
4,000	−140	3,860		+1,200	5,200
5,000	−290	4,710		+ 700	5,700
6,000	−450	5,550		+ 200	6,200
6,400[b]	−511	5,889		0	6,400
7,000	−603	6,397		− 300	6,700
7,920[c]	−760	7,160		− 760	7,160
8,000	−772	7,228		− 772	7,228

[a] On the assumption that the government would provide a minimum family income of $3,200, with a marginal income tax rate of 50 percent to supplement the regular tax system.

[b] End of government direct subsidy.

[c] Point of after-tax equality with 1977 tax system.

NIT, Incrementalism, and the Political Process

Neither Nixon's nor Carter's NIT proposals ever got out of the Senate Finance Committee. Their fates are instructive in the ways of the political process. The bureaucrats administering welfare in Washington and throughout the country opposed the change, which threatened their jobs. Many welfare recipients were opposed because the proposed uniform NIT benefits were below the benefits they received from existing multiple programs. Northern liberals opposed it on the same grounds. Conservative senators of both parties opposed NIT because they generally disapproved of paying people who do not work, and because it might raise federal expenditures. Representatives of wealthier northern and western states were opposed because the benefits would go disproportionately to the poorer southern states, which now have low welfare benefits. An undercurrent of racism was important, because blacks bulked large among the poor who would be helped by NIT. A more unlikely coalition could hardly be imagined. Yet the sweeping reform of NIT drew the fire of everyone whose interests were threatened by any part of the reform, even though their reasons were often contradictory. The opposition was strong; the potential beneficiaries were diverse, widely scattered, unorganized. Taking away established benefits or jobs is very difficult in our political process.

Experienced political observers suggest that no massive single welfare-reform program has much chance of success, that only incremental changes to improve particular parts of the program can hope to divide the opposition and get the votes for passage. But piece-by-piece reform of the complex, overlapping structure of welfare has little chance of producing a rational, integrated welfare program in place of the existing melange. Public-sector processes are not calculated to produce efficient results; claims of equity, justice and entitlement, and narrow group self-interest tend to dominate the goal of efficiency in Congress and the bureaucratic agencies that line Constitution Avenue.

How Much Aid for the Poor?

Table 25-1 reported a total of $240 billion of federal benefit payments to individuals in 1980, many of them originally justified as aid to the poor. Yet of this total, only about $40 billion went directly to the poor, with payment conditioned on the recipients' meeting poverty standards. In 1978, the budget reported $179 billion of "income security" payments, of which $120 billion were Social Security or related retirement benefits that went mainly to the vast middle classes. Table 25–3 summarizes the main federal aid programs for the poor in that year, but it understates the amount somewhat, since it includes only programs specifically providing aid for poor people; it excludes, for example, the share of general Social Security benefits, education, unemployment payments, and the like that help the poor along with other beneficiaries. And it omits state and local programs for the poor, totaling at least $10 billion in 1978. But the central fact is clear, that only a small fraction of federal benefit payments to individuals go to the poor, whatever their original rationalization.

We shall look at these issues more broadly in the following section. Economic analysis cannot tell you which distribution of income is most equitable. That depends on each person's own value judgments. But economic analysis *can* tell you that, if a major goal of the government's vast income transfer system in Table 25–1 is to abolish poverty, the present hodgepodge of antipoverty measures is a highly inefficient way of achieving that goal.

INEQUALITY, EQUITY, AND EFFICIENCY

Going beyond the poverty issue, how much inequality in incomes is consistent with equity and efficiency in our economy? Few issues create more social tensions. How high taxes should I pay to provide a higher real income for you, if I am a prosperous lawyer or businessman and you are a lower-income store clerk, factory worker, or student?

During the post–World War II decades, persistent movement toward more government intervention to transfer income from higher- to lower-income groups reflected widespread feeling that large income disparities were inequitable. But as growth has slowed and inflation has

TABLE 25–3
Federal Aid to the Poor, 1978

	AMOUNT (IN BILLIONS)
Public assistance (AFDC, etc.)	$ 6.7
Medicaid	14.0
Food (mainly food stamps)	11.1
SSI, earned-income tax credits, etc.	6.2
Housing	2.1
	$40.1

Source: Budget of the United States, Fiscal Year 1980.

pushed the large "middle classes" into higher income tax brackets, protests against ever-bigger government, "welfare," and more progressive taxation have swollen. Increasing numbers have questioned whether equity and more equality are necessarily the same thing.

Most Americans subscribe to the basic proposition that "all men are created equal." From this, you may conclude that all men should be economically equal—but this does not necessarily follow. Economic analysis cannot tell you what definition of equity is best. But it is useful to explore some of the main alternatives. Three different definitions of equity (or fairness) are commonly stated, or implied, in discussions of income equality and inequality.

1. Everyone should have an equal start in the economic race. Thus, equality of opportunity is the central notion. If, from an equal start, some obtain larger incomes than others (by working harder, being smarter, being luckier, or producing more of what others will buy), so much the better for them. There's nothing unfair about that kind of inequality, in this view. This concept of equity implies government action to ensure equality of opportunity, but not government action to reduce inequality based on winning the economic race from a fair start. Whatever inequality arises from differing economic contributions to the general welfare, as measured by the market test (see number 3 below) is fair, if everyone has an equal start. Inequality reflecting personal choice (to be a minister rather than a lawyer) would be acceptable. Some questions, if you accept this concept: How should we ensure equal opportunity to babies born with white and black skins, into poor and rich families, in urban slums and on Western ranches? Will equal expenditure on education for all do the job? How much, if any, transfer of accumulated wealth from parents to children should be permitted?

2. Everyone should have an equal income. Equality of results is what counts. If you accept this notion of equity, the implications are clear. To produce an equitable society, government should tax the rich and subsidize the poor until all incomes are equal, however much or little each individual contributes to producing the income distributed. This is presumably the foundation of socialist doctrine: "From each according to his abilities, to each according to his needs." Many will not go to this extreme, but accept without questioning the general proposition that taxes that bear more heavily on higher-than on lower-income families are fairer than those that don't. "Progressive" taxes are fairer than "regressive" ones. This is often taken for granted. Why?

One line of argument in support of the position is that the marginal utility of one dollar is always less to a rich man than to a poor man; therefore, total utility will always be increased by taxing the rich and subsidizing the poor. But this is clearly unacceptable reasoning. We have no objective way of comparing the marginal utilities of different individuals, and many challenge the proposition. Consider a millionaire and a $5,000-a-year waiter. The first dollar transferred from the former to the latter may plausibly be assumed to hurt the millionaire less than it pleases the waiter. But what of the situation when the rich man has already paid out nearly half his income in taxes, while the waiter has now become rich beyond his wildest dreams? There is no objective way of comparing marginal utilities and disutilities between the two, but it now intuitively seems far from clear that the once-millionaire's marginal disutility is less than the now-rich waiter's marginal utility from the transfer of one more dollar. One may prefer this concept of equity, but he should not kid himself

that its preferability can be logically demonstrated by such reasoning.[4]

3. Everyone should have the income he earns by contributing to consumer wants in a market-directed society, unless he voluntarily chooses to transfer part of it to others. This can be combined with concept 1 above requiring an equal start for all in the economic race. Some apply this principle only to income earned by working, and do not consider inequality based on earnings from capital as justified. The main thrust of this concept, whether or not income from capital is included, is that inequality is acceptable, indeed desirable, on both efficiency and equity grounds, when it reflects merit in contributing to producing what others want to buy.

Equity vs. Incentives

Suppose you believe that equity calls for more equal incomes. How much of a person's income can the state tax away without seriously reducing his incentive to earn more? Part of the current "taxpayers' revolt" reflects this concern—that we are seriously eroding the incentives that provide the progress and hard work that make us all better off economically. There is head-on conflict, the protesters say, between this concept of equity, economic incentives, and efficiency in getting produced the goods and services we want.

We shall examine the evidence on this conflict between more equality and economic incentives in the next chapter. In principle, we may be able to have both the efficiency of a market-directed, individual-incentive economy to get the goods and services that we want produced most efficiently, and the equity of whatever income distribution seems fairest—by transferring incomes from rich to poor once they have been earned in the market and letting the market respond to the spending of the redistributed income.[5] But this will work only if the required

---

[4]Suppose a stock-market crash cuts the wealth and income of all rich people by half, but does not change the income of others. Clearly, incomes are now more equal. Is the result more equitable?

[5]For a micro example of such a combination, see Case 24, "The Voucher Education Plan."

taxes do not seriously reduce incentives to earn. If they do, we face a painful choice between equity and efficiency. Many observers believe they see serious strains on this score today in some of the major West European economies, especially the U.K. and Scandinavia. And the debate rages increasingly in the United States over each budget and tax-reform bill.

Social Security—an example. Social Security benefits alone already exceed $100 billion annually. Although Social Security is commonly thought of as insurance, with benefits financed by each individual's contributions while he is employed, its benefits bear no direct relationship to each individual's contributions, and no large "reserve fund" has been built up, as with private insurance, to finance future benefit payments. Instead, Social Security is a massive income-transfer program, from the working population to the elderly who no longer work. Payroll taxes on workers each year finance the payments to retired beneficiaries that year. The small accumulated "reserve fund" totals less than one year's benefits. Today and in the future, anything like the level of benefits specified by existing law will be feasible only if current workers annually pay the taxes to provide the benefits.

As of 1979, each worker paid a special payroll tax of about 6 percent on the first $22,900 of his earnings, and the employer paid an equal tax (which is probably passed on to the workers by reducing his salary), making a total of about 12 percent. There was no tax on earnings above $23,000. Therefore, the typical workers whose wages are less than $23,000 pays 6 (or 12) percent of his total income, while those with incomes over $23,000 pay a smaller percentage of their total incomes.[6] Thus the payroll tax, second in size only to the personal income tax, is regressive. And benefit payments are scheduled to rise persistently, with escalation to offset any inflation that occurs. By 1990, annual taxes and

benefit payments will exceed a quarter of a trillion dollars. Will you be willing to pay your share to support those who have retired? (For more details see Case 25.)

Equality of Opportunity vs. Equality of Results

Equal opportunity has been at the core of American mores through our history. Every mother could think that her son, or daughter, could become president. Abraham Lincoln, studying by the light of the fireplace, was perhaps our greatest hero. And education for all was seen as the open door to progress. But increasingly in the post–World War II decades, more and more Americans found that not enough. Research findings suggest that the home and general environment have more force in molding the young than does their schooling, so the route up for the poor through better schools was far from sure. Moreover, as our living standards rose, so did our aspirations, and more and more people came to argue that equality of results (in health, housing, living standards, and so on) was the only true test of equity in a free society; equality of opportunity sounded good, but it wasn't fast and sure enough.

This led to important government policy changes. Government regulations to implement affirmative-action hiring, safer working conditions, better products for consumers, and cleaner air, intruded further and further into the day-to-day lives of individuals and the operations of business firms. Taxes were larger to finance the welfare state, and most of the increases in real GNP went into the public sector, especially transfer payments. Conservatives, who mistrusted government intervention generally, viewed with alarm this increased intrusion, and blamed it for lowered individual incentives, lower investment, and the gradual slowdown in U.S. (and Western European) economic growth during the 1970s. The prestigious *London Economist* ran a widely discussed series on America's third century (1976–2076), predicting a gradual decline in U.S. economic and political world leadership, reflecting the replacement of tradi-

---

[6]The tax is scheduled to rise to 7.15 percent (or 14.3 percent including the employer's share) on the first $42,600 of income by 1987. This would be an annual tax of just over $3,000 ($6,000) on each employee.

tional American drive and economic initiative by the growing government security blanket.[7]

What income transfers will be supported by the public as equitable, and the growing clash betwen equity, incentives, and efficiency, will predictably be major issues of public policy over the decade ahead. More on them in the following case, and in Chapter 26, which examines growing taxpayer resistance to these developments in the so-called "tax revolt" of the late 1970s.

---

[7]Reprinted in N. Macrae, *America's Third Century* (New York: Harcourt Brace Jovanovich, 1976).

SUMMARY AND REVIEW

1. Since World War II, the public sector's biggest activity has increasingly been the redistribution of income through taxes and transfer payments. These transfers are partly from rich to poor but are primarily within the large middle- and upper-middle-income groups.

2. About 24 million Americans are officially classified as "poor" in government statistics. This number fell steadily with economic growth over the past half century, but has been relatively stable over the past few years.

3. The poor include many different groups (minorities, farmers, elderly people, fatherless families, and others), and there are many causes for poverty (e.g., inadequate aggregate demand, slow growth, low productivity, market imperfections, discrimination, and absence from the labor force).

4. Antipoverty measures include both steps to increase productivity and jobs for the poor (which increase total output), and measures to redistribute income from upper- to lower-income groups. The present "welfare" system, designed to transfer income to the poor, is widely criticized as inequitable, full of disincentives to work, and administratively expensive and inefficient. Of total federal benefit transfer payments of $240 billion to individuals in 1980, only about $40 billion went specifically to the poor.

5. The "negative income tax" is supported by many economists to replace much of the present welfare system, but it runs against political forces blocking such change. The political process tends to react more to arguments of personal "equity" and "justice" than to arguments of efficiency.

6. How far government should go toward equalizing incomes through transfer payments depends on issues of both equity and efficiency-incentives. Three major definitions of equity often (consciously or subconsciously) used are: (a) equality of opportunity; (b) equality of incomes (results); and (c) the income distribution produced by competitive market processes. (b) implies extensive government intervention to redistribute incomes earned in competitive markets. (c) implies limited, or no, government intervention to redistribute incomes earned in competitive markets.

7. The huge Social Security program (see Case 25) illustrates redistribution of income from workers to nonworkers, rather than rich to poor. It also illustrates the disincentives to work, earn, and save that may be caused by heavy taxes to finance income transfers.

8. Government redistribution of income from successful workers and investors to nonworkers and lower-income groups has grown rapidly since the 1930s in most major Western industrialized countries. Some critics feel that this move toward a "welfare state" is seriously undermining the incentives to work and invest that underlie our rapid growth and rising living standards. The "tax revolt" of the late 1970s, examined in the next chapter, may mark a major shift in public attitudes on redistribution issues.

For Analysis and Discussion

1. How unequal should incomes be? What criteria do you use in deciding?

2. Should government aid to the poor be primarily in money or in kind? Is your answer consistent with analysis of individual utility maximization in Chapter 4?

3. "The simplest and cheapest approach to eliminating poverty would be simply to give a tax-financed cash subsidy to each poor individual big enough to raise his income above the poverty level, perhaps through the negative income tax. This would avoid the waste and misdirection of elaborate programs and would give each individual freedom to spend his income as he pleases." Do you agree? Why, or why not?

4. "A strong aggregate-demand policy to ensure high employment would solve the poverty problem and eliminate the need for the hodgepodge of government measures adopted over recent years." Do you agree?

5. What is your program to reduce or eliminate poverty in the United States?

6. How good a living can the current workers in our society afford to provide for nonworkers, such as the aged and the unemployed? What criteria do you use in answering?

7. What is your test of fairness in the distribution of income? Does it lead to any conflict with attaining the most efficient production of wanted goods and services?

8. Which of the "income-security benefits" listed in Table 25–1 do you consider justified? Which ones not? Would you be willing to pay $100 more in personal taxes to increase any of them?

9. Can you suggest a politically practical way to get Congress to adopt a major simplification like the negative income tax in place of the present complex, overlapping set of antipoverty measures?

CASE 25

HOW MUCH SOCIAL SECURITY CAN WE AFFORD?

The American Social Security system was set up in 1936, during the Great Depression, to provide some protection against poverty after retirement for wage and salary earners. The early benefits were about $30 a month for retired workers; these benefits were financed by a payroll tax of 2 percent on the first $3,000 of each worker's wages, matched by an equal tax on the employer. The plan was seen as a forced saving, or compulsory public retirement-insurance plan for workers who might not otherwise save enough to provide a living postretirement income for themselves.

Since the 1930s, Congress has repeatedly extended the coverage of the system and raised benefits and taxes to finance them. In 1965, it added basic medical benefits for all participants over 65, through Medicare. (There are special provisions for wives, disabled workers, and other special cases.) Today, the Social Security system has become a financial giant, with over 100 million participants, and tax collections and benefit payments of more than $100 billion annually. It covers nearly all private workers (most public employees are covered by parallel systems), and minimum cash-income payments are guaranteed for all aged poor. Social Security was originally conceived as roughly parallel to private insurance, accumulating a reserve fund with the payments made by participating individuals. But the insurance principle was soon discarded, and the system is now essentially a massive annual transfer of income from working taxpayers to nonworking retirees and their spouses. Although there is a small reserve fund of about $40 billion, this equals less than one year's liabilities to retirees, while the present actuarial value of future liabilities to participants in the system is between $2 and $3 trillion.

Benefits vary somewhat, according to how long the individual has worked. Annual benefits in 1980 totaled about $6,000 for a couple where the husband had worked for a long period at good pay in covered occupations. Under Supplementary Security Income (SSI) a minimum income of about $3,000 is guaranteed to every couple over 65, whether or not they have contributed to the plan. In addition, most medical costs are covered for those over 65, with a minimum payment by the individual on each illness. Participants between 65 and 70 receive reduced benefits, however, if they continue to work and earn over $4,500; for each dollar earned over that amount, Social Security benefits are reduced by 50 cents and the individual must pay Social Security tax on his earnings.

By law, both taxes and benefits are scheduled to rise as average real wages rise and as inflation occurs. In 1979, the annual tax per worker was about $2,800 (including the employer share, which is passed on to the workers in most cases—see Chapter 26). By 1989,

it will be $6,000. Benefits will rise roughly in proportion, under present law.

Recently, two developments have led to widespread alarm concerning the state of the Social Security system. First, in spite of the large increases planned for annual tax collections, they will probably not be enough to finance all the benefits promised. And the payroll taxes already are very large.

Second, there is growing recognition that the Social Security system is not an insurance plan at all, and that there is no accumulated reserve fund to guarantee each participant's benefits at retirement time. Recognition that future benefits are dependent on the willingness of Congress to levy the current taxes needed to pay the benefits has come as a major shock to many. What if congressmen (the voters) decide they are unwilling to levy the required heavy taxes on themselves, the workers, to support the retired nonworkers in the future?

As benefits and taxes rise, how to finance the system has been widely debated. The payroll taxes used to finance Social Security are regressive. Critics argue that this regression should be eliminated by raising the limit on taxable income, or alternatively, by giving up the whole pretense of "insurance" and simply providing retirement and related medical payments for everybody out of general tax funds. If the president of General Motors has a salary of $800,000, they say, let him pay the 7 percent tax on all of it, making a tax of $56,000, which would still only be the same tax *rate* as that on lower-income workers. A shift to general-tax-system financing would go even further, making the burden of financing retirement benefits progressive (see Figure 23–4). But opponents protest that retirement benefits are limited to about $6,000 annually, no matter how much one contributes in taxes. To make the $800,000 businessman pay $56,000 annually when he will collect only the same modest retirement benefit as low-income workers seems a perversion of equity. Indeed, the higher-income person is likely to collect even less, since he is more likely to keep on earning more than the permissible amount after age 65, and hence to receive no retirement benefits at all until he is 70.

Another attack on the present system is that it provides disincentives for older people to work and for all participants to save and invest in the private economy. To get the full Social Security retirement benefits, people must now stop working at age 65. Maybe this made sense in a depression like the 1930s, when we were trying to spread the few jobs around, but now it merely help to guarantee that the human resources of older people will be wasted, even though they may want to work. On the macro level, if the public views its payments into the Social Security system as saving to accumulate retirement benefits, this will substitute at least in part for private saving, which could otherwise have been channeled on into private investment. Thus, Social Security may play a major role in explaining why the American economy has had a low investment rate and grown so slowly in recent years. For the government uses the Social Security tax collections for transfer payments, not to build new factories and machines that increase productive capacity and productivity.

One last set of facts: When Social Security was adopted, there were very few workers eligible for retirement benefits, and the ratio of taxpaying workers to beneficiaries was large. By the 1950s, the ratio of workers to beneficiaries was about 4 to 1. Reflecting the low birthrates of the 1930s and 1940s, the ratio of workers to older people has fallen steadily and is now about 3.2 to 1. If present demographic trends continue, in fifty years, the ratio will be down to about 2 to 1.

What, if anything, should be done to reform the nation's Social Security system? In particular:

1. Are benefits too large, or too small? Should they be indexed to rise with inflation and with rising real wages of workers?

2. Who should pay—the workers, or general taxpayers? Should taxes be directly related to the benefits each individual will receive on retirement, as in private insurance?

3. Should we abandon the position that Social Security is different from other government income transfers (welfare payments, unemployment insurance, food stamps, etc.), and simply merge it into the annual federal budget-making process?

4. How much work are you willing to do now to support the retired nonworkers in society? How much should the next generation be willing to do to support you when you reach 65?

5. Should the government accumulate a reserve fund from current workers' tax payments to finance future benefit payments, as private insurance companies do? (In answering, think back to the likely effects on aggregate demand, real output, and prices.)

Taxes,
the "Tax Revolt,"
and Tax Reform

Chapter 26

veryone complains about high taxes. But if we want public goods and services, we must get resources transferred from private to public use. If we assume full employment, taxes are the most straightforward way to get the necessary funds, since they take private incomes that would otherwise bid directly for the productive resources. With full employment, more government spending without more taxes means increased total spending and inflation; then resources are taken away from those whose incomes fall behind during inflation. If we divert more resources to the public sector, there is no escape from paying for them in such a case.

With government spending over $700 billion annually and headed higher, toward $1 trillion, an efficient and equitable tax system is very important. The multi-billion-dollar federal budget may not mean much to you—the figures are just too big. But the fact that when you leave college with an average, middle-class income of perhaps $15,000, you will start turning over to Uncle Sam and to state and local government units about $4,000 each year (see Figure 23–4) puts the dollars and cents in more meaningful terms. And in the late 1970s, taxpayers nationwide staged a virtual revolt against further growth in government, inflationary government deficits and ever-rising taxes. Fighting inflation and cutting back the size of government became the nation's top economic objectives.

Let us look first briefly at some criteria for good and bad taxes, and then at the broader question of the total tax burden.

GOOD AND BAD TAXES

You can't judge intelligently what are good and what are bad taxes until you've clarified the criteria by which you judge them. Since many people don't bother to do this, it is little wonder that they often disagree violently on what taxes should be.

The same broad social objectives we have used before can be pointed up conveniently in three questions in analyzing the tax system:

1. Progress. Do the taxes encourage or hinder savings and investment, employment, and stable economic growth?

2. Freedom and individual choice. Do the taxes hinder or aid the allocation of resources in accordance with consumer preferences? Do they interfere with the free choices of individuals and businesses in earning and spending?

3. Equity. How equitably is the tax burden distributed? Government taxing and spending significantly affect the distribution of income. Unless government tax collections exactly equal the benefits provided to each family (that is, unless all government services are sold at cost), the issue is not whether the government will redistribute income, but how.

Progress: Stable Economic Growth

Economic growth depends on an intricate complex of factors, but especially on technological advance, saving and investment, education, and hard work by the labor force. Any tax is a drain on someone's incomes from work or investment, and in general, taxes will deter economic growth. But some taxes deter growth more than others.

Theory tells us that taxes that fall on savings, profits, and other returns from investment will discourage growth, compared to taxes that fall on personal income and consumption. Similarly, taxes that give special advantages to expenditures on investment, research and development, and education are incentives to faster growth. Lower corporate tax rates, the "investment tax credit" of 1962, and more generous depreciation guidelines for taxing plant and equipment are examples.

Tax contribution to stability is also important. We want taxes that help to keep after-tax incomes growing stably, not fluctuating sharply. Individual and corporate income taxes, for example, provide built-in tax flexibility. When national income rises, these tax liabilities rise even more rapidly, because individual income tax rates are progressive and because corporate profits subject to taxes rise sharply in business expansion. The opposite is true when national income falls. This built-in flexibility tends to damp the swings in private incomes and spending. By contrast, a tax that is insensitive to income changes (for example, the property tax) makes no contribution to stabilizing private spending.[1]

Noninterference with Free Choices

If we want free private choices to determine the allocation of resources and the distribution of income, a "good" tax system should be neutral in the sense that it does not affect these results. But a tax system as pervasive as ours cannot be completely neutral. In a few cases—for example, tobacco and liquor—we consciously discourage the use of particular products through taxation. In these cases, the tax is used to bring resource allocation into line with our social preferences.

But in most cases, the distortions produced by taxes on individual commodities (excise taxes) are unfortunate. These distortions occur because higher taxes on particular commodities lead people to buy less of that commodity than they otherwise would, relative to other commodities. Or they lead people to work less in particular occupations than they would otherwise choose. By distorting resource use this way, a tax produces a "deadweight" loss to the economy—a cost against which there is no offsetting gain. Such a cost is in excess of the resources given up by the private sector through taxation to finance public expenditures. The economy is misled into producing the wrong combination of goods.

To minimize this deadweight loss while raising any given amount of revenue, we should use taxes that produce the smallest changes in private production and consumption behavior (excluding cases with externalities). A "head tax" (a lump-sum tax on each person regardless of income or expenditure) would rate high on this criterion. Because no one could avoid it, it would not affect his economic behavior much, if at all. Taxes on commodities with very inelastic demand (for example, a salt tax) are similar, since people buy about as much of the product at the higher (taxed) price as before. Conversely, excise taxes on commodities with elastic demand are apt to be highly distorting in their effects.

---

[1]Remember, however, that built-in flexibility tends to damp down any changes in GNP, whether or not we want the upswing or downswing checked. Thus, such built-in flexibility may produce undesirable as well as desirable results.

"Equity" in Taxation

A tax system should be equitable, as well as nondistorting and conducive to stability and growth. Three different broad concepts of equity were outlined in the final section of Chapter 25, and these can be related specifically to tax policy. Those who believe in a more equal distribution of income than is provided by the market generally stress "ability to pay" as the main guide to equity in taxation. Those who believe the results of the market are generally equitable favor "benefit received" as the criterion of who should pay the taxes. Nearly everyone adds the further principle of equity, "equal treatment of those equally situated."

The "ability-to-pay" principle. Taxation according to ability to pay is widely favored by those who favor more equality. This generally means to them that people with higher incomes should pay more than those with lower incomes. The underlying presumption is that a more equal after-tax distribution of income would be more equitable.

But even if we agree on income as the best measure of ability to pay, how much more should higher-income people pay? At what rates should different incomes be taxed to meet the ability-to-pay criterion? Some argue that the rate should be proportional—that is, the same percentage of each person's income. For example, the tax rate might be 1 percent, giving a $10 tax on $1,000; $100 on $10,000; $1,000 on $100,000. More argue that rates should be progressive—that is, a higher-percentage tax on high incomes than on low (for example, $5 on $1,000; $100 on $10,000; $2,000 on $100,000). All ability-to-pay advocates argue against regressive taxation, which takes a larger percentage of income from the lower-income groups.

It is important to see that there is no objective way of deciding whether rates should be proportional or progressive, or, if progressive, how steeply progressive. As Chapter 25 stressed, there is no way of comparing objectively interpersonal disutilities of taxes paid by different people at different income levels. Some presume that the marginal disutility of a dollar paid in taxes will always be less for a higher- than a lower-income taxpayer. But such comparisons are not logically defensible; and even at an intuitive level, the proposition seems very doubtful as more taxes on the rich reduce their after-tax incomes toward equality with the rising lower incomes (see the final section of Chapter 25 for the reasoning).[2]

Progressive taxation of income and estates represents the primary applications of the ability-to-pay principle. In the last analysis, the issue of how much progression is "equitable" boils down to the question of who should get how much of the national-income pie—a fundamental and explosive question. This issue of relative tax burdens at different income levels is often called the issue of "vertical" equity. Look back at Figure 23–4 for estimates of how progressive the present tax system is.

The "benefit" principle.   The second concept of equity is that each individual should have the income that he earns by helping to produce what consumers choose to buy. This implies that an equitable tax system will leave that distribution of income undisturbed, except insofar as each individual chooses to spend his money. It leads toward the proposition that people should be taxed only to pay for the benefits they choose to buy from the government. The public sector would then roughly approximate the working of the market, except for cases of public goods and externalities.

One obvious problem is how the principle could be applied practically. If a city is putting in a new sewer, it's easy to see who the primary beneficiaries will be and to assess the cost against these property owners through a "special assessment." But how can the benefits derived from national defense, or highways, be divided up among the citizens?

Consider education, for example. Now we have free public schools for all. Suppose we put all education on a benefit-tax basis. Then each parent would have to pay a special school tax equal to the cost of educating each child he has in school—for example, $1,000 per child. This pol-

icy might be fine for the local banker and doctor. But how about the poor family on the other side of the tracks, with eight school-age children? The well-to-do could continue sending their youngsters to school (and more cheaply than now), but millions of poor children would be priced out of the market, or get a very inferior, low-cost education. Government activities like welfare would be completely ruled out by the benefit principle, since there would be little point in imposing special taxes on the poor just to return the funds to them.

Broad use of the benefit principle would thus be far more revolutionary than it sounds at first. It would mean, in effect, direct sale of government services to the user, and would preclude any redistribution of income through the public economy.

"Equal treatment of those equally situated."   A third principle of equity states that people equally situated should be taxed equally. This is a powerful guide to tax policy, and one that is accepted by most observers. But what is "equally situated"? Are two people with the same income always equally situated? For example, is a disabled man with an annual pension income of $10,000 equally situated with a healthy young man with the same income? Are both equally situated with the $10,000-a-year laborer who has a wife and five children to support? Does it matter where the income comes from? For example, is a factory superintendent who earns $25,000 a year equally situated with an investor who gains $25,000 on General Motors stock that has gone up in price between his buying and selling it? Our tax laws give a special advantage to the disabled man and the one with children, and they tax the "capital gain" on GM stock less than regular income. Should they? This is the issue of "horizontal" equity. It obviously involves some highly subjective judgments.

SHIFTING AND INCIDENCE OF TAXATION

Often, the person who hands the funds over to the government does not actually bear the burden of the tax. The federal tax on liquor, for

---

[2]Note that strict application of the principle would require that all taxes should be applied to the richest taxpayer first, until his income was just equal to the next richest; then to both of them till their incomes were reduced to just equal to the third richest; and so on until all after-tax incomes were equal.

example, is paid to the government by distillers; but it is largely "shifted" forward to consumers through higher prices. The final "incidence" of a tax may be far from the person who turns the money over to the government.

It is safe to assume that a taxpayer will shift a tax whenever he can. The question generally is, therefore, When can a tax be shifted? A tax can be shifted only when, as a result of the tax, the taxpayer is able to obtain a higher price for something he sells or to pay a lower price for something he buys. A price transaction is essential if shifting is to occur.

Generally, taxes do nothing to increase demand for taxed commodities (remember that we are examining the impact of the tax, apart from what is done with the money collected). But many taxes do raise costs and prices. If, as a result of a tax (for example, on cigarettes), the price is higher than it otherwise would have been, the tax has been shifted to that extent.[3]

Because tax shifting depends on the prices charged and paid, it is largely an application of the general supply-and-demand analysis of Part 2. But a warning is necessary. A rise in price following the imposition of a tax in the real world is not necessarily proof that the tax has been shifted. The price rise may have come from some other cause. (Remember the fallacy of post hoc, propter hoc.) Empirical verification of tax shifting is very difficult, since it is hard to isolate one cause and its effects in the multitude of forces simultaneously at work in economic life. Analytically, however, we can trace through the effects of any tax assuming *"other things equal"*—that is, assuming the tax to be the only new element in the situation.

Three Examples

Personal income tax. The personal income tax, which accounts for nearly half of all federal tax revenues, is an example of a nonshiftable tax. The tax does not increase the demand for the services of the people taxed, nor does it probably greatly decrease the supply of labor. (The latter

---

[3]See, for example, the analysis of the excise tax on whiskey, in the concluding section of Chapter 6.

statement may not be accurate; some people may work less because their earnings are taxed. But even though the government takes some of your earnings, you still have more left when you work than when you don't, and for most people, there's no nontaxed way of earning a living.) Thus, there is no effective way the taxed individual can raise his price to shift the tax forward, and there is no one onto whom he can shift it backward.

You may ask, How about unions? Won't they demand bigger wage increases if their taxes are raised? They may ask, but nothing has increased the demand for their labor to permit them to get a bigger wage increase without cutting the number of jobs. If they get more money after the tax, we must ask, why didn't they get it before? Price theory says the tax won't be shifted except possibly in cases of monopsony or oligopolies that are protected by barriers to entry. But in the dynamics of inflation and business cycles, the picture is less clear.

Payroll taxes. Payroll taxes, levied on both workers and employers to finance Social Security benefits, are the second biggest and fastest-growing tax, totaling nearly $200 billion in 1978. The portion levied on the worker is like the income tax; it can't be shifted, for substantially the same reasons. But the part levied on the employer generally is shifted—back onto the worker. Consider the reasoning. The tax on the employer increases the effective wage cost of the employee. Since cost per unit of output is now higher, unless the employer can reduce the wage rate he pays, he will have to raise prices, which will reduce output; and he wil substitute machinery for labor to maximize his profits. If wage rates are flexible, wages will fall as the demand for labor falls. If wage rates are inflexible downward, some workers will be laid off. Either way, the burden is largely shifted onto the workers, although some of it may be shifted forward to consumers through higher prices.

A simple diagram makes it clear that the incidence of both halves of the payroll tax is on the worker. In Figure 26–1, let D^L be the demand for labor and S^L its supply, fixed in amount. Part A shows that the wage will be W^1 without any tax. Now suppose a payroll tax is imposed on all

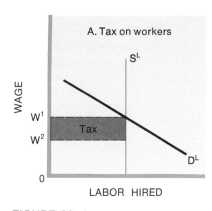 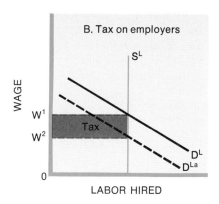

FIGURE 26–1
Payroll Tax Borne by Employees
Payroll taxes are generally borne by employees, whether they are imposed on employees or employers.

workers, which they must pay to the government. Neither demand nor supply is changed, so the wage paid by employers is unchanged. Unhappily, workers' wages *after taxes* are only W^2, lower by the amount of the tax they must pay.

Part B starts with the same S^L and D^L curves, and the same wage, W^1. Now the government imposes the same wage tax *on employers*. Workers are worth no more than before to employers, so the employers' demand curve shifts down at all outputs by the amount of the tax, to D^{La}. Each worker now costs the old wage plus the tax, so employers will demand fewer workers at any wage level. If the wage is flexible, it will fall to a new equilibrium level at W^2, just as in Part A. In both cases, employment stays constant and the wage after tax is reduced by just the amount of the tax. It should be easy to see that the critical factor underlying the full incidence on workers is the fixed stock of labor, the perfectly inelastic labor-supply curve. The same result would follow for a tax imposed on the wage (or rent) of any other fixed resource. (If the wage rates is fixed at W^1, say by a union contract, work out for yourself what will happen to employment.)

If we want workers to bear the cost of old-age and unemployment insurance, payroll taxes may be a good means of financing Social Security. But levying half the tax on the employer, even though you *want* him to pay, doesn't necessarily mean that he *will* pay it.

Property taxes. Property taxes, the third most important revenue source, are levied on both residential and business property. They are often considered regressive on the theory that they are shifted to renters, but in part they fall on capital and are to that extent more progressive. Consider separately the main parts of the tax.

The part of the tax that falls on land mainly stays there—on the landowner. Note that the supply of land is fixed. The first effect of the tax is to reduce the net after-tax yield on the land. Thus, future buyers will be willing to pay less for the land after the tax. Since the capital value of the land has been reduced by the tax, we say the tax has been "capitalized." No future buyer of the land will invest unless the price falls enough to provide a net return *after taxes* equal to that obtainable on other comparable investments. The burden of the new tax is placed permanently on the owner at the time of first taxation; he has no way to shift it by transferring his investment and reducing the supply. Future owners buy free of the special land tax.

The part of the tax on residences is probably partly shifted, partly borne by capital. The tax will be gradually shifted to renters if the tax drives investment out of housing into other areas where taxes are lower, thereby reducing the supply and raising the rents on taxed buildings. This effect is plainly visible in big-city slums, where effective property-tax rates rise as buildings age but assessments are not reduced. Property owners just let their buildings depreciate and transfer their investment elsewhere. But insofar as alternative investment opportunities are also taxed so property owners have no real alternative to keeping their investment in housing, they are stuck with the tax; it cannot be shifted.

One last point on the incidence of real-property taxes: Low-priced buildings are widely overassessed relative to high-priced ones; assessment practices are regressive. Thus, the actual incidence depends on a combination of basic tax and administrative factors.

Taxes on business property like inventories and machinery are business costs, quite similar to excise taxes on business products. They are usually shifted, but sometimes partly borne by owners of the business.

The incidence of the property tax is complex. To the extent that it falls on renters, it makes the tax system more regressive for very low income receivers, who pay a large part of their incomes for rent. This would raise the average tax burden for very low incomes in Figure 36–4. But modern analysis is moving toward allotting much of the burden to the capital.

THE "TAX REVOLT" OF THE 1970s

Congress and the administrative bureaucracy of government often respond slowly to the wishes of the voters back home, especially when organized interest groups are pushing for contrary ends. But the so-called "tax revolt" of the late 1970s provides an interesting case study in political economy of an uprising of the general public to cut back taxes and government spending, reversing a trend of government expansion that has run since the Great Depression of the 1930s.

The three decades after the Great Depression and World War II saw a persistent growth of government spending and taxes, and general reliance on government to handle our pressing social problems. As was noted in Chapter 36, federal, state, and local government spending all rose persistently as percentages of GNP. Keynesian fiscal policy was widely acclaimed as the answer to both unemployment and inflation

problems. "Welfare" and other "income-security" transfer payments came to dominate the federal budget. Government regulation of economic life spread apace, and the regulation involved far more direct government interference with personal economic life than had been true earlier (see Chapter 16).

But somehow, it didn't all work satisfactorily. The Johnson "Great Society" failed to eliminate poverty and other social ills. Government deficits soared to incredible billions, yet unemployment persisted. Worse, inflation took off after the mid-1960s in a jagged, upward peacetime path that reached double-digit levels in both the mid- and late-1970s. Economic growth slowed after the 1960s, reflecting lower saving and investment rates and slower productivity growth, with little improvement in average American private living standards during the decade. Nearly all the lagging growth in real output went to more government. Inflation further eroded the buying power of the money-income increases households and businesses did receive. Many people saw government "income-security" transfer payments as subsidies to those who didn't work from those who did. Although the consumerism and environmental-protection movements scored many successes, Jimmy Carter ran for the presidency on less regulation, smaller government, and a balanced budget.

In 1977, California voters overwhelmingly approved a controversial constitutional amendment slashing property taxes and setting a permanent upper limit on such taxes at 1 percent of the property's value. Within a year, 28 states had voted that Congress call an unprecedented constitutional convention to consider a constitutional amendment requiring that the budget be balanced each year. Public-opinion polls showed that six out of seven Americans favored a balanced-budget requirement and saw the government deficit as a—or the—major cause of inflation. A parallel amendment requiring that total government spending be limited to a fixed or falling percent of GNP received widespread support. President Carter sent Congress an "austere" budget for 1980, and congressmen hopped on the austerity bandwagon, calling for even further cuts in government spending. The obsolescence of Keynesian economics was proclaimed in many

"Other folks have to pay taxes, too, Mr. Herndon, so would you please spare us the dramatics!" (Drawing by Booth; © 1975. The New Yorker Magazine, Inc.)

universities and newspaper editorials. Less government, fewer taxes, and a smaller deficit were the overwhelming spirit of the day, and government responded—at least in part.

How much difference the taxpayers' revolt actually made you will know by the 1980s. Some observers saw it as a transient set of attitudes engendered by special events of the 1970s. But others saw a basic change in the role of government in economic life. They stressed the slowdown in the rate of economic growth and productivity. Nearly all the modest increase in national output was diverted to governments. With our highly progressive income tax system, inflation rapidly pushes almost everyone into higher tax-rate brackets as their dollar incomes rise. Governments get more money without legislatures' having to raise tax rates: each 1 percent increase in GNP raises tax receipts about 1.6 percent. Government is the big gainer from

inflation, and many congressmen and bureaucrats know it. One equitable way to correct this would be to "index" the tax system, adjusting rates downward to offset rising inflation. Then government could get a bigger share of the nation's output only by openly raising tax rates.

How effectively did the "tax revolt" of the 1970s reflect the public's wishes as to the size and role of government? How effectively did the government respond to those wishes?

TAX REFORM

Recent years have produced many complaints about the inequity of the present tax system. These charges have been leveled mainly against "loopholes" and special privileges allegedly enjoyed by the rich and powerful, and against the tax burdens borne by the poor and middle

357

classes. Other critics charge that our taxes destroy incentives to work, save, and invest. With taxes as big as they are, it is important to consider these criticisms.

As Figure 23–4 showed, the tax system's progression comes largely from the federal income taxes, which mainly miss the poor and hit the wealthy with high marginal rates. Payroll taxes for Social Security, state–local sales, excise, and (possibly) property taxes produce regressive offsets on the poor and middle-income classes. The result is a roughly flat or slightly progressive overall tax burden of around 30 percent for the lower- and middle-income classes (with perhaps a regressive burden on the very poor if the residential-property tax is largely shifted to renters). But, even though their tax rates are relatively low, it is the great middle classes who in the aggregate pay the bulk of the taxes, because that's where the bulk of the income is. The cry of the radicals that we should make the rich pay the taxes and lift the burden from the back of the common man makes fine rhetoric, but it runs up against the fact that even a confiscatory 100 percent tax on all untaxed income over $1 million per family would yield less than $10 billion additional, compared to total federal tax collections exceeding $500 billion. Most of the well-to-do already pay substantial taxes. In 1975, for example, the top 1 percent of all families (those with taxable incomes over $60,000) paid 19 percent of all federal income taxes; the lowest 25 percent (with taxable incomes below $5,000) paid only .4 of 1 percent of all such taxes. If the government needs big increases in tax revenue, they will have to come from the general public, not just a super-rich few. But that doesn't say we may not want tax reform to close some loopholes that especially help the rich.

Loopholes and "Tax Expenditures"

Oil depletion allowances, cattle ranches, and tax-exempt bonds make the headlines as tax loopholes. The federal Internal Revenue Code is full of special deductions, exemptions, and provisions that permit some citizens and businesses to pay less than others. For example, nearly all transfer payments, such as Social Security, unemployment payments, and "welfare" benefits, are exempt from income taxes. Interest on state and municipal bonds is exempt. Capital gains are taxed at lower rates than regular income. Taxes paid to states and localities, interest on mortgages and other borrowed money, and losses on personal businesses, like farming, can be deducted from taxable income. The aged and the blind are given other special exemptions. Poor families are now completely exempt if their income is under $7,200 for a family of four.

These legal loopholes can be looked at as federal government subsidies to the affected taxpayers. They are sometimes called "tax expenditures." Table 26–1 shows the magnitude of these federal tax expenditures, or loopholes. They totaled $182 billion in 1980, $140 billion for individuals and $42 billion for corporations, according to rough Treasury estimates. This table does not include the additional personal deductions available to all taxpayers ($1,000 exemption for each individual), omission of imputed rent on owner-occupied homes, and the like. Addition of these further concessions would add another $100 billion or so to the tax expenditures. It is obviously a hazy line that divides general reductions (like the $1,000 personal exemption) from "loopholes."

You may be struck by the fact that most of the big "loopholes" in Table 26–1 aren't quite what you expected. They're exemptions and deductions that obviously help you and most other middle-income taxpayers, not just the rich few— exemption of Social Security and unemployment benefits, deduction of property and sales taxes and of interest payments on mortgages, and the like. Some of the "loopholes" mainly benefit the rich (for example, the lower tax rates on capital gains and the exemptions of interest on state and local bonds). But a big portion of the total goes to reduce the taxes of the vast middle and upper-middle classes. You read in the newspaper each year of a few super-rich individuals who somehow managed to pay very low income taxes. They managed this mainly by holding tax-exempt state and local bonds (where the exemption is intended mainly to help those governments borrow at lower interest rates), by having large deductible interest payments on money borrowed for personal business purposes (like real estate and cattle feeding), and by

TABLE 26–1
Federal Tax Loopholes, or Tax Expenditures, 1980

	AMOUNTS (IN BILLIONS)	
	CORPORATIONS	INDIVIDUALS
Lower tax rate on capital gains	$ 1.0	$ 22.3
Deductibility of state–local taxes paid		17.7
Deductibility of medical and health costs		15.7
Investment tax credit	15.4	3.1
Exemption of contributions to pension funds		15.1
Deductibility of consumer- and mortgage- interest payments		14.9
Exemption of Social Security and similar benefits		14.2
Deductibility of charitable gifts	1.0	8.0
Lower corporate tax for smaller firms	6.9	
Exemption of state–local bond interest	4.7	3.0
Other	13.5	25.7
Total	$42.5	$139.7

Source: Special Analysis of the U.S. Budget for 1980. Totals shown are of dubious validity because of interactions among the loopholes shown, which would change amounts of some if others were eliminated.

having large losses carried over from earlier years. But these are a tiny fraction of 1 percent of all high-income taxpayers, and to make them pay more will do more to assuage our feelings of inequity than to raise more money. The tax law now requires that such large-income receivers pay a minimum tax even though their exemptions and deductions would otherwise completely free them from tax.

Many Americans are outraged by such legal tax avoidance by the very rich. But it is no accident that Congress shows little enthusiasm for closing the big loopholes, in spite of the vivid rhetoric about their injustice to the common man. Most of the exemptions were put in to help special groups or causes—the Social Security exemption to help the elderly, the pension contribution exemption to help nearly all workers, and so on—and the many beneficiaries are understandably unenthusiastic about losing them. But it seems unlikely that Congress or the public would support annual subsidies of those amounts to all the groups concerned if they were openly visible cash grants.

Just about everyone agrees that the federal income tax code has become such a thicket of special provisions, understandable only to tax lawyers and accountants, that sweeping reform is desirable. Some observers propose eliminating all exemptions, and then applying a flat tax rate to all income, from whatever source received. Calculations vary, but with such a reform, a flat tax rate of about 18 percent on total income would produce as much revenue as the present tax with its rates ascending to 70 percent. Few Americans would advocate a flat federal tax rate for all income levels, but the example highlights the position we have got ourselves into through the increasing complexity of the tax code.

Taxes and Inflation

Inflation increases nearly everyone's real tax burden, unless Congress reduces tax rates. Inflation raises money incomes, thus moving income into higher tax brackets. For example, using 1979 personal income tax rates, your tax would have been about $3,500 on a $20,000 taxable income. But if the price level doubles over the next decade as it did over the last and your money income doubles to $40,000, your new tax would be about $11,000, although your real income is unchanged. You are subject to a 45 percent marginal tax rate, not the 28 percent one that Congress passed for $20,000 incomes in 1973.

Corporations' real taxes are similarly increased by inflation, even though real profits do not rise. Business's problem is compounded by two standard corporate accounting practices, which overstate profits even further in inflation. First, businesses can only charge depreciation equal to the original cost of their buildings and equipment. But with inflation, the cost of replacing the worn-out building or machine exceeds the original cost. Thus, businesses have undercharged their real costs, and must pay corporate income taxes on inflated "paper" profits. Second, inventories of materials bought today appreciate in price as inflation raises the price of the final product into which they are incorporated. Thus, the business, charging as a cost only the original low cost of the materials incorporated, records a juicy profit, and it pays a tax on this profit. But the profit is only a "paper" profit. When the firm replaces the materials inventory for the next round of production, it must pay a new, higher price for the replacement inventory, roughly equal to the increase in product price that generated the inflation-period profit. Thus, again the firm has had to pay a real tax on inflation-period paper profits.[4]

Inflation thus serves as a hidden tax increase on both individuals and businesses. Tax liabilities increase 16 percent for each 10 percent increase in the national income, without the unpleasant necessity of the government's having to raise tax rates. If we want to avoid this presumably unintended effect, we should "index" the tax system by increasing tax exemptions and adjusting tax brackets to eliminate inflation's effect of raising the real effective tax rate. And we should permit businesses to adjust their depreciation and inventory accounting practices to eliminate tax increases produced by inflation-induced paper profits. When inflation soars, as during the past decade, the distorting effects can be very large. For example, in 1977,

Harvard's Martin Feldstein estimated that inflation raised taxes on nonfinancial corporations by $32 billion, 69 percent of their real after-tax profits. In 1978, $43 billion of $178 billion of reported corporate profits were paper profits, unreal but subject to federal income tax. The impact varied among different corporations. For some, it raised the effective real tax rate to nearly 100 percent of profits.[5]

Canada, Israel, and Brazil have indexed their personal income tax laws to eliminate most of such inflation-induced real-tax increases, and accountants in many nations are moving toward at least informing the public how much of stated profits are real and how much paper in inflation periods. But this country has taken no steps to index our tax system. Instead, government spending has grown persistently, and Congress has periodically passed tax-reduction bills, lowering rates or raising exemptions for some taxpayers. Inflation-induced tax revenues have thus recently greatly reduced tax pressures for government fiscal restraint.

Taxes, Savings, Investment, and Growth

Keynes's ideas in the 1930s mobilized economists into a war on underconsumption and oversaving. Ever since the Great Depression, many economists and policymakers have treated saving as a kind of unlovely stepchild. More aggregate demand was the answer to the pervasive problem of unemployment, and saving diverted funds from spending on consumption.

But the modern neoclassical economists say it was a big mistake. Shortage of total aggregate demand is surely not now the economy's main problem. We need more saving, they say, to finance the investment in machines and factories that will keep the economy growing and the standard of living rising. A chronic high federal deficit drains away savings that would otherwise go into private investment, and inflation still further undercuts the incentives to save and invest. The U.S. saving rate (for consumers as a

---

[4]For accounting students: U.S. tax law now permits corporations to use LIFO (last-in, first-out) accounting for inventories, which eliminates part of the overtaxing problem on inventories when FIFO (first-in, first-out) accounting is used, as the text here describes.

[5]However, net debtors tend to gain from inflation, and, on average, nonfinancial corporations are net debtors. This effect, therefore, partially offsets the adverse tax effects of inflation on many businesses.

percent of disposable personal income and for consumers plus businesses as a percent of GNP) is the lowest since World War II, and the lowest by far of the major Western capitalist countries. U.S. consumer saving in the 1973–78 period was 6.2 percent of disposable income, in the United Kingdom 14 percent, in West Germany 15.3 percent, and in Japan 24.2 percent.

Many of these critics see the American tax system as loaded against saving and investment, and hence significantly responsible for our lackluster growth. We rely on progressive personal and corporate income taxes for far more of our tax revenue than do most other advanced nations, which rely more heavily on sales, excise, and related transactions taxes like the "value-added tax" (VAT).[6] These indirect taxes bear primarily on expenditures and consumption, leaving saving untaxed. Many other nations have no substantial corporate income tax, thus eliminating the double taxation of corporate profits, and many exempt capital gains completely or tax them very lightly. European companies are also given more freedom on how they handle depreciation, which reduces their effective tax rates.

There is little doubt that the U.S. tax system does bear relatively heavily on saving, investment, and business profits. But defenders of the present system argue that steps to lighten taxes on saving, investment, and profits would make the system less progressive and hence, at least to them, less equitable. If progressivity is the test of equity, then we face a real tradeoff between equity and incentives to save and invest, the foundations of economic growth.

The Limits to Taxation

Heavy taxation, and especially use of the wrong taxes, can seriously deter saving, investment, and economic progress. Some conservatives go further, and argue that we have reached the limit of our ability to pay taxes. Is there some definite limit to how much taxation the country can stand? If so, are we near it?

The general answer to both questions is no. But heavy taxation can indeed produce undesirable effects, and it is worthwhile to consider these possible effects more specifically. Economic analysis suggests that if more taxes are going to bring disaster, it will probably be through one or more of the following effects:

1. Heavier taxes may reduce the incentive to work. If the government takes too big a share of the incomes people earn, they may just quit working—or at least work less. But as long as something remains after taxes and most people still have much less than they want, the incentive to earn is a powerful one, even when earnings must be shared with the government. Still, for well-to-do people who feel less income pressure, the amount of work may fall off as tax rates rise. And as Chapter 25 noted, high effective marginal tax rates certainly may reduce the incentive of the poor on welfare to give up government benefits and take relatively low-pay jobs. The evidence we have doesn't settle the question. Most formal studies find little evidence that higher income taxes seriously reduce work until marginal rates become very high, as in the antipoverty programs we now have. But insensitivity to high rates runs contrary to many people's intuitive notions.

2. Heavier taxes may reduce the incentive to invest, especially if the taxes fall heavily on savings and profits, as the preceding section emphasized. If taxes fall differentially on one type of investment, investors will flee from it in droves. But taxation on all personal and corporate income leaves few alternatives to which investors can escape. They may turn to partnerships or individual enterprises, or to tax-exempt state and municipal bonds. But corporations are the only practical form of organization for most big businesses, partnership possibilities are limited (although widely used for real estate investments), and government bonds have limited appeal to profit-seeking investors. There's little evidence that wealthy individuals just consume more instead of investing. More likely, they complain bitterly about the low return on investment, and go on investing—*if* profits are good (which is the most fundamental stimulus to investment). But Yale's Bill Nordhaus has found

---

[6]VAT is similar to a general sales tax, but it is partially collected at each stage of manufacture instead of all from the final consumer. It is a major revenue source in most European nations.

that the *real after-tax* rate of return on capital has fallen from 10 to 5 percent during the generally inflationary post–World War II years, a fact that can hardly avoid being discouraging to investors.

3. Heavier taxes may lead to legal tax "avoidance." The law provides many loopholes for people who feel taxes heavily enough to hire a good tax lawyer. At last count, the Treasury listed about 100,000 tax counselors and tax lawyers whose business is to help on income tax returns. And the effort pays off. In spite of the 70 percent peak rate on incomes over $200,000, Treasury statistics show that less than 40 percent of all income above that level is collected in personal income taxes. What is worse, desire to avoid high tax rates often leads to distortions in investment and diversion of earning activities into special channels (like cattle feeding and oil drilling) that permit wealthy people to avoid peak tax rates under the law.

4. Heavier taxes may lead to illegal tax "evasion." The cases of France and Italy are often cited, where for years the government has been able to collect only a modest fraction of the taxes due because of the expense and energy required to run down the individuals who just don't pay. By and large, we Americans report and pay our taxes without being pursued. No good data are available. But one National Bureau of Economic Research estimate suggested that 5 percent of all wages and 30 percent of unincorporated-business incomes (farmers,

doctors, lawyers, and so on) went unreported. How much harder it would become to collect taxes at higher rates nobody knows. Introduction of widespread employer reporting and computerized checking of tax returns has made tax evasion increasingly difficult for most people, and most dividend and interest income is probably now caught.

5. Higher taxes may lead to inflation. This seems a perverted argument, since modern fiscal policy rests on the premise that higher taxes check inflation. But this argument is that if taxes get too high, everyone will raise his asking price to offset them—unions, businessmen, lawyers, farmers, everyone—especially as part of an inflationary spiral. You should quickly recognize that this behavior can result in continuing inflation only if the government helpfully puts in more money to validate the higher wages and prices by increasing total purchasing power. But there are great pressures on government to do just that, if the price of inaction or restraint is unemployment and recession.

What do all these points add up to? Not a conclusion that we can't stand any more taxation. Clearly, we can. Our standard of living is so high that we could readily divert more resources to the public sector and still have one of the highest private-consumption standards in the world. But more taxes and a bigger public sector may mean slower growth and a lower standard of living than we might otherwise have.

SUMMARY AND REVIEW

1. With taxes taking over 30 percent of the GNP annually, it is important to consider what taxes should be used and what the costs are of such a large tax burden. To judge intelligently, we must first clarify the criteria used in judging. Many economists suggest

emphasizing the effects of taxes on progress, freedom of individual choice, and equity.

2. All taxes tend to deter economic growth, but those bearing on saving, investment, and profits are

especially deterrent. Taxes should also tend to stabilize the growth of aggregate demand; personal and corporate income taxes are best on this score.

3. Taxes should be as nondistorting as possible on individuals' and businesses' spending decisions. Taxes that change relative prices tend to be most distorting.

4. "Ability to pay" is a widely accepted criterion of equity in taxation. It is generally consistent with use of progressive taxation (primarily personal and corporation income taxes) and with movement toward a more equal distribution on income. The "benefit" principle stresses that people should have to pay taxes only for benefits received. This is consistent with primary reliance on markets to produce an equitable distribution of income. Nearly everyone favors equal treatment of persons equally situated, but there are no generally agreed-on, objective measures of equality.

5. Many taxes are shifted by those who pay them to others—for example, the cigarette tax paid by manufacturers but mainly shifted on to consumers, who bear its final "incidence." Generally, a tax can be shifted only when, as a result of the tax, the taxpayer is able to obtain a higher price for what he sells, or to pay a lower price for something he buys. Personal income taxes and payroll taxes on employees are hard to shift; property, sales, and excise taxes are easier to shift, at least in part.

6. In the late 1970s, taxpayers across the nation "revolted" against ever-higher taxes and growing government. Observers disagree whether this reflected merely a transient unhappiness with higher taxes and big government, or marked the beginning of a new trend toward restraint on taxes and government economic activities. Inflation, slowing productivity increases, slowing real growth, and diversion of most of the increase in real output to government through inflation-induced tax increases all appear to have been important in causing widespread public dissatisfaction.

7. Tax reform has focused heavily on closing tax "loopholes" (or tax expenditures) in recent years. Although the public impression is that these mainly help the rich avoid paying their share of taxes, in fact most of them provide large benefits for the middle- and upper-middle income classes (see Table 26-1). which explains why Congress is reluctant to close many of the loopholes.

8. Rapid inflation has had a major impact on the tax system. By pushing money incomes into higher tax brackets, inflation increases personal and business tax liabilities without the need for Congress to raise tax rates. Inflation also increases the real tax burden on most corporations, because depreciation and inventory accounting rules lead to overstatement of taxable profits. Government is thus the major beneficiary of inflation.

9. There is considerable evidence that the current U.S. tax structure and government intervention in economic affairs are partly responsible for our reduced rates of saving and investment, and our slower economic growth during the past decade.

10. There is no simple limit to how much taxation any economy can stand, but a number of significant costs of heavy taxation can be identified.

New Concepts to Remember	benefit principle ability-to-pay principle progressive taxation regressive taxation "deadweight loss" incidence	tax shifting vertical equity horizontal equity incentive effects "tax expenditures" capital gain tax capitalization

For Analysis and Discussion

1. Are taxes too high? What is your criterion?
2. In raising funds for government expenditures, is it always more equitable to use taxes that bear more heavily on higher- than on lower-income groups? Would you impose all new taxes on the rich?
3. Some tax experts argue that taxes should be highly visible (like the personal income tax) in order to make citizens keenly aware of the taxes they are paying. Others argue that indirect and hidden taxes (for example, excise and sales taxes) are better because taxpayers don't feel the burden so strongly and are less unhappy about the costs of government services. Analyze these arguments. What are the main issues, and where do you stand on them?
4. What are tax loopholes? Should all tax loopholes be closed by Congress? (See Table 26-1 in answering.)

5. Should all tax rates be automatically reduced and all exemptions be automatically increased to eliminate inflation's increase in real-tax burdens? Do you see any disadvantages?

6. Suppose a new excise tax were imposed on the following products, at the producer's level:

   a. Steel (where there is mixed price leadership and competition, plus strong labor unions)

   b. Potatoes (where the market is highly competitive and little unionized labor is involved)

   c. Ladies' garments (where the market is highly competitive and there is a strong labor union)

   d. Refined oil and gasoline (where the market is oligopolistic and little strongly unionized labor is involved)

   Explain in each case whether you would expect the incidence of the tax to be on the consumer, labor in the industry, the producing firm, or some combination. (Remember your price theory from Chapters 6, 10, and 13–14.)

7. Assume a period of strong inflationary pressures as a result of government arms spending. Which of these alternatives would you consider the more equitable, and why?

   a. A general sales tax to balance the budget

   b. Inflation

8. Given a full-employment situation and the need for more taxes to finance increased government spending on national defense, what tax program would you propose to raise an additional $10 billion? Defend your program against likely criticism from those who would bear the major burden.

CASE 26   PROPOSED CONSTITUTIONAL AMENDMENT TO BALANCE THE BUDGET

The "tax revolt" of the late 1970s spawned a variety of proposals to amend the Constitution to require that the federal budget be balanced each year. Public opinion polls showed voters 6 to 1 in favor of a balanced budget. By 1979, 32 states had adopted some version of such a proposal, most of them directing Congress to propose a constitutional amendment for a balanced budget, some proposing a constitutional convention to develop such a proposal in case Congress did not do so. The details of such proposals varied widely. However, the following summary includes some of the major provisions included in many of the proposals.

Proposed constitutional amendment.

SECTION 1.   To protect the people of the United States against excessive taxation and government spending and to promote sound fiscal and monetary policies, the budget of the government of the United States shall be balanced each year, except as provided below.

1. The President shall submit to Congress each year a balanced budget for the forthcoming fiscal year.
2. Congress shall enact outlays for each fiscal year only to the extent that they will be covered by receipts from taxes enacted by Congress for that year.

SECTION 2.   In the event of a domestic or international emergency, the President may declare an emergency under the provisions of this amendment and Congress may authorize, by a 2/3 vote of both houses, a specified amount of emergency outlays in excess of regularly budgeted taxes for the current and immediately following fiscal years.

SECTION 3.   This article may be enforced by one or more members of the Congress in an action brought in the United States District Court for the District of Columbia, and by no other persons. The action shall name as defendant the Secretary of the Treasury of the United States [in some proposals, the President], who shall have authority over outlays by any part or agency of the government of the United States when required by a court order enforcing the provisions of this article. The order of the court shall not specify the particular outlays to be made or reduced. Changes in outlays necessary to comply with the orders of the court shall be made no later than the end of the second full fiscal year following the court order.

Criticisms.   Critics of the proposed amendment argued that it would do more harm than good. Among their main points were the following:

1. Requiring that the federal budget be balanced annually would often destabilize rather than stabilize the economy. It would remove the possible effectiveness of built-in cyclical stabilizers that now tend to keep the economy from swinging widely one way or the other, because tax collections rise or fall automatically as the economy expands or contracts. The proposed amendment would require the president and Congress to increase taxes and decrease spending whenever the economy went into a recession, and to decrease taxes and increase spending when it went into a boom. These are precisely opposite what is needed for stabilization.

2. State and local budgets have become very important in recent decades. This proposal would relate only to the federal budget, so it would omit about one-third of all government taxes and spending.

3. A balanced-budget amendment would impede the federal government's ability to deal with national emergencies in a timely and effective manner. It is impossible to anticipate the nature, timing, and costs of national security problems, natural catastrophes, and even development of booms and depressions. Under the proposal, urgent outlays would be delayed until the constitutional provisions involving two-thirds votes of each house, following special proclamations by the president, were carried out. There would be opportunity for disastrous, time-consuming logrolling, political haggling, and filibusters. The balanced-budget amendment would thus compromise U.S. leadership in the free world and our ability to maintain a healthy, growing economy.

4. Implementing the balanced-budget amendment would be extremely complex. (a) The president and Congress could plan for a balanced budget; there is no way they could be sure of attaining one. Thus the constitutional provision would not guarantee the desired objective. (b) The president submits in January of each year a budget for the following fiscal year, which begins in October and runs for twelve months thereafter. Thus, he is planning ahead 21 months in his proposals. There is no way of planning precisely a balanced budget with such a long lead time in a fluctuating and uncertain economy. (3) What budget should be balanced? Specifically, what expenditures should be included in the budget? How about budgeting for long-term construction projects, which will take several years for completion? (c) How could we be sure that Congress would in good faith try to balance the budget when it is so easy to estimate large tax revenues simply by assuming optimistic economic developments?

5. The amendment would carry serious enforcement problems. If, as would be inevitable, Congress did not succeed in balancing the budget, any congressman could throw the entire budget problem into the courts, which could then place on the secretary of the Treasury, or the president, the entire responsibility for altering federal outlays to balance the budget. This would give that individual enormous power in such cases. Would this concentration of power in the hands of the secretary of the Treasury or the president be either desirable or workable?

Your senator asks your advice on whether he should support or oppose this constitutional amendment. What is your advice?

CASE 27

SHOULD TAXES ON CORPORATE PROFITS BE REDUCED?

The following editorial appeared in the *Wall Street Journal*.[7]

Growth and ethics. Treasury Secretary Simon's specific proposals to reform the taxation of corporate dividends, offered to the Ways and Means Committee last week, represent a milestone in an absolutely vital national debate that ranges far beyond the technicalities of the tax code. Ultimately the question is whether society should emphasize economic growth or redistribution of income.

Speeding economic growth is the purpose of Secretary Simon's proposals. There is an extraordinarily strong relationship between capital investment and productivity; see Chart 1. Various compilations of these statistics show that, with the possible exception of Great Britain, the United States has the lowest rate of capital investment in the developed world. It needs to boost capital formation in order to provide jobs for the baby-boom workers now entering the labor market, to make the investments necessary for clean air and water, to pay the huge commitments of Social Security and private pensions, and to provide an increasing standard of living.

Secretary Simon proposes to boost capital formation by reducing the taxes on returns from capital. A greater after-tax return on investment will induce people to save more and invest more, thus providing the funds for future growth. Even in today's recession, an increase in after-tax return would provide a better yield on capital. It would not only speed the construction of productive resources for the future; it would also speed the rate at which existing resources are put back to work.

[7] The *Wall Street Journal*, August 5, 1975. Reproduced by permission.

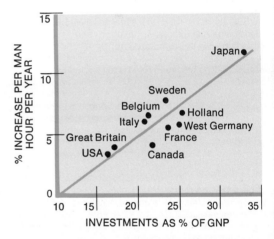

CHART 1
Production Increases and Investments
(Average values 1960–1970)
(Source: *Monthly Labor Review*, November 1973, OECD Economic Surveys.)

Specifically, the Secretary proposes to allow corporations a partial tax deduction for dividend payments, and to allow dividend recipients a partial tax credit. The effect would be to "integrate" the corporate and personal taxes, so that the shareholder would in effect be taxed as if he personally earned a pro rata share of the corporate earnings. At present, the income stream from the shareholder's invested capital is taxed twice, once through the corporate tax and again through the personal income tax on dividends.

366

Integration of corporate and personal taxes is already widespread in Europe. Indeed, the European Economic Committee has passed a resolution specifically urging all of its members to adopt such a system. It is one of a number of ways in which European nations tax returns from capital less heavily than does the United States. And their lower taxes on capital no doubt have much to do with their higher rates of capital formation.

When you want to reduce taxes on returns from capital, however, you are by definition talking about reducing the taxes of people who hold capital. Obviously, these will tend to be relatively wealthy people (though Secretary Simon pointed out that lower-income people living on savings would also receive some net benefit from his proposals). Thus the new proposals were immediately attacked as tax breaks for the rich. Rep. James Burke called them "a bonanza for the wealthy."

The nation is faced, then, with a trade-off between growth and redistribution. Does it want to split a smaller pie more equally or a larger pie less equally? We notice that for guidance on such matters, our liberal friends recently have been recommending *A Theory of Justice,* by Harvard philosopher John Rawls. The heart of his book is "the difference principle," which holds that inequality can be justified only if it works to the absolute benefit of the least advantaged.

For the record, we have little use for Professor Rawls' ideas, which stand in the dubious tradition of trying to draw morality from *a priori* principles rather than from reality as it exists. We do not believe a society can be meaningfully judged by any single criterion, and if forced to choose we would not pick Professor Rawls' criterion of equality but the ultimately opposing criterion of freedom. For all this, we do hope that his liberal followers apply his "difference principle" in judging Secretary Simon's proposals.

In helping the poor, economic growth has proved itself far more important than income redistribution. Even without changes in distribution over the last decade, growth has helped millions lift themselves out of poverty. In seeking more incentives for capital investment, Secretary Simon is pointing the way toward maintaining future growth. And an important result of those incentives, just as Mr. Rawls' recipe demands, will be a more rapid increase in the standard of living of the poor.

Do you favor or oppose Secretary Simon's proposal to integrate the personal and corporation income taxes, eliminating "double taxation" of dividends and reducing the effective tax rate on capital?

Part 5

The International Economy

International Trade and Lending

CHAPTER 27

n the "one world" of today, the close interdependence among nations is painfully obvious. The big economic issues fill the newspapers. Should we "buy American" and shut out foreign goods? Do Japanese-made imports threaten U.S. jobs? Do low foreign wages threaten our standard of living? Is the dollar weak, or strong?

Since prewar days, our sales of goods and services abroad have soared—from $4 billion in 1939 to $142 billion in 1978. Our imports grew even more—from $3 billion to $172 billion over the same period. The best estimates indicate that perhaps 7 to 9 million American workers owe their jobs directly to export sales, and exports come from every state in the union. Our exports of goods and services total only 9 percent of GNP, but to many industries, foreign trade is the blood of life—we export half our cotton crop and import almost all the tin and nickel we use. In manufacturing, one job out of eight produces for export. So does one acre of every three of our farmland. To most of the world, foreign trade is more urgent than it is to us. England must import most of her food or starve, and she can pay for these imports only by selling her exports abroad. And so it is with other nations—their living standards depend heavily on foreign trade.

In spite of the importance of foreign trade, governments have long followed policies that restrict rather than encourage such trade—tariffs, quotas, exchange controls. Prima facie, the case for international division of labor and exchange is as clear as it is in domestic affairs. On the surface, there would appear to be no reason to suppose that human welfare could be improved by obstructing the processes of specialization and exchange. Why, then, do laymen and lawmakers so often distrust foreign trade and favor the

FIGURE 27–1
Chief Merchandise Exports of the United States, 1978
Agricultural products and high-technology manufactures (machinery, autos, and chemicals) dominate our exports. (Source: U.S. Department of Commerce.)

RANK	COMMODITY	VALUE (BILLIONS OF DOLLARS)	% OF TOTAL EXPORTS	BILLIONS OF DOLLARS
1	Agricultural products	$29.9	21	
2	Nonelectrical machinery	29.8	21	
3	Automobiles and parts	14.5	10	
4	Chemicals	10.4	7	
5	Mfd. consumer goods (ex. autos)	9.8	7	
6	Computers and scientific equipment	7.3	5	
7	Electrical machinery	6.8	5	
8	Aircraft and parts	8.1	6	
9	Iron, steel and other metals	4.5	3	
10	Fuels and lubricants	8.7	6	

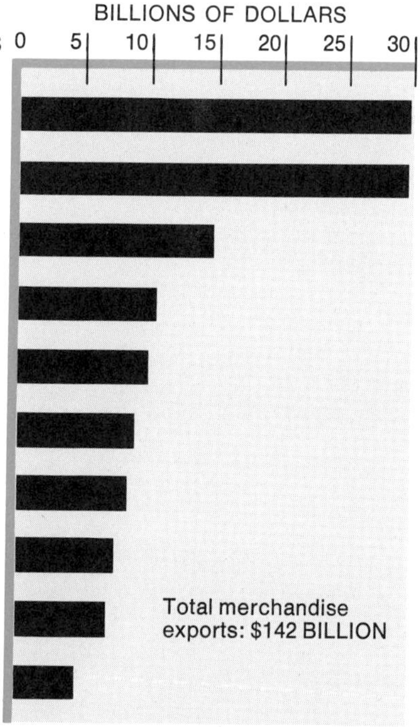

Total merchandise exports: $142 BILLION

tariff? Why have nations so often flown in the face of apparent economic reason? Nowhere in economics is there a better opportunity to apply relatively simple economic analysis to popular fallacies.

THE BALANCE OF TRADE

First consider our exports and imports of commodities. Figure 27–1 summarizes the goods we exported in 1978. The figures speak for themselves. They show the huge sales abroad by many of our basic industries, especially high-technology manufactured goods and farm products. It's easy to see why a lot of American farmers, businessmen, and workers are in favor of foreign trade. Figure 27–2 shows the huge volume of goods we imported in 1978. From this, it's equally easy to see why some businessmen and workers are opposed to foreign trade, which competes directly with them. But note too the huge expenditure on oil imports, reflecting the quintupling of oil prices by the OPEC countries.

Figure 27–3 throws more light on this comparison of exports and imports. During the prosperous 1920s, about 7 percent of all goods and services produced in the United States were exported. During the depression, this figure fell to around 4 percent. After World War II, the ratio rose sharply, then fell back, and has since climbed back up to 7–9 percent. Imports have usually been less than exports, but this has changed radically in the last few years, reflecting especially the oil situation.

In recent years, the pattern of U.S. foreign trade has changed significantly. Overall, the U.S.

FIGURE 27–2
Chief Merchandise Imports of the United States, 1979
Petroleum dominates our imports, followed by lower-technology consumer goods, raw materials, and foods. (Source: U.S. Department of Commerce.)

RANK	COMMODITY	VALUE (BILLIONS OF DOLLARS)	% OF TOTAL IMPORTS
1	Petroleum and products	$39.5	23
2	Automobiles and parts	24.3	14
3	Mfd. consumer goods (ex. autos)	14.6	8
4	Nonelectrical machinery	12.1	7
5	Iron and steel products	7.5	4
6	Electrical machinery	5.9	3
7	Coffee	5.1	3
8	Paper and pulp	4.0	2
9	Chemicals	3.8	2
10	Sugar	3.7	2

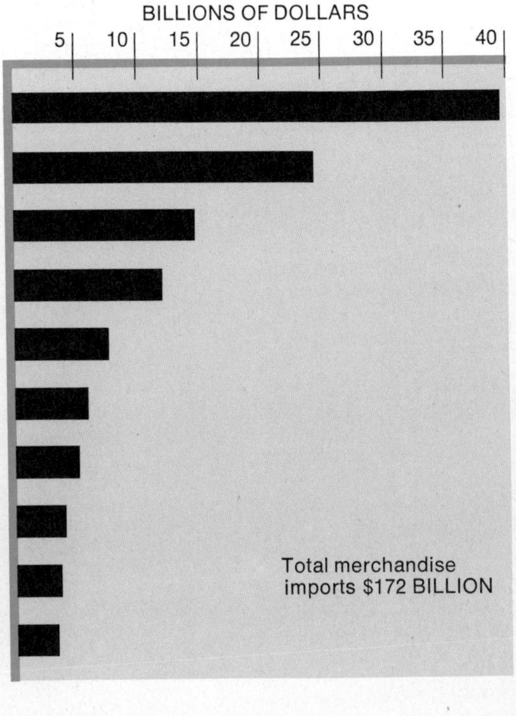

Total merchandise imports $172 BILLION

share has declined from about 20 to 10 percent of total world exports. Our exports have been increasingly concentrated in farm products (where we use the most advanced technology and heavy capital investment) and in high-technology manufactured products (computers, automatic machine tools, aircraft, and the like). Markets for lower-technology manufactures (textiles, iron and steel, and consumer durables) have been increasingly usurped by other nations with lower labor costs than ours.

There is still another interesting way of looking at our foreign-trade picture: Who are our main customers and suppliers? Figure 27–4 provides the answer. Canada dominates the list, and all Western Hemisphere nations combined constitute about 40 percent of our customers. But the OPEC (oil-producing) countries have shot up in importance since their spectacular price increases in 1974. Western Europe and Japan are the other major trading partners. Trade with the so-called developing countries, except for oil, accounts for only about one-fifth of the total.

The commodities we buy and sell abroad are the most visible part of our foreign trade, and the part most directly related to American jobs. But in Figures 27–3 and 27–4, $35 billion of American services abroad (shipping, banking, and the like) were added to the $142 billion of merchandise exports. To get a complete picture of the international "balance of payments," we will need to add "capital movements" (the transfer of short- and long-term investments). But first, let us consider the basic analytical case for free international trade and lending.

THE CASE FOR INTERNATIONAL TRADE

Florida produces oranges; Iowa produces corn and hogs; Pittsburgh produces steel. Each sells its products to the others. When each specializes in what it does best, we produce more in total and we all have more to consume than if we each tried to be self-sufficient. In the same way, Brazil sells coffee to us, we sell computers to England, England sells cloth to Brazil. When each nation specializes in what it does best and then exchanges with others, we produce more in total and we all end up consuming more than if we each tried to be self-sufficient.

The advantages to all in the first case—to Florida, Iowa, and Pittsburgh—are obvious. No one would question them. For each area to try to live alone, barring trade with the others, would be foolish. The advantages to nations from specialization and exchange are identical; more is produced for all to consume. The case for free international trade is that simple and that powerful. By using its total resources most efficiently through specialization and exchange, the world can move all the way out to its combined production-possibilities frontier. But it seems very hard for voters and legislators to see and to remember this simple truth.

FIGURE 27–3
U.S. Exports and Imports as a Percentage of GNP
U.S. exports of goods and services have exceeded imports, with rare exceptions. During recent years, both have risen substantially as percentages of GNP, and we have had a large import surplus. (Source: U.S. Department of Commerce.)

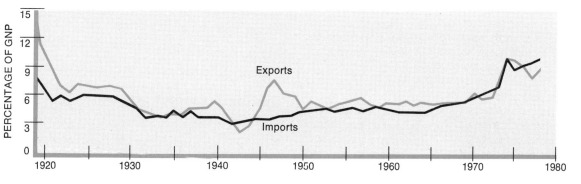

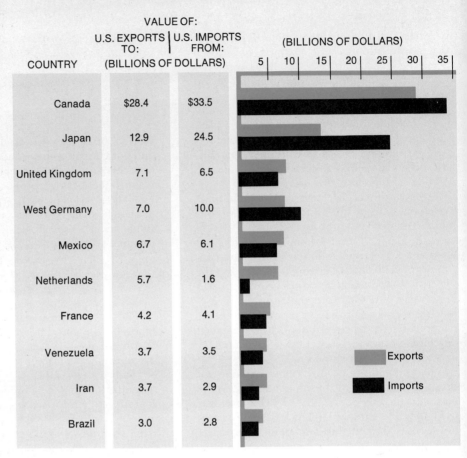

COUNTRY	VALUE OF: U.S. EXPORTS TO: (BILLIONS OF DOLLARS)	U.S. IMPORTS FROM: (BILLIONS OF DOLLARS)
Canada	$28.4	$33.5
Japan	12.9	24.5
United Kingdom	7.1	6.5
West Germany	7.0	10.0
Mexico	6.7	6.1
Netherlands	5.7	1.6
France	4.2	4.1
Venezuela	3.7	3.5
Iran	3.7	2.9
Brazil	3.0	2.8

FIGURE 27—4

U.S. International Trade, 1978

Canada is by far our best customer, followed by Japan. The European Common Market and Latin America are about equally important. "Developing" countries accounted for nearly 40 percent of our imports with oil included, only about 15 percent without oil. (Source: U.S. Department of Commerce.)

Interregional and International Trade

Nations (like regions within a nation) vary greatly in efficiency in producing different goods, differences that persist largely because of international immobility of resources. These differences arise largely out of five considerations:

1. Over the face of the earth, climatic and geographical conditions vary widely. Brazil is admirably suited for raising coffee, the lower Nile valley for cotton production. Texas and Oklahoma are great oil-producing centers. Chile has rich nitrate deposits. Such geographical and climatic differences alone would justify worldwide specialization.

2. Human capacities vary over the globe. Some groups are large and strong, suited for physical labor. Others excel at dexterity and manual skills. Still others stand out in enterprise and organizational ability. These differences may be due to long-standing racial characteristics, or to the varying political, social, and economic environment. Whatever the causes, they constitute a reason why international specialization and trade will be beneficial.

3. The accumulated supply of capital goods, as well as the kinds of capital, varies greatly from nation to nation. In some countries, centuries of accumulation have produced large supplies of capital—railroads, buildings, machinery,

and so forth. Examples are the United States and England. In other countries—for example, Greece and Nigeria—capital is scarce; they specialize in simple production that requires little elaborate equipment.

4. The proportions among different resources vary widely among nations. Australia has vast plains but relatively few people and capital goods. Therefore, she specializes in farm products that require a high proportion of natural resources to labor and capital goods. In England, land is scarce relative to human beings and capital. Therefore, she is best fitted for manufacturing and industry, even though her soil may be as good as Australia's for wheat growing.

5. In addition to these "economic" considerations, great differences exist in the political and social climates in different countries. In countries with stable government, vast industrial organizations requiring large long-period capital commitments are likely to grow. In less-developed, badly governed areas, conditions virtually prohibit mass-production industry. A hustling, mechanically minded nation like the United States could hardly be expected to be satisfied again with a small-unit, predominantly rural economy, any more than we would expect South Sea islanders to be happy, efficient auto makers.

The Principle of Comparative Advantage

Given these differences among nations, it is clear that some international trade will be advantageous. But how far each nation should specialize and how much international trade is to its advantage is not so obvious. Disregard costs of transport between nations for the moment in answering that question.

The greatest possible advantage for all from trade will be obtained if each nation specializes in what it can do relatively most cheaply. In the simple case of Iowa and Florida, where the cost advantage of each in its representative products is clear and large, and with only two products, Iowa should raise all the corn, Florida all the oranges. The greatest total of corn plus oranges will be obtained in that way. But such money-cost comparisons don't provide much guidance when it comes to comparing costs between different nations with different monetary units, different proportions of the factors of production, different qualities of labor, and different productive techniques. Perhaps as between coffee and computers, Brazil has an "absolute" advantage in the former, the United States in the latter. But even in such an extreme case, it is hard to be precise on just what these absolute advantages mean. When less-striking differences are considered, such as textiles in the United States and in England, the difficulty of such comparisons becomes insurmountable. Monetary comparisons mean little, because different monetary units are used in the two countries.

But fortunately, as David Ricardo demonstrated a century and a half ago, the advantages of international trade don't depend on such absolute-cost calculations. Even if one nation were more efficient than another in the production of everything, it would still be to the advantage of both to specialize and engage in international trade. Each, and both combined, will gain most when each specializes in producing those commodities for which its comparative, or relative, costs of production are lowest.

Let us first illustrate this "principle of comparative advantage" with a case involving only two countries and two commodities—the United States and France, producing wheat and cloth. To simplify, let us assume that labor is the only factor of production (or that a day of labor is a shorthand measure of a bundle of land, labor, and capital used in producing things). Assume further that in the United States, one man-day can produce one bushel of wheat or one yard of cloth. Thus, in the United States we can obtain one bushel of wheat by giving up the production of one yard of cloth, and vice versa.[1]

Assume that in France, one day of labor also produces one bushel of wheat, but only a half yard of cloth. In this sense, American labor is more productive than French labor, but, as we shall see, this is not the critical factor. The critical factor is that in France, two bushels of wheat must be given up to produce one more yard of cloth. This situation is shown in Table 27–1.

---

[1]Temporarily assume that wheat and cloth are industries of constant costs both here and abroad. That is, unit costs of production do not increase or decrease as output in the country changes. This is sometimes called the assumption of constant returns to scale.

TABLE 27–1
Comparative Costs of Production, in Man-Days

	U.S.	FRANCE
Wheat (1 bushel)	1	1
Cloth (1 yard)	1	2

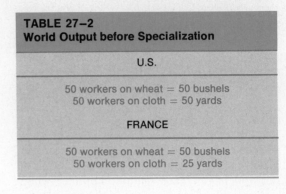

TABLE 27–2
World Output before Specialization

U.S.
50 workers on wheat = 50 bushels
50 workers on cloth = 50 yards

FRANCE
50 workers on wheat = 50 bushels
50 workers on cloth = 25 yards

First suppose that there is no trade between France and the United States; each country produces all its own wheat and cloth. Will it pay them to begin specializing and trading? The answer is yes. In the United States, we can obtain one more bushel of wheat by giving up one yard of cloth. But in France they can obtain two more bushels of wheat by giving up one yard of cloth. Therefore, there will be an increase in total world output if the United States uses more of her labor to produce cloth while resources in France are shifted to raising wheat.

A simple example may help demonstrate this point. Assume that there are 100 workers each in the United States and France. At the beginning, in each country, half are producing wheat and half cloth. Total world output is 100 bushels of wheat and 75 yards of cloth, as in Table 27–2.

Now suppose that we specialize completely in cloth and France specializes completely in wheat, as the principle suggests. As Table 27–3 shows, the result is 100 bushels of wheat and 100 yards of cloth, an increase of 25 yards of cloth to divide between us.

It might appear from these tables that the United States has an absolute advantage in efficiency over France, since in France it takes two man-days to produce a yard of cloth, whereas here it takes only one. But it is easy to show that these absolute differences are not the critical point at all. Suppose, instead, that we had begun with the assumption that French labor was the more efficient—that one man-day in France would produce two bushels of wheat or one yard of cloth. Total world output can be larger because of the higher productivity of French labor. But work out the new example, and you will see that it pays each country to specialize where its comparative advantage is higher, just as before, and then to exchange part of its production.

The principle is that gain in total world output is possible from specialization and trade if the cost ratios of producing two commodities are different in different countries. This same principle would have applied in the example above had the cost ratios for producing wheat and cloth been 3 to 2 in the United States and 5 to 1 in France, or any other set of different ratios. To repeat, absolute costs in the two countries are not relevant. It would make no difference, for example, if U.S. labor were vastly more efficient than French. Total output could be increased by further U.S. specialization in cloth, because our comparative advantage is greater in producing cloth. This is the principle of comparative advantage: Total output will be maximized when each nation specializes in the lines where it has the greatest comparative advantage or the least comparative disadvantage.[2]

From this statement we can also tell how far it is advantageous to carry specialization and trade. Gain from trade is possible until the cost ratios of producing the two commodities are the same in both the United States and France. With constant costs, complete specialization would occur; the cost ratios never become equal, because they are fixed by the constant-cost as-

---

[2]Note that we use this principle all the time in our domestic economic life. Suppose that in a business firm, the president is better at typing than any of the secretaries are. Should he do his own typing? Obviously not. He should specialize where his comparative advantage is greatest, in managing the firm, leaving the typing to his secretary even though she types more slowly than he does. Or suppose a fine surgeon is also the best driver in the community. Should he drive the hospital ambulance instead of spending all his available time in the hospital operating room?

TABLE 27–3
World Output after Specialization

U.S.
100 workers on cloth = 100 yards

FRANCE
100 workers on wheat = 100 bushels

sumption. But now, realistically, drop the assumption of constant costs. As production of cloth increases in the United States, the cost of producing cloth will rise relative to that of producing wheat. In France, as it produces more wheat, the cost of producing wheat will rise relative to that of producing cloth. Finally, at some levels of output, the cost ratios will become identical in the two countries. Thereafter, there is no advantage in further specialization and exchange, since no further increases in total output can be obtained. (Realistically, we should introduce transport costs between nations, which would correspondingly reduce the potential gains from international exchange.)

When the law of comparative advantage is generalized to many countries and thousands of products, no new principles are introduced, but the picture becomes more complex. Gain will still be maximized if each country specializes in those goods and services where its comparative advantage is greatest or its comparative disadvantage least, and if this specialization is carried to the point where the cost ratios involved are equal in all countries producing the products. In any given country, production of many products will never take place, because the country's comparative disadvantage in their production is so great and because of international transportation costs. Most nations will find it advantageous to produce a variety of products.

You may have noted that thus far we have said nothing about the division of the gains from international trade. For example, in the case of Table 27–3, will France or the United States get the extra 25 yards of cloth obtained by specialization, or will they be divided between the two nations? In most cases, the gain will be divided, based on a complex set of considerations, mainly the relative cost structures of the countries involved. In extreme cases, it is possible to demonstrate logically that all the gain would accrue to one country, but this requires some highly unlikely assumptions.

The Law of Comparative Advantage, Free Trade, and the Price System

In world markets, the search for profits and the price system tend to bring about this international specialization and optimal allocation of resources in each country automatically. If we are relatively inefficient in producing coffee but very efficient in producing computers, American producers are going to have a tough time competing with Brazil in the world's coffee markets, but we'll beat out other computer manufacturers in the marketplace. Under an international free-trade system, in each country the greatest profits can be obtained by producing those commodities most desired by consumers at home and abroad where our costs are relatively lowest. If our comparative advantage is great in producing computers, this fact will be reflected in high returns to resources in the computer industry. If our comparative advantage is low in producing spices, American spice producers will be unable to pay wages high enough to bid resources away from the more efficient computer industry, since world prices for spices are set by relatively efficient East Indian production. Thus, under free trade, the resources of each nation would be drawn into its most efficient industries. No one would manage or direct international trade. Each producer would simply try to maximize profits, and each buyer would simply buy where the price was lowest. The central mechanism is the same as domestically with Adam Smith's "invisible hand." The principle of comparative advantage is central in both domestic and international trade.

Worldwide Multilateral Trade

To provide the full advantages of international specialization and exchange, trade must be multinational or "multilateral." That is, goods and services must move freely among all nations. This eliminates the necessity that the exports and imports between any two nations must be in balance, which would severely restrict the degree of international specialization. Vis-à-vis all other countries combined, a nation's exports and imports must roughly balance (omitting capital movements), but with multinational trade, this balance may result from a combination of export and import imbalances with different individual nations, taking full advantage of the individual-country comparative advantages involved.

This fact is illustrated by Figure 27–5, which shows the pattern of multinational trade among the major areas of the world. The United States, for example, exports more to Europe, Canada, and nontropical Latin America than it imports from them. But our imports from the tropical nations exceed our exports to them. Our international trade is multinational, in fact much more complex than the patterns of exchange shown in Figure 27–5.

U.S. FOREIGN LENDING

A major development of the postwar world has been the massive growth of U.S. lending abroad. Our large postwar balance-of-payments deficits have been attributable mainly to our heavy private foreign investments and to government loans and foreign-aid programs (including military aid), since we had an export surplus on trade and services consistently until 1972. U.S. investors have acquired ownership of a huge volume of assets abroad—factories, oil refineries, assembly plants—through foreign securities and multinational corporations.

Figure 27–6 shows how U.S. investment abroad has burgeoned since 1929. The three lower areas in each bar are direct American investments. The area at the top is investment in foreign securities, including short-term investments. Even allowing for inflation, the rise has been phenomenal.

Figure 27–7 shows the picture in terms of annual new U.S. investments abroad and annual earnings on our investments abroad. The earnings bars show that our earnings each year on investments abroad now clearly exceed new investments abroad. Foreign investments are profitable business. As with domestic firms, a big part of new U.S. investment abroad each year consists of plowing back earnings on the investments already there. About three-fourths of U.S. private investment since World War II has been in the developed nations (mainly Canada and Western Europe), about one-fourth in the less-developed economies.

Figure 27–7 also suggests a central fact about foreign lending. To collect earnings and amortization on loans and investments abroad, we must either accept payment through importing

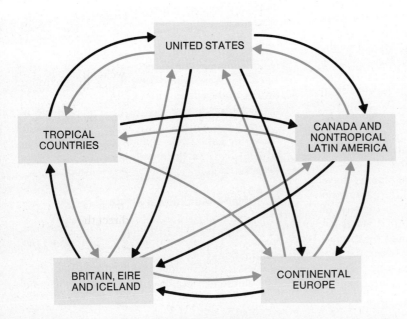

FIGURE 27–5
The Complex Pattern of Multilateral World Trade
The grey arrows show the directions of flow of exports where they exceed imports, while the blue arrows represent the net imports moving in the opposite directions. (Source: United Nations.)

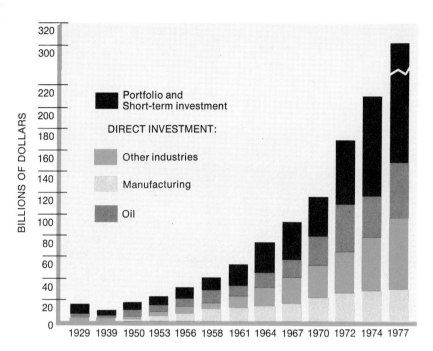

FIGURE 27–6
Total U.S. Private Investment Abroad
Since the 1930s, U.S. private investment abroad has soared. Petroleum is the biggest single industry, but manufacturing has grown much faster in recent years, and total manufacturing far exceeds oil investment. (Source: U.S. Department of Commerce.)

goods and services or be prepared continually to reinvest the principal and earnings abroad. Government and private lending abroad has been a major factor in permitting us to continue our traditional export surplus of goods and services. If we ever stop our annual net lending abroad, we will be able to collect our earnings and repayments on principal only by running a large net import surplus of goods and services.

Foreign investments in the United States have also grown rapidly recently, especially since the OPEC oil price increases since 1974. Excluding foreign official dollar holdings, foreign investments here totaled about $175 billion in early 1978, compared to about $350 billion of private U.S. investments abroad.

THE CASE FOR INTERNATIONAL LENDING

Society benefits when individuals and institutions save and invest, because useful capital

goods are thereby accumulated. The saver gains individually from the return on his investment, and society gains from the increased efficiency of mechanized production. Both the saver and society gain most when savings are invested where their productivity is highest.

In the domestic economy, we mainly trust the price system to allocate savings to the most desirable investments. Those who save invest their funds (either directly or through such institutions as banks) where the combination of safety, liquidity, and rate of return seems most attractive. Because the rate of return tends to be highest where investments fulfill the strongest consumer demands, savings are drawn into those industries where consumers most want output increased. Consumer choices direct the allocation of savings among investments.

Internationally, as domestically, society is generally best off if savings are allocated where their marginal productivity is greatest. International loans are "better" than domestic loans when the anticipated rate of return on them

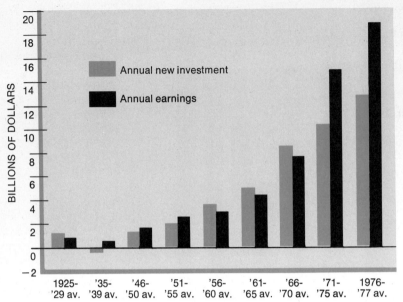

FIGURE 27–7
Annual New Investment and
Earnings on U.S. Private
Capital Abroad
Annual new U.S. private
investment abroad has grown
rapidly, but returns on such
investments abroad have grown
even faster in recent years.
(Source: U.S. Department of
Commerce.)

(including liquidity and risk allowance) is greater. For decades, both England and the New World gained from heavy loans by Britishers to the rapidly developing Western Hemisphere. British lenders gained by receiving good returns on their investments; U.S. borrowers gained by getting capital to combine with the plentiful natural resources of the New World. The overall result was a faster growth in world output, divided between the United States and Britain. Today, the United States is the big international lender, but the general result is similar. Internationally, as domestically, lending may be unwise if the loan is unsafe or undesirably illiquid, and the risk is often greater on international investments. But here again, national political boundaries do not invalidate basic economic principles: We gain as individuals and as nations from having savings invested where their marginal productivity is highest.

THE FOREIGN-TRADE MULTIPLIER AND DOMESTIC EMPLOYMENT

Thus far, we have implicitly assumed that full employment prevails, and that the problem is to allocate our fully employed resources most efficiently. But in the real world of intermittent underemployment and inflation, international trade can affect the level of domestic employment and output as well.

Export sales provide jobs, just as domestic sales do. Conversely, imports replace domestic jobs. Thus, the net excess of exports over imports ("net exports" in the GNP accounts) is one component of aggregate demand that calls forth production and employment. And like any other autonomous expenditure, such as private investment, it may have a multiplier effect on GNP. Thus, the net export balance produces jobs in its own right and also has a further multiplier effect, creating additional income and jobs.

But this "foreign-trade multiplier" is smaller than the regular domestic-investment multiplier, because our increased exports, by increasing domestic income, will indirectly induce more imports into the United States. We import more when our incomes rise, and the foreign-trade multiplier is reduced by the extent to which induced imports offset the original export balance. Imports are a "leakage" in addition to saving and taxes when we add the foreign-trade multiplier to the domestic multipliers.

This reasoning makes it easy to see why nations with unemployment want to increase their net export balances, by increasing exports and/or reducing imports. Either way, the result will be more jobs at home. Creation by this country of a net export surplus is a way of exporting unemployment to the nation that buys more U.S. goods or has its exports to the United States cut. For this reason, it is often called a "beggar-my-neighbor" policy for increasing domestic employment.

But if any nation tries to export its unemployment in a world of widespread unemployment (as in the 1930s)—say, by raising its tariffs to shut out imports—it is easy to predict the result. Rather than import unemployment, other nations will retaliate by raising their tariffs too. Obviously, it is not possible for all nations to increase their export surpluses, for each export is someone else's import. Thus, the main result of import restrictions aimed at exporting unem-

ployment is likely to be retaliation abroad and a shrinking total volume of international trade, with no more than transient gains to any nation. This was exactly the result in the 1930s, when snowballing trade restrictions cut world trade to a small fraction of its level during the 1920s, and everyone was worse off. But the lure of creating jobs by shutting out imports is great, and nearly every nation has tried it sometime during the post–World War II period.

THE BALANCE OF PAYMENTS

Table 27–4 summarizes the complete U.S. balance of payments in 1978, including international investments and short-term capital move-

TABLE 27–4
U.S. Balance of International Payments, 1978[a]

	AMOUNT (IN BILLIONS)	
I. U.S. exports (payments due United States):		
Merchandise	$141.8	
Services and foreign travel in U.S.	34.7	
Income from investments abroad and misc.	41.5	
Total exports		$218.0
II. U.S. imports (payments due to foreigners):		
Merchandise	−176.0	
Services and U.S. travel abroad	− 31.3	
Income on foreign investments here and misc.	− 21.6	
Total imports		−228.9
III. U.S. government grants		− 5.1
IV. Balance on current account		**−16.0**
V. Foreign assets in U.S.: Official	31.0	
Private	29.3	
Total		63.3
VI. U.S. assets abroad: Official	− 3.4	
Private	−55.0	
Total		−58.7
VII. Balance on capital account		**4.6**
VIII. Errors and unrecorded transactions		11.4
Memoranda: Increase in foreign official claims on U.S. dollars		31.1
Increase in foreign private short-term claims on U.S. dollars		20.4
Increase in total dollar balances of foreigners		$ 51.5

[a]Minus sign shows payment from the United States. Minor items are omitted. Some items do not add to totals, because of omissions and errors totaling $11.4 billion.
Source: U.S. Department of Commerce, preliminary data

ments, as well as exports and imports of goods and services. Basically, the table shows what we paid to foreigners and what they paid to us. The minus items are payments from the United States to foreigners; the other items, payments from foreigners to us.

The lines are largely self-explanatory. The top section shows our exports, then our imports, of goods and services. Then V and VI show capital movement (short- and long-term investments) by foreigners in the United States and by U.S. individuals and businesses abroad.

Lines IV and VII show major "balances" in our international affairs during 1978. We imported $16 billion more goods and services than we exported; thus, we had a $16 billion deficit "on current account," involving an outflow of $16 billion to pay for that difference. Addition of $4.6 billion net of capital movements to the U.S. completes the balance of payments. We could also have shown separately the "trade deficit"; on merchandise alone, we imported $30.2 billion more than we exported, although note that the trade deficit is already included in the current-account deficit on line IV.

The memorandum items at the bottom show the way foreign central banks (official government institutions) and private individuals and businesses used the billions of dollars they received in 1978. After paying for U.S. exports to them and making $5.6 billion new long-term investments in the United States, both foreign central banks and private individuals and businesses built up their dollar balances—by $31 and $20 billion, respectively. (Short-term investments in U.S. Treasury bills, bank accounts, and others having a maturity of less than one year are often

called "dollar balances.")[3] These dollar balances, of course, represent future foreign purchasing power over U.S. current output or investment in U.S. factories, land, and other businesses. Foreigners held most of their increased assets in the United States in the form of dollar balances.

You may be struck by the fact that gold does not appear on the table. Until recently, foreigners might have chosen to convert part or all of their dollar balances into gold at the U.S. Treasury. But in 1973, the U.S. government announced it would no longer convert dollars into gold. The government now simply holds its gold stock as part of its monetary reserves.

The Balance of Payments and the Balance of Trade

Table 27–4 points up the importance of being clear about the difference between the "balance of payments" and the "balance of trade." The balance of payments includes all payments between the countries concerned (all of Table 27–4). The balance of trade includes only merchandise imports and exports. Popular discussion, which generally runs in terms of balance of trade, is often confused because of the failure to consider the entire balance of payments. U.S. capital outflows (short- and long-term investments overseas) have been huge since World War II. Even when netted against private investment flows to the United States, they have frequently exceeded our balance-of-trade surplus, thus producing an overall U.S. balance-of-payments deficit. Individual components of the balance of payments may be in deficit for long periods, depending on the behavior of other components.

---

[3]Foreigners would earn no interest on their dollar balances if they simply held dollars. Instead, they invest their dollars in

highly liquid short-term investments or bank accounts that draw interest.

SUMMARY AND REVIEW

1. U.S. exports total about 8–9 percent of our GNP. Imports are roughly equal. But foreign trade is vitally important to some industries and areas. We import about half our petroleum, nearly all our tin and

nickel. We export about one-third of our total farm production, and a big portion of the products of our high technology, capital intensive industries. Some 7–9 million U.S. jobs depend on the export market.

2. Canada and the Western Hemisphere countries generally are our best customers, but our exports go all over the world, and the sources of our imports are equally widespread.

3. The basic case for free international trade is the same as for free domestic specialization and division of labor, followed by voluntary exchanges of wanted goods and services. When each nation specializes in what it does best and then exchanges with others, total production is maximized and there is more to be consumed by all than if each nation tries to be partially or completely self-sufficient. According to the "principle of comparative advantage," total output of wanted goods will be maximized when each nation specializes in producing those products where it has the greatest comparative, or relative, advantage—that is, where its comparative, or relative, costs of production are lowest. In principle, further specialization and trade will be advantageous as long as the cost ratios of producing different commodities are different in different countries.

4. Optimal specialization and exchange will tend to occur under a free-market, competitive price system, internationally as domestically.

5. To provide the full advantages of international specialization and exchange, trade must be multinational (multilateral).

6. The case for free international lending and investment of capital across national boundaries is the same—that total wanted output will be maximized when each dollar (resource) is used where its expected marginal productivity is greatest, and this will tend to be achieved by investors seeking to maximize returns in free markets.

7. Increased net exports (through increased exports or decreased imports) may create more jobs in the exporting country, directly and through a foreign-trade multiplier. But "beggar-my-neighbor" attempts to create domestic jobs by taking jobs away from workers in other countries are likely to call forth retaliation and result in less trade and fewer jobs in both countries.

8. The balance of payments sums up all the international payments made by and to a nation. The main categories are goods and service ("current account") items, and capital movements (short- and long-term international investments). Economists often calculate a nation's "deficit" or "surplus" of payments for each of these categories and for all payments combined. A U.S. deficit in total payments on current account plus private capital movement will lead other nations to accumulate dollar balances received in payment for these deficits. In recent years, the United States has run large payments deficits, and both central banks and private individuals and businesses abroad have accumulated large dollar balances.

9. It is important to distinguish between the balance of trade (goods only) and the entire balance of payments.

New Concepts to Remember

International economics is essentially basic economics applied to the international scene. But there are some important new terms and concepts.

principle of comparative
   advantage
comparative costs
balance of payments
balance of trade

foreign-trade multiplier
multilateral trade
capital movements
beggar-my-neighbor policies
dollar balances

For Analysis and Discussion

1. State the basic case for specialization, division of labor, and free exchange. Are there reasons why this case applies differently within a nation and across national boundaries?
2. "Large, multinational, profit-seeking firms like the auto and oil companies obviously cannot be counted on to invest internationally so as to maximize the interest of the general public." Analyze this argument. What is your test of optimal choice among investments?
3. What industries in your area are most affected by international trade? (See Figures 27–1 and 27–2.) How important is such trade to your immediate area?
4. Suppose U.S. imports were reduced by one-half due to new tariffs or import quotas. What effect would this probably have on jobs in export industries in your area? (See Figure 27–1.)
5. Explain the difference between the balance of payments and the balance of trade. On which do the data in Figure 27–1 through 27–4 throw the most light?

6. "Anyone who believes in free trade ought to believe in free international migration of labor, unrestricted by immigration barriers." Do you agree? Why, or why not?

7. What is the principle of comparative advantage? How does it relate to your answer to question 1 above?

8. Why is multilateral trade more advantageous than bilateral trade?

9. If you were wealthy, would you invest any of your money abroad? Why, or why not?

10. Why is the foreign-trade multiplier different from the domestic-investment multiplier?

11. "Although other nations may understandably object if we raise tariffs on their products to create jobs here, they should have no objection if the U.S. government provides special tax benefits to U.S. exporters, who will then reduce product prices to buyers abroad." Do you agree with this argument? Analyze it.

CASE 28

ROBINSON CRUSOE, FRIDAY, AND THE GAINS FROM TRADE

Frederick Bastiat was one of the liveliest of the nineteenth-century economic liberals. He delighted in little vignettes that exposed the essence of economic issues. The following, focused on the problem of gains from international trade, is one of these.

In Bastiat's tale, Robinson Crusoe and Friday are marooned on their island. Each morning, they hunt for six hours and bring back four baskets of game. In the evening, they work in the garden for six hours and obtain four baskets of vegetables.

One day a longboat lands on the Isle of Despair. A handsome foreigner disembarks and is admitted to the table of our two recluses. He tastes and highly praises the products of the garden, and, before taking leave of his hosts, he addresses them in these words:

"Generous islanders, I dwell in a land where game is much more plentiful than it is here, but where horticulture is unknown. It will be easy for me to bring you four baskets of game every evening, if you will give me in exchange only two baskets of vegetables."

At these words, Robinson and Friday withdraw to confer, and the debate they have is too interesting not to report here in full:

FRIDAY: Friend, what do you think of it?

ROBINSON: If we accept, we are ruined.

FRIDAY: Are you quite sure of that? Let us reckon up what it comes to.

ROBINSON: It has all been reckoned up, and there can be no doubt about the outcome. This competition will simply mean the end of our hunting industry.

FRIDAY: What difference does that make if we have the game?

ROBINSON: You are just theorizing? It will no longer be the product of our labor.

FRIDAY: No matter, since in order to get it, we shall have to part with some vegetables.

ROBINSON: Then what shall we gain?

FRIDAY: The four baskets of game cost us six hours of labor. The foreigner gives them to us in exchange for two baskets of vegetables, which take us only three hours to produce. Therefore, this puts three hours at our disposal.

ROBINSON: You ought rather to say that they are subtracted from our productive activity. That is the exact amount of our loss. *Labor is wealth,* and if we lose one-fourth of our working time, we shall be one-fourth less wealthy.

FRIDAY: Friend, you are making an enormous mistake. We shall have the same amount of game, the same quantity of vegetables, and—into the bargain—three more hours at our disposal. That is what I call progress, or there is no such thing in this world!

ROBINSON: You are talking in generalities! What shall we do with these three hours?

FRIDAY: We shall do *something* else.

ROBINSON: Ah! I have you there. You are unable to mention anything in particular. *Something else, something else*—that is very easy to say.

FRIDAY: We can fish; we can decorate our cabin; we can read the Bible.

ROBINSON: Utopia! Who knows which of these things we shall do, or whether we shall do any of them? . . . Moreover, there are political reasons for rejecting the selfish offers of the perfidious foreigner.

FRIDAY: Political reasons!

ROBINSON: Yes. First, he is making us these offers only because they are advantageous to him.

FRIDAY: So much the better, since they are so for us too.

ROBINSON: Then, by this traffic, we shall make ourselves dependent upon him.

FRIDAY: And we will make himself dependent on us. We shall have need of his game; and he, of our vegetables; and we shall all live in great friendship.

ROBINSON: You are just following some abstract system.

The dispute goes on for a long time and leaves each one, as often happens, unchanged in his convictions. However, since Robinson has great influence over Friday, he makes his view prevail; and when the foreigner comes to learn how his offer has been received, Robinson says to him:

"Foreigner, in order for us to accept your proposal, we must be very sure about two things:

"First, that game is not more plentiful on your island than on ours; for we want to fight only *on equal terms.*

"Second, that you will lose by this bargain. For, as in every exchange there is necessarily a gainer and a loser, we should be victimized if you were not the loser. What do you say?"

"Nothing," says the foreigner. And, bursting into laughter, he reembarks in his longboat."[4]

---

1. Who is right, Crusoe or Friday?
2. Do you see any fallacies in Friday's reasoning?
3. Is it true that in every exchange, there is necessarily a gaining and a losing party?

---

[4]Adapted from Frederic Bastiat, *Economic Sophisms* (New York: Van Nostrand Reinhold, 1964), pp. 245–48.

CASE 29 MULTINATIONAL CORPORATIONS

The years since World War II have seen a spectacular growth in the importance of multinational corporations, which have been called the most successful innovation in international relations since Adam Smith. "Multinational" corporations are companies with production and distribution facilities in several or many countries; often, ownership of the subsidiaries in different countries is shared with nationals of those countries. Thus, multinationals (sometimes called "transnationals") differ from the "international" companies that for many years have exported part of their production for sale abroad. In 1950, for example, U.S. direct investment abroad through multinationals was $11 billion; today, it is nearly $175 billion. Ford Motor Company, for example, has some 40 foreign-based subsidiaries, which produce and sell about 30 percent of its total output and provide jobs for about 30 percent of its 465,000 employees.

In 1977, the fifty largest industrial companies in the world, nearly all multinationals, had sales exceeding a half-trillion dollars, equal to about 10 percent of the world's total GNP. General Motors' sales are greater than the GNPs of most of the world's smaller nations. The table shows the ten largest industrial multinationals. Strikingly, seven of the top ten were oil companies. Seven of the top ten were headquartered in the United States, but only 22 of the top 50 were American. British, German, and Japanese companies were prominent on the list. The world's largest banks are similarly multinational.

On profits, the ten top multinationals did better than other industrial companies. But this was due partly to the performance of National Iranian Oil, the only government-owned, nonmultinational on the list. Of every dollar of sales, 87 cents was profit. This compared to about 5 or 6 cents for the private oil giants.

Why? Why have multinationals grown so? Why do they produce abroad rather than producing at home and exporting part of their products? Fundamentally, because it's cheaper the multinational way. Adam Smith might disapprove of the huge size of some multinationals, but he would surely commend their efficiency in shifting capital and production around the world to those areas where they promise the highest return. The multinational has proved a powerful ally of the principle of comparative advantage.

Fifty or a hundred years ago, most direct business investment abroad was from rich to poor countries, focused on exploiting natural resources, building railways, and developing manufacturing that used cheap local labor. The postwar multinational boom has fundamentally changed this pattern. Recent multinational investment has been predominantly in other developed countries—in Western Europe, Canada, Japan, and the United States. Immediately after World War II, about 55 percent of all U.S. direct investment abroad was in the less-developed ("Third World") countries. Today, 75 percent of the total is in the developed nations.

Some problems. Are the multinationals good for everyone? Not necessarily. After World War II, they were welcomed nearly everywhere—in Western Europe as their investments helped rebuild war-torn economies, and in less-developed nations as they provided scarce capital needed to develop industrial capabilities. But as the war-torn economies regained their health and American-based multinationals took over more and more local industries—especially high-technology products that seemed vital to rapid economic growth and military preparedness—local sentiment began to shift against the multinationals,

		SALES	PROFITS
The Largest Multinationals, 1977			
COMPANY	HEADQUARTERS	(IN BILLIONS)	
1. General Motors	Detroit	$55	$ 3.3
2. Exxon	New York	54	2.4
3. Royal Dutch/Shell	London/The Hague	40	2.4
4. Ford	Dearborn, Mich.	38	1.7
5. Mobil Oil	New York	32	1.0
6. Texaco	New York	28	.9
7. National Iranian Oil	Tehran	22	19.3
8. British Petroleum	London	21	.5
9. Standard Oil of California	San Francisco	21	1.0
10. IBM	Armonk, N.Y.	18	2.7

Source: Fortune, August 1978.

especially in France. A prominent French writer, Servan-Schreiber, created a sensation with his *American Challenge,* in which he predicted that the American-based multinationals might well become the world's greatest international power, after only the United States and the USSR. Three problems have received most attention.

THE MULTINATIONALS VS. NATIONALISM. Huge multinational companies may pose a basic challenge to the supremacy of national economic, and even political and military, power. Sometimes, the multinational is larger than the entire host country. When national interests of the host country conflict with those of the multinational company, which will dominate? Most host governments suspect it will be the parent company's. The host country clearly has the legal power to require the multinational to obey national laws if it operates within the host's boundaries; at the extreme, the host can expropriate the multinational's properties and expel the company. But to do so may have high costs. Future investors will think twice before coming, and the expelled multinational may have skills, technology, and capital that the host country badly needs.

Recently, host nations have increasingly asserted their power over visiting multinationals. Wholesale expropriation of multinational oil properties is the most visible example; but the cards are seldom all on one side. Companies like IBM, which has technology, management skills, and capital that are badly needed in many nations, bargain from a very strong position. But few nations are willing to see outside companies in a position to dominate their national economic and even military developments. It is a rare case now where the multinational can maintain 51 percent ownership of its foreign subsidiary.

TAX PROBLEMS AND TRANSFER PRICING. When multinationals operate in many countries, and especially when they produce components and final products in different countries, they can substantially control where they make their profits by the "transfer prices" their component subsidiaries charge the final-assembly subsidiary. Since taxes vary widely among countries, multinationals often have a major incentive to set transfer prices that show the company's profits as being made largely in low-tax countries. This may be great for the company's stockholders and the low-tax country, but it is sure to raise hackles in the other countries to which the multinational pays few taxes. For example, the big American oil multinationals have long paid only small taxes to the United States, because a big part of the price paid to the oil-producing nations has been formally levied as a tax there. But here again, the problem is complex. Suppose the United States did not give multinational companies credit for income taxes paid abroad against their U.S. income tax liabilities. The companies could readily end up with tax rates over 100 percent. Would this be good for the companies and the United States?

BALANCE-OF-PAYMENTS PROBLEMS. When multinationals make profits abroad, they often want to bring them home to the stockholders. This is sure to cause resentment—and when multinational investment is large, profit repatriation may mean a large annual balance-of-payments outflow for the host country.

Moreover, the multinational is almost certain to face difficult decisions on currency management. If it expects the host country's currency to weaken, shall it convert its holdings into dollars to avoid the loss—thereby, of course, helping to drive down the value of the host country's currency? If it does, the multinational will be seen as speculating against the host's currency. But if it does not, it is clearly imposing a loss on its stockholders that it could have avoided by selling the local currency. To whom is the multinational's subsidiary first responsible—the parent company, or the host nation?

The problem is even more complex. If an American-based multinational moves its production to Europe or Singapore, the American labor movement protests that this steals jobs from American workers and gives them to lower-wage foreign workers. At the same time, the capital outflow weakens the U.S. balance of payments. Worse, the multinational may begin to export goods from its new facility abroad back to the United States, which both competes with American-made products and increases the flow of dollars abroad. The offset, of course, is the flow of profits that will soon be established to the United States if the investment abroad has been a wise one. Contrary to widely held beliefs, modern research suggests that multinationals neither create nor destroy a substantial number of American jobs, and that they have little net effect on the U.S. balance of payments.[5]

MULTINATIONALS AND THE LESS-DEVELOPED COUNTRIES. The strongest criticisms of the multinationals come from the less-developed countries, which often see themselves as the victims of imperialist exploitation by multinationals based in the highly developed, rich nations. The imperialism charge raises complex issues, which we will consider in Chapter 29. As we shall see, by and large the multinationals have raised the living standards of the less-developed countries in which they have made direct investments. But they have sometimes made very large profits in the process, with most of the gain going to the multinational's stockholders and only a little to the host country. The principle again is that of comparative advantage; and the multinationals have generally channeled resources to those areas where the potential rate of return is highest. Even critics have stated that American multinationals have done more to raise LDC living standards than all our AID programs. But

[5]See F. Bergisten, T. Horst, and T. Moran, *American Multinationals and American Interests.* (Washington, D.C.: Brookings Institution, 1978), especially Chap. 3.

the overriding issue, in the developed nations, is often that of nationalism, national pride, and resentment of foreign control. Economic analysis alone cannot solve the imperialism controversy.

Multinationals and a new world order?   Today's huge multinational corporations seem to some the framework for a new world order. They see the managers of such corporations as true citizens of the world, international civil servants advancing the interests of the people of the world, not the individual interests of the nation-states that have so long dominated international affairs. Multinational rationalization of world production could, they argue, serve as the foundation for advancement of international economic efficiency and the world interest, replacing the narrow nation-state jealousies that have led to so much international friction and conflict in the past. But others counter that the multinationals constitute a threat to the common people. How can huge, oligopolistic corporations, dedicated to profit making as their primary goal, provide the basis for a stable world where the interests of individual citizens and groups are the ultimate good?

Try a combination of analysis and speculation on the following questions:

1. Why would Adam Smith, if he were here today, approve or disapprove of the development of multinational corporations?

2. If an American-based multinational producing computers (say, IBM) invests in France by buying up a French computer company, what is the probable effect on U.S. and French investors, workers and standards of living? (Use the principle of comparative advantage in thinking through your answers.)

3. Should America welcome investments here by foreign-based multinationals—say, by the National Iranian Oil Company? Would your answer be different if the foreign company planned to buy control of U.S. steel mills, computer companies, banks, or farmland?

4. Would you favor a plan whereby multinationals would become truly transnational—say, based on some independent island rather than in any existing nation?

5. If you managed the British subsidiary of an American-based multinational auto company and you strongly expected the British pound to be devalued against the dollar, would you continue to hold the pounds you now have, or would you convert them into dollars?

6. Should the world's nations try—say, through the UN—to agree on ways to encourage the rapid growth of multinational corporations? Is your answer different for the developed and the less-developed nations? Explain your answer to a non-economist.

Tariffs,
Import Quotas,
and Free Trade

CHAPTER 28

Adam Smith's *Wealth of Nations* in 1776 was a major attack on barriers to free international trade. The case for free trade internationally is the same as the case for free trade domestically, Smith argued. It is that specialization and division of labor with free exchange of the resulting products makes possible a higher standard of living for everyone. Tariffs, import quotas, or other barriers to free international trade impede such mutually advantageous specialization and exchange and reduce living standards throughout the world, just as would barriers to free trade within a nation.

Yet from Smith's day to this, many have remained unconvinced. Support for tariffs and import quotas to protect American jobs, the American standard of living, and the high wages of American workers is still widespread. Recently, criticism has been focused on Japanese imports—autos, TV sets, electronic equipment, and many other products—which have won many American markets. Why? Why should we not welcome such imports if they are cheaper than their American counterparts?

THE TARIFF

A tariff is a tax on imports, whose major goal is to restrict imports. Figure 28–1 shows average U.S. tariff rates on dutiable imports since 1820. From peak rates of about 60 percent under the Tariff Act of 1833 and the Smoot-Hawley Tariff of 1930, average tariff rates on covered products have been cut to below 10 percent in the last two decades, including a major downward push by the "Kennedy round" in the 1960s. The "Tokyo Round," signed in 1979, will reduce average tariffs another 40 percent, and significantly reduce other trade barriers. These figures understate the real restrictive effect of the tariff, because some products are shut out completely by the tariff, and they don't show up in Figure 41–1. But any way you look at it, major progress has been made in reducing U.S. tariff barriers since the early 1930s. The United States, after a spotty history of restrictionism, has been a leader in a worldwide push toward freer trade.

The history books are full of accounts of the tariff acts battled through Congress over nearly two centuries, and of the regional and political

FIGURE 28–1
Average U.S. Tariff Rates since 1820
U.S. tariff rates have fluctuated with changing times and attitudes. Since 1934, they have been reduced sharply, to the lowest levels in our history. (Source: U.S. Department of Commerce.)

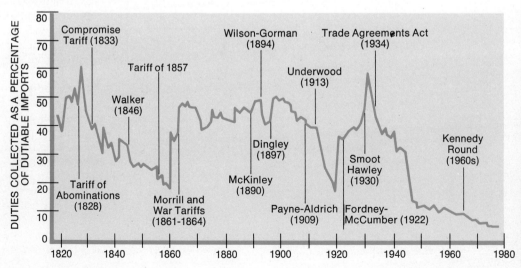

logrolling and compromises underlying them. Our job is to look objectively at the economics of tariffs—to apply the economic analysis of the preceding chapters to the major arguments advanced in support of tariffs. And the central principle to use is the law of comparative advantage.

Some Partially Valid Arguments

Nations may use tariffs to stimulate the development of "infant industries," to ensure the continued operation of industries deemed essential to the national defense, and to stimulate more diversification of industries in order to avoid too much reliance on one or a few industries to foreign trade. All these arguments may be valid, if the nation wants to achieve these goals even though it incurs a lower standard of living at least temporarily by doing so. All involve shutting out lower-cost foreign products, and hence paying higher prices for domestically produced products. A nation may choose to do this in order to achieve other goals. But it should recognize the costs involved.

Recently, in the United States, these partially valid arguments have carried little weight in tariff controversies, except perhaps the national-defense case for protecting such key industries as steel. Let us now turn to the arguments that have been the most important ones in support of the tariff. As we shall see, they turn out to be largely fallacious.

Jobs

The protectionist argument claims that, at least in the short run, raising tariffs will create more jobs as domestic firms begin selling to the customers who previously bought imported goods. And the foreign-trade multiplier will amplify the creation of domestic jobs.

But this is a shortsighted argument. Suppose America puts on a tariff to shut out foreign goods and to export our unemployment. What would you do if you were Belgium, or England, or France? You'd come right back with higher tariffs or quotas against American exports. And that's just what they did during the 1930s. If we

can increase our exports relative to imports in a period of unemployment, this may temporarily raise employment and real GNP. But it's likely that the main result will just be less trade for everyone, as other nations defend themselves against our "beggar-my-neighbor" attempts to export our unemployment.

Even if foreign nations did not respond with higher tariffs or more import quotas, our new jobs would probably be only temporary. *In the long run,* as we shall see presently, we can sell abroad only if we buy abroad, unless we are willing to continuously give or lend foreigners the money to buy our exports. Considering only the current account for the moment, if we shut out foreign goods with a tariff or quota, this may temporarily create American jobs as U.S. goods replace imports. But as foreigners stop receiving dollars in payment for their exports to us, they will have to stop buying American goods. Thus, Americans employed in our export industries will lose their jobs, roughly offsetting the jobs gained by shutting out foreign imports into this country. In the long run, a protective tariff neither increases nor decreases employment. It merely shifts labor (and other productive resources) from more-efficient to less-efficient industries, as we shall demonstrate in the next section.

Note that, although import restrictions are unlikely to succeed in creating many jobs for very long, they have quite different effects on different industries. A new import quota limiting Japanese TV sets into the United States might indeed create jobs in the American TV industry (although TV sets would cost U.S. consumers more). But workers in U.S. export industries (especially farming and high-technology manufacturers) would see their jobs vanish as our exports of such products were reduced.

In the complex real world, when international capital movements are added, the account above is oversimplified, as we shall see presently. But the main point stands: Creating domestic jobs by restricting imports is, at best, a doubtful policy to gain short-term advantages. In the longer-run, temporary job gains are lost and the total volume of foreign trade is reduced, to the disadvantage of all countries involved.

Let us turn now to other arguments advanced in support of tariffs and other import restrictions.

The Favorable-Balance-of-Trade Argument

Most naive of all the tariff arguments is the desire for a "favorable balance of trade" for its own sake. It goes back to the old mercantilist desire to gain more gold and silver as national treasure. Two major fallacies are involved.

First, there is nothing generally favorable about a "favorable" balance of trade (that is, an export surplus of goods and services). A continued "favorable" balance means that we continually give foreigners more goods and services than they give us; we receive in exchange gold (often to be held idle at considerable storage expense),[1] foreign currencies, or investments abroad. Thus, it means a reduced standard of living for the country sending away goods and services, certainly in the short run, and indefinitely if the "favorable" balance of trade continues without willingness to accept goods from abroad. We don't eat gold or foreign currencies. Our standard of living is made up of the goods and services we obtain and consume.

Second, a favorable balance of trade is impossible as a continuing policy, if we consider only the goods-and-services portion of the balance of payments. Foreigners can't buy from us unless they get dollars to pay for our products. The way they get dollars is by selling us their goods and services. It is only by buying from foreigners that we can expect to sell to them.

There is no point more fundamental than this: We can sell abroad only if we buy abroad. It is basic to understanding the fallacy in nearly every argument for protective tariffs and other trade-restriction policies. Figure 28–2 shows where other countries obtained the dollars to buy our exports from 1929 to 1978 (U.S. exports are indicated by the heavy black line). Private investments abroad and government aid helped foreigners finance their purchases from us. But our purchases of foreign goods and services have always been the big source of dollars with which foreigners bought our exports. To sell abroad, we must buy abroad. We cannot shut out foreign imports and continue to export, unless we give or lend to foreigners the money to pay for their purchases.

The Protect-Home-Industry Argument

Perhaps the most popular argument for the tariff is that we need it to protect American industry against low-cost foreign competition.

A domestic industry asking for tariff protection argues that without protection, its market will be lost to foreign competitors. This will force the domestic industry to reduce output, throwing American workers out of jobs. Suppose that the industry is right; if it does not receive protection, it will lose its market to foreign competitors. What are the effects of giving the tariff protection the industry wants?[2]

The first effect is that domestic consumers must pay more for the protected product than if it had come in free. If sugar comes in over the tariff, consumers must pay the regular price of the foreign sugar plus the tariff duty. If the tariff shuts out foreign sugar, domestic consumers must pay a higher price for domestic sugar. We know it's higher because domestic producers cannot, without tariff protection, produce and sell at a price low enough to meet foreign competition. If they could, they wouldn't need the tariff.

Second, domestic sugar producers are subsidized by the tariff; they are enabled to charge higher prices than would have been possible if foreign competition had not been shut out. It's clear that domestic producers are the great gainers from a tariff on their product.

In effect, therefore, a tariff is a subsidy to domestic producers, financed by consumers through higher prices for the protected product. Moreover, the more inefficient domestic producers are, the higher tariff they need to protect them against foreign competition and the larger subsidy they receive.

Indeed, industry's argument for a tariff is often for a "scientific" tariff that would just

---

[1] Since gold is no longer generally used in settling international accounts, presumably the export-surplus nation would accumulate foreign currencies or investments abroad.

[2] Often, industries seeking protective tariffs would be able to retain their markets without tariffs; tariffs enable them to raise domestic prices with lessened fear of foreign competition. Indeed, the tariff has been called "the mother of monopolies," because it helps domestic monopolies to exist by shutting out foreign competition.

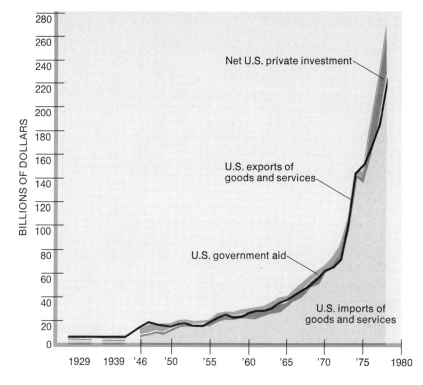

BILLIONS OF DOLLARS

Net U.S. private investment

U.S. exports of
goods and services

U.S. government aid

U.S. imports of
goods and services

1929 1939 '46 '50 '55 '60 '65 '70 '75 1980

FIGURE 28–2
How Other Countries Get
Dollars to Buy U.S. Exports
Other countries get dollars with
which to buy U.S. exports mainly
through our payments for imports.
But net U.S. investments abroad
and government foreign aid also
provide a good many dollars.
(Source: U.S. Department of
Commerce. Military aid and
exports excluded.)

"equalize domestic and foreign costs of production." A suggestion in Congress that special taxes be levied on consumers to finance subsidies to producers, the size of each subsidy to be determined by the producer's inefficiency, would horrify everyone. Yet this is substantially the result of a "scientific" protective tariff designed to equalize foreign and domestic costs of production.

The same economist, Frederic Bastiat, who was responsible for Case 28, put the free-trade case against protection tellingly over a century ago, in his satirical "Petition of the Candlemakers." We need protection, said the candlemakers of Paris in their petition. Foreign competitors are bad enough, but it is the sun that is the most unfair competitor of all. Each day it shines and throws light over all, at no cost at all. If you only shut out the sun, pleaded the candlemakers, we can have a magnificent candle industry, giving jobs to untold numbers of workers.

Should we protect American domestic industry against cheap foreign competition today,

using the same arguments that Bastiat's candlemakers did a century ago?

The Protect-Our-High-Wages Argument

American wages are among the highest in the world. Therefore, it is argued, unless we have a protective tariff, competition from low-wage nations will pull down high American wages to the level of wages abroad.

The "Petition of the Candlemakers" should suggest a fallacy here. Would the real wages of French workers have been raised by shutting out the sun? Would the French people have been better off? Look at the argument in detail.

First, why are wages now higher in the United States than in other countries? Fundamentally, because of the high productivity of American workers. Anything that raises their productivity makes it possible for them to receive higher real wages. And each worker can receive his highest-possible wage when he works where his marginal productivity is highest.

393

What happens when a tariff is passed to "protect" high American wages? The tariff shuts out foreign products and permits relatively inefficient American industries to grow up where they could not otherwise have existed, giving new jobs to American workers. But, as a result, American exports will fall off, because foreign countries cannot buy from us unless we buy from them. (See Figure 28–2 above.) Therefore, fewer workers are employed in the export industries. The net result is a shift of workers from relatively efficient export industries (where they would be situated under free trade) into less-efficient protected industries. As workers move to lower-marginal-productivity positions in protected industries, the wages they can receive in the new jobs are necessarily lower than they could have been before the shift. The long-run result of a protective tariff is to lower real wages, not to raise them. People earn the most when they work where they are most efficient.[3]

To be sure you understand this point, consider an extreme example cited by proponents of a tariff to protect American wages. Suppose that Japanese labor is paid only one-half as much as U.S. workers and we remove all tariffs on Japanese imports. Won't American workers be forced to take much lower wages to compete?

In analyzing this case, we first need to recognize that even though Japanese daily wages are much lower, it is not necessarily true that the labor costs of Japanese producers are correspondingly lower. The Japanese worker gets lower wages, but he also produces less in a day. Therefore, the labor cost per unit of output may be as much, or more, for the Japanese producer as for the American. For example, suppose the average hourly wage of Japanese industrial workers is $4, that in America $8. But suppose that in the chinaware industry, the hourly output per worker in Japan is 100 plates; then the labor cost per plate is 4 cents. If the hourly output per

American worker is 200 plates, the labor cost per plate would be only 4 cents too. Wage cost per plate (per unit of output) is the one that counts.

The evidence is clear that although U.S. wages are high, U.S. unit costs are highly competitive in many industries. Our $140 billion worth of annual merchandise exports is impressive evidence. Wages and unit labor costs have risen rapidly everywhere in the Western world during the post–World War II period, but faster in almost every other industrialized nation than in the United States. U.S. average hourly compensation in manufacturing in 1978 was $8.50, below the $10.00 and $9.60 figures for Sweden and West Germany, but well above France's $5.30 and Japan's $4.30. Two decades earlier, the U.S. average of $2.50 per hour was more than three times that in France and Germany, and nearly ten times that in Japan. Unit labor costs grew in the United States at about 5 percent a year over the last decade; in Germany, Japan, and France, at 10–12 percent. Note that what happens to unit labor costs depends on changes in both wage rates and labor productivity.

Suppose, to continue the hypothetical example above, that even when productivity differences are taken into account, Japan can far undersell us on china plates, and that we remove the tariff on china. This move, of course, would throw workers in the American chinaware industry out of jobs. But since Japan would then be selling more to us, she could now buy more from us. She would buy from us those goods that we are able to produce most efficiently—say, computers. Workers thrown out of jobs in making china would gradually be drawn into the computer industry. But since the United States is, by assumption, comparatively more efficient in producing computers than china, workers can receive higher wages in the computer industry. Workers in the china industry would surely be temporarily unemployed and, if personally unadaptable, might never be reemployed. But the general public would gain by obtaining cheaper china, and more workers would be drawn into the high-productivity industries where wages are highest. Removal of an existing tariff may ruin protected producer groups; yet in the long run,

---

[3]This is not to deny that a protective tariff on a product may temporarily raise the real wages of workers *in that industry* by increasing the demand for labor there, as long as there are immobilities in the domestic labor market that keep other workers from moving in to take advantage of the higher labor demand provided there by protection.

"Don't be childish, man! Kicking Toyotas is no answer to the balance-of-trade gap."
(Drawing by Donald Reilly; © 1971. The New Yorker Magazine, Inc.)

average wages and the standard of living for the economy as a whole will be raised.

This reasoning, however, rides easily over some tough short-run adjustment problems. Higher average wages for the economy don't help the 50-year-old china maker thrown out of work by the new imports. Where will he get another equally good job, or even one at all? The offsetting new jobs, in industries producing for export, may not come immediately. The Japanese may temporarily accumulate dollars, or spend them elsewhere.[4] Sooner or later, our expanded imports will mean new export markets. But with these uncertainties and the pain felt in the displaced industries, it's easy to understand why some labor opposition to tariff cuts is bitter. Nor does the higher average national standard of living help those china-company stockholders whose investment is destroyed by cheap imports. Both workers and businesses have been badly hurt by foreign competition. The opposition to lower tariffs, and the arguments for more protection, come from investors and businessmen as well as from workers.

---

[4]For example, in 1977–78, Japan ran a $12 billion export surplus vis-à-vis the United States, while our total import surplus vis-à-vis all countries was over $30 billion.

Summary

From this analysis, we can draw a broad summary of the economic effects of tariffs. In the long run, a protective tariff lowers real wages and the standard of living. It diverts resources from self-sustaining export industries to less-efficient, protected domestic-consumption industries; and it forces consumers to pay higher prices. In the short run, advantages may be gained from imposing tariffs to aid infant industries or to reduce unemployment. However, new tariffs will increase domestic employment only if almost inevitable retaliatory steps are not taken by other nations.

IMPORT QUOTAS AND EXPORT SUBSIDIES

Since World War II, import quotas and other nontariff trade barriers have been used increasingly, at the same time that tariffs have been substantially reduced. Import quotas set fixed limits to imports of different products. Sometimes they are specified by legislation; often they are bargained directly between two countries' governments on a bilateral basis. The most notable recent case is United States–Japan negotiations on major products, in an attempt to reduce the huge Japanese export surplus and American trade deficit in the late 1970s. But import quotas on such diverse products as chickens, wine, and steel have also been subjects of intense negotiations vis-à-vis the European Common Market recently. U.S. unions and businesses in areas exposed to foreign competition have become strong advocates of tougher U.S. quotas, and have pressed for Japanese and West European agreements to limit exports to the United States. The United States now has import quotas for 67 major product categories, ranging from oil, steel, and textiles to minor consumer items like brooms. Japan and most European nations have roughly similar import quota structures.

Import quotas are more disruptive to free trade than are tariffs. With a quota, additional foreign goods cannot enter, no matter how much more efficient foreign producers may be. With a tariff, at least foreign goods may enter if their cost advantage is large enough to overcome the tariff barrier.

Bargaining on import quotas has become a more important means of adjusting competitive trade positions than are tariff negotiations.

Export subsidies are another device widely used to give domestic producers a special advantage over foreign competitors in world markets. Many governments provide such subsidies, sometimes through government operation of the industry—for example, airlines, steel, and auto production. U.S. farm-price-support programs are considered by many foreigners to provide, in effect, a large export subsidy to U.S. farm exporters. U.S. legislation also permits the use of "countervailing duties" against such subsidies given by foreign nations that sell in this country. Such countervailing duties have recently been levied on a variety of food imports from Europe, and on specialty steels.

A variety of other nontariff barriers are commonplace. Many governments, including the United States, forbid foreign bids on government contracts. On a less formal level, customs and health authorities can make import clearance slow and expensive. Nontariff barriers of all sorts have become the main barriers to international trade over the past two decades.

THE POLITICAL ECONOMICS OF TRADE RESTRICTION

If protective tariffs and import quotas are open to such serious criticism, and if they benefit only particular groups at the expense of the rest of society, why have we had protective tariffs so long? There are two chief answers.

First, public opinion on the tariff has been greatly influenced by special-interest groups, and many citizens are uninformed on the nature of international trade. Groups seeking protection have presented their case vigorously to Congress and to the general public, and the appeal to nationalism against foreigners is a potent rallying cry.

Second, the benefits of freer trade are diffuse—lower prices, higher wages, and more jobs in export industries tomorrow. But the costs are concentrated and direct—on the businesses and workers that lose out to cheaper foreign imports. The threatened interests are alarmed, organized, and vocal. Consumers as a whole are not organized to speak effectively. Congress passes acts covering thousands of products, and most of the actual decisions are made by small subcommittees in the House and Senate. Each congressman is pressed by his constituents to vote for protection for the goods that they produce. Thus, the congressman from one state will vote for a tariff on shoes if his colleague from another state will vote for one on sugar. The tariff is the classic example of congressional logrolling. (Remember the "political failures" of Chapter 24.) Thus, the big tariff reductions since 1930 have come through congressional delegation of tariff-cutting authority to the president.

Recent trade-expansion legislation has included an important special provision. The International Trade Commission (formerly the Tariff Commission) can recommend to the president, where imports are a "substantial cause of serious harm" to a domestic industry, either imposition of tariffs, import quotas, or dollar "adjustment assistance" to workers and companies in the injured industry. If the president does not accept the recommendation of the commission, Congress can override him and impose the commission's recommendation directly. Recently, for example, the commission recommended new import quotas on specialty steels, and the president imposed the recommended quota, against vigorous protests by free traders. But he refused to accept a divided commission recommendation for similar action on shoes (which total over $1 billion of imports annually), ordering instead that adjustment assistance be made available to both displaced workers and companies that lost markets to imports. He emphasized that import restrictions would raise prices to American consumers. How much adjustment assistance is provided in such cases depends on the president's and Congress's willingness to provide funds. Aid to workers has been mainly unemployment insurance. Little aid has been provided thus far to businesses.

The Tokyo Round

In 1979, all the major Western noncommunist nations signed a major agreement to reduce further a wide range of trade restrictions. This so-called Tokyo Round of negotiations, begun in Tokyo in 1973, called for average tariff reductions of about 40 percent, liberalized import quotas on major products, an end to trade-distorting export subsidies, a common code governing the use of countervailing duties, simplification of customs procedures, and the opening up of more government purchases to bids from abroad. All told, over $100 billion of annual trade was affected by the agreement, which will take effect over a period of eight years. The Tokyo Round marks a major step indeed toward expansion of international trade.

But the less-developed nations boycotted the signing of the agreement, although they had participated in the negotiations. They said the final agreement did not include enough special concessions to imports from the LDCs, which they argued are essential to raising living standards in the less-developed parts of the world. The developed nations replied that the agreement does open the door to such special treatment of LDC exports. This is part of a long-standing dispute over how far the richer nations of the world should go to help the poor ones. We shall examine it in more detail in Chapter 29, on growth in the less-developed nations. Internationally as domestically, politics and economics are inextricably intertwined in the issues of international trade.

THE EUROPEAN COMMON MARKET

After World War II, the spirit of internationalism was strong. All the victorious nations except the USSR moved to extend their wartime collaboration into economic cooperation that would reverse the restrictionist wave of the 1930s. Within the framework of the United Nations, the General Agreement on Tariffs and Trade (GATT) was created. It provides for regular discussion of means to reduce international trade barriers among members, and each member nation agrees to work toward freer trade practices, insofar as these practices are not in conflict with the country's national legislation. The Tokyo Round discussions took place within the framework of GATT.

But the biggest postwar move toward international economic cooperation is the European Common Market, and a major move it is. After earlier cooperation on coal, iron, and atomic energy, in 1958 six European nations—Belgium, France, Italy, Luxembourg, the Netherlands, and West Germany—banded together in the European Economic Community (EEC), generally called the Common Market. This precedent-shattering agreement has eliminated all tariff and similar trade barriers against one another and has gradually equalized all their restrictions on trade with nations outside the six, so they present a common tariff to the outside world. Barriers against internal movement of capital and labor are being abolished. Other economic policies will be "harmonized." A common antitrust policy is provided to reduce restrictions on competition, although here, considerable freedom is left for national differences. In essence, the Common Market is a new, huge, free-trade area.

In 1973, Denmark, Ireland, and the United Kingdom joined the Common Market. "The Nine" now have a total population of 260 million, larger than either the United States or the USSR. Their combined GNP was $1.8 trillion in 1978, far more than the USSR's and nearly 90 percent that of the United States. Combined, The Nine are by far the largest exporter and importer in the world; their 1978 exports and imports (including intercountry trade) were nearly $400 billion each, nearly triple those of the United States. Their combined international monetary reserves were over $80 billion, far in excess of ours. The EEC is a huge economic bloc.

The member nations have also attempted to cooperate on international monetary policies, but have faced major difficulties in doing so. In 1979 they formed a new European Monetary Union (EMU), although the U.K. did not join. The EMU countries agree to cooperate in maintaining substantially stable exchange rates among them.

While the Common Market has been a powerful force toward free trade among its member countries, its push toward freer world trade is less clear. The Nine agree to have a common external tariff against other countries, but the agreement says nothing about the level of that external tariff. This situation confronts American business firms and American trade policy with a new challenge. American export markets inside the Common Market are in serious danger, because our products must pay the common external tariff while competitive products made within the Common Market pay no tariff. Intra–Common Market trade has grown far more than EEC trade with other nations. Recently the EEC has faced serious internal political and monetary strains that have slowed its progress. But we negotiate with the EEC on roughly equal economic terms.

America's response thus far has been a combination of public and private action. The U.S. government has bargained hard with the Common Market countries for lower tariffs against U.S. commodities (especially farm products) in exchange for larger European exports to the United States. But the private-market response has been stronger. Many American-based multinational companies have established plants or subsidiaries inside the Common Market, thus escaping the external tariff. Indeed, American investment by large multinational firms has grown so large that some European nations, especially France, have increasingly controlled U.S. direct investment there. (See Case 29.)

SUMMARY AND REVIEW

1. A tariff is a tax on imports whose major goal is to restrict those imports.

2. Although tariffs violate the basic case for specialization and exchange, they have long been used by most nations. Since the 1930s, the United States has taken leadership in reducing tariff barriers.

3. Tariffs may logically be used to stimulate infant industries, diversify national economies, and support a nation's defense capabilities, although they may involve substantial costs in doing so.

4. Raising tariffs can create jobs at home by shutting out foreign products only if other countries do not retaliate by shutting out our exports to them. Even if there is no retaliation (very unlikely), new jobs created will be only temporary, since we can continue to sell abroad only if we buy abroad, unless we give or lend foreigners the money to pay for our exports.

5. Arguments that tariffs will protect high American wages and living standards are largely invalid. In the long run, tariffs shift workers from more-efficient to less-efficient industries, where their productivity will be lower. Since real wages depend on the real marginal productivity of the workers, tariffs will reduce workers' wages.

6. Since World War II, import quotas and other nontariff barriers have been increasingly used to restrict imports and create export surpluses. Export subsidies have been used to stimulate exports, and many countries use countervailing tariff duties or import quotas to offset such subsidies. The net result is to reduce foreign trade and raise prices for consumers in both countries.

7. The benefits of freer trade are diffuse—lower prices, higher wages, and more jobs in export indus-

tries tomorrow. Costs are concentrated and direct—on businesses and workers that lose out to cheaper foreign imports. Thus, special-interest groups seeking protection tend to be strong and well-organized, and use logrolling effectively in Congress. Tariff and other import restrictions have been eliminated only when the power to negotiate lower barriers has been delegated to the president, as for the Kennedy and Tokyo Rounds of the 1960s and 1970s.

8. The Tokyo Round agreement of 1979 marks a major step toward freer international trade, reducing both tariff and nontariff barriers.

9. The European Common Market is another major step toward expanded international trade. The EEC is nearly as large a free-trade area as the United States. But it retains tariff barriers against non-EEC nations. The U.S. response has been to negotiate lower tariffs and other barriers, and to establish plants of U.S.-based multinational firms inside the EEC to serve customers there.

For Analysis and Discussion

1. Recently, when France raised her import barriers against U.S. chickens, the United States raised its tariff on French brandy. Who gained and who lost by these actions? Are such retaliatory tariff increases good for the country making them?
2. What is the fallacy in the "Petition of the Candlemakers" for protection against the sun? Is the same fallacy present in other arguments for protective tariffs?
3. List the factors that explain the high wages received by American workers in the auto and chemical industries. Which, if any, would be affected, and in which direction, if American tariffs were raised on autos and chemicals?
4. Presidents Kennedy, Nixon, Ford, and Carter have all supported "adjustment assistance" for workers and firms that suffer because U.S. tariffs that previously protected them are removed. Do you agree? How large should such assistance be, and who should pay for it?
5. Are there any industries in the United States today that seem clearly to deserve tariff protection as "infant industries"?
6. Can you suggest any ways whereby, in a period of depression, the United States could raise its tariffs against foreign goods and avoid probable retaliation?

CASE 30

IMPORTS: BANE OR BOON

The following are excerpts from a statement of I. W. Abel, president, United Steelworkers and Industrial Union Department, AFL-CIO, in *Tariff and Trade Proposals,* Hearings before the House Ways and Means Committee:[5]

We are here today because many of our members have already been hurt by imports, and many more live in apprehension, with the fear that in the not too distant future they too will be elbowed out of a job by the growing flood of foreign imports. We are here to voice these deep-rooted concerns.

The world has changed. . . .

First, there has been a revival of the war-devastated economies, a revival which we helped. Japan is a most remarkable example of this recovery. . . . The Japanese expect—in five years—to be producing more steel than the United States. . . .

Another change is that technology has become international. It has become international because of improved communications and a sharp rise in United States investment in foreign countries—investment not only of money but of American technology.

Another startling new phenomenon on the world scene is the multinational corporation. . . .

As Fortune magazine has pointed out, these multinational firms like to buy cheap and sell dear—producing where costs are lowest and selling where prices are highest. The operations of American firms on the Mexican side of the border are another example of the problem of the multinational corporation. . . . They take advantage of Mexican law for its border area, U.S. tariff regulations, and low-wage Mexican labor, then ship the goods back to the United States, and sell them at U.S. prices. . . .

To put it bluntly, these American corporations which use components and complete units made overseas—at sweatshop wages—and sold here with no reduction in price—commit a kind of fraud against the American consumer.

In some circles, efforts are made to perpetuate the myth that American consumers benefit from such arrangements. But the truth is that in most cases, American consumers pay American prices. . . .

Delegate after delegate at our [last] convention arose to describe the impact of these new world trade conditions upon his members. . . . In the textile industry, for example, we learned that imports more than doubled between 1964 and 1968. Today, the textile

---

⁵ May 22, 1970, pp. 1776–81.

industry is up against the wall because of imports. The glass workers, too, are seriously concerned about imports. In one Pennsylvania county alone, imports have caused the loss of 1,500 jobs in the county's glass industry. . . .

Also in the electronics field, some 60 percent of black-and-white TV sets and 17 percent of the color TV sets last year were made in foreign countries, and virtually all transistors are now made overseas. . . .

The shoe workers, like the textile workers, are living in a nightmare of an increasing flood of imports that is washing out factories and jobs. Since 1955, the number of foreign-made shoes imported in 1969 were equivalent to the exportation and the loss of 65,000 job opportunities. . . .

Some will make the charge that we are putting on the cloak of protectionism. Those who do so fail to recognize that old concepts and labels of "free trade" and "protectionism" have become obsolete. . . .

I would also say to those who charge us with seizing the banner of protectionism: We still believe in a healthy expansion of trade with other nations. But our support for the balanced expansion of trade does not mean we believe in the promotion of private greed at public expense. It does not mean that such expansion of trade should undercut unfairly the wages and working standards of Americans. . . .

That international trade is a two-way street is a truism which has long been neglected. The very countries, like Japan, which most strongly criticize our movement toward import restrictions, themselves are among the most protectionist in the world. That is, we open our markets to them while they close their markets to us.

Here are a few suggestions:

1. Industries, large and small, which have been seriously hurt by unrestricted tides of foreign imports include: textiles, including man-made fibers and rugs; autos, radios, TVs, and other consumer electronic products; shoes, sheet glass, furniture, pianos, apparel, ceramics, stainless-steel flatware, and so forth. The list is by no means complete, and it is growing.

We believe these industries to be of basic importance to the American economy. We believe our more seriously affected industries must be assured of at least a modest share in the total economy's growth. This means that future import increases in such industries must be regulated and that their import growth, whether from foreign firms or from U.S.-owned offshore production facilities, must be proportionate to the total growth of the domestic market. . . .

Sound policy also means we must adopt measures to limit and tax the export of capital which finances the establishment, acquisition, or expansion of U.S.-owned manufacturing facilities abroad.

2. Truth-in-import-labeling legislation to identify the manufacturer and nation of origin of all imported products would serve an important purpose.

3. It is important that there be a clearly defined international crash program to quickly raise substandard wage levels to acceptable minimums, together with a longer-range program to raise such wages closer to our own domestic legal minimums within prescribed periods of time. There is a clear need for the creation of international fair labor standards, and the U.S. government should take aggressive leadership in such efforts. . . .

4. There should be more effective adjustment assistance for all workers displaced by a rise in imports, where it is a major or significantly contributing cause of such displacement. . . .

Your congressman is a member of the House Ways and Means Committee. He has just read Mr. Abel's testimony, and is intrigued by the analysis and suggestions. He asks your advice. Write him a letter explaining why he should accept or reject Abel's proposals. If you favor any of the recommendations, indicate what specific steps you believe Congress should take.

Part 6

The Changing Economic World

The Developing
Economies

Chapter 29

For more than 2 billion people who live in the economically less-developed countries (LDCs), economic growth is a necessity if they are to escape from the bitter poverty that has been their lot throughout history. U.S. per capita GNP in 1978 was $9,600. In the less-developed countries it averaged $260, and perhaps 30 percent of these people were living on less than $100 a year.

Table 29–1 classifies the nations of the world into four groups, depending on their per capita annual GNPs in 1977. Highly developed countries are those with per capita GNPs above $2,500. The intermediate group comprises countries where the figure was between $500 and $2,500. The less-developed nations are those with per capita GNPs below $500. Of the 65 LDCs, about half (sometimes called the "Fourth World") have been able to make little or no progress in raising living standards and still have per capita GNPs below $200. The other half (sometimes called the "Third World") have somewhat higher incomes, in the $200–$500 range, and most appear to be making some progress toward development. But the line between the two groups is hazy, and both are very poor by our standards. Many writers lump together these third and fourth groups as the "Third World."

The figures in Table 29–1 are very rough, and there is little meaning to precise quantitative comparison between widely differing living standards—for example, that the average American living standard is ten times as high as in Zambia. The figures in the table probably substantially underestimate income levels in the poorer nations on two counts. First, incomes in the LDCs may be relatively underestimated because so much home-produced food and clothing does not go through the market; accurate estimates are very difficult. Second, the staples that form the standard of living of the masses there are generally very cheap compared to other items, including imports. However, conversion of, say, Indian rupee incomes into U.S. dollars at the official exchange rate reflects prices of all internationally traded goods and services (plus capital movements), most of which are not bought by low-income Indian families. Thus, the conversion implies higher dollar prices than most families actually pay for what they consume. But even if per capita incomes in the poor nations were doubled to adjust for these possible underestimates, the less-developed nations would still appear desperately poor. For most of the world, poverty is far and away the number one economic problem.[1]

Worse, this huge gap between rich and poor nations is widening rapidly, not closing. Table 29–2 tells the story for the United States and India since 1960. Although it shows the extremes, it suggests the rapid rate at which the Western industrial nations are pulling away from the less-developed world. A 2 percent annual increase on the U.S. base of $10,000 means a $200 increase in one year, more than the *entire* per capita GNP in India. In India, the same 2 percent increase, if it could be achieved, would be about $3 per capita.[2]

Why do these vast differences in living standards exist? Why is the gap between the rich and the poor widening even further? The theory of economic growth can help answer these questions, and most of this chapter is devoted to applying that theory to the LDCs.

Development of these economically less-developed countries has become the most explosive socioeconomic problem of our times. Poverty is a source of acute discontent for hundreds of millions of people, aroused by their leaders. In China and India alone, there are 1.6 billion people. But in literally a hundred other nations, people are awakening to the fact that poverty and misery

---

[1]The comparisons of Table 29–1 among high-income nations are also very sensitive to the exchange rates used to convert local currencies to dollars. The dollar depreciation of the mid- and late 1970s sharply raised foreign incomes in dollar terms, especially for Switzerland, Sweden, West Germany, and Japan. Only limited weight should be placed on such international comparisons. The United Nations has released new data for leading countries, based on prices of only widely used commodities in each country. These estimates, shown in Table 1–1, show U.S. per capita income as still substantially ahead of all other major countries (i.e., excluding some of the small oil-producing nations like Kuwait).

[2]Two good general references on the less-developed areas and their problems are C. Kindleberger, *Economic Development* (New York: McGraw-Hill, 1978); and E. E. Hagen, *The Economics of Development* (Homewood, Ill.: Richard D. Irwin, 1975).

TABLE 29–1
Countries Grouped by 1977 GNP Per Capita—in 1977 U.S. Dollars[a]

DEVELOPED COUNTRIES (ABOUT 1.1 BILLION PEOPLE)
(OVER $2,500 PER CAPITA)

Kuwait	$12,700	Netherlands	$7,160	Spain	$3,190
Switzerland	9,960	Libya	6,680	Poland	3,150
Sweden	9,250	Finland	6,150	USSR	3,010
United States	8,640	Austria	6,140	Israel	2,920
Norway	8,540	Japan	5,640	Singapore	2,890
Canada	8,450	Saudi Arabia	4,980	Ireland	2,880
West Germany	8,160	East Germany	4,940	Venezuela	2,820
Denmark	8,050	United Kingdom	4,430	Greece	2,810
Belgium	7,580	New Zealand	4,370	Bulgaria	2,590
Australia	7,340	Czechoslovakia	4,090	Hong Kong	2,590
France	7,290	Italy	3,450	Hungary	2,570

INTERMEDIATE COUNTRIES (ABOUT 600 MILLION PEOPLE)
($500–$2,500 PER CAPITA)

Puerto Rico	$2,460	Mexico	$1,190	Guatemala	$790
Trinidad and Tobago	2,380	Taiwan	1,180	Ecuador	770
Iran	2,180	Chile	1,170	Paraguay	760
Yugoslavia	1,960	Turkey	1,110	Colombia	710
Portugal	1,850	Algeria	1,110	Jordan	710
Argentina	1,730	Malaysia	930	Ivory Coast	710
Romania	1,580	Cuba	900	North Korea	700
Iraq	1,530	Syria	900	Albania	610
Uruguay	1,450	Tunisia	860	El Salvador	570
Brazil	1,390	Dominican Republic	840	Morocco	570
South Africa	1,340	Mongolia	830	Bolivia	540
Panama	1,240	Nicaragua	830	Congo	500
Jamaica	1,220	Peru	830	Rhodesia	500
Costa Rica	1,150	South Korea	810		

LESS-DEVELOPED COUNTRIES—"THIRD WORLD" (ABOUT 1.4 BILLION PEOPLE)
($200–$500 PER CAPITA)

Papua New Guinea	$480	Ghana	$380	Kenya	$270
Philippines	450	Cameroon	340	Uganda	260
Honduras	450	Angola	330	Central African Empire	250
Liberia	430	Yemen	320	Haiti	230
Nigeria	420	Egypt	310	Guinea	230
Senegal	420	Indonesia	300	Madagascar	210
Thailand	410	Togo	300	Sierra Leone	200
China	410	Sudan	300	Sri Lanka	200
Yemen	390	Mauritania	270	Tanzania	200

LESS-DEVELOPED COUNTRIES—"FOURTH WORLD" (ABOUT 1.2 BILLION PEOPLE)
(LESS THAN $200 PER CAPITA)

Pakistan	$190	Bangladesh	$90	All of Africa	
India	150	Bhutan	80	not listed above	about $120

[a] Figures are estimated GNP for each nation, divided by population and converted to 1977 U.S. dollars at official exchange rates. Estimates for less-developed countries are generally understated compared to developed countries. Conversion to dollars is *very rough*; see text. Table 1–1 provides more accurate data for highly developed countries. Estimates for Communist-bloc countries are rougher than for others. Some small nations are omitted.

Source: International Bank for Reconstruction and Development, *World Bank Atlas,* 1978.

TABLE 29–2
Per Capita Real GNP in the United States and India^a

	1960	1978
United States	$4,800	$9,600
India	140	160

^a Data in 1978 U.S. dollars. Figures for India are probably understated relative to the United States, but the 1960–78 change is roughly accurate.

may not be the inescapable lot of the masses. A great change is moving Asia, Africa, and Latin America, a change compounded of growing nationalism and a desire for economic progress and power. A revolution of rising expectations—of economic progress, individual status, and national prestige and power—is sweeping the less-developed nations. We hear of it at every meeting of the United Nations and other international organizations. We will hear more in the future.

THE ANATOMY OF UNDERDEVELOPMENT

Poverty is the central economic fact of the less-developed areas. But there are many differences among them. Some are primitive; others, like India and China, boast civilizations that are far older than those of the Western world. Some have generous natural resources; others are bitterly poor in the endowments of nature. Some have a high ratio of population to land; others have vast open spaces. Some are clearly on the way to development; others seem mired in poverty. The poverty of a beggar on the streets of Calcutta is different from that of the Bushman of Africa, or the desert nomad of the Middle East. But in spite of these differences, there are some strong resemblances.

Patterns of Economic Activity

First, a brief summary look at the economies of the less-developed nations as a backdrop for analysis of why they are poor, and of what can be done to raise their production.

Poverty and the dominance of low-productivity agriculture. In the less-developed countries, food is the main item of production and consumption. It has to be, for starvation hovers uncomfortably near. For the poorest (Fourth World) group of LDCs, about 70 percent of all production is food. In the United States, the comparable figure is below 20 percent. Although diets in most nations are adequate to preserve life, they are often inadequate to fend off disease or, even, allowing for the small bodily stature of many peoples, to provide enough energy for continued hard work.

A mud or thatched hut and some simple clothing make up most of the rest of the consumption pattern in the poorest nations. Remember that only about $5 per month per capita is left to cover everything except food. Hospitals, plumbing, highways, and other services that we take for granted have no place in such standards of living. The masses in these nations save little or nothing at all. In Calcutta, between a quarter- and a half-million people have no homes or jobs, so they simply wander the streets.

Because human labor is very cheap and capital scarce, hard work and laborious details are done by hand. Tractors and other mechanized farm equipment are scarce, and would often be unusable even if available, because of lack of fuel, maintenance facilities, and sufficient education to use them. Figure 29–1 shows vividly how little the poor nations rely on nonhuman energy (electricity, water, and minerals) compared to the developed nations. (In this and the following figures, income per capita is always shown on the vertical axis. Both income and energy use are plotted on ratio, or logarithmic, scales to facilitate relative comparisons.)

The nonagricultural population is often crowded into a few large cities, where small-scale industry, services for the wealthy, and government employment provide most of the jobs. Unemployment is rampant. Simple textiles are important in many less-developed economies; the cloth is used for clothing and home furnishings. In the more developed countries, modern large-scale industry (steel, chemicals, fertilizers) has begun to appear in the major cities.

Dual economies: limited development of markets. Thus, many LDCs are, in essence, "dual economies." One part is a money, market-

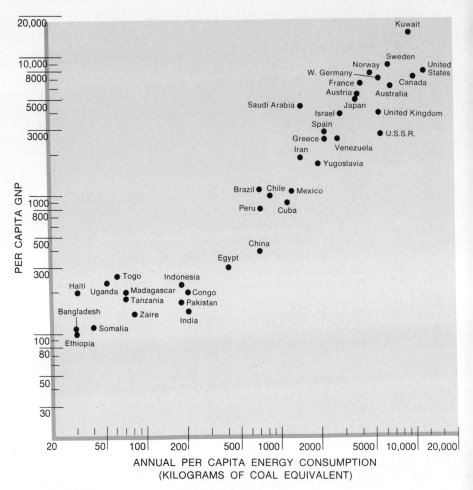

FIGURE 29–1

Energy Consumption Per Capita in Different Countries

Energy consumption per capita is closely correlated with the degree of economic development. (Source: United Nations World Bank, *World Development Report,* 1978. Data for 1976.)

oriented economy centered in a few large cities, with modern industry mixed with crowded slums. The other part is a subsistence-level, rural, barter-type economy of hand labor and primitive superstitions, comprising 75 percent or so of the population, substantially isolated from the markets and industry of the cities. Incomes are far higher in the industrial than in the agricultural sectors. To go from one to the other is to go from one world to another, from the present to the dark ages.

Transportation is crude. The highways of the cities rapidly dwindle to dirt roads and to mere paths a hundred miles away. Religious and cultural barriers fragment the nation. One can scarcely call them "economies"—for economic life as we know it exists only around the cities and towns. Without roads and communication, there is little chance for a market economy to develop.

In some nations, profitable one-product export economies have developed—copper in Chile, oil in Saudi Arabia. In many ways, these are the fortunate LDCs. But much of the investment to develop these export enclaves is often foreign, and resentment against foreign ownership and operation is common. Often it leads to expropriation, whether or not there is a native competence to operate the industry.

Unequal distribution of income. In most less-developed countries, income is very unequally distributed—far more unequally than in the highly developed, capitalist economies. In Honduras, Ecuador, sand Iraq, for example, the bottom 40 percent of the population receives less than 7 percent of the income. There are often a few rich landholders, sometimes a few industrialists. The masses are dismally poor, mainly living just above the subsistence level on farms or in villages, often as tenant farmers who keep little of what they raise. There is no substantial "middle class" of shopkeepers, professionals, and skilled workers, who make up a major portion of Western populations.

Weak governments. A few LDCs have well-established democratic institutions, but they are the exception. Governments are typically unstable, revolutions are commonplace. There can be little long-range planning of basic government services such as schools, highways, and the like. Equally important, there is no basis for long-run planning by investors and businessmen. Often governments are dominated by the entrenched "haves," who block social and political change that might endanger them.

Governments, which must provide leadership in development, are usually weakly staffed, reflecting the newness of the nations and the lack of education and traditions of honest civil service. Government jobs are often political perquisites, which mainly provide an accepted position for corruption. Confusion, red tape, and bungling often characterize government "programs." There is little chance for such governments to establish and administer effective tax systems to collect the funds needed to provide schools, highways, and sanitation. Overissue of money and rampant inflation are commonplace.

Theoretical Model

So much for a general, if discouraging, overview. Now let us look more analytically at the problem. The theory predicts that low per capita output in the less-developed nations will reflect a high ratio of population to natural resources and to capital; a slow rate of capital accumulation and technical advance; an uneducated, low-productivity labor force; and a general environment unconducive to initiative, enterprise, and organized economic activity. And in fact, this is a reasonable model of most of the LDCs. Look now at these factors one at a time.

Natural Resources

Lack of natural resources explains little of the plight of the less-developed nations. Switzerland has one of the world's highest per capita incomes on virtually no natural resources; Africa and Asia have some of the lowest on vast natural resources. The ratios of population to arable land for Switzerland, Belgium, and the Netherlands are about the same as those for Bolivia, Peru, and Egypt.

Nonetheless, plentiful natural resources can certainly help. The United States, Canada, and Australia all have rich resources and low ratios of population to land. Surely the vast western frontier helped to speed our early growth. Many poor nations would be much worse off without generous resources—the copper and nitrates of Chile, the oil of the Middle East. Perhaps climate, rather than natural resources in the usual sense, is critical. Most of the world's well-to-do nations lie in the temperate zone, none of them in the tropics. But within the temperate zone, there are wide variations in economic development. Nor does primary reliance on agriculture necessarily characterize poor nations. Denmark and New Zealand demonstrate that agricultural countries need not be poor. The poor nations are poor not because they are agricultural, but because productivity in their agriculture is so low.

Shortage of Capital and Primitive Technology

The stock of capital explains much more. No less-developed country has a large stock of capital goods per capita; every well-to-do nation does. Modern factories, machinery and equipment, highways, hospitals—all are scarce in the LDCs. Without them, high output per capita is very difficult.

The reason is easy to see. When nations are poor, they find it hard to save. Saving in India or

Somalia means cutting back an already pitifully low standard of living. Saving in America is easy. Yet without capital goods, the poor nation can never hope to raise the standard of living of the masses very much.

Capital investment of over $40,000 per factory worker in America was cited above. In the poorest nations, the comparable figure is only a few dollars. Gross capital formation is only 10–15 percent of gross national product in such poor nations as Paraguay and Nigeria. In the well-to-do nations, it generally runs 20–25 percent, and in very rapidly growing nations, like Japan, up to 30–40 percent. It is easy for the rich to become richer. The poor, like the queen in *Through the Looking Glass,* must run as fast as they can merely to stay in the same place, as population grows constantly.

As a closely related factor, most less-developed countries have little modern technology. Human beings and beasts do virtually all the work in agriculture. Handicraft methods dominate in small-scale industry in the towns and cities. To the illiterate native of Tanzania or Yemen, Detroit's mass-production methods have little relevance. Where economic development is beginning, sometimes wild contrasts exist in the dual economies. In the cities of India and Venezuela, modern oil refineries and chemical plants loom against the sky. A hundred miles away, there is the most primitive agriculture, unchanged for a thousand years.

Overpopulation and the Labor Force

In one fundamental sense, overpopulation is the crux of the less-developed economies' problems. The population is so large that, given the natural resources and capital available, there is barely enough output per person to maintain life. And when total output increases because of improved technology or capital accumulation, population increases nearly as fast, so there is little improvement in the average standard of living. This is not the picture in all the LDCs, but it is in many.

In recent years, total production has risen at substantial rates in many LDCs—4 to 5 percent per annum in Latin America, Africa, and south-east Asia. This is near the growth rate of total output, so income per capita and equal standard of living have shown little improvement in the industrialized countries. But population has grown nearly as fast as output.

In most less-developed economies, the annual birth rate is between 30 and 50 per thousand people; in the United States and Western Europe, the comparable rate has generally declined to around 15 to 20 per thousand. But in the LDCs, until recently death rates typically ran from 25 to 35 per thousand, compared to 10 or below in the Western world. Thus, population growth rates in the two types of economies were roughly similar, running around 10 to 15 per thousand (1–1.5 percent per year).

Since World War II, Western methods of disease prevention have drastically reduced the death rate in many LDCs, especially the rate of infant mortality. DDT alone is estimated to have saved 50 million lives through checking the spread of infectious disease. The result is a population explosion. In Latin America, Asia, and Africa, population is doubling every 20 to 25 years.

Figure 29–2 shows this contrast dramatically. Note the high birth rates in most less-developed countries, and the rapid rates of population growth implied by the big spread between their birth and death rates.

The world population problem is thus centered in the less-developed countries. In the developed nations of the Western world, population is generally stable or growing 1 percent or less per year. But given the explosive growth rates in the rest of the world, total world population may nearly double—from about 4 to 7.5 billion—in the next 25 years. If that rate should continue, it would imply a world population of over 30 billion a century from now.

Such a population would make the earth into a human anthill, but we are unlikely to reach it or anything like it. Malthus's famine would probably check the growth before then, if nothing else did. Although food production has been rising rapidly, and there are still periodic food "surpluses" in developed nations that lead governments to support prices and restrict output, over half the world's population today has less

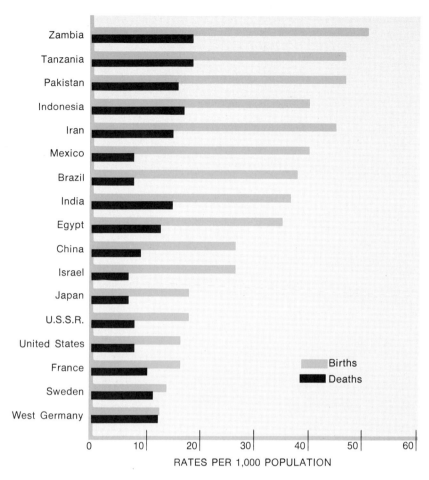

FIGURE 29–2
Birth and Death Rates in Different Countries
The less-developed countries have the fastest-growing populations. For the whole world, the birth rate is about 33 per thousand, and the death rate about 11. (Source: United Nations World Bank, *World Development Report*. Data for 1975.)

than what most experts consider an "adequate" diet.[3]

The population problem is all the more serious because in many less-developed nations, much of the population is illiterate. New methods that involve even the simplest changes often meet barriers of superstition and inadequate understanding. In Africa, only about 30 percent of all children between 5 and 18 go to school, about 40 percent in Asia. In the United States, the figure is over 95 percent. Figure 29–3 shows the high correlation between literacy and living standards.

Environment and Initiative

Rapid economic growth has occurred mainly in the Western world, where the social and economic groundwork was laid centuries ago. Nowhere has there been rapid, continuing growth without reasonably stable government and fi-

---

[3]For authoritative analyses of the population and world food problems, see P. Hauser, ed., *The Population Dilemma* (Englewood Cliffs, N.J.: Prentice-Hall, 1969), and W. W. Cochrane, *The World Food Problem* (New York: Crowell Collier and Macmillan, 1969), which draw heavily on United Nations studies.

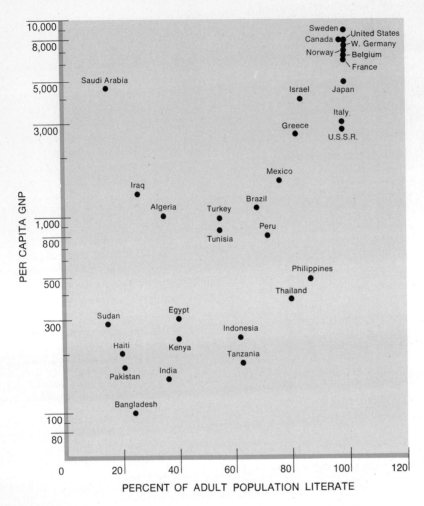

FIGURE 29–3
Literacy and Per Capita GNP
The degree of literacy is highly correlated with the extent of economic development, as both cause and effect. (Source: United Nations World Bank, *World Development Report*, 1978. Data for 1975.)

nancial and economic institutions. In all the top countries of Table 29–1, the profit motive and individual initiative have played a central role.

On these scores, the problems faced by the less-developed economies are enormous. Apathy and ignorance characterize the great mass of their populations. Except for government leaders and small educated groups, there is often little effective impetus for economic development; and all too often, even the leaders appear more concerned with their own status than with economic progress for the masses. In central Africa, the medicine man or witch doctor is still the most influential member of some tribes. In some nations, manual labor is considered beneath the dignity of a man, and is left entirely to women. In

many LDCs, few of the peasants own much, if any, land. They see little reason to work harder to produce more when most of it must be given up to the absentee landlord.

Many LDCs attempting to industrialize face backward-bending labor-supply curves. Ordinarily, higher wages will call forth more labor. But native workers, used to only low living standards and unacquainted with the Protestant work ethic, may be content with what seem to them adequate money incomes and simply stop working to take it easy or go spend their new wealth when they reach some weekly or monthly income level. Thus, offers of higher wages call forth less, not more, work, since workers reach the "big enough" income level sooner with higher wage rates. The labor-supply curve, as shown back in Figure 19–2, is backward-bending above some (often low) income level.

Thus, it is not surprising that the LDCs lack entrepreneurs—individuals with imagination and initiative to seize economic opportunities and to develop them. In the traditional societies, such attitudes and activities are often frowned upon. Caste systems bar occupational changes, and class hierarchies prevent vertical mobility. Things have been done the same way since time immemorial.

Nor can such nations expect to surge upward without what economists call an "infrastructure" of "social overhead capital"—highways, schools, communications, hospitals, sanitation. These all require capital and planning. Government tax collections is the only practical way to finance them. Thus, stable, established governments, capable of collecting taxes and spending efficiently, are essential—but rare.

Absence of stable governments and established tax systems leads to persistent government deficits and to inflation. There are vast needs. But subsistence living standards make taxes very difficult to collect. The predictable result is government spending without matching taxes, and inflation in the market sector of their economies.

The resulting inflations are bad partly because of the inequities they work on the masses, who have no way to protect themselves from the higher prices of essentials. Inflation thus becomes a kind of "forced saving" that substitutes for tax collections. But worse, inflation and financial instability repel foreign investors, whose capital is desperately needed, and exacerbate balance-of-payments problems.

The Vicious Circle of Poverty

The less-developed nations vary widely. But in most, a central problem seems to be a vicious circle of poverty. Incomes and living standards are so low that productivity is low and saving is impossible for the mass of the population. But without more capital goods, highways, and education, output per capita cannot be increased. If total output increases, population grows nearly as fast.

Throughout the LDCs, a significant part of the farm population is "surplus" in the sense that

it could be removed from the farms of the countries concerned without any reduction in *total* farm output. But to move this surplus population to productive employment seems impossible. What will keep them from starving until they become established in industrial jobs? How can uneducated people be made into effective industrial workers? Who will provide the factory equipment, and the capital to establish new concerns? How could the newly made industrial goods be sold either domestically or abroad without an established market and without adequate transportation and commercial facilities?

Last, government planning and taxation are required to enforce saving and to channel investment into socially desirable uses; yet governments are weak, inefficient, unstable. Inefficient bureaucracies bungle rules and frustrate businessmen with red tape. Inflations and financial instability are commonplace. It seems that everywhere they turn, the LDCs face insoluble dilemmas. Their leaders may know the prescriptions, but what shall they do?

POLICY FOR ECONOMIC DEVELOPMENT

How can the LDCs break out of the vicious circle of poverty and take off into self-sustaining growth? There is no simple answer.

Environment and Institutions for Economic Development

It is striking that all the top ten countries in the highly developed group of Table 29–1 are either in Western Europe or have inherited much of Western European culture and traditions.[4] Max Weber, a famous sociologist, in his *Protestant Ethic and the Spirit of Capitalism*, argued that the rapid economic development of Western Europe was linked intimately with what he called the "Protestant ethic"—the belief that work is good for its own sake and that the individual should be free to seek after his own welfare through work.

Weber emphasized the institutions of capitalistic society that have accompanied rapid

---

[4]Except for Kuwait, which has been described as a tiny nation sitting on an oil well.

economic development in the West: (1) private ownership and control of the means of production; (2) freedom of the market from such restrictions as guild monopolies, social-class barriers, and government price-fixing; (3) the reign of calculable law, enabling people to know in advance what rules they operate under in economic life; (4) freedom of individuals to work for wages; (5) "commercialism" of economic life through a market system of wages and prices to mobilize and allocate productive resources; and (6) speculation and risk taking (which had been largely forbidden in the preceding feudal and guild societies).

Were the Protestant ethic and the institutions of capitalism essential to the rapid economic growth of today's richest countries? The facts fit Weber's description reasonably well, but there are important exceptions.

Everyone agrees that sustained rapid economic growth is unlikely without a stable government, law, and order. Without them, neither domestic nor foreign investors are willing to risk their funds; the essential economic infrastructure of highways, communications, and other public utilities is unlikely to come. But revolution and instability have been common in the LDCs. Struggles for power by competing factions have been common. Illiterate, superstitious people find it hard to make democracy work effectively after they wrest power from rich dictators or foreign rulers. But difficult as it may be, establishment of stable government appears to be a *sine qua non* for the takeoff into economic growth.

Development of individual initiative and an entrepreneurial class, plus acceptance of a market economy, also seem very important (although China may be a counterexample). Individuals who take leadership, who see potential gains in taking risks, who manage to mobilize capital, who have the drive to push ahead through difficulties and to organize the work of others play a key role in most successful development. Often, immigrants from a different culture, who are materialistic, experimental, industrious, and ambitious for their families, have provided entrepreneurial leadership.

How initiative, a market, and an entrepreneurial class develop in traditional tribal or village societies is far from clear. Sociologists, economists, and anthropologists have studied dozens of cases and find no single explanation. In some instances (Japan, for example), an entrepreneurial class seems to develop from pressures of social and cultural change. Dissatisfied groups outside the ruling elite see trading and business as a way to rise to higher status. In other cases (Egypt, for example), the spirit of entrepreneurship is imported through colonial rule, which is later thrown off. Increasing awareness of the outside world seems everywhere to be important. In many cases, the development of an entrepreneurial class has been a revolt against prevailing tribal or village mores, a social as well as an economic revolution.

Capital Accumulation and Industrialization

As our theory would lead us to expect, substantial capital accumulation has marked every major case of rapid economic development. To rise from poverty, every nation faces the central problem of increasing saving and investment as a share of total output. Figure 29–4 shows the wide variation among countries in the ratio of gross investment to GNP. Although a few nations with very high investment ratios have relatively low per capita incomes (for example, Nigeria and Yugoslavia), they are now growing rapidly. The United States has a relatively low savings–investment ratio but also a relatively slow rate of growth over recent years; we had a high savings ratio during the nineteenth century.

There is some evidence that it takes about $3–$4 of new capital goods to increase current income by $1 annually in these countries (a "capital–output ratio" of 3 : 1 or 4 : 1). With a 4 : 1 marginal capital–output ratio, an economy that saves 4 percent of its income to accumulate capital will, other things equal, increase its national income by 1 percent annually. Then, if population grows at, say, 1 percent annually, per capita income is just held constant. To raise its living standard, the economy must either save more or slow its population growth. Any saving rate below 4 percent of income will mean decreasing per capita incomes.

This relationship between the capital–output ratio and the rate of saving is illustrated by Table 29–3. If 4 percent of total income is saved, there will be a 1.33 percent annual increase in output in case the capital–output ratio is 3 : 1, but only a 1 percent increase if the ratio is 4 : 1. Obviously, both higher savings ratios and lower capital–output ratios are good for economic growth. A few countries have apparently managed a capital–output ratio of 2 : 1, which has permitted them to expand output rapidly with modest savings ratios.

Many LDCs have turned to government investment programs (financed by taxes or inflationary money-issue) to force more saving and investment, especially in economic infrastructures—roads, schools, and dams that aid development throughout the nation. When the mass of the population is barely above the subsistence level, to obtain more voluntary saving is very difficult. Recent research emphasizes the importance of developing financial institutions to gather together small savings and channel them to useful investments.

Foreign Investment and Imperialism

Some nations—for example, India, Taiwan, Israel, and the oil countries of the Middle East—have obtained substantial portions of their growth capital from abroad, through both private investment and government aid. The United Nations estimates that the annual provision of capital by the developed to the less-developed nations rose from $2 billion in 1950 to $40 billion in 1976. About 40 percent was loans or grants from other governments or international agencies; 60 percent was private investment from the developed nations. Twelve billion dollars came from the United States. In 1976, the IMF sold off one-sixth of its gold stock, and provided the proceeds to the LDCs.

Poor nations desperately need capital from abroad. Economic analysis says that there will be benefit to both borrower and foreign lender if the expected rate of return on the capital in the developing nation exceeds the one the lender can obtain elsewhere. Nonetheless, many developing nations have invited foreign private investment only with stringent restrictions. With burgeoning national pride, they want no part of foreign control, and they distrust foreign investors who may try to exploit them. The memories of many decades of colonialism are still strong. Thus, as badly as they need foreign capital, many of the poor nations have hedged foreign capital and companies around with restrictive controls reaching into day-to-day operations.

Are these fears of foreign imperialism and multinational corporations irrational? Over the past century, some foreign investors have exploited native resources and workers, making large profits with little concern for the welfare of the less-developed nations. This economic domination was often paralleled by ruthless political and social repression of native populations. Although native living standards may well have been higher than they would have been with no foreign capital at all, bitter resentment was a predictable consequence.

But since the emergence of national independence for nearly all people since World War II, the pendulum has swung. Foreign companies (for example, in petroleum) that formerly paid only 25 percent of their profits to local nations for the privilege of extracting natural resources first watched their share cut to 50 percent, and then outright expropriation of their property, often with inadequate compensation. Restrictions on foreign operations have been steadily tightened. Prospective foreign businesses have often been turned away because offers were considered inadequate, sometimes with the result that nothing happens—no foreign capital, no jobs for native people.

Socialist doctrine says that foreign "imperialist" investment will exploit the natives by paying low wages to workers and low prices for raw materials, and will bleed the economy by withdrawing the profits it extorts from the native population.

TABLE 29–3
Capital–Output and Savings Ratios

SAVINGS–INCOME RATIO	ANNUAL INCREASE IN OUTPUT (PERCENTAGE) WITH:	
	CAPITAL–OUTPUT RATIO = 3:1	CAPITAL–OUTPUT RATIO = 4:1
.04	1.33	1.0
.05	1.67	1.25
.10	3.33	2.5
.15	5.0	3.75

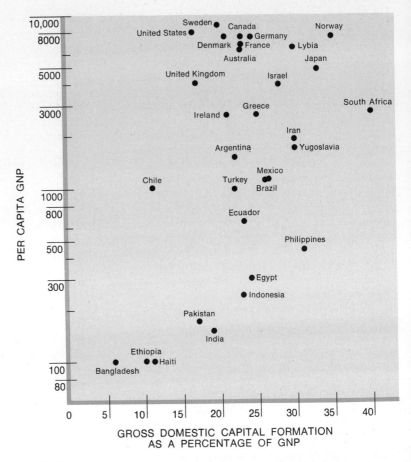

FIGURE 29–4

Capital Formation as Percentage of GNP

High per capita GNPs and high rates of capital formation generally go together, as interacting cause and effect. But there are exceptions; note Japan, Singapore, the Phillipines, and the United States. (Source: United Nations World Bank, *World Development Report,* 1978. Data for 1976.)

What are the facts? *Answer:* Complex, and varied from case to case. Wages in the developing countries are much lower than in the developed nations, but so are skills and training. If there is effective competition, wages will be bid up to roughly the marginal productivity of the local workers; if there is not, exploitation is clearly possible. The same reasoning applies to the prices foreign corporations pay for local materials. Most companies require higher expected rates of profit on LDC projects because of the higher risks involved. On the average, the profit rates on

investments in the LDCs have been somewhat higher than on domestic investments, but failures and expropriations have been common.

What of the argument that foreign corporations bleed the LDCs by withdrawing the profits they make, also causing serious balance-of-payments problems? Analysis suggests counterarguments.

First, although withdrawal of profits and interest has grown steadily with the cumulation of foreign investments in the LDCs, reinvested earnings plus new U.S. investments in the LDCs have been even larger, so net U.S. investment in the LDCs has grown persistently.

Second, even if all profits were withdrawn by the foreign investor, the developing nation might well gain from the investment. Remember the desperate need for capital to raise output and provide jobs for the surplus native population. If native workers take jobs voluntarily in the foreign business, they presumably prefer that to their other alternatives. If local customers voluntarily buy the foreign product, they presumably prefer it to other alternatives, even though its price may have yielded a large profit to the foreign company. Hard-boiled realism would ask, Whether I like the foreigner or not, am I better off with his capital invested here, or without it? Clearly, the developing nation would be still better off if part or all of the profits were reinvested there. But what if the alternative is no foreign investment at all?[5]

Most of the developing nations have attempted to compromise this dilemma. They seek foreign capital, but on terms they dictate. Some compromises have been effective in attracting foreign capital; others have not. To the outsider, restrictions that lead foreign investors to turn away may seem shortsighted, for the less-developed nation ends up with its restrictions and no capital for development. But fear of foreign exploitation is strong in many of the less-developed nations.

Technical Advance and Education

Technological advance and development of an educated, skilled labor force have played a central role in the development of the Western economies. How can the poor nations achieve such technical advance?

Their problem may look easy—just borrow the technology of more advanced nations. The USSR after World War II adopted industrial methods and techniques wholesale from the West. Japan has adopted foreign technology even more effectively. But such importation often requires heavy capital investment; skilled laborers, technicians, and managers; and mass markets to justify many modern methods—conditions not met in most poor nations.

Think, for example, how you would go about introducing modern technology into Somalia, an emerging African nation of about 3 million people, many of them illiterate nomads. Literacy: perhaps 20 percent. Total college graduates in the country: about 300. Per capita income: about $100 a year. Politics: longstanding bitter rivalry among tribal groups.

In fact, the biggest promise for technical change probably lies in agriculture rather than in industry. Primitive, low-productivity agriculture is the greatest millstone around the necks of the poorest economies. Improving productivity in agriculture has led the way in nearly every case of growth. Here, technology can be introduced in small stages, and with modest capital costs—simple tools, fertilizers, improved irrigation.

More sophisticated advance requires an educated labor force and willingness to accept change. Thus, mass education and development of a core of skilled technicians and teachers are goals of virtually every LDC. Investment in education may not pay a fast return. But Figure 29–3 speaks for itself. The long-run payoff is big. But schools are expensive and teachers are very scarce. Thus, educational efforts have been concentrated on the young. It will be generations before half the population in many of the less-developed nations is even literate.

But the task is not hopeless. Steps toward mass education in some LDCs have been spectacular since World War II. Some of the LDCs—the new Third World—have broken out of the circle of poverty and are on the road to development. Mexico and Brazil, for example, now have per capita incomes of $1,000, functioning mass-education systems, and hundreds of modern, technologically sophisticated factories—and millions of peasants little touched by the development. Countries like Ghana, Egypt, and Ecuador are further back on the development ladder, but they have apparently broken out of the backwater of the Fourth World. For them, food and agriculture probably remain the key problem for development, but every country's problem is different.

---

[5]For a more complete analysis, see C. Bergsten and others, *American Multinationals and American Interests* (Washington, D.C.. Brookings Institution, 1978), especially Chap. 10.

Population Policy

Many LDCs in the last two decades have shown growth rates in total production exceeding those of the highly developed nations. But until most LDCs slow their rates of population growth, they are unlikely to escape far from Malthus's dire predictions. Even high growth rates in aggregate output cannot outdistance high rates of population growth.

Many LDCs' first reaction to Western suggestions that population growth be limited was resentment. They accused the developed nations of plotting to hold down the numbers of the poor who might overtake them, of advocating genocide for the Third World peoples. And some of the resentment remains. But the pressure of exploding populations has made the point unmistakably, and increasing numbers of the LDCs are inaugurating population-limitation programs. China and India, the world's two most populous nations, provide striking examples.

If China's statistics are correct, her recent efforts are the spectacular success of family-planning history. She reports a drop in the birth rate from 32 per thousand to only 19 per thousand between 1970 and 1975. Chinese family planning is part of the total planning process. The rule is straightforward. Each couple is entitled to, but should not have more than, two or three children. Late marriage is encouraged. It is stressed that women can be men's equals only if they are freed from an endless round of childbearing. Contraceptive information and methods are provided by the state. Family planning is the responsibility of numerous small planning groups in factories, neighborhoods, and villages. Just how these planning groups get people to agree and cooperate is not entirely clear.

India, whose population is growing about 15 million people per year, has had only limited success. For over a decade, the Gandhi government included large expenditures for birth control in its annual budgets. In 1976, some of the individual Indian states adopted experimental legislation requiring sterilization of couples who have more than two children, although with many exceptions in the law. The national government withdrew housing benefits from large families, increased outlays on education, and threatened increasingly drastic measures. But these measures sparked violent objections, and were apparently a major factor in Gandhi's defeat as prime minister. The government since is moving with more caution.

Population limitation is easier said than done, and the programs of most LDCs have had limited success. In Asia, Indonesia has been quite successful, but Pakistan and Bangladesh have made little headway. A mixed picture prevails elsewhere too. Providing effective bases for family planning among hundreds of millions of illiterate, widely scattered people is very difficult. Religious barriers appear to be less formidable than was previously believed. But in most poor societies, the family is the main economic and social unit, and parents must look to their children for support in old age. Some people in the poor nations now recognize that with modern death rates, they need not have seven or eight children to be reasonably sure three or four will survive, and perhaps birth control will be more readily accepted. But overturning centuries-old beliefs and practices is not easy, and progress is far from certain.[6]

Balanced vs. Unbalanced Growth

In the less-developed nations and among the experts, the debate rages as to whether poor nations can grow faster by concentrating on the development of either industry or agriculture alone, or by striving to develop both sectors in balance.

Sooner or later, industrialization is necessary for full economic development. Every high-income nation in Table 29–1 has a major industrial and commercial sector. Transport and steel play prominent roles in industrialization. Adequate transport facilities and communication permit specialization and underlie mass production and mass markets. Steel is used in nearly every facet of modern industrial activity, and every growing nation longs for its own modern steel mill, as a symbol of national pride. Moreover, if a nation can develop its own industry, it

[6]For a generally optimistic survey, see L. Brown and B. Stokes, "World Gains in Family Planning," *Challenge*, November 1977.

can then substitute domestic products for essential but expensive imported goods (machinery, fertilizer, food), for which there is never enough foreign exchange. Thus, "import substitution" is always an alluring goal for the developing nations. Getting more foreign exchange to pay for imports is a top priority of every LDC.

However, large industrial plants in the developing nations have often proved costly and inefficient, with their products costing far more than the imports for which they are supposed to substitute. So they generally require heavy subsidies and tariff or import protection to get started. Often, little foreign exchange is saved.

Thus, mounting experience suggests that improving agricultural productivity is the first need if LDCs are to break out of their vicious circle. This is particularly true for the very poor nations, in the "Fourth World." With 70–80 percent of the population in agriculture, that's where the first problem is.

Some simple arithmetic dramatizes the importance of improving farm productivity. Suppose a nation wants to increase total output 5 percent annually but finds it impossible to raise agricultural productivity. If the "modern," non-agricultural sector produces 20 percent of total output, *its* productivity would have to increase 25 percent a year in order to provide the desired overall 5 percent increase. Such a spectacular performance is hardly likely.

Thus, allocation of scarce capital to raising agricultural output makes sense. Improving agricultural efficiency through fertilizer, simple tools, and improved methods requires little capital compared to mass industrialization. It requires less social disruption, less transfer of people, less infrastructure than does movement to a modern industrial sector. But as development progresses, the case for some industrialization grows, as does that for more emphasis on international trade. Balanced growth becomes increasingly important for countries in the middle-income group.

The Crucial Role of Foreign Trade

As the preceding section indicates, nearly every LDC faces a critical shortage of foreign exchange to pay for essential imports of food, fertilizer, and capital goods. The LDCs can get foreign exchange only by selling their own exports, unless they can borrow abroad, attract foreign investors, or obtain gifts from the developed nations or international institutions.

Typically, LDCs can compete effectively in world export markets only when they have supplies of scarce natural resources (oil, nitrates, copper, bauxite, and so on), special advantages in agriculture (as with coffee in Brazil, long-staple cotton in Egypt), or relatively efficient, labor-intensive, simple manufactured products where they can take advantage of their plentiful, cheap labor (cotton textiles). Thus, developed-country markets for these products are essential to the development of many LDCs, and they have understandably exerted increasing pressure through international organizations on the richer nations to guarantee markets for such products at high prices, and to provide preferential tariff treatment for them. In the "Tokyo Round" international trade agreement of 1979, numerous basic products of the developing nations were given preferential tariff rates by the highly developed nations, but the LDCs complained bitterly that the preferences were too small. They have also attempted cartel arrangements, like OPEC, to achieve the same purposes. Import substitution through industrialization, as noted above, is an ever-beguiling possibility, but one that often, alas, turns out to be costly rather than helpful. The need to export is a never-ending pressure on most LDCs. (See Case 31 at the end of this chapter.)

Growth and Poverty

Raising the living standards of the poorest people in the less-developed countries is a major goal of most development programs, and it is clear that only by substantially increasing output per capita in the LDCs can we hope to make major progress toward that goal. Merely redistributing income from the rich to the poor is neither feasible in most cases nor sufficient to raise the great masses of the poor to significantly higher levels. But economists have recently suggested a related, discouraging hypothesis: As the very poor nations rise gradually to higher income levels, all the gains may at first go to the middle-

and upper-income groups that lead the growth sectors. Indeed, in some cases—for example, India—it appears that the relative (even the absolute) incomes of the very poor actually fell. There is widespread debate as to why this occurs and whether it is necessary to getting development started, but economists increasingly agree that early income improvements may help the poor very little. Some have suggested that only after an income level of perhaps $400–$500 per capita is reached will the income share of the poor begin to rise.[7]

Many economists reject this argument because we have data on too few cases to permit generalizing. Others accept the analysis and data, and say this should make us rethink our whole approach toward development. They suggest focusing directly on programs to raise the basic living standards of the poor, rather than trying to stimulate growth of the whole economy. Class the whole issue as "unsettled" for the time being.

Economic Planning or the Price System?

Many Americans, seeing the success of our essentially private-enterprise, market-directed economy, argue that the LDCs should rely on private initiative and the marketplace. But this view has found little sympathy in the LDCs. There is so much to be done and so little time to do it. These nations do not trust the "unseen hand" of Adam Smith to guide the complex process of growth, to assess the long-range importance of alternative uses of resources. They want roads, schools, fertilizers, and industrial plants now. Thus, government intervention on a wide scale is the active agent in less-developed nations. The main issue is whether it shall involve complete government control over economic life (as in Communist China) or merely government direction of broad lines of activity, with wide scope left to private initiative (as in India).

Nearly everywhere, it is agreed that government must provide infrastructure. Even where most of the economy stays private, basic investment priorities have become the province of the government. Nearly everywhere, foreign exchange is under government control, so that scarce foreign currencies are used for high-priority imports rather than for private luxuries.

But in recent years, the experts have turned back to the crucial importance of individual initiative, and the role of self-interest in providing that initiative. There is disenchantment with government planning to solve all the problems. Many government planners and native bureaucrats have proved incompetent; corruption is commonplace. Some LDCs now try to regulate the behavior of individuals to a degree unknown in the Western world since mercantilism. All foreign trade and use of foreign exchange is regulated in detail; new businesses require government licenses. Rents, wages, and basic commodity prices are controlled; internal shipments of grains and other basic commodities require government permits. The amount of red tape horrifies both native entrepreneurs and foreign businessmen. With the best of intentions, such complex regulations plus incompetence in their administration can stifle business rather than speed development.[8] Many countries are learning that government control per se is no answer to the real problems of development, even though government planning is needed to supplement markets and individual initiative. Only Communist China and Cuba have adhered closely to a communist complete-planning approach, and even they make substantial use of markets.

Monetary-Fiscal Policy and Economic Growth

Why don't the governments of the poor nations use deficit-financed spending to set up factories, provide jobs for the city unemployed, and lure the surplus farm population away from disguised

---

[7]See T. N. Srinivasan, "Development, Poverty, and Basic Human Needs," *Stanford Food Research Institute Studies,* April 1977. One major explanation is that growth primarily increases the demand for relatively skilled labor, so those incomes rise while wage rates for the unskilled (poor) are not bid up.

[8]See W. Dick, "Authoritarian versus Nonauthoritarian Approaches to Economic Development," *Journal of Political Economy,* July 1974. But Communist China has developed rapidly under economywide planning; see below.

unemployment into useful work, thereby increasing output and improving everyone's welfare?

The answer is that the main result would be inflation rather than increased output. As in the United States, raising the long-term growth rate is basically a *real* "supply" problem, not one of inadequate demand.

Suppose the government of Peru or Afghanistan prints money to lure workers into industry. There are no idle factories where output can be increased by calling the unemployed back to work. The critical shortage is real capital (factories, machinery, transport), not aggregate money demand. The situation is very different from the depression period in advanced countries, with vast unused productive capacity.

With this barrier to increasing real output, government spending without corresponding tax collections is likely to lead mainly to inflation as spending rises and output does not. Rapid inflation may endanger the stability of the government. Sound government finances are the first thing outside investors look for. And inflated domestic costs and prices make it harder to sell in world markets, a major blow when foreign exchange is badly needed to finance imports. To repeat, the problems of the less-developed economies are basically *real* problems.

Two Important Cases: India and China

One third of all the people in the world live in two countries: nearly a billion in China, and over 600 million in India. These countries exemplify dramatically different approaches to economic development.[9]

In many respects India and China face similar problems. They are both vast land masses, heavily populated in many areas but with great

---

[9]Informative overviews of the two economies in action are provided by *China: A Reassessment of the Economy* (Joint Economic Committee of Congress, 1975), especially Introduction and Chapter 1; A. Eckstein, *China's Economic Revolution* (New York: Cambridge University Press, 1977); G. Myrdal, *Asian Drama* (New York: Pantheon, 1968); and J. Mellor, *The New Economics of Growth* (Ithaca, N.Y.: Cornell University Press, 1976). For a brief summary of recent Chinese developments, see J. S. Prybyla, "Industrial Development in China," *Challenge,* September 1978.

reaches of mountains and wasteland. Both, in 1950, had per capita incomes below $100. In both, about 75 percent of the total population is engaged in agriculture. And both, since World War II, have undertaken vigorous planned programs of economic development.

India. In her six "five-year plans" since 1951, India has chosen an essentially democratic approach. This has left considerable freedom to private enterprise under government planning, while using government projects in such major areas as irrigation, transportation, and steel. Over one-third of total investment has been private, and in spite of India's claim to be a "socialist" state, the great bulk of her economic activity remains in private hands. Government taxes and spending remain only about half as large a percentage of GNP as in the United States and Western European nations. The plans pushed both industrialization and agricultural productivity—primarily the former at first, with more stress on agriculture recently. Industrial investment concentrated on both small-scale industry, such as textiles, and on larger projects, such as power development, fertilizers, coal, and heavy manufacturing. The plans called for increased capital accumulation in both agriculture and industry, plus added government services.

Results of the plans have been mixed. Real national income rose 3–4 percent per annum and population about 2.5 percent, giving perhaps a 1 percent annual increase in per capita income—a pitifully small $1 a year. It is not clear that the living standard of many Indian peasants is much higher than it was a thousand years ago. Industrial improvement is more encouraging. Industrial production has quadrupled since 1950. Net investment rose from about 5 to 10 percent of net national product, and saving is apparently rising.

But the achievements have fallen far short of India's optimistic goals, and per capita income has risen very little in the 1970s. Moreover, unemployment has risen from probably 10 to 20 million people in the cities, perhaps many more; no one has reliable statistics. Agriculture has been the great problem sector. And all the plans would have foundered had not large-scale foreign aid, mainly from America, eased India's desperate foreign-exchange shortages as she tried to finance the imports required for food and capital investment. Heavy military expenditures, reflecting concern over Indian relations with both China and Pakistan, have cut the supply of civilian-type goods.

India has wavered uncertainly as to the amount of government control she wants. In the second and third plans, government regulation of investment, foreign trade, and other aspects of economic activity became more and more detailed. Complaints of bureaucratic red tape and corruption multiplied, from Indians, foreign businesses in India, and potential investors. The major shortfalls of the third plan were attributed by many to this increasing bureaucracy and government inefficiency. Detailed government planning is thus less prominent in the later plans. Detailed industry targets have been replaced by planning estimates, except for a few key industries. More stress is placed on encouraging initiative of individual farmers.

The hopeful view is that India is on the verge of her takeoff into self-sustaining growth. But her successes have been modest, and the plans have made little progress in raising per capita incomes—especially because population-control programs have fallen far short of hopes. Foreign investment faces strict Indian controls. Bureaucracy, indecision, and red tape frustrate foreign businessmen and visitors who try to do business in India. Today, India remains a restless giant, unsure of the success of her individualistic, humanistic program of mixed public and private enterprise.

China. China's first five-year plan, covering 1952–57, called for drastic increases in industrialization, collectivization of agriculture, and ruthless suppression of consumption to obtain the resources required for capital accumulation. The plan centralized economic control in the Communist government. High government taxes on the masses and "profits" on government-monopolized necessities were used to seize a larger portion of total income for government investment. Large-scale external aid was received from the USSR. Hard work and long hours were forced on the Chinese people. The result was a substantial pickup in the rate of economic growth, which had been zero or negative during the preceding war decade.

The second five-year plan called for a further "great leap forward" with the primary focus on heavy industry, although food targets were also upped substantially. In 1958, government seizure of huge land masses and forced concentration of millions of agricultural families in huge "communes" virtually abolished individual family units. Women were pressed into all areas of work, and children were placed in state nurseries. Communist dictation of thought patterns made George Orwell's *1984* seem very real indeed.

But Mao's great leap forward turned out to be China's great failure. After an initial surge, industrial output collapsed. In the years 1959–61, both industrial and agricultural output fell radically—food production apparently by nearly one-half, as bad weather compounded the troubles. The strains of the previous decade's massive conversion to industry and of the Communists' ruthless abolition of traditional family values apparently forced a massive retreat from the "communes" policy that had seized all private land and forced families into closely regulated agricultural communes. Some land was returned to individual family ownership, and some degree of family life was restored. More stress was placed on food production, and industrialization plans were revised downward radically.

After the failure of the great leap forward, China followed a more moderate development policy. The 1960s were devoted to restoring more orderly growth, and it was not until the mid-1960s that food and industrial production again reached the levels of a decade earlier.

China's forward progress was again interrupted by the great "cultural revolution" of the late 1960s, which involved a massive social, economic, political revolution to assure the dominance of Maoist thought. Group planning and supervision of all activities was established. Income differentials were reduced. Intellectuals were banished to work in the farms and factories. Universities were closed. Mao was almost deified.

But the "cultural revolution" proved little more successful economically than had the "great leap forward," and after Mao's death, China's new leaders moved rapidly to reestablish more orderly and sophisticated economic planning and operation of the economy—to modernize China. Many of the former elite were returned to positions of influence. Skilled workers were recalled, and wider income differentials were established for managers and production workers. The universities were reopened. China moved to reopen its channels of trade and communication with the Western world.

Today, China is the world's most completely communist nation—a rapidly growing, dual economy with substantially more progress in the industrial than the agricultural sector. Over the entire 1952–78 period, real GNP has apparently grown at an average of about 5 percent annually, with large swings above and below that figure. Industrial production has apparently grown at 10 percent per annum during the 1970s. The impressive growth in industrial output, absolutely and relative to India, is shown in Table 29–4. Visitors are impressed by the hard work of the Chinese people, by the clean cities, and by the obviously improving standard of living. China has launched space satellites, built atomic bombs, and mounted a major military force. She is clearly no longer a typical less-developed nation.

But China is still a very poor nation, and the differences between the cities and agriculture are great. Nearly 80 percent of all Chinese live on the land, and most still spend their lives at back-breaking labor, with little help from modern machinery or even animals. As in most LDCs, farm incomes are apparently only about one-third to one-half those in the cities. The farm sector, the backbone of the Chinese economy, is organized into people's communes, which are both local government subdivisions and economic units for production, including some non-agricultural output. The communes vary in size from 5,000 to 40,000 people. They are in turn divided into production brigades of about 1,000 members, and these into production teams of 150–200. The team is responsible for cultivating its assigned land, and for carrying out all the associated activities. The Maoists emphasized the importance of group participative decision making at this level, but the new look puts more stress on individual initiative. Part of the output is allocated to local public and social services, and taxes are paid to the central government. Each team is given delivery goals for sales to the state at state-established prices. As long as it meets these goals, it is apparently free to consume what it wants of what more it produces. Peasants are allowed small plots for their own cultivation, and there are small private markets for their output, as in most other communist economies, reflecting what are termed "spontaneous forces" for the rural economy.

Although communism stresses equality of incomes, there are substantial income differentials. In the late 1970s, the average factory worker's wage was about 60 yuan per month, while a beginning, low-output worker got about half that amount. (A yuan equals about 45 cents in U.S. money.) High-skilled workers got about 100

TABLE 29–4
Economic Growth in India and China

	INDIA		CHINA	
	1950	1975	1950	1975
GNP (in 1975 U.S. dollars)	24	85	60	300
GNP per capita (in 1975 dollars)	90	140	90	350
Industrial production (1950 = 100)	100	480	100	1050
Electrical power (million kilowatt hrs.)	4	63	5	115
Cement (million tons)	1	16	1	36
Steel (million tons)	1	8	.1	26
Cotton cloth (billion meters)	1	5	2	9
Grain (million ton)	55	105	135	260
Fertilizers (million tons)	1	12	1	26

Source: United Nations, reports by Indian and Chinese governments, and CIA estimates. Figures are rough estimates and may be overstated in some cases.

yuan, and engineers and technicians earned up to 130–140 yuan. Some physicians and surgeons apparently earned 200–300 yuan. In the post-Mao changes, incomes were raised, especially for the higher skills, and income differentials were widened somewhat. Thus, incomes are considerably more equal than in the Western capitalist societies, because there are no high incomes from capital, but high-skilled experts may still earn ten times what common workers do, and perhaps twenty times as much as farm workers. The Chinese apparently find that monetary rewards can be important, as have the Russians and other communist societies.

The Future of the Less-Developed Nations

Clearly, many of the less-developed nations are economies in motion. During the 1960s, labeled by the UN the "decade of development," real GNP for all developing countries combined grew at a surprising 5.6 percent per annum. Some countries—Libya (oil), Greece, Taiwan, Israel, Iran (oil), Korea, and Brazil—averaged 7 percent or better. Oil-producing LDCs are the big success stories of the 1970s. Although special factors, like oil, explain some of the success, the overall picture is reasonably encouraging.

Most nations are learning from experience. A leading American economist has summarized the lessons of development policy over the past two decades:

Both the practical and theoretical emphasis is now more on agriculture and less exclusively on industry, more on human and relatively less on physical capital investment, more on private enterprise and less on state industries, more on reducing birthrates and less on increasing national output, and more on cultural and technological change instead of making foreign loans and grants called "capital." The lack of real managers and technical specialists is seen as especially acute in the recently decolonized nations. The importance of efficient and honest government is becoming more appreciated.[10]

There is no chance that the LDCs will catch up with the developed-nation per capita in-

comes in the foreseeable future. Even on the most optimistic assumptions of annual growth rates in the LDCs, the absolute gap between rich and poor nations is widening at a breakneck pace. A 2 percent annual increase on $10,000 (roughly the present U.S. per capita figure) is $200, more than the total present annual per capita income in India. Even if the Indian growth rates were to be double ours (say, 4 percent per capita as against 2 percent)—a most unlikely situation—by the end of the century, U.S. per capita GNP would still be about $15,000, Indian per capita GNP less than $500. Clearly, the less-developed nations can raise their living standards. But even if success surpasses their wildest dreams, the absolute gap between the "haves" and "have-nots" in our ever-smaller world seems certain to widen spectacularly over the years ahead. But countries like Brazil, Mexico, Taiwan, and Argentina, with per capita GNPs over $1,000, show that progress is possible.

What would you advise the prime minister of India to do to raise the standard of living of the Indian people?

U.S. POLICY

Mankind is passing through the most pervasive revolution it has ever known—the revolt of two-thirds of the world's people against the poverty, misery, and degradation of their present conditions of life, and against the domination of the industrialized, wealthy Western powers. The speed and force of this revolution are hard to perceive by someone sitting in the comfort of an American home or classroom. But they may well do more than any other force to determine the kind of world in which we will live a half century hence.

What should American policy be? As the proud leaders of a democratic, humanitarian tradition, what should we do? What interests do we have in the less-developed nations, many of whose names we scarcely recognize?

First, an unhappy, resentful world of LDCs will be politically unstable. Rising living standards can give hope to the world's undernourished billions, even though they certainly cannot guarantee friendship or quiescence.

---

[10]Stephen Enke, "Economists and Development," *Journal of Economic Literature,* December 1969, p. 1135.

Second, we have economic interests. It would be foolish to overstress this element. Trade with *all* the LDCs amounts to only about 2 percent of U.S. GNP. But trade with the LDCs looks favorable for both us and them. We need their raw materials, and they need our food and manufactures.

Third, and perhaps most important, many Americans feel that we have a humanitarian interest in the relief of starvation, the lessening of disease and misery, and the improvement of education and living standards of the billions of people in the less-developed areas. There but for the grace of God go I, they say. We are very rich and they are very poor, and they need our help. Others disagree, especially when the time comes to pay the taxes to finance help to the LDC. Here, obviously, is a moral issue on which you must make up your own mind.

Channels of American Aid

If we want to help, for political, economic, or humanitarian reasons, we should first ask the question, Can we really make any difference? The task of helping 1 or 2 billion people to a better life is a huge one. And the preceding pages surely show that the task is not simply one of providing more dollars of foreign aid.

Yet we should remember some facts. The total income of all the billion people in the non-Communist less-developed nations in 1978 was less than $250 billion. The GNP of the United States was $2.1 trillion. In 1978, we spent over $100 billion on military purposes; total arms spending in the world was over $300 billion. Elimination of these war expenditures could have doubled the living standard of each of the billion people.

The United States and the other developed nations have the economic ability to help significantly. What have we done? What should we do?

In 1976, total government loans, grants, and private investments from the developed countries to the LDCs totaled $40 billion, including $12 billion from the United States. About 60 percent was private long-term investment, presumably made in search of profits. The rest was government aid, either bilaterally or through international organizations. The U.S. $12 billion was $4.3 billion government aid, including "Food for Peace," with the remainder private investment,

mainly in Latin America and the Middle East. (These totals do not include military aid.) Although the United States dominated total grants and investments, our $4.3 billion of government aid was only one-quarter of 1 percent of our GNP, below the .33 percent average for all developed nations.

Since World War II, U.S. government loans and gifts to other nations have totaled $190 billion, about two-thirds in military aid and one-third in civilian aid. India has received by far the largest amount of civilian aid (nearly $10 billion), followed by South Vietnam, South Korea, and Pakistan. Most such aid was originally on a government-to-government basis, but in recent years, more U.S. official aid has been channeled through international institutions, such as the World Bank and the Inter-American, Asian, and African Development Banks.

After the postwar burst of enthusiasm for aid to the less-developed economies came the sobering recognition that many of the crucial problems were internal ones. "Technical assistance" programs to help local governments and local peoples help themselves thus grew in popularity, partly because they seem to work well, partly because they are far cheaper than mass capital-investment grants. Assistance in establishing better schools, efficient local government administration, sanitation and public-health projects, and better farming techniques are examples. U.S. and multinational technical-assistance programs stress training natives to take over essential jobs themselves at the earliest possible moment. In most cases, U.S. technical assistance has been provided on a matching basis, with half the cost of the joint programs being borne by local governments. Technical assistance is a bright spot in our foreign-aid program.

In order to grow, most LDCs must sell basic products abroad if they are to secure foreign exchange with which to finance needed imports. Many of their economies are centered around one or two basic products—oil, rubber, nitrates, coffee, tin. Trade barriers that shut these products out of American markets strike a serious blow to the economies concerned. Contrary to the "imperialism" argument that we are bleeding the LDCs of their natural resources, those nations bitterly resent barriers to their sales in U.S. markets. The United States has led the way in reducing tariff barriers and in helping to provide stable international markets for such basic commodities.

The LDCs and a New World Order?

Not long ago, most LDCs were polite supplicants for development aid from the richer nations. But no more! Third and Fourth World countries want a new international economic order, with a massive sharing of the world's wealth. Using a variety of international organizations in which they can now outvote the highly developed nations, the LDCs have demanded vastly increased low-interest loan facilities with funds provided by the richer nations; an indefinite moratorium on existing debts owed to the developed nations; international cartel-like commodity price-stabilization agreements covering raw materials, with prices guaranteed by the developed nations; preferential tariff treatment in Western markets; freer transfer of technology. Much of the flavor is conveyed by a quotation from a recent U.N. speech by President Houari Boumediène of Algeria:

Europe and the U.S. have plundered the natural wealth of the Third World. We should consider whatever contribution the industrialized countries make to be a simple restitution of a tiny part of the debt contracted by their odious exploitation.

What should be the response of the United States and other developed nations to such demands? We have repeatedly led the way toward establishment of new international organizations to support Third and Fourth World development, especially through international lending plans. But in case after case, the LDCs have demanded more generous aid programs than the United States has supported, and have amassed the votes, on a one-country-one-vote basis, to substitute theirs for the Western nations' proposals. Since the charters of world financial organizations generally allocate votes roughly on the basis of contributions, the poorer nations cannot force contributions by the Western nations. Nor can they force us to participate in commodity price-support agreements and the like. But the successful OPEC escalation of oil prices strengthened their hand, and the industrialized countries find themselves increasingly outvoted by the LDCs, usually with the support of the Communist bloc.

Economic analysis can tell you a lot about the problem of raising living standards for the world's impoverished billions. It can give some guidance on how our help can do the most lasting good. But the problem of aid is moral and political as much as economic. It is one of the biggest issues on which this nation will repeatedly take a stand over the decades ahead. How, and how much, shall we aid the less-developed countries?

SUMMARY AND REVIEW

1. Living standards differ widely in different countries. Perhaps half the world's population is desperately poor by our standards. About 2 billion people live in what are often called the "Third World" or "Third and Fourth World" countries, with per capita GNPs below $500 per annum. Income estimates for these countries are very rough, and precise comparisons of their living standards are impossible.

2. The less-developed countries differ widely, but they are similar in some important respects. Nearly all have predominantly poor, low-productivity, agricul-

tural economies, with food the major product. They have dual economies, with development and rising incomes concentrated in the urban areas. There is often limited development of markets, and very unequal distribution of incomes. There is no large "middle class," as in the developed economies. There is a low ratio of capital to labor, low saving and capital accumulation, and slow technical progress. Governments are often weak, and the environment is poor for stable economic activity and long-range business planning. There are overpopulation in the sense of very high ratios of population to capital, and high growth rates of population. With low income, it is very difficult to save and invest enough to break out of the vicious circle of poverty.

3. There is no one simple answer as to how the LDCs can break out of poverty into self-sustaining economic growth. Probably, the best policy varies for different nations. Development economists generally stress improvement of the environment for work and development; faster capital accumulation, based on more saving; more education and more modern technology in both agriculture and industry; family planning to slow population growth; and development of export industries to earn more foreign exchange.

4. Foreign investment can help greatly in deepening capital in the LDCs, and most major LDC successes have depended at least partly on foreign capital. But many LDCs fear exploitation and place elaborate controls on foreign investment. There is much dispute over the importance and effects of foreign investment, especially between Marxists and supporters of private enterprise.

5. Expansionary monetary-fiscal policy is of limited value in stimulating growth and eliminating unemployment in the LDCs, because the basic problems there are real—lack of capital, absence of skills,

etc. More spending under these circumstances produces inflation rather than more output and jobs.

6. How much government planning and control is optimal is debated by the experts. In recent years, many experts have stressed the inefficiencies of government planning and bureaucracy, and the potentialities of individual initiative and markets.

7. China and India, the world's two most populous nations, provide interesting contrasts in their approaches to development. In recent decades, China has clearly shown faster development.

8. Even if the LDCs are highly successful in speeding their growth rates, the absolute per capita GNP gaps between them and the present highly-developed nations will widen, probably rapidly.

9. The United States has been the largest source of external aid to the LDCs ($3–$4 billion annually in the late 1970s, plus $6–$10 billion of private investment), but this official aid has been only about .25 of 1 percent of our GNP, a lower ratio than for most of the other highly developed nations. U.S. official aid has been increasingly channeled through international organizations, like the World Bank and the regional development banks. Recently, many LDCs have demanded more help in the form of international commodity agreements and tariff preferences for their basic exports.

For Analysis and Discussion

1. How well do the theories of Adam Smith and Malthus explain the plight of the less-developed nations? Has modern growth theory added much to their analyses?

2. To develop rapidly, a nation must save and invest a substantial portion of its income. What steps would you advise the Indian government to take to increase India's saving rate when the majority of the population is on the brink of starvation? How about Mexico, where GNP per capita is $1,100?

3. Suppose the U.S. government sends you to a less-developed nation to assess its development prospects over the next decade. What would be the key information you would seek for your report?

4. Nearly everyone agrees that slower population growth is essential to reducing poverty in the LDCs. Suppose you were prime minister of India or Kenya; how would you bring this about?

5. Development of an entrepreneurial class seems critical for nations trying to break out of the vicious circle of poverty. If you were a government official in Peru or Zaire, what would you do about this problem?

6. Modern economics tells us to pump in purchasing power in order to eliminate unemployment when depression occurs in the Western world. How well will this policy work in the less-developed nations?

7. Will the gap between U.S. and less-developed nations' living standards narrow or widen over the next quarter century?

8. Are large-scale U.S. purchases of raw materials from the LDCs a sign of U.S. exploitation at work, or an aid to development through providing badly needed foreign exchange?

9. If the United States wishes to provide development aid to the LDCs, should it do so directly on a government-to-government basis, or through international organizations like the World Bank or the regional development banks?

CASE 31

COFFEE, CARTELS, AND U.S. DEVELOPMENT AID

Basic commodity prices (of agricultural products and minerals) have long fluctuated sharply, reflecting sharp variations in supply and fluctuating (often inelastic) demands. During the 1930s, nearly all basic commodity prices nosedived, and a number of international intergovernmental commodity agreements were established (for example, on sugar and coffee), somewhat parallel to the New Deal agricultural price and income stabilization programs in the United States (see Chapter 24). Under these agreements, producing countries agreed to maintain reasonably stable output levels, and both producing and consuming governments agreed to keep prices reasonably stable by export and import controls, stockpiles, and production-control plans. Without such agreements, the LDCs, which were the primary producing countries, suffered wild fluctuations in their supplies of foreign exchange.

During the World War II inflations, commodity prices shot up, and since then, international commodity agreements have had a checkered history. In general, producing countries have sought them in depressed times, and output and trade restrictions have withered in boom periods. By the early 1970s, most such plans had been abandoned.

In 1973, the international coffee agreement expired, as Brazilian producers held out for higher coffee prices than the United States (the number one consumer) was willing to accept. Two-thirds of the world's coffee is produced by Brazil, Colombia, the Ivory Coast, and Angola, with the rest scattered among several countries, many of them in Latin America. Brazil and other producing countries argued that they desperately needed the foreign exchange provided by good coffee prices, and they reminded the United States and other developed nations of their promises to aid in economic development. They were also keenly aware of the spectacular success of the OPEC countries in quadrupling oil prices.[11] The United States said that the concessions demanded by the producers were just too much, and other major consumers agreed.

When the international agreement regulating prices, exports, and imports expired, the four main producers formed a cartel, and by mid-1974, world coffee prices hit an all-time peak, reflecting in part at least the major producers' agreement to hold 20 percent of the 1974–75 crop off the world market. But a year later, coffee prices were back down to their 1973 levels and falling. While Brazil was holding back coffee

[11]Several other international cartels (bauxite, phosphates, bananas, copper, and tin) were activated at about the same time.

to support the higher prices, several of the smaller exporters, which had never stockpiled coffee before, couldn't resist the temptation to capitalize on the high prices, and started selling heavily. The weather was good, and coffee surpluses piled up. Farmers in Angola, uncertain about the revolution in Portugal, also decided that the best policy was to take profits when they could be had, and finally Colombia also broke ranks. As Chapter 27 emphasized, cartel prices are hard to maintain without close control over supply.

By mid-1975, top Brazilian and Colombian officials were back in the United States, exploring the possibility of renewing a worldwide coffee pact.

Put yourself in two different roles in this case:

1. Suppose you were a Brazilian or Colombian government official. What position would you take?
   a. Let your individual coffee producers battle it out in the free market, winning customers away from other nations as best they could by price cuts or other competitive moves?
   b. Try to re-form the coffee cartel among the major producers, building in stronger safeguards against price cutters?
   c. Try to get the United States, other large consumers, and other producers to join in a new international coffee agreement in the hope that it would both stabilize coffee prices and keep them at a moderately higher level than would be produced by cutthroat competition?

   Whichever position you take, specify the arguments you would use to convince others to support it, and explain how you would implement the plan.

2. Suppose you are the U.S. assistant secretary of state for economic affairs. Would you support formation of a new international coffee agreement? Explain your recommendation to a congressional committee, including how you would compromise the interests of U.S. consumers and the LDC producers. If you oppose renewal of the coffee agreement, indicate how you would explain this country's position to Brazil, Colombia, and other Latin American producers when we claim that we want to be a good neighbor and help the Latin American nations develop economically.

An Overview: Comparative Economic Systems and Ideologies

Chapter 30

What type of economic system serves man best? On the evidence of Tables 1–1 and 29–1, it is private-enterprise, market-directed capitalism. Of the top ten nations in real income per capita, every one (except tiny, oil-rich Kuwait) has basically this type of economy. But all now mix in a liberal dose of government planning and regulation. Moreover, one-third of the world's people live in Communist nations (mainly China and the USSR), and Soviet Russia is the world's second great industrial and military power. Many of the smaller nations are still hovering as to the type of economy they prefer.

At the end of a long book, devoted mainly to our type of largely private-enterprise system, it is well to look briefly at what other ideologies have to say, and how other types of economic systems work. The USSR is perhaps the most interesting comparison, because it is the world's second most powerful economy and because it exemplifies modern socialism in action in a developed, industrial economy, even though it is far from Karl Marx's dreams. But a look at Japan is also appropriate, because it has been the world's great economic success story since World War II and because it exemplifies a more planned capitalist economy than does the United States. Add to these China, India, and the other LDCs from Chapter 46 and you have the spectrum of economic systems currently on trial, although there are many variations among the other nations.

CAPITALISM, COMMUNISM, AND MIXTURES

To look at the economic side of any "ism" alone is to miss its essence. Communism has become inseparably associated with political and economic dictatorship because we see them together in Russia and China, today's predominant Communist countries. Yet in its original form, Marxian socialism was highly democratic in spirit. Karl Marx's famous *Das Kapital,* the foundation of modern communism, provided a detailed critique of capitalism, but he was conveniently vague when it came to blueprinting the communist economy. Still Marx surely wasn't looking for any political or economic dictatorship except the dictatorship of the proletariat—of the whole working class.

From an economic viewpoint, there are two big differences between capitalism and communism. Under private-enterprise capitalism as we know it, most productive resources are privately owned, and economic activity is largely directed by the interaction of supply and demand in the market in response to individual interests. Under communism, conversely, most productive resources are publicly owned, and economic activity is directed largely by central planning; this type of economy is often called a "command economy." The two critical questions, then, are, (1) Are productive resources privately or publicly owned? and, (2) Is economic activity directed by individual preferences and the price system, or by government planning?

Obviously, both are matters of degree. Not all productive resources are privately owned under American capitalism—governments own land, highways, dams, buildings, and so on. Nor are all resources publicly owned in Russia. Also, an economy can have private ownership of resources and nevertheless be centrally planned. The American economy during World War II was a partial example. Hitler's fascism in Germany was a more complete example. India makes substantial use of central planning today, with primarily private ownership of resources.

Thus, economic systems fall along a spectrum on both these conditions, something like the arrangement shown in the diagram. The location

| Private ownership | Japan / U.S.————————India————————————————USSR—China | Public ownership |
| Price-directed | U.S.————Japan————————India————————USSR————————China | Centrally planned |

of the countries is only approximate, but it suggests the variation on both. The American and Russian systems differ widely on both. But don't forget that most of the world's economies lie in between, on one or both of the spectrums shown.

Neither Marx nor the modern Marxist "New Left" have spelled out in detail how a large, modern, industrial communist economy would operate. Thus, we have no operational way of comparing "ideal" communist and capitalist societies. Instead, we may, in conclusion, look at the USSR economy as a practical example of a large, industrial communist-type economy in action and compare it with the United States. Marxists protest bitterly that the USSR is not a fair example of communism in action—that it falls far short of communist ideals. It is ruled by the Communist party elite, not by the masses; it has adopted many capitalist techniques, such as profits, money-wage incentives, interest rates, elitism, and inequality. But these may be responses to precisely the main practical problems of making communism work, and the USSR may be as reasonable an example of communism in action as the United States is of capitalism. China, while nearer to a true communist pattern, is so poor and less-developed an economy that it faces problems quite different from those of highly developed industrial economies like the United States and USSR.[1]

COMMUNISM AND CAPITALISM IN PERSPECTIVE

How well have modified communism and capitalism done in the USSR and the United States? To answer, we must specify criteria for judgment. It may be convenient to use the five suggested in Chapter 1. But it may also be interesting to add some criteria used by today's radical "New Left" economists, mainly but not entirely disciples of Marx. For example, they ask, Which system provides the more rational allocation of resources to meet society's real needs? Which leads to greater inequality of economic and political

power? Which produces greater exploitation of workers?

Progress—Rising Living Standards

Which economic system has provided the higher standard of living for its people? However you measure, the United States is far out in front. In 1978, the U.S. GNP was $2.1 trillion. The USSR's, with a vastly larger area and 40 million more people, was only about 35–45 percent as large. Per capita GNP, a more significant measure of individual economic well-being, was $9,600 in the United States, $3,500–$4,500 in the USSR. Such comparisons may be substantially off because of measurement problems and currency-conversion difficulties, and some observers put Russian per capita incomes as high as half ours, but not more.

The Soviets have made substantial headway since they took over in the 1920s. Table 30–1 presents data comparing U.S. and USSR performance on a variety of scores. While total USSR output is less than half ours, in 1978, Soviet steel, coal, and oil production surpassed ours, reflecting the longtime Soviet emphasis on expanding industrial output. But on food, consumer goods, and just about everything else, the U.S. lead is large. Some important variables are hard to summarize in a simple table. Soviet housing is appallingly poor. Over a third of all city families still live in a single room, sharing a kitchen and bath with others. Food is adequate, but has little variety. Life in the USSR is repeatedly described as drab.

The Soviet growth rate in real GNP was 6–6½ percent from World War II to the 1960s. Since then, the rate has dropped to around 4 percent for the 1970s; and even the official Russian plan now calls for only 4½–5 percent, about the rate expected by the West European non-Communist countries. In perspective, the earlier rapid communist growth reflected very high investment while consumption was suppressed; a large increase in the industrial labor force as workers shifted from low-productivity agriculture and most women entered the labor force; and widespread borrowing of technology from the Western economies. But a more open society has recently led to more consumer goods and lower investment. By the 1960s, over 90 percent of the able-bodied population, including women, was

---

[1] The appendix to this chapter presents a brief overview of the Soviet economy. It provides more information underlying the evaluation of this section, and should be read here if it is used.

TABLE 30–1
How the Giants Compare (1978)

	UNITED STATES	USSR
Gross national product (bil. U.S. dollars)	2,100	900–1,200
Per capita GNP (U.S. dollars)	9,600	3,500–4,500
Grain production (million tons)	294	259
Electricity (bil. kw-hours)	2.1	1.1
Steel production (mil. tons)	135	166
Crude-oil production (mil. tons)	474	629
Coal production (mil. tons)	654	796
Telephones per capita	.69	.08
National defense (bil. U.S. dollars)	110	140 (est.)
Autos per hundred people	50	2
TV sets per family	2.6	.8
Doctors per 100,000 population	178	365
Months' earnings to buy a car	4.3	51
Residential living space (sq. ft. per person)	450	133
Average workweek (hours)	36.0	40.6

either in the labor force or going to school; the labor force grew from 97 million in 1950 to 135 million in 1975; further increases will be much slower. As Soviet industry caught up in technology with other nations, this source of growth also faded. Explanation of the high Soviet postwar growth rate thus appears to be much like that for capitalist countries, and the reasons for the recent Soviet slowdown also look much like those found in maturing capitalist nations. With the end of their special growth advantages, the Soviets' rate of growth will depend heavily on their ability to maintain high growth in productivity (output per man-hour).

Some critics argue that GNP per capita is an inadequate measure of economic well-being. They are right. GNP doesn't take into account leisure, such real costs as pollution, and a variety of other factors. But as far as we can tell, the USSR is no better off than we are on these unmeasured factors. Their press and their officials complain about water, air, and noise pollution, much as we do. Inclusion of leisure in GNP would clearly *worsen* Russia's relative position. Although the industrial work-week is about the same in both countries, a much larger proportion of the total population, including women, works in Russia. No other non-GNP factor would appear to change the relative standard of living comparison much. If we could construct a Russian measure of net economic welfare, it would probably relate to GNP about the way ours does.

No simple measures of efficiency of the two systems are available. Per capita or per-worker output provides a very rough approximation, but it reflects many different variables. For what it is worth, it shows U.S. real output per capita more than twice that of the Soviets. Most Western observers have been struck by the examples of obvious inefficiency under Soviet planning— parts that don't fit, production halted by the absence of required parts or materials, and the like. The accompanying cartoon shows the Russian wryly observing their problem. In a market system, the profit incentive continually pushes managers to avoid such inefficiencies. Under quotas and physical planning, the manager's goal is to meet the quotas, not to question why. A standard Russian joke has a factory turning out one huge one-ton nail as the cheapest way to meet its quota of one ton of steel nails.

Individualism and Consumer Control— Dispersion of Economic Power

In Russia, the Communist central planners, not the consumers, decide what is to be produced. Consumers have substantially free choice in spending their money—but they can spend it only on goods available and at the prices set by the planners. The American system surely responds more directly to consumer demands if we take their dollar votes as guides. About three-

— Наверное, в проекте произошла неувязка...

Рисунок В. ТИЛЬМАНА

In this cartoon from a Soviet humor magazine, one construction worker says to the other, "A slight mistake in the plans, perhaps."

fourths of our GNP is allocated through the private economy, pretty much in response to consumers' dollar demands.

But this talk of consumer sovereignty is fantasy, modern Marxists say. Under capitalism in America today, they argue, what gets produced is what capitalists think they can sell for the largest profit—whether or not it makes any sense economically, aesthetically, morally, or otherwise. Capitalists need not produce what consumers want or need. Instead, the giant corporations decide what they want consumers to want, and then use modern advertising, television, and other "demand creation" techniques to develop the markets they need to maximize profits. Thus, not only are consumers not sovereign, but the big corporations produce air-polluting autos, luxury apartments, expensive jewelry, and atomic bombs, while workers desperately need simple, healthy foods, decent housing and clothing, and healthy, clean sites in which to live. War spending is the most extreme example of this irrationality. There is no rational, national planning of

the goods and services that society really needs.

The capitalist defenders have two main answers. First, it is true that the American market-directed system responds to consumer demands far from perfectly. But overall, consumer choice is *the* powerful director of economic production in our basically market-directed, unplanned economy.

Second, imperfect though the market system may be, the consumer has a far stronger voice than under the Soviet system, where power to decide what to produce lies in the hands of the Communist party central planners. Will the output of a society be more "rational" if it is determined by such central planners than by the give-and-take of consumers and businesses in the American market system? Who is to say what is most rational and where the power is to lie? It is one of the market's greatest virtues that it so widely disperses economic power over what is to be produced, where, how, and by whom. General Motors and General Electric are very big, and perhaps they should be smaller, but their con-

433

centration of economic power is far from that of the Politburo in Moscow.

Last, what of the substantial public sector of the American economy? Does it respond to individual choices better or worse than the Communist planners in Russia do? Chapters 23 and 24 emphasized that our political democracy is far from perfect in meeting the one-man-one-vote ideal. But most Americans clearly feel it comes closer than the Soviets do to democratic control over resources allocated through the public sector. And many argue that the massive concentration of economic power that is inevitable with centralized economic planning is per se incompatible with the maintenance of individual freedom and democratic political processes.

Equity and Inequality

Which system does a better job in slicing up the national economic pie equitably among competing claimants? By substantially eliminating incomes from property, the Communists have eliminated most of the very high incomes of capitalistic systems. *Worker* money incomes, on the other hand, are apparently more unequally distributed than in the United States, but then somewhat equalized by subsidized government services and pricing policies. This fact reflects the heavy emphasis placed on both monetary work incentives and government assurance of essentials by the Communists.

America has a few very rich, and a lower tenth who are poor by our standards, although well off by the standards of most nations. But the emergence of a huge, reasonably well-to-do middle class is the most striking development of recent American economic history. Claims that workers are exploited and driven to poverty do not match the facts of the income statistics.

More equality of incomes has many American supporters. But many others prefer a mixture of more equality of opportunity and reward for services rendered. They stress the danger that higher taxes on large incomes reduce incentives to work, earn, and invest. And they want a path for themselves to higher incomes. Table 29–1 showed how growth in the Western market-directed economies has dominated all distributional issues. Even the poor at the bottom of the income scale in the highly productive Western economies have higher incomes than the middle-income citizens in the command-type economies. Individual initiative motivated by individual reward has been the foundation of most successful economic growth in the nineteenth- and twentieth-century world. Any income redistribution that reduces total output is very hard to defend.

Individual Freedom

The American economy provides almost complete freedom on where to work, where to live, how to spend your money, and other economic choices. The freedom to go into business for yourself is completely unmatched in the Soviet system. American unions are a powerful device for equalizing the economic power of employers and employees, lacking in the USSR. Government taxes are substantial in the United States, and to this extent, economic freedom may be said to be curtailed—although less so than in Russia and in other "command" nations.

How much "economic freedom" the Soviet economy provides for the individual depends on what you mean by the phrase. Today, the Soviet citizen has considerable freedom to move to another job and to spend his income on whatever he can find to buy. But the government determines what goods will be available for purchase and often tells him where he should work through housing allocations. Russian unions have no voice in determining the wages at which the citizens will work. Nor have the Soviets shown concern for their minorities and dissenters that compares favorably with the American record. Concern for human rights goes far beyond economics, but the economic component is an important one.

Security

Is economic security freedom from the fear of unemployment? of arbitrary discharge? of poverty and disaster in old age or ill health? Is economic security separable from political security? The possible collapse of capitalism in mass depressions plays a central role in all Marxist criticism of modern capitalism.

By one test, the Soviet citizen is secure economically. He is assured of a minimum of public services and of a job if he works reasonably hard and conforms to the rules of the leaders in power. In a planned economy, workers aren't planned into unemployment (although Westerners observe apparent widespread "hidden" unemployment where excess labor is allocated to particular jobs or industries).

The United States has moved a long way toward similar security (see Chapter 25). Our Social Security system, with Medicare and Medicaid, now offers protection against most types of economic insecurity likely to strike older people; and private pension plans are now widespread. But beyond these, the great protection of economic security in the American system is the jobs and high per capita income that make it possible for workers to look out for themselves. Modern monetary and fiscal policy appear to have massive booms and depressions under control, and unemployment insurance, welfare, food stamps, and other aids greatly reduce the burden of temporary unemployment. Still, persistent inflation and unemployment plague capitalism in America and the other major Western nations.

FOUR FUNDAMENTAL QUESTIONS

Professor Assar Lindbeck, one of Sweden's most distinguished economists and a friendly but sharp critic of the Marxist New Left in America, has suggested four fundamental questions that summarize the key issues in the controversy.[2]

1. How should economic activity be organized—through markets, or through a political bureaucracy? Marxists and the New Left vigorously criticize the use of markets to organize what shall be produced, how, and who shall get it. They criticize equally the "capitalist-dominated political bureaucracy" that, they say, runs the government. But if we reject both the market and political bureaucracy, how shall the millions of interlocking decisions about what is to be

produced, how resources are to be used, and how products are to be distributed be decided? On this, the critics are strikingly silent. They apparently hope that somehow, 200 million people will beam their thoughts to a wise and thoughtful socialist state that, with no concentration of bureaucratic power in Washington, will produce what everybody wants or "needs" in the right amounts at the right time.

But 200-million-person town meetings to develop consensus are wildly impractical. And even if some sort of majority vote could be arranged on major economic issues, it is highly doubtful that this would satisfactorily reflect the multiple minority interests that characterize most major economic issues. (Remember Chapter 24.) If we don't use the market, political bureaucracy appears to be the only practical alternative. But experience tells us that placing major power to organize the economy in bureaucratic hands will lead to increasingly concentrated power in the government.

By contrast, it is the genius of the price system that it somehow manages to reflect and compromise the diverse, often conflicting wishes of millions of individuals in a complex economy. It collects information on preferences; allocates resources at least roughly in accordance with these preferences, including minority wishes; creates incentives to satisfy these complex wants, coordinating and compromising the actions of millions of different individuals; and simultaneously allocates incomes roughly in accordance with the contribution each makes to meeting consumer demands. Lindbeck looks in vain for a New Left solution to all this if we reject both bureaucracy and the market.

2. Shall decision making be centralized or decentralized? As a closely related matter, the Marxists and New Left bitterly criticize the concentration of power in the hands of the big corporations and the government in the United States. Look back over the course and judge for yourself how much basis there is for these criticisms. But whatever your answer, if we reject the market and turn to central planning, the concentrated power of the planners will be greater than under the market alternative. Mankind has found no way to concentrate vast economic

---

[2] *The Political Economy of the New Left* (New York: Harper & Row, 1977).

power in the hands of a central government without having this power strongly used, and often abused. Indeed, perhaps the strongest argument for a market-directed economy is precisely the dispersion of economic and political power that it assures, by reserving to millions of individual consumers, businessmen, and others in society the power to participate actively in the decision-making process.

3. Who shall own capital, and how shall we manage incentives and the distribution of incomes? The Marxist and New Left critics argue that capital should be owned by the state, not by private individuals, and that incomes should be distributed on the basis of need, not as rewards for work done. Above all, private ownership of capital should not be a source of individual incomes.

The radical literature says virtually nothing about the importance of providing adequate incentives for work and saving in the ideal communist society, or about initiatives in a society without private ownership of capital or substantial income inequalities. Strikingly, as a practical matter all the major Communist industrial states have introduced more use of income inequality, more monetary and economic rewards for work done, to provide incentives. Lindbeck writes, "This problem—of encouraging initiative—is probably the basic unsolved problem of nationalized economies, along with the problems of avoiding bureaucratization and concentration of economic, political and military power in the same hands."[3]

Perhaps cooperation and concern for others' welfare ought to be the strongest motivating force in inducing human beings to work hard, produce more, and save more for the future. But apparently self-interest, personal income, and personal accumulation of property are, as a practical matter, powerful incentives, even in communist-based states like the USSR.

4. Shall we have competition or cooperation as the basis for organizing society? The Marxist–New Left argument against competition seems to be primarily an ethical one; competition is less moral than cooperation. It would be a "better" society if we would cooperate rather than compete in it. This argument is closely related to many New Left arguments that further economic growth and "development" are unnecessary—indeed, in many ways bad. People should not want more GNP, but instead should prefer a better "quality" of life. They should be content cooperating with others to assure such a good life for all. America has no real need for more output, if only we would make "rational" use of existing resources.

Again, the practical question of incentives and actual behavior comes center stage. Most evidence in America seems to be that, although we vigorously criticize overemphasis on growth, most of us still want more, as well as a better quality of life. We want less pollution and a more pleasant, healthy environment—but we want more goods and services too. Elimination of personal competition has much appeal to some. But "cooperation" instead of market competition has yet to show that it offers a workable way of organizing a vast, complex economy, or provides incentives that get people to work hard and produce the goods and services that most Americans want.

PLANNING WITH PRIVATE ENTERPRISE: THE NEW LOOK?

Most of the world's economies lie somewhere between America's private enterprise and Russia's communism. Some, like Japan, are basically private enterprise but with extensive government–industry cooperation and joint planning. Others, like Yugoslavia, are near the communist end of the spectrum, but with a new twist that allows widespread individual initiative and market guidance, with collective ownership of productive resources. Still others, like Sweden and Denmark, are experimenting with limited joint government–private planning and extensive equalization of incomes through government real and money transfers. Most of the world's economies can only be classified as mixed, and to most Americans these mixtures (not communism) are the likely alternatives if we want to change. Japan is worth special attention, because of her spectacular rise to third place among the world's economies during the past half century.

---

[3] *Political Economy of the New Left*, p. 69.

JAPAN

Japan is the economic success story of the post-war world. Her growth rate since World War II has been a spectacular 10 percent, and she grew at a rapid, although slower, rate over the preceding century. Before the Meiji era, beginning in 1868, Japan was an isolated, backward, feudal economy. To analyze the Japanese growth performance since would take a book itself. Here, we are primarily interested in the role played by Japan's economic organization—a uniquely Japanese mixed economy.

Growth experts suggest that Japan's recent performance reflects an unusual set of forces, woven together in a planned national growth policy. (1) Her postwar saving–investment rate has averaged a huge 30–35 percent of GNP, producing an annual growth of 12 percent in the capital stock, while consumption grew relatively slowly. (2) There was a massive shift of labor from low-productivity agriculture to industry, producing a nearly 4 percent annual growth in the nonagricultural labor force. (3) Japan was extraordinarily effective in adapting new technology from the United States and West European economies. (4) She devoted virtually no resources to national defense, and very few to the "welfare" programs that burgeoned in other Western democracies, so taxes were low. (5) She began from a very low post–World War II level. (6) Both laborers and management demonstrated an extraordinarily high level of hard work and skill development. (7) Business–government joint efforts proved especially effective in selling Japanese exports. (8) An unusual program of joint government–industry planning and operations facilitated growth as the nation's number one economic objective. This peculiarly Japanese combined growth effort is worth examination, including some reasons why it seems already to be giving way to more traditional problems.

National Commitment to Growth

Japan (government officials, industrialists, bankers, workers, just about everyone) has been committed to rapid growth as a keystone of national economic policy. Just how this commitment was achieved is unclear to most Westerners, but it provided the framework for the entire interlinked, coordinated Japanese growth effort. Many outsiders have reported the extraordinary commitment to common goals of the Japanese, their hard work, and their focus on achieving the goals they set. Private goals are important; the national goal of growth seems equally so.

Government–Business Relations

The relations between big business and government are very close, peculiarly Japanese, and difficult to describe in Western terms. The giant industrial combines that dominate the economy (*zaibatzu*) both compete vigorously and work together and with the government on plans for domestic and (especially) foreign markets. Japanese profit rates have been high. Direct government intervention in day-to-day business activities has been moderate, probably less than in the United States, although the Japanese government does operate the railroads, the major airline, telecommunications, and the cigarette and salt monopolies. But the government ministries and the Bank of Japan on the one hand and the major business groups on the other constitute a planning net, which interacts closely on major economic decisions for the economy.

Broad economic plans are developed by the Economic Planning Agency, working with business organizations. Some 300 consultative committees of government and trade-association officials work out detailed implementation of these plans. All Japanese industry is organized into trade associations, which in turn combine into a prestigious federation of economic organizations, which represents all industry. Neither government nor business is monolithic. Different government ministries and different industries have different needs and approaches, and the overall plan for the economy carries less weight than do individual industry plans. Yet Japanese business and government plan and operate closely together; some American businessmen call the result "Japan, Inc.," as if the nation were one big integrated economic firm.

Japan's spectacular success in world markets shows this cooperation most clearly. The Japanese export offensive produced a 15 percent annual increase in exports during the 1960s. The Japanese Supreme Trade Council is headed by the premier himself; top business executives and government officials personally set export goals. The government backs corporations with special tax incentives and credit facilities. Cartels of Japanese exporters are encouraged to fix prices and make collaborative plans for invading foreign markets. Giant trading companies market Japanese products throughout the world, sometimes at prices substantially below Japanese domestic prices. At the same time, the government has imposed import quotas on a wide range of products and limits foreign investment in Japan to protect Japanese firms. Little wonder that businessmen in the United States and Europe complain that competing with Japanese exports is very difficult, and that they too need governmental help to let them compete on even terms.

Monetary-Financial Policies for Growth

Adequate financing is a first requirement for capital investment. Japanese firms finance most (up to 85 percent) of their investment through bank loans, an extraordinarily high figure. This heavy debt ratio leaves them badly exposed in case the banks ever run short of funds and call their loans. The banks in turn operate with nearly 100 percent of their deposits offset by loans. How can the economy operate so precariously? The answer is that the Bank of Japan (fundamentally, the Japanese government) stands firmly committed to financing rapid growth and to providing the reserves needed to support it through bank loans. This financing system works especially well for the giant *zaibatzu*. Each industrial group is tied closely to a major bank or financial group. Because only a few *zaibatzu* dominate much of Japanese industry, it is easy for them and the big banks to work directly with the government and the Bank of Japan in making their plans for expansion and national economic growth. The monetary support for rapid growth has produced persistent inflation, but it is a cornerstone of the Japanese growth policy.

Employment Practices and Work Habits

Japan is the only non-Western economy to industrialize so successfully, but in the process, she has become only partly Westernized. When the typical Japanese factory worker, clerk, or minor manager is employed, it is for life. His salary depends almost entirely on age, education, and seniority, not on his job or productivity. In effect, he becomes a member of that business family for the rest of his life, with both benefits and responsibilities. Strikingly, the system produces high labor productivity. Workers identify closely with their companies, and the Japanese tradition of hard, careful work is strong. Although union membership is about as widespread as in the United States, and union leaders are often left-wing, strikes are rare and generally mild. Since pay and status do not depend on job assignments, managers have great freedom in moving workers among jobs, and employment flexibility is high, in spite of the apparent rigidity of the traditional arrangement. Union work rules and "featherbedding" are almost unknown. Clearly, this employment system can work only with continuing high-level employment; firms would go bankrupt rapidly if they had to keep on paying workers when markets vanished. Again, the system depends on the government's commitment and ability to maintain high employment and rapid growth.

The Future of Japanese Growth

Has Japan found the key to success through its own brand of mixed economy? The record is impressive, but the OPEC oil crisis and worldwide recession of 1974 hit Japan hard, and for the first time since World War II, her real GNP growth rate fell precipitously, from $+10$ to -2 percent. Domestic sales, exports, and profits all nosedived. Two large industrial firms actually failed and some workers lost their jobs, partly because the central bank sharply reduced the growth rate in the money stock from 30 to 10 percent in order to restrain the inflation that reached 25 percent per annum. Retrenchment became the order of the day. Businessmen, financiers, and government officials were shaken.

Although Japan recovered quickly from her recession, most experts predict slower growth for the future. Inflation has proved a persistent problem to the Japanese as they operate their high-pressure economy. Consumers increasingly press for a bigger share of the growing national output, and the personal savings rate is falling. Workers are less content to follow traditional patterns of work, promotion, and pay. Large supplies of excess farm labor are no longer available. Technology can no longer be borrowed wholesale from the West. Pollution and urban crowding will require investment resources, as in the United States. Stronger retaliation by other nations in foreign markets seems likely. Leftist critics challenge big-business—government domination of economic life, and demand more welfare benefits for the poor. Japan, although still growing lustily, is very unlikely to overtake the United States in total or per capita output, as some journalists have predicted by extrapolating postwar growth rates.[4]

ASPIRATIONS AND ACHIEVEMENTS

Looking back over two centuries, any reasonable observer must be impressed with the achievements of the American economy. But our aspirations have risen as fast as our achievements. What was only a hope fifty years ago is taken for granted today, as we insist on ever-higher performance. As fast as total output has grown, our aspirations have grown even faster—for health, national defense, education, housing, consumer goods, electric power, entertainment, travel, social security, clean air, consumer protection, minimum incomes, leisure. The list could go on and on.

These swelling aspirations make economic scarcity still the number one problem of the American and the world economies. They generate economic, social, and political frictions that threaten domestic stability and international peace, and jeopardize the ability of aggregate-demand measures to ensure both high employment and stable prices. Most of us feel that fairness entitles us to more, to an improving life. But all the "mores" add up to more than the economy produces, given the constraints we place on it. It is no accident that the "tax revolt" of the 1970s came after a decade in which per capita after-tax incomes had risen very little, with most of the improvement going to the

public sector. How we resolve the problem of these excess "entitlements," or income claims, is one of the major unanswered questions of American democratic capitalism—and probably of the other Western industrial democracies as well. Indeed, the big economic problems facing the United States today are strikingly similar to those facing the other major democracies. The need to provide adequate monetary demand, which was the great economic lesson of the 1930s, is no longer a major problem. The supply side of the aggregate-demand-and-supply equation is again the central problem in modern economic policy.

Some nations, like Sweden and Denmark, appear to have compromised these competing socioeconomic claims reasonably effectively, at least for the time being. Others, like the United Kingdom and Italy, currently face disruptive economic and social tensions that may precipitate major changes in the country's traditional political and economic arrangements. Some thoughtful observers question whether democratic capitalism can survive the strains of excess claims by powerful competing groups, and suggest that more authoritarian political and economic systems are inevitable. But others point to the great achievements of the modern democratic economies as the path toward higher living standards and a higher quality of life for all.

CONVERGENCE OF ECONOMIC SYSTEMS?

Each nation has tried its own approach to economic "rationalization" over the postwar period. Sweden has combined private management with moves to share control between owners and workers, and with extensive government welfare programs to reduce income inequality. Britain has moved toward a pervasive government-sponsored "incomes policy" prescribing growth rates for wages and profits, although without detailed government planning. The French have their own brand of "indicative planning."

Some observers say that these experiments are the new look for the democratic societies—planning combined with private enterprise. Others fear that such planning will be an entering wedge for more government control over the private

---

[4] A good study of the postwar Japanese economy is H. Patrick and H. Rosovsky, eds. *Asia's New Giant: How the Japanese Economy Works* (Washington, D.C.: The Brookings Institution, 1976).

economy. At first, the plan is voluntary. But after a while, when some private firms or unions decide not to play the roles assigned them under the plan, it is a short step to government mandatory controls. And informal planning sooner or later requires agreement on an "incomes policy," which specifies the shares of the growing GNP that should go to labor and to profits. Cooperative planning has repeatedly collapsed when unions and firms refuse to accept the wage and price holddowns provided in the official plans. What then? is an unsolved problem.

Economists debate whether capitalist and communist economies are converging on a middle ground. No one argues that all nations will soon have identical mixed economies. It is unlikely that Sweden, Russia, Yugoslavia, Japan, and the United States will soon look the same. But after a survey of European economies, Stanford's J. E. Howell and UCLA's Neil Jacoby advance the following two hypotheses:

1. Optimum performance by advanced economies requires a judicious and probably changing blend of central economic management and decentralized competitive market direction.
2. There is an increasing appearance of convergence among the economic management systems of advanced countries.[5]

Do these hypotheses point the optimal path for the United States?

CONCLUSION

Since the beginning of recorded history, men have sought the perfect society. In the books that fill the libraries, many of these utopias promise peace and plenty for all. But it is a long step from dream to reality. In the real world, the utopias that look best in the writing sometimes turn sour for quite unforeseen reasons.

Over the years, some economists have worked out the details of an "ideal" democratic economy. In it, resources would be allocated in accordance with consumer market demands, in-

dividuals would be free to work and spend as they wish, state-owned capital resources would be devoted to producing what consumers want, and the proceeds from state enterprises would be distributed among the people to provide as much income equality as the public desired. This is much like the utopia of the early socialists, with state ownership of resources and operation of enterprise, with political democracy, and with economic implementation through the price system. Its advocates claim it combines the best features of private enterprise and socialism.

But in the real world, are centralized economic control and democratic freedom in fact compatible? The Russian official blueprint looks surprisingly like this model, but in operation it looks very different. Wise observers have noted that dispersed economic and political power are usually handmaidens to each other—that centralized economic power and political democracy seldom live long together. If this is true, the attempt to plan and centrally control economic activity toward the goals we want may be a false dream, likely to lead to political and economic slavery rather than to organized plenty.

The economic system must be our servant, not our master, in an effective society. If the society has fundamentally democratic, individualistic ideals, most people must be at heart satisfied with the way the system works—not in detail and all the time, but by and large. Lewis Carroll, in *Alice in Wonderland*, puts his finger tellingly on the basic problem:

. . . the Dodo suddenly called out, "The race is over!" and they all crowded round it, panting, and asking, "But who has won?"
This question the Dodo could not answer without a great deal of thought, and it stood for a long time with one finger pressed upon its forehead . . . while the rest waited in silence. At last the Dodo said, *"Everybody* has won, and *all* must have prizes."

In a working democratic society, most must win, and most must have prizes. What shall the prizes be, and how can the economic system keep everyone satisfied with his reward? The American economy provides prizes in abundance, compared with the other nations of the world. And its ability to adapt, without revolution, to the changing demands of the people has been one

---

[5] *European Economics: East and West* (New York: World Publishing Company, 1967).

of its most impressive qualities. Any reasonable evaluation must count it highly successful. But to be pleased should not make us smug. The American economic system is far from perfect. And it will change further over the years ahead, as it adapts to shifting demands and objectives.

You should now be able to do a good share of your own thinking on how the American economy should steer over the years ahead. Economic analysis alone cannot give you answers to the hard problems we face. But it can help greatly to illuminate the way in a changing world.

SUMMARY AND REVIEW

1. Under capitalism in America, most productive resources are privately owned, and economic activity is largely directed by the interaction of supply and demand in markets in response to individual interests. Under communism in the USSR, most productive resources are publicly owned, and economic activity is mainly directed by central planners.

2. The United States and the USSR are the leading examples of the two types of systems, but each deviates widely from the "pure" form of its system. (The chapter appendix provides information on the USSR in action as a modified communist economy.)

3. Using the five criteria specified in Chapter 1 for evaluating any economy, the United States appears to meet these goals better than does the USSR. Although American democratic capitalism has many flaws, pointed out throughout the book, it provides higher living standards and stronger incentives to work and invest, produces more efficiently, responds more fully to free consumer choices, disperses economic and political power more widely, and provides more individual freedom and meaningful security than does the Soviet system. Whether it provides a more equitable distribution of income depends on your definition of equity; most Americans apparently believe the system should, as it does, provide opportunities to obtain high incomes to individuals with high marginal productivities.

4. As a practical matter, we must probably choose between markets and political bureaucracy to organize our economic activities in complex economies, although Marxists and the "New Left" reject both. A major advantage of markets is the wider dispersion of power they offer. A second basic choice is how to provide effective incentives to work and save—invest. Capitalists generally argue that these will be provided best by individuals' self-interests—higher incomes and accumulation of capital—while Marxists and the New Left object to such competition and advance cooperation as the main incentive.

5. Japan exemplifies a new look in economic organization—planning with private enterprise. She has been very successful in raising Japanese output per capita, but appears now to be having greater difficulty in sustaining her high growth rate.

6. In America, and in many other well-to-do nations, our aspirations for a better life economically have risen even faster than our progress in raising living standards, producing intermittent economic and social tensions when different groups' achievements fall short of their aspirations. A working democratic system must provide results that seem reasonable to most participants in relation to what they feel they are entitled to.

For Analysis and Discussion

1. In the light of your study of the American economic system and alternative systems, make a careful list of the major defects, if any, you see in the American system. What, if any, reforms do you think are needed, and how feasible do you think each of your reforms is?

2. During the past half century, the economic climate of the world has shifted toward central economic planning. What factors do you think have been most important in bringing about this change?

3. If you don't like either markets or a political bureaucracy as the major way for making our economic decisions, what alternative do you suggest? Is the Japanese system an attractive alternative?

4. Recently, the USSR has apparently moved toward a limited profit motive for managers. If this experiment is broadened, do you think it will be compatible with central planning for the rest of the economy? Explain your answer.

5. Since World War II, four nations showing high growth rates have been Russia (a communist state), West Germany (a basically private-enterprise economy), Japan (a mixed capitalist economy with extensive government intervention), and Yugoslavia (a modified socialist country). How do you account for this fact? Does it indicate that the two types of economic organization are equally fitted for producing continued, rapid growth?

6. In Russia, wages are set by the central planners to keep total purchasing power about in line with the supply of goods to be bought. Would some variant of this plan be a good approach to our problem of avoiding wage-push inflation? If you think so, defend your answer against the likely attack of a union member.

7. Make a list of those attributes of present-day communist Russia that seem most objectionable to you. How many of these attributes are economic, how many social, how many political?

8. Do you believe the United States should adopt some of the cooperative government—business planning approach of Japan? What would be the main advantages and disadvantages?

APPENDIX   The Soviet Economy

Goals. Although Marx never specified how an ideal communist society would work, its key characteristics would apparently be the following:[6]

1. True equality—to each according to his needs
2. Cooperation, rather than competition, in meeting the needs of society
3. All productive resources owned by the state, with the proceeds distributed to the masses (the workers)
4. Power to direct production, and to allocate resources and incomes, in the hands of the masses
5. Small and declining government

The day-to-day goals stressed by modern Soviet leaders look very much like those stated by Americans—improved living standards, economic growth, more leisure, freedom, security, elimination of poverty, and political democracy. From these words, it is

hard to distinguish Russia from the Western democratic societies. But in fact, the USSR appears to be a "command" economy. The Politburo (Communist party leaders) decide what they want to happen, and they use a comprehensive system of plans and controls to make it happen.

(1) Deciding what to produce, and
(2) Getting it produced.[7]

MAKING THE PLAN. The broad goals for the economy are set by the Praesidium and the Central Committee of the Communist party. Since 1928, the goals have been contained in a series of comprehensive five-year plans. The tenth plan, for 1976–80, called for an annual growth rate of 6 percent in industrial production and 4½ to 5 percent in national income. Although early plans concentrated on military output

[6]For a brief summary of Marx's analysis of capitalism, see the appendix to Chapter 22.

[7]A good study of the Russian economy is Robert Campbell, *Soviet Economic Power* (Boston: Houghton Mifflin, 1973).

and industrial growth, recently more weight has been given to satisfying consumer wants.

Within these broad objectives, the plan for each year is developed by the Gosplan (State Planning Commission), working with a huge Central Statistical Administration, which provides data on available resources and productive capacities. Their job is immense. Suppose you had to plan only aircraft. How would you plan production of all the hundreds of thousands of components that go into a modern airplane, scheduling each to be on hand when it was needed? Now back up and decide how you would plan the production of all the subcomponents to produce the parts you need for the airplanes. By now you'll be up in the millions of individual decisions, just for one major product. And the complexities multiply geometrically when you add other products, because of all the interlinkages among materials, labor, and manufacturing facilities needed. And this complexity has led the Soviets into more and more trouble as their economy has grown. How do they do it now?

First, they don't start from scratch each year. They use last year as a bench mark, which greatly simplifies the task. Second, the Gosplan apparently focuses each year primarily on some fifty basic products and industtries that are of critical importance in attaining the prime goals of the overall plan.[8] They apparently then construct for some 1,500 major commodities (industries) a materials balance, a labor balance, and a geographical balance. These show the materials, labor, and other resources needed to produce the desired output throughout the economy. By combining these balances for all major products, they have a reasonably complete input-output picture of the overall materials, labor, facilities, and regional balances for the entire economy.

Once the broad outline of an annual plan is completed, it is sent to regional and industry councils throughout the economy. They check their quotas against the productive capacities in their region or industry to see whether the plan appears feasible. If they think the quotas are too high, or if they believe their tentative allocations of materials and equipment would be inadequate to meet them, they have the right to protest—and they do! Local plant managers often argue that the goals are too high and that inadequate raw materials and machinery are being allocated to meet them. The Soviet planning process involves a lot of talk. Some observers have called it the most gigantic collective-bargaining process in history.

---

[8]During World War II, when the U.S. industrial economy was extensively but by no means completely planned, the whole planning process hinged largely on allocation of three major materials—steel, copper, and aluminum.

Finally, all this information gets reflected back to Moscow, where the Gosplan must settle on the final plan so that everything balances out for the whole economy. The planners do the best they can, using some modern mathematical and electronic computer techniques, and making adjustments to accommodate the major goals.

We know the planners make mistakes. Plans are continuously adjusted. If the small-machinery plan runs into labor shortages while that for electric light globes turn up a surplus, the planners don't wait until next year to make an adjustment. This doesn't make for a quiet life among Gosplan employees or for managers throughout the economy, and the number of adjustments has apparently snowballed in recent years as the Russian economy has grown in complexity. Complaints from below have increased. Industry plans are changed dozens of times a year. These crises have led the pragmatic rules in the Kremlin to delegate more responsibility and freedom to local managers in carrying out the broad goals handed down from above.

CARRYING OUT THE PLAN.   How do the Soviets get their plans carried out? In essence, by telling people what to do and by paying them for doing it.

MANAGERIAL INCENTIVES.   Under the early plans, each plant manager received a production *quota,* together with detailed information on the supply of materials he would receive, the equipment that would be allocated to him, the labor he was to use, and so on. Then it was up to him to get the final product out. His job was to meet the quota, not to question why.

Good managers are very important under communism, the Soviets have found, just as they are under capitalism.

But the Soviets have had major problems on managerial incentives. Managers concealed production possibilities in order to get lower quotas, hoarded materials, and avoided doing too well lest quotas be raised for the next year. There was no penalty for wasteful use of materials or manpower as long as it didn't violate the plan.

Innovation has been another special managerial problem. New ideas involve risks, and the Soviet system has lacked effective rewards for risk taking. In the Soviet climate, doing reasonably well is more conducive to the manager's peace of mind than taking a chance on a new idea that may flop. There's nothing like the American private-enterprise entrepreneur out to make a million (or go broke) on a new product or new method. Soviet criticism of managers for lack of imaginative innovation has been bitter.

"PROFITS" AND THE NEW LOOK IN SOVIET PLANNING. As the central planning process increasingly bogged down and as inefficiencies piled up at the local level, in the 1960s the Soviets began to question whether more reliance on a kind of "profit motive" for individual managers couldn't help the planners avoid the local wastes of physical planning and increase total output. In 1965, the Communists announced an experiment that freed managers in the shoe and food-processing industries from planned quotas, and directed them to maximize their profits, much as in America, with their own bonuses based on the profits they made. Each manager was substantially free to set the price of his product and the wages he paid, and to choose his own production methods. The profits themselves, above the special awards to the successful manager, of course reverted to the state. In the following years, about one-third of all consumer-goods production was shifted to such a plan.

But the new look inevitably raised basic issues. Local managers free to bid resources away from others came into conflict with central-plan allocations. Thus, in 1973 another major reform was announced. The Soviets combined much of the economy into intermediate-level industry corporations, or production associations. Managers of these industry production centers apparently now have some freedom to attempt to maximize "profits" for their industries, and they have assumed much of the planning function for their industries.

The problem of how much decentralization of decision-making and operating authority is optimal remains unsettled in the USSR. The problem is similar to that faced by a large American corporation like GM. In America, decentralizing decision making and authority to local "profit centers," under only broad rules from headquarters, is now widely accepted as the best way to maintain local managerial initiative and to couple the advantages of central corporate planning with local, firsthand management. But in the USSR, Gosplan still makes the basic plans and the blueprints for carrying them out for most of the economy.

LABOR INCENTIVES AND LABOR UNIONS. How do the Soviets get the workers to carry out their plans? Just as in the United States, money is the big incentive, but it is supplemented by continuous emphasis on national pride and party loyalty for members.

The planners decide how much should be paid for each type of work, and they do it so as to get the plan carried out effectively. The biggest pay goes to scientists, artists, inventors, and managers who overproduce their quotas. Over half of all industrial workers are on "piece rates," whereby each worker gets paid according to how much he turns out. This is a much higher percentage than in the United States. Money wages thus play much the same role in pulling labor into jobs and stimulating good performance as they do in America, except that in Russia they are set by the planners to channel workers where the planners want them, rather than by market supply and demand.

Most Soviet workers belong to unions. But Soviet unions have nothing to do with setting wages. The unions are worker organizations that are expected to help in implementing government plans. They are more like workmen's clubs than like the unions we know. Make your own comparison with the role of unions in America, where there is far more union power—and far more conflict.

CHECKING ON PERFORMANCE: THE GOSBANK AND THE STATE CONTROL COMMISSION. The Gosplan also makes up a complete set of "value" (or financial) plans to parallel the basic physical plans. Using these financial plans, the Gosbank (state banking system) provides money to managers to pay for labor and materials to carry out the production plans. For example, if the annual plan calls for 10 million pairs of shoes, the Gosbank provides shoe-plant managers just enough rubles to pay for the labor, leather, and so on, allocated to the production of those shoes. It does the same for all other products. And managers must deposit their receipts in the Gosbank, except for cash payments made to workers.

The Gosbank plays two significant roles. First, it provides a financial control over managers. If they run out of money, this is a sign they are buying more than the inputs allocated to them under the physical plan. And because they can get materials and labor only by paying for them, the control is close. When the manager deposits his receipts in the Gosbank, this provides an automatic check on whether he has produced the amount specified in the plan. Second, the Gosbank provides a regular banking function, transferring funds, advancing working capital, and creating money for the economy.

How does this checking compare with the private-enterprise process? In America, too, the availability of funds controls what is done and who does it. The firm continuously gets funds from selling its product; thus, consumers exercise a continuous check on whether any firm is doing its job effectively. If a firm wants to expand, it must either have stored up its own profits or it must go to the competitive capital market for funds. There, its project is evaluated by bankers, private investors, and other lenders against alternative demanders of funds. If the firm's prospects look good, it will get loans; if they look bad, it will have trouble raising funds. The capital market controls who can expand and who cannot.

Which process is more effective? Who should check on whom? The Soviet procedure gives direct control to the planners through the Gosbank and the control commission. In America, we place most of our faith in the impersonal market, where consumers, lenders, and business firms are counted on to look out for their own capital and incomes and thereby to get resources allocated most effectively.

THE RECALCITRANT PROBLEM OF AGRICULTURE. Agriculture has been the Communists' knottiest problem. Their early attempts to collectivize Russian agriculture, carried through by bloody force during the 1920s and 1930s, met bitter and sullen resistance. Forced to work on collective farms, farmers produced less than before and kept crops and animals for themselves rather than turning them over to the authorities for export to the cities. Frustrated Communist planners tried one tack, then another—but with little success.

In theory, a collective farm is a cooperative, democratic association of farmers who have pooled their land, tools, and labor to make a large farm, which they operate in common. Proceeds are shared in proportion to the quantity and quality of work they do. Large-scale operation produces the economies of large-scale mechanized farming, eliminating the waste and inefficiency that for centuries characterized Russian agriculture.

It sounds fine, but not to the peasants. Soviet planners found crops vanishing into farm consumption and total production declining. Bloody reprisals brought only temporary compliance and smoldering resentment. Over millions of acres and widely scattered farmers, effective control was impossible.

There are now some 100,000 collective and state farms, compared to perhaps 25 million small peasant farms four decades ago. About 5,000 of these are huge state farms of many thousand acres, operated outright as "business" firms by the Ministry of Agriculture in much the same pattern as prevails for industrial production. The rest are collective farms, ranging from a few "communes" (which involve complete sharing of property, labor, and results) to many cases where the collective farm is scarcely more than a sharing of major machinery and some exchange of labor. In most cases, part of the land is farmed collectively but each family retains a small plot for its own individual operation. These private plots make up only 5–10 percent of the total land under cultivation, but they apparently produce nearly one-third of total farm output of vegetables, eggs, meat, milk, and other products that are suited to labor-intensive

production and that can be sold in small lots on uncontrolled markets, which exist throughout Russia. Private initiative is far from dead in Russian agriculture.

Agricultural output has persistently lagged far behind the plan goals, in spite of one reform after another. A quarter of the Russian labor force is in agriculture—over 30 million compared to only 3 million in the United States. Yet U.S. total farm output exceeds Russia's. One American farmer can feed nearly 60 people, one Russian farmer only seven. Low productivity in agriculture is the Communists' number one production problem.

(3) Deciding how income is to be distributed. Marxist doctrine says, "To each according to his need." The Soviet leaders today season this liberally with, "To each according to how hard he works and how much he contributes." Incomes are more equally distributed than in the United States, because in Russia income from property is very limited. But money incomes derived from work are about as unequally distributed in Russia as in America. Thus inequality reflects the strong use of incentive payments to achieve the central planners' goals.

Scientists, artists, professors, managers, and party officials receive the highest incomes. As in America, common labor is at the bottom of the totem pole—except for farmers, many of whom in Russia take much of their incomes in kind from their farms. Within the ranks of factory workers and comparable laborers, apparently the ratio of the lowest to the highest monthly income is nearly 1 : 10, wider than in America.

The Soviets adjust wage rates up and down frequently for different occupations and industries, to help implement the overall plan. The planners may be good Marxists on paper, but their behavior on wages suggests that they have learned a good deal about the power of monetary incentives.

Government services and income redistribution. The state provides widespread free social services to help the masses. Soviet authorities claim that one-third of the income of low-income groups is provided by free government services. Nearly all housing is government-owned, and rents are extremely low; on the average, Soviet citizens apparently pay only about 2–3 percent of their income for housing, far under the 15–25 percent common in America. A Moscow two-bedroom apartment rents for $20–$30 a month—if you can find one. Russian housing is generally bad, but it's very cheap. Paid vacations, government nurseries, special grants to large families, free education, and extensive health services all supplement money incomes.

Who pays for these government services? A general sales (turnover) tax accounts for over half of all government income. Profits on state enterprises provide most of the rest. Increases and decreases in the turnover tax are used to adjust the prices of individual products up and down to discourage or to stimulate consumption. This way, the planners make consumer demand match the goods produced. This tax, therefore, substantially offsets the apparent big government supplement to low incomes.

On the other hand, the Soviets use especially low prices on some major commodities in addition to housing to subsidize low-income consumers. This means that such goods are sold below "cost." Prices are set very high on such luxuries as autos. Here again, pricing is used to promote the goals that seem important to the planners.

(4) Deciding between current consumption and economic growth. In America, the choice between current consumption and economic growth depends on consumer and business saving, business investment decisions, private educational and research decisions, private educational and research decisions, and government tax and investment behavior. In Russia, the decision is made and implemented by the central planners. And their choice has been in favor of rapid industrialization and growth, at the expense of current consumption.

Since the early 1920s, Russia's GNP has grown at about 4 percent annually. Soviet growth during the 1950s was spectacular—nearly double that rate—but it has slowed since then. To press its postwar growth, the USSR allocated an extraordinarily large portion of its output to capital formation, and Soviet military expenditures now exceed ours, although their GNP is less than half ours. Soviet consumption was so repressed that per capita real consumption was no higher in 1958 than it had been in 1928; only since about 1960 has the average Russian benefitted much through higher consumption from the last half century of economic growth. But this Soviet policy produced an average annual increase of 10 percent in the Russian capital stock, which went far to account for rapid Soviet growth—aided by her ability to borrow a large amount of technology from the West, and by rapid growth in the industrial labor force.

The decline in Russian growth since 1960 has reflected in substantial part a decline in the growth of the labor force for industry, and in the capital accumulation rate, as more resources were allocated to satisfying consumer wants. Even with central planning and control rather than individual choice and the price system, Russia faces the same fundamental problem in growth as does any other economy—she must divert scarce resources from consumption to investment, improve her technology, and step up the ability and performance of her labor force. There is no other way, for either communism or capitalism. As post-Stalin liberalization has opened up the Soviet economy to Western standards and Western ideas, the pressure has intensified on Communist leaders for more consumption goods.[9]

Government monetary and fiscal policy and economic stabilization. The Soviet central planners do not program men or machines into unemployment. If there is unemployment, it is because planning has gone awry or because someone is not behaving according to plan. And there has been very little official unemployment in the USSR. But there is much evidence of disguised unemployment in the form of excess labor allocated to some industries. And there is still the problem of keeping total spending power roughly equal to goods available for purchase. If buying power gets too large, inflationary pressures will mount. If buying power is too low, prices must be cut or unsold inventories and excess labor will pile up.

The Soviets manage this balance largely through the turnover tax (fiscal policy) and the Gosbank (monetary policy), the same two tools we use. In Russia, most of the burden falls on the turnover tax. If total demand is excessive, the turnover tax is raised all along the line, or on those products where demand seems most excessive, raising prices and siphoning off income to the government. If total demand is inadequate, turnover taxes are lowered. In a real sense, the Russians have adopted "functional finance" as the core of their stabilization and allocation mechanism.

Inflation has been an intermittent problem for the Soviets. The Russians are human beings too, and when there isn't enough to go around, they apparently tend to plan a little more resources for all the demands than there are to parcel out. The result is a demand pressure that tends to bid up prices as shortages occur; black markets spring up. The basic pressures that make for inflation—shortage of goods relative to the purchasing power provided by incomes paid out—are the same in communist and capitalist societies.

---

[9]Under Marxist doctrine, only labor is truly productive. Thus, interest on money or real capital plays no role in communist doctrine. Western economists properly point out that this position, if followed, will lead Soviet planners to improper decisions in allocating resources—to waste capital if they underprice it. But the pragmatic Soviet planners are now slipping the interest rate into their calculations through the back door.

Mathematical appendixes

NOTE: These appendixes were prepared in collaboration with Professor Michael Lovell of Wesleyan University.

In economics, as in many other disciplines, mathematics has important uses. Mathematics provides a convenient, concise language for stating complicated ideas and relationships. It facilitates the analysis of complicated interrelationships and helps in reaching "correct" conclusions from sets of assumptions or premises. It provides a language for stating "models" or theories in a precise way that makes them testable by rigorous statistical analysis of empirical data ("econometrics").

Since an increasing number of college students know some mathematics, these brief appendixes use mathematics (through elementary calculus) to state precisely and rigorously some of the concepts and arguments developed verbally or graphically in the text. Each appendix relates directly to the chapter or section of the text indicated. If you know some mathematics, and especially if you find the language of mathematics a helpful one, the following appendixes may prove a useful supplement to the verbal and graphical exposition of the same ideas in the relevant chapters.

The appendixes show, in very elementary form, how mathematical language and mathmatical reasoning can simplify and illuminate the sometimes complex interrelationships with which economic analysis must deal. Although a half century ago there were virtually no economists interested in applying mathematical analysis to economic problems, today use of mathematics in economics has become commonplace; and *econometrics* (the use of mathematically stated models as the basis for quantitative measurement in analysis of economic variables) has become the fastest growing branch of modern economics. The following appendixes give a small indication of how mathematics can help in stating clearly and precisely some of the important concepts and relationships in economics.[1]

---

[1] If you find these appendixes interesting and want to investigate mathematical economics a bit further, R.G.D. Allen, *Mathematical Economics* (New York: Macmillan, 1956) provides an excellent introduction for students who know calculas. Lawrence Klein's *Introduction to Econometrics* (Englewood Cliffs, N.J.: Prentice-Hall, 1974) is a comparable introduction to the field of econometrics, although it is designed primarily for readers who have also had a course in elementary statistics.

The demand curve for any commodity shows how many units will be bought at each price. Looked at another way, it represents the function indicating how price responds to changes in the quantity of a commodity offered for sale, given buyer preferences and incomes, and may be denoted as $p(q)$. [This function might also be denoted by p, or by $f(q)$.] It will be assumed that this function is differentiable.

As is explained in Chapter 4, demand curves are ordinarily negatively sloped; that is, $dp/dq < 0$. This information does not tell precisely how the total revenue obtained by the sellers will respond to changes in price and quantity sold, but simple analysis of the demand function can provide an answer to this important question.

Total revenue, denoted by $r(q)$, is simply price times quantity:

$$r(q) = p(q)q \tag{I.1}$$

Differentiating with respect to quantity yields

$$\frac{dr}{dq} = p(q) + \frac{dp}{dq}q \tag{I.2}$$

This derivative, which economists call marginal revenue, may be either positive or negative (remember, $dp/dq < 0$). Selling more at a lower price will reduce total revenue if the fall in price is not offset by the increase in the quantity of the commodity purchased; that is, if the demand is inelastic. (Note that this is the same as saying that a reduction in price will increase the number of units sold less than proportionately.)

What level of output with its resulting price would maximize total revenue (but not necessarily profits)? We can tell by examining the demand function with the aid of a few rules of elementary calculus. Remember that a necessary condition for a maximum is that the first derivative of revenue with respect to quantity be zero.

$$\frac{dr}{dq} = p(q) + \frac{dp}{dq}q = 0 \tag{I.3}$$

This maximum can be defined in terms of the elasticity of the demand function. Economists, fol-lowing the reasoning on elasticity in Chapter 4, customarily denote elasticity more precisely as[2]

$$\eta = -\frac{dq}{dp} \cdot \frac{p}{q} \tag{I.4}$$

Thus, when elasticity of demand is unity, revenue is maximized.

If demand is inelastic ($\eta < 1$), note that a reduction in the quantity of the commodity offered on the market would increase total revenue. Thus, a businessman with control over his selling price and output would be foolish to produce at a point where the demand for his commodity is inelastic, for then he could obtain more revenue by producing and selling less!

It is easy to determine graphically the elasticity of demand. Consider the demand curve q^*p^*, first graph on page 693. To find the elasticity of demand at any point a (corresponding to price p and quantity q), we note that $-dq/dp = (q^* - q)/p$; hence

$$\eta = -\frac{dq}{dp} \cdot \frac{p}{q} = \left(\frac{q^* - q}{p}\right)\frac{p}{q} = \frac{q^* - q}{q} \tag{I.5}$$

From the last equality we see that for a linear demand curve, the elasticity of demand is simply the ratio of the excess of the quantity that could have been sold at a zero price over actual sales [i.e., $(q^* - q)$, divided by quantity sold (q)]. Note that, although this demand curve has a constant slope, it is not characterized by a constant elasticity. The elasticity changes along the curve. If q^* units were sold at zero price, the elasticity of demand would be zero; for higher prices, less is sold and elasticity increases without bound as the price approaches p^*.

To determine the elasticity of demand at some point on a nonlinear demand curve, such as point a on curve DD on the second graph, draw a straight line tangent to the demand curve at that point, and from it determine the location of point q^*. Since at point a the

---

[2]If, as for the individual seller under perfect competition, $\frac{dq}{dp} = \infty$, then we say elasticity is infinite.

demand curve and the tangent line have the same slope, as well as the same p and q values, they also have the same elasticity at that point; hence, formula I.5 again applies.

$$\eta = \frac{q^* - q}{q}$$

Is it possible for a demand curve to have constant elasticity throughout its entire length? Yes. Suppose that $q = \alpha p^{\beta}$, $\beta < 0$; then

$$dq/dp = (\beta \, \alpha p^{\beta-1}) = \beta \frac{q}{p}$$

and

$$\eta = -\left(\beta \frac{q}{p}\right)\frac{p}{q} = -\beta$$

That is, the parameter $-\beta$ of the demand curve is the elasticity of demand. For example, a rectangular hyperbola has a constant elasticity equal to 1.

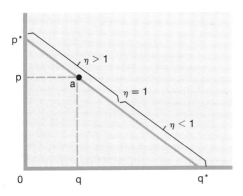

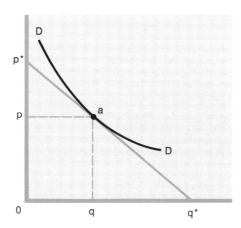

⊂ᴩᴩEND𝗂X 2

(to Chapters 8–9)

Cost Curves
and Profit Maximization

To determine what level of output will maximize profits, production costs in relation to demand considerations must be analyzed. This appendix mathematically analyzes this interrelationship.

A. Key cost concepts. In Chapter 8, the dependence of production costs upon the level of output was examined in detail, and a number of basic concepts were explained. Table 8–1 reported hypothetical cost figures for a firm producing a single commodity. In such cases, the total cost function, $c(q)$, reveals how the total costs incurred by the firm depend on the level of output; we assume that the function is differentiable. Other costs concepts discussed in the text may be

expressed in terms of $c(q)$, as shown in the following list:

Fixed costs:	$c(0)$
Variable costs:	$c(q) - c(0)$
Total unit cost:	$c(q)/q$
Variable unit cost:	$[c(q) - c(0)]/q$
Fixed unit cost:	$c(0)/q$
Marginal cost:	$\dfrac{dc(q)}{dq}$

B. Maximizing profits. Profit, at any level of output, $\pi(q)$, is simply the excess of total revenue over total cost,

$$\pi(q) = r(q) - c(q) \qquad (\text{II}.1)$$

where $r(q)$ is the total revenue function discussed in Mathematical Appendix I; the three curves are plotted in Figure 9–1. From elementary calculus we know that if profits are maximized at some level of output $q > 0$, it is necessary that

$$\frac{\partial \pi(q)}{\partial q} = \frac{\partial r(q)}{\partial q} - \frac{\partial c(q)}{\partial q} = 0 \qquad (\text{II}.2)$$

Equation II.2 implies:

$$\frac{\partial r(q)}{\partial q} = \frac{\partial c(q)}{\partial q} = 0 \qquad (\text{II}.3)$$

This mathematically states the fundamental proposition that a necessary condition for profit maximization at $q > 0$ is that marginal cost equals marginal revenue.

It is essential to note that condition II.2 does not necessarily yield a level of output, q, at which profits will be positive. In the short run, before the firm can liquidate its fixed investment, it may be worthwhile to operate at a loss rather than shut down. Remember that zero output involves fixed cost, $c(0)$, in the short run. Would a zero output minimize losses (negative profits) when there are fixed costs? Not if

$$\pi(q) = r(q) - c(q) > \pi(0) = -c(0) \qquad (\text{II}.4)$$

or equivalently:

$$r(q) - [c(q) - c(0)] > 0 \qquad (\text{II}.5)$$

In other words, the firm will produce a positive output at a loss if revenue exceeds total variable costs. Dividing both sides of II.5 by q yields, since $r(q)/q = p$, an equivalent condition:

$$p - [c(q) - c(0)]/q > 0 \qquad (\text{II}.6)$$

This is the condition (in Chapter 9) that the firm will minimize losses by shutting down altogether only if there is no positive level of output where price would exceed average variable cost.

C. Some observations on competitive equilibrium.
Under competitive conditions, the output of the individual firm constitutes an insignificant contribution to the total market sales of the commodity.

Consequently, the price the firm receives for its output is unaffected by variation in the quantity it offers for sale; its demand curve is horizontal ($dp/dq = 0$), and from equation I.2 we have marginal revenue equal to price ($dr/dq = p$). Hence, equation II.3 implies that if firms maximize profits under competitive conditions, they produce at the point where marginal cost equals price.

This constitutes a basic proposition of economic theory that explains the general presumption of economists in favor of competition: When firms maximize profits under competitive conditions, the increment to total cost incurred in producing the last unit sold is exactly equal to the price, which is precisely as it should be. For the price reflects the consumer's evaluation of the benefits he will obtain from the purchase of that last unit; if the benefits were less, he wouldn't buy the unit, and if they were greater, he would buy more units.

Chapter 10 points out that in long-run competitive equilibrium, price is equal to the minimum point on the total-unit-cost curve. This must be the case, for a higher price would encourage new firms to enter the industry in search of profits, while a lower price would yield continued losses and induce firms to leave the industry. But if price is to be equal to the minimum point on the total-unit-cost curve, can we be sure it also equals marginal cost, as required under competition (condition II.3, with $dr/dq = p$)? It is easy to show that the answer is, necessarily, yes. If output is at the minimum total-unit-cost level, then marginal cost will be equal to total unit cost. To establish this proposition, we note that the condition that output be at the minimum total-unit-cost level implies:

$$\frac{d\left[\frac{c(q)}{q}\right]}{dq} = \frac{\frac{dc(q)}{dq}}{q} - \frac{c(q)}{q^2} = 0$$

Multiplying through by q yields:

$$\frac{dc(q)}{dq} = \frac{c(q)}{q}$$

Thus, marginal cost is equal to average cost if output is at the firm's lowest average-unit-cost point. The marginal-cost curve cuts the average-total-cost curve at the latter's minimum point.

Most firms have alternative ways to produce any given output. Thus, within limits, the services of machinery may be substituted for labor in the production of steel, or vice versa. A "production function," which states the relationship between various combinations of inputs and the resulting outputs (products), can be a helpful concept for exploring the way in which technological considerations influence the distribution of income among different factors of production (labor, capital, and so on).

A. Simple production functions. For simplicity, suppose that only two factors of production, labor (L) and machinery (M), are used in producing a commodity. The output (q) produced each period depends on the quantity of labor and machinery services employed. We assume that this production function can be described by a differentiable function of the two inputs:

$$q = f(L,M) \tag{III.1}$$

Such functions can be estimated empirically from business and engineering production data or derived from engineering or physical principles.

We wish to determine the optimal (highest-profit) mix of labor and machinery to produce any output. We will maximize profits (π) by maximizing the excess of revenue over cost. If we assume that labor and machinery services are purchased on competitive markets at prices w and p_m, we have:

$$\pi = r(q) - wL - p_m M \tag{III.2}$$

or, substituting from III.1,

$$\pi(L,M) = r[f(L,M)] - wL - p_m M \tag{III.3}$$

If the optimal quantity of labor is indeed being employed, it must be impossible to increase profits by either increasing or decreasing the amount of labor used. Consequently, a necessary condition for profit maximization is that:

$$\frac{\partial \pi(L,M)}{\partial L} = \frac{dr}{dq} \cdot \frac{\partial q}{\partial L} - w = 0 \tag{III.4}$$

Similarly, if the optimal quantity of machinery services is being employed,

$$\frac{\partial \pi(L,m)}{\partial M} = \frac{dr}{dq} \cdot \frac{\partial q}{\partial m} - p_m = 0 \tag{III.5}$$

As Chapters 18 and 19 indicate, economists call

$$\frac{\partial r}{\partial q} \cdot \frac{\partial q}{\partial L}$$

the marginal-revenue product of labor. Thus, equation III.4 shows that to maximize profits, a firm hiring on a competitive market must hire additional workers just to the point where the marginal-revenue product of labor equals the wage rate.

It follows from III.4 and III.5 that

$$\frac{\partial q / \partial m}{p_m} = \frac{\partial q / \partial L}{w} \tag{III.6}$$

The economist calls

$$\frac{\partial q}{\partial L}$$

the marginal productivity of labor; similarly,

$$\frac{\partial q}{\partial m}$$

is the marginal productivity of machinery services. Equation III.6 thus shows that under profit-maximizing equilibrium conditions in competitive markets, each factor of production is rewarded in proportion to its marginal productivity.

B. The Cobb-Douglas production function: an example. As an illustration, let us consider a much discussed conjecture of Professors C.W. Cobb and Paul H. Douglas (later U.S. senator) that the total industrial output of the American economy may be described by a simple production function of the form:

$$q(L,M) = aL^\lambda M^{1-\lambda} \tag{III.7}$$

Statistical investigations have disclosed that a function of this form fits the historical data quite closely when $\lambda = .75$. Note that this function is characterized by constant returns to scale; that is, if the initial inputs are all multiplied by some scale factor, $\rho > 0$, then output will also increase by ρ; more precisely:

$$q(\rho L, \rho M) = \rho q(L, M) \text{ for all } \rho \geqslant 0 \qquad \text{(III.8)}$$

What are the implications of the Cobb-Douglas analysis for the shares of labor and machinery (capital) in the national income? Not only did Cobb-Douglas find that equation III.7 provides a reasonable explanation of how capital and labor contribute to the generation of industrial output. They also found that this function, in conjunction with equation III.4, embodying the assumption of competition, helps to explain an important observed fact—that labor income (wages and salaries) has been a roughly stable percentage of total income over many decades.

Their explanation of the rough constancy of labor's share can be appreciated if we first observe that the marginal productivity of labor is

$$\frac{\partial q}{\partial L} = \lambda a L^{\lambda-1} M^{1-\lambda} = \lambda \frac{Q}{L} \qquad \text{(III.9)}$$

Similarly, the marginal productivity of capital services is

$$\frac{\partial q}{\partial M} = (1 - \lambda) a L^{\lambda} M^{-\lambda} = (1 - \lambda) \frac{Q}{M} \qquad \text{(III.10)}$$

If output is sold on a competitive market at price p (so that $dr/dq = p$), then condition III.4 implies:

$$p\lambda \frac{Q}{L} = w \qquad \text{(III.11)}$$

Hence

$$\frac{Lw}{Qp} = \lambda \qquad \text{(III.12)}$$

Now remember that Lw is labor income, while Qp is the value of total output; consequently, equation III.12 implies that the ratio of labor income to total income, labor's share, is equal to the parameter λ of the Cobb-Douglas production function.

Suggestions for Analysis of Cases

This section includes suggestions to help you with the analysis of each case in the book. The cases are primarily designed to get you to use the concepts and principles in the chapter that each case follows. You will generally benefit the most if you work each case through for yourself, or in discussion with others, before you check against these suggestions.

In some cases, especially the earlier ones, the suggestions are quite explicit and detailed. In others, especially the later ones, they are brief, often consisting more of questions you should be asking yourself than of specific suggestions on how to proceed and what principles to use. Even in the former, you will seldom find simple "answers" to the cases. The purpose is to get you to think through your own answers, and many of the cases are designed so that there is no one "right" answer that is unambiguously superior to all others. In many cases, you will have to combine your value judgments with economic analysis. (Case 1 is a good example.) Especially on such cases, but on the others as well, you will usually gain by discussing the problem and your answer with other students, in or out of class. One of the tricks in thinking through such real-world cases is to be sure that you see the problem from different points of view, and your friends are almost certain to see some of the cases from different angles from the one that appears to you. But never forget that a major goal is to practice your economic analysis. Even though your value judgments differ, you should be able to agree on the relevant economic concepts and principles, and on the economic analysis involved.

CASE 1: HOW MUCH FOR AUTO SAFETY? Auto passenger safety legislation poses sharply the issue of priorities and resource allocation by individual choice through the market as against collective action through the political process and government regulation. Supporters of the legislation say that everyone "should" be protected against death or serious injury in case of accident; obviously, the protection is worth far more than $100 in case of a serious accident, and the only way to be sure everyone will have it is for Congress to make it mandatory on all new cars.

Opponents counter that each individual should be free to decide for himself how much the protection is worth to him, and to buy only as much auto safety as he wants to pay for. They argue that this case is quite different from other auto safety legislation that is designed to protect innocent people against injury by others, such as speed laws, requirements for operating head- and taillights, and so on. Everyone agrees that laws are needed to protect innocent people against injury by others, but seat belts and air bags protect only their users. They do nothing to lessen the risk of injury for others. And opponents of the legislation point out that car purchasers could buy a lot of other things with the $2–$3 billion they would be required to spend on air bags—things they might value more highly, such as ski trips to Squaw Valley, new clothes, T-bone steaks, health insurance, or any of thousands of other goods and services available on the market.

Thinking through this controversy should help you sort out the issues as to when individual free choice in the market, and when "collective" (governmental) action that is binding on everyone, should control our priorities. In the process, consider the following two related questions: (1) Should Congress pass a law requiring everyone who goes out in below-freezing weather to wear warm clothing? (2) Should Congress pass a law requiring steel mills to reduce the amount of smoke and dirt they emit? How, if at all, do these two cases differ from each other and from the auto passenger safety case? (*Hint*: How does the action affect innocent third parties in each case?)

CASE 2: CAMPUS PARKING.   Stanford faces the central problem that is always faced when the supply of some desirable good is limited (scarce): how to allocate the scarce goods or services among those who want them—in this case, good parking spaces. At Stanford, the past method has combined tradition and "command" (by the central administration) to solve the problem. Four additional alternatives are suggested in the case, and obviously there are a number of further possible combinations and permutations. In deciding which is best, it may be useful to use at least two criteria—equity and efficiency.

On the first, what is your criterion of equity? Should everyone have an equal chance at the best spaces, regardless of his status? Should seniority on the campus count? age? distance of residence from the central campus? Would giving everyone an equal chance under first-come, first-serve be fairest? How about giving the best spaces to those who are willing to pay the most for them?

On the efficiency criterion, what are the critical points? Is it important to ensure that professors get to class on time? Should preference be given to those who stay all day, in contrast to those who come for just two or three classes? In satisfying parking needs, is willingness to pay for a sticker a good measure of how badly an individual needs a close-in parking place? Would a parking charge be an efficient way of discouraging professors, staff, and students who now drive to work although they live nearby and could readily walk or bicycle?

How do the four approaches suggested in the case fare under these tests of equity and efficiency? Tradition, first-come first-served, prices, and the political process are quite different ways of allocating parking spaces. Think who would get the spaces under each arrangement, and how the results would meet your criteria of equity and efficiency. And if equity and efficiency conflict, as they may well do, which should dominate?—for example, if you believe everyone should have an equal chance at the best spaces but know that to follow that policy would make professors late frequently and would give spaces to some people who live close by and would only use them the first few hours of each day.

Last, *how* should Stanford *determine* its parking policy (as distinct from what you believe the policy should be)—by decision of the president, by a democratically elected committee, or some other way? If by voting, who should get to vote, and how, if at all, should minority interests (for example, those of the faculty) be protected? Stanford's problem, if you look at it closely, is similar to the nation's problem when it must decide how to allocate its scarce productive resources. Would you apply your conclusions on the parking problem to the allocation of Jaguar sports cars? raincoats? education on the national scene?

CASE 3: THE PRICE OF PEARS.   This is essentially a simple exercise in applying the price-elasticity-of-demand concept. The pear growers, if they have studied their elementary economics, obviously must be assuming that the demand for their pears is *inelastic*. By reducing the quantity offered for sale, they presumably think the price per ton will be raised more than proportionately, and total consumer expenditure on pears will be increased. If their judgment about the elasticity of demand is correct, they will get more dollars for the smaller quantity of pears, even if they throw away 30,000 tons of good pears. If they are wrong and demand is *elastic*, dumping the 30,000 tons of pears will raise pear prices less than proportionately, and their total sales revenue will be less than if they had marketed the whole crop.

If your goal is maximizing the pear producers' sales revenue, presumably your advice to them will hinge on your elasticity-of-demand estimates, as explained in the preceding paragraph. If demand *is* inelastic (as it probably is), can you suggest any way of increasing producers' total revenue without reducing the amount of pears offered for sale?

If you are ethically outraged at the idea of destroying 30,000 tons of pears when there are so many poor people in the world who would like them, how about (1) giving the 30,000 tons free directly to poor families; (2) getting the government to buy up the 30,000 tons and give them or sell them at a very low price to poor families; or (3) proposing to apply the antitrust laws to the pear producers for conspiring to raise the price of pears? (They are now exempt under special agricultural-cooperative provisions.) How would you expect the pear producers to react to either (1), (2), or (3)? Although you won't have all the analytical tools needed to evaluate these proposals until Chapter 6, how would consumers, pear producers, and the government (taxpayers) fare under each?

CASE 4: GENERAL ELECTRIC COMPANY. The suggestions for analysis of this case are given in the appendix to Chapter 5.

CASE 5: CONSUMER CREDIT AND USURY LAWS. Simple supply-and-demand analysis can help on this problem. The new laws are fixing a price ceiling (interest rate) on loans, below the free-market price. Suppose the supply and demand curves for consumer credit in your state are as on the following chart. Then the free-market interest rate would be 20 percent per year, and $300 million would be offered and borrowed per month. The supply curve, sloping upward, says that lenders would offer more at higher interest rates, less at lower ones. Why? Because at higher interest rates on consumer loans, it will pay to divert more credit from other potential borrowers, and because at higher rates, it will pay to lend to higher-risk borrowers. The demand curve, sloping downward, says that more will be borrowed at lower than at higher rates. Obviously the "finance charge" (of which the interest rate is a big part) helps determine whether or not people can afford a new refrigerator or a new car. The lower the interest rate, the lower the monthly payments and the effective price of the product to people who buy on credit rather than paying cash.

Suppose, now, the state legislature decrees that no lender shall charge consumers more than 1 percent monthly—12 percent per year. At that rate, lenders will lend only $225 million monthly, but consumers will want to borrow $400 million. Clearly, there is a large excess demand—$175 million of unsatisfied consumer wants for credit. There's a "shortage" of credit for consumers. The first effect of the new law is that some consumers get cheaper credit, but some who were previously borrowing at 20 percent now get nothing. Seventy-five million dollars less is lent and an additional $100 million of demand goes unsatisfied. We can be sure there are going to be a lot of angry consumers who get a friendly but firm "no" from auto dealers, banks, finance companies, department stores, and credit-card companies. And the lenders are not

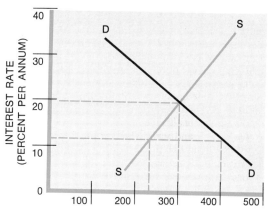

CREDIT PER MONTH (MILLIONS OF DOLLARS)

going to be very happy about alienating their present and potential customers.

But the law is the law. Who gets the limited supply of consumer credit at 1 percent a month? Probably the well-established, low-risk customers of the lenders. But pity the consumer who applies for a new credit card, or charge account, or finance-company loan in your state, especially if his income is low and he does not look like a top-notch credit risk. If you were a lender, you would stick with your established, sure-pay customers for what credit you have to lend—and that is just what lenders did in Arkansas, Minnesota, Washington, and Wisconsin. If the free price system does not decide who gets the available credit, lenders will have to ration it out on some other basis—unhappy customers or not.

What other effects would you expect? Rejected borrowers who live near the state boundary can reasonably be expected to take their business next door where credit is available. This is not calculated to make your home-state merchants very happy. Some borrowers and lenders may cheat a little—some of those rejected potential borrowers may offer to slip the finance man, auto dealer, or credit-card manager a little something on the side to get credit, or a new credit card. "Black markets" can develop in credit just as they did in butter and gasoline when they were price-fixed. For sure, angry customers turned away will complain bitterly to their legislators that they are being treated unfairly—they were supposed to get cheaper credit, but in fact they are getting none. It is those greedy moneylenders trying to gouge them again, especially the poor, minority groups, and others who need the credit most if they are to buy.

Next, and a bit outside our assumptions, the whole supply curve (*SS*) is likely to move to the left—because big consumer lenders, like the nationwide finance companies, may essentially drop out of business in your state. Why suffer the criticisms and take the lower interest rates there if they can make more money with happier customer relationships in other states? Move the *SS* curve to the left and see what that does to the problem in your state.

Who has gained and who has lost from the new law? Should your state legislature be next to put a 1 percent monthly ceiling on customer credit rates?

Last, apply your analysis to Senator Tunney's proposal. (For a relevant news account of what happened in Tennessee, see "Voters End Tennessee's Credit Crunch," *Business Week,* March 20, 1978. The results of Tennessee's 10 percent ceiling were just what you would have predicted above, and the electorate voted the ceiling out when Tennessee lenders laid off many of their employees, and funds became very difficult for consumers to borrow in the state.)

CASE 6: CASH OR FOOD STAMPS FOR THE POOR?

One main issue here is, Which form of aid is more efficient? That is, which increases the well-being of the poor more, $182 worth of food stamps monthly, or $182 in cash? Economic analysis cannot decide the ethical issue of how much, if any, aid should be given, or whether those giving the aid have an ethical right to determine in which form it should be given. But economic analysis can help judge the consequences of different policies.

If a poor family is given cash, we can assume it will spend the money to maximize its satisfaction by so allocating its income that the last dollar spent on each good yields about the same marginal utility. If, instead, the family receives food stamps, its freedom to allocate its income is restricted. If the amount of the food stamps is less than the amount that would have been spent on food anyhow, the food stamps would be equivalent to cash because the household could spend the money saved on food for anything else it wanted (including more food). But if the food stamps are more than the family would otherwise have spent on food, under the food-stamp program the family consumes more food than it prefers relative to other goods; it is forced to take a lower total satisfaction than it could have obtained from an all-cash income. On grounds of economic efficiency, cash aid is likely to be better than food stamps.

But many people do not believe that economic efficiency is the most important consideration in this case. They believe that Congress does know better than the poor what is best for them. Or they are simply not interested in maximizing the satisfaction of the poor; they just want to assure poor people, especially children, a minimum diet. And they doubt that many recipients will resist the temptation to waste the money on nonessentials, instead of adequately feeding their youngsters. These are matters of ethics, however, not economics. Chapter 7 does not have much to say about ethics, but it is important to separate clearly the ethical from the economic arguments. You should also recognize that in making the actual decision, Congress must decide on both types of issues.

Make up your own mind. Then ask yourself whether your arguments hold equally for cash aid versus in-kind subsidies of public housing, health services, and public education.

CASE 7: POLLY POET'S PROBLEM:

Professor Poet's first inclination is to say that if she can get anything more than $405 per month, she'll be better off to rent the house. She's stuck with paying $405 anyway, so anything she gets above that will help her all-too-small bank account. But one of her friends points out that this seems wrong, because there will clearly be more wear and tear on the house and furnishings if a renter lives in the house: The minimum rent to charge is $485.

Actually, neither Polly nor her friend is right, if you think it through. The right answer is, rent for anything over $40, if all that matters are the costs listed in the table. The reasoning, which is far from intuitively obvious, is this.

Suppose Polly keeps the house empty. She is clearly out $405 per month, the amount of her inescapable costs; they are sunk costs. If she rents the house, how much additional (marginal) cost does she incur? The answer is $40, the additional wear and tear on the place. Suppose she rents the house for $45 per month. Her costs are then $445 per month, or $40 higher. But when she uses the $45 rent to apply on the $445, she has only $400 left to pay out-of-pocket on her inescapable $405 sunk costs. She's $5 better off than with the house empty, even at such a low rent.

Obviously, she will be still better off if she can rent for more than $45, which presumably she can for such a nice house. If she can get $345 rent, for example, she can apply it against the $445 of costs, thus leaving only $100 she must pay of her own bank account on her sunk costs. If she can rent for more than $445, of course, she will actually make a profit on her house for the year, covering all her costs and having something left over.

Principles: If your additional cost from renting (your marginal cost) is more than covered by your additional income (marginal revenue), you'll be better off by renting, even though you don't cover all your sunk costs. Marginal cost is the key concept here, and marginal cost doesn't include sunk costs.

How much rent should she ask for her house?

Answer: As much as she can get, as long as it's $40 or more.

CASE 8: AIRLINE TAKES THE MARGINAL ROUTE. The main lesson is pointed up in the box in the case. As long as the marginal cost is below marginal revenue, it pays Continental Airlines to increase its output (add more flights), even though the extra income (marginal revenue) may not cover the full average total cost of production (ATC). Continental's total profit is larger with the flights in question than without them. Mr. Whelan gets an A in Economics I.

But there is a second lesson, too, which Mr. Whelan recognizes in the tenth paragraph. Some flights can add to total profits even though they do not cover *full* costs, but clearly, for all flights together, income must cover full costs if the firm is to make a profit and to stay in business. Those marginal Continental flights are good business because the company has the planes, airport docks, reservation clerks, and other needed facilities on hand anyway. For purposes of this analysis, these are *fixed* (*sunk*) costs; they go on whether or not Continental adds the marginal flights in question. As Whelan says, the out-of-pocket (marginal) approach comes into play only after the airline's basic schedule has been set—but income from some flights obviously has to cover all these costs if the company is to make a profit.

CASE 9: SHOULD BUSINESS SERVE THE PUBLIC INTEREST OR MAXIMIZE PROFITS? Should business serve the public interest rather than attempt to maximize profits? Question 2 is the critical one in this little case: "Is there a conflict between businesses' trying to maximize profits and serving the public interest?" Chapter 10, following Adam Smith, argues that, *given highly competitive markets*, the attempts of businessmen to maximize their profits would redound to the maximum benefit of consumers and society as a whole. Then, as Friedman suggests in his statement, as long as pure competition prevails to channel the profit motive to the common good, there is no conflict between the public interest and the attempt of businesses to maximize profits; on the contrary, there is a profound common interest, even though businessmen in fact succeed in making only "normal" profits in the long run in such a society.

Most supporters of the private-enterprise system

will accept the three kinds of "market failures" listed at the end of the chapter as requiring special governmental action, and much of the criticism of business profit-seeking activities is based on these kinds of market failures. But another criticism of business, which has developed rapidly in the last few decades, is that it ought to be more "socially responsible" in helping to solve the nonbusiness problems of society—renovating the central cities, eliminating discrimination against minorities and women, reducing pollution, reducing poverty, and the like. Many of these goals are now in fact embedded in the law, and business should surely obey the law. But should it go further? If so, how much further, at what cost? Who should decide? And who should pay—customers or stockholders?

Questions 3 and 4 have no simple right or wrong answers. They are designed to make you think about the role of business and of profits in a basically private-enterprise, market-directed economy. Consider number 4 especially. Friedman asks, What special wisdom do business managers have to decide what is good for society, once they go beyond responding to consumer demands? Do you have an answer?

Clearly, if Friedman's general position is accepted, completely or in large part, it must be on the presumption that business operates in competitive markets, where its profit-seeking activities are constrained by competition. A lot of people don't believe this is true. They argue, instead, that business has large monopoly powers that it can and does use to benefit its managers and stockholders, at the expense of the public. This concern is examined at length in Chapters 12–16. After those chapters, it will be useful to raise the four questions in this case again.

CASE 10: EGGS, COPPER, AND COFFEE. The California case is a microcosm of the problems raised by federal farm policy on major products. The analysis in the chapter should be directly applicable. Make up your own mind after you have analyzed the gains and costs to producers, consumers, and any others concerned. Would we be better off to let competition work its will?

Existence of the California Egg Advisory Board to monitor policies of the egg producers raises a question that will be considered at length in Chapters 15 and 16—how effective government agencies and boards are likely to be in compromising the interests of consumers and producers in such cases. Looking ahead, the answer is, Mixed, but not very effective in many cases. The urgent problems of producers tend to override the less concentrated concerns of consumers.

Such industry agreements to restrict production are generally called cartels, and often government-monitored cartels have worked effectively for the producers involved (for instance, in agriculture) where purely private agreements would have been both illegal and unworkable.

The international copper and coffee cartels raise the same issues as do the domestic ones involving eggs or hi-fis, except that the consumers and producers are in different countries in the various cases—leaving aside balance-of-payments considerations from international transactions until Part 5. (See Case 31.)

The hi-fi producers' proposal, again, raises the same issues. Should farmers be treated differently from nonfarm businesses by the government and by consumers? Most hi-fi producers are relatively small firms. Would you want to distinguish between large and small businesses in judging such cases? If so, why? (Use the analysis of Chapter 10 here.)

CASE 11: *U.S. V. ALUMINUM COMPANY OF AMERICA.*
There are no suggestions for analysis for this case. Use your basic analysis of competition and monopoly, especially from Chapters 10 and 12, to develop your own answers to the questions.

CASE 12: SHOULD LAWYERS, DOCTORS, AND DENTISTS ADVERTISE?
No suggestions for analysis on this one. The answers are essentially judgmental, and the main issues for consideration are indicated in the case itself and in the material directly bearing on the case in Chapter 13.

CASE 13: ADVERTISING AND CONSUMERISM.
The concepts and analysis of the preceding chapters should help you decide on the proposed legislation. Try answering the following questions:

1. Who would gain? What would be the benefits to them?
2. Who would lose? What would be the costs to them? (Look at different groups of consumers and businesses.)
3. Would paragraphs 1 and 2 infringe in the freedom of individuals to seek profits as long as they do no harm to others?
4. How should the FTC decide what advertising is "useful" to consumers? what advertising is "misleading"? (If you don't think these terms are sufficiently clear, can you suggest better ones?)
5. Would you be concerned about concentration of power in the hands of the FTC?

6. Would consumers have more or less influence than now over what businesses produce?
7. Would you expect the price of newspapers and magazines to change if the legislation passed? How?
8. Would you expect TV programming and financing arrangements to change? How?
9. If triple damage suits under paragraph 3 involved large settlements, who would you expect to bear the cost? in the short run? in the long run?
10. If you see problems with this proposal, can you suggest an alternative that you think the country needs?

CASE 14: THE BATTLE OF THE SUPERMARKETS
This case illustrates both the managerial and the social problems of oligopoly. The questions at the end of the case point up some of the main issues. Questions 1–6 focus on management problems in this oligopoly; so viewed, this case is much like the ones you will face if you go on to a graduate school of business. Questions 7–9 focus on the social issues; who will gain and who will lose, what is the public interest here, and what, if any, government intervention is called for?

A&P's situation is a classic example of the problem faced by an oligopolistic market leader that is losing its share of the market. The A&P management surely knew that their price cutting would bring retaliation; presumably they decided that, nonetheless, this was their best chance of retaining their market share without such a serious price war that profits would be more than temporarily eroded. Possibly they were surprised at the vigor of the price war they started; many have criticized their managerial strategy. But it's not clear what other steps they could have taken to improve their deteriorating position; they had tried the obvious measures, such as more advertising, improved service, and the like.

The problem of the competitive chains is equally easy to understand, but no easier to solve. If they didn't meet the cuts, they would almost surely lose business to A&P, which would thus achieve its goal, at least in part. But meeting the cuts would clearly produce a price war, which would help no one's profits and would probably be hard to stop—and this is precisely what happened. One approach would have been to fight back through advertising and other sales techniques, instead of cutting prices. And advertising budgets did rise. But this raises costs, and there's no guarantee that you can convince housewives to buy your products if they can get substantially the same thing cheaper down the street. Or you might just sit it out in the hope that A&P will soon see the costs of cutting its own prices and profits. Do you have a better alternative?

Note, too, the strong market pressures in such a case toward open or covert collusion (illegal). If there were now some way to stop the price war, all firms would clearly be better off, especially some of the weaker ones that face extinction if their losses continue for long. But the law against price collusion is clear, and who dares risk being the leader in putting his prices back up to a profitable level and leaving them there to establish a new pattern without some assurance the others will go along? Only a strong, acknowledged price leader would dare to do so, and it's not obvious just which firm that is in this complex case. All things considered, from a managerial point of view, the case provides strong support for a price policy of leaving well enough alone in an oligopoly, as the text suggests is common practice in such markets.

Turning to the social issues, consumers seem to be the big gainers from the price war. But if the war ends up bankrupting many smaller, weaker firms, the long-run result is less clear. (Remember, that's what some smaller firms say A&P is trying to do.) With fewer firms, there's less certainty of effective competition to hold down prices in the future. Moreover, after "taking a bath" like this, you can be sure that every firm is going to think a long time before it risks starting another price war. And new investment in the industry is going to be unattractive unless there are both reasonably stable competitive relationships and reasonable returns on investment. The demand for food is growing steadily; unless investment in food retailing continues to grow, services to consumers will deteriorate.

Last, investors are part of society too. Price wars that benefit consumers can also bankrupt investors. Remembering that, what is "the public interest" in this case?

By 1978, A&P sales has fallen $5 billion behind Safeway's total of $12.5 billion; and A&P reported a net *loss* of $15 million for the year, compared to Safeway's profits of $140 million. Profits for the industry as a whole were only back up to 0.9 cents per dollar of sales. (Safeway earned about 1.1 cents per dollar of sales.)

If you want to check how A&P and the grocery industry have come out by the time you use this case, up-to-date sales and profit figures can be obtained from the July issue of *Fortune* each year, which provides summary information on each of the 50 largest retailing companies for the preceding year; or from Moody's, Standard & Poor's or Value Line's

investment manuals, probably available in your library.

CASE 15: SOME MANAGERIAL APPLICATIONS. These little cases are designed to illustrate the application of economic concepts and principles in relatively simple business situations. Because each example includes an explanation of the principles and concepts involved and how they apply, no further suggestions for analysis are needed.

CASE 16: *U.S. V. VON'S GROCERIES.* Just how many firms are needed to ensure the benefits of competition under different conditions is a complex issue. The purpose of this case is to pose this problem in a particular situation, and to let you see how the Supreme Court goes about analyzing such cases when it must decide them under the law. Although it is important to understand something of how the Court applies the broadly stated law to particular cases, the main purpose is to induce you to think through for yourself what would best serve the public interest here, using your economic analysis to do so.

In arriving at your answer, consider the following questions:

1. What do we want competition to accomplish for us?
2. How many grocery firms does it take in the Los Angeles market to ensure the benefits of competition? (Note the total number of firms in the Los Angeles market, the share of market covered by the merger, and the actual overlap in the markets served by Von's and Shopping Bag.)
3. How shall we balance the lower costs of supermarkets against the potentially greater competition among more small, but higher-cost, stores? Who or what should decide how many grocery stores there should be in Los Angeles?
4. Should the purpose of antitrust be to protect competition or small competitors?

CASE 17: TV ADVERTISING AND CHILDREN'S TEETH. This is a complex case. Economic analysis alone cannot give you an answer to the problem. Reaching a reasoned decision requires answering at least six questions—two on facts, two on value judgments, and two on economic analysis:

1. How harmful are sugar-coated cereals to children's teeth?
2. Are children in fact as susceptible to TV advertising as the FTC staff suggests?
3. What is the right of advertisers under the First Amendment to the Constitution to say what they

wish on television, and what is the right of listeners (especially children) to be protected against hearing TV material that may be harmful to them?

4. Should parents be held responsible for looking out for their children's interests by keeping them from watching TV programs that may be harmful to them?

5. Without advertising, would children's programs on television deteriorate or disappear completely? If so, how much of a loss would this be? Who would gain, and who would lose?

6. Is government protection of consumers justified here, on the ground that consumers are unable to understand the information required to make a wise purchase decision? Are the consumers in this case children or parents?

CASE 18: CONSUMER APPLIANCES. You're on your own for this one. Use the analysis suggested by Chapter 29, combined with your own set of values.

CASE 19: THE $66 BILLION MISTAKE: If you are an ardent environmentalist, you may be understandably wary of a proposal on auto-pollution control by one of the major oil companies. Clearly, you have no basis for judging the accuracy of Mobil's $66 billion estimate, and that is not the main point of the case. The $66 billion has been disputed, as has been the exact nature of the rising cost curve in Chart 2. If you prefer, assume that the $66 billion extra cost is only $33 billion and that the Chart 2 curve rises only half as fast between the California and national standards, figures that even Mobil critics would agree are reasonable. In analyzing the proposals, it may be useful to focus on these three broad questions (using whichever cost figure you prefer).

1. How clean is clean enough? Is meeting the 1976 clean-air standards for auto emissions worth $66 (or $33) billion over the next ten years? Note that economics can give no one "right" answers to this question; each person must decide for himself whether having air that is clean is worth the alternatives foregone. Marginalism and alternative cost are the key concepts here. Mobil is right in stressing the other things we could get with our $66 billion if we settle for the California standards on air cleanliness. But be careful about the figures; Mobil's $66 billion extra cost is spread over ten years, while most of the alternative gains given are for only one year.

2. Accepting the need for government controls, should the direct-regulation approach be used, as Mobil suggests, or would we be better served by an effluent-charge approach (for example, a special charge per unit of emission from each car, perhaps based on the type of car and mileage driven annually, or a special tax on gasoline)? Should every car owner pay the same amount (by buying an emission-control system for his car), regardless of how much and where he drives? Regulation versus stress on individual incentives is a big issue here.

3. If Congress accepts the Mobil proposal for large, modern mass-transit systems, who should pay the bill—the general taxpayer (as Mobil suggests), car drivers, mass-transit riders, local taxpayers in the areas served? What principle do you use in deciding who should pay?

CASE 20: ECONOMICS OF THE DRAFT. Supply and demand, marginal productivity, and opportunity cost are the basic economic concepts you need to analyze the two approaches to the draft. The figure shows the economics of the draft, using rough illustrative figures for supply and demand curves. The left-hand portion shows the draft. Military pay is plotted on the vertical axis, the number of servicemen in the army on the horizontal axis. Since both are set by law, the equilibrium point (E) shows 2.5 million people in the army at an average rate of $10,000 per year. The supply curve is vertical, indicating that the required number of men and women will be forthcoming at whatever wage the army offers to pay, in this case $10,000; the supply is perfectly inelastic. If Congress raises the average salary to $12,000, or lowers it to $8,000, the number of people in the army remains unchanged, while the tax bill for financing the army is increased or lowered correspondingly. (Assume that the salaries quoted include all living expenses paid by the armed services.)

The right-hand portion of the figure shows the supply and demand situation if we have an army in which people volunteer in response to the wage offered, just as they do for other jobs. Thus, the supply curve $(S'S')$ slopes upward to the right, indicating that more people would volunteer at a higher wage than at a lower one. In the same way, the demand for servicemen $(D'D')$ slopes downward to the right, indicating that with high service pay, it would pay the army to use civilians for many posts that uniformed personnel might fill under a draft; conversely, it would pay the army to use more servicemen relative to civilians at a lower service wage.

Given the army's demand curve in the figure, it would hire 2.5 million men and women at an average wage of $14,000. It could get more by raising the offered wage; if it wished to get along with less, it could get them at a lower wage. The equilibrium E' at $14,000 is a $4,000 higher annual wage than E in the

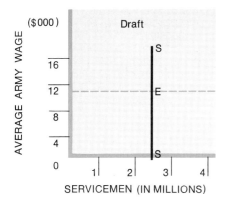

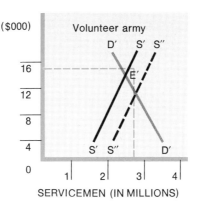

left-hand portion, indicating that in the draft, many people are required to enter the armed services who would not do so voluntarily at that wage.

Note that the supply curve ($S'S'$) will presumably shift with economic conditions. If a depression comes, with widespread civilian unemployment, more people will volunteer for military service at the same wage rates. For example, $S''S''$ might be the new supply curve, and the army could then get 2.5 million soldiers for a $7,000 average wage.

Which is the economically cheaper way? Given the facts shown, with volunteer supply curve $S'S'$, total army wages, and hence the nation's tax bill, are clearly less in the draft case. With the draft, the total wage bill for 2.5 million people is $25 billion; with the volunteer army, it is $35 billion. But from society's viewpoint, the *real* cost of the army is the opportunity cost of the civilian goods foregone by having 2.5 million people in the army—and that opportunity cost will partly depend on who the people in the army are.

The amount each individual could earn in the private marketplace (his marginal revenue product) is a measure of the civilian output society foregoes if he serves in the army instead. Suppose a star athlete, like Bill Walton, is drafted. He would have earned, say, $1 million in professional basketball, and that (not his army pay of $10,000) is the opportunity cost of his army service. Similarly, for every soldier drafted involuntarily at the army's going wage, the opportunity cost is presumably higher than his army wage. Clearly, to allocate these men and women to the army through the draft is to allocate them inefficiently in economic terms.

But if we don't draft Walton and others, the army still needs people. Would a volunteer army be cheaper in real (opportunity cost) terms? The answer is yes. $S'S'$ in the figure tells us that 2.5 million men and women would volunteer for army duty at a $14,000 wage. We can safely presume that these are people

who would have made less, or certainly not very much more, in civilian life. Thus, the total civilian output foregone by having the people in the army is $14,000 per person per year, or less. In terms of overall economic efficiency, resources are best allocated by the voluntary service plan, leaving the choice up to each individual as to whether he prefers a $14,000 job in the army to what he can earn in civilian life. We can safely assume that Walton and other high civilian-marginal-product people will not volunteer for the army. Those whose marginal product is higher in the army will go there, those with a higher civilian marginal product will take civilian jobs.

ECONOMICS AND ETHICS. Although a volunteer army would clearly be cheaper in terms of opportunity costs, that does not prove it would necessarily be better. Consider the ethical issues involved.

Presumably, the major equity of the draft is that everyone has an equal chance of being chosen in a lottery system. But note the related inequities. If Walton is drafted away from a $1 million civilian job at $10,000, the implied tax rate he pays to support the defense effort is 99 percent of his potential income. By comparison, a draftee with no civilian alternative above $10,000 pays no special tax at all, merely his regular income tax of a few percent of his income. Equitable? With a volunteer army, general taxpayers, not the luckless young people who happen to be drafted, would pay what it takes to fill the armed services.

But opponents of the volunteer system reply that as a practical matter, a volunteer army will end up with mainly low-income people, including a heavy representation of blacks and other minorities who have limited civilian employment opportunities. To be sure, they may be making more in the army than they could in civilian life—but why should they be the cannon fodder while higher-income whites remain civilians?

It is far from obvious which arrangement is more equitable, even if the volunteer army is clearly more efficient economically. Probably a lot depends on whether army service involves any serious danger of wartime death or injury. In a war, especially an unpopular one, the fundamental argument that everyone should have to face an equal chance of death in battle appears to dominate, and indeed it is not clear that any army wage would fill a volunteer army during a major war. But during peacetime, the case for a volunteer army, on both equity and economic grounds, looks strong.

A CONCLUDING QUESTION TO FOCUS THE ISSUES: If we use a military draft, should we use a similar draft to preempt men and women for police, postal, and all other public-service duties, at a wage equal to that paid in the armed forces draft? Or, at a more extreme level, should we preempt workers through a draft-like plan to make steel and to mine coal, rather than leaving it up to the private economy where firms clearly have to pay many workers more than army draft wage rates? A volunteer army would use the same method of getting people as do other industries in the United States.

CASE 21: THE ECONOMICS OF MINIMUM-WAGE LAWS. Minimum-wage legislation is an example of government price-fixing, with the legal minimum price (wage) above the market-clearing level. Draw a demand and a supply curve for labor, with the market equilibrium wage at, say, $2.50. Now set the minimum wage at $3.50, and assume the law is enforced rigorously. What are the likely results?

1. Clearly, there will now be an excess supply of labor—some previously employed workers will lose their jobs, and new labor-force entrants will seek jobs at the higher wage. In marginal-productivity language, the wage has gone up without any increase in labor's marginal productivity, so it will pay profit-seeking businesses to hire fewer workers, especially young, inexperienced, and low-skilled workers.

   What will happen to the unemployed workers? They may stay unemployed, or look for work in industries not covered by the minimum wage law. If they do the latter, they force wages down in the uncovered industries, since the supply of labor is increased without any increase in demand.

   Who is helped by the new law? Those who keep their jobs in the covered industries. This will presumably include some who were previously earning less than $3.50. Who is hurt? Obviously, those who lose their jobs, plus newcomers to the labor force who would have been hired into covered industries at a lower wage but whose marginal productivity is less than $3.50. Those hurt will be mainly unskilled workers, teenagers, school dropouts, minority workers—the very low-income people the law was designed to help. It will no longer pay businesses or others to hire workers whose marginal productivity is less than $3.50. The result is likely to make the "hardcore" unemployment problem worse.

2. If employers are now "exploiting" labor by paying wages below labor's marginal productivity, the minimum wage may boost wages without reducing employment. Wages would then get more of the consumer's dollar, profits less. This is the situation implicitly assumed in most of the ardent arguments for minimum wage legislation.

3. Even if there is no exploitation of labor, the law's upward pressure on wage rates may drive employers to more efficient methods, thereby absorbing the higher wages without reducing employment. This, too, is a favorite argument of minimum wage advocates. How often it works this way is not clear from the evidence. It depends mainly on how efficiently businessmen have been running their businesses without the pressures of the minimum wage law. If businesses were maximizing profits before, the results are as described in paragraph 1 above. If some businesses were failing to produce as cheaply as possible, the new minimum wage may simply push them to more efficient methods, which offset the higher wage costs. This latter case obviously implies the absence of effective competition. It is the other situation implicitly assumed by many minimum wage advocates.

4. Minimum-wage laws tend to redistribute incomes—from employers to labor, and mainly from workers who are shut out to those who keep their jobs at higher pay. What happens to the total labor share in the national income depends basically on the elasticity of demand for labor. If employers' aggregate demand for labor is inelastic, the law will mean higher total wage payments. Unfortunately, we don't know what the general elasticity of demand for labor is, although we do know that higher wages induce the substitution of capital for labor. The impact of a minimum-wage law is uneven, operating mainly against low-productivity workers wherever they are.

5. Although the analysis above is correct, as a practical matter the minimum-wage law has had only a limited effect thus far on the American economy. It

has repeatedly been repealed by inflation. By the time the original 30-cents-per-hour minimum went into effect, market wages in most covered industries had already risen above that level. Wages in some industries, especially in the South, lagged behind the minimum figures, but many of these were in industries not covered by the law—agriculture, services, local shops, and so on. Further inflation and rising wages robbed each increase in the legal minimum of much of its intended impact. If inflation continues, it would erode the effect of the new $3.50 minimum, as in the past—although even then, the $3.50 floor would affect low-wage pockets throughout the economy, and such low-productivity groups as unskilled workers and minority teenage school dropouts.

Given this analysis, what is your answer on the proposed $3.50 minimum wage?

Suggestions for analysis are provided in the case.

CASE 23: PROFITS FOR THE PICKING. The key to analysis of this case is suggested in the case. It is the search for profits and the ever-present competitive process that moves resources to those areas and industries where the prospective rate of profit is highest.

There are two related but different questions: (1) Who should pay for higher standards of quality, safety, and reliability in consumer products? This is an ethical question, at least in part. Your answer may well be, The rich corporations, who owe consumers better and safer products. (2) Who will pay for the higher standards if we require them? Here the answer is, In the long run, probably consumers, no matter where the law imposes them, unless the industry is making excess profits (above the normal rate of return), reflecting barriers to entry against other competitors. If there are such excess profits, a law requiring higher product standards may be able to seize some of the special profits by imposing higher costs. But if there is substantial freedom of entry into the industry, excess profits will have been eliminated. If a law increases costs, profits in the industry will be reduced below the normal rate of return, and either prices will be raised to reflect the higher costs, or resources will gradually be moved out of the industry to where at least a normal rate of return is available. In the latter case, price will rise in the regulated industry as supply is reduced, and the cost of higher quality will be passed on to consumers. Note that this conclusion follows in the long run in monopolistically competitive and oligopolistic, as well as in purely competitive, cases.

But two warnings. First, in the short run, firms may have to bear the cost of meeting the new, higher standards. It takes time for resources to shift out of low-return industries. Second, if an individual firm is failing to meet quality standards observed by the rest of the industry, legal (or informal consumer) action may force it to meet the prevailing industry standards—for example, where one firm is failing to meet pollution standards observed by the rest of the industry.

CASE 24: THE VOUCHER EDUCATION PLAN. At first, the idea of turning education over to profit-seeking business may shock you, but the plan has won many advocates.

Analytically, the voucher plan has two quite separate parts. First, it relies on the public sector to guarantee a minimum level of education for all children. This redistributes income; without the free vouchers for all, the poor would not be able to afford this much education, which, under the voucher plan as now, would be financed by general tax receipts that come more heavily from higher-income groups. The guarantee also rests on the widespread belief in positive externalities from general education. Most Americans believe that we have a better society when everyone has at least a minimum level of education.

Second, the plan relies on the private market to provide most efficiently the education parents want for their children. Advocates argue that it makes sense for private entrepreneurs to provide education, just as they produce clothing, hotels, highways, airplanes, food, and other goods and services. This is what the private sector has shown it can do best—produce efficiently the goods and services consumers demand in the market. Just because we need the government to guarantee a minimum level of education for all is no reason we should expect the government to actually produce the education, especially not in a monopoly status such as the present public education system provides.

What are the objections to the plan? First, and perhaps most important, many Americans feel that many (other?) parents really aren't competent to decide what is the best schooling for their youngsters, and that they would be easy picking for unscrupulous businessmen selling poor education. Make up your own mind. Should government give the poor money and let them decide how much to spend on food (education), give them vouchers but leave them free to decide what food (education) to buy, or prescribe in detail what food (education) they shall receive?

Second, some critics say the plan wouldn't guarantee the same education for everybody, poor and rich. They are correct; it would not. Nor does it claim to, any more than the present system does. Rich parents would still have the option, as now, of spending more than the voucher on education for their youngsters. But the voucher plan would guarantee the same *minimum* for each youngster within the area involved. If you stop to think about it, further legislation forbidding richer parents to spend more than the minimum on their children would be hard to justify, under the voucher plan or now, unless you favor eliminating all differences in income per se.

Third, isn't education too important to entrust to profit-seeking businesses? Would you make the same argument about food, drugs, medical services? Education is important, just as are many other goods and services now produced by private businesses. The issue is not how important the product is, but what kind of enterprise is likely to produce what consumers want most efficiently (at the lowest cost and price). We rely on private firms to train their employees in routine and highly technical skills; is education of youngsters more difficult? If so, why should non-profit-seeking schools be able to do it better? If the public feels there are some skills that should be guaranteed for all, let the state mandate them for all schools eligible to receive the vouchers. But, say the plan's supporters, be wary of getting too much government regulation into the picture lest you destroy the private initiative that the plan seeks.

Fourth, wouldn't many areas be too small to support enough schools to provide alternative programs to compete for parents' dollars? The answer is yes. Some would, just as some are now too small to support adequate schools. The youngster who lives in a small village out in the mountains isn't going to get the best education either way. It's a problem society must face, possibly with special subsidies, under any educational system.

Fifth, couldn't the plan be used to finance church schools, violating the constitutional separation of church and state? And sixth, might not it permit development of racially segregated schools? Voucher supporters answer that safeguards can and should be built in to forbid both religious and racial misuse of the plan, by refusal to certify such schools under the voucher plan. Indeed, they argue, the proposed voucher plan should speed integration by breaking present ties between the school attended and residential locations.

As a practical matter, the voucher plan is a long way from supplanting the present public school system. But it poses sharply the problem of where and how the private and public sectors can most effectively serve the public. Thinking it through is a valuable exercise. And don't think it's completely farfetched. Many governmental scholarships and fellowships for college and postgraduate education are given now in the form of vouchers, usable at any approved school. There are many partial voucher arrangements that may be attractive even though the complete plan may seem to go too far.

CASE 25: HOW MUCH SOCIAL SECURITY CAN WE AFFORD? This case raises an interesting combination of economic and ethical issues. Fundamentally, the problem is that we face limited resources, and that the more fully we use these resources, the larger will be the economy's total output. When people retire, they stop adding to society's output but continue as consumers. Thus, the earlier we require or permit people to retire, the smaller is the total real output on which we all depend for our standards of living.

Second, how much of any total output should be transferred to retired nonworkers is both an economic and an ethical issue. It is an economic issue because it may affect the incentives of both younger and older people to work, and hence affect society's total output. It is an ethical issue as to how much of their work younger people are willing to devote to supporting older nonworkers, who, it must be remembered, as parents earlier supported the present workers through their years of childhood and education.

The financing pattern used for Social Security determines who pays, again both an ethical and an economic (incentives) issue. It is also a political issue. If we throw Social Security into the regular annual federal budget process, will the result be higher or lower taxes and benefits for older people? Many supporters of the present system urge that it be kept in its present special status to avoid its becoming a political football, with annual battles over both taxes and benefits leading to unpredictable results and highly disruptive uncertainties for retired people.

Third, if the government were to accumulate a huge insurance-type reserve fund to finance future benefit payments, what would be the impact on current output and prices? If the fund were held uninvested, this would clearly impose a massive deflationary pressure on the economy—it would be an enormous annual government surplus. Suppose, therefore, the government set out to invest the fund, channeling it back into the income stream. In what would it invest? If in ventures like schools and highways, how would these be liquidated when the funds were later needed for benefit payments? Who would be the buyers to provide the funds needed then by the government? Alternatively, if the government invested the fund in business ventures, it would soon find itself massively engaged in the private business sector. The volume of funds is so huge that it would soon find itself dominating many markets and moving rapidly toward a socialist economy. Or if the government simply used the fund to cover part of its current budget expenditures, from a macroeconomic point of view there would be little change from the present pay-as-you-go system; no fund would be accumulated. If you think through the macroeconomic alternatives, it's easy to see why the government rapidly drifted into the present modified annual-income-transfer financing pattern.

Last, the next-to-last paragraph in the case is correct. If people view their Social Security taxes as savings, they will save less through private channels. Funds for private investment projects are therefore less than they would be without the present Social Security system. Thus, how we handle Social Security may have a significant effect on our rate of economic growth.

CASE 26: PROPOSED CONSTITUTIONAL AMENDMENT FOR A BALANCED BUDGET.

This case sums up many of the difficulties, both economic and political, of making a democratic government work effectively on complex economic issues. You have the analytical tools on fiscal policy to do the economic analysis. Do you want the federal budget balanced each year? If not, what amendment would you suggest to your senator for a better arrangement—for example, a balanced high-employment budget, or a plan for balancing the budget over the business cycle, or some other modification of the proposed amendment?

On the mixture of political and economic issues, would the requirement for budget balance keep taxes and expenditures under control, if that is your main objective? Would the amendment keep Congress from simply raising expenditures and raising taxes to go with them? Should we introduce major rigidities into the budget process by such a constitutional amendment, or simply leave the matter to the responsibility and judgment of Congress and the president? Should we completely give up efforts to "finetune" the economy through fiscal policy, and concentrate only on keeping the budget balanced?

A special inflation problem: Economic analysis suggests that balancing the high-employment budget would be more sensible economically than balancing the regular unified budget each year. But if inflation continues in the economy, the inflation increases the tax yield to the government substantially each year without any increase in tax rates. Thus, in an inflationary economy, the proposed annual budget balance (either unified or high-employment budget) would automatically provide for a steadily growing share of government in the national economy, unless the president and Congress chose to limit it by reducing tax rates. Since tax collections increase about 16 percent for each 10 percent increase in GNP, this would mean a rapid rise in total government spending and total tax payments by the public, unless the tax system were "indexed" to automatically reduce tax rates and raise exemptions in proportion to the amount of inflation.

Most economists had serious doubts about a constitutional amendment to require an annual balanced budget, although support increased when a high-employment budget and an indexed tax system were added. More economists, including some leaders in the profession, supported instead a constitutional amendment to limit government spending to some specific percent of GNP. Their argument was that this would directly keep federal expenditures under control, which is what the balanced-budget proposal tried to do indirectly. This expenditure-control amendment would also be simpler than the balanced-budget proposal. It would, however, have some of the same weaknesses, including the rigidity imposed by any constitutional provision (will we want just the same amount of government spending in relation to GNP 20 years from now as we want today?).

CASE 27: SHOULD TAXES ON CORPORATE PROFITS BE REDUCED?

This case raises both micro and macro issues, issues of both equity and incentives. The following questions may help organize your analysis:

On the incentives-growth issue:

1. Would reducing the effective tax rate on returns to capital (say, by integrating the personal and corporation income taxes to eliminate "double taxation") stimulate more investment and faster national economic growth? The answer is given partly by macro analysis, partly by the micro analysis of the behavior of the individual firm in Part 2 and this chapter.

On the equity issue:

2. If the answer to the preceding question is yes, will the increase in GNP be enough to increase the incomes of the lower- and middle-income classes, even though the first effect is to increase the after-tax incomes of the well-to-do?

3. Is more equality in after-tax incomes under the present tax system more "equitable" than would be the more unequal but higher absolute incomes

4. If personal and corporation income taxes were integrated, as Secretary Simon proposes, corporate profits would be taxed to the individual stockholder as earned, whether or not they are paid out

in dividends. The corporate income tax rate is proportional at about 46 percent for all large corporations, while personal income tax rates rise to a 70 percent maximum on very large incomes. Would the proposed change make the combined taxes more or less progressive? Is your answer changed by the fact that many corporate stocks are held by pension funds accumulated to pay future retirement benefits to lower- and middle-income workers?

CASE 28: ROBINSON CRUSOE, FRIDAY, AND THE GAINS FROM TRADE.

No suggestions for analysis should be necessary on this case. The analysis is presented directly in the middle portion of Chapter 27. It has also been presented repeatedly in the domestic sections of the text (Parts 1, 2, and 3) dealing with the advantages of specialization and exchange among freely consenting individuals or businesses.

CASE 29: MULTINATIONAL CORPORATIONS.

As the case suggests, answers to many of the questions here are open to debate. The fundamental thrust of the multinationals toward a more efficient allocation of world resources and against the restrictionism of nation-states is clear. Use the principle of comparative advantage, with specialization and exchange, as the central analysis. Multinationals will tend to increase total world output, and there will be more to divide up among all the nations involved.

But the balance-of-payments questions are more complex, and the question of how the increased total output is divided among the nations is uncertain. With Chapter 27, try tracing the effects of multinational investment and profit flows on the international payments of the different nations involved.

On the most explosive issue, nationalism versus multinational pressures, you're on your own. Economic analysis can suggest results, but it can only help to provide the answers.

CASE 30: IMPORTS: BANE OR BOON?

This case requires no extended suggestions for analysis. For the most part, Mr. Abel's statement is in head-on opposition to the reasoning supporting freer trade in Chapter 27. Apply that analysis to Abel's basic proposal for an import quota on each product, to keep imports from gaining a larger share of any market.

Note that Abel adds one argument to the usual case against free trade. He argues that the presumed advantages of free trade are not obtained when multinational corporations use cheap labor to manufacture abroad and then sell here, because they retain all the lower-cost advantages for themselves as profits. Consumers, he argues, do not benefit.

If Abel is right, clearly the presumed consumer gain from free international trade would be shortcircuited. How would you check up on his allegation? Note that there are two ways. One would be to look at profits of multinational firms compared to others; this would not be definitive, because many other factors also influence company profits. The other is to use your theory, which tells you to ask whether substantial competition exists in the areas discussed by Abel. If there is competition, and other firms selling in the United States are free to duplicate low-cost production overseas, we can be reasonably sure the multinational firms won't be able to hold onto their excess profits because competition will force prices down toward costs of production.

CASE 3: COFFEE, CARTELS, AND U.S. DEVELOPMENT AID.

Here it is the end of the course, and you should be able to be on your own at last. For the central issues and concepts to use, look back at Chapters 11 and 14, plus Cases 11 and 14, in addition to Chapter 29. This case, like the preceding one, provides an opportunity to use a substantial part of the tool kit you've been accumulating, and it leaves an important role for the differing value judgments that so often loom large in economic policy decisions.

Name index

N

Nader, R., 11, 175, 206, 212, 218n., 219, 307
Nichols, D., xiii
Nilsson, B., 289
Nixon, R. M., 143, 231, 341f.
Noll, R., 220n.
Nordhaus, W., 361

O

Opel, J., 57
Orwell, G., 422

P

Pareto, W., 136
Patrick, H., 439n.
Peltzman, S., 213n.
Phillips, A. W., 159n.
Posner, R., 216n.
Primeaux, W., 159n., 181n.
Prybyla, J. S., 421

R

Radner, D., 241n.
Rawls, J., 367
Reagan, B., 268n.
Rees, A., 264n.
Reilly, D., 395n.
Reynolds, L. G., 280n.
Reynolds, M., 30, 32
Ricardo, D., 108f., 375
Roosevelt, F. D., 275
Roosevelt, T., 201
Rosovsky, H., 439n.
Roos, W. S., 215n.
Ruff, L. E., 231n.

S

Saunders, P., xiii
Saving, T. R., 203
Scherer, F., 203f.

Schmid, J., xiii
Schultze, C., 230, 231n.
Schumpeter, J., 303
Schwartz, N., 186n.
Servan-Schreiber, J. J., 387
Sheehan, S., 341n.
Shieh, F., xiii
Shields, G., xiii
Shields, M., xiii
Siegfried, J., 199n.
Simon, W., 366f.
Smith, A., 29, 31ff., 52, 196, 206, 212, 225, 313, 388, 390
Smith, J., 241n.
Smith, M., 181n.
Srinivasan, T. N., 420n.
Steinke, S., xiii
Stieber, J., 281n.
Stigler, G., 181, 203, 216
Stokes, B., 418
Strober, M., xiii
Sweezy, P., 310n.

T

Taubman, P., 265n.
Teece, D., xiii
Thoman, L., xiii
Tiemann, T., 199n.
Tobin, J., 341
Truman, H. S., 143
Tunney, J., 80

V

Volkov, O., 226n.

W

Walras, L., 32n., 130n.
Walsh, L., 174
Walton, B., 2
Watson, D. S., 193n
Ways, M., 205n.
Weaver, P., 219n.
Weber, M., 413
Welch, A., xiii
Whelan, C. F., 119

Subject Index